# Read This First

The information in this book is as up to date and accurate as we can make it. But it's important to realize that the law changes frequently, as do fees, forms and other important legal details. If you handle your own legal matters, it's up to you to be sure that all information you use—including the information in this book—is accurate. Here are some suggestions to help you do this:

**First,** check the edition number on the book's spine to make sure you've got the most recent edition of this book. To learn whether a later edition is available, go to Nolo's online Law Store at www.nolo.com or call Nolo's Customer Service Department at 800-728-3555.

**Next,** because the law can change overnight, users of even a current edition need to be sure it's fully up to date. At www.nolo.com, we post notices of major legal and practical changes that affect a book's current edition only. To check for updates, go to the Law Store portion of Nolo's website and find the page devoted to the book (use the "A to Z Product List" and click on the book's title). If you see an "Updates" link on the left side of the page, click on it. If you don't see a link, there are no posted changes—but check back regularly.

**Finally,** while Nolo believes that accurate and current legal information in its books can help you solve many of your legal problems on a cost-effective basis, this book is not intended to be a substitute for personalized advice from a knowledgeable lawyer. If you want the help of a trained professional, consult an attorney licensed to practice in your state.

5th edition

# How to Get a
# Green Card

## Legal Ways to Stay in the U.S.A.

**by Loida Nicolas Lewis
and Len T. Madlansacay**

NOLO

| | |
|---|---|
| Fifth Edition | |
| Second Printing | SEPTEMBER 2003 |
| Editor | ILONA BRAY |
| Book Design | TERRI HEARSH |
| | JACKIE MANCUSO |
| Cover Design | TONI IHARA |
| Illustration | MARI STEIN |
| Production | SARAH HINMAN |
| Proofreading | JOE SADUSKY |
| Index | ELLEN DAVENPORT |
| Printing | ARVATO SERVICES, INC. |

Lewis, Loida Nicolas.
    How to get a green card : legal ways to stay in the U.S.A. / by Loida Nicolas Lewis
and Len T. Madlansacay ; illustrations by Mari Stein. -- 5th ed. / updated by Richard A. Boswell.
        p.  cm.
    Includes index.
    ISBN 0-87337-898-9
    1. Aliens--United States--Popular works. 2. Emigration and immigration law--United
States--Popular works. 3. Green cards. I. Madlansacay, Len T. II. Boswell, Richard A.
III. Title.

KF4840.Z9 L49  2003
342.73'082--dc21                                        2002190874

Quantity sales: For information on bulk purchases or corporate premium sales, please contact the Special Sales department. For
academic sales or textbook adoptions, ask for Academic Sales, 800-955-4775. Nolo, 950 Parker St., Berkeley, CA, 94710.

IN MEMORY OF

# REGINALD FRANCIS LEWIS

December 7, 1942 – January 19, 1993

husband, lover, counselor, friend, role model

and father to our children

Leslie Lourdes

and

Christina Savila

## ACKNOWLEDGMENTS-FIFTH EDITION

It has been several years since Nolo first published *How to Get a Green Card*. My co-author Len T. Madlansacay and I continue to derive a lot of satisfaction when lawyers and non-lawyers say they have been helped by this book.

In fact, my eldest daughter Leslie recently went into a large bookstore to inquire what would be the best book for a person wishing to immigrate to the United States, and she was given this book!

I am grateful to Nolo and its editors, Barbara Kate Repa, Spencer Sherman and Ilona Bray, because every year since 1993, they've helped ensure that this easy-to-read guidebook to U.S. immigration is fully updated and revised.

*Deo Gracias.*

*Loida Nicolas Lewis*

## ACKNOWLEDGMENTS-FIRST EDITION

After Bookmark Publishing Inc. published my book *101 Legal Ways to Stay in the USA* in 1992, I received a phone call from a publisher who wanted to buy the copyright.

It was Ralph "Jake" Warner of Nolo, whom I had previously written to with hopes of their publishing and distributing *101 Legal Ways*, a layman's comprehensive guide on how to obtain a green card. Needless to say, we signed the contract without much ado, with the understanding that the book would be updated and retitled *How to Get a Green Card*.

But circumstances beyond my control intervened, so that without the help of family and friends, *How to Get a Green Card* would not have been finished.

My co-author, Len T. Madlansacay of ManAsia, Inc., with his research techniques, sample immigration forms and practical experience with the INS bureaucracy, was invaluable in completing this revised edition.

My editor, Barbara Kate Repa, had the sharp mind and crisp writing skills to cut through the thicket of my legalese and give this book its clear and understandable format.

Alex L. Esteban provided up-to-date primary source materials in various immigration and labor certification applications. His contribution deserves high commendation, and is greatly appreciated.

My husband's mother, Carolyn E. Fugett, for her humane direction of the household staff (Dalma, Lucien, Estela, Margie, Olivia and Rena); his aunt, Beverly A. Cooper, for her comforting presence; his brothers, Jean S. Fugett for his able leadership of the business, Anthony S. Fugett for his deft management of the financial, and Joseph M. Fugett for his efficient administration of the personal; my sister Imelda M. Nicolas's wise counsel; all enabled me to spend time revising this book.

My husband's support staff, Deidra Wilson, Faye Jenkins, Norma Willis and Bimal Amin, and his professional staff, Rene "Butch" Meily, David Guarino, Kevin Wright, Alfred Fenster, Dennis Jones, Brenda Harper-Vandamme and Carl Brody, by following their "brief," helped me to revise according to my "brief."

My prayer warriors have sustained me with their intercessions: The Nicolas Family, Francis and Ching, Jay and Edith, Danny and Lilia; my school chums, Angie Cruz, Suzzette Bagaybagayan-Rutherford, Violy Calvo-Drilon, Davidica Endriga-Salaya; The Renew Group, Susan Farrarons, Carol Marechal, Nora Brady, Sally Brouard, Julia Jamison, Daniel Boys, Tina Enke, Rosel Kraebber, and many more relatives and friends who continue to pray for me.

My daughters, Leslie and Christina, with their innate grace, compassionate hearts and mature judgments, are my joy and consolation.

Most of all, recalling his admonition, "Keep going, no matter what," my dearest darling RFL remains my inspiration and my one true love.

*Loida Nicolas Lewis*
*Feast of St. Joseph*
*19 March 1993*
*Paris, France*

# CONTENTS

## HOW TO USE THIS BOOK

## 1

## A LOOK AT HISTORY

## 2

## GETTING A VISA

## 3

## KEEPING YOUR STAY IN THE U.S. LEGAL

## 4

## GETTING A GREEN CARD

# 5

## Quota Systems and Preference Categories

# 6

## Fiancé and Fiancée Visas

# 7

## Green Cards Through Marriage

# 8

## Adjustment of Status

# 9

## CONSULAR PROCESSING

# 10

## YOUR PARENTS AS IMMIGRANTS

# 11

## CHILD IMMIGRANTS

# 12

## ORPHAN IMMIGRANTS

# 13

## AMERASIAN IMMIGRANTS

# 14

## YOUR BROTHERS AND SISTERS AS IMMIGRANTS

# 15

## PRIORITY WORKERS

# 16

## PROFESSIONALS AND PEOPLE WITH EXCEPTIONAL ABILITY

# 17

## SKILLED AND UNSKILLED WORKERS

# 18

## LIVE-IN DOMESTIC WORKERS

# 19

## SPECIAL IMMIGRANTS AND RELIGIOUS WORKERS

# 20

## ENTREPRENEUR IMMIGRANTS

# 21

## REFUGEES AND POLITICAL ASYLEES

# 22

## GROUNDS OF INADMISSIBILITY

# 23

## VETERANS AND ENLISTEES

# 24

## GETTING AMNESTY

# 25

## REGISTRY: FOR THOSE IN THE U.S. SINCE 1972

# 26

## CANCELLATION OF REMOVAL

# 27

## PRIVATE BILLS

# 28

## INSIDE THE IMMIGRATION BUREAUCRACY

# 29

## IMMIGRATION FORMS: GETTING STARTED

# 30

## KEEPING, RENEWING AND REPLACING YOUR GREEN CARD

# 31

## HOW TO FIND AND WORK WITH A LAWYER

## ENDNOTE
### RESPONSIBILITIES OF THE NEW IMMIGRANT

# APPENDIX 1
## BCIS AND DOL OFFICES

# APPENDIX 2
## FORMS

| | |
|---|---|
| Form AR-11 | Alien's Change of Address Card |
| Form OF-169 | Instructions for Immigrant Visa Applicants |
| Form DS-230 (Parts I & II) | Application for Immigrant Visa and Alien Registration |
| Form ETA 750 Part A | Application for Alien Employment Certification |
| Form ETA 750 Part B | Statement of Qualifications of Alien |
| Form G-325A | Biographic Information |
| Form I-90 | Application to Replace Alien Registration Card |
| Form I-102 | Application for Replacement/Initial Nonimmigrant Arrival-Departure Document |
| Form I-129F | Petition for Alien Fiancé(e) |
| Form I-130 | Petition for Alien Relative |
| Form I-131 | Application for Travel Document |
| Form I-134 | Affidavit of Support |
| Form I-140 | Immigrant Petition for Alien Worker |
| Form I-360 | Petition for Amerasian, Widow or Special Immigrant |
| Form I-485 | Application to Register Permanent Residence or Adjust Status |
| Form I-485 Supp. A | Supplement A to Form I-485 |
| Form I-526 | Immigrant Petition by Alien Entrepreneur |
| Form I-539 | Application to Extend/Change Nonimmigrant Status |
| Form I-589 | Application for Asylum and for Withholding of Removal |
| Form I-600 | Petition to Classify Orphan as an Immediate Relative |
| Form I-600A | Application for Advance Processing of Orphan Petition |
| Form I-751 | Petition to Remove the Conditions on Residence |
| Form I-765 | Application for Employment Authorization |
| Form I-823 | Application—Alternative Inspection Services |
| Form I-824 | Application for Action on an Approved Application or Petition |
| Form I-829 | Petition by Entrepreneur to Remove the Conditions |
| Form I-864 | Affidavit of Support Under Section 213A of the Act |
| Form I-864A | Contract Between Sponsor and Household Member |
| Form I-864P | 2003 Poverty Guidelines |
| Form I-865 | Sponsor's Notice of Change of Address |
| Form N-400 | Application for Naturalization |
| Form N-600 | Application for Certificate of Citizenship |

## SAMPLE FILLED-IN FORMS

# HOW TO USE THIS BOOK

## WHEN YOU MAY NEED A LAWYER

The advice given in this book is for simple, straightforward cases. If your case is more complex, you may need to hire a lawyer to advise or represent you. It may be best to consult a lawyer if:

- you are required to go before an immigration judge for what are called "removal" proceedings because the immigration authorities do not believe that you have a legal reason to either enter or continue to stay in the United States
- you have a criminal record
- you have some other problems with your immigration paperwork, such as you have submitted forged documents, or
- if the bureaucratic requirements are too technical, for example, you must apply for political asylum or labor certification or you are appealing some decision made in your case by immigration authorities.

(See Chapter 31 for guidance in hiring and working with a lawyer.)

## PROCEEDING THROUGH THE BOOK

You need not read every chapter in this book—only those that pertain to your specific situation. Here is some guidance.

Read Chapter 1 if you're interested in a summary of immigration trends and laws throughout history.

Everyone should read Chapters 2 and 3. They describe the requirements for obtaining a visa—legal permission for an alien to stay in the United States.

Everyone should also read Chapters 4 and 5. They explain the general forms and procedures required for obtaining a green card—and the quotas that may apply to allow set numbers of specific types of immigrants to come to the United States.

Then comes the time when you can choose and read the specific chapters that concern you. Look over the chapter headings for Chapters 6 through 27—and read the ones that make the most sense in your specific situation. For example, if you believe that you might qualify for a green card because you will be marrying a U.S. citizen or are already married to a U.S. citizen, begin reading Chapter 7. It may refer you to other chapters you should read to get a more complete picture. Each chapter contains samples of most of the forms you'll need to complete—and Appendix 4 contains blank copies of the forms you can fill out and file with the immigration authorities, using the sample form for guidance.

- After reading the information about various rules for specific types of immigrants, if you decide that you qualify to file for yourself or another person, read Chapters 28 and 29. They'll help you understand the rules for filling out the necessary forms and getting them into the right hands.
- If you lose your green card, read Chapter 30 to find out how to replace it.

## ICONS USED IN THE BOOK

 **CAUTION**
This icon alerts you to potential problems.

 **SEE AN EXPERT**
This icon alerts you to situations where you may need to seek the advice of an attorney.

 **TIP**
This icon gives you a useful tip. ■

# 1

• • • • • • • • • • • • • •

# A LOOK AT HISTORY

## America: A Nation of Immigrants

This country's history, people have come to its shores from other parts of the world.

—From *This American's Story*

## A. AMERICA'S EARLIEST SETTLERS

Long before Cristobal Colon—the Spanish name by which Christopher Columbus referred to himself—opened the Americas to the Europeans in 1492, the first inhabitants of what is now the United States were the Native American Indians, including the Eskimos. Over thousands of years, they traveled from Asia across the Bering Strait.

About the year 1000 A.D., around the same time that the Vikings reached the northernmost part of North America, the ancestors of today's Hawaiians sailed from Polynesia to the Pacific Islands. While the Viking settlements in America died out, the Polynesians prospered in Hawaii.

It was only in the 15th century that the Spaniards first explored, conquered and settled the southern and western parts of the United States, the Caribbean and South America. Although Portugal also sent explorers during that time, the only Portuguese legacy that remains in the Americas today is Brazil.

The French, not to be left behind in the conquest of the New World with its unimaginable riches, soon sent explorers to establish French power in Quebec and Montreal.

The Dutch came to the Hudson River and, in 1526, bought Manhattan from the Native Americans for the equivalent of 60 Dutch guilders, since it could not justify settlement by "discovery" alone.

England, more than a hundred years after John Cabot reached Newfoundland, sent explorers and established its first colony in Virginia in 1607 to yield profits for the crown and the ruling class.

The new continent became a magnet to different people in the world. These people saw the new world as a place to start a new life, to seek better opportunities, to practice their beliefs freely, to seek relief from natural or man-made disasters, or to avoid persecution in their home country.

The pilgrims landed in Massachusetts—although they intended to land in Virginia—where they founded their new Zion, free from the interference of the English government. The Quakers settled in Pennsylvania. Maryland was founded to provide a refuge for the Catholics persecuted in England.

And Spanish Jews, who had settled in Brazil after being expelled from Spain, arrived in New York when the Portuguese took over the former Spanish colony and started the Brazilian inquisition. After the Scottish rebellion was crushed, people from Scotland left for the colonies.

Other immigrants came in groups and provided their special skills to the new cities and settlements: Austrians from Salzburg made silk; Polish and Germans made tar, glass, tools and built homes. Later, Italians came and raised grapes. New Jersey was settled by the Swedes; northern Pennsylvania attracted a large number of Germans.

As the settlements grew in number, the colonies needed a large labor force to work the mines and plantations of tobacco, hemp and other agricultural products both in the North and the South.

### 1. Forced migration

But not everyone who came to the New World did so of their own free will. Many crossed the ocean as indentured servants—working as long as seven years for landowners in the English colonies in payment for their passage, or in exchange for their debts or jail terms.

And as cotton became the most important product in the South, the plantation owners turned to the inhuman trade of African people to create a huge and cheap workforce, while the businessmen of the North conducted the slave trade because it was highly profitable.

By the time the first census of the new republic was taken in 1790, the four million inhabitants were two-thirds English-speaking, and the rest were from other nations—of whom 59,000 were free African-Americans, while 698,000 lived in human bondage, mostly in the South.

Although the U.S. Congress amended the Constitution in 1808 to ban the importation of slaves, it took nearly half a century before the smuggling of human beings stopped. By the Civil War in 1861, the number of Americans of African descent had risen to 230,000 free and four million slaves taken forcibly from West Africa, where a very high form of culture had developed. Thus, people who had been miners, blacksmiths, metal workers, weavers, potters, traders, hunters, fishermen, farmers, scholars or religious teachers were brought in chains for the profit of the Western nations.

### 2. European exodus

Between 1820 and 1910, Europe experienced the greatest migration of people to the New World. During that time, at least 38 million Europeans arrived in the United States.

Several important events caused this great migration: the Napoleonic Wars; the political disturbances in Germany, Austria-Hungary, Greece and Poland; the Potato

Famine in Ireland; the religious persecutions of Protestants, Catholics and Jews in Czarist Russia and other parts of Europe; the Industrial Revolution, which created thousands of unemployed workers and peasants; the rigid social structure that supported a closed aristocracy and upper class. All these factors led millions to leave their homelands in search of a better life.

## B. Growth of the Continental U.S.

At the same time, the United States was expanding into the West and the Southwest all the way to the Pacific Coast. The country grew by purchase, such as the Louisiana Purchase from Napoleon I of France, which brought an expanse of land from the Mississippi to the Rocky Mountains and the purchase of Florida from Spain. It grew by war, such as the one waged with Mexico for California and Texas, or with Britain in 1812, which ended with a treaty granting the United States parts of Canada. The nation grew by treaty with, purchase from, or the outright massacre of, the Native American tribes for the possession of their ancestral lands.

In addition, the Industrial Revolution was shaping life in the United States throughout the 19th century. The factories, timberlands and manufacturing plants all needed workers. So the masses came—the adventurers, the pioneers, the settlers, the impoverished—mostly because the land was cheaper, the pay was higher and the opportunities were greater than they could hope for in their home country.

The railroads that were being constructed to connect the East with the West made the transport of people and products much easier. Thus, the Europeans crossed the Atlantic Ocean from Germany (5.3 million), Ireland (4.2 million), Austria (3.2 million), Italy (3.1 million), England and Scotland (2.7 million), Russia (2.4 million), Sweden and Norway (1.7 million), and came in the thousands from Switzerland, Holland, Poland, Romania, Yugoslavia, Hungary, Czechoslovakia, Greece and several other countries in Europe.

### 1. Racial restrictions on workers

In California, the Gold Rush of 1849 brought not only people from all over America but also the Chinese from across the Pacific Ocean. Chinese workers, contracted for very low wages, were shipped to America before and after the Civil War. Although they came in great numbers to provide cheap labor for the construction of the Union Pacific Railroad, they were not granted the right to become American citizens.

By 1882, there were approximately 300,000 low-wage Chinese laborers in America. Because they were different in color, in culture, in habits and in looks, these new workers were targeted by Americans for antagonism and racial hatred. As a result, the Chinese Exclusion Act was passed in 1882, completely banning non-citizen Chinese from immigrating to the United States. This law remained in effect until 1943.

The Japanese then took the place of the Chinese in agriculture, domestic work, lumber mills and salmon fisheries. By 1920, approximately 200,000 Japanese immigrants were found on the East Coast and 100,000 more on the sugar plantations in Hawaii. These Japanese workers also were subjected to racial hatred and were excluded from the United States in 1908 and prohibited from becoming U.S. citizens by the Immigration Act of 1924.

Also during this time, when America purchased the Philippines from Spain in 1898, the Filipinos were able to immigrate and were concentrated mostly on the East Coast and Hawaii as laborers on farms and sugar plantations, and in fish canneries and logging camps. These Filipinos were not spared the racial animosity that permeated American society—and they also were excluded from citizenship by the immigration laws passed in 1924.

This great influx of people in the late 19th and early 20th centuries brought the passage of several restrictive immigration laws. At various times, the U.S. Congress forbade people to enter it considered undesirable—paupers, drunkards, anarchists and people of various specific national origins.

In 1917, an Immigration Act was passed to restrict the entry of immigrants, especially the flow of illiterate laborers from central and eastern Europe. This law marked the beginning of a great change in American immigration policy. No immigration was permitted to the United States from the Asiatic Barred Zone. In addition to China and Japan, this zone included India, Siam (Thailand), Indochina (Vietnam, Cambodia and Laos), Afghanistan, parts of Siberia, Iran and Arabia, and the islands of Java, Sumatra, Ceylon, Borneo, New Guinea and Celebes.

After World War I, America faced economic depression and unemployment, and the immigrant became the scapegoat for hard times. In 1921, a tight national-origins quota system was enacted as a temporary measure. Total immigration was limited to about 350,000 per year. Immigration from each country in a given year was limited to 3% of all nationals from that country who were living in the United States during the 1910 census.

This system was made permanent when the U. S. Congress approved the National Origins Act of 1924. Its purpose was "to arrest a trend toward a change in the fundamental composition of the American stock." Based on the ethnic composition of the United States as recorded in the 1920 census, it limited the entry of aliens from any one country to 2% of the number of their people living in the United States. In one stroke, the law reduced the total immigration of aliens from all countries to 150,000 per year.

The object of the law was not simply to limit immigration but to favor certain kinds of immigrants and keep out others. More immigrants were permitted from western Europe and fewer from southern and eastern Europe. The law totally excluded Asians. It was intended mainly to prohibit Chinese, Japanese and Filipinos from acquiring U.S. citizenship.

The American door, for so long left wide open to "all the tired, the poor, the huddled masses yearning to breathe free," was all but closed against future immigrants for the next 40 years.

## 2. Restrictions relaxed

After World War II, the door would again open—this time, for a few carefully selected groups of immigrants.

For one thing, a new category of naturalized Americans was admitted: thousands of alien soldiers had earned citizenship by serving with the U.S. Armed Forces overseas during the war.

Congress also passed the War Brides Act in 1945 to facilitate the reunion of 118,000 alien spouses and children with members of the U.S. armed forces who had fought and married overseas.

The Displaced Persons Act of 1948 allowed 400,000 refugees to be admitted to the U.S. over the next two years. Most of them had been displaced during the war from Poland, Romania, Hungary, the Baltic area, the Ukraine and Yugoslavia, and had been placed in refugee camps in Germany, Italy and Austria.

When the Iron Curtain fell on eastern Europe, the Refugee Relief Act of 1953 allowed 214,000 refugees from the Communist countries to be admitted into the United States. The Anti-Soviet fighters from Hungary, after the suppression of their revolution in 1956, were paroled into the United States—that is, allowed to enter without a visa.

## C. Legal Controls Consolidated

When the Immigration and Nationality Act was passed in 1952, it brought all the immigration laws into one and formed the basic immigration law as we know it now. However, it was not until President Lyndon Johnson signed the 1965 amendments into law that the racially-biased National Origin Quota was abolished.

The amendments introduced two general ways of becoming an immigrant: by family relationship and by the employment needs of the United States. The legislation established a preference system—giving priority to some groups of immigrants over others. For example, spouses and children of American citizens had higher priority than business workers.

Aliens from the eastern hemisphere—Asia, Europe and Africa—were limited to 170,000, and applicants from this group were subject to the preference system. The quota for immigrants from North and South America was 120,000, and applicants were not subject to the preference system.

The law also provided a separate category for refugees from communism and the Middle East—with an annual limit of 10,000.

## 1. The brain drain begins

Under the 1965 amendments, skilled workers, who had a higher preference than unskilled workers, moved more easily to the United States, so that the departure of doctors, lawyers, engineers, scientists, teachers, accountants, nurses and other professionals caused a "brain drain" not only in Europe, but also in Asia, the Pacific Rim and developing countries.

People from Mexico, the Caribbean Islands and Central and South America also began crossing the border into the United States in search of economic advantages.

In 1976 and 1978, the immigration law was modified again. The separate quotas for the Eastern and Western Hemispheres were eliminated and a worldwide quota of

290,000 immigrants every year was established. Each country was given a yearly quota of 20,000 immigrants; Hong Kong, as a colony of Great Britain, was given 5,000.

## 2. Refugees and political asylum

The end of the Vietnam War resulted in a flow of refugees from the Indochinese peninsula.

In 1980, Fidel Castro declared that the Port of Mariel was open to anyone who wanted to leave. Cuban refugees arrived on the shores of Florida by the thousands. These included some criminals and mentally ill people who had been forced by Castro to leave the jails and mental hospitals.

In response, the U.S. Congress passed the Refugee Act of 1980, which removed the preferential treatment of refugees from Communist countries. Under that law, a refugee was defined as someone who fears persecution in his or her home country because of religious or political beliefs, race, national origin or ethnic identity.

## 3. Amnesty for the undocumented

The door opened wider with the Immigration Reform and Control Act of 1986, more commonly known as the Amnesty Law. This law benefited a large number of Mexicans and other aliens who had entered and had been living without legal status in the United States since January 1, 1982. More than two million aliens were granted legal residency.

At the same time, the Amnesty Law attempted to control the future influx of undocumented aliens into the United States—and those controls still exist today. Any employer who hires or recruits an alien, or who, for a fee, refers an alien to another employer without first verifying the alien's immigration status, is subject to a fine ranging from $200 to $10,000 for each undocumented alien employed.

## 4. Immigration acts since 1990

With the Immigration Act of 1990, the U.S. Congress approved its most comprehensive overhaul of immigration law since 1965.

This Act provided for a huge increase of immigrants, to 700,000 annually in 1992, 1993 and 1994, and to 675,000 from 1995. It aimed to attract immigrants who have the education, skills or money to enhance the economic life of the country, while at the same time maintaining the immigration policy of family reunification. The law therefore makes it easier for scientists, engineers, inventors and other such highly skilled professionals to enter the United States. Millionaire entrepreneurs have their own immigrant classification.

Citizens of nations which have had little immigration to the United States for the past five years are allocated 55,000 immigrant visas yearly under the "lottery" system. The spouses and children of illegal immigrants who were granted amnesty under the 1986 law are also entitled to become permanent residents.

Temporary protections were added for people fleeing war or natural disasters, such as earthquakes. Refugees from the civil war in El Salvador were the first beneficiaries.

Such provisions made the Immigration Act of 1990 the most humane legislation for immigrants in the past century. However, more recent changes again closed America's doors to many immigrants. These changes included 1996's Antiterrorism and Effective Death Penalty Act (AEDPA) and Illegal Immigration Reform and Immigrant Responsibility Act (IIRIRA). And a variety of legislative and regulatory changes have been added since the terrorist attacks of September 11, 2001, tightening controls on would-be immigrants as well as those who are already here. The most notable of these were the USA PATRIOT Act of 2002, which expanded the definition of terrorism and increased the government's authority to detain and deport immigrants, and the November 2002 legislation establishing the new Department of Homeland Security (DHS) and breaking the Immigration and Naturalization Service (INS) into three agencies under the DHS's power. These three new agencies include the Bureau of Citizenship and Immigration Services (BCIS), which took over the most public INS functions such as deciding on applications for immigration benefits; the Bureau of Immigration and Customs Enforcement (BICE), which now handles enforcement of the immigration laws within the U.S. borders; and the Bureau of Customs and Border Protection (BCBP), which now handles U.S. border enforcement (including at land borders, airports and seaports). These changes further illustrate that the immigration policy of the United States constantly shifts according to the needs and national purpose of its multi-ethnic and multi-racial people.

## D. Looking Forward

Immigration law policies have become a subject of ongoing Congressional scrutiny, change, and then reverse change. With every shift in the U.S. economy and sense of security, public attitudes toward immigrants shift as well.

But the opening lines of the Declaration of Independence of the United States of America, so eloquently written by Thomas Jefferson some 200 years ago, remain both an inspiration and a challenge:

*We hold these truths to be self-evident, that all men are created equal, that they are endowed by their Creator with certain unalienable Rights, that among these are Life, Liberty and the pursuit of Happiness.* ■

# 2

# GETTING A VISA

## Why Do I Need So Many Documents?

If you are not a citizen of the United States, the U.S. government refers to you as an alien. But try not to think of being branded as the monster in a science fiction movie. The U.S. Congress has used this term ever since it began to restrict the flow of non-citizens into the country, long before Hollywood began producing films. Aliens must receive permission to stay and work in the United States—and that's where a visa comes in.

## A. WHAT IS A VISA?

The basic rule is that you may enter the United States only after receiving permission from the U.S. government, through the U.S. Embassy or Consulate in your own country. The permission or authority to enter the United States is called a visa, and is stamped in your passport by the U.S. consul. The exception is if you are eligible to enter under the Visa Waiver Program; see discussion in Section C, below.

If you enter the United States without permission, without a visa or a visa waiver and without being examined by the immigration authorities, you are called an "undocumented alien" within the immigration laws and an "illegal alien" by the general public.

## B. TYPES OF VISAS

There are two kinds of visas an alien can receive from the U.S. Embassy or Consulate: an immigrant visa and a nonimmigrant visa.

### 1. Immigrant visas

The immigrant visa gives you the right to enter the United States, claim your permanent residency and live and work permanently anywhere in the United States. If you qualify to become an immigrant—and the most common ways to qualify are that you are related to a U.S. citizen or an immigrant, or you have an employer who petitions for you—you will be granted an immigrant visa by the Immigration Service or by an American Embassy. Getting a visa is just one step away from getting a green card—the documentation you'll need to travel into and out of the United States freely and to work here legally. Sometime after you've entered the United States, your actual green card will be mailed to you.

### 2. Nonimmigrant visas

A nonimmigrant visa gives you the right to stay in the United States temporarily with limited rights.

For example, a nonimmigrant visa (B-1) allows a businessperson to work only for his or her company's business concern and not for any other company while in the United States. A tourist visa (B-2) does not allow an alien to work. A student visa (F-1 or M-1) does not allow a student to stop studying to work. A temporary worker's visa (H-1B), given to a professional worker such as an accountant or engineer, does not authorize an alien to change employers without permission.

Therefore, for the unlimited right to work and live in the United States, you must take the steps necessary to get a green card. (See Chapter 4.) With it, you will gain a new title: lawful permanent resident.

**ADVANTAGES AND DISADVANTAGES OF GETTING A GREEN CARD**

Advantages
- Unlimited right to work in the U.S.
- Unlimited right to live anywhere in the U.S.
- Eligible to become a U.S. citizen

Disadvantages
- Must make your home within the U.S.
- Must pay U.S. taxes on income earned anywhere in the world
- Cannot remain outside the U.S. for more than one year without special permission

## 3. Nonimmigrant Visa Classifications

You will often hear visa classifications referred to in short-hand by a letter followed by a number. The following list explains the nonimmigrant visa classifications available.

| | |
|---|---|
| A-1 | Ambassadors, public ministers, consular officers or career diplomats and their immediate families |
| A-2 | Other foreign government officials or employees and their immediate families |
| A-3 | Personal attendants, servants or employees and their immediate families, of A-2 visa holders |
| B-1 | Temporary business visitors |
| B-2 | Temporary tourist visitors |
| C-1 | Foreign travelers in immediate and continuous transit through the U.S. |
| D-1 | Crewmembers (sea or air) |
| E-1 | Treaty traders and their spouses or children |
| E-2 | Treaty investors and their spouses or children |
| F-1 | Academic or language students |
| F-2 | Spouses or children of F-1 visa holders |
| G-1 | Designated principal resident representatives of foreign governments coming to the U.S. to work for an international organization, their staff members and immediate families |
| G-2 | Other representatives of foreign governments coming to the U.S. to work for an international organization, and their immediate families |
| G-3 | Representatives of Foreign Governments and their immediate families who would ordinarily qualify for G-1 or G-2 visas except that their governments are not members of an international organization |
| G-4 | Officers or employees of international organizations and their immediate families |
| G-5 | Attendants, servants and personal employees of G-1 through G-4 visa holders, and their immediate families |
| H-1B | Aliens working in specialty occupations requiring at least a bachelor's degree or its equivalent in on-the-job experience |
| H-2A | Temporary agricultural workers coming to the U.S. to fill positions for which a temporary shortage of American workers has been recognized by the U.S. Department of Agriculture |
| H-2B | Temporary workers of various kinds coming to the U.S. to perform temporary jobs for which there is a shortage of available qualified American workers |
| H-3 | Temporary trainees |
| H-4 | Spouses or children of H-1A/B, H-2A/B or H-3 visa holders |
| I | Representatives of the foreign press coming to the U.S. to work solely in that capacity, and their immediate families |
| J-1 | Exchange visitors coming to the U.S. to study, work or train as part of an exchange program officially recognized by the U.S. Information Agency |
| J-2 | Spouses or children of J-1 visa holders |
| K-1 | Fiancé(e)s of U.S. citizens coming to the U.S. for the purpose of getting married |
| K-2 | Children of K-1 visa holders |
| K-3 | Spouses of U.S. citizens awaiting approval of their immigrant visa petition or the availability of a green card |
| K-4 | Children of K-3 visa holders |
| L-1 | Intra-company transferees who work as managers, executives or persons with specialized knowledge |
| L-2 | Spouses or children of L-1 visa holders |
| M-1 | Vocational or other nonacademic students |
| M-2 | Immediate families of M-1 visa holders |
| N | Children of certain special immigrants |
| NATO-1 | Principal permanent representatives of member states to NATO—including any subsidiary bodies, residents in the U.S. and resident official staff members, secretaries general, assistant secretaries general and executive secretaries of NATO, other permanent NATO officials of similar rank, or their immediate families |

NATO-2  Other representatives to member states to NATO—including any subsidiary bodies, including its advisers and technical experts of delegations, members of Immediate Article 3, 4 UST 1796 families; dependents of members of forces entering in accordance with the Status-of-Forces Agreement or in accordance with the Protocol on Status of International Military Headquarters; members of such a force if issued

NATO-3  Official clerical staff accompanying representatives of member states to NATO—including any subsidiary bodies, or their immediate families

NATO-4  Officials of NATO—other than those who can be classified as NATO-1, or their immediate families

NATO-5  Experts—other than officials who can be classified as NATO-1, employed on missions in behalf of NATO, and their dependents

NATO-6  Members of civilian components accompanying forces entering in accordance with provisions of the NATO Status-of-Forces Agreement; members of civilian components attached to or employed by allied headquarters under the Protocol on Status of International Military Headquarters set up pursuant to the North Atlantic Treaty, and their dependents

NATO-7  Attendants, servants or personal employees of NATO-1 through NATO-6 classes or their immediate families

O-1  Aliens of extraordinary ability in the sciences, arts, education, business or athletics

O-2  Support staff of O-1 visa holders

O-3  Spouses or children of 0-1 or O-2 visa holders

P-1  Internationally recognized athletes and entertainers

P-2  Artists or entertainers in reciprocal exchange programs

P-3  Artists and entertainers coming to the U.S. to give culturally unique performances in a group

P-4  Spouses or children of P-1, P-2 or P-3 visa holders

Q-1  Participants in international cultural exchange programs

Q-2  Immediate family members of Q-1 visa holders

R-1  Aliens in religious occupations

R-2  Spouses or children of R-1 visa holders

S-1  Certain aliens supplying critical information relating to a criminal organization or enterprise

S-5 or S-6  Certain aliens supplying critical information relating to terrorism

S-7  Immediate family members of S-1 visa holders

T  Women and children who are in the United States because they are victims of trafficking, who are cooperating with law enforcement and who fear extreme hardship (such as retribution) if returned home

TN  NAFTA professionals

TD  Spouses or children of NAFTA professionals

V  Spouses and children of lawful permanent residents who have been waiting for three years or more to qualify for a green card.

## C. Exemptions From the Visa Requirement

The U.S. Department of State (DOS) started a Visa Waiver Pilot Program in 1989. It allows the citizens of certain countries—that the DOS chooses—to visit the United States without first having a tourist visa stamped on their passports. The program was made permanent in October 2000.

The Visa Waiver Program was originally set up to eliminate the useless paperwork involved in processing tourist visas for applicants who were clearly temporary visitors. All that is required is a passport and a round-trip ticket.

**EXAMPLE:** You want to visit the United States for two months. If you live in a country that is included in the Visa Waiver Program, you can take a plane to the United States without a tourist visa and enter without any problem. You will, however, be required to show a round-trip ticket as evidence that you are simply visiting and that you will return to your country within the 90-day limit.

### 1. Countries exempted

Under the Visa Waiver Program, citizens of the following countries who can present a machine-readable passport are exempted from getting visas before entering the United States:

| | | |
|---|---|---|
| Andorra | Holland | Norway |
| Australia | (Netherlands) | Portugal |
| Austria | Iceland | San Marino |
| Belgium | Ireland | Singapore |
| Brunei | Italy | Slovenia |
| Denmark | Japan | Spain |
| Finland | Liechtenstein | Sweden |
| France | Luxembourg | Switzerland |
| Germany | Monaco | |
| Great Britain | New Zealand | |
| (United Kingdom) | | |

To be included in the Visa Waiver Program, the country must have:

- a very low rate of refusals of tourist visa applications, and
- few violations of U.S. immigration laws.

In short, countries whose citizens are least likely to stay too long or work illegally in the United States are most likely to be included in the Visa Waiver Program.

## 2. Procedure required

While on the plane to your U.S. destination, you will be handed Form I-94W, Arrival/Departure Record for the Visa Waiver Program, which asks for simple information, including your:

- name
- birthdate
- country of citizenship
- passport number
- airline and flight number
- country where you live
- city where you boarded the airplane, and
- address while staying in the United States.

You must use an ink pen to fill out the form. Print neatly, in all capital letters. The questions on Form I-94W are straightforward, and you should have no trouble answering them. However, if you do have questions or problems when filling out the form, a flight attendant should be able to help you—or ask immigration officers for assistance when you land.

On the bottom half of Form I-94W, you will write in your name, birthdate and country of citizenship. That portion of the form will later be stamped by immigration officers with the port of entry, the dates you were admitted and the date by which you must leave the U.S. and the type of visa—and will be attached to your passport.

---

### DISADVANTAGES OF ENTERING WITHOUT A VISA

There may be disadvantages to entering the U.S. under the Visa Waiver Program without first getting a visa.

You cannot change your tourist status to another nonimmigrant status, such as that of student or temporary worker, nor can you request an extension of your 90-day stay.

Unless you marry an American citizen, it will be almost impossible to change your status to a lawful permanent resident.

In addition, should the border officials deny you entry into the United States for any reason, you have no right to appeal. Political refugees who are fleeing persecution and who apply for asylum in the United States are the sole exceptions. (See Chapter 21.)

---

For more information on the process of obtaining student or tourist visas, see *Student & Tourist Visas: How to Come to the U.S.*, by Ilona Bray & Richard Boswell (Nolo).

## D. FREQUENT FLYERS: SPECIAL RULES

During peak hours of travel, people complained that they were processed together with first-time arrivals and were delayed in their important appointments. To answer this criticism, the government instituted a procedure using biometric technology called INSPASS identifying the frequent flyers by the geometry of their hands.

If you qualify as a frequent flyer, you will be processed faster upon arriving at the airport. You will be directed to an automated inspection booth where you will insert a card into a machine and then place your hand into a scanning device to establish your identity—and at once, you are out of the inspection area. The machine will print an I-94 card or receipt for you.

You qualify as a frequent flyer for INSPASS if you travel on business at least three or more times each year to the United States. In addition you must be:

- a citizen of the United States, or
- a permanent resident of the United States who is also a national of Bermuda, Canada or one of the countries participating in the Visa Waiver Program, or
- a nonimmigrant holding a B-1, E or L-1 visa, who is a national of Bermuda, Canada or one of the countries participating in the Visa Waiver Program. (See C1 above.)

You can apply for an INSPASS upon arriving at a designated port of entry by using Form I-823, "Application—Alternate Inspection Services." The application asks you to provide simple information, including your:

- name
- birthdate
- country of citizenship
- passport number and expiration date
- permanent address
- company name
- position with the company
- number of trips to or from the U.S. each year
- average length of trip, and
- contact address in the United States.

You must have and carry with you a valid passport—and visa, if you do not belong to the Visa Waiver countries. And you must not be an inadmissible alien—drug addict, convicted felon, infected with a communicable disease, spy, terrorist or Nazi.

Applying for an INSPASS may require a little time and patience. You must complete the application form, make a hand geometry print using biometric technology at the airport and answer a few questions from the immigration officer to determine whether you indeed qualify as an INSPASS frequent flier.

The INSPASS is valid for a year or until the traveler's passport or visa expires, whichever is less.

INSPASS service is now available at a number of airport locations, including Kennedy Airport in New York, Newark Airport in New Jersey, Washington (Dulles), Miami Airport, San Francisco Airport and Los Angeles Airport, as well as at pre-clearance sites at Pearson International Airport in Toronto and Vancouver International Airport in British Columbia. INSPASS is scheduled to be offered at airports in Seattle-Tacoma, Honolulu, Atlanta, Boston, Chicago, Cincinnati, Dallas–Fort Worth, Detroit, Houston and Montreal. ■

# 3

# KEEPING YOUR STAY IN THE U.S. LEGAL

## I Only Came to Visit, But I Need More Time

The Immigration and Nationality Act of 1952, revised by later legislation such as the Immigration Act of 1990, controls who may enter and leave the United States if they are not American citizens. The law provides various ways for such people to stay and work legally in the United States—most of them discussed in detail in later chapters of this book.

If you entered the United States as a tourist, a student, temporary worker, entertainer or any immigrant catagory, you should maintain your legal status and not violate the conditions of your stay in the United States. Do not overstay the limits of your visa. Do not work when you are not authorized to work. Do not change schools or employers without first requesting and receiving permission from the immigration authorities.

## A. The Importance of Keeping Legal

By making an effort to keep your status legal, you will be free from the anxiety that the immigration authorities are watching your every move. The consequences for breaking the rules controlling immigration may be quite serious: You could be detained in an immigration jail; deportation proceedings could be brought against you; and, if deported, you could be barred from returning to the United States for the next five years. Even if you are not deported, if you overstay your status by six months and then leave the United States, you will have to stay outside for three years before being admitted again. If you overstay by 12 months and then leave, the waiting period is ten years before you will be allowed to return. (See Chapter 26.)

More to the point, by staying within the law, you can make use of almost all the ways enumerated in this book to stay in the United States for as long as your status is legal.

The immigration laws allow some flexibility in changing your status from tourist to temporary worker as long as your immigration status is legal, you are not an overstaying visitor and you have not worked illegally. But once you become an undocumented alien by remaining in the United States beyond the period of time given to you, you risk getting in trouble with immigration authorities and losing your rights to certain immigration benefits. If you overstay the period written on your I-94 card, your visit will be automatically void—even if it is a multiple entry, indefinite visa. You will then be required to apply for a new visa at the consulate in your home country, unless you can prove "exceptional circumstances."

In any case, it is best to stay out of trouble with the law. If there is some question in your case, seek professional advice from an immigration support group, specialized clinic or experienced immigration lawyer. (See Chapter 31.) Do not depend on advice from your friends or relatives, or you may make decisions based on wrong information.

## B. How to Extend a Visitor Visa

Temporary business or tourist visitors—those who hold B-1 or B-2 visas—once admitted to the United States, can apply for an extension of stay. Under current law, the basis can be business circumstances or other family reasons. However, be warned: Before the restructuring, the INS had proposed limiting extensions of stay to visitors who can demonstrate "compelling humanitarian reasons," such as "situations involving an alien's new or continued medical treatment, the need of an alien parent to stay with his or her minor child receiving medical treatment or specialized education in the United States or the need of an alien adult to attend to an acutely ill immediate family member who is receiving medical treatment." After the INS got broken up, the BCIS withdrew this proposal, but some worry that it will be brought back again. This doesn't seem to encompass visitors who just want to enjoy a longer stay. For further information, keep your eye on the BCIS website (www.bcis.gov) and the Updates to this book on Nolo's website (www.nolo.com).

For example, if a tourist decides to visit different locations, or to spend more time with relatives, he or she can seek an extension. The Application for Extension must be mailed directly to the BCIS Service Center closest to where the applicant lives. (See the BCIS website at www.bcis.gov for contact details.)

The application must include the following:

• Form I-539, Application to Extend/Change Nonimmigrant Status

- Form I-94; a copy may be submitted
- A filing fee of $140; either personal check or money order will be accepted
- a company letter or other supporting documentation, stating the reason for the extension request—for example, more business consultations, continuing medical reasons, extended family visit with a complete itinerary
- evidence to show that the visit is temporary—particularly evidence of continued overseas employment or residence and a return ticket, and
- evidence of financial support, such as the purchase of travelers' checks or a bank letter including amounts in accounts.

Also attach an itinerary or a letter explaining your reasons for requesting the extension.

Be sure you have attached Form I-94, Arrival/Departure Record to your application. (See Chapter 2, Section C2.) It is proof that you arrived in the United States lawfully. Also attach information showing when and how you will depart the United States after your extension, such as a copy of a new plane ticket.

The extension may not give you as much time as you'd like. Even under the old rules, extensions of more than six months were rare. Under the proposed new rules, extensions would be limited to a mere 30 days.

## 1. When to file

You can file for an extension up to 60 days before the expiration date of your stay, which is shown on your Form I-94—the white paper as proof of inspection and attached to your passport when you entered the United States. If you are prone to procrastination, file the request for extension at least 15 days before the expiration date shown on your Form I-94.

## 2. If your I-94 is missing or destroyed

Your completed Form I-94 or Form I-95 (Crewman's Landing Permit, issued to crews on ships and airlines)—which is your proof of lawful arrival in the United States—may have been lost, stolen or damaged. Or perhaps you were not issued the proper form when you entered.

To get the proper documentation, file Form I-102, Application for Replacement/Initial Nonimmigrant Arrival-Departure Document. (See the sample at the end of this chapter.) It costs an additional $100 to file this form.

This form must accompany your Form I-539, Application to Extend/Change Nonimmigrant Status. Your check

or money order should be sufficient to cover filing fees for both forms.

If you are applying to replace a lost or stolen Form I-94 or Form I-95, submit a copy of the original form if you have it, or submit a copy of the biographic page from your passport and a copy of the page indicating admission as claimed.

If you have none of these documents because your passport was lost or stolen, you will have to submit other evidence of your admission. The BCIS may accept your ticket and an affidavit, which is a written statement that you have sworn to before a notary public, explaining why you cannot provide any of the documents requested. Submit this affidavit with some proof of identity, such as a copy of your work identification card, credit card or driver's license.

If your Form I-94 has been damaged, attach it anyway.

If you were not issued a Form I-94 when you were admitted to the United States, submit a copy of your passport and the page showing that you were admitted as it was stamped by the border officials when you first arrived.

## C. Changing Your Reason for Staying

If you wish to request a change of status from one category to another, do not apply for the change within the first two months after arriving in America.

If you do so, the BCIS may deny your application based on the theory of "preconceived intent." Preconceived intent simply means that you lied about your reasons for coming to the United States.

For example, if you attempt to change your status from tourist to student soon after arriving in the United States, the BCIS will conclude that you had the preconceived intent of studying in the United States when you applied for a tourist visa from the American Embassy. Your failure to reveal your actual reason for going to the United States when you first requested a visa would be considered to be fraud. Since your intention was to study, you should have applied for the proper student visa (or at least explained that your reason for traveling was to look at possible schools, and had a "prospective student" notation made in your tourist visa). Your only hope to obtain a student visa after being accused of such misrepresentation would be to return to your country and apply for a student visa all over again.

If, however, you have told the American Consul that you were planning to go to college but had not yet selected a particular college to attend, your visitor's visa would have noted this. This is a policy of most Consular Offices. You would also be allowed to change your status—that is, apply for student status—in the United States.

## D. WHAT TO DO IF YOUR APPLICATION IS DENIED

If the BCIS denies your request for an extension of your stay in the U.S., you could contest the denial and attempt to show that you required a different visa because you have a true change of heart that only happened after arriving here. This can involve complicated legal rules that will require you to get help from an experienced immigration lawyer. (See Chapter 31. )

You may simply have to leave the U.S. and apply for a new visa from overseas. This is far safer that staying in the U.S. illegally.

## E. TIPS ON FILLING OUT FORM I-539

On Part 4 of Form I-539, Additional Information, Questions 3a through f may act as time bombs if you answer "yes" to any one of them—that is, they may explode and prove fatal to your application. A denial of your application means that your authorized stay will be limited to the time given when you first entered the country.

Do not lie and misrepresent your answer as "no" when the truthful answer is "yes." But if you have to answer yes to any of these six questions, it is best to consult with an immigration lawyer or other experienced immigration professional.

EXAMPLE: The first question on this part of the form is: Are you or any other person included in this application an applicant for an immigrant visa or adjustment of status to permanent residence? Do not answer "no" if your U.S. citizen brother filed a relative visa petition for you ten years ago and your immigrant visa is still pending. In all probability, the BCIS would find out your fraudulent answer and you might never get your green card as a result.

---

### DO NOT BRING THIS BOOK WITH YOU

Because this book tells you how to stay and work legally in the United States, you should not have it—or any other book about immigrating to the U.S.—with you when you enter the United States on a tourist or other nonimmigrant visa.

If the border officials suspect that you are not a bona fide tourist, they may detain and question you at the airport or border about your purpose in coming to the United States.

The theory of preconceived intent once again rears its ugly head. The fact that you have this book in hand may create the impression that you deceived the American consul into believing that you wished to be a temporary visitor when you had actually intended to stay permanently in the United States.

For the same reason, you should not board the plane with letters from your Aunt Mary or cousin John stating that employment has been arranged for you as soon as you arrive in the United States, a wedding dress or a stack of resumes. Should the border officials find such things when you land, you will not be admitted as a tourist; you may, in fact, be sent back to your home country without being allowed to set foot outside the airport of your port of entry in the United States.

If the border offficials do question your intention of entering the country as a tourist, they can exclude you from the U.S., require you to return home immediately and refuse to let you return to the U.S. for five years.

## APPLICATION FOR REPLACEMENT/INITIAL NONIMMIGRANT ARRIVAL-DEPARTURE DOCUMENT, SAMPLE FORM I-102

OMB No. 1615-0079; Exp. 2/29/04

### I-102, Application for Replacement/Initial Nonimmigrant Arrival - Departure Document

**U.S. Department of Homeland Security**
Bureau of Citizehsip and Immigration Services

**START HERE - Please Type or Print**

**FOR BCIS USE ONLY**

### Part 1. Information about you.

| Family Name | Given Name | Middle Name |
|---|---|---|
| Khanmohammad | Parirokh | Jamal |

**Address** - In care of -
Hossein Lofti

| Street Number and Name | Apt./Suite # |
|---|---|
| 17241 Fulton Street | 101 |

| City | State or Province | Zip/Postal Code | Country |
|---|---|---|---|
| New York | NY | 10038 | U.S.A |

| Date of Birth (mm/dd/yyyy) | Country of Birth |
|---|---|
| Sept. 24, 1966 | France |

| Social Security # (if any) | A # (if any) |
|---|---|
| None | None |

| Date of Last Admission (mm/dd/yyyy) | Expires on (mm/dd/yyyy) |
|---|---|
| 8/27/2003 | 11/26/2003 |

| Current Nonimmigrant Status | I-94, Arrival/Departure Document # |
|---|---|
| B1 | 112 113 124 |

**For BCIS Use Only:** Returned, Receipt, Date, Resubmitted, Date, Reloc Sent, Date, Reloc Rec'd, Date, Date. ☐ Applicant Interviewed on ____. New I-94 #. Action Block.

### Part 2. Application type. (check one)

a. ☑ I am applying to replace my lost or stolen Form I-94 (I-94W).
b. ☐ I am applying to replace my lost or stolen Form I-95.
c. ☐ I am applying to replace Form I-94 because it is mutilated. I have attached my original I-94.
d. ☐ I am applying to replace Form I-95 because it is mutilated. I have attached my original I-95.
e. ☐ I was not issued a Form I-94 when I entered as a nonimmigrant, and I am filing this application together with an application for an extension of stay/change of status.
f. ☐ I was not issued a Form I-94 when I entered as a nonimmigrant member of the military and I am filing this application for an initial Form I-94.
g. ☐ I was issued a Form I-94 or Form I-95 with incorrect information, and I am requesting the BCIS to correct the document.

### Part 3. Processing information.

Are you filing this application with any other petition or application?
☐ No  ☑ Yes - Form # I-539

Are you now in removal proceedings?
☑ No  ☐ Yes (Attach an explanation on a separate sheet of paper.)

If you are unable to provide the original of your Form I-94, give the following information:

| Class of Admission: | B1 | Place of Admission: | Newark, NJ |
|---|---|---|---|

Your name exactly as it appears on Form I-94 or I-95, if known
Parirokh J. Khanmohammad

**To Be Completed By Attorney or Representative, if any.**
☐ Fill in box if G-28 is attached to represent the applicant.
ATTY State License #

### Part 4. Signature.
Read the information on penalties in the instructions before completing this section. You must file this application while in the United States.

I certify, under penalty of perjury under the laws of the United States of America, that this application and the evidence submitted with it is all true and correct. I authorize the release of any information from my records which the Bureau of Citizenship and Immigration Services needs to determine eligibility for the benefit I am seeking.

| Signature | Daytime Telephone Number (with area code) | Date (mm/dd/yyyy) |
|---|---|---|
| Parirokh J. Khanmohammad | 212-555-1212 | 09/19/2003 |

### Part 5. Signature of person preparing form, if other than above. (Sign below)

I declare that I prepared this application at the request of the above person and it is based on all information of which I have knowledge.

| Signature | Print or Type Your Name | Fax Number (if any) | Date (MM/DD/YYYY) |
|---|---|---|---|

Firm Name and Address | Daytime Telephone Number (with area code)

Form I-102 Form (Rev. 04/04/03)N (Prior versions may be used until 09/30/03)

**APPLICATION TO EXTEND/CHANGE NONIMMIGRANT STATUS, SAMPLE FORM I-539**

---

**U.S. Department of Justice**
Immigration and Naturalization Service

OMB No. 1115-0093; Expires 7/31/04

## Application to Extend/Change Nonimmigrant Status

**START HERE - Please Type or Print.**　　　　　　　　　　**FOR INS USE ONLY**

### Part 1.　Information about you.

| | | |
|---|---|---|
| Family Name　Martino | Given Name　Tony | Middle Initial　F. |

Address -
In care of - Antero Martino

| Street Number and Name　3746 81st St. | Apt. #　2D |
|---|---|

| City　Jackson Heights | State　NY | Zip Code　11372 | Daytime Phone #　718-555-1212 |
|---|---|---|---|

| Country of Birth　Philippines | Country of Citizenship　Philippines |
|---|---|

| Date of Birth (MM/DD/YYYY)　Aug. 2, 1969 | Social Security # (if any)　None | A # (if any)　None |
|---|---|---|

| Date of Last Arrival Into the U.S.　Feb. 5, 2003 | I-94 #　334533908 03 |
|---|---|

| Current Nonimmigrant Status　B-2 | Expires on (MM/DD/YYYY)　Aug. 4, 2003 |
|---|---|

**FOR INS USE ONLY**

| Returned | Receipt |
|---|---|
| Date | |
| Resubmitted | |
| Date | |
| Reloc Sent | |
| Date | |
| Reloc Rec'd | |
| Date | |

### Part 2. Application type. *(See instructions for fee.)*

1. I am applying for: *(Check one.)*
   a. ☑ An extension of stay in my current status.
   b. ☐ A change of status. The new status I am requesting is: _____
   c. ☐ Other: *(Describe grounds of eligibility.)* _____
2. Number of people included in this application: *(Check one.)*
   a. ☐ I am the only applicant.
   b. ☑ Members of my family are filing this application with me.
      The total number of people (including me) in the application is: __2__
      *(Complete the supplement for each co-applicant.)*

☐ Applicant Interviewed on _____ Date

☐ *Extension Granted to (Date):* _____

*Change of Status/Extension Granted*
New Class: From *(Date):* _____
_____ To *(Date):* _____

### Part 3. Processing information.

1. I/We request that my/our current or requested status be extended until (MM/DD/YYYY): January 15, 2004
2. Is this application based on an extension or change of status already granted to your spouse, child or parent?
   ☑ No ☐ Yes, Receipt # _____
3. Is this application based on a separate petition or application to give your spouse, child or parent an extension or change of status? ☑ No ☐ Yes, filed with this I-539.
   ☐ Yes, filed previously and pending with INS. INS receipt number: _____
4. If you answered "Yes" to Question 3, give the name of the petitioner or applicant:

   | |
   |---|
   | |

   If the petition or application is pending with INS, also give the following information:

   | Office filed at _____ | Filed on (MM/DD/YYYY) _____ |
   |---|---|

If Denied:
☐ Still within period of stay
☐ S/D to: _____
☐ Place under docket control

**Remarks:**

**Action Block**

### Part 4. Additional information.

1. For applicant #1, provide passport information:
   Country of Issuance　Philippines
   Valid to: (MM/DD/YYYY)　Jan. 16, 2005
2. Foreign Address: Street Number and Name　66 Felix Manalo St.　Apt. #

| City or Town　Cubao, Quezon City | State or Province |
|---|---|

| Country　Philippines | Zip/Postal Code　1111 |
|---|---|

**To be Completed by**
***Attorney or Representative,* if any**

☐ Fill in box if G-28 is attached to represent the applicant.

ATTY State License # 

Form I-539 (Rev. 09/04/01)N *Prior versions may be used until 3/30/02*

## SAMPLE FORM I-539 (PAGE 2)

### Part 4. Additional information.

| 3. Answer the following questions. If you answer "Yes" to any question, explain on separate sheet of paper. | Yes | No |
|---|---|---|
| a. Are you, or any other person included on the application, an applicant for an immigrant visa? | | ✔ |
| b. Has an immigrant petition ever been filed for you or for any other person included in this application? | | ✔ |
| c. Has a Form I-485, Application to Register Permanent Residence or Adjust Status, ever been filed by you or by any other person included in this application? | | ✔ |
| d. Have you, or any other person included in this application, ever been arrested or convicted of any criminal offense since last entering the U.S.? | | ✔ |
| e. Have you, or any other person included in this application, done anything that violated the terms of the nonimmigrant status you now hold? | | ✔ |
| f. Are you, or any other person included in this application, now in removal proceedings? | | ✔ |
| g. Have you, or any other person included in this application, been employed in the U.S. since last admitted or granted an extension or change of status? | | ✔ |

- If you answered "Yes" to Question 3f, give the following information concerning the removal proceedings on the attached page entitled "**Part 4. Additional information. Page for answers to 3f and 3g.**" Include the name of the person in removal proceedings and information on jurisdiction, date proceedings began and status of proceedings.
- If you answered "No" to Question 3g, fully describe how you are supporting yourself on the attached page entitled "**Part 4. Additional information. Page for answers to 3f and 3g.**" Include the source, amount and basis for any income.
- If you answered "Yes" to Question 3g, fully describe the employment on the attached page entitled "**Part 4. Additional information. Page for answers to 3f and 3g.**" Include the name of the person employed, name and address of the employer, weekly income and whether the employment was specifically authorized by INS.

### Part 5. Signature. (*Read the information on penalties in the instructions before completing this section. You must file this application while in the United States.*)

I certify, under penalty of perjury under the laws of the United States of America, that this application and the evidence submitted with it is all true and correct. I authorize the release of any information from my records which the Immigration and Naturalization Service needs to determine eligibility for the benefit I am seeking.

| Signature *Tony F. Martino* | Print your Name Tony F. Martino | Date 6/29/03 |
|---|---|---|

*Please note: If you do not completely fill out this form, or fail to submit required documents listed in the instructions, you may not be found eligible for the requested benefit and this application will have to be denied.*

### Part 6. Signature of person preparing form, if other than above. (*Sign below.*)

I declare that I prepared this application at the request of the above person and it is based on all information of which I have knowledge.

| Signature | Print your Name | Date |
|---|---|---|
| Firm Name and Address | Daytime Phone Number (Area Code and Number) | |
| | Fax Number (Area Code and Number) | |

**(Please remember to enclose the mailing label with your application.)**

Form I-539 (Rev. 09/04/01)N - *Prior editions may be used through 03/30/02:* Page 2

## SAMPLE FORM I-539 (PAGE 3)

**Part 4.  Additional information.  Page for answers to 3f and 3g.**

**If you answered "Yes" to Question 3f** in Part 4 on page 3 of this form, give the following information concerning the removal proceedings. Include the name of the person in removal proceedings and information on jurisdiction, date proceedings began and status of procedings.

**If you answered "No" to Question 3g** in Part 4 on page 3 of this form, fully describe how you are supporting yourself.  Include the source, amount and basis for any income.

My brother, Antero Martino, will provide my lodging and other support. See attached Form I-134 Affidavit of Support.

**If you answered "Yes" to Question 3g** in Part 4 on page 3 of this form, fully describe the employment.  Include the name of the person employed, name and address of the employer, weekly income and whether the employment was specifically authorized by INS.

## SAMPLE SUPPLEMENT TO FORM I-539

**Supplement -1**
**Attach to Form I-539 when more than one person is included in the petition or application.**
*(List each person separately. Do not include the person named in the form.)*

| Family Name | Martino | Given Name | Eduardo | Middle Name | L. | Date of Birth (MM/DD/YYYY) | Dec. 1, 1991 |
|---|---|---|---|---|---|---|---|
| Country of Birth | Philippines | Country of Citizenship | Philippines | Social Security # (if any) | None | A # (if any) | None |
| Date of Arrival (MM/DD/YYYY) | Feb 5, 2003 | | | I-94 # | 334 533 909 03 | | |
| Current Nonimmigrant Status: | B-2 | | | Expires On (MM/DD/YYYY) | Aug. 4, 2003 | | |
| Country Where Passport Issued | Philippines | | | Expiration Date (MM/DD/YYYY) | March 8, 2006 | | |

| Family Name | Martino | Given Name | Miranda | Middle Name | C. | Date of Birth (MM/DD/YYYY) | April 2, 1967 |
|---|---|---|---|---|---|---|---|
| Country of Birth | Philippines | Country of Citizenship | Philippines | Social Security # (if any) | None | A # (if any) | None |
| Date of Arrival (MM/DD/YYYY) | Aug. 4, 2003 | | | I-94 # | 334 533 910 03 | | |
| Current Nonimmigrant Status: | B-2 | | | Expires On (MM/DD/YYYY) | Aug. 4, 2003 | | |
| Country Where Passport Issued | Philippines | | | Expiration Date (MM/DD/YYYY) | Jan 16, 2005 | | |

| Family Name | | Given Name | | Middle Name | | Date of Birth (MM/DD/YYYY) | |
|---|---|---|---|---|---|---|---|
| Country of Birth | | Country of Citizenship | | Social Security # (if any) | | A # (if any) | |
| Date of Arrival (MM/DD/YYYY) | | | | I-94 # | | | |
| Current Nonimmigrant Status: | | | | Expires On (MM/DD/YYYY) | | | |
| Country Where Passport Issued | | | | Expiration Date (MM/DD/YYYY) | | | |

| Family Name | | Given Name | | Middle Name | | Date of Birth (MM/DD/YYYY) | |
|---|---|---|---|---|---|---|---|
| Country of Birth | | Country of Citizenship | | Social Security # (if any) | | A # (if any) | |
| Date of Arrival (MM/DD/YYYY) | | | | I-94 # | | | |
| Current Nonimmigrant Status: | | | | Expires On (MM/DD/YYYY) | | | |
| Country Where Passport Issued | | | | Expiration Date (MM/DD/YYYY) | | | |

| Family Name | | Given Name | | Middle Name | | Date of Birth (MM/DD/YYYY) | |
|---|---|---|---|---|---|---|---|
| Country of Birth | | Country of Citizenship | | Social Security # (if any) | | A # (if any) | |
| Date of Arrival (MM/DD/YYYY) | | | | I-94 # | | | |
| Current Nonimmigrant Status: | | | | Expires On (MM/DD/YYYY) | | | |
| Country Where Passport Issued | | | | Expiration Date (MM/DD/YYYY) | | | |

**If you need additional space, attach a separate sheet(s) of paper.**
*Place your name, A # if any, date of birth, form number and application date at the top of the sheet(s) of paper.*

**4**

•••••••••••••

# GETTING A GREEN CARD

## But, It Isn't Even Green!

---

The official name for the green card is the Alien Registration Receipt Card. It has been called a green card because, when it was first introduced in the 1940s, the color of the plastic identification card with the alien's photo, registration number, date of birth and date and port of entry was green.

The card was blue in the 1960s through the 1970s. In the 1980s, the government changed it to white. In the 1990s, it has become pink. Even so, this sought-after plastic card continues to be called the green card.

### Front of New-Style Card

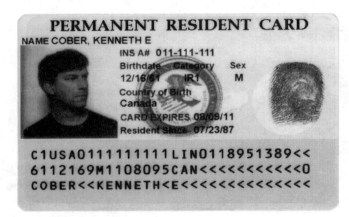

### Back of Old-Style Card

Once you have a green card, you can go in and out of the United States. So it serves as your entry document and your identity document for employment.

There are several ways an alien can obtain a green card—that is, become a lawful permanent resident. The most popular ones are through family and work. However, there are a number of other ways, such as proving that you're fleeing from persecution, making large investments or others.

## A. FAMILY-BASED RELATIONSHIPS

Recognizing that the family is important in the life of the nation, the U.S. Congress has created ways for family members to be reunited with their relatives who are U.S. citizens or lawful permanent residents.

### 1. Related or engaged to a U.S. citizen

If you are the spouse, child, brother or sister or parent of, or if you are engaged to be married to, a U.S. citizen, you can become a lawful permanent resident if the person to whom you're related or engaged files a petition with the BCIS or the U.S. Embassy of your country of residence.

If you are the widow or the widower of an American citizen with whom you have lived for at least two years, you can petition for a green card for yourself, provided you file the application within two years of the death of your spouse.

For more information, see Chapters 5 through 7.

### 2. Related to a lawful permanent resident

If you are the spouse or unmarried child of a lawful permanent resident, you can obtain a green card if the relative who has the green card files a petition with the BCIS or the U.S. Embassy of your country of residence. However, you won't get it right away, as explained in Chapter 5.

### 3. Other relatives

If you are the aunt, uncle, niece, nephew, cousin, grandmother or grandfather of an American citizen, or if you are the brother, sister, parent, or fiancé of someone who holds a green card, you do not qualify for a green card based on a "family relationship." Understandably, the U.S. Congress had to draw the line on what constitutes a family for the purpose of immigration.

## B. EMPLOYMENT-BASED RELATIONSHIPS

If you do not have a close family member who is an American citizen or who holds a green card, you may be able to obtain a green card through a job offer from an employer in the United States—as either a priority or a non-priority worker.

### 1. Priority workers

Because it appears that the United States may chronically lack a sufficient number of skilled professionals, Congress created a new immigration classification in the Immigration Act of 1990: priority workers.

Priority workers are people with extraordinary ability (such as an internationally known artist), or outstanding professors and researchers or multinational executives and managers.

Such highly skilled aliens are not required to go through the difficult labor certification process by which the Department of Labor determines that there are no Americans or lawful permanent residents available and willing to do the job for which the immigrating alien wishes to apply.

For more information, see Chapter 15.

### 2. Non-priority workers

Other aliens who seek employment in the United States need certification from the Department of Labor to obtain green cards. (This process is described in Chapter 18, Section B.)

Congress was able to meet the objections of the labor unions by keeping this requirement of labor certification for the other groups of alien workers and by giving the unions the right to notify the Labor Department that an American or permanent resident is available, willing and able to do the work of the alien. In this way, both the unions and the aliens are given the opportunity to safeguard their interests.

As long as this requirement is met, applicants who have graduate degrees in the arts or sciences or a profession (such as lawyers), or those with a master's degree in business administration (MBA), or those having a bachelor's degree plus five years of specialized experience equal to a graduate degree, are eligible for immigrant visas.

But the Department of Labor also requires businesses that need ordinary professionals (without graduate degrees), or skilled or unskilled workers (factory workers, plumbers, domestic workers, carpenters) to apply for labor certification.

For more information, see Chapters 16 through 18.

### BE READY TO WAIT

It may take you a long time to become a permanent resident under some of the immigrant visa categories described in this book. Once you file under any of these categories it will be very difficult for you to come to the United States as a tourist or other nonimmigrant or be able to have your status as a nonimmigrant extended.

The only groups who need not be concerned with this warning are diplomats (A visas), employees of international organizations (G visas), intracompany transferees (L-1 or L-2) or workers in specialty occupations that require a baccalaureate degree or its equivalent (H-1B).

In order to immigrate to the United States at some time in the future, you must choose one or more of the immigration categories. You must understand, though, that applying for a green card might prevent you from entering the United States while you wait for your permanent visa.

## C. ENTREPRENEUR IMMIGRANTS

An alien entrepreneur from any country who invests at least one million dollars in a business (or $500,000 if the business is in an economically depressed area) and who employs at least ten American citizens or lawful permanent residents is eligible for a green card. Each year, 10,000 immigrant visas are set aside for this millionaire immigrant category, which is designed to create employment. (See Chapter 20.)

The legislators evidently intended to attract wealthy investors, particularly from Asia and the Middle East. Canada and Australia, among other countries, have had successful programs of this kind for several years now.

## D. SPECIAL IMMIGRANTS

Certain categories of people may obtain a green card by special laws—in addition to certain provisions of the Immigration Act of 1990—intended to benefit limited groups. These include, for example:

- Priests, nuns, pastors, ministers, rabbis, imams and other workers of recognized religious denominations. (See Chapter 19.)

- Former employees of the U.S. government, commended by the U.S. Secretary of State for having performed outstanding service to the government for at least 15 years. (See Chapter 19.)
- Medical doctors who have been licensed in the United States and have worked and lived in the United States since January 1978. (See Chapter 19.)

## E. ASYLUM AND REFUGEE STATUS

Political refugees and asylees who can prove that they fled their country for fear of persecution owing to their race, religion, nationality, membership in a particular social or political group, or political opinions, may apply for green cards even though they are not strictly defined as immigrants. A person who gains U.S. government approval as a refugee or asylee can apply for permanent residence status one year after being admitted to the United States as a refugee or one year after their petition for asylee status is granted. There is no yearly quota or limit on the number of refugees who can be granted permanent residency. But only 10,000 asylees each year can obtain permanent residency.

Since the number of asylees applying for permanent residence is currently over 10,000, there is a waiting list.

(For more information on applying for refugee or asylee status, see Chapter 21.)

## F. AMNESTIES

Once in a while, Congress gives blanket green card eligibility to people who have been living in the United States illegally. Recent amnesties have covered:

- Aliens who applied for amnesty under the Immigration Reform and Control Act of 1986—having been in the United States out of status since January 1, 1982. Their spouses and unmarried children under 21 years of age were also eligible to become permanent residents.
- Nicaraguans, Cubans, Guatemalans, El Salvadorans and certain Eastern Europeans, under the NACARA law (see Chapter 24).

While the deadline for both these amnesties have passed, many people's cases are still being decided by the BCIS and the courts. ■

# 5

## QUOTA SYSTEMS AND PREFERENCE CATEGORIES

### Waiting for the Green Card

I filed the papers for my brother five years ago. Why is it taking so long for the U.S. Embassy in India to give him his immigrant visa?

My ten-year-old daughter was born in Hawaii, where I was a graduate student at the University of Hawaii. Since she is an American citizen, can I get a green card by having her claim me as her mother?

Three years ago, I sponsored our live-in domestic help who comes from St. Vincent. She is still waiting for her green card. What is the problem?

These questions are often asked by people who may have expected some delay in getting their green cards, but who can't believe how many years it's taking.

The cause of many long delays in being lawfully admitted to the U.S. lies in the quotas imposed by the immigration laws. These quotas determine how many immigrants worldwide, as well as how many aliens from a particular country, can be given immigrant visas every year. You cannot get a visa until your "Priority Date," that is the date when your relative or employer first filed a petition for you, appears on the State Department's chart.

The Immigration Act of 1990 increased the current worldwide annual quota of immigrants to 675,000 yearly. The Act of 1990 also increased the country quota of immigrants to the U.S. to 25,620 visas annually. Still, the demand is greater than the supply. Naturally, immigrants from countries with huge numbers of applicants have to wait longer than those in countries with substantially fewer applicants.

**EXAMPLE:** Because the demand for immigrant visas from mainland China, India, Korea, Mexico, the Philippines, the Dominican Republic and Hong Kong is so far over the quota allowed to them each year, applicants from these countries may have to wait longer—from two years to 15 years—than those from countries with a smaller number of immigrant visa applicants, such as Great Britain, France or Brazil—where the wait is from three months to ten years, depending on the category.

## A. Immediate Relatives of Americans: No Waiting

Immigrant visas are immediately available for one group of eligible aliens: Immediate Relatives of American citizens. They have the highest priority in immigration law because of the congressional intent to encourage families of U.S. citizens to live together and stay together.

Members of this group have only to wait two to 12 months for their green cards, depending on the number of applications at the U.S. Embassy or the Bureau of Citizenship and Immigration Services (BCIS, formerly called the INS).

For purposes of immigration law, you are the Immediate Relative and eligible for an immigrant visa without waiting if you are:
- the husband or wife of a U.S. citizen
- the parents of a U.S. citizen, if the citizen is at least 21 years of age
- children under 21 years of age (including stepchildren and children adopted before they reach the age of 16) of a U.S. citizen, or
- the widow or widower of a U.S. citizen who died after living with you for at least two years.

## B. Relatives in Preference Categories: Longer Waits

The Immigration Act of 1990 modified the classification of intending immigrants into several major groupings, as discussed in Chapter 4. The first two major groups—the family-based and the employment-based immigrant visas—have their own preference categories.

### 1. Family-based preferences

In all family-based preference categories, petitions from U.S. citizens generally have higher priority than those of lawful permanent residents.

**Family First Preference: unmarried sons or daughters of U.S. citizens.** The children must be either 21 years old or older and not married—meaning either single, divorced or widowed. A son or daughter who is under 21 years old and not married would be classified as an Immediate Relative. A maximum of 23,400 immigrant visas are now available worldwide for the Family First Preference category, reduced from the previous quota of 54,000 visas given yearly. A longer waiting period for this group of relatives should therefore be expected—from one to nine years, depending on how many people apply in one country under this preference.

**Family Second Preference: spouses and unmarried children of permanent residents.** This category includes:

- husbands and wives of a lawful permanent resident and their unmarried children who are under 21 years old (category 2A), and
- unmarried (meaning single, divorced or widowed) sons or daughters (over 21 years old) of a lawful permanent resident (category 2B, which waits somewhat longer than category 2A).

A total of 114,200 immigrant visas worldwide are given to Second Preference aliens. However, 77% (87,934) of the total is intended for the spouses and minor children of green cardholders (2As), while 23% (26,266) of the total is meant for the unmarried children over 21 years of age (2Bs).

**Family Third Preference: married sons and daughters of U.S. citizens.** This category provides a fall-back position if an unmarried son or daughter in the Family First Preference category gets married before entering the U.S. as a lawful permanent resident. Only 23,400 visas worldwide are made available every year for married sons and daughters of U.S. citizens. Therefore, there may be a considerable wait—up to ten years—for those who come from countries in which many immigrants in the category are waiting.

**Family Fourth Preference: brothers and sisters of U.S. citizens.** The brother or sister of a U.S. citizen has to wait until the American sibling turns 21 years of age before a petition can be filed for the alien brother or sister. A total of 65,000 visas worldwide are available each year for this category. The waiting list is always very long, from ten to 24 years.

## 2. Employment-based preferences

Employment-based preferences are also built on a system in which a limited number of visas are given to a specific group of aliens each year. Most employment-based aliens must obtain Labor Certification—a complex procedure in which the Department of Labor verifies that no American worker is available and qualified to take the job. (See Chapter 18, Section B.)

**Employment First Preference: people of extraordinary ability in science, art, education, business or athletics, and outstanding professors, researchers and multinational executives and managers.** A total of 40,000 immigrant visas are allocated

each year for this group of employment-based aliens who are exempt from Labor Certification. (See Chapter 15.)

**Employment Second Preference: professionals with advanced degrees or people of exceptional ability in science, arts or business.** Forty thousand immigrant visas, including visas not used by the Employment First Preference group for the year, are set aside for this category. Most need Labor Certification for the visa. (See Chapter 16.) However, people in some occupations are considered "pre-certified" and do not need individual Labor Certification. The Department of Labor generally grants this exemption to those whose occupation serves the national interest. Employers of workers who are pre-certified may file permanent residence papers directly with the BCIS.

**Employment Third Preference: skilled and unskilled workers, recently graduated professionals and those with a bachelor's degree.** A total of 40,000 immigrant visas—10,000 of which are for unskilled workers—plus the unused visas from the First and Second Preference groups are available every year for this group of employment-based applicants. They also need Labor Certification. (See Chapter 17.)

**Employment Fourth Preference: special and religious workers.** This group, given 10,000 visas yearly, includes religious workers of an affiliate organization in the United States. Ministers, pastors, rabbis, ayatollahs, nuns and lay people involved in religious work are also included. No Labor Certification is needed for this group. (See Chapter 19.)

**Employment Fifth Preference: entrepreneurs.** The millionaire immigrant or alien entrepreneur category is given its own quota of 10,000 immigrant visas. Immigrants do not need Labor Certification to apply for this category. (See Chapter 20.)

## C. How Long Must You Wait?

If you belong to a preference category in which there are many hopeful immigrants waiting—for example, in Mexico, there are 60,000 brothers and sisters of U.S. citizens on file—you may have to wait several years for your immigrant visa number.

If, during these years, you want to come to the United States as a nonimmigrant—as a tourist, businessperson, student or official of your government's Foreign Service Department—the U.S. Embassy in your country will probably not approve your application for a nonimmigrant visa. This is because you already have an application on file for an immigrant visa. The U.S. government interprets that filing as a statement that you intend to live permanently in the United States.

Of course, there are exceptions to every rule. If you can convince the U.S. Consul that you will not remain illegally in the United States waiting for your immigrant visa number to come up, and that you will return to your country once the period of your nonimmigrant stay is over, you may be granted a nonimmigrant visa. Also, spouses of U.S. citizens may qualify for the newly expanded "K" visa. And even if you've already lived illegally in the U.S., if you're the spouse or minor child of a permanent resident, and have already waited three years for a green card, you may qualify for the new "V" visa.

However, people with certain temporary work statuses (H and L visas) need not worry about this happening to them. Although they may have an approved visa petition by reason of their American spouse, child, parent, brother or sister or a lawful permanent resident spouse or parent, the U.S. Embassy is supposed to issue them an H or L visa if they qualify for that nonimmigrant visa, while waiting for their Priority Date to arrive.

If you are not in the Immediate Relative category, you can track when your application is likely to be processed if you pay special attention to the Priority Date and the cut-off date that apply to your visa application.

## 1. The Priority Date

The Priority Date is the date on which your relative filed a petition for you with the BCIS (or INS as it was formerly called) or with the U.S. Embassy, or the date your employer filed an application for you with the Department of Labor.

It is very important to keep the receipt of the fee paid to the BCIS and the registered mail return receipt card from the post office. The date on the BCIS receipt is the Priority Date of your application or petition. That date should also be shown on your approval notice, which is the next piece of paper you'll get from the BCIS—and which is even more important to keep.

The Department of State keeps careful count of how many immigrant visas are issued for each country in each Preference category. If the quota has been reached in one category before the fiscal year is over (in October), the Department will not issue any immigrant visas in that category for the rest of the fiscal year and will, in addition, state that visas are temporarily unavailable for that category, either for a particular country or worldwide.

October 1 of each year marks the beginning of another fiscal year for the federal government—and the count of the immigrant visas issued begins all over again for each country in each Preference category.

## 2. Visa cut-off date

Each month, the Department of State issues a *Visa Bulletin,* which sets out the immigrant visa cut-off date of each preference.

The cut-off date simply announces which Priority Dates in each category are being processed by the Department of State for issuance of an immigrant visa. Anyone whose Priority Date falls before this cut-off date will be given an appointment within a few months if they're overseas, or will be allowed to submit the next part of their application if they're in the U.S. and eligible to "adjust status" there. Anyone whose Priority Date falls after the cut-off date will have to wait.

**EXAMPLE:** You were born in Poland. Your brother, who is a naturalized American citizen, filed a petition for you on August 2, 1991, which becomes your Priority Date.

You are in the Fourth Preference category. The *Visa Bulletin* of July 2003 is processing those with a Priority Date of on or before August 15, 1991. Your appointment for your immigrant visa is currently available.

However, if you were from another country, the waiting period could be longer. For example:

| If born in | Your 4th Preference Priority Date is | What was being processed in July 2003 |
| --- | --- | --- |
| India | August 2, 1991 | March 22, 1990 |
| Mexico | August 2, 1991 | August 15, 1991 |
| Philippines | August 2, 1991 | February 1, 1981 |

The cut-off dates announced in the *Visa Bulletin* may not change much from one month to the next, depending on how many petitions have been filed during the same month. A cut-off date may move one week for one preference and two weeks for another preference every month, or it may not move at all for several months in your category. Be prepared to wait.

The *Visa Bulletin* is normally available in each embassy or consulate, or in the BCIS office. You can also call the Department of State in Washington, D.C., at 202-663-1541 for a tape-recorded message which gives the cut-off dates for each preference category being processed that month. You should have a copy of the *Visa Bulletin* when you call so you can keep track of what is being said. Or, visit the State Department website at www.state.gov. Under "Travel and Living Abroad," click "More," then "Visa Bulletins."

## D. SHIFTING PREFERENCE CATEGORIES

A special rule applies to family-based immigrant visas, which allows applicants to convert Priority Dates if they change from one preference category to another.

If you belong to one family preference, and some event (marriage, divorce, death of spouse or the simple passage of time) places you in a different preference category, your original Priority Date may remain unchanged—even if you have become eligible for a different preference.

---

### PETITIONS THAT AUTOMATICALLY CONVERT TO OTHERS BUT RETAIN THE ORIGINAL PRIORITY DATE

- Marriage of the son or daughter (over 21 years old) of U.S. citizen—changes First to Third Preference.
- Marriage of child (under 21 years old) of U.S. citizen—changes from Immediate Relative to Third Preference.
- Divorce of child or son or daughter—changes Third Preference to Immediate Relative or First Preference, depending on child's age at divorce.
- Naturalization of legal resident petitioner—changes Second Preference to Immediate Relative (if applicant is under 21 years old) or First Preference (if applicant is over 21 years old).
- Child of lawful permanent resident reaching age 21 before Priority Date becomes current—drops from category 2A to category 2B of the Second Preference. However, if the child reaches age 21 after his Priority Date has become current but before he has actually been approved for permanent residency, he can retain his 2A status as long as he applies within one year of the Priority Date having become current. (This represents a change in the law, as of 2002—formerly such children would have also dropped into category 2B, simply by virtue of not having received their approval on time, and therefore had to wait longer.)

---

### PETITIONS THAT ARE PROTECTED FROM CONVERSION

The Child Status Protection Act of 2002 allows certain children of U.S. citizens and permanent residents to retain their original visa eligibility even if they turn 21 while they're waiting for the process to finish up. (Formerly, turning 21 would have automatically dropped them into a lower preference category and caused them to have to wait longer for their visa or green card.) Those who benefit include:

- Children of U.S. citizens—will retain Immediate Relative status even if they turn 21 at any time after a visa petition has been filed on their behalf.
- Children of lawful permanent residents—will retain 2A status if they turn 21 after their Priority Date has become current, so long as they file for a green card within one year of becoming current.

---

These rules may sound technical and a little hard to follow, but because they can make a big difference in how quickly your application is processed, it is worth your time to understand which rules apply to your situation.

**EXAMPLE:** Your mother, a permanent resident, filed a Family Second Preference petition for you as her unmarried son on February 10, 1989. But she has recently been naturalized as an American citizen, so you could now move into the Family First Preference as the unmarried son of an American citizen. If the visa cut-off date for the Family First Preference is closer to your Priority Date than the cut-off date for the Family Second Preference, you are eligible to receive your immigration visa more quickly than if you remained in your Second Preference status.

**EXAMPLE:** A visa application is filed for the teenaged daughter of a U.S. citizen. When she turns 21 and her priority date has not yet become current, she moves into the First Preference but keeps the Priority Date assigned to the Immediate Relative petition filed by her American parent.

You must always call to the attention of the American Embassy or the BCIS this conversion of your preference category and your right to keep your old Priority Date. Write a letter with copies of the documents to prove your change of preference category. Enclose a copy of your previously approved petition to show your old Priority Date.

## E. Revocation of a Petition or Application

Here is a bit of scary information, but it's better to know it than not to know: After a petition or application has been filed on behalf of an alien, it can be revoked or canceled—even if it has already been approved by the INS or BCIS. This is usually based on a change in circumstances that makes the immigrant no longer eligible, but it can also be based on fraud.

The BCIS may revoke a petition if, for example:

- the person who filed the petition decides to withdraw it and informs the BCIS of this decision, or
- the person who filed the petition dies. However, the BCIS may decide not to revoke the petition if it is convinced that there are "humanitarian reasons" not to do so. (See Section E3, below.)

### 1. Revocations in family-based preferences

In preference categories that depend on marriage, if there is a divorce or annulment before the green card is approved, the BCIS will revoke the petition for the alien spouse.

If, in the case of the Family Second Preference, the unmarried son or daughter gets married before receiving a green card in the United States, the petition is automatically revoked.

---

**SPECIAL RULES FOR WIDOWS AND WIDOWERS**

If the beneficiary is the spouse of an American citizen, and the couple was married for at least two years, the petition will be granted as long as the widowed beneficiary applies within two years of the spouse's death and has not remarried.

---

### 2. Revocations in employment-based preferences

In the employment-based preferences, a petition will be automatically revoked if:

- either the employer or the alien dies
- the employer goes out of business
- the employer withdraws the petition

- the business is bought out by another company, unless the new company assumes all of the assets and liabilities of the company that petitioned
- the alien is no longer interested in the position—unless the petitioner requests substitution of another person, or
- there has been some fraud or misrepresentation in the process, such as an invalid Labor Certification.

### 3. Exception to the revocation rule

Consider this scenario: A permanent resident mother has brought all her children to the United States except her eldest son, who marries before she could petition for him. After five years, she becomes a naturalized American citizen and immediately files a petition for her married son, still living in the foreign country. The petition is approved, but before the son and his family come to the United States, the mother dies. The petition is automatically revoked and the son remains separated from his brothers and sisters, who have been living in the United States since their mother received her green card.

That application of the regulations seems cruel.

It is precisely for such cases that the regulations have been somewhat liberalized. The beneficiary of a petition filed by an American citizen, or by a permanent resident, who dies before the alien beneficiary could come to the United States, is no longer in an entirely hopeless situation.

A relative petition will be revoked upon the death of the petitioner unless the Attorney General determines that, "for humanitarian reasons, revocation would be inappropriate."

Pleading and proving that your petition should be granted because of humanitarian reasons may involve some complicated legal wrangling. If your situation seems to fit this exception, get advice at once from an immigration lawyer or other experienced immigration consultant. (See Chapter 31.) You will need to present strong evidence that you should be allowed to receive a green card for humanitarian reasons when the relative who petitioned for you to join him or her in the United States has passed away.

But you can always try the indirect approach. A little help from a U.S. representative or senator who can intercede on your behalf before your case is decided may prove effective. Call the office of your representative or senator and get the name of the aide in that office who is responsible for handling immigration matters and request an appointment to discuss your situation. Write the politician a letter summarizing why he or she should intercede on your behalf with the BCIS. This approach—depending on getting the strong backing of a busy politician—may be a long shot, but it may be your last hope. ■

# 6

# FIANCÉ AND FIANCÉE VISAS

## I Left My Heart in San Francisco

You are an American citizen who has fallen in love with your pen pal from Nigeria. After two years of letter-writing, the two of you decide to marry, but you are not able to go to Nigeria to marry her and the U.S. Embassy in Lagos will not give her a tourist visa to come to the United States. Can you petition for her to have a Fiancées Visa?

Bad news for long-distance love: The answer is no, not until you've met in person.

The Immigration Marriage Fraud Amendments were passed in 1986 to prohibit mail-order brides because of abuses of the "sweetheart's visa," now called the Fiancée (for women) or Fiancé (for men) Visa.

Aliens who wish to come to the United States for the sole purpose of marrying U.S. citizens may be given Fiancé or Fiancée Visas by the U.S. Embassy, on condition that their marriage occurs within 90 days from the date they arrive in the United States. However, the U.S. Consulate will deny your request for a visa if you, as the American citizen petitioner, have not personally met the person you intend to marry within two years before filing your petition.

## A. How to File

All the immigration forms required and prohibitions explained here are very unromantic. But because the immigration laws have been abused by people who used marriage simply to obtain a green card, romance takes a backseat when it comes to immigration procedures. Obtaining a Fiancée or Fiancé Visa—also called a K-1 Visa—requires time, patience and paperwork.

### 1. Documents required

To start the process, the American citizen must file the following with the BCIS:

- Immigration Form I-129F, Petition for Alien Fiancé(e). (See the sample at the end of this chapter.)
- Separate color photographs of the American citizen and the alien fiancé(e)
- one Form G-325A, Biographic Information, for each person. (See the sample at the end of Chapter 7.)
- Proof of U.S. citizenship, such as a copy of a passport or birth certificate.

- Proof that any previous marriages have been terminated by death, divorce or annulment.
- Written affidavit from the U.S. citizen stating how the couple met, how they decided to get married and the plans for the marriage and the honeymoon.
- Proof that the American and the alien fiancé(e) have met each other within the past two years: photographs, plane tickets, letters.
- Proof that there is an intention to marry within 90 days after the alien fiancé(e) arrives in the United States: letters, long-distance telephone bills, letter from the religious or civil authority who will officiate at the wedding, letter from the place where the reception will be held, and engagement or wedding announcement or invitation.

There is a filing fee of $110, payable to the BCIS, in the form of a money order or bank check.

All of these documents must be sent by certified mail, return receipt requested, to the BCIS Regional Service Center nearest the residence of the American petitioner. (See the BCIS website for contact details; make sure to get the right P.O. Box.)

The American petitioner may be called in for an interview by an BCIS officer. Bring all original documents to the interview. If the documents and the interview convince the BCIS that true romance is behind the planned marriage, the petition will be approved and a Notice of Action, Form I-797, will be mailed to the U.S. citizen. The form will contain instructions for the next step to take—and may include a request for additional information or documentation. When the file is considered complete and approved, it will be sent to the U.S. Embassy or Consulate at which the alien will apply for the visa. The Embassy or Consulate will then take over, communicating directly with the alien fiancé(e).

## ADVICE TO THE ALIEN FIANCÉ(E)

While waiting for the Notice of Action to arrive, start gathering all the documents required by the American Embassy so that you are ready to proceed with the case as soon as notified.

These documents include:

- a current passport for yourself and for all of your unmarried children under 21 years of age, if they are coming with you or following you to the United States
- birth certificates for yourself and all children mentioned above
- documents to prove termination of any previous marriage (death certificate, divorce decree, annulment decree)
- police clearance from all places you have lived for more than six months (except from the United States, where the BCIS gathers the information)
- originals of all documents, copies of which were submitted by your American fiancé(e) with Form I-129F (see the sample at the end of this chapter)
- three photographs of yourself and each of any children applying with you for a visa (see Chapter 29, Section E)
- report of your own medical examination and those of all children over 14 years of age to verify that no one has a communicable disease, and
- Form I-134, Affidavit of Support, filled out by your American fiancé(e). (See the sample at the end of Chapter 9.)

- documents showing the value of any of the following property, if owned: bonds and stocks, real estate and mortgage information or life insurance.

The fiancé(e) will also need to have a medical exam done. The fiancé(e) can't just go to the family doctor, but will have to go to a clinic specified by the consulate. The doctor will do an exam, ask questions about medical history and drug and alcohol use, take X-rays and withdraw blood. The fiancé will be asked to show records of having received all appropriate vaccinations, and will have to get any vaccinations that are lacking. The cost is usually around $150.

Most of the forms and documents must be filed for you and for any minor children who will also be going to the United States.

Because of new and increased security procedures, it is unlikely that you will receive your visa on the same day as you attend your interview. It can take several weeks for the consulate to run security checks on you—and even longer if you come from a country that the United States suspects of supporting terrorism.

If the American consul is ultimately convinced that you and your American fiancé(e) are truly engaged to be married and will marry upon your arrival in the United States, your passport will be stamped with the K-1 Visa, signifying that you are the fiancé(e) of an American citizen; the passports of your accompanying minor children will be stamped with the K-2 Visa, meaning that they are dependent upon you for their immigration status.

## 2. Filing at the embassy

The American Embassy or Consulate will schedule the alien fiancé(e) for an interview, to which he or she should take all the documents that have been collected according to the instructions. There will be an application fee of $100.

One of the most important of the documents will be Form I-134, Affidavit of Support (see the sample in Chapter 9), along with proof that the petitioner is willing and able to take financial responsibility for the beneficiary including:

- bank statements of the petitioner
- recent tax returns and W-2s
- employment certification of the petitioner (normally a letter from the employer detailing salary, hours and whether the position is temporary or permanent), and

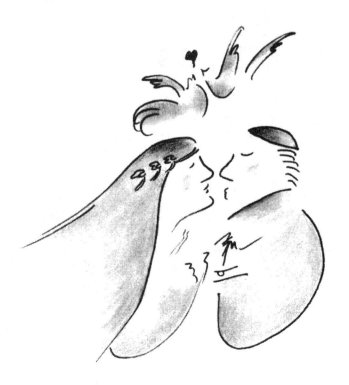

The Fiancé(e) Visa is considered a nonimmigrant visa because you are simply promising to marry a U.S. citizen. You are not yet an immigrant.

### 3. Permission to work in the U.S.

When you arrive in the United States, you can apply at once for an Employment Authorization card that will enable you to work legally. The proper paperwork to complete for this is Form I-765. (See Chapter 8, Section D.)

However, you'll have to submit your application to a BCIS Service Center, and the service centers are famous for delays of many months. Submitting this application may not be worth the effort since the maximum time the work permit will be good for is three months (based on the length of your fiancé visa). You may be better off getting married, then submitting your green card application together with an application for a work permit. This allows you to submit the work permit application to a local BCIS office, receive an answer more quickly and have more time to work before the card expires (it will last for approximately one year).

---

**WEDDING CAKE**

4 lbs. of love
1 lb. of patience
1/2 lb. understanding
1 lb. sweet temper
1 lb. of blindness to faults
1 lb. of self-forgetfulness
1 lb. of pounded wit
1 lb. of good humor
2 tbsp. of sweet argument
1 pint of rippling laughter
1 wine glass of common sense
1 oz. of modesty

Put the love, understanding and sweet temper into a warm house. Beat the patience into a cream, mix well together with the blindness to faults and self-forgetfulness. Stir the pounded wit and good humor into the sweet argument, then add the rippling laughter and common sense. Sprinkle with modesty. Work the whole together until everything is well-mixed and bake gently forever.

---

### B. MARRIAGE AND AFTER

You must marry within 90 days after arriving in the United States. It's best to get married as soon as possible after you arrive. That's because you've got only 90 days to apply for your green card; and at that time, you'll have to prove to the BCIS that you really got married. The BCIS won't accept a mere church certificate—it needs the official marriage certificate prepared and stamped by your local government office. However, it can take your local government several weeks to prepare this certificate and get you a copy, so plan ahead.

If you cannot get married because of some emergency or circumstances beyond your control, you must submit an affidavit to the BCIS stating the reasons for the delay and request an extension of time to marry.

If you fail to marry your American fiancé(e) at all, the BCIS will start deportation proceedings against you and all children who came with you on a Fiancé(e) Visa.

If you marry someone other than your American fiancé(e), you will lose your right to receive your green card in the United States—and so will all of your minor children who are attempting to immigrate with you.

If you do marry your American fiancé(e) within 90 days, there is one more important step you must take in order to get a green card. You must file for Adjustment of Status (see Chapter 8), for yourself and all your minor children who came on the Fiancé(e) Visa at the BCIS office closest to your new home in America.

---

 **BEWARE OF THE TWO-YEAR TIME LIMIT**

Going through the Adjustment of Status procedure will confer upon you and your minor children conditional permanent residence status, and you will acquire a green card which is valid only for two years. You must follow the procedures which pertain to a conditional permanent resident whose green card is based on marriage. (See Chapter 7, Section F.)

---

# PETITION FOR ALIEN FIANCÉ(E), SAMPLE FORM I-129F (PAGE 1)

OMB No. 1115-0071

**U.S. Department of Justice**
Immigration and Naturalization Service

## Petition for Alien Fiancé(e)

### DO NOT WRITE IN THIS BLOCK

| Case ID# | Action Stamp | Fee Stamp |
|---|---|---|

A#

G-28 or Volag #

The petition is approved for status under Section 101(a)(15)(k). It is valid for four months from date of action.

AMCON: _____
☐ Personal Interview      ☐ Previously Forwarded
☐ Document Check
☐ Field Investigations

Remarks:

## A. Information about you.

**1. Name** (Family name in CAPS)    (First)    (Middle)
SMITH    John    Gibbs

**2. Address** (Number and Street)    (Apartment Number)
114 Fulton Street    6E

(Town or City)    (State/Country)    (Zip/Postal Code)
New York    New York    10038

**3. Place of Birth** (Town or City)    (State/Country)
White Plains    New York

**4. Date of Birth** (Mo/Day/Yr) 12/28/66

**5. Sex** ☒ Male   ☐ Female

**6. Marital Status** ☐ Married   ☒ Single   ☐ Widowed   ☐ Divorced

**7. Other Names Used** (including maiden name)
N/A

**8. Social Security Number** (if any) 127-32-1322

**9. Alien Registration Number** (if any) N/A

**10. Names of Prior Husband/Wives** None

**11. Date(s) Marriages(s)** N/A

**12. If you are a U.S. citizen, complete the following:**
My citizenship was acquired through (check one)
☒ Birth in the U.S.    ☐ Naturalization
Give number of certificate, date and place it was issued

☐ Parents
Have you obtained a certificate of citizenship in your own name?
☐ Yes    ☐ No
If "Yes," give number of certificate, date and place it was issued.

**13. Have you ever filed for this or any other alien fiancé(e) before?** ☐ Yes    ☐ No
If you checked "yes," give name of alien, place and date of filing, and result.

## B. Information about your alien fiancé(e).

**1. Name** (Family name in CAPS)    (First)    (Middle)
RAMIREZ    Brenda    Flores

**2. Address** (Number and Street)    (Apartment Number)
4-E Avalon Condominium, 95 Greenhills

(Town or City)    (State/Country)    (Zip/Postal Code)
San Juan    Metro Manila    1502

**3. Place of Birth** (Town or City)    (State/Country)
La Union    Philippines

**4. Date of Birth** (Mo/Day/Yr) 10/17/73

**5. Sex** ☐ Male   ☒ Female

**6. Marital Status** ☐ Married   ☒ Single   ☐ Widowed   ☐ Divorced

**7. Other Names Used** (including maiden name)
N/A

**8. Social Security Number** (if any) N/A

**9. Alien Registration Number** (if any) N/A

**10. Names of Prior Husbands/Wives** None

**11. Date(s) Marriages(s)** N/A

**12. Has your fiancé(e) ever been in the U.S.?** ☐ Yes    ☒ No

**13. If your fiancé(e) is currently in the U.S., complete the following:**
He or she last arrived as a (visitor, student, exchange alien, crewman, stowaway, temporary worker, without inspection, etc.)

N/A

**Arrival/Departure Record (I-94)**    **Date arrived** (Month/Day/Year)

**Date authorized stay expired, or will expire, as shown on Form I-94**

| INITIAL | RESUBMITTED | RELOCATED | | COMPLETED | | |
|---|---|---|---|---|---|---|
| | | Rec'd | Sent | Approved | Denied | Returned |
| | | | | | | |

Form I-129F (Rev.11/20/01) Y Page 1

## SAMPLE FORM I-129F (PAGE 2)

---

**B.  Information about your alien fiancé(e)            (Continued)**

**14.  List all children of your alien fiancé(e)** (if any)

| (Name) | (Date of Birth) | (Country of Birth) | (Present Address) |
|---|---|---|---|
| N/A | | | |

**15.  Address in the United States where your fiancé(e) intends to live**

| (Number and Street) | (Town or City) | (State) |
|---|---|---|
| 136 Lake Avenue | Yonkers | New York |

**16.  Your fiancé(e)'s address abroad**

| (Number and Street) | (Town or City) | (Province) | (Country) | (Phone Number) |
|---|---|---|---|---|
| same as in Part B  #2 | | | Philippines | 876-3214 |

**17.  If your fiancé(e)'s native alphabet uses other than Roman letters, write his or her name and address abroad in the native alphabet:**

| (Name) | (Number and Street) | (Town or City) | (Province) | (Country) |
|---|---|---|---|---|
| N/A | | | | |

**18.  Is your fiancé(e) related to you?**     ☐ Yes    ☒ No

If you are related, state the nature and degree of relationship, e.g., third cousin or maternal uncle, etc.

**19.  Has your fiancé(e) met and seen you?**     ☒ Yes    ☐ No

Describe the circumstances under which you met.  If you have not personally met each ether, explain how the relationship was established, and explain in detail any reasons you may have for requesting that the requirement that you and your fiancé(e) must have met should not apply to you.

We met at a hotel in Hongkong as were both tourists/guests billeted at the same hotel during one of my trips abroad last year.

**20.  Your fiancé(e) will apply for a visa abroad at the American Consulate in**     Manila            Philippines

                                                                                                (City)                    (Country)

(Designation of a consulate outside the country of your fiancé(e)'s last residence does not guarantee acceptance for processing by that consulate. Acceptance is at the discretion of the designated consulate.)

---

## C.  Other information

**If you are serving overseas in the Armed Forces of the United States, please answer the following:**

N/A

I presently reside or am stationed overseas and my current mailing address is _____

I plan to return to the United States on or about _____

**Penalties:  You may, by law, be imprisoned for not more than five years, or fined $250,000, or both, for entering into a marriage contract for the purpose of evading any provision of the immigration laws and you may be fined up to $10,000 or imprisoned up to five years, or both, for knowingly and willfully falsifying or concealing a material fact or using any false document in submitting this petition.**

**Your Certification:**

I am legally able to and intend to marry my alien fiancé(e) within 90 days of his or her arrival in the United States.  I certify, under penalty of perjury under the laws of the United States of America, that the foregoing is true and correct.  Furthermore, I authorize the release of any information from my records which the Immigration and Naturalizaton Service needs to determine eligibility for the benefit that I am seeking.

Signature  *John Smith*                    (Date) 8/29/03    (Phone Number) (212) 285-1012

**Signature of Person Preparing Form, If Other Than Above:**

I declare that I prepared this document at the request of the person above and that it is based on all information of which I have any knowledge.

Print Name  N/A            (Address) _____ (Signature) _____ (Date) _____

**G-28 ID**    _____            Volag        _____

# 7

# GREEN CARDS THROUGH MARRIAGE

## I'm Getting Married in the Morning

Yes are getting desperate. You have already gone to several employment agencies. You have gone as far as the interview with an interested employer. But each time, you are asked the same question: "Do you have a green card?"

You have heard from other job seekers, undocumented aliens like you, that the easiest way to get a green card is to marry an American citizen.

To make that idea very tempting, a friend who is a U.S. citizen has offered to marry you, provided you give this friend a round-trip ticket to your home country. You will not live together. The marriage would be a matter of convenience to enable you to obtain a green card and your American friend to have a vacation. It may turn out to be less convenient than you thought.

## A. WHO QUALIFIES

You are eligible for a green card if you have entered into a bona fide, legal marriage with a U.S. citizen or lawful permanent resident. Bona fide means that the marriage is based on your desire to create a life together with your new spouse, not merely on your desire to obtain a green card. Legal means that it is valid and recognized by the laws of the state or country in which you live. It doesn't matter whether you hold the marriage ceremony in the United States or overseas, but you do need to abide by local laws—and obtain a document, such as a marriage certificate, to prove that you've done so.

- **Marriage to a U.S. citizen** makes you an Immediate Relative and eligible to receive a green card just as soon as you can get through the application process.
- **Marriage to a U.S. permanent resident,** unfortunately, will not yield such fast results. Your new spouse can file a visa petition for you right away, but then you'll be placed in category 2A of the second visa preference and have to wait, probably several years, before a green card becomes available to you. Only after that waiting period is over and you've applied for your green card will you be legally permitted to live in the United States.

---

**THE INCONVENIENCES OF MARRIAGES OF CONVENIENCE**

In the early 1980s, the U.S. government claimed that half the petitions based on marriage were fraudulent, as the marriages were thought to be entered into solely for the purpose of obtaining a green card. In 1986, the U.S. Congress passed a law called the Immigration Marriage Fraud Amendments, to eliminate as many "paper marriages" as possible.

Both American citizens and permanent residents who conspire with an alien to evade immigration laws by means of a fraudulent marriage can be charged with a federal crime. Those found guilty can be imprisoned for up to five years, fined up to $250,000, or both imprisoned and fined. In addition, permanent residents can be deported, as can those who are undocumented.

Before you even entertain the idea of entering a sham marriage, consider the following…

Do you want to live with the possibility of being blackmailed, emotionally, psychologically and financially?

Do you want to be prosecuted for a federal crime with a penalty of five years in prison, a fine of up to $250,000, or both?

If the BCIS discovers that you have entered into a marriage or even helped someone else enter into a marriage to evade the immigration laws—or if you have submitted papers to the BCIS based on such a marriage—you will almost certainly forever lose the possibility of getting a green card, no matter what relationships you may have in the future.

---

## B. SPECIAL RULES IN COURT PROCEEDINGS

Assume that removal—formerly called deportation or exclusion—proceedings have already been started against you because the immigration authorities have found that you are out of status or that you entered the U.S. without the proper documentation. While the proceedings are pending, you marry a U.S. citizen. You now may file your marriage-based petition and the application for Adjustment of Status with the judge, assuming you are eligible to do so. (See Chapter 8.)

However, because you married while removal proceedings were going on, your marital status is suspect. After all, you did get married with the "shotgun" of a possible removal order facing you. You, the newly married alien, will have to provide clear and convincing evidence showing that the marriage was entered into in good faith and not solely for the purpose of getting a green card, and that no fee or financial arrangements were given for filing the petition. (This is apart from money you might have paid an attorney or other person to help you.)

You will have to clearly establish that you married to establish a life together—for love and with a real commitment—not simply to evade your removal from the United States. (See Section E, below, for more guidance on gathering this evidence. Also seek help from an experienced attorney.)

## C. GETTING A GREEN CARD

A green card may be obtained through marriage to a U.S. citizen (Immediate Relative) or to a permanent resident (Family Second Preference). (See Chapter 4, Section A.)

The legal term for the American citizen or permanent resident who is signing the immigration papers for the alien spouse is petitioner. The legal term for the alien spouse is beneficiary.

### 1. Beginning the process

The following papers and procedures set the process in motion within the BCIS:

- Form I-130, Petition for Alien Relative. (See the sample at the end of this chapter.) This form must be signed by the U.S. citizen or permanent resident spouse. It gives information about both the husband and the wife.
- Two copies of Form G-325A, Biographic Information—one for the husband and the other for the wife. Each person must fill out a separate form and sign it. (See the sample at the end of this chapter.) The form contains information about the parents, places of residence, employers of both spouses during the past five years and any previous foreign residences. Both of these forms are used mainly for checking on the alien spouse's background in case an investigation is ordered.
- Both spouses must provide one color photograph that has been taken within 30 days before the filing. The photos must be shot in the manner and style required by the BCIS. (See Chapter 29, Section E.)

- Documents to prove that there is a valid marriage, including copies of the documents listed below.
  **Marriage certificate.** Submit the civil registry certificate and not the marriage license or the church certificate, unless your country accepts a church marriage certificate as an official document. Marriage by proxy, a cultural practice in certain countries, is not acceptable to the immigration authorities.
  **Previous marriages.** If either person was previously married, attach proof of the termination of the previous marriage—a divorce decree, annulment decree or death certificate. Some foreign divorces may not be recognized by the BCIS. The law provides that at least one of the parties must be living in the place where the divorce was granted. In addition, when the divorcing pair is living in the U.S., they should obtain a divorce in a local court, not at their embassy.
- Filing fee of $130 in the form of a money order, or certified check to the BCIS.

When you've completed and assembled all these items, make a complete copy for yourself. What you'll do with it next depends on where you are living, how you entered the U.S. and whether you're eligible to adjust status here, your spouse's status and where your spouse is living, as detailed on the table below.

## FROM VISA PETITION TO GREEN CARD APPLICATION

| YOUR SITUATION | WHERE TO MAIL THE APPLICATION | WHAT'S NEXT |
|---|---|---|
| You're living overseas and your spouse is a U.S. citizen living in the U.S. | Send the I-130 visa petition via certified mail with a return receipt requested to the BCIS Service Center that serves your spouse's geographic region. Find the correct address and Post Office Box on the BCIS website at www.bcis.gov. | As soon as the visa petition is approved, you'll be able to apply for your immigrant visa and green card through an overseas U.S. consulate. |
| You're living overseas and your spouse is a U.S. lawful permanent resident living in the U.S. | Send the I-130 visa petition via certified mail with a return receipt requested to the BCIS Service Center that serves your spouse's geographic region. Find the correct address and Post Office Box on the BCIS website at www.bcis.gov. | Approval of the visa petition will give you a Priority Date, but you'll have to wait until that date is current to apply for your green card. You'll need to wait overseas during that time, after which you'll apply for your immigrant visa and green card through a U.S. consulate. |
| You're presently in the U.S. and your spouse is a lawful permanent resident. | Send the I-130 visa petition via certified mail with a return receipt requested to the BCIS Service Center that serves your spouse's geographic region. Find the correct address and Post Office Box on the BCIS website at www.bcis.gov. | Approval of the visa petition will give you a Priority Date, but you'll have to wait until that date is current to apply for your green card. Unless you have a separate visa to remain in the U.S. for those years, or will be eligible to adjust status in the U.S., you may have to leave soon to avoid the three and ten years' time bars for having lived in the U.S. illegally. |
| You're presently in the U.S., your spouse is a U.S. citizen but you entered illegally. | See an immigration attorney for help—you may not be able to adjust status without leaving the United States, which would probably expose you to a three or ten year bar on returning. | |
| You're presently in the U.S., your spouse is a U.S. citizen and you entered legally (with a visa or on a visa waiver, no matter if your expiration date passed). | You are eligible to Adjust Status in the United States. Submit your I-130 visa petition in combination with your adjustment of status application (described in Chapter 8) to your local BCIS office. | Await fingerprinting and later an interview at your local BCIS office. |

## 2. Marrying a U.S. citizen

When you marry an American citizen, you have certain immigration benefits not available to other aliens. The most obvious benefit is that you are entitled to a green card much more quickly and, if you entered the U.S. legally, without returning to your country or waiting for an immigration quota number to be given to you. You are the Immediate Relative of a U.S. citizen and are given the red-carpet treatment in terms of obtaining your permanent residence.

In legal terms, this process of remaining in the United States and not having to get the green card outside the country is called Adjustment of Status (to the status of permanent resident). It is known as a one-step procedure. Instead of having to file the Form I-130 at the BCIS Service Center, and then later file the green card application (Form I-485) at the local BCIS office, Immediate Relatives (spouse, parent or minor unmarried child of a U.S. citizen) can file both forms at once at the local BCIS office.

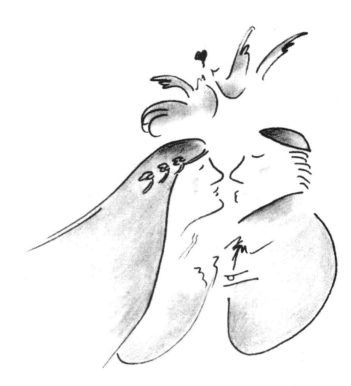

 **IF YOU ENTERED THE U.S. ILLEGALLY, IT'S ANOTHER STORY.**

Except in rare circumstances (described in Chapter 8), people who entered the United States illegally (for example, by crossing the border away from an inspection point) do not have the right to adjust status in the United States. Attempting to turn your application in at a local BCIS office could get you deported. Your best course is to get help from an experienced immigration attorney in evaluating and completing your application.

## 3. Marrying a permanent resident

You cannot apply for a green card as a Second Preference alien until your Priority Date is current. There will be a long waiting period for your Priority Date to become current. For example, as of July 2003, the Department of State listed the waiting period for the Second Preference 2A category as about five years. The law expects that you will spend this period outside the United States, and get your visa through a U.S. consulate.

Once your Priority Date is current, and if you are in status and otherwise eligible, you may apply for Adjustment of Status in the United States. Being "in status" means that the expiration date on your I-94 hasn't passed and you haven't violated the terms of your visa. You'll need to pay the filing fee for Form I-485, which is $255 for anyone 14 and older and $160 for anyone 13 and younger.

However, during the many years you were waiting for your Priority Date to become current, it's quite likely you reached the expiration date of your permitted stay in the U.S.—in other words, fell out of status. And, a family member who is out of status or who has worked without authorization or entered the country without inspection is eligible to apply for Adjustment of Status only if the spouse through which he or she is immigrating becomes a U.S. citizen or he or she comes under the old provision that allowed otherwise ineligible applicants to adjust if they agreed to pay a $1,000 penalty. To qualify under this penalty provision, an applicant must have had a visa petition or labor certification on file by January 14, 1998; or have been physically present in the U.S. on December 21, 2000, and had a visa petition or labor certification on file by April 30, 2001.

An additional problem is that if you were out of status for six months after April 1, 1997, leave the United States and seek to be admitted through a consulate or border, you will be subject to a three-year waiting period; the period is ten years if you were out of status for one year after April 1, 1997. There is a waiver available if you are the spouse or the son or daughter of a U.S. citizen or permanent resident, if you can show the U.S. citizen or resident would suffer extreme hardship. It's very difficult to get this waiver.

## D. PREPARING FOR YOUR INTERVIEW

Whether you are applying for Adjustment of Status or for an immigrant visa at a consulate abroad, start gathering documents for your green card interview. At the interview, you must present solid information showing who you are, that your spouse is a U.S. citizen or lawful permanent resident and that you have a valid marriage. This would include:

- marriage certificate
- birth certificates for the petitioner and beneficiary
- identification documents for the petitioner, such as a driver's license, alien registration card or proof of citizenship, employment ID, passport and credit cards
- current passport and Form I-94, Arrival Record, of the beneficiary (if you're in the U.S.)
- Social Security cards of both the petitioner and beneficiary if they are available
- birth certificates for all children of the petitioner and beneficiary
- leases on apartments that the petitioner and beneficiary have occupied, together with rent receipts
- hospital cards, union books, insurance policies, pay vouchers, bank accounts, telephone and gas and electric bills or charge cards containing the names of petitioner and beneficiary
- an Affidavit of Support (Form I-864) by the petitioner
- a letter on the company letterhead from the petitioner's employer stating when employment began, amount of salary, prospect of continuing employment, marital status, dependents claimed and the person to be notified in case of emergency (See the sample at the end of Chapter 18.)
- federal income tax returns, signed, dated and authenticated by the Internal Revenue Service, for the years that the beneficiary and petitioner have been married
- wedding pictures of petitioner and beneficiary, and
- any snapshots of petitioner and beneficiary together taken before the marriage and, more importantly, since the marriage.

Collect and make copies of as many of these documents as possible. If you cannot gather this documentation, be sure your explanation is consistent and truthful. Immigration officers are ordinary people with human experiences

similar to your own, but they are operating under severe time constraints and other pressures. If you and your spouse have married for love, you will eventually prevail. Nevertheless, you still have to present the required documentary proof.

Once you're approved, you won't be given a green card right away. If your interview was at a U.S. consulate, you'll be given an immigrant visa with which to enter the United States. If your interview was at a U.S. BCIS office, you'll be given a letter stating that you've been approved. In either case, the BCIS will send you your green card by mail, usually several months later. See Chapter 30 for important information on making sure you don't lose your right to the green card, for example, by failing to advise the BCIS of your changes of address.

## E. IF YOUR MARRIAGE IS LESS THAN TWO YEARS OLD

If you become a resident within two years of the date you were married, whether you were granted status by Adjustment of Status or by Consular Processing, your green card is only conditional and you are considered a "conditional permanent resident." It seems contradictory to be both "permanent" and "conditional" at the same time, but it actually makes sense in this situation. This is because once you remove the conditional basis, your two years of conditional residence will count as unconditional or permanent residence for naturalization and other intents and purposes.

To receive a green card without conditions that will be valid for more than two years, you could wait until you have been married at least two years before becoming a permanent resident. (If your marriage is already two years old at the time your permanent residence is granted, you are a full-fledged permanent resident and do not need to file papers to remove any conditions.) However, most people go ahead and become permanent residents, then wait two years minus 90 days and request the removal of the conditional status. Also, your alien sons or daughters who may have been petitioned by your spouse must likewise apply for removal of their conditional statuses.

The timing of the request is crucial. Mark on your calendar the third month before your second anniversary of becoming a conditional permanent resident.

**EXAMPLE:** Your date of admission as a conditional permanent resident was December 7, 2001, the date which is printed on your conditional green card. The second anniversary of your conditional permanent residence is December 7, 2003. And 90 days (three months) before the second anniversary of December 7, 2003, is September 7, 2003. Therefore, you must file for the removal of the conditional status any time after September 7, 2003, and before December 7, 2003.

## 1. Forms required for removal of conditions

Within the 90 days before the second anniversary of your conditional permanent residence, you must submit the following:

- Form I-751, Petition to Remove the Conditions on Residence, signed by both husband and wife (see the sample at the end of this chapter), or by the alien spouse alone, if seeking a waiver
- fee of $145 in the form of a money order or certified check, payable to the BCIS.

You must also present evidence of a true marriage. To do this, submit a sample of as many of the following documents as possible (from within the past two years):

- title to house or condo or co-op, or any other real property showing joint ownership
- lease to your apartment showing joint tenancy since the time of marriage, telephone or electric and gas bills showing both your names or addressed to you as Mr. and Mrs.
- bank books or statements showing evidence of a joint checking or savings account
- registration, with both names, of cars or any personal property
- insurance policies taken by husband or wife and showing the other as the beneficiary of any insurance benefits
- affidavits from your friends or relatives stating that they know your marriage was entered into in good faith and the reasons or facts they have to support this judgment. Your parents, employer, coworker, friend, priest, pastor, rabbi or imam should give details of times and places at which you appeared as husband and wife. This should only be required if you do not have sufficient proof of a true marriage—or for other unusual cases such as a waiver.

- birth certificate of any child born of the marriage, showing both parents' names
- current letter from employer of both husband and wife, on the company letterhead, stating present job and salary and the name of person to be notified in case of emergency, and
- current will showing one spouse as the beneficiary of the other's estate.

These documents should be sent by certified mail, return receipt requested, to the BCIS Regional Service Center nearest your residence. (See the BCIS website for the address.) You may receive a notice for an interview or it may be approved without one. While you're waiting, however, the receipt notice that you get from the BCIS Service Center will be your only proof that you are legally in the United States. You can use it in combination with your expired green card to prove your right to work. If you travel, however, it's best to visit a local BCIS office to get a stamp in your passport with which to reenter the United States. In any case, with or without an interview, your green card becomes permanent only when the BCIS decides to approve your joint petition.

## 2. If your spouse does not sign the joint petition

If your spouse, for one reason or another, does not sign the joint petition, do not despair. The BCIS allows you, as the conditional permanent resident alien, to file without your spouse's signature to have the conditional status removed from your green card.

You must fill out Form I-751, Petition to Remove the Conditions on Residence (see the sample at the end of this chapter) and mail it with a fee of $145 in money order or certified check. If you entered the marriage in good faith—that is, to establish a life with another person and not just to get a green card—the form sets forth other ways to get permanent residence even if the marriage has deteriorated or ended. These ways are called waivers. They require an alien spouse to show that:

- his or her spouse died
- he or she was the victim of battery or abuse
- the marriage was valid when it occurred but is now legally terminated, or
- he or she would suffer extreme hardship if removed.

These waivers require the assistance of an experienced immigration attorney. (See Chapter 31.)

**BEWARE OF THE EXPIRATION DATE**

Since the conditional green card is valid for only two years, it cannot be used after it expires. In short, it self-destructs at the end of its term.

The saving grace is that once you and your spouse, or you alone, file Form I-751, your receipt gives you a one-year extension on your green card. (See the sample at the end of this chapter.) During this year, the BCIS is supposed to either approve or to deny your petition.

If you must travel, keep the receipt with your expired or soon-to-expire green card and passport with you so that your reentry into the United States will be smooth. Also, visit our local BCIS office and ask for an I-551 stamp in your passport.

### 3. People married two years or more

If the original date of your admission as a permanent resident is more than two years after your marriage, you are not considered a conditional permanent resident. You are a full-fledged permanent resident and not subject to the conditions on residence.

**EXAMPLE:** You married a permanent resident on February 14, 1990, and a visa petition was filed on your behalf shortly thereafter in the Second Preference category. However, your visa number was not immediately available and you had to wait a few years. You finally received your green card and were admitted as a permanent resident on July 4, 1992, more than two years after your date of marriage.

## F. IF YOU REMARRY

If your marriage ends in divorce or annulment after you receive your permanent green card, and then you marry an alien, it will be difficult for you to sponsor your alien spouse for a green card.

To obtain permanent residence for your alien spouse during the first five years after you received your green card through marriage, you'll have to show by "clear and convincing evidence" that your first marriage—the one by which you got your green card—was not fraudulent and was entered into in good faith. Again, this means showing you got married because you wanted to establish a life together, not just to get a green card.

In addition to the other proof required (see Section E, above), you will be asked to explain:

- why and when you got the previous divorce
- how long you lived with your first spouse
- how, when and where you met your intended spouse, and
- facts about your courtship.

However, after you have been a green card holder for five years—the number of years required for naturalization—you can file a petition for your second spouse without providing such evidence.

Again, Congress provided this restriction because a number of alien couples had obtained green cards fraudulently. One of them would marry either an American citizen or a permanent resident. After getting the immigrant visa, the marriage to the American or the permanent resident would be ended by divorce or annulment. The alien, then in possession of a valid green card, would then marry the original spouse to give him or her a green card, too. To eliminate this nefarious practice, a law was passed requiring that a green card be valid for five years before a petition to marry another alien, after divorce from an American citizen or green card holder, could be approved, unless the permanent resident can show very clearly that the first marriage was a good one.

*Dura lex, sed lex.* The law is harsh, but such is the law.

## G. COMMON QUESTIONS ABOUT MARRIAGE AND IMMIGRATION

The answers to most immigration questions depend on timing and the specific history of those involved, so it is difficult to give one correct response in solving a problem. There are, however, a number of questions that are asked over and over.

### 1. Before marriage

**Q:** My boyfriend, who is a U.S. citizen, is getting a divorce soon. Can he file a petition for me to get a green card?

**A:** No—because he has not yet legally ended his previous marriage, he cannot marry you now. He can marry you as soon as his previous divorce petition is finalized.

**Q:** I intend to marry a U.S. citizen, but because work obligations will require us to live in different states for a while, we will not be living together for the first six months or so after we're married. Can he file for me to get a green card?

**A:** Yes. But you will have to prove to the BCIS examiner that your marriage is true and not a sham. Good evidence of that would be ticket stubs from visits to one another, telephone bills showing frequent calls to one another, stubs from social events you attended together such as movies, theater performances and meals, copies of joint bank accounts and bills bearing both of your names.

### 2. After marriage

**Q:** I entered the U.S. with another name. Now I am married to a U.S. citizen using my real name. Can I get my green card?

**A:** Yes. But you may need to request that the misrepresentation be waived, or forgiven, before the BCIS will approve your case. You should see a lawyer in this case.

**Q:** Can I get a green card right after my marriage to a U.S. citizen?

**A:** Yes—if your American spouse files the petition and your marriage is bona fide, that is, sincere and not merely for the purpose of evading immigration laws. However, because of administrative delays and backlogs at various immigration offices, it may be nearly a year before you get your green card. You might also face problems if you've been living in the U.S. illegally and don't have the right to adjust status (file your green card application) in the United States. When you leave the U.S. to attend your green card interview at a U.S. consulate, you could be prevented from returning to the U.S. for three or ten years. If you've lived in the U.S. illegally for six months or more since April 1, 1997, see an immigration attorney for help.

**Q:** I have a minor child living with me in the U.S. and two more young children now living outside the U.S. Can I get green cards for all of them?

**A:** Yes—if your American citizen spouse files separate petitions for them. If your spouse is a permanent resident, not a citizen, he or she can simply include the children on your visa petition.

**Q:** What will happen if my marriage legally ends before the conditional status of my green card is removed?

**A:** A conditional resident can file an application for a Waiver of Condition with the BCIS. However, because there are complicated matters of proof, it is best to consult an experienced immigration lawyer for help.

---

### SECRET OF AN ENDURING MARRIAGE

What makes some marriages fail and others succeed?

St. Paul gave the answer to that questions some two thousand years ago when he wrote to the Corinthians (1 Cor. 13:4) about what is true love. To paraphrase his letter:

If you truly love your spouse so that no matter what, you will remain faithful to your mate, you should be patient. You should be kind. You should not be jealous or conceited or proud.

You should not be ill-mannered; always say "Please, thank you, good morning, good night." You should not be selfish.

You should not be irritable. Keep watch over the door of your mouth. Harsh words stir up anger. A soft answer turns away wrath.

You should not keep a record of wrongs. Avoid repeating, like a broken record, your spouse's faults or wrongs done to you. Be forgiving.

You should not be happy with evil—leave if you are being physically abused—but be happy with the truth. Seek the truth always, and accept it, if you cannot change things.

You must never give up. You must have faith in your mate. Your hope and patience should never fail.

If you love in the manner described above, your marriage will always be alive, and ever fresh, until death do you part.

And even after death, true love never ends.

## PETITION FOR ALIEN RELATIVE, SAMPLE FORM I-130 (PAGE 1)

**U.S. Department of Justice**
Immigration and Naturalization Service

OMB #1115-0054
### Petition for Alien Relative

| DO NOT WRITE IN THIS BLOCK - FOR EXAMINING OFFICE ONLY | | |
|---|---|---|
| A# | Action Stamp | Fee Stamp |

**Section of Law/Visa Category**
- [ ] 201(b) Spouse - IR-1/CR-1
- [ ] 201(b) Child - IR-2/CR-2
- [ ] 201(b) Parent - IR-5
- [ ] 203(a)(1) Unm. S or D - F1-1
- [ ] 203(a)(2)(A)Spouse - F2-1
- [ ] 203(a)(2)(A) Child - F2-2
- [ ] 203(a)(2)(B) Unm. S or D - F2-4
- [ ] 203(a)(3) Married S or D - F3-1
- [ ] 203(a)(4) Brother/Sister - F4-1

Petition was filed on: _____ (priority date)
- [ ] Personal Interview
- [ ] Pet. [ ] Ben. " A" File Reviewed
- [ ] Field Investigation
- [ ] 203(a)(2)(A) Resolved
- [ ] Previously Forwarded
- [ ] I-485 Filed Simultaneously
- [ ] 204(g) Resolved
- [ ] 203(g) Resolved

Remarks:

## A. Relationship     You are the petitioner; your relative is the beneficiary.

**1. I am filing this petition for my:**
[X] Husband/Wife  [ ] Parent  [ ] Brother/Sister  [ ] Child

**2. Are you related by adoption?**
[ ] Yes  [X] No

**3. Did you gain permanent residence through adoption?**
[ ] Yes  [X] No

## B. Information about you

**1. Name** (Family name in CAPS) (First) (Middle)
NGUYEN    May    Thanh

**2. Address** (Number and Street) (Apt.No.)
1640 Lincoln Park
(Town or City) (State/Country) (Zip/Postal Code)
Beaverton    Oregon    97006

**3. Place of Birth** (Town or City) (State/Country)
Saigon    Vietnam

**4. Date of Birth** (Month/Day/Year)
4/12/70

**5. Gender**
[X] Male  [ ] Female

**6. Marital Status**
[X] Married  [ ] Single  [ ] Widowed  [ ] Divorced

**7. Other Names Used** (including maiden name)
None

**8. Date and Place of Present Marriage** (if married)
May 22, 2002 – Salem, Oregon

**9. Social Security Number** (if any)
756-91-0637

**10. Alien Registration Number**

**11. Name(s) of Prior Husband(s)/Wive(s)**
None

**12. Date(s) Marriage(s) Ended**

**13. If you are a U.S. citizen, complete the following:**
My citizenship was acquired through (check one):
- [X] Birth in the U.S.
- [ ] Naturalization. Give certificate number and date and place of issuance.
- [ ] Parents. Have you obtained a certificate of citizenship in your own name?
  [X] Yes. Give certificate number, date and place of issuance. [ ] No

**14a. If you are a lawful permanent resident alien, complete the following:** Date and place of admission for, or adjustment to, lawful permanent residence and class of admission.

**14b. Did you gain permanent resident status through marriage to a United States citizen or lawful permanent resident?**
[ ] Yes  [X] No

## C. Information about your relative

**1. Name** (Family name in CAPS) (First) (Middle)
NGUYEN    Lea    Nadres

**2. Address** (Number and Street) (Apt. No.)
1640 Lincoln Park
(Town or City) (State/Country) (Zip/Postal Code)
Beaverton    Oregon    97006

**3. Place of Birth** (Town or City) (State/Country)
Quezon City    Philippines

**4. Date of Birth** (Month/Day/Year)
7/18/69

**5. Gender**
[ ] Male  [X] Female

**6. Marital Status**
[X] Married  [ ] Single  [ ] Widowed  [ ] Divorced

**7. Other Names Used** (including maiden name)
Pebet

**8. Date and Place of Present Marriage** (if married)
May 22, 2002 – Salem, Oregon

**9. Social Security Number** (if any)

**10. Alien Registration Number**

**11. Name(s) of Prior Husband(s)/Wive(s)**

**12. Date(s) Marriage(s) Ended**

**13. Has your relative ever been in the U.S.?** [X] Yes  [ ] No

**14. If your relative is currently in the U.S., complete the following:**
He or she arrived as a::
(visitor, student, stowaway, without inspection, etc.)

Arrival/Departure Record (I-94)
| 1 | 4 | 6 | 0 | 7 | 7 | 1 | 2 | 2 | 1 | 0 |

Date arrived (Month/Day/Year)
12/23/99

Date authorized stay expired, or will expire, as shown on Form I-94 or I-95
Manilla, Philippines
06/23/00

**15. Name and address of present employer** (if any)
Sunshine Day Care, 10 Avenue E, Beaverton, OR 97006

Date this employment began (Month/Day/Year)
Dec. 8, 2001

**16. Has your relative ever been under immigration proceedings?**
[X] No  [ ] Yes  Where _____ When _____
[ ] Removal  [ ] Exclusion/Deportation  [ ] Recission  [ ] Judicial Proceedings

| INITIAL RECEIPT | RESUBMITTED | RELOCATED: Rec'd | Sent | COMPLETED: Appv'd | Denied | Ret'd |
|---|---|---|---|---|---|---|

Form I-130 (Rev. 06/05/02) Y

## SAMPLE FORM I-130 (PAGE 2)

### C. Information about your alien relative (continued)

**17. List husband/wife and all children of your relative.**

| (Name) | (Relationship) | (Date of Birth) | (Country of Birth) |
|---|---|---|---|

N/A

**18. Address in the United States where your relative intends to live.**

| (Street Address) | (Town or City) | (State) |
|---|---|---|
| 1640 Lincoln Park | Beaverton | Oregon |

**19. Your relative's address abroad.** (Include street, city, province and country)

1678 Trout Chautoco Roxas District, Q.C., Philippines        Phone Number (if any)

**20. If your relative's native alphabet is other than Roman letters, write his or her name and foreign address in the native alphabet.**

(Name)        Address (Include street, city, province and country):

N/A

**21. If filing for your husband/wife, give last address at which you lived together.** (Include street, city, province, if any, and country):

1640 Lincoln Park        Beaverton, Oregon        **From:** 5/02 (Month) (Year)   **To:** Present (Month) (Year)

**22. Complete the information below if your relative is in the United States and will apply for adjustment of status**

Your relative is in the United States and will apply for adjustment of status to that of a lawful permanent resident at the office of the Immigration and Naturalization Service in ___Portland___ ___Oregon___ . If your relative is not eligible for adjustment of status, he or she
(City) (State)

will apply for a visa abroad at the American consular post in ___Manila, Philippines___ _____
(City) (Country)

NOTE: Designation of an American embassy or consulate outside the country of your relative's last residence does not guarantee acceptance for processing by that post. Acceptance is at the discretion of the designated embassy or consulate.

### D. Other information

**1. If separate petitions are also being submitted for other relatives, give names of each and relationship.**

**2. Have you ever filed a petition for this or any other alien before?** ☐ Yes ☒ No
If "Yes," give name, place and date of filing and result.

**WARNING:** INS investigates claimed relationships and verifies the validity of documents. INS seeks criminal prosecutions when family relationships are falsified to obtain visas.

**PENALTIES:** By law, you may be imprisoned for not more than five years or fined $250,000, or both, for entering into a marriage contract for the purpose of evading any provision of the immigration laws. In addition, you may be fined up to $10,000 and imprisoned for up to five years, or both, for knowingly and willfully falsifying or concealing a material fact or using any false document in submitting this petition.

**YOUR CERTIFICATION:** I certify, under penalty of perjury under the laws of the United States of America, that the foregoing is true and correct. Furthermore, I authorize the release of any information from my records which the Immigration and Naturalization Service needs to determine eligibility for the benefit that I am seeking.

### E. Signature of petitioner.

*May Thanh Nguyen*        Date June 11, 2002   Phone Number (503) 730-1493

### F. Signature of person preparing this form, if other than the petitioner.

I declare that I prepared this document at the request of the person above and that it is based on all information of which I have any knowledge.

Print Name _____   Signature _____   Date _____

Address _____   G-28 ID or VOLAG Number, if any. _____

Form I-130 (Rev. 06/05/02) Y Page 2

## PETITION TO REMOVE THE CONDITIONS ON RESIDENCE, SAMPLE FORM I-751

**U.S. Department of Justice**
Immigration and Naturalization Service

OMB No. 1115-0145

### Petition to Remove the Conditions on Residence

**START HERE - Please Type or Print**

### Part 1.   Information about you.

| Family Name | Wang | Given Name | Meijin | Middle Initial |
|---|---|---|---|---|

Address - C/O:

| Street Number and Name | 81 Lake St. | Apt. # 114 |
|---|---|---|

| City | Chicago | State or Province | IL |
|---|---|---|---|

| Country | USA | ZIP/Postal Code | 60499 |
|---|---|---|---|

| Date of Birth (month/day/year) | September 20, 1973 | Country of Birth | Singapore |
|---|---|---|---|

| Social Security # (if any) | 063-74-6969 | A# 028753489 |
|---|---|---|

Conditional residence expires on (month/day/year)   May 20, 2003

Mailing address if different from address listed above:

| Street Number and Name | N/A | Apt. # |
|---|---|---|

| City | | State or Province | |
|---|---|---|---|

| Country | | ZIP/Postal Code | |
|---|---|---|---|

### Part 2.   Basis for petition *(check one).*

a. ☑ My conditional residence is based on my marriage to a U.S. citizen or permanent resident, and we are filing this petition together.

b. ☐ I am a child who entered as a conditional permanent resident and I am unable to be included in a Joint Petition to Remove the Conditional Basis of Alien's Permanent Residence (Form I-751) filed by my parent(s).

My conditional residence is based on my marriage to a U.S. citizen or permanent resident, but I am unable to file a joint petition and I request a waiver because: (check one)

c. ☐ My spouse is deceased.

d. ☐ I entered into the marriage in good faith, but the marriage was terminated through divorce/annulment.

e. ☐ I am a conditional resident spouse who entered into the marriage in good faith, or I am a conditional resident child, who has been battered or subjected to extreme cruelty by my citizen or permanent resident spouse or parent.

f. ☐ The termination of my status and removal from the United States would result in an extreme hardship.

### Part 3.   Additional information about you.

| Other Names Used *(including maiden name):* None | Telephone # (630) 555-1212 |
|---|---|

| Date of Marriage | March 10, 2001 | Place of Marriage Chicago, IL |
|---|---|---|

If your spouse is deceased, give the date of death. (month/day/year)   N/A

- Are you in removal or deportation proceedings?   ☐ Yes  ☑ No

- Was a fee paid to anyone other than an attorney in connection with this petition?   ☐ Yes  ☑ No

*Continued on back.*

**FOR INS USE ONLY**

| Returned | Receipt |
|---|---|

Resubmitted

Reloc Sent

Reloc Rec'd

☐ Applicant Interviewed

**Remark**

**Action**

**To Be Completed by Attorney or Representative, if any**

☐ Fill in box if G-28 is attached to represent the applicant

VOLAG#

ATTY State License #

Form I-751 (Rev. 06/05/02)Y Page 1

## SAMPLE FORM I-751 (BACK)

### Part 3. Additional information about you. (continued)

- Since becoming a conditional resident, have you ever been arrested, cited, charged, indicted, convicted, fined or imprisoned for breaking or violating any law or ordinace (excluding traffic regulations), or committed any crime for which you were not arrested?  ☐ Yes  ☑No

- If you are married, is this a different marriage than the one through which conditional residence status was obtained?  ☐ Yes  ☑No

- Have you resided at any other address since you became a permanent resident? *(If yes, attach a list of all addresses and dates.)*  ☐ Yes  ☑No

- Is your spouse currently serving with or employed by the U.S. government and serving outside the United States?  ☐ Yes  ☑No

### Part 4. Information about the spouse or parent through whom you gained your conditional residence.

| Family Name | Long | Given Name | Winston | Middle Initial | S. | Phone Number | 630-555-1212 |
|---|---|---|---|---|---|---|---|

Address  81 Lake St., Chicago, IL  60499

| Date of Birth (month/day/year) | June 3, 1972 | Social Security # (if any) | 163-62-6150 | A# | N/A |
|---|---|---|---|---|---|

### Part 5. Information about your children. *List all your children. Attach another sheet(s) if necessary.*

| Name | Date of Birth (month/day/year) | If in U.S., give A number, current immigration status and U.S. address. | Living with you? |
|---|---|---|---|
| 1.  Aimee Long | 6/3/02 | U.S. citizen; 81 Lake St., Chicago, IL 60499 | ☑Yes ☐No |
| 2. | | | ☐ Yes ☐No |
| 3. | | | ☐ Yes ☐No |
| 4. | | | ☐ Yes ☐No |

### Part 6. Signature. *Read the information on penalties in the instructions before completing this section. If you checked block " a" in Part 2, your spouse must also sign below.*

I certify, under penalty of perjury under the laws of the United States of America, that this petition and the evidence submitted with it is all true and correct. If conditional residence was based on a marriage, I further certify that the marriage was entered into in accordance with the laws of the place where the marriage took place and was not for the purpose of procuring an immigration benefit. I also authorize the release of any information from my records that the Immigration and Naturalization Service needs to determine eligibility for the benefit sought.

| Signature | *Meijin Wang* | Print Name | Meijin Wang | Date | 2/28/03 |
|---|---|---|---|---|---|
| Signature of Spouse | *Winston Long* | Print Name | Winston Long | Date | 2/28/03 |

**Please note:** If you do not completely fill out this form or fail to submit any required documents listed in the instructions, you cannot be found eligible for the requested benefit and this petition may be denied.

### Part 7. Signature of person preparing form, if other than above.

I declare that I prepared this petition at the request of the above person and it is based on all information of which I have knowledge.

| Signature | | Print Name | | Date | |
|---|---|---|---|---|---|

Firm Name
and Address

## Biographic Information, Sample Form G-325A

**U.S. Department of Justice**
Immigration and Naturalization Service

OMB No. 1115-0066

**BIOGRAPHIC INFORMATION**

| (Family name) | (First name) | (Middle name) | ☐ MALE ☑ FEMALE | BIRTHDATE (Mo.-Day-Yr.) | NATIONALITY | FILE NUMBER |
|---|---|---|---|---|---|---|
| SALONGA | Fe | Valdez | | 3-7-63 | Filipino | A- |

ALL OTHER NAMES USED (Including names by previous marriages)
Fe Agnes Salonga

CITY AND COUNTRY OF BIRTH
Manila, Philippines

SOCIAL SECURITY NO. (If any) 210-76-9478

| | FAMILY NAME | FIRST NAME | DATE, CITY AND COUNTRY OF BIRTH (If known) | CITY AND COUNTRY OF RESIDENCE |
|---|---|---|---|---|
| FATHER | SALONGA | Amando | Manila, Philippines, 6-9-39 | Manila, Philippines |
| MOTHER (Maiden name) | VALDEZ | Lourdes | Manila, Philippines, 12-5-42 | -do- |

| HUSBAND (If none, so state) OR WIFE | FAMILY NAME (For wife, give maiden name) | FIRST NAME | BIRTHDATE | CITY & COUNTRY OF BIRTH | DATE OF MARRIAGE | PLACE OF MARRIAGE |
|---|---|---|---|---|---|---|
| | None | | | | | |

FORMER HUSBANDS OR WIVES (if none, so state)

| FAMILY NAME (For wife, give maiden name) | FIRST NAME | BIRTHDATE | DATE & PLACE OF MARRIAGE | DATE AND PLACE OF TERMINATION OF MARRIAGE |
|---|---|---|---|---|
| None | | | | |

APPLICANT'S RESIDENCE LAST FIVE YEARS. LIST PRESENT ADDRESS FIRST

| STREET AND NUMBER | CITY | PROVINCE OR STATE | COUNTRY | FROM MONTH | YEAR | TO MONTH | YEAR |
|---|---|---|---|---|---|---|---|
| 741 12th Ave. | White Plains, | NY | U.S.A. | 9 | 01 | PRESENT TIME | |
| 676 W. Houston Street | New York, | NY | U.S.A. | 8 | 99 | 8 | 99 |

APPLICANT'S LAST ADDRESS OUTSIDE THE UNITED STATES OF MORE THAN ONE YEAR

| STREET AND NUMBER | CITY | PROVINCE OR STATE | COUNTRY | FROM MONTH | YEAR | TO MONTH | YEAR |
|---|---|---|---|---|---|---|---|
| 52-50 MBLA Court, Malaya St. | Marikina | Metro Manila | Philippines | since birth | | 8 | 99 |

APPLICANT'S EMPLOYMENT LAST FIVE YEARS. (IF NONE, SO STATE) LIST PRESENT EMPLOYMENT FIRST

| FULL NAME AND ADDRESS OF EMPLOYER | OCCUPATION (SPECIFY) | FROM MONTH | YEAR | TO MONTH | YEAR |
|---|---|---|---|---|---|
| Griffith School, 560 Lexington Avenue, NY, NY 10118 | Teacher | 3 | 00 | PRESENT TIME | |
| Embassy of Japan, Buendia Ave., Makati, Metro Manila, Philippines | Secretary | 5 | 92 | 8 | 99 |

Show below last occupation abroad if not shown above. (Include all information requested above.)
see above

| THIS FORM IS SUBMITTED IN CONNECTION WITH APPLICATION FOR: | SIGNATURE OF APPLICANT | DATE |
|---|---|---|
| ☐ NATURALIZATION ☑ STATUS AS PERMANENT RESIDENT ☐ OTHER (SPECIFY): | *Fe Valdez Salonga* | 2/26/03 |

**Submit all four pages of this form.**

If your native alphabet is other than roman letters, write your name in your native alphabet here:

PENALTIES: SEVERE PENALTIES ARE PROVIDED BY LAW FOR KNOWINGLY AND WILLFULLY FALSIFYING OR CONCEALING A MATERIAL FACT.

## APPLICANT: BE SURE TO PUT YOUR NAME AND ALIEN REGISTRATION NUMBER IN THE BOX OUTLINED BY HEAVY BORDER BELOW.

| COMPLETE THIS BOX (Family name) | (Given name) | (Middle name) | (Alien registration number) |
|---|---|---|---|
| SALONGA | Fe | Valdez | |

**(OTHER AGENCY USE)**

**INS USE (Office of Origin)**
OFFICE CODE:
TYPE OF CASE:
DATE:

(4) Consul

Form G-325A (Rev. 09/11/00) Y Page 4

# 8

**ADJUSTMENT OF STATUS**

## Getting a Green Card While in the U.S.

**Y**ou arrived at Logan International Airport in Boston as a transit passenger to Spain, where you have a permanent job. But since all your relatives and your boyfriend live in Boston, you managed to evade the immigration authorities by going to the ladies' room. You took a taxi later to your American boyfriend's apartment. After the two of you are married, can you get your green card in the United States?

Maybe. It depends on whether your visa petition was filed before or after certain new laws took effect. These new laws force many people who are now in the United States illegally to leave before they can apply for a green card—but then face long time bars to returning.

As an alien beneficiary of either a family-based or employment-based petition, you can become a permanent resident in one of two ways:

- You can receive your lawful status without leaving the United States. In BCIS language, you can "Adjust your Status" from that of a nonimmigrant to that of a permanent resident.
- You can go back to your original country of residence and apply for an immigrant visa through Consular Processing (see Chapter 9).

If you are in the United States illegally, you can only adjust your status while remaining in the country if you had a visa petition or labor certification on file before April 30, 2001 or before April 30, 2001 if you were present in the U.S. on and around December 21, 2000, or if you entered legally and your spouse is a U.S. citizen (not a green card holder). Otherwise you'll have to leave the United States and attempt Consular Processing—as long as you are not inadmissible and not subject to a waiting period of three or ten years.

Based on a 1996 immigration law, aliens who were unlawfully present in the United States after April 1, 1997 for more than 180 days but less than one year and who left cannot be readmitted to the United States within three years. Aliens who were unlawfully present for one year or more and who left cannot be readmitted to the country within ten years.

---

**HOW DO YOU DECIDE?**

If you are eligible for both Adjustment of Status in the United States or Consular Processing abroad, it is usually best to choose Adjustment of Status, because:
- you will save the expense of traveling back to your home country
- if your application to adjust your status is denied, you can remain and work in the U.S. while you appeal that decision
- if you go for Consular Processing and your application is denied, there is no right to appeal, and
- there is no risk of being kept out for three or ten years due to past illegal stays in the U.S.

---

## A. WHO QUALIFIES

Two groups of aliens are eligible for Adjustment of Status so that they can be admitted as permanent residents in the United States.

### 1. Those not required to pay penalty fee

The following people are eligible for Adjustment of Status without paying an additional fee of $1,000:

- Immediate relatives (spouses, parents and minor unmarried children) of a U.S. citizen (see Chapter 4, Section A), who entered the United States with a visa and were inspected by the U.S. government authorities or entered on a Visa Waiver. (See Chapter 2, Section C.)
- People who entered the United States legally, have never been out of lawful status (for example, their visa hasn't expired and they haven't violated its terms), and have never worked without INS or BCIS authorization.

There is a special exception for certain immigrants who are applying for permanent residence based on an employer. If you apply for a green card under First, Second or Third Preference employment categories—or as a special immigrant religious worker under the Fourth Preference category—you may still apply for Adjustment of Status without having to pay the $1,000 penalty discussed earlier. To do this, however, you must have been legally admitted to the United States when you last arrived—and your total period of unauthorized work or unlawful status cannot have exceeded 180 days when you file your green card application.

## 2. Those required to pay penalty

Some aliens may also qualify for Adjustment of Status if they had a visa petition or labor certification filed by either January 14, 1998 (no requirement that they were in the U.S.) or by April 30, 2001 (in which case they must have been in the U.S. on December 21, 2000). They must pay an additional fee of $1,000.

You can adjust your status under these rules even if:

- you entered the United States without permission from the government or without a valid visa—that is, you crossed the border without first being inspected by immigration officials; this is called Entering Without Inspection, or EWI
- you have a transit visa that allows you to pass through the United States while on your way to another country—a C-1 Visa—but you violated that visa by staying too long or by working in the United States
- you are a crewmember of a ship or an airplane who has a D-1 Visa, or
- your sponsoring relative is a permanent resident and you have entered the United States with a visa, but overstayed your permitted time or worked without authorization from the INS or BCIS.

If you don't fall into any of these categories, you do not qualify. This means that someone who only recently became eligible to immigrate—for example, by marrying a U.S. citizen—but who entered the U.S. illegally, and had no visa petitions filed for him or her by any of the important 1998 or 2001 dates, will be ineligible to adjust status. Unfortunately, this person is in a difficult trap, because if he or she has spent more than six months in the U.S. illegally, leaving the U.S. to try to apply through an overseas U.S. consulate could result in being barred from returning for three or ten years. See a lawyer if you're in this situation.

## B. WHO IS BARRED FROM QUALIFYING

Some aliens cannot adjust their status in the United States no matter what. This includes people who:

- were stowaways
- were admitted to the U.S. with a Fiancé(e) Visa, but who do not marry the person who petitioned for them
- are subject to the two years foreign residence requirement under a J-1 Visa who have not obtained a waiver of that requirement

- failed to appear at a scheduled removal proceeding or asylum interview
- failed to depart as required by a deportation order
- failed to meet a voluntary departure date, or
- married while exclusion or deportation hearings were pending (and are trying to get a green card based on that marriage), unless they can show that the marriage was entered into in good faith and not for the purpose of obtaining immigrant status.

## C. HOW TO FILE

If you are one of the lucky people who can Adjust Status in the U.S., there are a number of picky rules that control how and when you can submit your various application forms. It is important to follow them exactly so that you will be sure that your paperwork can be processed quickly and properly.

## 1. Special timing for filing

If you are the spouse, parent or minor child of an American citizen (an "Immediate Relative"), or if you are over 21 years old and the unmarried child of a U.S. citizen and you have maintained your legal status and never worked illegally and your Priority Date is current, then you can file the following documents at the same time:

- Form I-130, Petition for Alien Relative, with accompanying documents. (See the sample at the end of Chapter 7.)
- Form I-485, Application to Register Permanent Residence or Adjust Status, with accompanying documents. (See the sample at the end of this chapter.)
- You must also file the other documents listed in Section C2, below.

If you are applying through a family member but do not match the description in the paragraph above, then your family member must file Form I-130 and accompanying documents at a BCIS Service Center first. Only after the I-130 is approved and your Priority Date is current can you continue with your application at a local BCIS office. However, unless your entire stay in the U.S. is legal or a separate visa petition was already on file for you by the dates described in Section A2, you will have to go through Consular Processing.

If you are an Employment Preference alien and you have received Labor Certification (See Chapter 18, Section B), you or your employer must first file Form I-140, Immigrant Petition for Alien Worker (see the sample at the end of Chapter 15), with the BCIS Regional Office. Only *after* that petition is approved and your Priority Date is current can you file Form I-485, Application to Register Permanent Residence or Adjust Status at a local BCIS office. (See the sample at the end of this chapter.) You must also file the other documents listed in Section C2, below.

---

## WHILE YOU WAIT ...

While waiting for your immigrant visa number to be available, according to the *Visa Bulletin*, it is important to maintain your legal nonimmigrant status. This could mean that you maintain your status as a student (F-1), as a treaty trader (E-1), as a nurse (H-1A) or as a professional (H-1B). If your legal status lapses, it will become more difficult—maybe impossible—to obtain permanent residence.

If you are an Immediate Relative as defined above, working without authorization or falling out of status will not prevent your application from being approved.

However, if you are married to a permanent resident or are the son or daughter of a permanent resident and you work without authorization or fall out of status, you will need to rely on the special rule that requires you to have a visa petition or Labor Certification filed by either January 14, 1998, or April 30, 2001 (with the added requirement that you have been in the U.S. on December 21, 2000), and to pay a $1,000 penalty. It doesn't matter who filed that visa petition for you, even if it's a different petitioner from the one through which you ultimately immigrate.

---

## 2. Additional forms

In addition to the forms mentioned above, an applicant for Adjustment of Status must submit the following forms to the BCIS:

- Form G-325A, Biographic Information. This form gives the information on where you have lived and worked since you were 16 years old, for background investigation. (See the sample at the end of Chapter 7.)

- Copy of Form I-94, Record of Arrival and Departure. This was attached to your passport when you entered the United States and is your proof that you had a visa and were examined by U.S. authorities. If you have lost it, your passport should have an entry notation stamped by the U.S. border officials. This stamp should be acceptable as proof of legal entry.

- Form I-864, Affidavit of Support. (See the sample at the end of Chapter 9.) If you're applying through a family member, not an employer, you must submit this sworn statement from the petitioner (an American citizen or lawful permanent resident who is sponsoring you) who has sufficient income and who promises to support you and to refund the U.S. government certain types of public benefits if you become destitute and receive public assistance after receiving your permanent residence. The latest three years' tax returns of the citizen or permanent resident should be attached to the affidavit as proof of financial capacity. (See Chapter 4.) Proof of the sponsor's employment should also be attached. If your petitioner doesn't earn enough to meet the government requirements you'll have to find an additional financial sponsor or another member of the sponsor's household who can add income and/or assets to the mix.

- Job letter. If you are working, you can submit a job letter from your employer in the United States stating your work history, when you started to work, whether your employment is permanent and how much you earn along with a payroll statement showing your earnings.

If you are married, the job letter must include your marital status, name of spouse, and name and telephone number of person to be notified in case of an emergency.

## SAMPLE JOB LETTER

ABC Company
123 Main Street
Anytown, Anystate  12345

April 24, 200_

Bureau of Citizenship and Immigration Services
26 Federal Plaza
New York, NY  10278

Dear Sir or Madam:

This letter is to certify that Jon Fratellanza has been employed by this company since March 1992 as a widget inspector.

His salary is $850/week and he is employed on a full-time, permanent basis. His prospects for continued employment with this company are excellent.

Our personnel records indicate that this employee is married. In case of emergency, his spouse, Danielle Fratellanza, must be notified at their home telephone: 111/222-3456.

Sincerely,

*Milton Mutter*

Milton Mutter
Personnel Director, ABC Company

- Form I-693, Medical examination of aliens seeking Adjustment of Status may or may not have to be submitted at the time of filing; it depends on the BCIS office where the filing takes place. If it is not required when you file, you will need to bring it to your interview.
- Four color photographs. Be sure they are taken according to INS requirements. (See Chapter 29, Section E.)
- Filing fee. The fee to file Form I-485 is $255 if the petitioner is 14 years old or over, $160 if under 14 years old—in money order or certified check made payable to the BCIS. In addition, you have to file Form I-485 Supp. A if you'll have to pay the penalty fee of $1,000 (see Section A2); and if you apply for a work permit (Form I-765) the fee is $120. Fingerprints are an additional $50.

It is best to file these forms in person to be sure that the BCIS receives them and issues a receipt for them. However, this may not be possible. Check the BCIS website instructions under Form I-485 to see where and how to file your application. Also check your local BCIS office's website—procedures vary between offices. The BCIS will send you an appointment date after your filing is processed—often eight months to a year from the time of filing, depending on how backed up they are.

Spouses' cases require a brief personal interview; other cases may or may not require one.

Also, if you have applied for Employment Authorization, you may be given an appointment to pick up your Employment Authorization card—usually about one month after you file with the BCIS.

## TRAVEL OUTSIDE THE U.S. RESTRICTED

You or your minor children should not leave the United States while waiting for your Adjustment of Status interview without first applying for and receiving advance permission to reenter the United States; this is called Advance Parole. You can apply for Advance Parole at the BCIS when you file your Adjustment of Status application or later, by submitting Form I-131.

If you leave without this permission, the BCIS will cancel your Adjustment of Status application. It will assume that your departure shows your lack of interest in receiving your green card in the United States and that you have abandoned your application.

However, if you have a real personal or business reason to leave, the BCIS may give you Advance Parole, which will allow you to leave and reenter the United States without affecting your application for Adjustment of Status. You must pay a fee of $110.

Note that if you have been out of status for six months or more after April 1, 1997, before filing your green card application, you should not travel until your application is approved. In this case, according to BCIS interpretation, you must wait for three years to return to the United States—or ten years if you were out of status for over 360 days. Not even an Advance Parole document will protect you.

## D. GETTING EMPLOYMENT AUTHORIZATION

If you want to work in the United States while your application is awaiting an interview, you must ask for permission. It's also a good thing to request because the work permit card serves as a photo I.D. File Form I-765, Application for Employment Authorization. (See the sample at the end of this chapter.) Pay a filing fee of $120 with Form I-765 in money order or certified check.

## E. APPROVAL OF YOUR GREEN CARD APPLICATION

If everything is in order, your application for Adjustment of Status should be approved. If you are not approved at your interview, you will later be notified of the approval and requested to bring your passport to the nearest BCIS office. It will be stamped with a temporary approval, good for one year, authorizing you to stay in the United States.

Your green card—which is actually pink—will be sent by mail to your address in several months. Be sure to inform the BCIS of any change of address, because your green card might not be forwarded to you by the post office. Even after you get your green card, you are obligated to send the BCIS written word every time your address changes—see Chapter 30 for this and other important rules on keeping your right to a green card.

It's wonderful! You are now a lawful permanent resident who is authorized to work and stay in the United States legally.

If your application is denied, consult an experienced immigration attorney. Unless you have some other visa or legal status in the United States, your file will be transferred to the Immigration Court for removal proceedings.

---

### INTERVIEW TIPS FOR SPOUSES

If you are requesting an Adjustment of Status as the spouse of a U.S. citizen or permanent resident, the BCIS will require a personal interview with you both before granting your application. If you know in advance that you have an out-of-town trip on your interview date, go to the BCIS personally to ask for a new interview date or write a letter in advance requesting another date.

Arrive on time for your interview. Bring copies of all the forms relevant to your application, along with evidence of a bona-fide marriage—such as wedding pictures. (See Chapter 7.)

And be prepared to wait. The BCIS may have scheduled a lot of people for Adjustment of Status interviews on the same day as yours. If you miss your turn because you step out to have a bite to eat, you may find that your pleas to be reinstated fall on deaf ears. Immigration employees are simply following procedures and they usually will not try to decide whether your absence was justified or not.

At your interview, an immigration officer will review your forms and will ask you questions based on all of the documents you have submitted. Most interviews last about 20 minutes. During the interview, answer truthfully and courteously all questions asked by the immigration officer. If you're unsure about any answer, say so.

Above everything else, immigration officers are human and understand human conditions and problems. If you cannot understand a question, request clarification. If you need a foreign language interpreter, be sure you bring a friend or hire one—the BCIS does not provide interpreters.

## APPLICATION TO REGISTER PERMANENT RESIDENCE OR ADJUST STATUS, SAMPLE FORM I-485

OMB No. 1115-0053

**U.S. Department of Justice**
Immigration and Naturalization Service

**Form I-485, Application to Register Permanent Resident or Adjust Status**

### START HERE - Please Type or Print

FOR INS USE ONLY

| | Returned | Receipt |
|---|---|---|

#### Part 1. Information About You.

| Family Name | MICHELSKI ANDA | Given Name | M. | Middle Initial |
|---|---|---|---|---|

Address - C/O GRUN MICHELA

| Street Number and Name | 68 WATERTOWN BOULEVARD | Apt. # 12 |
|---|---|---|

City ERIE

| State PENNSYLVANIA | Zip Code 19380 |
|---|---|

| Date of Birth (month/day/year) JUNE 28, 1978 | Country of Birth BULGARIA |
|---|---|

| Social Security # 128-46-9255 | A # (if any) |
|---|---|

| Date of Last Arrival (month/day/year) NOVEMBER 4, 2003 | I-94 # 123 123 123 |
|---|---|

| Current INS Status B-1 | Expires on (month/day/year) DECEMBER 1, 2003 |
|---|---|

**INS use column:**
Returned _____
Resubmitted _____
Reloc Sent _____
Reloc Rec'd _____
Applicant Interviewed

#### Part 2. Application Type. *(check one)*

I am applying for an adjustment to permanent resident status because:

a. ☑ an immigrant petition giving me an immediately available immigrant visa number has been approved. (Atttach a copy of the approval notice-- or a relative, special immigrant juvenile or special immigrant military visa petition filed with this application that will give you an immediately available visa number, if approved.)

b. ☐ my spouse or parent applied for adjustment of status or was granted lawful permanent residence in an immigrant visa category that allows derivative status for spouses and children.

c. ☐ I entered as a K-1 fiance(e) of a U.S. citizen whom I married within 90 days of entry, or I am the K-2 child of such a fiance(e). [Attach a copy of the fiance(e) petition approval notice and the marriage certificate.]

d. ☐ I was granted asylum or derivative asylum status as the spouse or child of a person granted asylum and am eligible for adjustment.

e. ☐ I am a native or citizen of Cuba admitted or paroled into the U.S. after January 1, 1959, and thereafter have been physically present in the U.S. for at least one year.

f. ☐ I am the husband, wife or minor unmarried child of a Cuban described in (e) and am residing with that person, and was admitted or paroled into the U.S. after January 1, 1959, and thereafter have been physically present in the U.S. for at least one year.

g. ☐ I have continuously resided in the U.S. since before January 1, 1972.

h. ☐ Other basis of eligibility. Explain. (If additional space is needed, use a separate piece of paper.)
_____

**Section of Law**
☐ Sec. 209(b), INA
☐ Sec. 13, Act of 9/11/57
☐ Sec. 245, INA
☐ Sec. 249, INA
☐ Sec. 2 Act of 11/2/66
☐ Sec. 2 Act of 11/2/66
☐ Other _____

**Country Chargeable**

**Eligibility Under Sec. 245**
Approved Visa Petition
Dependent of Principal Alien
Special Immigrant
Other _____

**Preference**

**Action Block**

I am already a permanent resident and am applying to have the date I was granted permanent residence adjusted to the date I originally arrived in the U.S. as a nonimmigrant or parolee, or as of May 2,1964, whichever date is later, and: *(Check one)*

i. ☐ I am a native or citizen of Cuba and meet the description in (e), above.

j. ☐ I am the husband, wife or minor unmarried child of a Cuban, and meet the description in (f), above.

**To be Completed by**
*Attorney or Representative, if any*
☐ Fill in box if G-28 is attached to represent the applicant.
VOLAG #

ATTY State License #

*Continued on back*

Form I-485 (Rev. 02/07/00)N Page 1

## SAMPLE FORM I-485 (PAGE 2)

### Part 3. Processing Information.

**A.** City/Town/Village of Birth  SOFIA | Current Occupation  LANGUAGE TEACHER

Your Mother's First Name  ANASTASIA | Your Father's First Name  LISKI

Give your name exactly how it appears on your Arrival /Departure Record (Form 1-94)

ANDA MICHELSKI

Place of Last Entry Into the U.S. (City/State)

JFK AIRPORT, NEW YORK | In what status did you last enter? (*Visitor, student, exchange alien, crewman, temporary worker, without inspection, etc.*)

Were you inspected by a U.S. Immigration Officer?  ☑ Yes  ☐ No

VISITOR

Nonimmigrant Visa Number  1062745139652 | Consulate Where Visa Was Issued  SOFIA

Date Visa Was Issued (month/day/year)  JULY 2, 2002 | Sex: ☐ Male ☑ Female | Marital Status ☐ Married ☑ Single ☐ Divorced ☐ Widowed

Have you ever before applied for permanent resident status in the U.S.? ☐ No ☑ Yes  If you checked "Yes," give date and place of filing and final disposition.

**B.** List your present husband/wife and all your sons and daughters. (If you have none, write "none." If additional space is needed, use a separate piece of paper.)

| Family Name | Given Name | Middle Initial | Date of Birth (month/day/year) |
|---|---|---|---|
| Country of Birth | Relationship | A # | Applying with You? ☐ Yes ☐ No |
| Family Name | Given Name | Middle Initial | Date of Birth (month/day/year) |
| Country of Birth | Relationship | A # | Applying with You? ☐ Yes ☐ No |
| Family Name | Given Name | Middle Initial | Date of Birth (month/day/year) |
| Country of Birth | Relationship | A # | Applying with You? ☐ Yes ☐ No |
| Family Name | Given Name | Middle Initial | Date of Birth (month/day/year) |
| Country of Birth | Relationship | A # | Applying with You? ☐ Yes ☐ No |
| Family Name | Given Name | Middle Initial | Date of Birth (month/day/year) |
| Country of Birth | Relationship | A # | Applying with You? ☐ Yes ☐ No |

**C.** List your present and past membership in or affiliation with every political organization, association, fund, foundation, party, club, society or similar group in the United States or in other places since your 16th birthday. Include any foreign military service in this part. If none, write "none." Include the name(s) of the organization(s), location(s), dates of membership from and to, and the nature of the organization (s). If additional space is needed, use a separate piece of paper.

NONE

Form I-485 (Rev. 02/07/00)N Page 2

## SAMPLE FORM I-485 (PAGE 3)

## Part 3.   Processing Information. *(Continued)*

Please answer the following questions. (If your answer is **"Yes"** to any one of these questions, explain on a separate piece of paper. Answering **"Yes"** does not necessarily mean that you are not entitled to adjust your status or register for permanent residence.)

1. Have you ever, in or outside the U. S.:

   a. knowingly committed any crime of moral turpitude or a drug-related offense for which you have not been arrested?   ☐ Yes   ☒ No

   b. been arrested, cited, charged, indicted, fined or imprisoned for breaking or violating any law or ordinance, excluding traffic violations?   ☐ Yes   ☒ No

   c. been the beneficiary of a pardon, amnesty, rehabilitation decree, other act of clemency or similar action?   ☐ Yes   ☒ No

   d. exercised diplomatic immunity to avoid prosecution for a criminal offense in the U. S.?   ☐ Yes   ☒ No

2. Have you received public assistance in the U.S. from any source, including the U.S. government or any state, county, city or municipality (other than emergency medical treatment), or are you likely to receive public assistance in the future?   ☐ Yes   ☒ No

3. Have you ever:

   a. within the past ten years been a prostitute or procured anyone for prostitution, or intend to engage in such activities in the future?   ☐ Yes   ☒ No

   b. engaged in any unlawful commercialized vice, including, but not limited to, illegal gambling?   ☐ Yes   ☒ No

   c. knowingly encouraged, induced, assisted, abetted or aided any alien to try to enter the U.S. illegally?   ☐ Yes   ☒ No

   d. illicitly trafficked in any controlled substance, or knowingly assisted, abetted or colluded in the illicit trafficking of any controlled substance?   ☐ Yes   ☒ No

4. Have you ever engaged in, conspired to engage in, or do you intend to engage in, or have you ever solicited membership or funds for, or have you through any means ever assisted or provided any type of material support to, any person or organization that has ever engaged or conspired to engage, in sabotage, kidnapping, political assassination, hijacking or any other form of terrorist activity?   ☐ Yes   ☒ No

5. Do you intend to engage in the U.S. in:

   a. espionage?   ☐ Yes   ☒ No

   b. any activity a purpose of which is opposition to, or the control or overthrow of, the government of the United States, by force, violence or other unlawful means?   ☐ Yes   ☒ No

   c. any activity to violate or evade any law prohibiting the export from the United States of goods, technology or sensitive information?   ☐ Yes   ☒ No

6. Have you ever been a member of, or in any way affiliated with, the Communist Party or any other totalitarian party?   ☐ Yes   ☒ No

7. Did you, during the period from March 23, 1933 to May 8, 1945, in association with either the Nazi Government of Germany or any organization or government associated or allied with the Nazi Government of Germany, ever order, incite, assist or otherwise participate in the persecution of any person because of race, religion, national origin or political opinion?   ☐ Yes   ☒ No

8. Have you ever engaged in genocide, or otherwise ordered, incited, assisted or otherwise participated in the killing of any person because of race, religion, nationality, ethnic origin or political opinion?   ☐ Yes   ☒ No

9. Have you ever been deported from the U.S., or removed from the U.S. at government expense, excluded within the past year, or are you now in exclusion or deportation proceedings?   ☐ Yes   ☒ No

10. Are you under a final order of civil penalty for violating section 274C of the Immigration and Nationality Act for use of fradulent documents or have you, by fraud or willful misrepresentation of a material fact, ever sought to procure, or procured, a visa, other documentation, entry into the U.S. or any immigration benefit?   ☐ Yes   ☒ No

11. Have you ever left the U.S. to avoid being drafted into the U.S. Armed Forces?   ☐ Yes   ☒ No

12. Have you ever been a J nonimmigrant exchange visitor who was subject to the two-year foreign residence requirement and not yet complied with that requirement or obtained a waiver?   ☐ Yes   ☒ No

13. Are you now withholding custody of a U.S. citizen child outside the U.S. from a person granted custody of the child?   ☐ Yes   ☒ No

14. Do you plan to practice polygamy in the U.S.?   ☐ Yes   ☒ No

## SAMPLE FORM I-485 (PAGE 4)

**Part 4.  Signature.** *(Read the information on penalties in the instructions before completing this section. You must file this application while in the United States.)*

I certify, under penalty of perjury under the laws of the United States of America, that this application and the evidence submitted with it is all true and correct. I authorize the release of any information from my records which the INS needs to determine eligibility for the benefit I am seeking.

**Selective Service Registration. The following applies to you if you are a man at least 18 years old, but not yet 26 years old, who is required to register with the Selective Service System:** I understand that my filing this adjustment of status application with the Immigration and Naturalization Service authorizes the INS to provide certain registration information to the Selective Service System in accordance with the Military Selective Service Act. Upon INS acceptance of my application, I authorize INS to transmit to the Selective Service System my name, current address, Social Security number, date of birth and the date I filed the application for the purpose of recording my Selective Service registration as of the filing date. If, however, the INS does not accept my application, I further understand that, if so required, I am responsible for registering with the Selective Service by other means, provided I have not yet reached age 26.

| *Signature* | *Print Your Name* | *Date* | *Daytime Phone Number* |
|---|---|---|---|
| *Anda Michelski* | Anda Michelski | 12/19/03 | 314-276-9440 |

***Please Note:*** *If you do not completely fill out this form or fail to submit required documents listed in the instructions, you may not be found eligible for the requested benefit and this application may be denied.*

**Part 5.  Signature of Person Preparing Form, If Other Than Above.** *(Sign Below)*

I declare that I prepared this application at the request of the above person and it is based on all information of which I have knowledge.

| *Signature* | *Print Your Name* | *Date* | *Daytime Phone Number* |
|---|---|---|---|

*Firm Name and Address*

Form I-485 (Rev. 02/07/00)N Page 4

## APPLICATION FOR EMPLOYMENT AUTHORIZATION, SAMPLE FORM I-765

**U.S. Department of Justice**
Immigration and Naturalization Service

OMB No. 1115-0163; Expires 04/30/05

## Application for Employment Authorization

**Do Not Write in This Block.**

| Remarks | Action Stamp | Fee Stamp |
|---|---|---|
| A# | | |

Applicant is filing under §274a.12 _____

☐ Application Approved. Employment Authorized / Extended *(Circle One)*   until _____ (Date).
                           _____ (Date).

          Subject to the following conditions: _____
☐ Application Denied.
      ☐ Failed to establish eligibility under 8 CFR 274a.12 (a) or (c).
      ☐ Failed to establish economic necessity as required in 8 CFR 274a.12(c)(14), (18) and 8 CFR 214.2(f)

I am applying for:
☑ Permission to accept employment.
☐ Replacement *(of lost employment authorization document).*
☐ Renewal of my permission to accept employment *(attach previous employment authorization document).*

1. Name (Family Name in CAPS)   (First)   (Middle)
MANZETTI    JULIET    ANNA

2. Other Names Used (Include Maiden Name)
JULIET STEFANO

3. Address in the United States (Number and Street)   (Apt. Number)
280 MOSHER STREET
(Town or City)   (State/Country)   (ZIP Code)
BALTIMORE   MARYLAND   21216

4. Country of Citizenship/Nationality
ITALY

5. Place of Birth (Town or City)   (State/Province)   (Country)
VERONA    ITALY

6. Date of Birth    7. Sex
DEC. 23, 1962    ☐ Male ☑ Female

8. Marital Status   ☑ Married   ☐ Single
               ☐ Widowed   ☐ Divorced

9. Social Security Number (Include all Numbers you have ever used) (if any)
NONE

10. Alien Registration Number (A-Number) or I-94 Number (if any)
45678910

11. Have you ever before applied for employment authorization from INS?
☐ Yes (If yes, complete below)    ☑ No
Which INS Office?    Date(s)

Results (Granted or Denied - attach all documentation)

12. Date of Last Entry into the U.S. (Month/Day/Year)
SEPTEMBER 1, 2002

13. Place of Last Entry into the U.S.
NEW YORK, NEW YORK

14. Manner of Last Entry (Visitor, Student, etc.)
PAROLEE

15. Current Immigration Status (Visitor, Student, etc.)
PAROLEE

16. Go to Part 2 of the Instructions, Eligibility Categories. In the space below, place the letter and number of the category you selected from the instructions (For example, (a)(8), (c)(17)(iii), etc.).

Eligibility under 8 CFR 274a.12

(   ) ( C ) ( 9 )

## Certification.

**Your Certification:** I certify, under penalty of perjury under the laws of the United States of America, that the foregoing is true and correct. Furthermore, I authorize the release of any information which the Immigration and Naturalization Service needs to determine eligibility for the benefit I am seeking. I have read the Instructions in Part 2 and have identified the appropriate eligibility category in Block 16.

| Signature | Telephone Number | Date |
|---|---|---|
| *Juliet Manzetti* | (301) 123-4567 | MAY 25, 2003 |

**Signature of Person Preparing Form, If Other Than Above:** I declare that this document was prepared by me at the request of the applicant and is based on all information of which I have any knowledge.

| Print Name | Address | Signature | Date |
|---|---|---|---|
| | | | |

| Initial Receipt | Resubmitted | Relocated | | Completed | | |
|---|---|---|---|---|---|---|
| | | Rec'd | Sent | Approved | Denied | Returned |
| | | | | | | |

Form I-765 (Rev. 5/09/02)Y

# 9

# CONSULAR PROCESSING

## Leaving the U.S. to Get a Green Card

If you are outside the United States and wish to come to the U.S. as a permanent resident, you can do so by applying for an immigrant visa at a consulate abroad, as long as you have an approved employment-based or family-based preference petition which has become current. This is called Consular Processing. Even if you are in the United States, you may have no choice but to complete your application process at an overseas consulate.

---

### Choosing the Best Procedure

While the requirements for Adjustment of Status (getting a green card at a U.S. BCIS office) are rather restrictive, if you qualify, there are a number of advantages to that procedure over Consular Processing. If you are currently in the U.S. or have a current visa allowing you to go there, read Chapter 8 carefully to see whether you qualify to get a green card through Adjustment of Status.

---

## A. Who Qualifies

Assuming you're otherwise eligible for a green card, which you can research using other chapters of this book, you may be able to get an immigrant visa through Consular Processing if:

- you have an approved visa petition, or
- you are the derivative beneficiary—such as the spouse, sibling or child—of someone who holds an approved visa petition, and
- you are not subject to the three-year or ten-year waiting periods imposed on people who have lived in the U.S. illegally. Also, be sure you are admissible as an immigrant before leaving the United States if you are in this country and wish to proceed with Consular Processing. (See Chapter 22.)

## B. Filing the Petition or Application

The first step to Consular Processing is to have a visa petition on Form I-130 filed by your relative (see the sample at the end of Chapter 7) or one on Form I-140 filed by your employer (see the sample at the end of Chapter 15) at a

BCIS Regional Service Center. We discuss visa petitions in the chapters concerning particular categories of eligibility. As a reminder, the technical term for the American citizen, resident or employer filing the visa petition is the petitioner. The alien on whose behalf the visa petition is filed is called the beneficiary.

An important part of the petition is the part asking to which U.S. Consulate the beneficiary plans to apply for an immigrant visa. Normally, you choose the consulate located where you currently live. For a complete list of U.S. consulates, with links to their websites, go to the State Department website at www.state.gov. On the homepage, click "U.S. Embassies and Consulates." If your country does not have diplomatic relations with the United States, ask the immigration office to direct you to where Consular Processing is being done for your country.

## C. Starting the Process

When the U.S. Consulate receives the approved visa petition, the beneficiary will be notified.

If you are an Immediate Relative or your Priority Date becomes current, you will receive an instruction packet of documents from the Department of State's National Visa Center. The packet contains some forms and tells you what documents you must have before you can be given an appointment for your immigrant visa interview.

If you are a preference alien whose Priority Date is not yet available, you will receive a letter informing you that you will have to wait a longer time for your immigrant visa to be ready. When it is ready, you will receive the instruction packet.

### 1. Complete and send your application

Included in your instruction packet from the National Visa Center will be Form DS-2001 (formerly "OF-169") and Form DS-230 Part I, Application for Immigrant Visa and Alien Registration. The first part of Form DS-230 asks for information about your family and personal history, your past and present residences, places of employment and your membership in any organizations. Answer all questions as accurately as possible. (See the samples at the end of this chapter; note, however, that because the new form DS-2001 was not yet available, we've shown a sample of the old version, Form OF-169.)

Complete and mail these forms as soon as possible. The U.S. Consulate will not begin working on your immigration papers until it receives completed forms from you. Once the forms are received, government officers will begin a background security check.

## 2. Other documents to prepare

You should also begin gathering a number of other documents, including:

- current passports for you and for everyone in your family who is getting an immigrant visa (they must not expire earlier than six months after your interview date)
- birth certificates for you and for your spouse or children, with English translations
- a police clearance certificate for each person over 16 years of age from every country in which the person has lived for more than six months
- marriage certificate, death certificate, divorce or annulment decree—whichever shows your current marital status
- military record of any service in your country, or any country, including certified proof of military service and of honorable or dishonorable discharge
- a certified copy of court and prison records if you have been convicted of a crime
- evidence of your own assets, including titles or deeds to any real estate, condominium or co-op apartment, or bank account statements to show that you are not destitute and will not be a financial burden to the U.S. government, and
- if you are immigrating through a family petition, a job letter from your petitioner's employer in the United States, which gives their work history and salary and explains whether the employment is permanent. (See the sample in Chapter 8, Section C2.)
- Form I-864 (with $65 fee), or Form I-134, both of them called Affidavit of Support. (See the samples at the end of this chapter.) Which form you must submit depends on your situation. You must file Form I-864 if your petition is family-based—or if it is employment-based, but your relatives submitted your visa petition or own at least 5% of the petitioning company. On both Form I-134 and I-864, a U.S. citizen or permanent resident promises to repay the U.S. government if you become impoverished and go on public assistance after you arrive in the United States. Your sponsor who fills out the form must also include financial documents, including an employer letter or other proof of income, U.S. income tax returns and W-2s for the last three years and bank statements or other proof of assets. In certain exceptional cases, however, a Form I-864 need not be filed. One of these is where the beneficiary is a child (adopted or natural born) who will become a U.S. citizen automatically upon entering the United States (see Chapter 11 for details). The other is where

### THE TRUTH IS... THEY PROBABLY WON'T FIND YOU

Unless you come to the attention of the immigration authorities, you can stay in the United States while you are waiting to be called for Consular Processing. But if you have no separate immigration status, then you are not entitled to work in the United States—and staying here is a violation of the law. You run the risk of being deported if the INS decides to start deportation proceedings against you. And, if you have been in the United States for more than six months without INS permission, you could be prevented from reentering the United States for three years. If you spend one or more years out of status, you may not be eligible to return for ten years. In either case, you may require a lawyer and should consult Chapter 22.

Although filing a petition on your behalf with the BCIS brings your presence in the United States to the notice of the U.S. government, the BCIS computer system has not yet reached such a level of sophistication that it will automatically flash red to indicate the illegal status of any beneficiary.

Until the BCIS installs a more comprehensive system or hires more personnel, you can hope to remain unnoticed until the State Department's cut-off date includes your Priority Date and the American Embassy assigns you an interview date for your immigrant visa. You could then return to your country when your immigrant visa interview is imminent. But it will then be up to you to prove that you weren't living in the U.S. illegally. If you fail, you could be barred from returning for three or ten years.

the beneficiary, or the beneficiary's spouse or parent, has worked 40 "quarters" (about ten years, as defined by the Social Security Administration) in the United States.

You will also be required to submit to fingerprinting, for a background check by the FBI. (See Chapter 29, Section F.)

As soon as you have all the documents required by the consulate, complete Form DS-2001. Sign, date and mail it to the consulate that is processing your application. This informs the consulate that you—and all people immigrating with you—now have all the documents required and are ready to attend the interview.

You will then be sent a final packet, which gives you the date of your interview with the Chief of the Immigrant Visa Branch. On this form, you will also be directed to where you must go to get a required medical examination. During that exam, your blood will be tested and you will be X-rayed. You may be barred from immigrating if these tests show that you have a contagious disease of public health concern such as AIDS or tuberculosis, or if you have a severe mental disorder.

## D. Personal Interview

Bring with you to your interview the following documents, including:

- Three color photographs. These must be taken in the manner required by the U.S. Consulate. (See Chapter 29, Section E.)
- Medical examination report.
- Form DS-230 Part II, Application for Immigrant Visa and Alien Registration (Sworn Statement). (See the sample at the end of this chapter.) Each applicant must submit one. After your interview, you must sign it in the presence of the U.S. consular officer.
- U.S. income tax returns. All those who have worked in the U.S. and intend to immigrate must present proof that they have filed income tax returns for every year they have worked, as reported on Form OF-230.
- Filing fee. The fee is $335 per person. The charge for a Fiancé(e) Visa is $65.

 **Unmarried Children Beware**

If you are an unmarried son or daughter of a permanent resident or an American citizen, and you marry before you have your immigration visa interview, be prepared for a shock: Your visa will be denied because you are no longer in the Immediate Relative Preference category under which you were petitioned.

If you married after your visa interview but before you entered the U.S. with your immigrant visa, you may also be in serious trouble. Although you may be admitted into the United States because the BCIS has no way of knowing that you are no longer eligible, the agency could discover this fact if you later apply to bring your spouse or try to become a U.S. citizen. It will not matter that you have been admitted as a permanent resident.

Deportation proceedings will be started against you. You and your spouse will not be reunited in the United States. And you will eventually have to go back to your country and start all over again in the preference category of the married son or daughter of an American citizen. You could completely lose your immigrant eligibility if your parent is only a green cardholder.

If you fall into this category, you should see an attorney.

## TIPS FOR THE INTERVIEW

The most important thing to do is relax. The interviewer will ask you only about information you have already given in response to questions on your immigration forms and other documents.

Most interviews are brief—less than 30 minutes.

If you have overstayed your visa in the U.S., you can expect questions about why you have done so.

Sometimes, questions will be repeated—especially if your employer has filed the petition for you. If you have worked as a housekeeper or nanny for a private employer, you may be asked for photos taken at your workplace.

Answer all questions truthfully. If you cannot understand a question, be brave and ask for an interpreter. It is better to be embarrassed about not understanding English very well than to be denied your immigrant visa because you misunderstood the question.

## E. APPROVAL OF YOUR IMMIGRANT VISA

If everything is in order, if you have all the documents required and if you are not inadmissible according to immigration law—you have no criminal record, terrorist affiliations or communicable disease, for example—your application for an immigrant visa should be approved.

You will be given a final document, your Immigrant Visa and Alien Registration, which bears your photograph and a stamp of approval. You will also be given your original Form DS-230, supporting documents and your medical X-rays. You will carry all these documents with you during your trip to the United States and give them to immigration authorities when you arrive.

Your immigrant visa is valid for six months, and you must arrive in the United States within those six months.

If you are unable to leave for the United States and your visa is about to expire, you may apply for an extension of your immigrant visa by means of an affidavit, or written statement signed before a notary public, explaining why you are unable to leave on time. But unless you have a very good reason, the U.S. Consulate will be reluctant to approve an extension.

## F. ARRIVING IN THE UNITED STATES

When you arrive at the first American city, which is now your port of entry, the American citizens who were on the plane with you will be admitted in one line while all the noncitizens will be queuing in another line.

When it is your turn, the immigration officer will take your immigrant documents and keep them—all but your X-rays—and make them part of your permanent record in the BCIS office. Your passport will be stamped to show that you have entered as a lawful permanent resident and your Form I-94, Record of Arrival and Departure, will be stamped with an Employment Authorization, good for six months from your date of entry.

Your green card will be mailed to you within several months. Be sure to inform the BCIS if you change addresses, using Form AR-11, available in this book (but see the BCIS website for full instructions). You must tell them within ten days of your move. Otherwise, you may not receive your green card until you have made several trips to the BCIS office and filled out countless forms. See Chapter 30 for more information on keeping your right to a green card.

At last. You are now a bona fide immigrant—able to live and work legally in the United States. Welcome.

## OF-169

# INSTRUCTIONS FOR IMMIGRANT VISA APPLICANTS

This office has received evidence entitling you to immigrant visa status. While no assurance can be given regarding the date of your visa interview appointment, you should now prepare for that appointment by taking the following three steps:

**FIRST:** Complete and send immediately to the consular office processing your case the enclosed Form OF-230 Part I, APPLICA TION FOR IMMIGRANT VISA AND ALIEN REGISTRATION (Biographic Data). The consular office cannot process your case until this form is received.

**SECOND:** Obtain the following documents on this checklist which pertain to you. As you obtain each document, check the box before each item. Do NOT send them to the consular office.

☐**1. PASSPORTS:** A Passport must be valid for travel to the United States and must have at least six months validity beyond the issuance date of the visa. Children may be included on a parent's passport, but if over the age of 16, they must have their photographs attached to the passport.

☐**2. BIRTH CERTIFICATES:** One certified copy of the birth certificate of each person named in the application is required. Birth records must be presented for all unmarried children under age 21, even if they do not wish to immigrate at this time. (If children are deceased, so state giving year of death.) The certificate must state the date and place of birth and the names of both parents. The certificate must also indicate that it is an extract from official records. If you, or any children were adopted, you must submit a certified copy of the final adoption decree. Photostatic copies are acceptable provided the original is offered for inspection by the consular officer.

　　**UNOBTAINABLE BIRTH CERTIFICATE:** In rare cases, it may be impossible to obtain a birth certificate because records have been destroyed or the government will not issue one. In such cases, you should obtain a statement to that effect from the civil registrar's office and proceed to obtain secondary evidence of birth. A baptismal certificate may be submitted for consideration provided it contains the date and place of the applicant's birth and information concerning parentage and provided the baptism took place shortly after birth. Should a baptismal certificate be unobtainable, a close relative, preferably the applicant's mother, should prepare a notarized statement giving the place and date of the applicant's birth, the names of both parents, and the maiden name of the mother. The statement must be executed before an official authorized to administer oaths or affirmations. In such cases, please bring any secondary evidence you might have concerning your birth.

☐**3. POLICE CERTIFICATES:** Each visa applicant aged 16 years or over is required to submit a police certificate from the police authorities of each locality of the country of the applicant's nationality or current residence where the applicant has resided for at least six months since attaining the age of sixteen. Police certificates are also required from all other countries where the applicant has resided for at least one year. A police certificate must also be obtained from the police authorities of any place where the applicant has been arrested for any reason, regardless of how long he or she lived there. Police certificates must cover the entire period of the applicant's residence in any area. A certificate issued by the police authorities where you now reside must be of recent date when presented to the consular officer. The term "police certificate" as used in this paragraph means a certification by appropri　ate police authorities stating what their records show concerning each applicant, including all arrests, the reasons for the arrests, and the disposition of each case of which there is a record.

Police certificates from certain countries are considered unobtainable. See the attached list on form DSL-1083. If specific questions arise regarding police certificates, please consult the consular office.

☐**4. COURT AND PRISON RECORDS:** Persons who have been convicted of a crime must obtain a certified copy of each court record and of any prison record, regardless of the fact that they may have benefited subsequently from an amnesty, pardon, or other act of clemency.

☐**5. MILITARY RECORDS:** A certified copy of any military record, if applicable and obtainable, is required.

☐**6. PHOTOGRAPHS:** Two (2) color photographs with white background on glossy paper, unretouched, and unmounted are required. The photograph must be a three-quarter frontal portrait with the right side of the face and right ear visible. The dimensions of the facial image must measure about one inch (30 mm) from chin to top of hair. No head covering or dark glasses should be worn.

☐**7. EVIDENCE OF SUPPORT:** Form I-864, a contractual affidavit of support, must be submitted for most family-based applicants and employment-based applicants when a relative is the petitioner or has ownership interest in the petitioning business. The enclosed information sheet provides guidance for preparing the I-864. Other applicants must show evidence that they are not likely to become public charges while in the United States.

OPTIONAL FORM 169 (CPC) 4-98
DEPARTMENT OF STATE

# OF-169 (PAGE 2)

☐**8. MARRIAGE CERTIFICATES:**   Married persons are required to present a certified copy of their marriage certificate. Proof of the termination of any previous marriage must also be submitted (e.g., death certificate of spouse, final decrees of divorce or annulment).

☐**9. ORIGINAL DOCUMENTS:**   If you are the beneficiary of a family-based immigrant visa petition, you must be prepared to present the **originals** of all civil documents which establish your claimed relationship to the petitioner.

☐**10. TRANSLATIONS:**   All documents not in English, or in the official language of the country in which application for a visa is being made, must be accompanied by certified English translations. Translations must be certified by a competent translator and sworn to before a Notary Public. (   <u>All</u> documents in Japanese must be translated.)

ONLY ONE COPY OF EACH DOCUMENT, EXCEPT PHOTOGRAPHS, MUST BE SUBMITTED WITH THE VISA APPLICATION. YOU ARE ADVISED, HOWEVER, TO OBTAIN THE NECESSARY DOCUMENTS IN DUPLICATE, AS THIS WILL ENABLE YOU TO PROVIDE IDENTICAL COPIES IN THE EVENT THE FIRST SET IS LOST OR DAMAGED.

**PLEASE READ THE FOLLOWING CAREFULLY**

**THIRD:**  As soon as you have obtained all of the documents that apply to your case, carefully read the statement at the bottom of this page, sign and date it, and send the form to the consular office processing your case. You will not be scheduled for an appointment until you sign and return the checklist.

After this form has been sent to the consular office, you will be scheduled for a visa interview at the earliest possible date. It is not possible to predict when this will be since it depends upon when the priority date for your visa category and country becomes current. You will receive an appointment letter along with instructions for a medical examination approximately one month before your scheduled interview with a consular officer. You may not receive any further correspondence from the consular office until the appointment is scheduled.

The total fee for an immigrant visa is U.S. $325, or the local currency equivalent. Each applicant must be prepared to pay this fee on the appointment date.

You need not check with the consular office unless you have to report a CHANGE OF ADDRESS or change in your situation such as marriage, death of petitioner, or birth of children. Please do not send any documents to the consular office unless you are specifically requested to do so.

Enclosures:
1.  Optional Form 230 Part I, Application for Immigrant Visa and Alien Registration - Biographic Data
2.  Form DSL-l083, Immigrant Visa Supplemental Information Sheet
3.  Form I-864, Affidavit of Support and Checklist

## APPLICANT'S STATEMENT

I have in my possession and am prepared to present all the documents listed in items 1 through 10 which apply to my case, as indicated by the check mark I have placed in the appropriate boxes. I fully realize that no advance assurance can be given when or whether a visa will actually be issued to me and I also understand that I should NOT give up my job, dispose of property, or make any final travel arrangements until a visa is actually issued to me. When it is possible for me to receive an appointment to make formal visa application, I intend to apply: (check appropriate boxes)

☐1. Alone
☐2. Together with my spouse (Print first name: _____ )
☐3. Together with my spouse and the following minor children: (Print first names of each child

who will accompany  you)

_____          *DATE:* _____

_____          *CASE NUMBER:* _____

_____          *SIGNATURE:* _____

_____          *PRINT NAME :* _____

_____          *CURRENT ADDRESS:* _____

_____          _____

## APPLICATION FOR IMMIGRANT VISA AND ALIEN REGISTRATION, SAMPLE FORM DS-230

U.S. Department of State

# APPLICATION FOR IMMIGRANT VISA AND ALIEN REGISTRATION

OMB APPROVAL NO. 1405-0015
EXPIRES: 05/31/2004
ESTIMATED BURDEN: 1 HOUR*
(See Page 2)

### PART I - BIOGRAPHIC DATA

**INSTRUCTIONS:** Complete one copy of this form for yourself and each member of your family, regardless of age, who will immigrate with you. Please print or type your answers to all questions. Mark questions that are Not Applicable with "N/A". If there is insufficient room on the form, answer on a separate sheet using the same numbers that appear on the form. Attach any additional sheets to this form.

**WARNING:** Any false statement or concealment of a material fact may result in your permanent exclusion from the United States.

This form (DS-230 PART I) is the first of two parts. This part, together with Form DS-230 PART II, constitutes the complete Application for Immigrant Visa and Alien Registration.

| 1. Family Name | First Name | Middle Name |
|---|---|---|
| Mancini | Terese | Maria |

2. Other Names Used or Aliases *(If married woman, give maiden name)*
Terese Brabantio

3. Full Name in Native Alphabet *(If Roman letters not used)*
n/a

| 4. Date of Birth *(mm-dd-yyyy)* | 5. Age | 6. Place of Birth (City or town) | *(Province)* | *(Country)* |
|---|---|---|---|---|
| Feb. 02, 1969 | 33 | Venice | | Italy |

| 7. Nationality *(If dual national, give both)* | 8. Gender | 9. Marital Status |
|---|---|---|
| Italian | ☐ Male　☒ Female | ☐ Single *(Never married)*　☒ Married　☐ Widowed　☐ Divorced　☐ Separated<br>Including my present marriage, I have been married ___one___ times. |

10. Permanent address in the United States where you intend to live, if known *(street address including zip code)*. Include the name of a person who currently lives there.

800 Broadway
Linderhurst, NY 11757

Telephone number:　212 222-2121

11. Address in the United States where you want your Permanent Resident Card *(Green Card)* mailed, if different from address in item #10 *(include the name of a person who currently lives there)*.

Telephone number:

12. Your Present Occupation
Freelance writer

13. Present Address *(Street Address) (City or Town) (Province) (Country)*
108 Piazza d'Azeglio
Venice, Italy

Telephone number: Home　764-290-7645　Office　none

| 14. Name of Spouse *(Maiden or family name)* | First Name | Middle Name |
|---|---|---|
| Mancini | Alberto | Ilario |

Date *(mm-dd-yyyy)* and place of birth of spouse:　3/30/58, Los Angeles, CA

Address of spouse *(If different from your own)*:
800 Broadway
Linderhurst, NY 11757

Spouse's occupation:　cook　　　　Date of marriage *(mm-dd-yyyy)*:

| 15. Father's Family Name | First Name | Middle Name |
|---|---|---|
| Brabantio | Francisco | Noffo |

| 16. Father's Date of Birth *(mm-dd-yyyy)* | Place of Birth | Current Address | If deceased, give year of death |
|---|---|---|---|
| August 2, 1941 | Venice, Italy | deceased | 1979 |

| 17. Mother's Family Name at Birth | First Name | Middle Name |
|---|---|---|
| Gallo | Magdalena | Alcine |

| 18. Mother's Date of Birth *(mm-dd-yyyy)* | Place of Birth | Current Address | If deceased, give year of death |
|---|---|---|---|
| April 24, 1948 | Venice, Italy | 90 Piazza d'Azeglio, Venice, Italy | |

DS-230 Part I
05-2001

**THIS FORM MAY BE OBTAINED FREE AT CONSULAR OFFICES OF THE UNITED STATES OF AMERICA**
**PREVIOUS EDITIONS OBSOLETE**

Page 1 of 4

# FORM DS-230 PART I (PAGE 2)

**19. List Names, Dates and Places of Birth, and Addresses of ALL Children.**

| NAME | DATE (mm-dd-yyyy) | PLACE OF BIRTH | ADDRESS (If different from your own) |
|---|---|---|---|
| Giovana Moreno | 6/01/90 | Florence, Italy | |

**20. List below all places you have lived for at least six months since reaching the age of 16, including places in your country of nationality. Begin with your present residence.**

| CITY OR TOWN | PROVINCE | COUNTRY | FROM/TO (mm-yyyy) |
|---|---|---|---|
| Venice | | Italy | 1969 present |

**21a. Person(s) named in 14 and 19 who will accompany you to the United States now.**

Giovanna Moreno

**21b. Person(s) named in 14 and 19 who will follow you to the United States at a later date.**

**22. List below all employment for the last ten years.**

| EMPLOYER | LOCATION | JOB TITLE | FROM/TO (mm-yyyy) |
|---|---|---|---|
| Self-employed | 108 Piazza d'Azeglio Venice, Italy | Writer | Aug. 1995 present |

In what occupation do you intend to work in the United States? Writer

**23. List below all educational institutions attended.**

| SCHOOL AND LOCATION | FROM/TO (mm-yyyy) | COURSE OF STUDY | DEGREE OR DIPLOMA |
|---|---|---|---|
| Venice University, Italy | 9/1986 6/1990 | Linguistics | B.A. |
| Venice High School, Italy | 9/1982 6/1986 | | Diploma |
| Venice Primary School | 9/1970 6/1982 | | Certificate |

Languages spoken or read: Italian, English

Professional associations to which you belong: Italian Writer's Guild

**24. Previous Military Service** ☐ Yes ☒ No

Branch: ___ Dates (mm-dd-yyyy) of Service: ___

Rank/Position: ___ Military Speciality/Occupation: ___

**25. List dates of all previous visits to or residence in the United States. (If never, write "never") Give type of visa status, if known. Give INS "A" number if any.**

Never

| FROM/TO (mm-yyyy) | LOCATION | TYPE OF VISA | "A" NO. (If known) |
|---|---|---|---|
| | | | |

SIGNATURE OF APPLICANT
*Terese Mancini*

DATE (mm-dd-yyyy)
7/30/03

## AFFIDAVIT OF SUPPORT, SAMPLE FORM I-134

OMB No. 1115-0062

**U.S. Department of Justice**
Immigration and Naturalization Service

**Affidavit of Support**

*(Answer All Items: Fill in with Typewriter or Print in Block Letters in Ink.)*

I, __Alberto Mancini__ residing at __800 Broadway__
(Name) (Street and Number)

__Linderhurst__ __New York__ __11757__ __U.S.A.__
(City) (State) (Zip Code if in U.S.) (Country)

**BEING DULY SWORN DEPOSE AND SAY:**

1. I was born on __March 30, 1958__ at __Los Angeles, California__ __U.S.A.__
(Date) (City) (Country)

   If you are **not** a native born United States citizen, answer the following as appropriate:
   a. If a United States citizen through naturalization, give certificate of naturalization number _____
   b. If a United States citizen through parent(s) or marriage, give citizenship certificate number _____
   c. If United States citizenship was derived by some other method, attach a statement of explanation.
   d. If a lawfully admitted permanent resident of the United States, give "A" number _____

2. That I am __44__ years of age and have resided in the United States since (date) __1958__

3. That this affidavit is executed in behalf of the following person:

| Name | Gender | Age |
|---|---|---|
| Terese Mancini | F | 33 |

| Citizen of (Country) | Marital Status | Relationship to Sponsor |
|---|---|---|
| Italy | Married | Wife |

| Presently resides at (Street and Number) | (City) | (State) | (Country) |
|---|---|---|---|
| 108 Piazza D'Azeglio | Venice | | Italy |

Name of spouse and children accompanying or following to join person:

| Spouse | Gender | Age | Child | | Gender | Age |
|---|---|---|---|---|---|---|
| not applicable | | | | | | |
| Child | Gender | Age | Child | | Gender | Age |
| Giovana Moreno | F | 11 | | | | |
| Child | Gender | Age | Child | | Gender | Age |

4. That this affidavit is made by me for the purpose of assuring the United States Government that the person(s) named in item 3 will not become a public charge in the United States.

5. That I am willing and able to receive, maintain and support the person(s) named in item 3. That I am ready and willing to deposit a bond, if necessary, to guarantee that such person(s) will not become a public charge during his or her stay in the United States, or to guarantee that the above named person(s) will maintain his or her nonimmigrant status, if admitted temporarily and will depart prior to the expiration of his or her authorized stay in the United States.

6. That I understand this affidavit will be binding upon me for a period of three (3) years after entry of the person(s) named in item 3 and that the information and documentation provided by me may be made available to the Secretary of Health and Human Services and the Secretary of Agriculture, who may make it available to a public assistance agency.

7. That I am employed as, or engaged in the business of __Merchant Shipping__ with __Duke of Venice__
(Type of Business) (Name of concern)

   at __100 Piazza D'Azeglio__ __Venice Italy__
   (Street and Number) (City) (State) (Zip Code)

   I derive an annual income of *(if self-employed, I have attached a copy of my last income tax return or report of commercial rating concern which I certify to be true and correct to the best of my knowledge and belief. See instructions for nature of evidence of net worth to be submitted.)* $ __50,000.00__

   I have on deposit in savings banks in the United States $ __25,000.00__

   I have other personal property, the reasonable value of which is $ __0,000.00__

OVER

Form I-134 (Rev. 10/12/00)Y

## AFFIDAVIT OF SUPPORT, SAMPLE FORM I-134 (PAGE 2)

I have stocks and bonds with the following market value, as indicated on the attached list, which I certify to be true and correct to the best of my knowledge and belief. $ _none_

I have life insurance in the sum of $ 1,000,000-

With a cash surrender value of $ 25,000-

I own real estate valued at $ 200,000-

With mortgage(s) or other encumbrance(s) thereon amounting to $ _____

Which is located at _800 Broadway_ _Lindenhurst_ _New York_ _11757_
(Street and Number)   (City)   (State)   (Zip Code)

8. That the following persons are dependent upon me for support: *(Place an "x" in the appropriate column to indicate whether the person named is **wholly** or **partially** dependent upon you for support.)*

| Name of Person | Wholly Dependent | Partially Dependent | Age | Relationship to Me |
|---|---|---|---|---|
| Terese Mancini | X | | 33 | Wife |
| | | | | |
| Giovana Moreno | X | | 12 | Stepdaughter |

9. That I have previously submitted affidavit(s) of support for the following person(s). If none, state **"None."**

| Name | Date submitted |
|---|---|
| None | |

10. That I have submitted visa petition(s) to the Immigration and Naturalization Service on behalf of the following person(s). If none, state none.

| Name | Relationship | Date submitted |
|---|---|---|
| Terese Mancini | Wife | This Affidavit |

11. **(Complete this block only if the person named in the item 3 will be in the United States temporarily.)**
That I ☐ intend ☐ do not intend, to make specific contributions to the support of the person named in item 3. *(If you check "intend," indicate the exact nature and duration of the contributions. For example, if you intend to furnish room and board, state for how long and, if money, state the amount in United States dollars and state whether it is to be given in a lump sum, weekly or monthly, or for how long.)*

_Not Applicable_

### Oath or Affirmation of Sponsor

*I acknowledge at that I have read Part III of the Instructions, Sponsor and Alien Liability, and am aware of my responsibilities as an immigrant sponsor under the Social Security Act, as amended, and the Food Stamp Act, as amended.*

**I swear (affirm) that I know the contents of this affidavit signed by me and the statements are true and correct.**

**Signature of sponsor** _Alberto Mancini_

**Subscribed and sworn to (affirmed) before me this** _6_ **day of** _January_ , _2003_

**at** _Venice   Italy_ . **My commission expires on** _____

***Signature of Officer Administering Oath*** _John Doe_ **Title** _Vice Consul American Consulate_

**If affidavit prepared by other than sponsor, please complete the following: I declare that this document was prepared by me at the request of the sponsor and is based on all information of which I have knowledge.**

| (Signature) | (Address) | (Date) |
|---|---|---|

## AFFIDAVIT OF SUPPORT UNDER SECTION 213A OF THE ACT, SAMPLE FORM I-864

OMB No. 1115-0214

**Affidavit of Support Under Section 213A of the Act**

**U.S. Department of Justice**
Immigration and Naturalization Service

START HERE - Please Type or Print

### Part 1.    Information on Sponsor  (You)

| Last Name | First Name | Middle Name |
|---|---|---|
| Mancini | Alberto | Ilario |

Mailing Address *(Street Number and Name)*
800 Broadway

Apt/Suite Number
N/A

City
Linderhurst

State or Province
New York

Country
U.S.

ZIP/Postal Code
11757

Telephone Number
212 222-2121

Place of Residence if different from above *(Street Number and Name)*
same as above

Apt/Suite Number

City

State or Province

Country

ZIP/Postal Code

Telephone Number

Date of Birth *(Month, Day, Year)*
3-30-58

Place of Birth *(City, State, Country)*
Los Angeles, CA, U.S.

Are you a U.S. Citizen?
☒ Yes  ☐ No

Social Security Number
222-22-2222

A-Number *(If any)*
none

**FOR AGENCY USE ONLY**

This Affidavit        Receipt

[ ] Meets

[ ] Does not meet

Requirements of Section 213A

Officer or I.J. Signature

Location

Date

### Part 2.    Basis for Filing Affidavit of Support

I am filing this affidavit of support because *(check one)*:

a. ☒  I filed/am filing the alien relative petition.

b. ☐  I filed/am filing an alien worker petition on behalf of the intending

immigrant, who is related to me as my _____ .
*(relationship)*

c. ☐  I have ownership interest of at least 5% _____ .
*(name of entity which filed visa petition)*

which filed an alien worker petition on behalf of the intending

immigrant, who is related to me as my _____ .
*(relationship)*

d. ☐  I am a joint sponsor willing to accept the legal obligations with any other sponsor(s).

### Part 3.    Information on the Immigrant(s) You Are Sponsoring

| Last Name | First Name | Middle Name |
|---|---|---|
| Mancini | Terese | Maria |

Date of Birth *(Month, Day, Year)*
2-15-69

Sex
☐ Male  ☒ Female

Social Security Number *(If any)*
none

Country of Citizenship
Italy

A-Number *(If any)*
none

Current Address    *(Street Number and Name)*
108 Piazza D'Azeglio

Apt/Suite Number
none

City
Venice

State/Province

Country
Italy

ZIP/Postal Code
99999

Telephone Number
764 290-7645

List any spouse and/or children immigrating with the immigrant named above in this Part:    *(Use additional sheet of paper if necessary.)*

| Name | Relationship to Sponsored Immigrant | | | Date of Birth | | | A-Number *(If any)* | Social Security *(If any)* |
|---|---|---|---|---|---|---|---|---|
| | Spouse | Son | Daughter | Mo. | Day | Yr. | | |
| Giovana Moreno | | | x | 06 | 01 | 90 | none | none |
| | | | | | | | | |
| | | | | | | | | |
| | | | | | | | | |

Form I-864 (Rev. 11/05/01)Y

## SAMPLE FORM I-864 (PAGE 2)

---

**Part 4.**      **Eligibility to Sponsor**

To be a sponsor you must be a U.S. citizen or national or a lawful permanent resident. If you are not the petitioning relative, you must provide proof of status. To prove status, U.S. citizens or nationals must attach a copy of a document proving status, such as a U.S. passport, birth certificate, or certificate of naturalization, and lawful permanent residents must attach a copy of both sides of their Permanent Resident Card (Form I-551).

The determination of your eligibility to sponsor an immigrant will be based on an evaluation of your demonstrated ability to maintain an annual income at or above 125 percent of the Federal poverty line (100 percent if you are a petitioner sponsoring your spouse or child and you are on active duty in the U.S. Armed Forces). The assessment of your ability to maintain an adequate income will include your current employment, household size, and household income as shown on the Federal income tax returns for the 3 most recent tax years. Assets that are readily converted to cash and that can be made available for the support of sponsored immigrants if necessary, including any such assets of the immigrant(s) you are sponsoring, may also be considered.

The greatest weight in determining eligibility will be placed on current employment and household income. If a petitioner is unable to demonstrate ability to meet the stated income and asset requirements, a joint sponsor who *can* meet the income and asset requirements is needed. Failure to provide adequate evidence of income and/or assets or an affidavit of support completed by a joint sponsor will result in denial of the immigrant's application for an immigrant visa or adjustment to permanent resident status.

### A. Sponsor's Employment

I am:    1. ☒ Employed by ___Bob's Diner_____ *(Provide evidence of employment)*

               Annual salary __20,000____ or hourly wage $ _____ *(for _____ hours per week)*

   2. ☐ Self employed _____ *(Name of business)*

               Nature of employment or business _____

   3. ☐ Unemployed or retired since _____

### B. Sponsor's Household Size

| | Number |
|---|---|
| 1. Number of persons (related to you by birth, marriage, or adoption) living in your residence, including yourself *(Do NOT include persons being sponsored in this affidavit.)* | 2 |
| 2. Number of immigrants being sponsored in this affidavit *(Include all persons in Part 3.)* | 2 |
| 3. Number of immigrants **NOT** living in your household whom you are obligated to support under a previously signed Form I-864. | 0 |
| 4. Number of persons who are otherwise dependent on you, as claimed in your tax return for the most recent tax year. | 0 |
| 5. Total household size. *(Add lines 1 through 4.)*      **Total** | 4 |

List persons below who are included in lines 1 or 3 for whom you previously have submitted INS Form I-864, *if your support obligation has not terminated.*

*(If additional space is needed, use additional paper)*

| Name | A-Number | Date Affidavit of Support Signed | Relationship |
|---|---|---|---|
| | | | |
| | | | |
| | | | |
| | | | |
| | | | |
| | | | |

## SAMPLE FORM I-864 (PAGE 3)

---

**Part 4.     Eligibility to Sponsor**          *(Continued)*

### C. Sponsor's Annual Household Income

Enter total unadjusted income from your Federal income tax return for the most recent tax year below. If you last filed a joint income tax return but are using only your *own* income to qualify, list total earnings from your W-2 Forms, or, *if* necessary to reach the required income for your household size, include income from other sources listed on your tax return. If your *individual* income does not meet the income requirement for your household size, you may also list total income for anyone related to you by birth, marriage, or adoption currently living with you in your residence if they have lived in your residence for the previous 6 months, or any person shown as a dependent on your Federal income tax return for the most recent tax year, even if not living in the household. For their income to be considered, household members or dependents must be willing to make their income available for support of the sponsored immigrant(s) and to complete and sign Form I-864A, Contract Between Sponsor and Household Member. A sponsored immigrant/household member only need complete Form I-864A if his or her income will be used to determine your ability to support a spouse and/or children immigrating with him or her.

*You must attach evidence of current employment and copies of income tax returns as filed with the IRS for the most recent 3 tax years for yourself and all persons whose income is listed below. See "Required Evidence " in Instructions.* Income from all 3 years will be considered in determining your ability to support the immigrant(s) you are sponsoring.

☒ I filed a single/separate tax return for the most recent tax year.
☐ I filed a joint return for the most recent tax year which includes only my own income.
☐ I filed a joint return for the most recent tax year which includes income for my spouse and myself.

  ☒ I am submitting documentation of my individual income (Forms W-2 and 1099).
  ☐ I am qualifying using my spouse's income; my spouse is submitting a Form I-864A.

| **Indicate most recent tax year** | <u>  2002  </u> |
|---|---|
| | *(tax year)* |
| Sponsor's individual income | $ <u>  20,000  </u> |
| **or** | |
| Sponsor and spouse's combined income<br>*(If spouse's income is to be considered, spouse must submit Form I-864A.)* | $ <u>  20,000  </u> |
| Income of other qualifying persons.<br>*(List names; include spouse if applicable. Each person must complete Form I-864A.)* | |
| <u>                              </u> | $ <u>   0   </u> |
| <u>                              </u> | $ <u>   0   </u> |
| <u>                              </u> | $ <u>   0   </u> |
| **Total Household Income** | $ <u>  20,000  </u> |

Explain on separate sheet of paper if you or any of the above listed individuals were not required to file Federal income tax returns for the most recent 3 years, or if other explanation of income, employment, or evidence is necessary.

### D. Determination of Eligibility Based on Income

1. ☒ I am subject to the 125 percent of poverty line requirement for sponsors.
   ☐ I am subject to the 100 percent of poverty line requirement for sponsors on active duty in the U.S. Armed Forces sponsoring their spouse or child.
2. Sponsor's total household size, from Part 4.B., line 5     <u>   4   </u>   .
3. Minimum income requirement from the Poverty Guidelines chart for the year of   <u>  2003  </u>   is $  <u>  23,000  </u>
   for this household size.       *(year)*

**If you are currently employed and your household income for your household size is equal to or greater than the applicable poverty line requirement (from line D.3.), you do not need to list assets (Parts 4.E. and 5) or have a joint sponsor (Part 6)** unless you are requested to do so by a Consular or Immigration Officer. You may skip to Part 7, Use of the Affidavit of Support to Overcome Public Charge Ground of Admissibility. **Otherwise, you should continue with Part 4.E.**

## SAMPLE FORM I-864 (PAGE 4)

### Part 4.    Eligibility to Sponsor        *(Continued)*

### E. Sponsor's Assets and Liabilities

Your assets and those of your qualifying household members and dependents may be used to demonstrate ability to maintain an income at or above 125 percent (or 100 percent, if applicable) of the poverty line *if* they are available for the support of the sponsored immigrant(s) and can readily be converted into cash within 1 year. The household member, other than the immigrant(s) you are sponsoring, must complete and sign Form I-864A, Contract Between Sponsor and Household Member. List the cash value of each asset *after* any debts or liens are subtracted. Supporting evidence must be attached to establish location, ownership, date of acquisition, and value of each asset listed, including any liens and liabilities related to each asset listed. See "Evidence of Assets" in Instructions.

| Type of Asset | Cash Value of Assets *(Subtract any debts)* |
|---|---|
| Savings deposits | $ 25,000 |
| Stocks, bonds, certificates of deposit | $ none |
| Life insurance cash value | $ 25,000 |
| Real estate | $ 5,000 |
| Other *(specify)* | $ |
| **Total Cash Value of Assets** | $ 55,000 |

### Part 5.    Immigrant's Assets and Offsetting Liabilities

The sponsored immigrant's assets may also be used in support of your ability to maintain income at or above 125 percent of the poverty line *if* the assets are or will be available in the United States for the support of the sponsored immigrant(s) and can readily be converted into cash within 1 year.

The sponsored immigrant should provide information on his or her assets in a format similar to part 4.E. above. Supporting evidence must be attached to establish location, ownership, and value of each asset listed, including any liens and liabilities for each asset listed. See "Evidence of Assets" in Instructions.

### Part 6.    Joint Sponsors

If household income and assets do not meet the appropriate poverty line for your household size, a joint sponsor is required. There may be more than one joint sponsor, but each joint sponsor must individually meet the 125 percent of poverty line requirement based on his or her household income and/or assets, including any assets of the sponsored immigrant. By submitting a separate Affidavit of Support under Section 213A of the Act (Form I-864), a joint sponsor accepts joint responsibility with the petitioner for the sponsored immigrant(s) until they become U.S. citizens, can be credited with 40 quarters of work, leave the United States permanently, or die.

### Part 7.    Use of the Affidavit of Support to Overcome Public Charge Ground of Inadmissibility

Section 212(a)(4)(C) of the Immigration and Nationality Act provides that an alien seeking permanent residence as an immediate relative (including an orphan), as a family-sponsored immigrant, or as an alien who will accompany or follow to join another alien is considered to be likely to become a public charge and is inadmissible to the United States unless a sponsor submits a legally enforceable affidavit of support on behalf of the alien. Section 212(a)(4)(D) imposes the same requirement on an employment-based immigrant, and those aliens who accompany or follow to join the employment- based immigrant, if the employment-based immigrant will be employed by a relative, or by a firm in which a relative owns a significant interest. Separate affidavits of support are required for family members at the time they immigrate if they are not included on this affidavit of support or do not apply for an immigrant visa or adjustment of status within 6 months of the date this affidavit of support is originally signed. The sponsor must provide the sponsored immigrant(s) whatever support is necessary to maintain them at an income that is at least 125 percent of the Federal poverty guidelines.

> *I submit this affidavit of support in consideration of the sponsored immigrant(s) not being found inadmissible to the United States under section 212(a)(4)(C) (or 212(a)(4)(D) for an employment-based immigrant) and to enable the sponsored immigrant(s) to overcome this ground of inadmissibility. I agree to provide the sponsored immigrant(s) whatever support is necessary to maintain the sponsored immigrant(s) at an income that is at least 125 percent of the Federal poverty guidelines. I understand that my obligation will continue until my death or the sponsored immigrant(s) have become U.S. citizens, can be credited with 40 quarters of work, depart the United States permanently, or die.*

## SAMPLE FORM I-864 (PAGE 5)

---

**Part 7.** **Use of the Affidavit of Support to Overcome Public Charge Grounds**          *(Continued)*

---

### Notice of Change of Address.

Sponsors are required to provide written notice of any change of address within 30 days of the change in address until the sponsored immigrant(s) have become U.S. citizens, can be credited with 40 quarters of work, depart the United States permanently, or die. To comply with this requirement, the sponsor must complete INS Form I-865. Failure to give this notice may subject the sponsor to the civil penalty established under section 213A(d)(2) which ranges from $250 to $2,000, unless the failure to report occurred with the knowledge that the sponsored immigrant(s) had received means-tested public benefits, in which case the penalty ranges from $2,000 to $5,000.

> *If my address changes for any reason before my obligations under this affidavit of support terminate, I will complete and file INS Form I-865, Sponsor's Notice of Change of Address, within 30 days of the change of address. I understand that failure to give this notice may subject me to civil penalties.*

### Means-tested Public Benefit Prohibitions and Exceptions.

Under section 403(a) of Public Law 104-193 (Welfare Reform Act), aliens lawfully admitted for permanent residence in the United States, with certain exceptions, are ineligible for most Federally-funded means-tested public benefits during their first 5 years in the United States. This provision does not apply to public benefits specified in section 403(c) of the Welfare Reform Act or to State public benefits, including emergency Medicaid; short-term, non-cash emergency relief; services provided under the National School Lunch and Child Nutrition Acts; immunizations and testing and treatment for communicable diseases; student assistance under the Higher Education Act and the Public Health Service Act; certain forms of foster-care or adoption assistance under the Social Security Act; Head Start programs; means-tested programs under the Elementary and Secondary Education Act; and Job Training Partnership Act programs.

### Consideration of Sponsor's Income in Determining Eligibility for Benefits.

If a permanent resident alien is no longer statutorily barred from a Federally-funded means-tested public benefit program and applies for such a benefit, the income and resources of the sponsor and the sponsor's spouse will be considered (or deemed) to be the income and resources of the sponsored immigrant in determining the immigrant's eligibility for Federal means-tested public benefits. Any State or local government may also choose to consider (or deem) the income and resources of the sponsor and the sponsor's spouse to be the income and resources of the immigrant for the purposes of determining eligibility for their means-tested public benefits. The attribution of the income and resources of the sponsor and the sponsor's spouse to the immigrant will continue until the immigrant becomes a U.S. citizen or has worked or can be credited with 40 qualifying quarters of work, provided that the immigrant or the worker crediting the quarters to the immigrant has not received any Federal means-tested public benefit during any creditable quarter for any period after December 31, 1996.

> *I understand that, under section 213A of the Immigration and Nationality Act (the Act), as amended, this affidavit of support constitutes a contract between me and the U.S. Government. This contract is designed to protect the United States Government, and State and local government agencies or private entities that provide means-tested public benefits, from having to pay benefits to or on behalf of the sponsored immigrant(s), for as long as I am obligated to support them under this affidavit of support. I understand that the sponsored immigrants, or any Federal, State, local, or private entity that pays any means-tested benefit to or on behalf of the sponsored immigrant(s), are entitled to sue me if I fail to meet my obligations under this affidavit of support, as defined by section 213A and INS regulations.*

### Civil Action to Enforce.

If the immigrant on whose behalf this affidavit of support is executed receives any Federal, State, or local means-tested public benefit before this obligation terminates, the Federal, State, or local agency or private entity may request reimbursement from the sponsor who signed this affidavit. If the sponsor fails to honor the request for reimbursement, the agency may sue the sponsor in any U.S. District Court or any State court with jurisdiction of civil actions for breach of contract. INS will provide names, addresses, and Social Security account numbers of sponsors to benefit-providing agencies for this purpose. Sponsors may also be liable for paying the costs of collection, including legal fees.

## SAMPLE FORM I-864 (PAGE 6)

---

**Part 7.     Use of the Affidavit of Support to Overcome Public Charge Grounds** *(Continued)*

*I acknowledge that section 213A(a)(1)(B) of the Act grants the sponsored immigrant(s) and any Federal, State, local, or private agency that pays any means-tested public benefit to or on behalf of the sponsored immigrant(s) standing to sue me for failing to meet my obligations under this affidavit of support. I agree to submit to the personal jurisdiction of any court of the United States or of any State, territory, or possession of the United States if the court has subject matter jurisdiction of a civil lawsuit to enforce this affidavit of support. I agree that no lawsuit to enforce this affidavit of support shall be barred by any statute of limitations that might otherwise apply, so long as the plaintiff initiates the civil lawsuit no later than ten (10) years after the date on which a sponsored immigrant last received any means-tested public benefits.*

### Collection of Judgment.

*I acknowledge that a plaintiff may seek specific performance of my support obligation. Furthermore, any money judgment against me based on this affidavit of support may be collected through the use of a judgment lien under 28 U.S.C 3201, a writ of execution under 28 U.S.C 3203, a judicial installment payment order under 28 U.S.C 3204, garnishment under 28 U.S.C 3205, or through the use of any corresponding remedy under State law. I may also be held liable for costs of collection, including attorney fees.*

### Concluding Provisions.

I, _____Alberto Mancini_____, *certify under penalty of perjury under the laws of the United States that:*

    *(a) I know the contents of this affidavit of support signed by me;*

    *(b) All the statements in this affidavit of support are true and correct,*

    *(c) I make this affidavit of support for the consideration stated in Part 7, freely, and without any mental reservation or purpose of evasion;*

    *(d) Income tax returns submitted in support of this affidavit are true copies of the returns filed with the Internal Revenue Service; and*

    *(e) Any other evidence submitted is true and correct.*

_____*Alberto J. Mancini*_____          _____7-6-03_____

      *(Sponsor's Signature)*                                  *(Date)*

Subscribed and sworn to (or affirmed) before me this

__6th_____ day of ___July_____ ,_2003_____

               *(Month)*        *(Year)*

at_New York, New York_____.

My commission expires on _____1/1/04_____.

_Ralph Benotti_____

*(Signature of Notary Public or Officer Administering Oath)*

Notary Public

_____

               *(Title)*

---

**Part 8.     If someone other than the sponsor prepared this affidavit of support, that person must complete the following:**

I certify under penalty of perjury under the laws of the United States that I prepared this affidavit of support at the sponsor's request, and that this affidavit of support is based on all information of which I have knowledge.

| Signature | Print Your Name | Date | Daytime Telephone Number |
|---|---|---|---|
|  |  |  |  |

Firm Name and Address

## ATTACHMENT TO AFFIDAVIT OF SUPPORT

U. S. Department of Homeland Security
Bureau of Citizenship and Immigration Services

OMB# 1115-0214
Poverty Guidelines

### 2003 Poverty Guidelines*
### Minimum Income Requirement For Use in Completing Form I-864

**For the 48 Contiguous States, the District of Columbia, Puerto Rico, the U.S. Virgin Islands, and Guam:**

| Sponsor's Household Size | 100% of Poverty Line<br>For sponsors on active duty in the U.S. Armed Forces who are petitioning for their spouse or child. | 125% of Poverty Line<br>For all other sponsors |
|---|---|---|
| 2 | $12,120 | $15,150 |
| 3 | 15,260 | 19,075 |
| 4 | 18,400 | 23,000 |
| 5 | 21,540 | 26,925 |
| 6 | 24,680 | 30,850 |
| 7 | 27,820 | 34,775 |
| 8 | 30,960 | 38,700 |
|  | Add $3,140 for each additional person. | Add $3,925 for each additional person. |

| Sponsor's Household Size | For Alaska | | For Hawaii | |
|---|---|---|---|---|
|  | 100% of Poverty Line<br>For sponsors on active duty in the U.S. Armed Forces who are petitioning for their spouse or child | 125% of Poverty Line<br>For all other sponsors | 100% of Poverty Line<br>For sponsors on active duty in the U.S. Armed Forces who are petitioning for their spouse or child | 125% of Poverty Line<br>For all other sponsors |
| 2 | $15,140 | $18,925 | $13,940 | $17,425 |
| 3 | 19,070 | 23,837 | 17,550 | 21,937 |
| 4 | 23,000 | 28,750 | 21,160 | 26,450 |
| 5 | 26,930 | 33,662 | 24,770 | 30,962 |
| 6 | 30,860 | 38,575 | 28,380 | 35,475 |
| 7 | 34,790 | 43,487 | 31,990 | 39,987 |
| 8 | 38,720 | 48,400 | 35,600 | 44,500 |
|  | Add $3,930 for each additional person. | Add $4,912 for each additional person. | Add $3,610 for each additional person. | Add $4,512 for each additional person. |

### Means-tested Public Benefits

**Federal Means-tested Public Benefits.** To date, Federal agencies administering benefit programs have determined that Federal means-tested public benefits include Food Stamps, Medicaid, Supplemental Security Income (SSI), Temporary Assistance for Needy Families (TANF), and the State Child Health Insurance Program (SCHIP).

**State Means-tested Public Benefits.** Each State will determine which, if any, of its public benefits are means-tested. If a State determines that it has programs which meet this definition, it is encouraged to provide notice to the public on which programs are included. Check with the State public assistance office to determine which, if any, State assistance programs have been determined to be State means-tested public benefits.

**Programs Not Included:** The following Federal and State programs are *not* included as means-tested benefits: emergency Medicaid; short-term, non-cash emergency relief; services provided under the National School Lunch and Child Nutrition Acts; immunizations and testing and treatment for communicable diseases; student assistance under the Higher Education Act and the Public Health Service Act; certain forms of foster-care or adoption assistance under the Social Security Act; Head Start Programs; means-tested programs under the Elementary and Secondary Education Act; and Job Training Partnership Act programs.

* These poverty guidelines remain in effect for use with the Form I-864 Affidavit of Support from April 1, 2003 until new poverty guidelines go into effect in the Spring of 2004.

Form I-864P (Rev. 03/10/03)N

## CONTRACT BETWEEN SPONSOR AND HOUSEHOLD MEMBER, SAMPLE FORM I-864A

| U.S. Department of Justice<br>Immigration and Naturalization Service | OMB No. 1115-0214<br>**Contract Between Sponsor and Household Member** | |
|---|---|---|
| Sponsor's Name *(Last, First, Middle)*<br>Alberto J. Mancini | Social Security Number<br>222-22-2222 | A-Number (If any)<br>none |

### General Filing Instruction

Form I-864A, Contract Between Sponsor and Household Member, is an attachment to Form I-864, Affidavit of Support Under Section 213A of the Immigration and Nationality Act (the Act). The sponsor enters the information above, complete Part 2 of this form, and signs in Part 5. The household member completes Parts 1 and 3 of this form and signs in Part 6. A household member who is also the sponsored immigrant completes Parts 1 and 4 (instead of Part 3) of this form and signs i Part 6. The Privacy Act Notice and information on penalties for misrepresentation or fraud are included on the instructions to Form I-864.

The signatures on the I-864A must be notarized by a notary public or signed before an immigration or consular officer. A separate form must be used for each household member whose income and/or assets are being used to qualify. This blank form may be photocopied for that purpose. A sponsored immigrant who qualifies as a household member is only required to complete this form if he or she has one or more family members immigrating with him or her and is making his or her *income* available for their support. Sponsored immigrants who are using their *assets* to qualify are not required to complete this form. This completed form is submitted with Form I-864 by the sponsored immigrant with an application for an immigrant visa or adjustment of status.

### Purpose

This contract is intended to benefit the sponsored immigrant(s) and any agency of the Federal Government, any agency of a State or local government, or any private entity to which the sponsor has an obligation under the affidavit of support to reimburse for benefits granted to the sponsored immigrant, and these parties will have the right to enforce this contract in ar court with appropriate jurisdiction. Under Section 213A of Act, this contract must be completed and signed by the sponsor and any household member, including the sponsor's spouse, whose income is included as household income by a person sponsoring one or more immigrants. The contract must also be completed if a sponsor is relying on the assets of a househo member who is not the sponsored immigrant to meet the income requirements. If the sponsored immigrant is a household member immigrating with a spouse or children, and is using his or her income to assist the sponsor in meeting the income requirement, he or she must complete and sign this contract as a "sponsored immigrant/household member."

By signing this form, a household member, who is not a sponsored immigrant, agrees to make his or her income and/or assets available to the sponsor to help support the immigrant(s) for whom the sponsor has filed an affidavit of support and to be responsible, along with the sponsor, to pay any debt incurred by the sponsor under the affidavit of support. A sponsored immigrant/household member who signs this contract agrees to make his or her income available to the sponsor to help support any spouse or children immigrating with him or her and to be responsible, along with the sponsor, to pay any debt incurred by the sponsor under the affidavit of support. The obligations of the household member and the sponsored immigrant/household member under this contract terminate when the obligations of the sponsor under the affidavit of support terminate. For additional information see section 213A of the Act, part 213a of title 8 of the Code of Federal Regulations, and Form I-864, Affidavit of Support Under Section 213A of the Act.

### Definitions:

1) An "affidavit of support" refers to Form I-864, Affidavit of Support Under Section 213A of the Act, which is complete and filed by the sponsor.

2) A "sponsor" is a person, either the petitioning relative, the relative with a significant ownership interest in the petitionin entity, or another person accepting joint and several liability with the sponsor, who completes and files the Affidavit of Support under Section 213A of the Act on behalf of a sponsored immigrant.

3) A "household member" is any person (a) sharing a residence with the sponsor for at least the last 6 months who is related to the sponsor by birth, marriage, or adoption, *or* (b) whom the sponsor has lawfully claimed as a dependent or the sponsor's most recent federal income tax return even if that person does not live at the same residence as the sponsor, *and* whose income and/or assets will be used to demonstrate the sponsor's ability to maintain the sponsored immigrant(s) at an annual income at the level specified in section 213A(f)(1)(E) or 213A(f)(3) of the Act.

4) A "sponsored immigrant" is a person listed on this form on whose behalf an affidavit of support will be completed and filed.

5) A "sponsored immigrant/household member" is a sponsored immigrant who is also a household member.

## SAMPLE FORM I-864A (PAGE 2)

**Part 1.  Information on Sponsor's Household Member or Sponsored Immigrant/Household Member**

| Last Name Mancini | First Name Beatrice | Middle Name Stella |
|---|---|---|

| Date of Birth *(Month, Day, Year)* 3-6-72 | Social Security Number *(Mandatory for non-citizens; voluntary for U.S. citizens)* 206-45-9872 | A-Number *(If any)* none |
|---|---|---|

| Address *(Street Number and Name)*   Apt Number 800 Broadway | City Lindenhurst | State/Province NY | ZIP/Postal Code 11757 |
|---|---|---|---|

| Telephone Number ( 212 )222-9822 | I am: Relationship to Sponsor: daughter  ☒ The sponsor's household member. *(Complete Part 3.)*  ☐ The sponsored immigrant/household member. *(Complete Part* | Length of residence with sponsor 30 years, ____ months) |
|---|---|---|

**Part 2.  Sponsor's Promise**

**I, THE SPONSOR,** Alberto Mancini _____ , in consideration of the household member's promise to support the
*(Print name of sponsor)*
sponsored immigrant(s) and to be jointly and severally liable for any obligations I incur under the affidavit of support,
promise to complete and file an affidavit of support on behalf of the following 2 _____ sponsored immigrant(s):
*(Indicate number)*

| Name of Sponsored Immigrant *(First, Middle, Last)* | Date of Birth *(Month, Day, Year)* | Social Security Number *(If any)* | A-Number *(If any)* |
|---|---|---|---|
| Terese M. Mancini | 2-15-82 | none | none |
| Giovana Moreno | 06-01-90 | none | none |
| | | | |
| | | | |
| | | | |
| | | | |

**Part 3.  Household Member's Promise**

**I, THE HOUSEHOLD** _____ *Beatrice S. Mancini* _____ , in consideration of the sponsor's
*(Print name of household member)*
promise to complete and file the affidavit of support on behalf of the sponsored immigrant(s):

1)  Promise to provide any and all financial support necessary to assist the sponsor in maintaining the sponsored immigrant(s) at or above the minimum income provided for in section 213A(a)(1)(A) of the Act (not less than 125 percent of the Federal Poverty Guidelines) during the period in which the affidavit of support is enforceable;

2)  Agree to be jointly and severally liable for payment of any and all obligations owed by the sponsor under the affidavit of support to the sponsored immigrant(s), to any agency of the Federal Government, to any agency of a state or local government, or to any private entity;

3)  Agree to submit to the personal jurisdiction of any court of the United States or of any state, territory, or possession of the United States if the court has subject matter jurisdiction of a civil lawsuit to enforce this contract or the affidavit of support; and

4)  Certify under penalty of perjury under the laws of the United States that all the information provided on this form is true and correct to the best of my knowledge and belief and that the income tax returns I submitted in support of the sponsor affidavit are true copies of the returns filed with the Internal Revenue Service.

Form I-864A (11/05/01)Y Page 2

## SAMPLE FORM I-864A (PAGE 3)

**Part 4.  Sponsored Immigrant/Household Member's Promise**

**I, THE SPONSORED IMMIGRANT/HOUSEHOLD** _____

*(Print name o f sponsored immigrant)*

in consideration of the sponsor's promise to complete and file the affidavit of support on behalf of the sponsored immigrant(s) accompanying me:

1) Promise to provide any and all financial support necessary to assist the sponsor in maintaining any sponsored immigrant(s) immigrating with me at or above the minimum income provided for in section 213A(a)(1)(A) of the Act (not less than 125 percent of the Federal Poverty Guidelines) during the period in which the affidavit of support is enforceable;

2) Agree to be jointly and severally liable for payment of any and all obligations owed by the sponsor under the affidavit of support to any sponsored immigrant(s) immigrating with me, to any agency of the Federal Government, to any agency of a state or local government, or to any private entity;

3) Agree to submit to the personal jurisdiction of any court of the United States or of any state, territory, or possession of the United States if the court has subject matter jurisdiction of a civil lawsuit to enforce this contract or the affidavit of support; and

4) Certify under penalty of perjury under the laws of the United States that all the information provided on this form is tru and correct to the best of my knowledge and belief and that the income tax returns I submitted in support of the sponsor's affidavit of support are true copies of the returns filed with the Internal Revenue Service.

**Part 5.  Sponsor's Signature**

*Alberto J. Mancini* Date: 7-6-03
_____
*Sponsor's Signature*

Subscribed and sworn to *(or affirmed)* before me this __6th__ day of __July_____ , __2003__

*(Month)* *(Year)*

at New York, New York _____. My commission expires on __1/1/04____ .

*Ralph Berotti* Notary Public
_____ _____
*Signature of Notary Public or Officer Administering Oath* *Title*

**Part 6.  Household Member's or Sponsored Immigrant/Household Member's Signature**

*Beatrice S. Mancini* Date: 7-6-03
_____
*Household Member's or Sponsored Immigrant/Household Member's Signature*

Subscribed and sworn to *(or affirmed)* before me this __14th__ day of __July_____ , __2003__

*(Month)* *(Year)*

at New York, New York _____. My commission expires on __1/1/04____ .

*Ralph Berotti* Notary Public
_____ _____
*Signature of Notary Public or Officer Administering Oath* *Title*

Form I-864A (11/05/01)Y Page 3

## FORM DS-230 (PART II)

**U.S. Department of State**
# APPLICATION FOR IMMIGRANT VISA AND ALIEN REGISTRATION

OMB APPROVAL NO. 1405-0015
EXPIRES: 05/31/2004
ESTIMATED BURDEN: 1 HOUR*

### PART II - SWORN STATEMENT

INSTRUCTIONS: Complete one copy of this form for yourself and each member of your family, regardless of age, who will immigrate with you. Please print or type your answers to all questions. Mark questions that are Not Applicable with "N/A". If there is insufficient room on the form, answer on a separate sheet using the same numbers that appear on the form. Attach any additional sheets to this form. The fee should be paid in United States dollars or local currency equivalent, or by bank draft.

WARNING: Any false statement or concealment of a material fact may result in your permanent exclusion from the United States. Even if you are issued an immigrant visa and are subsequently admitted to the United States, providing false information on this form could be grounds for your prosecution and/or deportation.

This form (DS-230 PART II), together with Form DS-230 PART I, constitutes the complete Application for Immigrant Visa and Alien Registration.

| 26. Family Name | First Name | Middle Name |
|---|---|---|
| Mancini | Terese | Maria |

**27.** Other Names Used or Aliases *(If married woman, give maiden name)*

Terese Brabantio

**28.** Full Name in Native Alphabet *(If Roman letters not used)*

n/a

**29.** Name and Address of Petitioner
Alberto Mancini
800 Broadway
Lindenhurst, NY 11757
Telephone number:   (212) 222-2121

**30.** United States laws governing the issuance of visas require each applicant to state whether or not he or she is a member of any class of individuals excluded from admission into the United States. The excludable classes are described below in general terms. You should read carefully the following list and answer YES or NO to each category. The answers you give will assist the consular officer to reach a decision on your eligibility to receive a visa.

**EXCEPT AS OTHERWISE PROVIDED BY LAW, ALIENS WITHIN THE FOLLOWING CLASSIFICATIONS ARE INELIGIBLE TO RECEIVE A VISA. DO ANY OF THE FOLLOWING CLASSES APPLY TO YOU?**

a. An alien who has a communicable disease of public health significance; who has failed to present documentation of having received vaccinations in accordance with U.S. law; who has or has had a physical or mental disorder that poses or is likely to pose a threat to the safety  ☐ Yes  ☒ No

b. An alien convicted of, or who admits having committed, a crime involving moral turpitude or violation of any law relating to a controlled substance or who is the spouse, son or daughter of such a trafficker who knowingly has benefited from the trafficking activities in the past five years; who has been convicted of 2 or more offenses for which the aggregate sentences were 5 years or more; who is coming to the United States to engage in prostitution or commercialized vice or who has engaged in prostitution or procuring within the past 10 years; who is or has been an illicit trafficker in any controlled substance; who has committed a serious criminal offense in the United States and who has asserted immunity from prosecution; who, while serving as a foreign government official and within the previous 24-month period, was responsible for or directly carried out particularly severe violations of religious freedom; or whom the President has identified as a person who plays a significant role in a severe form of trafficking in persons, who otherwise has knowingly aided, abetted, assisted or colluded with such a trafficker in severe forms of trafficking in persons, or who is the spouse, son or daughter of such a trafficker who knowingly has benefited from the trafficking activities within the past five years.  ☐ Yes  ☒ No

c. An alien who seeks to enter the United States to engage in espionage, sabotage, export control violations, terrorist activities, the overthrow of the Government of the United States or other unlawful activity; who is a member of or affiliated with the Communist or other totalitarian party; who participated in Nazi persecutions or genocide; who has engaged in genocide; or who is a member or representative of a terrorist organization as currently designated by the U.S. Secretary of State.  ☐ Yes  ☒ No

d. An alien who is likely to become a public charge.  ☐ Yes  ☒ No

e. An alien who seeks to enter for the purpose of performing skilled or unskilled labor who has not been certified by the Secretary of Labor; who is a graduate of a foreign medical school seeking to perform medical services who has not passed the NBME exam or its equivalent; or who is a health care worker seeking to perform such work without a certificate from the CGFNS or from an equivalent approved independent credentialing organization.  ☐ Yes  ☒ No

f. An alien who failed to attend a hearing on deportation or inadmissibility within the last 5 years; who seeks or has sought a visa, entry into the United States, or any immigration benefit by fraud or misrepresentation; who knowingly assisted any other alien to enter or try to enter the United States in violation of law; who, after November 30, 1996, attended in student (F) visa status a U.S. public elementary school or who attended a U.S. public secondary school without reimbursing the school; or who is subject to a civil penalty under INA 274C.  ☐ Yes  ☒ No

### Privacy Act and Paperwork Reduction Act Statements

The information asked for on this form is requested pursuant to Section 222 of the Immigration and Nationality Act. The U.S. Department of State uses the facts you provide on this form primarily to determine your classification and eligibility for a U.S. immigrant visa. Individuals who fail to submit this form or who do not provide all the requested information may be denied a U.S. immigrant visa. If you are issued an immigrant visa and are subsequently admitted to the United States as an immigrant, the Immigration and Naturalization Service will use the information on this form to issue you a Permanent Resident Card, and, if you so indicate, the Social Security Administration will use the information to issue you a social security number and card.

*Public reporting burden for this collection of information is estimated to average 1 hour per response, including time required for searching existing data sources, gathering the necessary data, providing the information required, and reviewing the final collection. In accordance with 5 CFR 1320 5(b), persons are not required to respond to the collection of this information unless this form displays a currently valid OMB control number. Send comments on the accuracy of this estimate of the burden and recommendations for reducing it to: U.S. Department of State (A/RPS/DIR) Washington, D.C. 20520.

| DS-230 Part II | PREVIOUS EDITIONS OBSOLETE | Page 3 of 4 |
|---|---|---|

# FORM DS-230 PART II (PAGE 2)

g. An alien who is permanently ineligible for U.S. citizenship; or who departed the United States to evade military service in time of war. ☐ Yes ☒ No

h. An alien who was previously ordered removed within the last 5 years or ordered removed a second time within the last 20 years; who was previously unlawfully present and ordered removed within the last 10 years or ordered removed a second time within the last 20 years; who was convicted of an aggravated felony and ordered removed; who was previously unlawfully present in the United States for more than 180 days but less than one year who voluntarily departed within the last 3 years; or who was unlawfully present for more than one year or an aggregate of one year within the last 10 years. ☐ Yes ☒ No

i. An alien who is coming to the United States to practice polygamy; who withholds custody of a U.S. citizen child outside the United States from a person granted legal custody by a U.S. court or intentionally assists another person to do so; who has voted in the United States in ☐ Yes ☒ No

j. An alien who is a former exchange visitor who has not fulfilled the 2-year foreign residence requirement. ☐ Yes ☒ No

k. An alien determined by the Attorney General to have knowingly made a frivolous application for asylum. ☐ Yes ☒ No

l. An alien who has ordered, carried out or materially assisted in extrajudicial and political killings and other acts of violence against the Haitian people; who has directly or indirectly assisted or supported any of the groups in Colombia known as FARC, ELN, or AUC; who through abuse of a governmental or political position has converted for personal gain, confiscated or expropriated property in Cuba, a claim to which is owned by a national of the United States, has trafficked in such property or has been complicit in such conversion, has committed similar acts in another country, or is the spouse, minor child or agent of an alien who has committed such acts; who has been directly involved in the establishment or enforcement of population controls forcing a woman to undergo an abortion against her free choice or a man or a woman to undergo sterilization against his or her free choice; or who has disclosed or trafficked in confidential U.S. business information obtained in connection with U.S. participation in the Chemical Weapons Convention or is the spouse, minor child or agent of such a person. ☐ Yes ☒ No

31. Have you ever been charged, arrested or convicted of any offense or crime?
*(If answer is Yes, please explain)* ☐ Yes ☒ No

32. Have you ever been refused admission to the United States at a port-of-entry?
*(If answer is Yes, please explain)* ☐ Yes ☒ No

33a. Have you ever applied for a Social Security Number (SSN)?

☐ Yes    Give the number _____ ☒ No

Do you want the Social Security Administration to assign you an SSN (and issue a card) or issue you a new card (if you have an SSN)? You must answer "Yes" to this question and to the "Consent To Disclosure" in order to receive an SSN and/or card.

☒ Yes    ☐ No

33b. CONSENT TO DISCLOSURE: I authorize disclosure of information from this form to the Immigration and Naturalization Service (INS), the Social Security Administration (SSA), such other U.S. Government agencies as may be required for the purpose of assigning me an SSN and issuing me a Social Security card, and I authorize the SSA to share my SSN with the INS.

☒ Yes    ☐ No

The applicant's response does not limit or restrict the Government's ability to obtain his or her SSN, or other information on this form, for enforcement or other purposes as authorized by law.

34. WERE YOU ASSISTED IN COMPLETING THIS APPLICATION? ☐ Yes ☒ No
*(If answer is Yes, give name and address of person assisting you, indicating whether relative, friend, travel agent, attorney, or other)*

**DO NOT WRITE BELOW THE FOLLOWING LINE**
**The consular officer will assist you in answering item 35.**
**DO NOT SIGN this form until instructed to do so by the consular officer**

35. I claim to be:

☐ A Family-Sponsored Immigrant
☐ An Employment-Based Immigrant
☐ A Diversity Immigrant
☐ A Special Category *(Specify)* _____
(Returning resident, Hong Kong, Tibetan, Private Legislation, etc.)

☐ I derive foreign state chargeability under Sec. 202(b) through my _____

☐ Preference: _____

☐ Numerical limitation: _____
*(foreign state)*

I understand that I am required to surrender my visa to the United States Immigration Officer at the place where I apply to enter the United States, and that the possession of a visa does not entitle me to enter the United States if at that time I am found to be inadmissible under the immigration laws.

I understand that any willfully false or misleading statement or willful concealment of a material fact made by me herein may subject me to permanent exclusion from the United States and, if I am admitted to the United States, may subject me to criminal prosecution and/or deportation.

I, the undersigned applicant for a United States immigrant visa, do solemnly swear (or affirm) that all statements which appear in this application, consisting of Form DS-230 Part I and Part II combined, have been made by me, including the answers to items 1 through 35 inclusive, and that they are true and complete to the best of my knowledge and belief. I do further swear (or affirm) that, if admitted into the United States, I will not engage in activities which would be prejudicial to the public interest, or endanger the welfare, safety, or security of the United States; in activities which would be prohibited by the laws of the United States relating to espionage, sabotage, public disorder, or in other activities subversive to the national security; in any activity a purpose of which is the opposition to or the control, or overthrow of, the Government of the United States, by force, violence, or other unconstitutional means.

I understand that completion of this form by persons required by law to register with the Selective Service System (males 18 through 25 years of age) constitutes such registration in accordance with the Military Selective Service Act.

I understand all the foregoing statements, having asked for and obtained an explanation on every point which was not clear to me.

_____
Signature of Applicant

Subscribed and sworn to before me this _____ day of _____ _____ at: _____

_____
Consular Officer

**THIS FORM MAY BE OBTAINED FREE AT CONSULAR OFFICES OF THE UNITED STATES OF AMERICA**

# 10

**YOUR PARENTS AS IMMIGRANTS**

I Want My Mama ... And My Papa, Too

I was born in Hawaii when my parents were studying for their postgraduate degrees, after which we all returned to Italy. I have always known that I had dual citizenship and have never renounced my American citizenship.

I will soon celebrate my 21st birthday and am living in New York. As an American citizen, can I petition for my parents to become permanent residents?

Yes—you can.

## A. REQUIREMENTS FOR THE PETITIONER

Because the immigration laws generally encourage families to stay together, you can petition to get a green card for your parents—as long as you meet a couple of basic requirements.

### 1. You must be a U.S. citizen

You must be a U.S. citizen to file a petition on behalf of your parents. You are a citizen of the United States if you were:

- naturalized by a U.S. federal court
- born in any of the 50 states of the United States or its territories—U.S. Virgin Islands, Puerto Rico or Guam, or
- born outside the United States or its territories, if one or both of your parents were American citizens when you were born. This last situation can be complicated, because the immigration requirements differ, depending on what year you were born. If you have questions, contact the American Embassy, and if you are not satisfied, consult a lawyer or other experienced naturalization professional. (See Chapter 31.)

**Note:** If you were born in the United States and either of your parents were diplomats, you may not be a U.S. citizen even though you have a birth certificate from one of the states or territories. To be a citizen, a person born in the United States must also be subject to the laws of the United States at the time of their birth. A diplomat would not be "subject to the laws of the United States." However, the question of whether or not someone was born of diplomatic parents can be very complicated. Anyone in these circumstances should consult with an attorney.

### 2. You must be at least 21 years old

As an American citizen, you must be 21 years old or older to bestow the immigration benefit of a green card on your mother and your father as your Immediate Relatives.

Your mother and father may have no real interest in living in the United States, far away from their neighborhood, their friends, their extended families, the familiar customs and habits of their native country.

But they may agree to come anyway to get a green card. The obvious reason is that they want to be with you. The more subtle reason is that by becoming permanent residents of the United States, they can file for the immigration of all their unmarried children in their home country—as Family Second Preference or 2B petitioners. If they become naturalized as American citizens, they can petition even for their married children—in the Family Third Preference category.

Although as an American citizen, you may have filed for your brothers and sisters in the Family Fourth Preference category, your mother or father, after they have become American citizens, could secure a green card for them more quickly.

However, your parents must be aware that getting a green card does not automatically mean that their children can successfully obtain their own green cards. Your parents would also have to live (maintain residence) in the United States until their other children obtained their green cards.

The rules on maintaining residency are complicated and require that the person maintain the United States as their home. While the law allows them to travel overseas, their most important family and business ties should be in the United States. A person in this situation should compile documentation that would prove they maintained permanent residence. Good evidence to support a claim of permanent residency can include:

- a lease, rental agreement or title to property in the United States.
- utility bills
- a driver's license and/or car registration, and/or
- state and federal tax returns.

There are no clear rules on how to maintain permanent residency in the eyes of the U.S. government. But it is important to be able to show as much documentation as possible that you have a permanent residence in the United States. If you have questions about whether you have permanent residence, consult an immigration attorney.

## B. WHO QUALIFIES AS YOUR PARENT?

If you're from a traditional family, that is, you were born and raised by a married couple, you should have no problem petitioning for your parents to immigrate. However, the immigration law also recognizes some variations on the traditional family. Under certain circumstances, you can also petition for unmarried parents, stepparents and adoptive parents, as described further below. You can file a Petition for Alien Relative, Form I-130, for your parents as your Immediate Relatives. (See the sample at the end of Chapter 7.)

### 1. Natural mother

If your mother was not married to your father when you were born, so that your mother's maiden name appears on your birth certificate, you must present a copy of your birth certificate when you file the petition for your mother.

If your mother has changed her maiden name because she has married someone else, then also present her marriage certificate to show her change of name.

### 2. Natural father

If your biological father did not marry your mother either before or after you were born, you can still petition for him as your Immediate Relative by filing Form I-130. You must also provide some evidence of your relationship.

- Make a copy of your birth certificate, baptismal certificate or other religious records showing his name as your father. The BCIS may require both you and your father to take a blood test as proof of your relationship.
- If you and your father did not live together before you turned 18, you must present proof that, up to the time you turned 21 years of age, he maintained a father-child relationship with you by providing financial

### IF THE PETITIONER CHANGES NAMES

If you are a female U.S. citizen filing the petition for your alien parents as your Immediate Relatives, you may have changed your maiden name, which appears on your birth certificate. You may now be using your married name—that is, your husband's surname.

Therefore, in addition to your birth certificate to prove the parent-child relationship, you must also attach your marriage certificate to show your change of name when you send the Petition for Alien Relative, Form I-130, for your mother or father. (See the sample at the end of Chapter 7.)

If you have changed your name by petitioning the court, you must attach the final court judgment as proof of that change.

HAPPY THANKSGIVING LADIES

support, writing to you or your mother about your well-being, sending you birthday cards, Christmas cards, photographs, or perhaps naming you as a beneficiary to his life insurance, or

• If you lived with him before your 18th birthday, you must present proof that there was a father-child relationship, as evidenced by school records, photographs, letters, civil records or written statements from friends and relatives.

### 3. Stepmother or stepfather

If your father or mother marries somebody other than your biological parent before you turn 18 years of age, the person he or she marries becomes your stepmother or stepfather.

You can file a petition for your stepmother or stepfather as your Immediate Relative by submitting the usual petition Form I-130, and adding to it the following documents:

• your birth certificate showing the name of your mother or father, and

• the marriage certificate of your mother or father to show the name of her husband or his wife, who has become your stepparent.

For you to petition for your stepparent, the marriage must have occurred before your 18th birthday. If the marriage happened after your 18th birthday, then say, "I love you, but I cannot claim you as my Immediate Relative for immigration into the United States."

But all is not lost.

Your natural mother or father, after qualifying as your Immediate Relative and obtaining a green card, can petition for your stepparent, as the spouse of a permanent resident—2A, the Second Preference beneficiary. Unfortunately, however, the stepparent will have to wait a few years until a visa becomes available in this category.

### 4. Adopted mother and father

Suppose you were adopted by a non-U.S. citizen before your 16th birthday. If you are a U.S. citizen and you are now 21 years or older, you can petition for your adopted mother and father as your Immediate Relatives.

When you file Form I-130, you must also submit:

• the court decree of your adoption

• your birth certificate showing the name of your adopting parents as your father and mother, and

• a statement showing the dates and places you have lived together.

---

**NATURAL PARENTS ARE EXCLUDED**

When you were adopted, your natural parents gave up all parental ties with you. Therefore, you will never be able to petition for your natural parents as your Immediate Relatives. The adoption decree cuts off all legal ties between you and your natural parents.

---

### C. HOW TO FILE

The first step is to prepare:

• Form I-130, Petition for Alien Relative (see the sample at the end of Chapter 7)

• documents showing your U.S. citizenship

• birth certificate showing your name and your mother's name if filing for your mother; birth certificate showing your name and the names of both parents, if filing for your father

• marriage certificate of parents if you are filing for your father; your stepparents' marriage certificate, if you are filing for either stepparent, and

• the adoption decree, if you are filing for your adoptive parent.

If your parents are not in the United States, mail all these documents and the fee by certified mail to the nearest BCIS Regional Service Center. (See the BCIS website for contact details.) If they are in the United States, they may be able to file directly for Adjustment of Status (see Chapter 8).

There is a filing fee of $130, in a certified check or money order payable to the BCIS.

### D. FINAL STEPS TO GETTING A GREEN CARD

The next step in your parents' immigration process depends on where they're located. If they're in the United States, you need to start by figuring out whether they are eligible to Adjust Status (apply for their green card) here. See Chapter 8, Section A, "Who Qualifies," to determine this. (If they are on valid visas, then they are probably eligible. However, they must be careful—if they obtained a tourist or other visa with the secret intention of applying for a green card after they got here, that's visa fraud. They can be denied the green card based on this fraud.)

If they do qualify, then you can submit the I-130 visa petition in combination with an Adjustment of Status application to a local BCIS office (not a service center) as also described in Chapter 8. Eventually they will be fingerprinted, called in for an interview and hopefully approved for U.S. residency.

If your parents do not qualify to Adjust Status but are currently in the U.S., see a lawyer if any of that time has been unlawful—that is, after an illegal entry, past the date of their I-94 or in violation of their status. If so, leaving the U.S. could result in them being prevented from reentering for three or ten years, depending on the length of their unlawful stay.

If your parent's current stay in the U.S. has been lawful and they plan to leave on time, or if they're already living overseas, their next step is to await the BCIS approval of the Form I-130 visa petition and then go through consular processing, as described in Chapter 9. Eventually they will be called in for an interview at your local U.S. consulate, at which time they will hopefully be approved for an immigrant visa to enter the United States and claim their permanent residency.

See Chapter 30 for important information on how your parents can protect their right to keep the green card.

## IN DEFENSE OF THE ELDERLY

If your mother or father is elderly, take some time to help them get acquainted with the customs and cultural habits of the country.

Introduce them to the senior citizen center located in their new neighborhood. Teach them how to use the public transportation system, including precautions to be taken if you live in a big city. Bring them to the cultural or popular entertainment activities available in your area.

It is cruel to relegate your parents to be merely baby-sitters for your young children. They have already done all the childrearing they were responsible for when they raised you. Pay them a decent amount if they take care of your children. Do not abuse their kindness by taking advantage of their presence in your home to do the work you should be doing.

Most of all, do not discard your own mother or father in thought and in deed, especially when they are less able to care for themselves than they once were. Even if you decide to ask someone else or an institution to care for their day-to-day needs, remain a thoughtful and caring son or daughter.

# 11

# CHILD IMMIGRANTS

## What Child Is This?

You are an American businessman who marries an Italian woman in Rome. She has two children by a previous marriage, one who is 19 and the other 15 years old at the time of your marriage. Can you petition for your two stepchildren at the same time as you petition for your wife?

You are an American soldier who fathered a son while you were stationed in Germany. You never married the mother of your son, but you have been sending her a monthly check for your son's maintenance. She has written to tell you that she is getting married soon. You want your son to live with you and your wife in the United States. What can you do?

You are a green cardholder and unmarried. Before you came to the United States, your niece had always lived with you. You would like to have her live with you in the United States. How do you go about it?

When Congress writes laws regulating immigration, it aims to keep families together. Alien children of American citizens or permanent residents are eligible to get a green card when a parent files for them. However, you need to look carefully at who qualifies as your "child."

## A. WHO CAN FILE

The Petition for Alien Relative, Form I-130 (see the sample at the end of Chapter 7) may be filed by:
- a U.S. citizen parent on behalf of an alien child under 21 years of age (Immediate Relative)
- a U.S. citizen parent on behalf of an alien son or daughter who is over 21 and not married (Family First Preference)
- a U.S. citizen parent on behalf of an alien son or daughter who is over 21 and married (Family Third Preference), or
- a lawful permanent resident on behalf of an alien child, who is not married and is under 21 (Family Second 2A Preference). If the son or daughter is over 21 years old and is not married, then he or she would come under the Family Second 2B Preference. If the alien child was married, but is now divorced or becomes a widow or widower, or if the marriage is an-

nulled, the parent who is a green cardholder can still petition for the son or daughter as an unmarried child in the 2B category.

---

### THE WAIT MAY BE LONG...

The Immigration Act of 1990 allocated worldwide around 88,000 immigrant visas per year to the spouses and unmarried children under 21 years of age of green cardholders and only 26,000 visas per year to their unmarried children over 21 years of age. But demand is far greater than supply. And the law placed no time limits on processing the applications—and most BCIS offices are bogged down.

The current waiting period for a spouse and unmarried children under the age of 21 is about five years. And adult children should be prepared not only to wait—five years or more—for their immigrant visas but also should be forewarned not to get married while waiting if they want to join the family as immigrants in the United States.

The green card-holding parent or spouse can hurry the process along by becoming a U.S. citizen.

---

## B. WHO QUALIFIES AS A CHILD

Immigration law recognizes many different meanings of the word "child" as it relates to obtaining a green card. The definition of the relationship is important because it determines what kind of documentation the BCIS will require when the petition is filed.

### 1. Natural child

A woman and man who conceive a child are that child's natural parents. Proving this relationship for immigration purposes requires extra steps if the woman and man are not married to one another.

**Proving through mother.** When a child is born of a woman who is not married to the child's father, the child is her natural child.

To establish the relationship of mother and child, the only document necessary is the birth certificate showing the name of the mother and the name of the child.

If the mother's maiden name as shown on the birth certificate of her child differs from her present name, the mother must present the document showing that her name was changed. Usually, she has changed her name after marrying. The marriage certificate will then verify that the mother named on the birth certificate and the mother on the immigration form are the same person.

Similarly, if the child is a daughter who has changed her name after marriage, her marriage certificate must be submitted with the immigration papers to show that the child on the birth certificate and the child on the immigration form are the same person.

**Proving through father.** Even if the father of the child is not married to the mother when the child is born, both the father and mother can petition for the child to immigrate into the United States.

But it may become complicated to prove the father-child relationship. First, the father must establish that he is really the biological father of the child. The birth certificate is the best proof, if his name appears as the father of the child.

If his name is not on the birth certificate, the father should apply to his civil registry requesting that his name be added to the birth certificate as the father of the child. He should do this before the child turns 18.

In some countries, the father may have to acknowledge before a civil court, government agency or civil registry that he is the father of the child. The BCIS requires such acknowledgment to occur before the child turns 18 years old.

If none of this proof is available, a blood test, accompanied by an affidavit from the mother stating that the man is the father of the child, may be acceptable.

In addition, the father must show that he was not simply the biological father, but that there was a father-child relationship. There must be proof that:

- the father and child lived together before the child turned 18, or
- that there was a true father-child relationship before the child turned 18 or got married.

This relationship can be shown by letters written by one to the other, canceled checks or other proof of money sent regularly to support the child, photos of both of them together, school records showing the father's name, affidavits from at least two people who know of the father-child relationship, U.S. income tax returns showing the child listed as a dependent, birthday cards or Valentine, Christmas or other holiday cards sent and received.

In short, almost any evidence may help show that the father did not abandon the child, but kept up paternal ties before the child turned 21 years old.

---

### SOME COUNTRIES REQUIRE NO PROOF

The governments in some countries, such as China, Haiti, Trinidad and Tobago and Jamaica, have passed laws erasing the legal distinction between children born to parents who are married to one another and those whose parents are not married.

But the father has to show the BCIS that the law was changed before the child turned 18 years of age. If he can show this, he need not submit all those letters, affidavits, school records and other proof mentioned above.

---

## 2. Legitimate child

When a child is born to a man and a woman who are married to each other, the child is, in legal terms, their legitimate child. To establish the relationship of mother and child, the only document necessary is the birth certificate showing the name of the mother and of the child.

To show the relationship of father and child, two documents are necessary:

- the birth certificate, which shows the name of the father and the child, and

• the marriage certificate, which shows that the mother and the father were married before the birth of the child.

### 3. Legitimated child

When a child is born to a man and a woman who are not married to each other when the child was born but who marry each other before the child turned 18 years of age, the child is considered to be a legitimated child.

For the relationship of mother and child, only the birth certificate is necessary.

For the relationship of father and child, two documents are needed: the birth certificate and the marriage certificate.

### 4. Stepchild

When the mother or the father of a child marries a person who is not the biological parent of that child, a step-relationship is created between the new parent and the child.

For there to be any immigration benefit, the marriage between the child's parent and stepparent must occur before the child turns 18 years of age. An American spouse can petition for an alien spouse's children as his or her stepchildren at any time as long as the children were under 18 years of age at the time of the marriage. The same benefits can be conferred by a parent who holds a green card.

In addition to the birth certificate of the child, a marriage certificate is necessary to show that the step-relationship was created by a marriage which occurred before the child's 18th birthday.

### 5. Adopted child

For immigration purposes, an adopted child is a child who has been adopted according to the laws of the country of his or her birth, or the American state of the adopting parents, as long as the adoption occurs before the child turns 16 years of age. Unlike an orphan child (discussed in Chapter 12), the adopted child is neither orphaned nor abandoned by his or her natural parents.

> **EXAMPLE:** If you were 17 years old when you were adopted by your naturalized American uncle, you may inherit his wealth, but you will not be able to obtain a green card as the adopted child of a U.S. citizen.

The BCIS requires two additional circumstances before a petition for an adopted child can be approved.
• The petitioner—who may be either an American citizen or a permanent resident—must have had legal custody of the adopted child for at least two years. This means that either a legal guardianship or an actual adoption decree must have been issued two years before the immigrant petition was filed, and
• The adopted child must have lived with the adopting parents at least two years before the petition was filed.

Because of these requirements, the only way the adopted child can get an immigrant visa is for one or both of the adopting parents to live in the foreign country with the alien child. This is practically impossible for lawful permanent resident parents, who must maintain their U.S. residences in order to keep their green cards. The other alternative may be to process the immigration papers required for an orphan child. (See Chapter 12.)

---

### NEW ADOPTION OPPORTUNITIES ON THE WAY

In October 2000, President Clinton signed into law the "Intercountry Adoption Act of 2000," which implements the Hague Convention on International Adoption. This is expected to streamline and broaden opportunities for adoption of children from overseas. However, it will probably be a few years before this law is actually implemented, since the government must first set up a Central Adoption Authority and issue regulations.

---

The child may live with the adopting parent, or may be under the legal custody of the adopting parent for two years, either before or after the adoption becomes final by court decree. It does not matter. However, the child must live with the adopting parents for two years and must be in the legal custody of the adopting parents for two years. When these two periods have occurred either simultaneously or successively, the immigrant petition can be filed.

The only other way to petition for a child under this provision is for the child to enter the United States as a nonimmigrant, such as a visiting student. Adoption proceedings may then be initiated in the United States. However, the adopting parents cannot file a petition for the child as a relative until two years after the adoption.

## C. HOW TO FILE

If the American citizen is filing for an unmarried child who is currently under 21 years old, the following forms and supporting documents must be filed:

- Form I-130: Petition for Alien Relative, to be signed by petitioner
- Form G-325A: Biographic Information, to be signed by beneficiary
- Form I-485: Application for Permanent Residence (U.S. Filing)
- Form DS-230 (consular filing)
- Form OF-169 or DS-2001 (consular filing)
- Form I-864: Affidavit of Support, to be signed by petitioner. If the beneficiary is employed in the U.S., a certificate of employment is recommended in addition (see sample copy, next page). In fact, if the beneficiary qualifies for automatic U.S. citizenship upon obtaining a green card, the I-864 is not necessary (see Section D, below). Or, if the beneficiary has already worked in the U.S. for 40 or more work quarters as defined by Social Security (about ten years), Form I-864 is also not required. Moreover, the beneficiary can count time worked by a parent while he was under the age of 18 toward these 40 quarters.
- Form I-765: Application for Employment Authorization (optional), to be signed by beneficiary if beneficiary desires to work before approval in the U.S.
- birth certificate of child
- petitioning parents' marriage certificate

- documents proving the parent's U.S. citizenship or permanent residence (see Chapter 29, Section D)
- three photographs of the child (see Chapter 29, Sections E and F), and
- passport with I-94 of child (if applying in the U.S.).

The filing fee for Form I-130 is $130 and for Form I-485 it is $150 for people under age 14 and $255 for people 14 and older; $50 for fingerprinting of applicants 14 years or older and (U.S. filing only), for Form I-765, $120.

In cases where the child is adopted, the following documents must be presented along with the forms and documents previously specified:

- the adoption decree showing adoption prior to 16 years of age
- documents showing legal custody for at least two years
- documents proving that the adopted child has resided with the adopting parent or parents for at least two years
- a birth certificate of the child showing the adopting parent as mother or father by reason of the adoption decree, and
- documents showing the marital status of the petitioning parent.

If the child is in the United States, and eligible to Adjust Status, then the I-130 and all the other forms and documents can be submitted to a local BCIS district office. If not, then the Form I-130 petition must first be submitted to a BCIS Service Center. Once the I-130 petition is approved, the beneficiary will be contacted by the U.S. Embassy, for Consular Processing. (See Chapter 9.)

## D. AUTOMATIC CITIZENSHIP FOR CHILDREN

In 2000, Congress passed important new legislation allowing many children living in the U.S. with green cards to become citizens automatically, if they have at least one U.S. citizen parent. Natural born as well as adopted children can benefit from these new laws.

The law is slightly less helpful for children living overseas, who must go through an application process in order to claim their U.S. citizenship.

### 1. Children living in the U.S.

For natural born children to qualify for automatic citizenship, one parent needs to be a U.S. citizen, the child must have a green card and be living in the legal and physical custody of the U.S. citizen parent and the child must still be under age 18 when all of these conditions are fulfilled.

For adopted children to qualify, one of the parents must be a U.S. citizen, a full and final adoption must have occurred, the child must be living in the United States after having entered on an immigrant visa (meaning the child would now be a green card holder) and the child must still be under age 18 at the time that all these things become true.

Though the process is automatic, such children will probably want to apply for U.S. passports as proof of their U.S. citizen status.

## 2. Children living overseas

For children who are living overseas, the process is somewhat more complex. Either natural born or adopted children may qualify, but they need to have one U.S. citizen parent; that parent or the parent's parent must have been physically present in the U.S. for five years after the age of 14; the child must be visiting the U.S. on a temporary visa or other lawful means of entry; the child must live in the legal and physical custody of the U.S. citizen parent in their overseas home; and the child must remain under the age of 18 and in valid visa status until the BCIS makes its decision on the citizenship application.

In practice, these conditions are very hard to meet. You might wish to consult with a lawyer. The application is made on Form N-600 for natural born children and N-643 for adopted children. For a sample of Form N-600, see the end of the chapter.

### SAMPLE CERTIFICATE OF EMPLOYMENT
[Typed on Employer's Letterhead]

[Date]
U.S. Department of Justice
Bureau of Citizenship and Immigration Services
[local BCIS address]

Re: [Last name, first name, middle initial]

Dear Sir or Madam:

This is to certify that ___[add name]___ is employed as ___[add type of employment]___ .

His/her annual salary is ___$ [add salary]___ .

The prospects of continued employment are excellent.

This certification is issued in connection with the application for adjustment of status to that of a permanent resident.

Very truly yours,

*Max Haxsim*

Max Haxsim
President [or Personnel Manager]

## APPLICATION FOR CERTIFICATE OF CITIZENSHIP, SAMPLE FORM N-600

OMB NO. 1115-0018

**U.S. Department of Justice**
Immigration and Naturalization Service

**Application for
Certificate of Citizenship**

**FEE STAMP**

Take or mail this application to:
**IMMIGRATION AND NATURALIZATION SERVICE**

Date January 15, 2003

*(Print or type)*   Besa Najada Reynolds
(Full, True Name, without Abbreviations)      nee _____
_____ (Maiden name, if any)

c/o Tomas Reynolds, 327 Main St.
(Apartment number, Street address, and if appropriate, "in care of")

Minneapolis, U.S.A   MN  55104
(City)      (Country)      (State)      (Zip Code)

**ALIEN REGISTRATION**
NO._____

218-555-1222
(Telephone Number)

## (SEE INSTRUCTIONS. BE SURE YOU UNDERSTAND EACH QUESTION BEFORE YOU ANSWER IT.)

I hereby apply to the Commissioner of Immigration and Naturalization for a certificate showing that I am a citizen of the United States of America.

(1) I was born in ___Tirana, Albania___ on ___March 9, 1995___
(City) (State or Country)                    (Month) (Day) (Year)

(2) My personal description is: Gender __F__ ; height __4__ feet __1__ inches;

Marital status: [X] Single; [ ] Married; [ ] Divorced; [ ] Widow(er).

(3) I arrived in the United States at ___Minneapolis, MN___ on ___January 12, 2003___
(City and State)                              (Month) (Day) (Year)

under the name ___Besa Najada Hoxha___ by means of ___Delta Airlines___
(Name of ship or other means of arrival)

[ ] on U. S. Passport No._____ issued to me at _____ on _____
(Month) (Day) (Year)

[ ] on an Immigrant Visa. [X] Other (specify) ___Nonimmigrant visa, B-2 visitor___

(4) FILL IN THIS BLOCK ONLY IF YOU ARRIVED IN THE UNITED STATES BEFORE JULY 1, 1924.

(a) My last permanent foreign residence was _____
(City)                          (Country)

(b) I took the ship or other conveyance to the United States at _____
(City)                          (Country)

(c) I was coming to _____ at _____
(Name of person in the United States)        (City and State where this person was living)

(d) I traveled to the United States with _____
(Names of passengers or relatives with whom you traveled, and their relationship to you, if any)

(5) Have you been out of the United States since you first arrived? [ ] Yes [X] No; If "Yes," fill in the following information for every absence.

| DATE DEPARTED | DATE RETURNED | Name of airlines or other means used to return to the United States | Port of return to the United States |
|---|---|---|---|
| | | | |
| | | | |
| | | | |

(6) I __have not__ filed a petition for naturalization. *(If "have," attach full explanation.)*
(have) (have not)

**TO THE APPLICANT. - Do not write between the double lines below. Continue on next page.**

| ARRIVAL RECORDS EXAMINED | | ARRIVAL RECORD FOUND | |
|---|---|---|---|
| Card index | _____ | Place | _____ Date _____ |
| Index books | _____ | Name | _____ |
| Manifest | _____ | Manner | _____ |
| _____ | | Marital status | _____ Age _____ |
| _____ | | (Signature of person making search) | |

Form N-600 (Rev. 10/11/00)Y

## SAMPLE FORM N-600 (PAGE 2)

**(CONTINUE HERE)**

**(7) I claim United States citizenship through my** *(check whichever applicable)*  [X] **father;**  [ ] **mother;**  [ ] **both parents;**

[ ] **adoptive parent(s);**  [ ] **husband**

**(8) My father's name is**  Joseph Reynolds _____ ; he was born on ____ July 10, 1969 ____

(Month)   (Day)   (Year)

at ____ Boston, MA U.S.A. _____ ; and resides at ____ 122 Dyrrah Way, Durres, Albania ____

(City)                  (State or Country)                              (Street address, city and State or country. If dead, write

He became a citizen of the United States by [X] birth; [ ] naturalization on _____

"dead" and date of death.)                                                                                       (Month)   (Day)   (Year)

in the _____ Certificate of Naturalization No. _____

(Name of court, city and State)

[ ] through his parent(s), and _____ **issued Certificate of Citizenship No. A or AA** _____

(was) (was not)

(If known) His former Alien Registration No. was _____

He _____ lost United States citizenship. *(If citizenship lost, attach full explanation.)*

(has)  (has not)

He resided in the United States from ____ 1969 ____ to ____ 1992 ____ ; from _____ to _____ ; from _____ to _____

(Year)         (Year)              (Year)    (Year)              (Year)    (Year)

from _____ to _____ ; from _____ to _____ ; I am the child of his _____ marriage.

(Year)      (Year)         (Year)      (Year)                            (1st, 2d, 3d, etc.)

**(9) My mother's present name is**  Ilira Naxhie Reynolds ____ ; her maiden name was  Ilira Naxhie Hoxha ____ ;

she was born on  August 17, 1972 ____ ; at  Tirana, Albania ____ ; she resides

(Month) (Day) (Year)                        (City)  (State or country)

at ____ 122 Dyrrah Way, Durres, Albania _____ . She became a citizen of the

(Street address, city, and State or country. If dead, write "dead" and date of death.)

United States by [ ] birth; [ ] naturalization under the name of ____ N/A _____

on _____ in the _____ ;

(Month) (Day) (Year)                          (Name of court, city, and State)

Certificate of Naturalization No. _____ ; [ ] through her parent(s), and _____ issued Certificate of

(was) (was not)

Citizenship No. A or AA _____ (If known) Her former Alien Registration No. was _____ .

She _____ lost United States citizenship. *(If citizenship lost, attach full explanation.)*

(has)  (has not)

She resided in the United States from _____ to _____ ; from _____ to _____ ; from _____ to _____ ;

(Year)    (Year)              (Year)    (Year)              (Year)    (Year)

from _____ to _____ ; from _____ to _____ ; I am the child of her _____ marriage.

(Year)      (Year)         (Year)      (Year)                         (1st, 2d, 3d, etc.)

**(10) My mother and my father were married to each other on** ____ June 5, 1993 ____ at ____ Boston, MA, U.S.A. ____

(Month) (Day) (Year)                  (City)   (State or country)

**(11) If claim is through adoptive parent(s):**

I was adopted on _____ in the _____

(Month) (Day) (Year)                        (Name of Court)

at _____ by my _____ who were not United States citizens at that time.

(City or town) (State) (Country)              (mother, father, parents)

**(12) My** _____ served in the Armed Forces of the United States from _____ to _____ and _____

(father) (mother)                                                (Date)         (Date)              (was) (was not)

honorably discharged.

**(13) I** ____ n/a ____ lost my United States citizenship. *(If citizenship lost, attach full explanation.)*

(have) (have not)

**(14) I submit the following documents with this application:**

| *Nature of Document* | *Names of Persons Concerned* |
|---|---|
| Birth Certificate | Ilira Naxhie Reynolds, Joseph Reynolds, Besa Najada Reynolds |
| Parent's Marriage Certificate | Ilira Naxhie Reynolds, Joseph Reynolds |
| Father's Birth Certificate | Joseph Reynolds |
|  |  |
|  |  |
|  |  |

## SAMPLE FORM N-600 (PAGE 3)

(15) Fill in this block if your brother, sister, mother or father ever applied to the INS for a certificate of citizenship.

| NAME OF RELATIVE | RELATIONSHIP | DATE OF BIRTH | WHEN APPLICATION SUBMITTED | CERTIFICATE NO. AND FILE NO., IF KNOWN, AND LOCATION OF OFFICE |
|---|---|---|---|---|
| | | | | |
| | | | | |
| | | | | |

(16) Fill in this block only if you are now or ever have been a married woman. I have been married _____ time(s), as follows:
(1, 2, 3 etc.)

| DATE MARRIED | NAME OF HUSBAND | CITIZENSHIP OF HUSBAND | IF MARRIAGE HAS BEEN TERMINATED: | |
|---|---|---|---|---|
| | | | Date Marriage Ended | How Marriage Ended (Death or Divorce) |
| | | | | |

(17) Fill in this block only if you claim citizenship through a husband. *(Marriage must have occurred prior to September 22, 1922.)*

Name of citizen husband _____ ; he was born on _____
(Give full and complete name) (Month) (Day) (Year)

at _____ ; and resides at _____ He became a citizen of the
(City) (State or country) (Street address, city, and State or country. If dead, write "dead" and date of death.)

United States by ☐ birth; ☐ naturalization on _____ in the _____ Certificate of
(Month) (Day) (Year) (Name of court, city, and state)

Naturalization No. _____ ; ☐ through his parent(s), and _____ issued Certificate of Citizenship No. A or AA
(was) (was not)

_____ . He _____ since lost United States citizenship. *(If citizenship lost, attach full explanation.)*
(has) (has not)

I am of the _____ race. Before my marriage to him, he was married _____ time(s), as follows:
(1,2, 3,etc.)

| DATE MARRIED | NAME OF WIFE | IF MARRIAGE HAS BEEN TERMINATED: | |
|---|---|---|---|
| | | Date Marriage Ended | How Marriage Ended (Death or Divorce) |
| | | | |

(18) Fill in this block only if you claim citizenship through your stepfather. *(Applicable only if mother married U. S. Citizen prior to September 22, 1922.)*

The full name of my stepfather is _____ ; he was born on _____ at _____ ;
(Month) (Day) (Year) (City) (State or country)

and resides at _____ He became a citizen of the United States by ☐ birth;
(Street address, city, and State or country. If dead, write "dead" and date of death.)

☐ naturalization on _____ in the _____ Certificate of Naturalization No. _____ ;
(Month) (Day) (Year) (Name of court, City and State)

☐ through his parent(s), and _____ issued Certificate of Citizenship No. A or AA _____ He _____ since lost United
(was) (was not) (has) (has not)

States citizenship. *(If citizenship lost, attach full explanation.)* He and my mother were married to each other on _____ at _____
(Month) (Day) (Year) (City and State or

_____ My mother is of the _____ race. She _____ issued Certificate of Citizenship No. A _____
country) (was) (was not)

Before marrying my mother, my stepfather was married _____ time(s), as follows:
(1, 2, 3.etc.)

| DATE MARRIED | NAME OF WIFE | IF MARRIAGE HAS BEEN TERMINATED: | |
|---|---|---|---|
| | | Date Marriage Ended | How Marriage Ended (Death or Divorce) |
| | | | |
| | | | |

(19) I _____ previously applied for a certificate of citizenship on _____ , at _____
(have) (have not) (Date) (Office)

(20) Signature of person preparing form, if other than applicant. I declare that this document was prepared by me at the request of the applicant and is based on all information of which I have any knowledge.

SIGNATURE _____

ADDRESS: _____ | DATE _____

(SIGN HERE) _____
(Signature of applicant or parent or guardian)

## SAMPLE FORM N-600 (PAGE 4)

APPLICANT. - Do not fill in or sign anything on this page

### AFFIDAVIT

I, the _____ , do swear
(Applicant, parent, guardian)
that I know and understand the contents of this application, signed by me, and
of attached supplementary pages numbered (     ) to (     ), inclusive;
that the same are true to the best of my knowledge and belief; and that
corrections numbered (     ) to (     ) were made by me or at my request.

_____
(Signature of applicant, parent, guardian)

Subscribed and sworn to before me upon examination of the applicant
(parent, guardian) at_____ ,
this _____ day of _____ , _____
and continued solely for:

_____
(Officer's Signature and Title)

### REPORT AND RECOMMENDATION ON APPLICATION

On the basis of the documents, records, and persons examined, and the identification upon personal appearance of the underage beneficiary, I find that
all the facts and conclusions set forth under oath in this application are _____ true and correct; that the applicant did _____ derive or acquire United
States citizenship on_____ , through
(Month) (Day) (Year)

and that (s)he_____ been expatriated since that time. I recommend that this application be _____ and that
( has ) (has not )                                                                              (granted)   (denied)
_____Certificate of citizenship be _____ issued in the name of _____
(A) (AA)
In addition to the documents listed in Item 14, the following documents and records have been examined:

| Person Examined | Address | Relationship to Applicant | Date Testimony Heard |
|---|---|---|---|
| _____ | _____ | _____ | _____ |
| | _____ | | |
| _____ | _____ | _____ | _____ |
| | _____ | | |

Supplementary Report(s) No.(s) _____ Attached.
Date _____ , _____

_____
(Officer's Signature and Title)

I do_____concur in the recommendation

Date _____ , _____

_____
(Signature of District Director or Officer in Charge)

# 12

●●●●●●●●●●●●●

# ORPHAN IMMIGRANTS

## Little Orphan Annie

You and your wife have a son but his birth was difficult. Her doctor warns that the next pregnancy may be dangerous to her health. You decide to adopt a child, but the local adoption agency has a long waiting list. You have heard that it is common to adopt abandoned children in a South American country. How do you go about it?

The immigration process and obtaining a visa for an abandoned child falls under a special section of immigration law called Adoption of an Orphan Child. This process does not require the parents to have legal custody and to live with the child for two years, as required by the adopted child regulations described in Chapter 11. However, it is a more complicated process. The regulations are at 8 C.F.R. §204.30.

## A. WHO QUALIFIES AS AN ORPHAN CHILD

A child under 16 years of age is considered an orphan if he or she meets any of the following conditions:

- both parents have died or have disappeared
- the sole or surviving parent is incapable of providing the proper child care and has, in writing, released the child for adoption and emigration, or
- both father and mother have abandoned the child, or have become separated or lost from the child—and the legal authorities in the child's country, recognizing the child as abandoned, have granted legal custody of the child to an orphanage.

However, if the child has been placed temporarily in the orphanage, or if one or both parents continue to maintain contact—sending gifts, writing letters or showing that they have not ended their parental obligations to the child—the child will not be considered an orphan by the U.S. government.

## B. REQUIREMENTS FOR PETITIONING

Only U.S. citizens are allowed to file a visa petition for an orphan child; lawful permanent residents may not do so. A number of other regulations also apply.

- If a couple is adopting, only one of them need be a U.S. citizen, but both have to sign the petition.
- If the U.S. citizen is not married, then he or she must be at least 25 years of age.
- The orphan child must be less than 16 years of age when the petition is filed.

- The adopting couple, or single person, must have completed certain pre-adoption requirements before filing the petition. (See Section C, below.)
- The adopting couple, or single person, must have seen the child in the orphan's country before or during the adoption proceedings, or show that they'll be able to "readopt" the child in the U.S.

 **BEWARE OF THE LAWBREAKERS**

In some developing countries, kidnapping poor children, then selling them for adoption to childless couples in the United States and Europe, has become scandalously rampant.

Your search for a child of your own should not cause the kidnapping or sale of another person's child. A situation in which a single parent gives up the child for adoption is fraught with possible emotional and legal complications, especially if money is involved. Before you sign up with any adoption organization, check its references with friends who have worked with the organization—or ask for the names of some former clients. Above all, avoid direct arrangements with the surviving parent or private individuals acting as brokers for a fee.

## C. PRE-ADOPTION REQUIREMENTS

To protect the child and to ensure that the adopting parent or parents will care for the child properly, the immigration laws require a Home Study before an adoption decree is finalized or before a petition for an orphan child will be approved. Many couples take care of this first as part of an Advance Processing application, described below in Section D1. The purpose of the Home Study is to allow the state agency handling adoptions to investigate the future home of the child and verify whether the adopting couple, or the single person, is psychologically and economically fit to adopt a child.

The Home Study must result in a favorable report recommending the proposed adoption. The report must be signed by an official of a state agency, or an agency licensed by the state in which the child will live with the adopting parent or parents. It's only good for six months.

This report must contain the following information:

- the financial ability of the parent or parents to raise and educate the child

- a detailed description of the living accommodations, and
- a factual evaluation of the physical, mental and moral ability of the adopting parent or parents, including observations made during personal interviews.

In addition to the Home Study, other pre-adoption conditions may be required by some states before an adoption petition may be filed with local courts. Therefore, if you are planning to adopt the orphan child in the United States, you must first comply with these state rules.

In every state, there is one main agency that oversees adoptions. To contact the local representative of your state agency, look in the telephone book under Adoption, Child Welfare, or Social Services. You may also get guidance from International Concerns for Children, Inc., 911 Cypress Drive, Boulder, CO 80303; telephone: 303-494-8333; website www.iccadopt.org.

## D. STARTING THE ADOPTION PROCESS

The first steps toward adoption depend on whether or not the orphan child has been identified.

### 1. When the child is not yet identified

If the child has not yet been identified and those who wish to adopt are going abroad to locate an orphan child for adoption, or for adoption after arrival in the United States, they should file an Advance Processing application, as follows:

- Form I-600A, Application for Advance Processing of Orphan Petition, signed by the U.S. citizen and, if married, the spouse.
- Proof of petitioner's U.S. citizenship. (See Chapter 29, Section D3.)
- Marriage certificate, divorce or annulment decree, or death certificate, as evidence of present and previous marital status.
- Fees of $50 each for fingerprints of the United States citizen and, if married, of the spouse. Also, all adults aged 18 years old or older who live in the household must also be fingerprinted. (See Chapter 29, Section F.)
- Evidence of petitioner's age, if unmarried.
- A favorable Home Study report. If the Home Study report is not yet available, it must be submitted within one year from the date of filing the advance application. Otherwise, the application will be considered to have been abandoned.
- proof of compliance with any pre-adoption requirements of the state in which the child will live if the adoption is to be completed in the United States (see Section C).

- A filing fee of $460. However, no filing fee is required if an Application for Advance Processing has been previously filed and if the petition has been filed within one year of the approval of the advance application. A copy of the receipt showing the filing fee has been paid is sufficient. Also include a copy of the approval notice.

The application is considered to be abandoned if the adopting parents are unsuccessful in locating an orphan child within one year. If the prospective parents wish to continue the process of adopting an alien child, a new Advance Processing application, with a filing fee of $460 if the child has not yet been identified, or a new petition with a filing fee of $460 if the child has been identified must be filed.

---

**CHILDREN ENTERING AS TOURISTS OR STUDENTS**

A child who enters the United States on a nonimmigrant visa as a tourist or a student cannot be adopted as an orphan child under the present immigration laws. You must explain to the consular officer in the American Embassy that you intend to adopt the child so that he or she will be given Advance Parole.

---

### 2. When the child is identified

When the adopting parent or parents have identified the orphan child they wish to adopt, they can immediately file a petition for the child at the nearest BCIS Regional Service Center. (See Appendix 1 for contact details and the BCIS website at www.bcis.gov for the exact P.O. Box.) This can be done even if the Advance Processing application has not yet been approved or has not yet been filed. If the Advance Processing application has been filed but not approved, include a copy of the filing receipt with the petition. If it has already been approved, include a copy of the approval notice.

You must file all the documents listed in Section D1 above (except Form I-600A), as well as:

- Form I-600, Petition to Classify Orphan as an Immediate Relative
- the birth certificate of the orphan child, who must be under 16 years of age when the petition is filed
- death certificates of the parents of the child or proof of legal abandonment by both the father and mother of the child, and

- the adoption decree or evidence that you have legal custody of the orphan and are working toward adoption.

## E. Where to File

The petition may be filed either with a BCIS Regional Service Center or with the U.S. Embassy in the country of the child's residence. When the American citizen, the spouse, or both of them together are traveling abroad to adopt the child or to identify the child, the petition may be filed at the U.S. Embassy or Consulate of the country in which the child lives.

Several countries have issued special rules on the adoption of their infant citizens by noncitizens. It is very important to be fully informed of these new regulations before proceeding to adopt an orphan child from one of these countries. Call the embassies of specific foreign counties in Washington, D.C., to begin your search for more information.

## F. After the Petition Is Approved

If the petition is filed and approved by the BCIS in the United States, the entire file is sent to the U.S. Embassy in the country in which the child lives.

If the petition is filed and approved by the Embassy, the entire file remains there until the next step in the immigration of the child is accomplished.

The consular officer then investigates the child. This may take either a few days or several months. The investigation aims to confirm that:
- the child meets the legal definition of an orphan, and
- the child does not have an illness or disability which has not been described in the orphan petition.

A long delay in the adoption process of an orphan child can cause would-be parents much anxiety. However, keep in mind that the investigation is performed as a service to protect adopting parents from the heartbreaking situation that could develop if the child later proved not to be available for adoption.

## G. Filing for a Visa

When the petition is approved, the U.S. citizen then files an Application for an Immigrant Visa with the U.S. Embassy on behalf of the orphan child who can enter the United States either as an immigrant or as a parolee. (See Chapter 9 on Consular Processing.)

### 1. Entering as an immigrant

The orphan child can then enter the United States as a permanent resident. If the child has not yet been adopted in the foreign country, the U.S. citizen, or couple, can proceed to adopt the child according to the laws of the state in which they live.

After adoption, the parents can then request a change of name on the green card (Immigration Form I-90) of the child to the name designated in the state or family court order of adoption.

### 2. Entering as a parolee

If the petition is not approved by the U.S. Embassy, you may be able to persuade the U.S. Consul to issue the orphan child Advance Parole. For example, you could argue that the child must come with you to the United States to complete the adoption process.

### 3. Adjusting status in the United States

Once the orphan child is in the United States as a parolee, the petition to classify the orphan as an Immediate Relative (Form I-130) and the Adjustment of Status Application (Form I-485) can be filed simultaneously. (See Chapter 8 for more information on Adjustment of Status.)

---

### Meeting Face-to-Face

The American individual or couple who wish to adopt need not have seen the child personally before filing the visa petition if the adoption is to be done in the United States. However, if you are going to adopt a child to raise as your own for the rest of your life, you will likely want to find out what the child looks like, how you react to one other, what his or her physical condition is and other imperceptible factors that only a face-to-face encounter can provide. Most people prefer to visit the child abroad before beginning adoption proceedings.

# 13

# **AMERASIAN IMMIGRANTS**

## I Am a GI Baby

In Vietnam, they are called "bui-doi," which means "dust of life."

In Korea, they are called "hon-hul," which means "mixed blood."

They are the children of American servicemen who have returned to the United States leaving behind the human results of the liaisons they had with the children's mothers. The children are often unclaimed, unrecognized and unwanted.

The U.S. Congress passed a law on October 22, 1982, allowing Amerasians to come to the United States as the sons or daughters of an American citizen. Because the shadow of the Vietnam War has receded with the passing of time, and most of those able to come to the United States have already come, the emigration of Amerasians to the United States has been reduced to a trickle.

## A. WHO QUALIFIES AS AN AMERASIAN

An Amerasian is a person who was:
- born in Korea, Vietnam, Laos, Kampuchea (formerly Cambodia) or Thailand
- born after December 31, 1950, and before October 22, 1982, and
- fathered by an American citizen.

## B. WHO CAN FILE

A number of groups can begin the immigrant petition process by filing Form I-360, Petition for Amerasian, Widow or Special Immigrant. (See the sample form at the end of this chapter.)
- If over 18 years of age, the Amerasian can file the petition on his or her own behalf.
- Any person of legal age, regardless of citizenship, can file the petition on behalf of the Amerasian.
- A business incorporated in the United States can also file the petition on behalf of the Amerasian.

The person filing the petition is called the petitioner. The Amerasian is called the beneficiary. Contrary to what you might assume, the American father does not have to be the petitioner. In fact, the American father's real name need not even be known as long as it can be proven that the father was an American citizen.

## C. EVERY PETITIONER MUST HAVE A SPONSOR

The Amerasian must have a sponsor who is either:
- an American citizen, at least 21 years of age and of good moral character
- a permanent resident in the United States who is at least 21 years of age and of good moral character, or
- an American organization that will arrange to place the Amerasian with a sponsor in the United States. The American organization filing the petition must be able to show that:
  - ▪ it is licensed in the United States and experienced in arranging to place Amerasian children
  - ▪ a sponsor has been identified, and is willing and able to accept the Amerasian in his or her home, and
  - ▪ if the Amerasian is under 18 years of age, a favorable Home Study of the sponsor has been conducted by a state agency and the organization has a plan to provide services (mediation, counseling, follow-up) to ensure that the placement is satisfactory.

 **SPONSORS ARE ESSENTIAL**

If the Amerasian cannot find an American family or citizen or permanent resident to sponsor his or her stay in the United States—someone who will take financial, emotional, cultural and social responsibility for him or her—the petition cannot be granted.

## D. HOW TO FILE

The procedure to be followed and documents required for filing are slightly different, depending on who files the petition.

### 1. If the petitioner files

No filing fee is required for Amerasians, but the petitioner should present the following documents to the BCIS office, Embassy, or Consulate:
- Form I-360, Petition for Amerasian, Widow or Special Immigrant. (See the sample form at the end of this chapter.)
- birth certificate of the Amerasian
- the identification card issued by the Vietnamese government if the Amerasian was born there. If the identification card is not available, an affidavit—a

written statement sworn to before a notary public—
should explain why, and

- documents to prove that the Amerasian was fathered
  by an American citizen. The name of the father is not
  required. The documents may include:

  - a birth certificate, baptismal certificate or any
    religious documents or church records
  - vital statistics on family members maintained by
    local civil authorities
  - affidavits from knowledgeable witnesses
  - letters, notes or proof of financial support from the
    father
  - photographs of the father, especially those taken
    with the Amerasian
  - evidence of the father's United States citizenship,
    such as military serial number

- photograph of the Amerasian

- documents to prove marital status of the Amerasian, if
  married, divorced or widowed, and

- a written release by the Amerasian's mother or guardian, sworn to before the American consulate or local
  court of minors, if the Amerasian is under 18 years of
  age.

The mother's release must state that she fully understands that she is giving up her child to emigrate to the
United States. It must also state whether she has been paid,
and if she was paid, how much money she received. She
must acknowledge whether she was or was not coerced into
signing the release. The statement must include the
mother's complete name, date and place of birth and permanent address.

## 2. If the sponsor files

After the petition is approved, the next phase involves the
sponsor, who must submit to either the BCIS or the American consulate the following documents:

- Form I-361, Affidavit of Financial Support and Intent
  to Petition for Legal Custody for Public Law 97-359
  Amerasian, signed by the sponsor. (Ask for a copy of
  this form from the nearest BCIS office or download it
  from www.bcis.gov.) Upon signing the affidavit, the
  sponsor becomes legally responsible for financially
  supporting the Amerasian. Therefore, unless the
  sponsor dies or becomes bankrupt, the Attorney
  General can sue the sponsor in federal court for
  enforcement of the support. This affidavit, which
  must be signed before an immigration or consular officer, states that the sponsor agrees:

  - to file for legal custody of the Amerasian through a
    state court within 30 days of the arrival of the child,
    if under 18 years of age, and
  - to financially support the Amerasian and any of his
    or her family members at 125% of the current offi-
    cial poverty line for the next five years, or until the
    Amerasian turns 21 years of age, whichever is longer.

- proof that the sponsor is over age 21

- proof of the sponsor's financial capability to support
  and maintain the Amerasian, such as income tax
  returns and bank statements

- proof of citizenship or lawful permanent residency of
  the sponsor

- fee of $50 for fingerprinting the sponsor (see Chapter
  29, Section F)

- if the Amerasian is under age 18, evidence that a licensed agency has arranged a placement in the United
  States, and has drafted a follow-up plan, and

- a favorable Home Study report, if the sponsor was
  identified by an American organization. (See Chapter
  12, Section C.)

**Filing for Amerasians under 21.** If the Amerasian is under 21 years of age, he or she qualifies as an Immediate Relative of an American citizen. Therefore, the documents mentioned above should be submitted together with the immigration papers required for Adjustment of Status (see Chapter 8) or Consular Processing (see Chapter 9).

**Filing for Amerasians 21 and over.** If the Amerasian is 21 years of age or older, he or she qualifies as an applicant in the Family First Preference (unmarried son or daughter of an American citizen) or Family Third Preference (married son or daughter of an American citizen) discussed in Chapter 5.

## E. WHERE TO FILE

Two places will accept the petition for the Amerasian: the BCIS office closest to the future residence of the Amerasian in the United States, and the American Embassy or Consulate in the country where the Amerasian now lives. For a complete list of U.S. consulates, with links to their websites, go the the State Department website at www.state.gov. On the homepage, click "U.S. Embassies and Consulates."

## PETITION FOR AMERASIAN, WIDOW OR SPECIAL IMMIGRANT, SAMPLE FORM I-360

OMB No. 1115-0117

**U.S. Department of Justice**
Immigration and Naturalization Service

**Petition for Amerasian, Widow(er), or Special Immigrant**

### START HERE - Please Type or Print

**Part 1. Information about person or organization filing this petition.** (Individuals should use the top name line; organizations should use the second line.) If you are a self-petitioning spouse or child and do not want INS to send notices about this petition to your home, you may show an alternate mailing address here. If you are filing for yourself and do not want to use an alternate mailing address, skip to part 2.

| Family Name | STUART | Given Name | ALICIA | Middle Initial | J. |

Company or Organization Name

Address - C/O
ALICIA AND SAM STUART

| Street Number and Name | 4602 G STREET, NW | | 4 | Apt. # |

| City | WASHINGTON | State or Province | DISTRICT OF COLUMBIA |

| Country | UNITED STATES | Zip/Postal Code | 20004 |

| U.S. Social Security # | 464-56-9217 | A # | N/A | IRS Tax # (if any) | N/A |

### FOR INS USE ONLY

| Returned | Receipt |
|---|---|
| | |

Resubmitted

Reloc Sent

Reloc Rec'd

☐ Petitioner/ Applicant Interviewed

☐ Benefitiary Interviewed

☐ I-485 Filed Concurrently
☐ Bene "A" File Reviewed

Classification

Consulate

Priority Date

Remarks:

### Part 2. Classification Requested (check one):

a. ☑ Amerasian
b. ☐ Widow(er) of a U.S. citizen who died within the past two (2) years
c. ☐ Special Immigrant Juvenile
d. ☐ Special Immigrant Religious Worker
e. ☐ Special Immigrant based on employrnent with the Panama Canal Company, Canal Zone Government or U.S. Government in the Canal Zone
f. ☐ Special Immigrant Physician
g. ☐ Special Immigrant International Organization Employee or family member
h. ☐ Special Immigrant Armed Forces Member
i. ☐ Self-Petitioning Spouse of Abusive U.S. Citizen or Lawful Permanent Resident
j. ☐ Self-Petitioning Child of Abusive U.S. Citizen or Lawful Permanent Resident
k. ☐ Other, explain:

### Part 3. Information about the person this petition is for.

| Family Name | NGUYEN SEAN T. | Given Name | | Middle Initial | |

Address - C/O
BANGKOK HOME

| Street Number and Name | 7 SINGLA MAI ROAD | | Apt. # |

| City | BANGKOK | State or Province | |

| Country | THAILAND | Zip/Postal Code | |

| Date of Birth (Month/Day/Year) | OCTOBER 1, 1981 | Country of Birth | THAILAND |

| U.S. Social Security # | NONE | A # (if any) | NONE |

Marital Status: ☑ Single  ☐ Married  ☐ Divorced  ☐ Widowed

Complete the items below if this person is in the United States:

| Date of Arrival (Month/Day/Year) | | I-94# | |

| Current Nonimmigrant Status | | Expires on (Month/Day/Year) | |

Action Block

### To Be Completed by Attorney or Representative, if any

☐ Fill in box if G-28 is attached to represent the applicant

VOLAG#

ATTY State License #

*Continued on back.*

Form I-360 (Rev. 09/11/00)Y Page 6

## Sample Form I-360 (page 2)

### Part 4. Processing Information.

Below give to United States Consulate you want notified if this petition is approved and if any requested adjustment of status cannot be granted.

| American Consulate: City    BANGKOK | Country    THAILAND |
|---|---|

If you gave a United States address in Part 3, print the person's foreign address below. If his/her native alphabet does not use Roman letters, print his/her name and foreign address in the native alphabet.

| Name | Address |
|---|---|
| | |

Sex of the person this petition is for. ☑ Male ☐ Female

Are you filing any other petitions or applications with this one? ☑ No ☐ Yes (How many? _____ )

Is the person this petition is for in exclusion or deportation proceedings? ☑ No ☐ Yes (Explain an a separate sheet of paper)

Has the person this petition is for ever worked in the U.S. without permission? ☑ No ☐ Yes (Explain an a separate sheet of paper)

Is an appilication for adjustment of status attached to this petition? ☑ No ☐ Yes

### Part 5. Complete only if filing for an Amerasian.

#### Section A. Information about the mother of the Amerasian

| Family Name    NGUYEN | Given Name    MALI | Middle Initial |
|---|---|---|

Living? ☑ No (Give date of death ___OCTOBER 14, 1993___ ☐ Yes (complete address line below) ☐ Unknown (attach a full explanation)

Address

#### Section B. Information about the father of the Amerasian: If possible, attach a notarized statement from the father regarding parentage.
Explain on separate paper any question you cannot fully answer in the space provided on this form.

| Family Name    ADAMCZEK | Given Name    SEAN | Middle Initial    C. |
|---|---|---|

Date of Birth (Month/Day/Year)    NOVEMBER 20, 1963 | Country of Birth    UNITED STATES

Living? ☐ No (give date of death _____ ) ☐ Yes (complete address line below) ☐ Unknown (attach a full explanation)

Home Address    N/A

| Home Phone #    N/A | Work Phone #    N/A |
|---|---|

At the time the Amerasian was conceived:

☑ The father was in the military (indicate branch of service below - and give service number here): UNKNOWN

    ☐ Army    ☐ Air Force    ☐ Navy    ☑ Marine Corps    ☐ Coast Guard

☐ The father was a civilian employed abroad. Attach a list of names and addresses of organizations which employed him at that time.

☐ The father was not in the military, and was not a civilian employed abroad. (Attach a full explanation of the circumstances.)

### Part 6. Complete only if filing for a Special Immigrant Juvenile Court Dependent.

#### Section A. Information about the Juvenile

List any other names used.

Answer the following questions regarding the person this petition is for. If you answer "no," explain on a separate sheet of paper.

Is he or she still dependent upon the juvenile court or still legally committed to or under the custody of an agency or department of a state? ☐ No ☐ Yes

Does he/she continue to be eligible for long term foster care? ☐ No ☐ Yes

Form I-360 (Rev. 09/11/00) Y  Page 7

*Continued on next page.*

## SAMPLE FORM I-360 (PAGE 3)

### Part 7. Complete only if filing as a Widow/Widower, a Self-petitioning Spouse of an Abuser, or as a Self-petitioning Child of an Abuser.

**Section A.** Information about the U.S. citizen husband or wife who died or about the U.S. citizen or lawful permanent resident abuser.

| Family Name | | Given Name | Middle Initial |
|---|---|---|---|

| Date of Birth (Month/Day/Year) | Country of Birth | Date of Death (Month/Day/Year) |
|---|---|---|

He or she is now, or was at time of death a (check one):

☐ U.S. citizen born in the United States.
☐ U.S. citizen born abroad to U.S. citizen parents.

☐ U.S. citizen through Naturalization *(Show A #)* _____
☐ U.S. lawful permanent resident (Show A #) _____
☐ Other, explain _____

**Section B. Additional Information about you.**

| How many times have you been married? | How many times was the person in Section A married? | Give the date and place you and the person in Section A were married. *(If you are a self-petitioning child, write: "N/A")* |
|---|---|---|

When did you live with the person named in Section A? From *(Month/Year)* _____ until *(Month/Year)* _____

If you are filing as a widow/widower, were you legally separated at the time of to U.S citizens's death? ☐ No ☐ Yes, *(attach explanation)*.

Give the last address at which you lived together with the person named in Section A, and show the last date that you lived together with that person at that address:

_____

If you we filing as a self-petitioning spouse, have any of your children filed separate self-petitions? ☐ No ☐ Yes *(show child(ren)'s full names)*

### Part 8. Information about the spouse and children of the person this petition is for. A widow/widower

or a self-petitioning spouse of an abusive citizen or lawful permanent resident should also list the children of the deceased spouse or of the abuser.

| A. Family Name | Given Name | Middle Initial | Date of Birth (Month/Day/Year) |
|---|---|---|---|
| Country of Birth | Relationship ☐ Spouse ☐ Child | | A # |

| B. Family Name | Given Name | Middle Initial | Date of Birth (Month/Day/Year) |
|---|---|---|---|
| Country of Birth | Relationship ☐ Child | | A # |

| C. Family Name | Given Name | Middle Initial | Date of Birth (Month/Day/Year) |
|---|---|---|---|
| Country of Birth | Relationship ☐ Child | | A # |

| D. Family Name | Given Name | Middle Initial | Date of Birth (Month/Day/Year) |
|---|---|---|---|
| Country of Birth | Relationship ☐ Child | | A # |

| E. Family Name | Given Name | Middle Initial | Date of Birth (Month/Day/Year) |
|---|---|---|---|
| Country of Birth | Relationship ☐ Child | | A # |

| F. Family Name | Given Name | Middle Initial | Date of Birth (Month/Day/Year) |
|---|---|---|---|
| Country of Birth | Relationship ☐ Child | | A # |

Form I-360 (Rev 09/11/00)Y Page 8

## SAMPLE FORM I-360 (PAGE 4)

| G. Family Name | | Given Name | | Middle Initial | Date of Birth (Month/Day/Year) |
|---|---|---|---|---|---|
| Country of Birth | | Relationship | ☐ Child | | A# |
| H. Family Name | | Given Name | | Middle Initial | Date of Birth (Month/Day/Year) |
| Country of Birth | | Relationship | ☐ Child | | A# |

### Part 9. Signature.

*Read the information on penalties in the instructions before completing this part. If you are going to file this petition at an INS office in the United States, sign below. If you are going to file it at a U.S. consulate or INS office overseas, sign in front of a U.S. INS or consular official.*

I certify, or, if outside the United States, I swear or affirm, under penalty of perjury under the laws of the United States of America, that this petition and the evidence submitted with it is all true and correct. If filing this on behalf at an organization, I certify that I am empowered to do so by that organization. I authorize the release of any information from my records, or from the petitioning organization's records, which the Immigration and Naturalization Service needs to determine eligibility for the benefit being sought.

| Signature  *Alicia J. Stuart* | Alicia J. Stuart<br>Print Name | Date  9/6/03 |
|---|---|---|
| Signature of INS or Consular Official | | Date |

Please Note: If you do not completely fill out this form or fail to submit required documents listed in the instructions, the person(s) filed for may not be found eligible for a requested benefit and it may have to be denied.

### Part 10. Signature of person preparing form if other than above. (sign below)

I declare that I prepared this application at the request of the above person and it is based on all information of which I have knowledge.

| Signature | Print Your Name | Date |
|---|---|---|
| Firm Name and Address | | |

# 14

# YOUR BROTHERS AND SISTERS AS IMMIGRANTS

## My Brothers and My Sisters All Over This Land

I was adopted by an American couple when I was in kindergarten. They were living in my old country. I had two brothers and two sisters younger than me who remained with my natural parents. I am now an American citizen and earning a good living. Could I petition for my biological brothers and sisters to come to the United States?

Yes, you could—as long as you are at least 21 years old when you file the petition. Because of the intention of the U.S. Congress to unite families, the brothers and sisters of an American citizen are given the immigration benefit of the Family Fourth Preference. (See Chapter 5, Section B1.) This is true no matter how you became a citizen. However, brothers and sisters of permanent residents do not have this privilege.

The immigration laws contain specific definitions setting out who qualifies as a brother and sister in every family.

## A. LEGITIMATE BROTHER AND SISTER

If your mother and father were married and had other children, all of them are your legitimate brothers and sisters.

You must submit your birth certificate and those of your brothers and sisters to show that you have the same mother and father when you file Form I-130, Petition for Alien Relative. (See the sample at the end of Chapter 7.) The fee for filing is $130.

If you are the American or alien sister and you are known by your married name, you must include your marriage certificate to show your change of name from that shown on your birth certificate.

**EXAMPLE:** Your parents raised your cook's baby as their own child. But to file a petition for that baby, you would have to present proof that your birth certificate and the other child's birth certificate show the same father and mother. Of course, you cannot do this. There is no way you can petition for this person as your brother or your sister.

The only way around this strict rule is for someone in the family to legally adopt the child before the child turns 16. If that is not possible, you will have to look for another way for the child to immigrate to the United States, such as an employment visa.

## B. HALF-BROTHER AND HALF-SISTER

If you and another person have the same mother or father, but not both parents in common, that other person is your half-brother or half-sister.

Along with Form I-130, Petition for Alien Relative (see the sample at the end of Chapter 7), you must include both of your birth certificates, showing that you and your half-brother or half-sister have the same mother or the same father. The fee for filing is $130.

It does not matter when the relationship of half-brother or half-sister occurred. As far as the immigration law is concerned, you can petition for them just as if they were your full-blooded brothers or sisters.

## C. STEPBROTHER AND STEPSISTER

If your mother or father has married somebody who had children from a previous marriage or relationship, the children of your stepfather or stepmother would be your stepbrother and stepsister.

However, for purposes of immigration into the United States, you can file a Petition for Alien Relative (Form I-130) for them only on one condition: Your mother or father must have married your stepparent before your 18th birthday.

You must also include the following documents:
- your birth certificate
- the birth certificate of your stepbrother or stepsister
- the marriage certificate of your mother or father and your stepparent, or documents showing that the marriage ended by death, divorce or annulment, and
- your own or your stepsister's marriage certificate, should either of you be using a married name instead of a maiden name.

## D. ADOPTED BROTHER AND ADOPTED SISTER

If your mother and father have adopted a child according to the laws of the state or country they are in, that child is your adopted brother or adopted sister. Or, you may have been adopted by parents who may have other legitimate children of their own. Their children became your brothers and sisters when you were adopted into their family.

However, the BCIS will accept your Form I-130, Petition for Alien Relative (see the sample at the end of Chapter 7) only if the adoption decree occurs before the 16th birthday of your adopted brother or sister if they are the petitioners; or before your own 16th birthday if you were the adopted child. The fee for filing is $130.

You must submit the adoption decree and the birth certificates to show you had the same parents along with the petition to give to your adopted brother or sister the immigration benefit of the Family Fourth Preference.

## E. WHAT HAPPENS AFTER FILING FORM I-130

It is highly unlikely that an immigration visa for someone in the Family Fourth Preference will be immediately available when you file a petition for your brother or sister. The reason is that, in many countries, there is often a huge backlog of applicants waiting in this category—from ten to 24 years.

Therefore, if your brothers or sisters are in the United States on nonresident visas when you file the petition, they cannot become permanent residents unless they remain in legal status during all the time that they are in the country. They will probably have to return to their home country and proceed with Consular Processing (see Chapter 9), unless they're lucky enough to qualify for Adjustment of Status in the U.S. (see Chapter 8).

If your brothers or sisters are in the U.S. illegally, they should talk to a lawyer about whether they'll be found inadmissible and barred from returning. Once the immigrant

visa is available to your brothers or sisters, they can extend the immigration privilege to their spouses and all unmarried children under 21 years of age at the same time, as "accompanying relatives."

Therefore, if your brother and sister are truly interested in working and living in the United States for their own benefit or for the benefit of their children who are your nephews and nieces, it may well be worth the wait of several years for you to file the petition on their behalf. This long wait is all the more reason it is very important to file the petition for your brothers and sisters as soon as you become an American citizen.

On the other hand, given the time that it takes for a person to immigrate as a brother or sister, the potential immigrant should consider whether it would be faster to apply under a different category, such as an employment or nonimmigrant visa category.

A brother or sister who wants to come to the United States to visit during the waiting period must disclose to the U.S. Consul when applying for a tourist or business visa that he or she has an approved visa petition. To be silent about this important fact will be looked upon as fraud in an immigrant visa file—and may mean a lost chance for a green card in the future. ■

# 15

. . . . . . . . . . . . . .

# PRIORITY WORKERS

## They're Superstars, No Matter Where They Are

Before the Immigration Act of 1990, most people who wanted to obtain a green card through employment had to go through a complicated process called Labor Certification.

With the passage of the Act of 1990, the Labor Certification requirement was eliminated for immigrants who have very valuable skills.

## A. WHO QUALIFIES

The U.S. Congress decided that infusions of highly skilled alien labor are needed for the continued economic progress of America. Many skilled workers are therefore to be given a welcome embrace because they belong to the superstar category. Those who qualify as Priority Workers are not required to go through the complicated and time-consuming procedure of obtaining Labor Certification. (See Chapter 18, Section D.)

Now, 40,000 visas are available every year on a first-come, first-served basis to a group of Employment First Preference immigrants: the Priority Workers.

There are three categories of Priority Workers.

### 1. Those with extraordinary ability

An alien with "extraordinary ability" may file a Priority Worker visa petition—or another person may file a petition on his or her behalf. To qualify, the alien must have risen to the very top of the field in science, arts, education, business or athletics.

Extraordinary ability must be documented by:
- proof of achievements that have brought national or international acclaim
- proof that this acclaim is sustained and not simply a flash-in-the-pan phenomenon
- proof of intent to work in the United States in the area of expertise which the alien claims (although a specific job offer is not required), and
- proof or arguments that the alien's extraordinary ability will substantially benefit the United States in the future.

If you are acclaimed in at least one country other than your own—as a scientist, a performing artist, a physicist, a painter, an author, an athlete, an economist, a computer whiz, a film or theater director or an actor—you may qualify as a Priority Worker.

**EXAMPLE:** An alien with extraordinary ability in the sciences and education would be a Nobel Prize winner; in the business world, the Sony magnate Akito Morita; in athletics, Arvydas Sabonis, Lleyton Hewitt or Pele; in the arts, the likes of Michelle Yeoh, Kiri Te Kanawa or Bob Marley.

People who are less famous may also qualify if they meet the requirements discussed here.

To qualify as a Priority Worker for immigration purposes, you must present proof of your achievements. This proof could include a one-time achievement—a major award that is recognized internationally—such as the Nobel Prize or the Olympic Gold Medal.

In lieu of such an award, present proof of at least three of the following:
- less acclaimed prizes or awards for excellence, such as the Magsaysay Award or a medal in the Asian Games
- membership based on merit in associations that require outstanding achievements of members, as judged by recognized national or international experts
- material published about the applicant in professional or major trade publications, international journals of scientific or scholarly works or other major media such as television or radio, relating to the applicant's work or achievements—include the title, date, author and any necessary translations
- participation as an international judge, individually or in a panel, of the work of others in the field

- the applicant's original scientific, scholarly, artistic, athletic or business-related contributions of major significance
- articles written by the applicant that have been published in professional or major trade publications or other major media outlets
- display of work in an artistic exhibition, showcase or competition
- performance in a leading or critical role for organizations or establishments that have a distinguished reputation
- high salary or other significantly high remuneration for services in relation to what others in the same field receive in the same country, and
- commercial successes in the performing arts, as shown by box office receipts or record, cassette, compact disk or video sales.

If you do not have any of these documents, or the criteria do not apply to your occupation, you may submit other evidence to try to convince the BCIS that you are extraordinary—even though you do not satisfy the regulations.

You need not have an offer of employment in the United States as long as you submit clear evidence that you are coming to the U.S. to continue work in your field of expertise, which may include:

- letters from a prospective employer
- a contract of employment from a present employer, or
- an affidavit detailing plans on how you intend to continue your work in the United States.

## 2. Outstanding professors and researchers

Stellar professors or researchers may petition on their own behalf, or the employing university or research center may file for this second group of Priority Workers. However, they must also submit proof that there has been an offer of employment in the United States.

The following additional documentation is also required.

- proof that the applicant has an "outstanding" reputation—meaning international recognition in a specific academic field, with the evidence consisting of at least two of the following:
- major prizes or awards for outstanding achievement
- membership in academic associations which require outstanding achievements of their members
- articles in professional publications about the applicant's work (mere citations in bibliographies are not enough)

- participation, either individually or in a panel, as the judge of others in the same or an allied academic field
- original scientific or scholarly research contributions to the academic field, or
- scholarly books or articles in journals with international circulation written by the applicant.
- proof of three years of experience in teaching or research—including teaching or research while working on an advanced degree if the research was outstanding or the student had full responsibility for the teaching position—shown by letters of previous employers describing the duties performed by the applicant
- proof that the job offer from a United States university or research institute or industry is for a tenured teaching or permanent research position, not simply for a temporary appointment, or
- proof, if the job offer is for research for a private university or research institute or industry, that the future employer has at least three other full-time researchers and has made significant achievements in research.

As you can see, the U.S. Congress wanted to attract the brains—the best professors and the top researchers of the world—to the universities and the research and development centers of the United States.

### JOB OFFER REQUIRED

There must be an institute of research or a university in the United States that is willing and able to employ you in your area of expertise. You cannot apply in the Priority Worker category as an outstanding professor or researcher without a job offer.

## 3. Corporate executives and managers

As a manager or executive of a multinational company, you are fortunate. Once the decision is made to assign you to work in the United States, your corporation will likely have the money needed to retain an experienced immigration lawyer to prepare and handle all your immigration papers and the necessary procedures. But first, you and your workplace must pass muster.

**Corporations.** A multinational corporation has a distinct meaning according to immigration law. It must be:

- a corporation with different branches located in two countries or more but owned and controlled by the same corporation or individual
- a corporation with a subsidiary or affiliate located in the United States but owned and controlled by the same group of individuals, each owning the same share
- foreign and U.S. corporations under the control of the same person or group, or the same company or group, or
- an internationally recognized accounting firm, organized in the United States and affiliated with a worldwide coordinating organization owned and controlled by the member accounting firms.

The multinational corporation should be doing business in the United States—providing goods or services systematically and continuously, and not merely present as an agent or an office.

The alien must be either an "executive" or "manager" within the corporation—both of which also have specific meanings according to immigration law.

**Executives.** To qualify for immigration purposes as an executive of a multinational corporation, the alien must:

- direct management of the corporation or a major component or function of the firm
- establish the goals and policies of the corporation component or function
- have broad discretion in decision-making regarding day-to-day operations, and
- receive only general supervision or direction from higher level executives, the board of directors or stockholders of the corporation.

**Managers.** To qualify for immigration purposes as a manager of a multinational corporation, the alien must:

- manage the organization or a department, subdivision, function or component of the corporation
- supervise and control the day-to-day work of other supervisory, professional or managerial employees or manage an essential function within the corporation or department or subdivision
- have the authority to hire, fire, promote or recommend such actions for personnel he or she supervises, or
- function at a senior level within the corporation if he or she has no direct supervisory authority.

**Additional requirements.** The executive or manager qualifies as a Priority Worker if he or she:

- has been employed as an executive or manager for at least one of the three years before the petition is filed by a multinational corporation, its affiliate or subsidiary abroad, and
- is planning to continue to work for the same multinational corporation, its affiliate, branch or subsidiary in the United States in the same role.

Also, the United States corporation or affiliate or subsidiary that will employ the executive or manager must have been doing business in the United States for at least a year.

 **JOB OFFER REQUIRED**

You cannot apply in the Priority Worker category as an executive or manager of a multinational corporation without a job offer.

The prospective employer in the United States must submit the job offer in the form of a letter indicating that the alien is to be employed in the United States in a managerial or executive capacity and describing clearly the duties to be performed.

## B. HOW TO FILE

To repeat, if you belong to these preferred groups of Priority Workers, you do not need a Labor Certification before you or your employer files a petition for your immigration to the United States. However, even if you are petitioning for yourself—except for the first group of superstars discussed earlier—you must have a job offer from an employer.

If you are not a multinational executive or manager, finding a job offer may be a challenge. Relatives, friends or employment agencies may be able to help you. This book only informs you of what you do after you have found an employer in the United States.

### 1. Forms required

You or your employer must fill out and file Immigration Form I-140, Immigrant Petition for Alien Worker. (See the sample at the end of this chapter.) The filing fee is $135.

Depending on your status and location, after your immigrant petition has been approved, you and your Immediate Relatives can either adjust your status while staying in the United States (see Chapter 8) or proceed with Consular Processing in the country in which you live. (See Chapter 9.) If you are in the U.S. illegally, however, consult with an attorney before going any further.

### 2. Documentation required

Include all the documentation described in this chapter to prove that you are indeed a superstar in the employment category. Collect those documents, college diplomas, university degrees, publications in international scientific journals, international or national prizes and awards, newspaper and magazine articles and book reviews of scientific or scholarly work to prove your extraordinary ability or your international reputation.

If you are not quite in the superstar league, you might still be able to immigrate to the United States under the Second or Third Preference of employment-based immigration. (See Chapters 16 and 17.)

## C. Spouse and Minor Children

As a Priority Worker, your immigrant visa may be extended to your spouse and unmarried children under 21 years of age—your Immediate Relatives.

## IMMIGRANT PETITION FOR ALIEN WORKER, SAMPLE FORM I-140

| | |
|---|---|
| **U.S. Department of Homeland Security**<br>Bureau of Citizenship and Immigration Services | OMB No. 1615-0015; Exp. 8-31-04<br>**I-140, Immigrant Petition for Alien Worker** |

| **START HERE - Please Type or Print.** | **FOR BCIS USE ONLY** |
|---|---|

**Part 1.    Information about the person or organization filing this petition.**
If an individual is filing, use the top name line. Organizations should use the second line.

| Family Name (Last Name) | Given Name (First Name) | Full Middle Name |
|---|---|---|
| | | |

Company or Organization Name
Duocorp, International

**Address:** (Street Number and Name)                                Suite #
123 Thornfield Road

Attn:
Edward W. Rochester, Esq.

City
Allenstown

State/Province
New Hampshire

Country
USA

Zip/Postal Code
03275

| IRS Tax # | Social Security # (if any) | E-Mail Address (if any) |
|---|---|---|
| 12-345789 | n/a | ewr@duocorp.net |

**FOR BCIS USE ONLY**

| Returned | Receipt |
|---|---|
| Date | |
| Date | |
| Resubmitted | |
| Date | |
| Date | |
| Reloc Sent | |
| Date | |
| Date | |
| Reloc Rec'd | |
| Date | |
| Date | |

**Part 2.    Petition type.**

**This petition is being filed for:** (Check one)

a. ☐ An alien of extraordinary ability.
b. ☒ An outstanding professor or researcher.
c. ☐ A multinational executive or manager.
d. ☐ A member of the professions holding an advanced degree or an alien of exceptional ability (who is **NOT** seeking a National Interest Waiver).
e. ☐ A skilled worker (requiring at least two years of specialized training or experience) or professional.
f. ☐ Item F- no longer available.
g. ☐ Any other worker (requiring less than two years of training or experience).
h. ☐ An alien applying for a National Interest Waiver (who **IS** a member of the professions holding an advanced degree or an alien of exceptional ability).

**Classification:**
☐ 203(b)(1)(A) Alien of Extraordinary
☐ 203(b)(1)(B) Outstanding Professor or Researcher
☐ 203(b)(1)(C) Multi-national executive or manager
☐ 203(b)(2) Member of professions w/adv. degree or exceptional ability
☐ 203(b)(3)(A)(i) Skilled Worker
☐ 203(b)(3)(A)(ii) Professional
☐ 203(b)(3)(A)(iii) Other worker

**Certification:**
☐ National Interest Waiver (NIW)
☐ Schedule A, Group I
☐ Schedule A, Group II

| Priority Date | Consulate |
|---|---|

**Remarks**

**Action Block**

**Part 3.    Information about the person you are filing for.**

| Family Name (Last Name) | Given Name (First Name) | Full Middle Name |
|---|---|---|
| EBERLY | Jane | Ann |

**Address:** (Street Number and Name)                                Apt. #
123 Thornfield Road

C/O: (In Care Of)
Edward R. Rochester, Esq.

City
Allenstown

State/Province
New Hampshire

| Country | Zip/Postal Code | E-Mail Address (if any) |
|---|---|---|
| USA | 03275 | ewr@duocorp.net |

| Daytime Phone # (with area/country code) | Date of Birth (mm/dd/yyyy) |
|---|---|
| 123-555-1212 | 09/07/1975 |

| City/Town/Village of Birth | State/Province of Birth | Country of Birth |
|---|---|---|
| Leeds | | England |

| Country of Nationality/Citizenship | A # (if any) | Social Security # (if any) |
|---|---|---|
| England | none | none |

| **IF IN THE U.S.** | Date of Arrival (mm/dd/yyyy) | I-94 # (Arrival/Departure Document) |
|---|---|---|
| | Current Nonimmigrant Status | Date Status Expires (mm/dd/yyyy) |

**To Be Completed By**
*Attorney or Representative*, if any.
☐ Fill in box if G-28 is attached to represent the applicant.

ATTY State License #

Form I-140 (Rev. 05/120/03)N (Prior versions may be used unitl 09/30/03)

## SAMPLE FORM I-140 (PAGE 2)

### Part 4. Processing Information.

**1.** Please complete the following for the person named in Part 3: *(Check one)*

[X] Alien will apply for a visa abroad at the American Embassy or Consulate at:

City | Foreign Country
--- | ---
London | England

[ ] Alien is in the United States and will apply for adjustment of status to that of lawful permanent resident.
Alien's country of current residence or, if now in the U.S., last permanent residence abroad

**2.** If you provided a U.S. address in Part 3, print the person's foreign address:

Loweed Institute, 1933 Loweed Lane, Yorkshire, England

**3.** If the person's native alphabet is other than Roman letters, write the person's foreign name and address in the native alphabet:

**4.** Are you filing any other petitions or applications with this one?  [X] No  [ ] Yes-attach an explanation

**5.** Is the person you are filing for in removal proceedings?  [X] No  [ ] Yes-attach an explanation

**6.** Has any immigrant visa petition ever been filed by or on behalf of this person?  [X] No  [ ] Yes-attach an explanation

If you answered yes to any of these questions, please provide the case number, office location, date of decision and disposition of the decision on a separate sheet(s) of paper.

### Part 5. Additional information about the petitioner.

**1.** Type of petitioner *(Check one)*.

[X] Employer  [ ] Self  [ ] Other (Explain, e.g., Permanent Resident, U.S. Citzen or any other person filing on behalf of the alien.)

**2.** If a company, give the following:

Type of Business | Date Established *(mm/dd/yyyy)* | Current Number of Employees
--- | --- | ---
Medical Research | 10/13/1985 | 120

Gross Annual Income | Net Annual Income | NAICS Code
--- | --- | ---
$6.2 million | $4 million | 1 2 3 4 5 6

**3.** If an individual, give the following:

Occupation | Annual Income
--- | ---
 | 

### Part 6. Basic information about the proposed employment.

**1.** Job Title

Biochemical Engineer

**2.** SOC Code

1 9 — 1 0 2 1

**3.** Nontechnical Description of Job

Head research in alternate chemicals

**4.** Address where the person will work if different from address in Part 1.

N/A

**5.** Is this a full-time position?

[X] Yes  [ ] No

**6.** If the answer to Number 5 is "No," how many hours per week for the position?

**7.** Is this a permanent position?

[X] Yes  [ ] No

**8.** Is this a new position?

[X] Yes  [ ] No

**9.** Wages per week

$ 2,500

## Sample Form I-140 (page 3)

**Part 7.   Information on spouse and all children of the person for whom you are filing.**

List husband/wife and all children related to the individual for whom the petition is being filed. Provide an attachment of additional family members, if needed.

| Name *(First/Middle/Last)* | Relationship | Date of Birth *(mm/dd/yyyy)* | Country of Birth |
|---|---|---|---|
| Nigel Eberly | husband | 12/04/1970 | England |
| | | | |
| | | | |
| | | | |
| | | | |
| | | | |

**Part 8.   Signature.** *Read the information on penalties in the instructions before completing this section. If someone helped you prepare this petition, he or she must complete Part 9.*

I certify, under penalty of perjury under the laws of the United States of America, that this petition and the evidence submitted with it are all true and correct. I authorize the release of any information from my records that the Bureau of Citizenship Immigration Services needs to determine eligibility for the benefit I am seeking.

**Petitioner's Signature**      **Daytime Phone Number** *(Area/Country Code)*      **E-mail Address**

| *Edward R. Rochester* | 123-555-1212 | ewr@duocorp.net |

**Print Name**                              **Date** *(mm/dd/yyyy)*

| Edward R. Rochester | 08/31/2003 |

**Please Note:** *If you do not completely fill out this form or fail to submit required documents listed in the instructions, you may not be found eligible for the requested benefit and this petition may be denied.*

**Part 9.   Signature of person preparing form, if other than above.**     *(Sign below)*

I declare that I prepared this petition at the request of the above person and it is based on all information of which I have knowledge.

**Attorney or Representative:** In the event of a Request for Evidence (RFE) may the BCIS contact you by Fax or E-mail? ☐ Yes ☐ No

**Signature**                  **Print Name**                  **Date** *(mm/dd/yyyy)*

**Firm Name and Address**

**Daytime Phone Number** *(Area/Country Code)*     **Fax Number** *(Area/Country Code)*     **E-mail Address**

# 16

## PROFESSIONALS AND PEOPLE WITH EXCEPTIONAL ABILITY

### Close to the Top

If you are not a Wernher von Braun, a Gabriel Garcia Marquez, or a Lea Salonga—the sort of person who belongs in the Priority Workers category—can you still obtain a green card by working in the United States?

All hope is not lost. The immigration laws also make special provisions for some talented professionals who have a lot to contribute in the sciences, the arts or in business.

## A. WHO IS QUALIFIED

Immigrants in the Second Preference group are granted 40,000 visas every year on a first-come, first-served basis. But they must first meet some strict requirements to qualify. There are two subcategories in this group:
- professionals with advanced degrees, and
- workers with exceptional ability in the sciences, arts or business.

### LABOR CERTIFICATION IS REQUIRED

If you belong to this group of immigrants, your prospective employer will have to prove to the Department of Labor that there are no Americans or permanent residents in the state in which you will be working who are ready, willing and able to do the work that you are being hired to do at the prevailing wage.

By attaching this requirement, Congress was able to satisfy the labor unions that the immigration gate will still be closed if an American worker is able to meet the job requirements.

Because this process of Labor Certification is quite detailed and complex, it is recommended that you find an immigration lawyer or other immigration professional to help with the process as soon as you have found an employer willing to hire you. (See Chapter 31.)

### 1. Professionals with advanced degrees

You must have not only a baccalaureate (also called Bachelor's, B.A. or B.S.) degree from an accredited college or university but also a graduate level degree, such as a master's or a doctorate degree.

**EXAMPLE:** Social workers, librarians, high school teachers with a master's degree in their fields and scientists with a master's degree or doctorate are among those qualified under this section.

If you have only a baccalaureate degree but you have five years of continuous experience in the specialty, you qualify as having the equivalent of a master's degree.

If you do not have an M.A. or a Ph.D., but your profession requires a four-year course of study before you can get your second diploma, you also qualify.

**EXAMPLE:** Lawyers with a bachelor of law degree are eligible in this category.

If your specialty customarily requires a doctorate degree, then a master's degree is not enough; you must have finished your doctoral studies to qualify.

**Documentation of advanced degree professional.** When you file the petition, you must include documents showing that you:
- have either a United States advanced degree or a foreign equivalent degree, or
- have a United States baccalaureate degree or a foreign equivalent degree plus evidence in the form of letters showing that you have at least five years of progressively responsible experience after graduating.

**Evaluation of your foreign degree.** For the INS to accept a diploma earned in your country, you must send your college and postgraduate transcripts of records—for a fee, ranging from $90 to $170—to an accredited academic evaluator. There are a number of them in the United States, such as:

World Education Services
P. O. Box 745 Old Chelsea Station
New York, NY 10113-0745
212-966-6311
Email: info@wes.org
Website: www.wes.org

Credentials Evaluation Service
International Education Research Foundation
P. O. Box 66940
Los Angeles, CA 90066
310-390-6276
Email: info@ierf.org
Website: www.ierf.org

You can also check the website of the National Association of Credential Evaluation Services, Inc. (NACES) at www.naces.org.

## 2. Those with exceptional ability

There are differences between the Priority Workers of "extraordinary ability" and this group of aliens of "exceptional ability." (See Chapter 15, Section A.) One difference between "extraordinary" and "exceptional" is the alien's reputation: Priority Workers are acclaimed and recognized not only in their own countries but also internationally. Aliens of "exceptional ability" are recognized only in their native lands.

Priority workers of extraordinary ability excel in the sciences, arts, education, business or athletics, while this second group—aliens of exceptional ability—are renowned in the sciences, arts or business; talent in athletics is not included.

Furthermore, aliens of extraordinary ability are generally of a higher caliber: it is said that they are in the top 2% to 5% of their fields. In contrast, a person may qualify under the exceptional ability Second Preference category without this degree of acclaim.

---

### THE BCIS MAY WAIVE LABOR CERTIFICATION

The BCIS may waive the Labor Certification requirement for professionals with advanced degrees and aliens of exceptional ability if it would be in the national interest to do so.

But the interest of the United States is sometimes difficult to define. The law provides that if, owing to their exceptional abilities in the sciences, arts or business, the petitioning immigrants will "substantially benefit the national economic, cultural, or educational interests or welfare of the United States," they can ask the BCIS for a waiver of the requirement of a job offer from an employer before filing a petition. You must submit evidence to support your claim that such exemption would be in the national interest before it will be granted.

It may be difficult to obtain a waiver. The best course of action for this group of prospective immigrants is to find employers willing and able to hire them and to be prepared to show that the national interest will be furthered by their employment. They should be able to show that the job will create jobs or improve working conditions for U.S. workers, will benefit the U.S. economy or culture, or will bring other benefits that are very significant and national in scope.

---

**Documentation of exceptional ability.** The immigrant petition should be accompanied by at least three of the following:

- an official degree, diploma, certificate or similar academic record from a college, university or school relating to the area of exceptional ability
- letters from current or former employers showing that you have at least ten years of full-time experience in the occupation for which you are being sought
- a license or certificate to practice the profession or occupation
- proof of a salary or other remuneration for services which shows exceptional ability
- membership in professional associations, or
- recognition for achievements and significant contributions to the industry or field by peers, governmental entities or professional or business organizations.

If these categories do not apply to your profession, you can try to submit other documentation by explaining that you are of exceptional caliber and by explaining why the evidence listed above does not apply to your particular situation.

Therefore, it is not required simply to have a degree, diploma or certificate from a college or university, or a license to practice a particular profession or occupation, to qualify as an alien of exceptional ability. In fact, holding a college degree may not be necessary at all as long as you have evidence that you have national recognition and acclaim in your field of expertise.

**EXAMPLE:** Performing artists, such as classical guitarists, lead singers in rock groups or popular actors or actresses in the cinema, must present playbills, reviews, magazine articles and awards.

Business executives or presidents of enterprises who do not have high school degrees could present articles by or about them and their success in business, testimonials from members of their peer group, awards as outstanding entrepreneurs or executives or annual reports of their companies.

Art exhibits, reviews of art magazines or favorable criticism in the cultural pages in a newspaper, and awards or prizes won in national competitions, are proof of exceptional ability for painters, sculptors or nationally recognized authors or writers.

Scientists may present magazine and newspaper articles about their research, accolades from scientific journals, books published about them or their study and proof of awards or fellowships that they have earned.

## B. HOW TO FILE

### 1. Labor certification

Your employer must file Form ETA 750 Part A and Part B, Applications for Alien Employment Certification (see the sample at the end of Chapter 18), for the Labor Certification.

Be prepared to wait two or more years until the Department of Labor (DOL) reaches a decision on your application if it is processed under the normal rules. However, the DOL allows expedited processing for cases in which employers can show six months prior recruitment for a position for which there is a shortage of workers, as long as market wage is offered for the position. Under these expedited procedures, processing time takes between three and six months.

Due to its complex bureaucratic requirements, however, it is recommended that you consult an expert on Labor Certification so that it is done right. (See Chapter 31.)

---

**SHORTCUT TO LABOR CERTIFICATION AVAILABLE FOR SOME**

The Department of Labor regularly specifies that certain professions are in short supply in the United States. Professionals are automatically granted Labor Certification if they belong to these occupations, listed in a document called Schedule A. Examples are registered nurses, physical therapists and people with exceptional ability in the arts or sciences.

You must have an employer who is willing to file Form I-140, Immigrant Petition for Alien Worker. If you qualify for Schedule A, your employer must mail to the BCIS Service Center Form ETA-750 in duplicate, together with Form I-140 and the documentation to show that you belong to a Schedule A profession. Be sure that the Job Offer portion of your completed ETA-750 form indicates that the job requires a professional described in Schedule A.

---

## 2. Immigrant petition

Only upon approval by the Department of Labor and after your Form ETA-750 has been marked with the red, white and blue Labor Certification stamp can your employer proceed to file the immigrant petition on your behalf, unless you qualify under the Schedule A or the national interest waiver provision.

Form I-140 is the primary form that must be completed and filed. (See the sample at the end of Chapter 15.) The filing fee is $135.

Attach the documentation required for your particular category as described in this chapter, together with the Department of Labor's certification on Form ETA 750, and mail it to the BCIS Service Center which has jurisdiction over your state. (See the BCIS website at www.bcis.gov for contact details; make sure to get the right P.O. box number.) It will take several months for the BCIS to make a decision. If it requests more information by sending you a Form I-767, then it could be even more time.

After you're approved, you'll have to wait until an immigrant visa becomes available before proceeding with the green card application.

## C. SPOUSE AND MINOR CHILDREN

When an immigrant visa becomes available for you under this category, your spouse and minor children are eligible to apply for an immigrant visa at the same time as you do. These immigrant visas are among the 40,000 given every year worldwide.

## D. THE GREEN CARD APPLICATION

If you are in the United States with an unexpired visa or status when your immigrant visa becomes available, you and your family members can apply for Adjustment of Status in the United States (see Chapter 8) or proceed for Consular Processing in your own country (see Chapter 9).

If you are here illegally, consult with an attorney; applying for Adjustment of Status could result in your deportation, while applying overseas could result in your being barred from returning for three or ten years. If you are currently overseas, your only choice is to apply through a U.S. consulate (see Chapter 9).

---

**CONCURRENT FILING OPTION**

If you're already in the U.S. on a temporary visa, and visas are immediately available in your category, then as of 2002, you have a new procedural choice. Instead of just submitting the Form I-140 petition and waiting for it to be approved before proceeding with your application, you can submit the I-140 petition concurrently with your Adjustment of Status (green card) application. If submitting concurrently, you would send the entire application package to the appropriate BCIS Service Center.

Concurrent filing offers many advantages, including giving you the right to stay in the U.S. while your application is pending (useful if your temporary visa is due to expire soon) and the right to apply for work permits for yourself and your immediate family members.

# 17

# SKILLED AND UNSKILLED WORKERS

## The Butcher, the Baker...

What about the butcher, the baker, the candlestick maker? College graduates with less than five years experience, or people who are not business entrepreneurs or performing artists—the skilled and unskilled workers—are they struck out of the immigration game?

No, they are still in the running.

The Immigration Act of 1990 continued the policy of ensuring the access of skilled and unskilled workers to the workforce in the United States, reclassifying them as Employment Third Preference.

## A. WHO QUALIFIES

Aliens who qualify for this Third Preference category will be allocated 40,000 immigrant visas every year. But first, they must meet some strict requirements. There are three sub-categories to the Third Preference:
- professionals without advanced degrees
- skilled workers, and
- unskilled workers

### 1. Professionals without advanced degrees

Some workers have only a baccalaureate or bachelor's degree from a college or university, but are working in a field that is generally classified as professional.

In simple terms, you belong to the category of professionals without advanced degrees if you:
- have a college degree
- are considered a member of a profession
- have less than five years' work experience, and
- are not acclaimed nationally—much less internationally.

**EXAMPLE:** An architect, accountant, business manager or executive, computer systems analyst, chemist, dietitian, fashion designer, insurance actuary, journalist, medical technologist, airline pilot, pharmacist, scientist, teacher, veterinarian or zoologist would likely be included in this category.

### 2. Skilled workers

If you are working in a specific field that requires special skills and you have had at least two years of training or experience, you may qualify for an immigrant visa as a skilled worker.

Normally, a skilled worker is a person working in industry or business in a position which does not require a college degree, but does require specialized training or experience of at least two years. The job must also be permanent—not seasonal or temporary.

### LABOR CERTIFICATION IS REQUIRED

To qualify as a skilled worker or unskilled worker entitled to immigrate, the Department of Labor requires that there be no American workers available, willing and qualified to do the job for which the alien has applied, for the prevailing wage—as determined by the State Employment Security Agency.

The necessary ingredient is a job offer from an employer in the United States who is not only willing and able to employ the alien applicant, but is also willing to cooperate in the recruitment process paperwork involved for the Labor Certification.

Because the Labor Certification process is quite detailed and complex, it is recommended that you find an immigration lawyer or other immigration expert to help with the process as soon as you have found an employer willing to hire you. (See Chapter 31.) For household workers, a sample Labor Certification procedure is explained in Chapter 18.

NO ONE MAKES STRUDEL LIKE YOU!

**CONSULT AN EXPERT**

The Department of Labor decides how much training or experience is necessary to be classified as a skilled worker—and unless you know from experience how the Department of Labor reaches this decision, you will be making a hit-or-miss attempt to get your Labor Certification. That is why it is better to find a lawyer experienced in Labor Certification to do the paperwork in this vital procedure.

## 3. Unskilled workers

If your present job does not require at least two years of training or experience and is not temporary or seasonal, you belong to the category of unskilled workers. No more than 5,000 visas may be allocated to this category per year, which means the waiting period is usually several years.

The U.S. Department of Labor has established a list of types of work, called Schedule B occupations, which will not be given Labor Certification because it is presumed that there are Americans and permanent residents who are available to take these jobs.

### Schedule B Occupations

Assemblers
Attendants—amusement and recreation service, parking lots and service stations
Bartenders
Bookkeepers
Caretakers
Cashiers
Charworkers and cleaners
Chauffeurs and taxicab drivers
Cleaners in hotels and motels
Clerks—general, grocery store and hotel and motel
Clerk typists
Cooks, short order
Counter and fountain workers
Dining room attendants or waiters
Electric truck operators
Floorworkers
Groundskeepers
Guards
Helpers, any industry
Household domestic service workers or housekeepers—unless they have one year of prior paid experience
Janitors
Keypunch operators
Kitchen workers
Laborers
Loopers and toppers
Material handlers
Nurses' aids and orderlies
Packers, markers and bottlers
Porters
Receptionists
Sailors and deck hands
Sales clerks, general
Sewing machine operators and handstitchers
Stockroom and warehouse workers
Streetcar and bus conductors
Telephone operators
Truck drivers and tractor drivers
Typists (lesser skilled only)
Ushers
Yard workers.

**Exception.** However, with every rule, there is an exception. If, after advertising, posting a notice with the labor union and other recruiting efforts have failed and your employer is truly unable to find an American citizen or permanent resident in your area to take the job, he or she may apply for your Labor Certification even if your job is listed as a Schedule B Occupation. The employer must file for a waiver at the same time.

The horse may talk.

Lightning may strike twice in the same place.

The Department of Labor may approve your employer's request for a waiver of a Schedule B Occupation.

## B. HOW TO FILE

Your employer must complete and file Form I-140, Immigration Petition for Alien Worker (see the sample at the end of Chapter 15) and pay a filing fee of $135 after your Labor Certification has been approved.

The employer will need to attach documents proving that it has made you a job offer, secured a labor certification and can pay you the prevailing wage and that you have the necessary skills or experience.

The petition must be filed with the BCIS Service Center serving your employer's geographic region. The addresses are on the BCIS website (www.bcis.gov). Responses can take several months or even years.

After you're approved, you'll need to wait until an immigrant visa becomes available before proceeding with the green card application (Section D).

## C. SPOUSE AND MINOR CHILDREN

When an immigrant visa is available to you under this Employment Third Preference, your spouse and any unmarried children under 21 years of age are also eligible to receive their immigrant visas at the same time you become eligible. As an immigrating alien, you have the right to have your family accompany you to, or join you in the United States.

## D. THE GREEN CARD APPLICATION

If you, your spouse and your minor children are already in the United States on a legal, unexpired visa or other status, each of you may be able to Adjust your Status in the United States (see Chapter 8) or proceed with Consular Processing in the American Embassy in your country (see Chapter 9). If you are in the United States illegally, consult an experienced immigration attorney before going any further.

If you are currently living overseas, you will get your immigrant visa (leading to a green card) at a U.S. consulate in your country (see Chapter 9).

# 18

## Live-In Domestic Workers

### Help Wanted: A Mary Poppins

I am a single parent with two school-age children. I have found a woman from Barbados who can help me with the children and the housework while I work part-time as a paralegal. How can I help her get a green card?

My father has Alzheimer's disease. My mother is not able to care for him. With our three children still living with us, our apartment is too small to accommodate my parents. A friend has recommended a mature woman from Mexico who has had experience working with the sick. How can I hire her legally?

The good news is, live-in domestic worker is one of the few occupations for which Labor Certification is usually approved by the Department of Labor.

The bad news is, only 5,000 visa numbers are annually allocated for this category of what are called unskilled workers. So it will be a long wait for a green card—even if your application is approved.

Also, if you're not careful, the Labor Certification could be denied on the grounds that the job falls into the "Schedule B" list of occupations for which there are sufficient U.S. workers. To avoid this, the worker must be either:

- coming to provide health or instructional services, or
- already have the equivalent of one year's full-time experience as a household domestic service worker, whether in the United States or elsewhere.

 **THIS IS A TRICKY AREA OF THE LAW— FULL OF NUANCES AND GRAY AREAS.**

If you intend to hire an alien domestic worker, it is best to first consult an experienced immigration lawyer. (See Chapter 31.)

## A. Filing for a Live-In Domestic

As a potential employer, there are three requirements in the Labor Certification process with which you must comply if you hire an alien domestic worker.

## Do You Have a Zoe Baird Problem?

When the newly elected President Bill Clinton sought to appoint an Attorney General, his first choice to fill the post was Zoe Baird—a highly paid corporate lawyer from Connecticut. During Senate confirmation hearings, Baird revealed that she had hired a Peruvian couple as a baby-sitter and driver in blatant violation of the immigration laws. After the public outrage over this revelation, Baird removed herself from the running.

Many people hire alien workers in technical violation of the law.

They pay no state and federal tax or disability.

They ignore the myriad of other tax and employment forms they are required by law to fill out and file.

The whispered question made its way from the Senate confirmation room to talks between neighbors over backyard fences: Do you have a Zoe Baird problem?

Baird's very public admission touched off an unexpected outcry throughout the nation: Crack down on immigration law violations by the rich and privileged—or reform the laws to reflect reality. And, years later, that fury has still not diminished.

### What is legal

You can apply to hire an alien live-in domestic worker if that person:

- now lives outside the United States, or
- has a valid temporary work visa or work authorization card—but keep in mind that the valid work time will also be very limited.

### What is not legal

You cannot get permission to hire an alien live-in domestic worker if that person:

- is currently in the United States and has no legal status or work authorization from the INS, or
- is currently in the United States and has remained here past the time his or her visa has authorized the stay.

## 1. Business need

The first and most important aspect of the application is proving the business necessity for having a live-in helper.

The BCIS is likely to question whether a day worker who will come to your house in the morning and leave in the late afternoon could do the same job as the alien worker you intend to hire as a live-in domestic. That may present you with the feeling of being between the devil and the deep blue sea. If you agree that a day worker can do the job, you should be able to find many Americans or permanent residents ready, willing and able to do the housework, care for the children, shop in the supermarket and have meals ready upon your return from work—and then go back to his or her own home. If that is the case, the Labor Certification for your alien to do day work will probably be denied.

You may insist on having a live-in household worker, but if you have no school-age children, if your office hours are the regular 9-to-5, if neither your work nor your spouse's justifies the need for a domestic helper who lives in the house with you around-the-clock, your Labor Certification for the alien worker will also be denied.

**Proof required.** In simple terms, look at what kind of work you do that requires another person to help. Ask yourself whether you truly require a household worker to live in the house with your family on a 24-hour basis.

If your profession or work—and your spouse's also—requires frequent travel out of town, business-related social engagements, irregular hours in the office, highway, hospital or airport, so that you are away from home in the evening, then your "business" needs a household worker to live with your family to take care of your young children. You must show that no other adult member in the family is able to perform the job of childcare while you and your spouse are not home.

The same principle applies if you have ailing parents who need the care and attention of an adult all the time. You must prove that you cannot provide this care because of the nature of your work so you need the live-in worker—who happens to be an alien in need of a green card—to live with your parents.

## 2. Your ability to pay

The second important thing to consider before filing for Labor Certification is your ability to pay the alien worker a salary that is comparable to similar jobs in your neighborhood and provide him or her with room and board, which are not included in the salary you are paying.

The acceptable rate of pay varies, depending on where you live. Ask the officer in charge of Labor Certification for live-in domestic workers to tell you the prevailing wage per hour and per week plus overtime for domestic workers in your locality.

In other words, you cannot offer $100 per month for the position of a live-in domestic helper because that salary is surely not the prevailing wage for household help in any area in the United States, and no American worker would bother to apply for the job. If that is all you can afford, your application will be returned—your Labor Certification will be denied and your alien worker will not get the green card.

Also, you must state on the application that you are prepared to provide room and board for the live-in domestic. If you live in a studio apartment, with no separate room for your live-in domestic, your application will be denied.

Finally, you must also submit proof that you can afford to pay the wage offered, including:

- copies of annual reports of your business
- federal tax returns
- accredited financial statements
- a statement from the financial officer of your organization establishing your ability to pay the offered wage
- profit/loss statements from the business
- bank account records, and
- personnel records.

If it appears to the INS that the amount you intend to pay the immigrant employee is too large a portion of your income, it may ask you to provide additional evidence of your ability to pay the offered wages.

## 3. No one else available

You must show that you tried to find an American worker or an alien with work authorization to fill the job of a live-in housekeeper and that no one else was available, qualified or willing to work as a live-in domestic.

**First proof.** Before filing the application for Labor Certification, the employer must:

- provide proof that notice has been given to the labor union, or
- if there is no labor union, and at least one other U.S. employee is working at the facility, provide proof that notice of the job has been posted conspicuously.

However, if it is a private household in which there may be only one person employed, and no other U.S. workers are working there, you can simply notify the state Department of Labor—and you will be exempt from the requirement of posting the job.

Therefore, if you already have an American employee working as a launderer, chef or gardener, you must state on your application:

- Notice has been posted in the laundry room, or
- Notice has been posted on the bulletin board, or

• Notice has been posted on the refrigerator door.

By complying with this notice requirement, you will satisfy the Department of Labor and the entire world that you have not denied a willing American worker a job.

Again, in a private house, the likelihood of a complaint from a neighbor regarding your labor standards or hiring practice is unlikely. But such a complaint may be sufficient to delay processing of your application for the Labor Certification of your live-in household worker—or have it denied.

**Second Proof.** After you file the application, the Department of Labor requires you to advertise the job in the local newspaper, and to give the Department's address so that anyone who answers the ad automatically sends his or her resume to the Department. Since few Americans or green cardholders wish to work as live-in domestics, you will probably not get any responses to the ad.

However, if the economy in your city is really bad and jobs are scarce, you must be prepared for the possibility of finding an American or green cardholder willing to do live-in work for your family. If you do not hire any of those who apply, you must give a good reason for rejecting the applications, such as failure to prove that they are qualified and otherwise appropriate to do the job, or that they were not available for the position.

## B. Step One: Getting Labor Certification

When you have found an alien you would like to hire, obtain two copies of Department of Labor Form ETA-750, Application for Alien Employment Certification. It's available in the Appendix or by contacting the Department of Labor. Answer the questions in Parts A and B. (See the sample at the end of this chapter.)

### 1. ETA 750 Part A: Offer of employment

Be sure you fully describe the job to be performed by the houseworker, including the days of work (for example, Monday to Friday, Saturday morning) and the hours of work (44 hours per week—8 a.m. to 8 p.m. with four hours off for lunch and rest on weekdays and 9 a.m. to 1 p.m. on Saturdays).

As for your prospective employee's education, training or experience, six years of education and three months of paid experience as a live-in household worker is the minimum permitted by the Department of Labor. Therefore, if a woman raised ten children of her own, but was never paid as a live-in domestic, she will not qualify.

Question 21 on the form asks you to describe your efforts at recruitment. Acceptable responses are that you have inquired among friends, relatives and employment agencies. (You'll have to do more recruitment later.)

### 2. ETA 750 Part B: Statement of qualifications of alien

The alien's experience must meet or exceed the minimum requirements for your job. Take care to be consistent. The Department of Labor is likely to question your application if you state in Part A that the worker must have an elementary education and in Part B, you state that the alien that you are petitioning for has finished only three years of school.

The most important part of Part B is documenting work experience. Your alien employee must have at least one year of paid experience with another employer. Be sure that your application reflects that.

All the information in the forms should be true and verifiable. Any fraudulent fact or false information written on the form will make both the employer and the alien subject to federal prosecution, and punishable by imprisonment, fine, or both. If the untruthful information is given for the purpose of evading the laws of the Department of Labor and the BCIS, the punishment is up to five years of imprisonment, a fine of up to $10,000, or a combination of both—and removal or deportation for the alien beneficiary.

### 3. Additional documents required

In addition to ETA-750, Parts A and B, two copies of the following documents should be also submitted:

• Documents showing the alien's previous paid experience—statements or letters from past employers giving the period of employment, the hours of work per day, number of days worked per week, detailed statements of duties performed on the job, equipment and appliances used and the salary paid per week or month.

▪ Unless the worker will provide primarily health or instructional services, the total paid experience must be equal to one full year's employment on a full-time basis. For example, if the past employment was on a half-day basis, then two years of experience working half-days would be equal to one year of experience.

▪ The name and address of the employer should be shown in the statement including the signature and the date when the statement was signed. There is no need to go to a notary public or the American consul for finalizing this letter of past experience.

• An employment contract between you and the alien, indicating the basic duties and responsibilities of both the alien and the employer. It must be signed and dated by you and the alien. You must provide your houseworker with a copy of the contract.

• Your statement on the business necessity of having a live-in domestic worker. Also include documents that back up your statement, such as a doctor's letter, records showing your frequent travel and evidence of the high cost of alternatives to live-in help.

- A statement specifying the household living arrangements referred to in Form ETA 750 Part A, Item 20. For example, give details on where in your house the live-in worker will sleep and how private the space will be.

---

### HURRY UP AND WAIT

Getting Labor Certification requires patience. The entire process may take two years or more to complete.

And after that, completing the procedures required for a green card may require a wait of as many as ten more years, since only 5,000 are granted in this category each year. If you're looking for childcare, your children could be in college by the time this process is completed.

---

## C. STEP TWO: ADVERTISING THE JOB

After your application is accepted, the Department of Labor will send you specific instructions about advertising the job.

### 1. Specifics of the ad

You must prepare a draft of your ad and submit it to the Department of Labor's Advertising Specialist or Case Manager as directed. The Help Wanted ad should show the address of the state employment agency and the job order number instead of your own telephone number, because the state agency will monitor the response to your ad and forward you the applications it receives.

You must also run an ad for three consecutive days in a daily newspaper, or for three consecutive weeks if it appears in a weekly paper. You must submit the entire newspaper page to the Department of Labor each time your ad appeared, unless you are specifically told that only one proof is required.

### 2. Interviewing applicants

The state employment agency will forward to you all resumes received in response to the Help Wanted ad you have placed. You may also receive responses from the ads you placed, and must carefully keep track of these as well.

You must have a solid, job-related reason for rejecting any applicants—not simply that you did not like the way they look or talk or dress. But if an applicant does not meet the

qualifications listed in the ad, lacks verifiable, stable work experience or has a history of mental illness or shows evidence of having an alcohol or drug problem, you are justified in not hiring that person for the job as a live-in domestic.

Make notes while you interview each of the applicants sent to you by the agency so that you can write a detailed statement about why you did not hire those who applied for the position.

## D. GETTING LABOR CERTIFICATION

If you have been thorough in collecting and presenting all of the documentation discussed here, your chances of getting Labor Certification are good.

### 1. Grounds for approving your application

Your application will be approved if the Department of Labor is satisfied that:

- you are offering the prevailing wage for the position of a live-in domestic worker
- your business and family responsibilities make it necessary for you to have a live-in domestic worker
- your efforts to locate a U.S. citizen or alien who already has a green card were not successful, and
- you complied with all other required procedures.

If you are asked to explain or change your application, do it promptly. Call the person who has signed the request letter you receive from the Department of Labor if you have any questions or problems. Never assume. Never presume. Follow the suggestions or instructions given to you by the Department of Labor and the BCIS. In this way, you will eventually reach your goal: getting approval of your application for Labor Certification.

## 2. Documents you will receive

If the Department of Labor approves your application, you will receive the following documents in the mail:

- a cover letter called "Final Determination" (Form 7145B) which is the Labor Certification
- one copy of the original application (Form ETA 750 Parts A and B) with the Department of Labor stamp of approval in the lower section of the first page, and
- one copy of all the documents including the contract of employment that you have submitted with the application. This explains why you have to submit two original applications for alien employment certification and two original copies of all documents attached.

If the Department of Labor does not approve your application, it will send you a letter titled Notice of Findings. You will then have the chance to provide more evidence or to explain your answers. If you do not respond, your application will be denied.

## E. Filing the Petition With the BCIS

The next step in the immigration process for many aliens who have an approved Labor Certification is for you, the employer, to prepare and file the following documents after the Labor Certification is granted:

- Petition for Alien Worker (Form I-140) (see the sample at the end of Chapter 15)
- Application for Alien Employment Certification (Form ETA-750 Parts A and B), which contains the Department of Labor's stamp of approval on the lower part of the front page
- certificate of employment from a previous employer—a copy of the letter you submitted earlier to the Department of Labor
- proof of your ability to pay the wages for the live-in domestic—your income tax, profit/loss statement or bank accounts for the year when you initially submitted the application to the Department of Labor, and
- a filing fee of $135 in the form of a certified check or money order, made payable to the BCIS.

Send the entire package by certified mail, with return receipt requested, to the nearest regional office of the BCIS. (See the BCIS website at www.bcis.gov for contact details.)

After the petition is approved, the worker will need to wait until his or her Priority Date becomes current and an immigrant visa becomes available. This can mean a long wait—in the past it's typically been as many as ten years. Having this petition on file does not give the worker any right to live in the United States while waiting for the next step.

After the Priority Date becomes current, you may have a problem if the worker has been living in the United States. If by some lucky chance the worker is still in valid visa status, or falls into certain exceptional categories, he or she can proceed to Adjustment of Status in the United States (see Chapter 8) and get a green card without hassle. However, the chances of the worker having a valid visa for all this time and qualifying for Adjustment of Status are slim. That means the worker's only choice may be to leave the country and do Consular Processing (see Chapter 9). However, if the worker has already lived in the United States illegally for six months or more, he or she will be barred from returning for three or ten years.

The easiest situation is where the worker has been living overseas during the wait. In that case, the next step is simply to go through Consular Processing in order to obtain the immigrant visa (see Chapter 9).

## F. Spouse and Minor Children

The spouse of a live-in domestic worker is given the same right to a green card as the domestic worker. The unmarried children under 21 years of age are also entitled to apply for an immigrant visa at the same time. As family members, they are entitled to accompany the immigrant to, or to join him or her in, the United States.

### Sample Letter From Previous Employer

August 30, 2003

To the Future Employer of Jane Eyre:

This is to certify that Jane Eyre has been employed as a household worker at the Lowood Institute located at Liverpool from July 1991 to June 2001.

She was educated at the Lowood Institute from the first grade until she graduated from High School. She began her employment while in her senior year.

Her responsibilities included cleaning the dormitory of the students, doing the laundry for the dining room, helping in the kitchen and looking after the younger student-boarders during recreation. She worked from 8:00 a.m. to 6:00 p.m., Monday to Friday and earned £250 per month.

She is intelligent, diligent and did her duties responsibly. I highly recommend her as a live-in housekeeper for your household.

Sincerely yours,

*John Reed*

John Reed
Headmaster
Lowood Institute

## APPLICATION FOR ALIEN EMPLOYMENT CERTIFICATION, SAMPLE FORM ETA 750, PART A

OMB Approval No. 44-R1301

U.S. DEPARTMENT OF LABOR
Employment and Training Administration

APPLICATION
FOR
ALIEN EMPLOYMENT CERTIFICATION

**IMPORTANT: READ CAREFULLY BEFORE COMPLETING THIS FORM**
*PRINT legibly in ink or use a typewriter. If you need more space to answer questions on this form, use a separate sheet. Identify each answer with the number of the corresponding question. SIGN AND DATE each sheet in original signature.*

*To knowingly furnish any false information in the preparation of this form and any supplement thereto or to aid, abet, or counsel another to do so is a felony punishable by $10,000 fine or 5 years in the penitentiary, or both (18 U.S.C. 1001).*

### PART A. OFFER OF EMPLOYMENT

1. Name of Alien *(Family name in capital letters, First, Middle, Maiden)*

SEPULCHRE, Bibiana Rafaela

2. Present Address of Alien *(Number, Street, City and Town, State, ZIP Code or Province, Country)*

1692 Newsome, San Francisco, CA 94102

3. Type of Visa *(If in U.S.)*

B2

The following information is submitted as evidence of an offer of employment.

4. Name of Employer *(Full name of organization)*

Raymond Bakker

5. Telephone *(Area Code and Number)*

415-261-7510

6. Address *(Number, Street, City or Town, County, State, ZIP Code)*

2100 Pacific View, San Francisco, CA 94115

7. Address Where Alien Will Work *(if different from item 6)*

same as above

| 8. Nature of Employer's Business Activity | 9. Name of Job Title | 10. Total Hours Per Week | | 11. Work Schedule *(Hourly)* | 12. Rate of Pay | |
|---|---|---|---|---|---|---|
| | | a. Basic | b. Overtime | | a. Basic | b. Overtime |
| Household | live-in housekeeper | 44 | N/A | 8:00 a.m. 8:00 p.m. | $ 260 per week | $6 if needed per hour |

13. Describe Fully the Job to be Performed *(Duties)*

General housekeeping, laundry, shopping, preparing meals and setting tables, washing dishes and caring for 6-year-old daughter of employer, supervising her personal needs and chaperoning trips to and from school and leisure outings.

14. State in detail the MINIMUM education, training, and experience for a worker to perform satisfactorily the job duties described in Item 13 above.

15. Other Special Requirements

not applicable

| EDU-CATION *(Enter number of years)* | Grade School | High School | College | College Degree Required *(specify)* |
|---|---|---|---|---|
| | 6 | 4 | | Major Field of Study |

| TRAIN-ING | No. Yrs. | No. Mos. | Type of Training |
|---|---|---|---|
| | | 3 | |

| EXPERI-ENCE | Job Offered | | Related Occupation | | Related Occupation *(specify)* |
|---|---|---|---|---|---|
| | Number | | | | |
| | Yrs. | Mos. | Yrs. | Mos. | |
| | | 3 | | | |

16. Occupational Title of Person Who Will Be Alien's Immediate Supervisor ► head of household

17. Number of Employees Alien will Supervise ► 0

◄ ENDORSEMENTS *(Make no entry in section - for government use only)*

| Date Forms Received | |
|---|---|
| L.O. | S.O. |
| R.O. | N.O. |
| Ind. Code | Occ. Code |
| Occ. Title | |

*Replaces MA 7-50A, B and C (Apr. 1970 edition) which is obsolete.*

ETA 750 (Oct. 1979)

## SAMPLE FORM ETA 750, PART A (PAGE 2)

| 18. COMPLETE ITEMS ONLY IF JOB IS TEMPORARY | | 19. IF JOB IS UNIONIZED   *(Complete)* | |
|---|---|---|---|
| a. No. of Open-ings To Be Filled By Aliens Under Job Offer | b. Exact Dates You Expect To Employ Alien | a. Number of Local | b. Name of Local |
| | From            To | | |
| | | | c. City and State |

### 20. STATEMENT FOR LIVE-AT-WORK JOB OFFERS    *(Complete for Private Household Job ONLY)*

| a. Description of Residence | | b. No. Persons Residing at Place of Employment | | | c. Will free board and private room not shared with any-one be provided?     *("X" one)* |
|---|---|---|---|---|---|
| *("X" one)* | Number of Rooms | Adults | Children | Ages | |
| ☑ House | | | BOYS | | ☑ YES   ☐ NO |
| ☐ Apartment | 24 | 1 | GIRLS     1 | 6 | |

**21. DESCRIBE EFFORTS TO RECRUIT U.S. WORKERS AND THE RESULTS.**  *(Specify Sources of Recruitment by Name)*

posted notice at supermarket and placed ads in local newspaper

**22.** Applications require various types of documentation. Please read PART II of the instructions to assure that appropriate supporting documentation is included with your application.

### 23. EMPLOYER CERTIFICATIONS

*By virtue of my signature below, I HEREBY CERTIFY the following conditions of employment.*

a. I have enough funds available to pay the wage or salary offered the alien.

b. The wage offered equals or exceeds the prevailing wage and I guarantee that, if a labor certification is granted, the wage paid to the alien when the alien begins work will equal or exceed the prevailing wage which is applicable at the time the alien begins work.

c. The wage offered is not based on commissions, bonuses, or other incentives, unless I guarantee a wage paid on a weekly, bi-weekly or monthly basis.

d. I will be able to place the alien on the payroll on or before the date of the alien's proposed entrance into the United States.

e. The job opportunity does not involve unlawful discrimination by race, creed, color, national origin, age, sex, religion, handicap, or citizenship.

f. The job opportunity is not:

(1) Vacant because the former occupant is on strike or is being locked out in the course of a labor dispute involving a work stoppage.

(2) At issue in a labor dispute involving a work stoppage.

g. The job opportunity's terms, conditions and occupational environment are not contrary to Federal, State or local law.

h. The job opportunity has been and is clearly open to any qualified U.S. worker.

### 24. DECLARATIONS

DECLARATION OF EMPLOYER ➤    Pursuant to 28 U.S.C. 1746, I declare under penalty of perjury the foregoing is true and correct.

| SIGNATURE | DATE |
|---|---|
| *Raymond Bakker, III* | Sept. 21, 2003 |

| NAME  *(Type or Print)* | TITLE |
|---|---|
| Raymond Bakker, III | Head of Household |

AUTHORIZATION OF AGENT OF EMPLOYER ➤    I HEREBY DESIGNATE the agent below to represent me for the purposes of labor certification and I TAKE FULL RESPONSIBILITY for accuracy of any representations made by my agent.

| SIGNATURE OF EMPLOYER | DATE |
|---|---|
| | |

| NAME OF AGENT  *(Type or Print)* | ADDRESS OF AGENT  *(Number, Street, City, State, ZIP Code)* |
|---|---|
| | |

## STATEMENT OF QUALIFICATIONS OF ALIEN, SAMPLE FORM ETA 750, PART B (PAGE 3)

| PART B. STATEMENT OF QUALIFICATIONS OF ALIEN |
|---|

**FOR ADVICE CONCERNING REQUIREMENTS FOR ALIEN EMPLOYMENT CERTIFICATION:** If alien is in the U.S., contact nearest office of Immigration and Naturalization Service. If alien is outside U.S., contact nearest U.S. Consulate.

**IMPORTANT: READ ATTACHED INSTRUCTIONS BEFORE COMPLETING THIS FORM.**

Print legibly in ink or use a typewriter. If you need more space to fully answer any questions on this form, use a separate sheet. Identify each answer with the number of the corresponding question. Sign and date each sheet.

| 1. Name of Alien (Family name in capital letters) | First name | Middle name | Maiden name |
|---|---|---|---|
| SEPULCHRE | Bibiana | Rafaela | |

| 2. Present Address (No., Street, City or Town, State or Province and ZIP Code | Country | 3. Type of Visa (If in U.S.) |
|---|---|---|
| 1692 Newsome    San Francisco    CA | USA | B2 |

| 4. Alien's Birthdate (Month, Day, Year) | 5. Birthplace (City or Town, State or Province) | Country | 6. Present Nationality or Citizenship (Country) |
|---|---|---|---|
| Sept. 7, 1980 | Bauko | Philippines | Filipino |

7. Address in United States Where Alien Will Reside

2100 Pacific View    San Francisco    CA    94115

| 8. Name and Address of Prospective Employer if Alien has Job offer in U.S. | 9. Occupation in which Alien is Seeking Work |
|---|---|
| same as above | Live-in housekeeper |

10. "X" the appropriate box below and furnish the information required for the box marked

| | | City in Foreign Country | Foreign Country |
|---|---|---|---|
| a. ☒ | Alien will apply for a visa abroad at the American Consulate in ——▶ | Manila | Philippines |
| b. ☐ | Alien is in the United States and will apply for adjustment of status to that of a lawful permanent resident in the office of the Immigration and Naturalization Service at ——▶ | City | State |

| 11. Names and Addresses of Schools, Colleges and Universities Attended (Include trade or vocational training facilities) | Field of Study | FROM Month Year | TO Month Year | Degrees or Certificates Received |
|---|---|---|---|---|
| Goran Institute | elementary | Sept. 1986 | June 1999 | high school |
| | high school | | | diploma |
| | | | | |
| | | | | |
| | | | | |

### SPECIAL QUALIFICATIONS AND SKILLS

12. Additional Qualifications and Skills Alien Possesses and Proficiency in the use of Tools, Machines or Equipment Which Would Help Establish if Alien Meets Requirements for Occupation in Item 9.

Knows how to use modern appliances, including washing machine, dryer, vacuum cleaner, rug shampoo machine, iron, clothes steamer

13. List Licenses (Professional, journeyman, etc.)

Not applicable

14. List Documents Attached Which are Submitted as Evidence that Alien Possesses the Education, Training, Experience, and Abilities Represented

Letter from principal, Goran Institute

| Endorsements | DATE REC. DOL |
|---|---|
| | O.T. & C. |
| (Make no entry in this section — FOR Government Agency USE ONLY) | |

*(Items continued on next page)*

## SAMPLE FORM ETA 750, PART B (PAGE 4)

15. WORK EXPERIENCE. *List all jobs held during past three (3) years. Also, list any other jobs related to the occupation for which the alien is seeking certification as indicated in item 9.*

a. NAME AND ADDRESS OF EMPLOYER

Goran Institute, 1750 Padadac, Baguio City, Philippines

| NAME OF JOB | DATE STARTED Month | Year | DATE LEFT Month | Year | KIND OF BUSINESS |
|---|---|---|---|---|---|
| Household helper | July | 1998 | June | 2001 | Boarding school |

DESCRIBE IN DETAILS THE DUTIES PERFORMED, INCLUDING THE USE OF TOOLS, MACHINES, OR EQUIPMENT | NO. OF HOURS PER WEEK

b. NAME AND ADDRESS OF EMPLOYER

| NAME OF JOB | DATE STARTED Month | Year | DATE LEFT Month | Year | KIND OF BUSINESS |
|---|---|---|---|---|---|
| | | | | | |

DESCRIBE IN DETAIL THE DUTIES PERFORMED, INCLUDING THE USE OF TOOLS, MACHINES, OR EQUIPMENT | NO. OF HOURS PER WEEK

c. NAME AND ADDRESS OF EMPLOYER

| NAME OF JOB | DATE STARTED Month | Year | DATE LEFT Month | Year | KIND OF BUSINESS |
|---|---|---|---|---|---|
| | | | | | |

DESCRIBE IN DETAIL THE DUTIES PERFORMED, INCLUDING THE USE OF TOOLS, MACHINES, OR EQUIPMENT | NO. OF HOURS PER WEEK

### 16. DECLARATIONS

DECLARATION OF ALIEN ► ►    *Pursuant to 28 U.S.C. 1746, I declare under penalty of perjury the foregoing is true and correct.*

| SIGNATURE OF ALIEN | DATE |
|---|---|
| *Bibiana Rafaela Sepulchre* | Sept. 23, 2003 |

AUTHORIZATION OF AGENT OF ALIEN ► ►    *I hereby designate the agent below to represent me for the purposes of labor certification and I take full responsibility for accuracy of any representations made by my agent.*

| SIGNATURE OF ALIEN | DATE |
|---|---|
| | |

| NAME OF AGENT *(Type or print)* | ADDRESS OF AGENT *(No., Street, City, State, ZIP Code)* |
|---|---|
| | |

# 19

# SPECIAL IMMIGRANTS AND RELIGIOUS WORKERS

## Practices to Follow Before You Preach

I am a catechist, working full-time for our parochial school in Calcutta, India, since last year. During my visit in New York I met the parish priest of Guardian Angel Church, who told me that the school needs a teacher of religion for the elementary grades. Can I get a green card even if I am not a nun?

I have worked as a receptionist for the Agudath Synagogue in Israel for the past ten years. The Reformed Judaism Synagogue in Miami, Florida, is willing to employ me in the same capacity. Can it sponsor my application for an immigrant visa?

The Immigration Act of 1990 has allocated 10,000 visas yearly for so-called Special Immigrants. These Special Immigrants, the Fourth Preference of the employment-based group, do not need to go through the extra hoop of securing a Labor Certification (discussed in Chapter 18).

## A. Who Qualifies As a Special Immigrant

Special Immigrants include the following groups:
- sons or daughters of employees of international organizations who have lived in the United States for seven years—and have been physically present for half of those seven years—between the ages of five and 21 years of age and who apply for immigrant visas before their 25th birthdays
- surviving spouses of deceased individuals, if the deceased was employed by an international organization for at least 15 years, who have lived in the U.S. for seven years—if the surviving spouse has been physically present for half of those seven years before applying. The surviving spouse must also apply for an immigrant visa within six months of the death of the deceased employee.
- retired employees of international organizations who worked for such organizations for at least 15 years, who have lived in the U.S. for at least seven years—and have been physically present for half of those seven years—before applying. They must apply for these immigrant visas within six months of retirement.
- foreign medical graduates with H or J visas, who were licensed to practice medicine in any U.S. state on January 9, 1978, and have been continuously present in the United States since January 10, 1978
- alien employees who have worked for the U.S. government overseas for at least 15 years whose immigration has been approved by the Secretary of State due to exceptional circumstances, as recommended by the principal officer of the Foreign Service
- alien employees or former employees of the Panama Canal Company or Canal Zone Government before June 16, 1978, and
- religious workers.

This chapter will focus on the religious worker category.

## B. Special Rules for Religious Workers

Religious workers are the largest group of Special Immigrants—allocated half of the immigrant visas available. This quota also includes visas allocated to the workers' spouses and minor children.

Again, while religious workers do not need Labor Certification, they must have a job offer in the United States.

### 1. Those who qualify as religious workers

To qualify as a religious worker, you must meet the requirements described below.
- You must be a member or a minister of:
  ■ a religious denomination, that is a group with a recognized creed, a form of worship, a code of doctrine

and discipline and established places of worship and congregation

- a bona fide group (must have some form of ecclesiastical government, assets and methods of operation, religious services and ceremonies) in the United States, and
- that has nonprofit standing in the United States, which means it must be incorporated and have tax-exempt status under U.S. laws (§501(c)(3)), or if it is not required by the IRS to apply for tax-exempt status, it must be eligible as a nonprofit organization by the IRS.

    An interdenominational religious organization, also tax-exempt by the IRS, such as the Billy Graham Evangelical Association, could be considered a religious denomination.

- You must have been paid to engage in a full time religious vocation or professional work—requiring at least a college degree or its equivalent—in the religious organization continually for at least two years before applying for an immigrant visa.
- You must have been offered a position by the U.S. religious affiliate to work in "a religious vocation, profession or occupation" in the United States—either the traditional religious functions of minister, priest, brother, nun and monk, or to perform the religious work done by liturgical workers, religious instructors, counselors, cantors and catechists, workers in religious hospitals or religious healthcare facilities, missionaries, religious translators or broadcasters.

## 2. Those who do not qualify as religious workers

You are not considered eligible if you are a worker who is:

- employed with a religious denomination in a clerical, janitorial, mechanical, nonprofessional capacity—that is, as a receptionist, secretary, janitor, chauffeur, carpenter, electrician, gardener or fundraiser of a religious organization
- employed for less than two years with the religious denomination immediately preceding the application; this provision is designed to eliminate those who might take advantage of this immigration category by joining and working for a short time
- employed with a religious denomination which has no affiliate in the United States, or which affiliate has no tax-exempt status and is not incorporated in the United States, or
- a volunteer.

## C. APPLICATION DEADLINE

If you are a non-minister religious worker (see Section B1, above), you or your employer must apply for a green card no later than September 30, 2004. For example, ministers, priests and rabbis remain eligible to obtain a green card under the Employment Fourth Preference after that date. Your spouse and your minor children are also eligible to immigrate at the same time as you.

## D. HOW TO FILE

Form I-360, Petition for Amerasians, Widows or Special Immigrants (see sample at the end of Chapter 13) must be filed either by the religious worker or the sponsoring religious organization. Although the worker may file the petition personally, the BCIS gives more weight to forms filed by the sponsoring organization.

The following documentation is also required:

- a letter from the authorized official of the religious organization in the United States that the person will perform services of a religious or professional nature, including terms of payment or other remuneration, clearly stating that the worker will not be solely dependent on supplemental employment or solicited funds for support
- proof that the religious organization or any affiliate in the United States that will employ the alien is a bona fide nonprofit religious organization, and is exempt from taxation by the U.S. Internal Revenue Service, or such proof as is required by the IRS to show nonprofit eligibility
- a letter from the authorized official of the religious organization in the foreign country stating the person's membership and explaining in detail the alien's religious work and employment within the organization during the past two years
    - for a minister (including Buddhist monks, commissioned officers of the Salvation Army, ordained deacons), attach the certificate of ordination or authorization to conduct religious worship as a member of the clergy
    - for a religious professional, include the baccalaureate degree (U.S. or foreign) required for entry into the religious profession, and
    - for a nun, monk, religious brother or a person called to religious life, proof that he or she is qualified in the religious vocation or occupation.

The filing fee is $130, in check or money order made payable to the BCIS.

Your employer will need to send this petition to the BCIS service center for the geographic region where you'll be working.

After your petition is approved, you can move forward with your application for a green card. If you're already in the United States legally, you can proceed to file your Adjustment of Status application (Chapter 8). If you're living overseas, you'll apply for your immigrant visa through Consular Processing (Chapter 9).

If, however, you're in the United States illegally, you should consult with an immigration attorney before going any further. Unless you fall into one of the exceptional categories described in Chapter 8, you are probably not eligible to adjust status in the United States. However, if you've already spent more than six months in the United States unlawfully, leaving the country for consular processing could result in a bar to your reentry to the United States of three or ten years.

## E. NONIMMIGRANT VISAS FOR RELIGIOUS WORKERS

Religious workers not only are eligible for an immigrant visa, but also for a nonimmigrant visa (R Visa, Form I-129) that allows them to work in the United States temporarily. The law also allows for their spouses and children to enter with them. The requirements for them are the same as for the immigrant visa of religious workers discussed earlier in this chapter.

The first difference between the immigrant and nonimmigrant visas is that the status of religious workers as nonimmigrants in the United States is valid for only five years. After five years, the alien religious workers, catechists, cantors or deacons have to go back to their home countries, unless they are eligible to change to another nonimmigrant status or apply for a green card.

The second difference is that the Special Immigrant category for religious workers requires two years of continuous work experience before the petition can be filed, while the nonimmigrant R visa requires only two years' membership in the particular religious order or denomination which has a counterpart religious nonprofit organization in the United States.

The third difference is that there is no quota on the number of nonimmigrant visas granted to religious workers, as long as those who apply have met the requirements. Every religious denomination in the United States that needs religious workers can sponsor individuals as nonimmigrants without regard to quotas.

The most important factor common to both the immigrant and nonimmigrant visa for religious workers is the religious vocation they have or the religious occupation or profession that they would perform in the United States with its affiliate religious denomination. ∎

# 20

# ENTREPRENEUR IMMIGRANTS

## Rich Man: Yes; Poor Man: No

A knock on the door—and you receive the most astounding news of your life. You are the sole heir to the fortune of your uncle who had gone to Argentina and made millions! You are suddenly a multimillionaire.

If you have always wanted to live in the United States, you can now get a green card based on your net worth.

The Immigration Act of 1990 added a new category of immigrants: the millionaire entrepreneur, the Fifth Preference category in employment-based immigration.

There are 10,000 immigrant visas allocated each year to millionaire entrepreneurs, including their spouses and minor children, as long as they plan to invest a significant amount of money in a business that creates jobs in the locality. This provision of the Immigration Act of 1990 reflects the intention of the U.S. Congress to create employment for American workers. It offers the carrot—a green card—to the millionaire alien who will engage in a commercial enterprise that will give jobs to American workers. Thus, the Bureau of Citizenship and Immigration Services (BCIS) calls this group of immigrants "employment creation aliens."

## A. WHERE TO INVEST

The alien millionaire can invest in any place in the United States. Out of the 10,000 immigrant visas allocated every year, however, 3,000 will be set aside for alien entrepreneurs who invest in "a targeted employment area" which can be either:

- a city or town of less than 20,000 inhabitants
- outside the boundaries of a city or town of more than 20,000 inhabitants, or
- any place that has high unemployment (150% of the national average).

---

 **CONSULT AN EXPERT**

This chapter explains the basic procedures for immigrating as an entrepreneur. But the process has many potential complications and getting your application approved may depend on a number of specific variables.

If you think you qualify as an immigrant under this category, it is best to get the advice of an experienced immigration lawyer who has prepared this particular type of case. (See Chapter 31.)

---

## B. HOW MANY EMPLOYEES TO HIRE

Aside from their spouses and children, the alien entrepreneurs must hire at least ten additional U. S. citizens or aliens with green cards or who have employment authorization.

The employees must each work at least 35 hours a week. Of course, if the business needs more workers, it follows that the alien entrepreneur could employ as many as he or she needs. But the minimum number of employees hired should be not less than ten American workers—excluding the spouse, sons and daughters of nonimmigrant aliens and excluding independent contractors.

## C. AMOUNT AND TYPE OF INVESTMENT

The investment must involve a business, such as a manufacturing plant or a service-oriented corporation, which requires the entrepreneur's participation or management skills to provide jobs to the community.

The general rule about the amount of money that the alien millionaire must invest is one million dollars. The investment or capital can take the form of cash alone, cash plus bank mortgage or a personal loan. The investment or capital can also include equipment, inventory or other tangible property.

---

### MILLIONAIRE ALIENS ENCOURAGED BY PILOT PROGRAM

In 1992, the U.S. Congress approved a Pilot Immigration Investor Visa Program to "promote economic growth, increase export sales, improve productivity, create jobs and increase capital investment."

The government had received only a few hundred petitions from alien entrepreneurs. So Congress set up this pilot program to allow 3,000 applicants to make investments that include jobs created indirectly through exports, or jobs from contracts or subcontracts with U.S. companies, in satisfaction of the ten-worker requirement.

The regulations controlling this pilot program require that the applicant also show that the qualifying investment is within one of the participating regional centers approved by the BCIS. To qualify as a regional center, the entity must establish that it will promote economic growth and that it focuses on a particular geographic region of the United States. See 8 C.F.R. §204.

---

## 1.  Restrictions on investments

The alien entrepreneur cannot buy an apartment worth $1 million, which produces income solely in rents, and then request an immigrant visa as an investor. For one thing, you do not need ten employees to run this operation. In short, there is no immigration break involved with real estate for speculation or personal residence.

But you could buy a building worth several hundred thousand dollars that requires several hundred thousand dollars more to be renovated. You could spend a million dollars to hire engineers, architects and construction workers to finish the project, which you then rent out or sell as cooperatives or condominium units.

You cannot buy stocks and bonds worth a million dollars and call yourself an alien entrepreneur when all you do is trade your own investments. Again, you do not need ten employees to run this sort of business.

But you can buy a brokerage firm that has at least ten American workers with a million or more dollars as a down payment.

## 2.  Exceptions to the $1 million rule

There are, however, exceptions to the rule requiring a $1 million investment.

- If the city or town chosen by the entrepreneur is one of those "targeted employment areas" designated by the Attorney General, the amount to be invested may be as low as $500,000.
- If the metropolitan area chosen by the entrepreneur has an unemployment rate significantly lower than the national average, the Attorney General may require that the investment be more than $1 million, though not in excess of $3 million.

## D.  SOURCE OF THE INVESTMENT MONEY

The source of the investment capital must be lawful. This requirement was added to prevent the Michael Corleones, the Scarfaces of the underworld—drug cartel kingpins, yakusas, La Cosa Nostra—from obtaining a green card through this category.

The investment dollars could be from savings, from selling stocks or real property in the foreign country, borrowed from banks with real property or stocks and bonds in the foreign country as collateral, borrowed from investors such as friends or relatives who believe in your business acumen, or an inheritance from your rich but childless uncle. In other words, the million dollars should come from legitimate sources of wealth.

---

### WHO IS AN INDEPENDENT CONTRACTOR?

Whether a worker is legally an independent contractor is determined primarily by who controls the work. To be considered an independent contractor, only the work product should be controlled by the company or person paying for the work. How, where and when that work is done—and whether anyone else is hired to do it—is up to the independent contractor.

The second major factor in being designated an independent contractor is that the worker must offer services to the entire public, not just to one company.

The Internal Revenue Service (IRS) is the federal government agency that sets the rules determining who is classified as an independent contractor and who is a regular employee. If you have questions, contact the IRS for its free booklet explaining the categories. Call 800-829-3676 or see www.irs.gov to obtain IRS Publication 937, "Employment Taxes and Information Returns."

---

### BANK LOANS PROBABLY WON'T DO IT

Realistically speaking, unless you buy the bank itself, no right-thinking banking institution will lend an alien entrepreneur several thousands of dollars without asking for collateral such as real estate, jewelry, major works of art, stocks or bonds or other forms of security. The projected assets of the new commercial enterprise are not acceptable as collateral, as far as the immigration rules are concerned.

Banks never seem to lend you the capital to start a business when you need it most. When you do not need it because you already have made your fortune and are financially successful, the banks can hardly wait to lend you the money.

### MAKING IT HAPPEN

While she was governor of Texas, Ann Richards delegated to the mayors of her state the power to certify that their cities or towns were areas of high unemployment for purposes of "employment creation" immigration. By doing this, she intended to attract investments from the millionaires of the world—especially Hong Kong, Taiwan, Singapore and South America.

## E. WHEN THE INVESTMENT MUST BE MADE

To qualify under this provision, alien entrepreneurs should have invested in a "new" business enterprise—that is, one created after November 29, 1990, which is the date the immigration bill was signed into law. (Formerly, the immigrant had to have been the one to establish the business enterprise, but that requirement was dropped in 2002.)

If you have an existing business, or if you began your investment in the United States before November 29, 1990, you cannot claim your ongoing enterprise as your million-dollar investment for immigration purposes, unless you refinance your old company or reorganize it so that you increase its net worth, or the number of employees, or both, by at least 40%.

## F. HOW TO FILE

The initial form required for investors to obtain immigrant visas as millionaire aliens is Form I-526, Immigrant Petition by Alien Entrepreneur. (See the sample at the end of this chapter.) The filing fee is $400, payable by a money order or a certified check. File the application at an BCIS Service Center. (See Appendix 1 for contact details and the BCIS website at www.bcis.gov for the correct P.O. box.)

## G. ADDITIONAL DOCUMENTATION REQUIRED

The law is quite clear concerning the amount of money required for investment, the legality of the source of the money and the number of employees your business should hire. It also specifies that you must be actively involved in the business. Thus, in addition to the immigration forms you have to fill out, you must also have supporting documentation to prove that you meet these four important requirements.

The following documentation should be included to prove that you fulfill the requirements of the millionaire entrepreneur:

- articles of incorporation, partnership, joint venture or business trust agreement, license or other official authorization to do business in the form of sole proprietorship, partnership, holding company, joint venture, corporation, business trust, public or private entity, including a holding company and its wholly-owned subsidiaries engaged in for-profit activity.
- in case of investment in an existing business, you must present proof (such as stock purchase agreements, investment agreements, certified financial reports, payroll records) that capital was transferred after November 29, 1990, which resulted in a substantial increase (at least 40%) in the net worth or number of employees of the existing business
- payroll records, personnel records including copies of Form I-9 of the ten or more employees, or the business plan showing when such employees will be hired
- copies of bank statements, purchase contracts, bank loan agreements, bank transfers, transfers of shares or stock or convertible debentures
- invoices, sales receipts and purchase contracts showing assets purchased for use in the U.S. enterprise
- transfers of foreign property to the United States, as shown by U.S. Customs Service commercial entry documents, bills of lading and transit insurance policies
- any loan or mortgage, promissory note, security agreement or other evidence of secured borrowing
- foreign business registration records, the corporate, partnership or personal income, franchise, property

- any loan or mortgage, promissory note, security agreement or other evidence of secured borrowing
- foreign business registration records, the corporate, partnership or personal income, franchise, property tax returns filed within five years in the U.S. or outside the U.S., including inheritance tax to show the invested capital was obtained by lawful means
- a certified copy of money judgments or any pending proceedings (criminal, civil or administrative actions) against the entrepreneur within the past 15 years
- statement of your position or title either as manager of day-to-day operations or executive officer for policy formulation and strategic planning, with a complete description of your duties, and
- if the business is in a targeted employment area, proof that it is doing business in a rural area or area of high unemployment, such as a letter from a state government, to that effect.

If everything is in order, the BCIS should approve your petition. Depending on your immigration status, you, your spouse and your minor children can obtain the immigrant visas either by Adjustment of Status (see Chapter 8) or Consular Processing (see Chapter 9).

## H. CONDITIONAL PERMANENT RESIDENCE

After going through the Adjustment of Status or Consular Processing proceeding, the millionaire investor, the spouse and the children are granted a "conditional" permanent resident status.

### 1. Initial green card is temporary

This conditional green card is valid for two years only, then it "self-destructs" if the alien entrepreneur fails to file the necessary papers or to appear for an interview with the BCIS.

To prevent fraudulent use of investments as a means of acquiring a green card, the U.S. Congress requires the millionaire immigrant to present proof that the investment is bona fide. Twenty-one months after receiving a green card, the alien entrepreneur must file the second set of immigration forms to make his or her status permanent. This is called removing the conditional basis of the green card. Although the BCIS may contact you to remind you of this requirement, it is your responsibility to remember.

The immigration form to remove the conditional status of the green card is Form I-829, Application by Entrepreneur to Remove Conditions. (See the Appendix for the form.) The filing fee is $395.

### 2. Becoming permanent

To remove the conditions on a temporary green card, the entrepreneur must present proof that, during the preceding 21 months:

- a commercial enterprise has been invested in which employs at least ten American workers or green cardholders
- the millionaire immigrant has invested or is actively in the process of investing the requisite capital, and
- the millionaire immigrant is sustaining or operating the business.

The alien entrepreneur must provide documents to demonstrate that the business is financially sound and that the solid state of the business is directly due to the millionaire alien's management. No visits or on-site inspection will be made by the BCIS unless the agency suspects that fraud has been committed and wants to prosecute the alien investor for a criminal or civil offense.

Documents to prove the continuing nature of the business include: income tax returns of the past two years of the corporation or partnership or single proprietorship, bank statements, financial statements from a licensed accountant, lease contract or title of ownership of the real estate, mortgage contract, invoices, salary statements and copies of the W-2 Forms of the employees and other evidence of a bona fide business enterprise.

 If the business fails, even for reasons that are not your fault, you will be denied the green card.

## I. INTERVIEW BY THE BCIS

Upon receiving the petition for the removal of the conditional status of the green card, the BCIS schedules a personal interview with the alien entrepreneur, the spouse and the children. The BCIS may waive this requirement.

During the interview, the millionaire immigrant should present all the documents that were submitted earlier to show management of the business enterprise for which the green card was granted. In addition to financial documents, the entrepreneur may present copies of advertisements in local newspapers, photos and newspaper clippings about the business or articles in magazines about the business.

If the immigration officer is satisfied that the documents presented are valid and the millionaire immigrant has truly invested in a business that employs at least ten American workers or aliens authorized to work, then the millionaire immigrant, the spouse and the minor children are granted permanent resident status, removing the conditional basis of their green cards.

The second green card, which should be received within several months after the date of interview, is now considered permanent. In addition, the immigrants can start counting their residency of five years to be eligible for American citizenship, beginning from the time they obtained their first, conditional green card.

**EXAMPLE:** If the millionaire immigrant was admitted to the United States on December 7, 1994, and was granted the removal of the conditional status of the green card two years later, the millionaire immigrant would be eligible to apply for naturalization on December 7, 1999, five years after the alien received the lawful, albeit conditional, green card.

## J. Penalties for Investment Fraud

If the alien entrepreneur is found to have filed fraudulent documents to obtain the green card, or to have diverted the initial investment to something contrary to the investment provisions of the Act of 1990, the penalty is a maximum of five years in prison or a maximum fine of $10,000, or both imprisonment and fine.

If the authorities decide to pursue the civil action, the millionaire immigrant can also be fined a maximum of $5,000 for each fraudulent document used. The government needs to present only a preponderance of evidence to find the alien guilty in a civil case, as opposed to the tougher standard of proof beyond a reasonable doubt required in a criminal case.

 ### Hire the Right Experts

The best advice for the alien millionaire who wants a green card is to hire a reputable immigration lawyer, an experienced business lawyer and a capable accountant. An alien investor must be able to rely on competent advisers to build and maintain a successful enterprise.

Since you are ready to invest a lot of money to start or buy a business, you should hire the right professionals who will see to it that the bureaucratic procedures are followed and your immigration and economic goals are achieved. Pay particular attention to the tax implications of your investment and other income outside the United States.

## IMMIGRANT PETITION BY ALIEN ENTREPRENEUR, SAMPLE FORM I-526

**U.S. Department of Homeland Security**
Bureau of Citizenship and Immigration Services

OMB #1615-0026: Exp. 2/28/05

### I-526, Immigrant Petition by Alien Entrepreneur

| DO NOT WRITE IN THIS BLOCK - FOR BCIS USE ONLY (Except G-28 Block Below) | | |
|---|---|---|
| Classification _____ | **Action Block** | Fee Receipt |
| Priority Date _____ | | **To be completed by Attorney or Representative, if any** ☐ G-28 is attached  Attorney's State License No. _____ |
| Remarks: | | |

**START HERE -  Type or Print in Black Ink.**

### Part 1.    Information about you.

| Family Name | Uldrian | Given Name | Joseph | Middle Name | Miroslav |
|---|---|---|---|---|---|

Address:
In care of   Belle Wichan

| Number and Street | 12 Post Lane | | Apt. # | 6 |
|---|---|---|---|---|

| City | Esto | State or Province | Florida | Country | U.S.A. | Zip/Postal Code | 32104 |
|---|---|---|---|---|---|---|---|

| Date of Birth (mm/dd/yyyy) | 04/24/65 | Country of Birth | Yugoslavia | Social Security # (if any) | none | A # (if any) | A42 111 989 |
|---|---|---|---|---|---|---|---|

| **If you are in the United States, provide the following information:** | Date of Arrival (mm/dd/yyyy) | 10/1/03 | I-94 # | 03123456789 |
|---|---|---|---|---|

| Current Nonimmigrant Status | B-2 | Date Current Status Expires (mm/dd/yyyy) | 4/1/04 | Daytime Phone # with Area Code | ( 123) 555-1212 |
|---|---|---|---|---|---|

### Part 2.    Application type (Check one).

a. ☑ This petition is based on an investment in a commercial enterprise in a targeted employment area for which the required amount of capital invested has been adjusted downward.

b. ☐ This petition is based on an investment in a commercial enterprise in an area for which the required amount of capital invested has been adjusted upward.

c. ☐ This petition is based on an investment in a commercial enterprise that is not in either a targeted area or in an upward adjustment area.

### Part 3.    Information about your investment.

| Name of commercial enterprise in which funds are invested | Truform Shirts, Inc. |
|---|---|

| Street Address | 92785 West Rural Post Road |
|---|---|

| Phone # with Area Code | 904-768-9216 | Business organized as (corporation, partnership, etc.) | Corporation |
|---|---|---|---|

| Kind of business (e.g. furniture manfacturer) | Shirtmaker, recycled linen | Date established (mm/dd/yyyy) | 06/28/03 | IRS Tax # | 62-1234567 |
|---|---|---|---|---|---|

RECEIVED: _____   RESUBMITTED: _____   RELOCATED: SENT _____   REC'D _____

Form I-526 (Rev. 05/09/03)N (Prior versions may be used until 09/30/03)

## SAMPLE FORM I-526 (PAGE 2)

**Part 3.  Information about your investment. (continued)**

| Date of your initial investment (mm/dd/yyyy) | 04/12/03 | Amount of your initial investment | $ 400,000 |
|---|---|---|---|

| Your total capital investment in the enterprise to date | $ 650,000 | Percentage of the enterprise you own | 75% |
|---|---|---|---|

If you are not the sole investor in the new commercial enterprise, list on separate paper the names of all other parties (natural and non-natural) who hold a percentage share of ownership of the new enterprise and indicate whether any of these parties is seeking classification as an alien entrepreneur. Include the name, percentage of ownership and whether or not the person is seeking classification under section 203(b)(5). **NOTE:** A "natural" party would be an individual person and a "non-natural" party would be an entity such as a corporation, consortium, investment group, partnership, etc.

If you indicated in **Part 2** that the enterprise is in a targeted employment area or in an upward adjustment area, name the county and state:  County  Hughes  State  Florida

**Part 4.  Additional information about the enterprise.**

**Type of Enterprise (check one):**

[✔] New commercial enterprise resulting from the creation of a new business.

[ ] New commercial enterprise resulting from the purchase of an existing business.

[ ] New commercial enterprise resulting from a capital investment in an existing business.

**Composition of the Petitioner's Investment:**

Total amount in U.S. bank account ................................................................ $ 65,000

Total value of all assets purchased for use in the enterprise........................... $ 250,000

Total value of all property transferred from abroad to the new enterprise........... $ 400,000

Total of all debt financing................................................................ $ 0

Total stock purchases........................................................................ $ 0

Other (explain on separate paper)........................................................... $ 715,000

$ 

**Total**

**Income:**

| | | | | | |
|---|---|---|---|---|---|
| When you made the investment.......... | Gross | $ 900,000 | Net | $ | 709,000 |
| Now....................................... | Gross | $ 1,200,000 | Net | $ | 900,000 |

**Net worth:**

| | | | | | |
|---|---|---|---|---|---|
| When you made investment................ | Gross | $ 1.9 million | Now | $ | 2.4 million |

## SAMPLE FORM I-526 (PAGE 3)

### Part 5. Employment creation information.

**Number of full-time employees in the enterprise in U.S.** (excluding you, your spouse, sons and daughters)

When you made your initial investment? | 6 | Now | 14 | Difference | 8

How many of these new jobs were created by your investment? | 6 | How many additional new jobs will be created by your additional investment? | 20-25

What is your position, office or title with the new commercial enterprise?

President

Briefly describe your duties, activities and responsibilities.

Oversee entire corporate operation and management of new manufacturing business in former hurricane destruction area.

What is your salary? $ To be determined | What is the cost of your benefits? $ To be determined

### Part 6. Processing information.

**Check One:**

☑ The person named in **Part 1** is now in the United States and an application to adjust status to permanent resident will be filed if this petition is approved.

☐ If the petition is approved and the person named in **Part 1** wishes to apply for an immigrant visa abroad, complete the following for that person:

Country of nationality:

Country of current residence or, if now in the United States, last permanent residence abroad:

If you provided a United States address in **Part 1**, print the person's foreign address:

242 1st St., Banja Luka, Serbia

If the person's native alphabet is other than Roman letters, write the foreign address in the native alphabet:

Is a Form I-485, Application for Adjustment of Status, attached to this petition? ☑ Yes ☐ No

Are you in deportation or removal proceedings? ☐ Yes (Explain on separate paper) ☑ No

Have you ever worked in the United States without permission? ☐ Yes (Explain on separate paper) ☑ No

### Part 7. Signature. *Read the information on penalties in the instrucitons before completing this section.*

I certify, under penalty of perjury under the laws of the United States of America, that this petition and the evidence submitted with it is all true and correct. I authorize the release of any information from my records which the Bureau of Citizenship and Immigration Services needs to determine eligibility for the benefit I am seeking.

Signature | *Joseph M Uldrian* | Date | 11/2/03

**Please Note:** *If you do not completely fill out this form or fail to the submit the required documents listed in the instructions, you may not be found eligible for the immigration benefit you are seeking and this petition may be denied.*

### Part 8. Signature of person preparing form, if other than above. (Sign below)

I declare that I prepared this application at the request of the above person and it is based on all information of which I have knowledge.

Signature | | Print Your Name | | Date

Firm Name | | Daytime phone # with area code | ( ) –

Address

Form I-526 (Rev. 05/09/03)N (Prior versions may be used until 09/30/03) Page 3

# 21

# REFUGEES AND POLITICAL ASYLEES

## America: A Safe Haven

I was an engineering student at the University in Shanghai. During the student demonstration at the Tiananmen Square, I participated by distributing the student newsletter and other literature to those attending the rally. I also joined the hunger strike. When the government crackdown began, I went into hiding and was able to elude the police successfully for several months. However, when I tried to enter Hong Kong, I was deported back to China and spent several years in prison. I managed to reach the United States through the help of friends by the backroads. I would like to apply for political asylum.

Since the Refugee Act of 1980 was passed by the U.S. Congress, people fleeing persecution from their own country, regardless of whether their country was considered communist or democratic, have found a permanent haven in the United States, in keeping with America's tradition and history. Those fleeing natural disasters or war do not receive this permanent protection, but may receive what is called Temporary Protected Status. (See Section K.)

---

 **Consult an Expert**

This chapter explains the basic procedures and describes the immigration forms required for those claiming status as refugees and political asylees. However, the full legal process is full of possible pitfalls. If, after reading the chapter, you decide that you may qualify as a refugee or political asylee, it is best to consult an experienced immigration lawyer or other immigration professional. (See Chapter 31.)

---

## A. Who Qualifies

To apply to be a refugee, you must be outside your country of nationality or country of residence but not within the borders of the United States. To apply to be a political asylee, you must be either at the border or already inside the United States.

In addition, the President of the United States is empowered to recognize as a refugee any person who is still residing in his or her own country and to fix the number of refugees eligible to be admitted to the United States during the year. (See Section C, below.)

However, both the refugee and the political asylee have one important thing in common: They are unable or unwilling to return to their countries because of actual persecution or a well-founded fear of persecution on account of their:

- race
- religion
- nationality
- membership in a particular social group, or
- political opinion.

Persecution can include such things as threats, violence, torture, inappropriate access or imprisonment, or a failure by the government to protect you from such things.

## B. Ineligibility for Refugee Status or Asylum

A number of people are prohibited from becoming refugees or asylees in the United States.

### 1. Those who have assisted in persecution

The opportunity for refugee or political asylum status is not open to anyone who has ordered, incited, assisted or participated in the persecution of any other person owing to race, religion, nationality, membership in a particular social group or political opinion.

For example, most of Saddam Hussein's military officers would be denied refugee status or political asylum because of his government's policy of persecution of the Kurds and the Shiite Moslems.

### 2. Those who threaten U.S. safety or security

No one who has been convicted of a "particularly serious crime" and is therefore a danger to the community of the United States will be granted refugee or asylee status. There is no list of particularly serious crimes—the decision is made case by case, depending on the facts surrounding the crime. However, all "aggravated felonies" are considered particularly serious crimes—and, because of the immigration laws' strict definitions of aggravated felonies, some crimes that may have been called misdemeanors when committed will be looked upon as aggravated felonies.

In addition, no one who has been convicted of a serious nonpolitical crime in a country outside the United States will be granted refugee or asylee status. However, people whose crimes were nonserious or political in nature may still qualify.

Furthermore, no one who has been involved in terrorist activity or who can reasonably be regarded as a threat to U.S. security will be granted refugee or asylee status.

### 3. Those who have resettled

Refugee status is also denied to refugees or political asylees who have become "firmly resettled" in another country. A person is usually regarded as firmly resettled if he or she has:

- been granted permanent residency or citizenship by that country
- made permanent housing arrangements and has traveled in and out of the adopted country, or
- achieved economic independence because of education, employment, exercise of profession or business affairs in the adopted country.

## C. PRESIDENTIAL PROCLAMATION

If you belong to a group that the President, in consultation with the U.S. Congress, has declared eligible for refugee status, you can apply for that status with the overseas BCIS office in charge of the area in which you are located. If no office has been designated, you can apply at the American Consulate or Embassy nearest your location.

## D. GETTING REFUGEE STATUS

For those who qualify as refugees, there are a number of documents you are required to file—and a number of steps you must follow.

### 1. Filing the application

You must submit the following forms:
- Form I-590, Registration for Classification as Refugee, which should include any documentation of persecution or a detailed affidavit supporting your request for classification as a refugee.

In addition, you must submit the following documentation:
- Form G-325C, Biographical Information—for applicants 14 years old or over
- Form I-134, Affidavit of Financial Support, from a sponsor (a responsible person or organization) for your transportation to the place of resettlement in the United States, and

- a medical examination report to ascertain that you are mentally sound and do not have a serious communicable disease.

The date on which you file the refugee status application is your Priority Date, and shall be the basis for determining when you will be allowed to enter the United States as a refugee. As stated earlier, the number of refugees allowed each year is limited and fixed by the President.

### 2. Interview

You will be interviewed by an overseas immigration officer who will verify that you have been persecuted or you have a well-founded fear of persecution because of your race, religion, nationality, political opinion or membership in a particular social group.

### 3. Action on your application

If the overseas immigration officer decides that you meet the requirements and may be designated as a refugee, the application will be granted and you will be given a "parole visa." After your application is approved, you have four months in which to enter the United States.

If the application is denied, there is no appeal. You have no further recourse because you are outside the United States and its legal mechanism of judicial review.

Once you have been granted status as a refugee, you will be granted work authorization for one year as soon as you enter the United States.

### 4. When you can apply for a green card

After one year of physical presence in the United States, during which you must not have violated certain laws or regulations, you, your spouse and children may apply for permanent residence (a green card).

If you are found to be eligible, you and your family will be given lawful permanent resident status. The date of your permanent residence will be the date that you first arrived in the United States as a refugee. You will be eligible to apply for citizenship five years from that date.

### 5. Removal proceedings

If you are found ineligible for permanent residency, removal proceedings may be started against you and your family and you will have to present your cases before an immigration judge. If this happens, consult with an experienced immigration lawyer who specializes in removal cases. (See Chapter 31.)

## E. GETTING POLITICAL ASYLUM

For people interested in applying for political asylum, you must fill out various forms and explain your case to a BCIS officer or judge.

### 1. Where to request asylum

You can request asylum:

- upon arrival at the border or port of entry, if you are an alien stowaway, a crewman, or a passenger seeking admission into the United States
- at a removal hearing before the immigration judge, or
- by sending an application to the BCIS, after which you'll be interviewed at one of the BCIS Asylum Offices. Under changes enacted by Congress in 1996, a person must apply for asylum within one year from the time of their arrival in the United States. Anyone who has not filed within that time will have to show either that conditions changed in his country or there were other compelling reasons for the failure to apply within one year. However, BCIS policy is not to count any time in which you had a valid visa or Temporary Protected Status against that year.

### 2. Filing your application for asylum

The following documents should be mailed to the BCIS Regional Service Center, if you are not in removal proceedings, or to the Immigration Court, if you are already in proceedings:

- Form I-589, Request for Asylum in the United States—one original and three copies. There is no filing fee for this form. Your spouse and children may be included in the application, as long as you have an additional copy for each (see the sample at the end of this chapter).
- One color photo of you and each family member applying with you, sized according to the instructions in Chapter 29, Section E. Write the person's name in pencil on the back.
- Copies of your passports (if you have them) and any other travel documents (including from the U.S. BCIS, such as an I-94 card).
- Copies of documents to prove your identity, such as a birth certificate, driver's license or national identity document ("cedula").
- Copies of documents to prove the relationships between the family members applying, such as birth and marriage certificates.
- Documentation of your experience in your country, showing why you fear to return, supported by your

own detailed written statement. If possible, also include statements of any witnesses, doctors, friends, relatives, respected leaders of your community; news reports; or letters from people in your country,

Some time after receiving your application, the BCIS will call you in to have your fingerprints taken (if you're over age 14). This is to make sure that you don't have a record of criminal or terrorist acts and that you haven't applied for asylum before.

### BCIS Asylum Offices—Where to File

There are four regional service centers that handle all asylum applications. Where you file depends on where you live. (See the BCIS website at www.bcis.gov for complete office addresses. Click on "Field Office Addresses and Information.")

- **California Service Center:** If you live in Arizona, California (southern part) or Nevada (southern part).
- **Nebraska Service Center:** Alaska, California (northern part), Hawaii, Idaho, Illinois, Indiana, Iowa, Kansas, Kentucky, Michigan, Minnesota, Missouri, Montana, Nebraska, Nevada (northern part), North Dakota, Ohio, Oregon, South Dakota, Territory of Guam, Washington or Wisconsin.
- **Texas Service Center:** If you live in Alabama, Arkansas, Colorado, District of Columbia, Florida, Georgia, Louisiana, Maryland, Mississippi, New Mexico, North Carolina, Oklahoma, Pennsylvania (western part), Puerto Rico, South Carolina, Tennessee, Texas, Utah, Virginia, Virgin Islands, West Virginia or Wyoming.
- **Vermont Service Center:** If you live in Connecticut, Delaware, Maine, Massachusetts, New Hampshire, New Jersey, New York, Pennsylvania (eastern part), Rhode Island or Vermont.

---

### APPLYING FOR A WORK PERMIT

If the 150 days pass with no decision, or if your application for asylum is approved, you'll need to apply for a work permit (more formally known as an employment authorization document.) Do so by filling out Form I-765 (in the Appendix and available on the INS website). Most of this form is self-explanatory. On Question 16, applicants who've been waiting for 150 days or more with no decision should enter "(c)(8)." Those whose asylum application has already been approved should enter "(a)(5)." Follow the instructions on the form regarding what to include and where to take or send it.

---

## 3.  BCIS interview

After your papers have been processed at the BCIS Service Center, you will be called in to have your fingerprints taken, then later get an appointment at one of the BCIS Asylum offices. There, you will be interviewed to determine whether you are eligible for political asylum. Interviews last around one half-hour.

An applicant is not automatically entitled to employment authorization, but may apply for work authorization only after the asylum application has been pending without a decision for five months. If an interview has not been held by the sixth month, the work authorization will be granted. If the application is denied by the asylum officer before a decision has been made on the employment authorization application, the BCIS will deny this application. If the BCIS has already sent a work permit, however, such permission terminates when the card is marked to expire or 60 days after asylum is denied, whichever is later. If the interview is held before six months, you will only be eligible for a work permit if and when your case is approved.

## 4.  Comments of the Department of State

When the BCIS receives your application, the officer may send a copy to the Bureau of Human Rights and Humanitarian Affairs (BHRHA) of the U.S. Department of State for comments on:

- the accuracy of the assertions on the conditions in the foreign country and the experiences described

- how an applicant who returned to the foreign country would be likely to be treated
- whether people who are similarly situated as the applicant are persecuted in the foreign country and the frequency of such persecution, and
- whether one of grounds for denial may apply to the applicant.

However, these comments are less important than they used to be, since the process usually goes faster than the BHRHA's ability to provide comments.

## 5.  Decision by the asylum officer

After interviewing you, the asylum officer has full discretion to approve or deny your application for political asylum. However, you won't be told the decision that day. You'll have to return to the Asylum office at an appointed time to pick up your decision from the front desk.

**Approval.** The asylum officer will approve your application if you can show that:

- you have a well-founded fear of persecution by reason of your race, religion, nationality, political opinion or membership in a particular social group
- there is a reasonable possibility of actually suffering such persecution if you were to return to that country, and
- you are unable or unwilling to return to that country because of such fear.

    You do not have to provide evidence that you would be singled out individually for persecution if you can establish that:

- there is a pattern or practice in your country of persecuting groups of people similarly situated to you
- you belong to or identify with the groups of people being persecuted so that your fear is reasonable
- your government persecutes its nationals or residents so that you had to leave your country without authorization or you have sought asylum in another country.

The persecution may have been by your government, or you can claim asylum by showing that you were persecuted by a group that your government is unable or unwilling to control, or that you fear such persecution.

---

### PROTECTION UNDER THE U.N. CONVENTION AGAINST TORTURE

Even if you don't qualify for asylum, you may be protected from deportation by the United Nations Convention Against Torture. This prohibits deporting anyone who can show that he or she is more likely than not to suffer torture at the hands of his or her home country's government. The asylum application has a place to mention whether you feel you qualify for this protection. However, it won't get you a green card—it will just stop the BCIS from deporting you. Whether the BCIS will also allow you a work permit is up to its discretion.

---

**Denial.** The asylum officer will deny asylum and your work authorization in the United States if your interview and your documentation show that:

- your fear of persecution is not well-founded
- you have been firmly resettled in another country
- you ordered, incited, assisted or participated in the persecution of any person
- you have, without a good reason that relates to your fear of persecution, circumvented the refugee process and entered the United States secretly or on a fraudulent passport
- you are dangerous to the American community because you have been convicted of a serious crime
- you may have committed a serious, nonpolitical crime outside the United States
- you are a danger to the security of the United States, or
- you have an outstanding offer of resettlement from a third nation in which you will not be persecuted.

Of course, if you deny any of the above charges after the BCIS alleges them, you have the burden of proving that such grounds do not apply to you.

## F. IF YOUR ASYLUM APPLICATION IS DENIED

If the asylum officer denies your application for political asylum, he or she will also serve you with papers to start your removal proceedings before the immigration court. Get an attorney to help you.

### 1. Removal proceedings

If you applied for political asylum at the border or the airport and your application was denied by the asylum officer, you may choose to accept an order to leave the United States voluntarily. Be sure to understand that an offer to withdraw your request to enter the United States is different from an order of deportation, which prevents you from reapplying for entry for five years. Under the summary exclusion rules, an inspector can order you to be deported if he or she thinks you are committing a fraud or asking for admission without having the proper documents to support your request.

If you choose to remain, then you should request that your case be heard by an immigration judge in a court proceeding. The immigration judge will promptly decide whether your case has merit. If the judge rules that it does have merit, you will be given the chance to explain your case at a full hearing.

If you were already living in the United States when your application was denied, you may choose to leave the United States or request that your case be heard by the immigration judge in a removal proceeding.

### 2. Hearing before the immigration judge

If you proceed on the hearing of your denied application or renew your application for political asylum before an immigration judge, you must demonstrate by documents, witnesses and your own testimony that your fear of persecution due to your race, religion, nationality, political opinion or membership in a social group is well-founded.

If you are able to convince the immigration judge that your fears are well-founded, your application for political asylum will be granted. If your documentation, any witnesses and your testimony are weak and unconvincing, your application will be denied.

**MISSING THE HEARING: AN EXPENSIVE MISTAKE**

If, after you have been notified orally and in writing of the time, place and date of the hearing, you fail to attend an asylum hearing before an immigration judge, you will be ordered deported and will never be able to adjust your status, or be given voluntary departure, or be granted suspension of deportation.

Thus, when you fail to appear at your asylum hearing, the immigration judge may hold the hearing without you being present—and issue an order of deportation if the evidence presented by the BCIS supports it. You will be unable to get a green card until after five years from the date of the asylum hearing which you failed to attend.

Only "exceptional circumstances beyond your control," such as your own serious illness or the death of an immediate relative are considered to be valid excuses for failing to appear before the immigration judge. A less compelling reason is not acceptable when your lawyer files a motion to reopen the order of your deportation.

## 3. Further appeals

Upon denial, you are free to pursue the case to the Immigration Board of Appeals and from there to the federal District Court. In the meantime, while your case or your appeal is pending, you are able to remain in the United States. If you have already received work authorization, it will continue to be granted for one year at a time.

## G. Getting a Green Card After Asylum Approval

One year after your asylum application has been approved, you and your family may apply to become permanent residents. (You can also wait more than a year, but it's safest to apply as soon as you can.) You will be given your green card if you:

- apply for Adjustment of Status (see Chapter 8)
- have remained physically in the United States for one full year after being granted asylum

- continue to be a refugee or asylee or the spouse or child of such a refugee or asylee (as defined in Section A, above)
- have not violated certain criminal laws of the United States, and
- have been assigned an immigrant visa number based on your Priority Date, which is the date you filed your application for asylum (you'll get this automatically, but it often causes delays).

## H. Extension of Asylee Status

If your Priority Date has not yet reached the top of the list of refugees, the BCIS may interview you and review your case from time to time to determine your continuing eligibility for asylum. If conditions in your home country remain unchanged, your asylee status will continue until your application for Adjustment of Status is approved and you finally receive your green card.

## I. Revocation of Asylee Status

Beware that if your country's political situation has improved or has changed so that you are no longer in danger of being persecuted, the BCIS may revoke your asylee status. However, it must first notify you and then convince the asylum officer that you:

- no longer have a well-founded fear of persecution upon your return due to a change of conditions in your country
- were guilty of fraud in your application so that you were not eligible for asylum when it was granted, or
- have committed any of the acts which would have caused your asylum application to be denied—such as a serious felony.

The Immigration Act of 1990 saved the day for asylees from Nicaragua, Poland, Panama and Hungary because the BCIS would have revoked their asylum status since their respective oppressive governments had been overthrown before the Act was passed in November 29, 1990. Thus, if you were granted asylum in the United States prior to November 29, 1990, and are no longer a refugee due to a change in circumstances in the country where you fear persecution, you may still apply for Adjustment of Status without proving that you still fear returning to your country.

## J. BACKLOG IN ASYLUM CASES

Due to budget limitations, and such things as the Haitian refugees in Guantanamo Bay, Cuba, the settlement of the cases favoring Salvadorans and Guatemalans, civil wars in South American and African countries and, most of all, the end of the Cold War and the resulting anarchy in many of the former Soviet Union satellites, the backlog of asylum cases may be as high as 300,000 applications.

The BCIS is making efforts to attend to this avalanche of applications—and cases that were filed recently are being decided within six months. However, cases filed in the past are still backlogged. And cases filed before January 5, 1995, are subject to different rules on some issues. For example, those applicants are entitled to work authorization automatically while their cases are awaiting decision at the Asylum Office.

## K. TEMPORARY PROTECTED STATUS

Temporary Protected Status (TPS) is a new legal category that was fashioned by the U.S. Congress to respond to situations when natural disasters, such as earthquakes, volcanic eruptions or tidal waves occur, or when war is being waged in a foreign country. It is a form of temporary asylum or safe haven for aliens whose country is in turmoil. Congress responded with this humanitarian gesture to avoid the deportation of aliens to countries where their personal safety is threatened or in which normal living conditions are substantially disrupted.

### 1. TPS benefits

A Temporary Protected Status offers several short-term benefits to an alien.

- **Stay of deportation.** The alien will not be placed in removal proceedings. If a removal case is already underway, the alien can claim TPS and the proceedings will be adjourned until the end of the disruption period.
- **Work authorization.** The alien, regardless of immigration status, will receive work authorization as long as the TPS is in effect.
- **Temporary Treatment (TT).** When the alien files for TPS with such documentary proof as a birth certificate showing that he or she is a national of the designated country, the benefits of a stay of deportation and work authorization will be granted immedi-

ately, pending the publication of the termination of the designation in the *Federal Register* or pending final determination of the application.

### 2. Who designates the TPS aliens?

The Attorney General, working through the BCIS, will designate the countries whose nationals deserve Temporary Protected Status. The following situations may give rise to this designation:

- ongoing armed conflict and civil war which pose a serious threat to the lives and personal safety of deported aliens who are nationals of that country
- earthquakes, floods, droughts, epidemics or other environmental disasters, resulting in a substantial disruption of living conditions and an inability to handle the return of its nationals, in a foreign country that has requested a TPS designation, and
- extraordinary and temporary conditions in the foreign country preventing its nationals in the United States from returning safely to their country.

### 3. Period of protected status

The Attorney General will designate the initial period of protection as being not less than six months or more than 18 months. Sixty days before the end of the period, the Attorney General will review the conditions of the foreign country to determine whether to end the TPS, or to extend it for a period of six, 12 or 18 months.

The termination or the extension will be published in the *Federal Register*. Termination will be effective 60 days after publication.

### 4. Who qualifies for TPS?

Nationals or native-born citizens of the designated foreign countries may apply for Temporary Protected Status if they:

- have been physically present in the United States continuously since the date of the designation
- have continuously resided in the United States since a certain date
- register for TPS during a registration period of not less than 180 days, and
- pay the filing fee.

---

## TPS-Designated Countries

At the time this book went to print, citizens from the countries on the list below could apply for TPS. However, this list changes rapidly, so keep your eyes on the news and the BCIS website at www.bcis.gov.

| | |
|---|---|
| Burundi | Nicaragua |
| El Salvador | Sierra Leone |
| Honduras | Somalia |
| Liberia | Sudan |
| Montserrat | |

---

## 5. Who is not eligible for TPS

TPS is not available to nationals or native-born citizens of a designated foreign country who are outside the United States. In addition, even if you are already in the United States, your application for TPS will be denied if you:

- have been convicted of any felony, or at least two misdemeanors, in the United States
- have ordered, incited, assisted or participated in persecuting any person
- have committed a serious nonpolitical crime outside the United States, or
- are regarded as a danger to the security of the United States.

## 6. No departure from the U.S. allowed

If a person who has been granted TPS leaves the United States without getting advance permission from the BCIS, the agency may treat the TPS status as having been abandoned.

Brief, casual and innocent absences from the United States—a few hours or days—shall not be considered as failure to be physically present in the United States. For humanitarian reasons, the BCIS recognizes emergency and extenuating circumstances, and may give Advance Parole or permission to depart for a brief and temporary trip without affecting the TPS.

## 7. How to file

The following forms should be filed with the BCIS local office nearest the applicant's place of residence (see the BCIS website at www.bcis.gov and Appendix 1 for contact details):

- Form I-821, Temporary Protected Status Eligibility Questionnaire. The filing fee is $50, plus an additional $50 for fingerprinting if you are age 14 or older.
- Form I-104, Address Report Filing

- Form I-765, Employment Authorization Application, with filing fee of $120. Work authorization, effective until TPS is ended, is granted for the TPS period or one year, whichever is shorter. The fee must be paid each time.
- documents showing physical presence during the period designated: passport used in entering the United States, Form I-94 (Record of Departure), rent receipts, school records, hospital records, pay stubs, banking records, employment records and affidavits of responsible members of your community (such as a religious officer, school director or employer)
- two kinds of documents showing personal identity: birth certificate, a passport, driver's license, employment ID, school ID, and
- two photographs.

## 8. Termination of protected status

After the U.S. government decides that the situation in the foreign country has improved and there is no longer any reason to retain the Temporary Protective Status for nationals of that country, the TPS designation will be lifted. However, your work authorization will continue until its expiration date. If you do not have any other legal right to be in the United States, you are expected to leave at that time. However, it does not appear that the immigration authorities will make efforts to deport people at the end of the TPS period—though there are no guarantees.

## 9. Deferred Enforced Departure (DED)

Another benefit which may be available for people from countries which have political or civil conflicts is known as Deferred Enforced Departure (DED). This is a temporary form of relief that allows designated individuals to work and stay in the United States for a certain period of time, during which the authorities will not try to deport them.

At the time this book went to print, no countries were currently designated under the DED program. (Liberia's designation expired on September 29, 2002, but Liberia was placed on the TPS list instead.)

Certain people are ineligible for DED, including those who have committed certain crimes, persecuted others, or been previously deported, excluded or removed from the United States.

If you are already in removal proceedings, you may ask the immigration judge to defer action on your case. If your case is already up on appeal after a decision by an immigration judge at the Board of Immigration Appeals, you should receive notice automatically about the administrative or temporary closure of your proceeding.

## REQUEST FOR ASYLUM AND FOR WITHHOLDING OF REMOVAL, SAMPLE FORM I-589

OMB No. 1115-0086

**U.S. Department of Justice**
Immigration and Naturalization Service

## Application for Asylum and for Withholding of Removal

*Start Here - Please Type or Print.* **USE BLACK INK. SEE THE SEPARATE INSTRUCTION PAMPHLET FOR INFORMATION ABOUT ELIGIBILITY AND HOW TO COMPLETE AND FILE THIS APPLICATION.** (Note: There is NO filing fee for this application.)

*Please* check the box if you also want to apply for withholding of removal under the Convention Against Torture. ☐

### PART A. I.   INFORMATION ABOUT YOU

| | |
|---|---|
| 1. Alien Registration Number(s)(A#'s)*(If any)*   A547505576 | 2. Social Security No. *(If any)*   999-99-9999 |

| | | |
|---|---|---|
| 3. Complete Last Name   Romero | 4. First Name   Luiz | 5. Middle Name   Manuel |

6. What other names have you used? *(Include maiden name and aliases.)*   None

| | |
|---|---|
| 7. Residence in the U.S.<br>C/O | Telephone Number<br>510-555-2222 |
| Street Number and Name   156 Arbol Lane | Apt. No. |
| City   Richmond    State   CA | ZIP Code   94666 |
| 8. Mailing Address in the U.S., if other than above   (same as above) | Telephone Number |
| Street Number and Name | Apt. No. |
| City    State | ZIP Code |

9. Sex ☒ Male   ☐ Female    10. Marital Status:   ☐ Single   ☒ Married   ☐ Divorced   ☐ Widowed

| | |
|---|---|
| 11. Date of Birth *(Mo/Day/Yr)*<br>4/7/65 | 12. City and Country of Birth<br>Quetzaltenango, Guatemala |

| | | | |
|---|---|---|---|
| 13. Present Nationality *(Citizenship)*<br>Guatemalan | 14. Nationality at Birth<br>Guatemalan | 15. Race, Ethnic or Tribal Group<br>Hispanic | 16. Religion<br>Catholic |

17. *Check the box, a through c that applies:*   a. ☒ I have never been in immigration court proceedings.
b. ☐ I am now in immigration court proceedings.   c. ☐ I am **not** now in immigration court proceedings, but I have been in the past.

18. *Complete 18 a through c.*
a. When did you last leave your country? *(Mo/Day/Yr)* Oct. 4, 2002   b. What is your current I-94 Number, if any? 02654000102

c. Please list each entry to the U.S. beginning with your most recent entry.
List date *(Mo/Day/Yr)*, place, and your status for each entry. *(Attach additional sheets as needed.)*

| Date | Place | Status | Date Status Expires |
|---|---|---|---|
| Oct. 4, 02 | San Francisco, CA | B-2 | April 4, 2003 |
| May 7, 99 | Los Angeles, CA | B-2 | |
| | | | |
| | | | |

| | | |
|---|---|---|
| 19. What country issued your last passport or travel document?   Guatemala | 20. Passport #<br>Travel Document #   775824 | 21. Expiration Date *(Mo/Day/Yr)*<br>1/1/07 |
| 22. What is your native language?<br>Spanish | 23. Are you fluent in English?<br>☐ Yes ☒ No | 24. What other languages do you speak fluently?<br>None |

| FOR EOIR USE ONLY | FOR INS USE ONLY |
|---|---|
| | **Action:**<br>Interview Date: _____ |
| | **Decision:**<br>__ Approval Date: _____ |
| | — Denial Date: _____ |
| | — Referral Date: _____ |
| | Asylum Officer ID# _____ |

Form I-589 (Rev. 10/18/01)N

## SAMPLE FORM I-589 (PAGE 2)

OMB No. 1115-0086

**PART A. II.     INFORMATION ABOUT YOUR SPOUSE AND CHILDREN**

**Your Spouse.** ☐ I am not married. (Skip to *Your Children, below.*)

| 1. Alien Registration Number (A#) *(If any)* | 2. Passport/ID Card No. *(If any)* | 3. Date of Birth *(Mo/Day/Yr)* | 4. Social Security No. *(If any)* |
|---|---|---|---|
| A54571570 | 775825 | 5/9/68 | 774-26-4954 |

| 5. Complete Last Name | 6. First Name | 7. Middle Name | 8. Maiden Name |
|---|---|---|---|
| Romero | Maria | Beatriz | Carcamo |

| 9. Date of Marriage *(Mo/Day/Yr)* | 10. Place of Marriage | 11. City and Country of Birth |
|---|---|---|
| Nov. 7, 1989 | Antigua, Guatemala | Panajachel, Guatemala |

| 12. Nationality *(Citizenship)* | 13. Race, Ethnic or Tribal Group | 14. Sex ☐ Male ☒ Female |
|---|---|---|
| Guatemalan | Hispanic | |

15. Is this person in the U.S.? ☒ Yes *(Complete blocks 16 to 24.)* ☐ No *(Specify location)*

| 16. Place of last entry in the U.S. ? | 17. Date of last entry in the U.S. *(Mo/Day/Yr)* | 18. I-94 No. *(If any)* | 19. Status when last admitted *(Visa type, if any)* |
|---|---|---|---|
| San Francisco, CA | Oct. 4, 02 | 02654000103 | B-2 visitor |

| 20. What is your spouse's current status? | 21. What is the expiration date of his/her authorized stay, if any? *(Mo/Day/Yr)* | 22. Is your spouse in immigration court proceedings? | 23. If previously in the U.S., date of previous arrival *(Mo/Day/Yr)* |
|---|---|---|---|
| B-2 | April 4, 2003 | ☐ Yes ☒ No | None |

24.     If in the U.S., is your spouse to be included in this application? *(Check the appropriate box.)*

☒ Yes *(Attach one (1) photograph of your spouse in the upper right hand corner of page 9 on the extra copy of the application submitted for this person.)*

☐ No

**Your Children.** Please list **ALL** of your children, regardless of age, location, or marital status.

☒ I do not have any children. *(Skip to Part A. III., **Information about Your Background.**)*

☐ I do have children. Total number of children _____

*(Use Supplement A Form I-589 or attach additional pages and documentation if you have more than four (4) children.)*

| 1. Alien Registration Number (A#) *(If any)* | 2. Passport/ID Card No. *(If any)* | 3. Marital Status *(Married, Single, Divorced, Widowed)* | 4. Social Security No. *(If any)* |
|---|---|---|---|
| | | | |

| 5. Complete Last Name | 6. First Name | 7. Middle Name | 8. Date of Birth *(Mo/Day/Yr)* |
|---|---|---|---|
| | | | |

| 9. City and Country of Birth | 10. Nationality *(Citizenship)* | 11. Race, Ethnic or Tribal Group | 12. Sex ☐ Male ☐ Female |
|---|---|---|---|
| | | | |

13. Is this child in the U.S.? ☐ Yes *(Complete blocks 14 to 21.)* ☐ No *(Specify Location)*

| 14. Place of last entry in the U.S.? | 15. Date of last entry in the U.S.? *(Mo/Day/Yr)* | 16. I-94 No. *(If any)* | 17. Status when last admitted *(Visa type, if any)* |
|---|---|---|---|
| | | | |

| 18. What is your child's current status? | 19. What is the expiration date of his/her authorized stay, if any?*(Mo/Day/Yr)* | 20. Is your child in immigration court proceedings? ☐ Yes ☐ No |
|---|---|---|
| | | |

21.     If in the U.S., is this child to be included in this application? *(Check the appropriate box.)*

☐ Yes *(Attach one (1) photograph of your child in the upper right hand corner of page 9 on the extra copy of the application submitted for this person.)*

☐ No

## FORM I-589 (PAGE 3)

OMB No. 1115-0086

### PART A. II.   INFORMATION ABOUT YOUR SPOUSE AND CHILDREN Continued

| 1. Alien Registration Number (A#) *(If any)* | 2. Passport/IDCard No. *(If any)* | 3. Marital Status *(Married, Single, Divorced, Widowed)* | 4. Social Security No. *(If any)* |
|---|---|---|---|
| 5. Complete Last Name | 6. First Name | 7. Middle Name | 8. Date of Birth *(Mo/Dayl/Yr)* |
| 9. City and Country of Birth | 10. Nationality *(Citizenship)* | 11. Race, Ethnic or Tribal Group | 12. Sex ☐ Male ☐ Female |

13. Is this child in the U.S.?   ☐ Yes *(Complete blocks 14 to 21.)*          ☐ No *(Specify Location)*

| 14. Place of last entry in the U.S.? | 15. Date of last entry in the U.S. ? *(Mo/Day/Yr)* | 16. I-94 No. *(If any)* | 17. Status when last admitted *(Visa type, if any)* |
|---|---|---|---|
| 18. What is your child's current status? | 19. What is the expiration date of his/her authorized stay,*(if any)?* *(Mo/Day/Yr)* | 20. Is your child in immigration court proceedings? ☐ Yes ☐ No | |

21. If in the U.S., is this child to be included in this application? *(Check the appropriate box.)*

☐ Yes *(Attach one (1) photograph of your child in the upper right hand corner of page 9 on the extra copy of the application submitted for this person.)*

☐ No

| 1. Alien Registration Number (A#) *(If any)* | 2. Passport/ID Card No.*(If any)* | 3. Marital Status *(Married, Single, Divorced, Widowed)* | 4. Social Security No. *(If any)* |
|---|---|---|---|
| 5. Complete Last Name | 6. First Name | 7. Middle Name | 8. Date of Birth *(Mo/Day/Yr)* |
| 9. City and Country of Birth | 10. Nationality *(Citizenship)* | 11. Race, Ethnic or Tribal Group | 12. Sex ☐ Male ☐ Female |

13. Is this child in the U.S. ?   ☐ Yes *(Complete blocks 14 to 21.)*          ☐ No *(Specify Location)*

| 14. Place of last entry in the U.S.? | 15. Date of last entry in the U.S.? *(Mo/Day/Yr)* | 16. I-94 No. *(If any)* | 17. Status when last admitted *(Visa type, if any)* |
|---|---|---|---|
| 18. What is your child's current status? | 19. What is the expiration date of his/her authorized stay, if any? *(Mo/Day/Yr)* | 20. Is your child in immigration court proceedings? ☐ Yes ☐ No | |

21. If in the U.S., is this child to be included in this application? *(Check the appropriate box.)*

☐ Yes *(Attach one (1) photograph of your child in the upper right hand corner of page 9 on the extra copy of the application submitted for this person.)*

☐ No

| 1. Alien Registration Number (A#) *(If any)* | 2. Passport/ID Card No. *(If any)* | 3. Marital Status *(Married, Single. Divorced, Widowed)* | 4. Social Security No. *(If any)* |
|---|---|---|---|
| 5. Complete Last Name | 6. First Name | 7. Middle Name | 8. Date of Birth *(Mo/Day/Yr)* |
| 9. City and Country of Birth | 10. Nationality *(Citizenship)* | 11. Race, Ethnic or Tribal Group | 12. Sex ☐ Male ☐ Female |

13. Is this child in the U.S.?   ☐ Yes *(Complete blocks 14 to 21.)*          ☐ No *(Specify Location)*

| 14. Place of last entry in the U.S.? | 15. Date of last entry in the U.S.? *(Mo/Day/Yr)* | 16. I-94 No. *(If any)* | 17. Status when last admitted *(Visa type, if any)* |
|---|---|---|---|
| 18. What is your child's current status? | 19. What is the expiration date of his/her authorized stay, if any? *(Mo/Day/Yr)* | 20. Is your child in immigration court proceedings? ☐ Yes ☐ No | |

21. If in the U.S., is this child to be included in this application? *(Check the appropriate box.)*

☐ Yes *(Attach one (1) photograph of your child in the upper right hand corner of page 9 on the extra copy of the application submitted for this person.)*

☐ No

# FORM I-589 (PAGE 4)

OMB No. 1115-0086

## PART A. III.    INFORMATION ABOUT YOUR BACKGROUND

1. Please list your last address where you lived before coming to the U.S.  If this is not the country where you fear persecution, also list the last address in the country where you fear persecution. *(List Address, City/Town, Department, Province, or State, and Country.)  (Use Supplement B Form I-589 or additional sheets of paper if necessary.)*

| Number and Street *(Provide if available)* | City/Town | Department, Province or State | Country | Dates From *(Mo/Yr)* | To *(Mo/Yr)* |
|---|---|---|---|---|---|
| 123 Avenida 7 | Guatemala City | Guatemala City | Guatemala | 11/14/85 | 10/4/02 |
| | | | | | |

2. Provide the following information about your residences during the last five years.  List your present address first. *(Use Supplement Form B or additional sheets of paper if necessary.)*

| Number and Street | City/Town | Department, Province or State | Country | Dates From *(Mo/Yr)* | To *(Mo/Yr)* |
|---|---|---|---|---|---|
| 123 Avenida 7 | Guatemala City | Guatemala City | Guatemala | 11/14/85 | 10/4/02 |
| 321 Calle de la Paz | Quetzaltenango | | Guatemala | birth | 11/4/85 |
| | | | | | |
| | | | | | |
| | | | | | |

3. Provide the following information about your education, beginning with the most recent. *(Use Supplement B Form I-589 or additional sheets of paper if necessary.)*

| Name of School | Type of School | Location (Address) | Attended From *(Mo/Yr)* | To *(Mo/Yr)* |
|---|---|---|---|---|
| San Carlos University | College | Guatemala City | 9/82 | 6/86 |
| Quetzal High School | High School | Quetzaltenango | 9/78 | 6/82 |
| Sta. Maria Academy | Elementary/Middle | Quetzaltenango | 9/70 | 6/78 |
| | | | | |

4. Provide the following information about your employment during the last five years.  List your present employment first. *(Use Supplement Form B or additional sheets of paper if necessary.)*

| Name and Address of Employer | Your Occupation | Dates From *(Mo/Yr)* | To *(Mo/Yr)* |
|---|---|---|---|
| Jose Torres Ramirez, Attorney | Legal Assistant | 8/7/94 | 10/2/02 |
| | | | |
| | | | |
| | | | |

5. Provide the following information about your parents and siblings (brother and sisters).  Check box if the person is deceased. *(Use Supplement B Form I-589 or additional sheets of paper if necessary.)*

| | Name | City/Town and Country of Birth | Current Location |
|---|---|---|---|
| Mother | Gloria Alcala de Romero | Quetzaltenango, Guatemala | ☐ Deceased  Quetzaltenango, Guatemala |
| Father | Jorge Romero | Quetzaltenango, Guatemala | ☒ Deceased |
| Siblings | Felipe Romero | Quetzaltenango, Guatemala | ☒ Deceased |
| | Laura Romero | Quetzaltenango, Guatemala | ☐ Deceased  Antigua, Guatemala |

Form I-589 (Rev. 10/18/01)N Page 4

# FORM I-589 (PAGE 5)

OMB No. 1115-0086

---

### PART B.    INFORMATION ABOUT YOUR APPLICATION

---

*(Use Supplement B Form I-589 or attach additional sheets of paper as needed to complete your responses to the questions contained in PART B.)*

When answering the following questions about your asylum or other protection claim (withholding of removal under 241(b)(3) of the Act or withholding of removal under the Convention Against Torture) you should provide a detailed and specific account of the basis of your claim to asylum or other protection. To the best of your ability, provide specific dates, places, and descriptions about each event or action described. You should attach documents evidencing the general conditions in the country from which you are seeking asylum or other protection and the specific facts on which you are relying to support your claim. If this documentation is unavailable or you are not providing this documentation with your application, please explain why in your responses to the following questions. Refer to Instructions, Part 1: Filing Instructions, Section II, "Basis of Eligibility," Parts A - D, Section V, "Completing the Form," Part B, and Section VII, "Additional Documents that You Should Submit" for more information on completing this section of the form.

1.  Why are you applying for asylum or withholding of removal under section 241(b)(3) of the Act, or for withholding of removal under the Convention Against Torture? Check the appropriate box (es) below and then provide detailed answers to questions A and B below:

I am seeking asylum or withholding of removal based on

- ☐ Race
- ☐ Religion
- ☐ Nationality
- ☒ Political opinion
- ☒ Membership in a particular social group
- ☒ Torture Convention

A.  Have you, your family, or close friends or colleagues ever experienced harm or mistreatment or threats in the past by anyone?

☐ No  ☒ Yes  If your answer is "Yes," explain in detail:

1) What happened;
2) When the harm or mistreatment or threats occurred;
3) Who caused the harm or mistreatment or threats; and
4) Why you believe the harm or mistreatment or threats occurred.

During the months of July through September 2002, jeeps with darkened windows have been circling our office and followed me home on at least two occasions. The neighbors told me that a military officer has been asking questions about me. I received a phone call on September 4, in which an anonymous voice said "drop the Diaz case or your wife will be a widow."

B.  Do you fear harm or mistreatment if you return to your home country?

☐ No  ☒ Yes  If your answer is "Yes," explain in detail:

1) What harm or mistreatment you fear;
2) Who you believe would harm or mistreat you; and
3) Why you believe you would or could be harmed or mistreated.

I believe that members of the Guatemalan military would torture, imprison or kill me because of my work assisting victims of human rights abuses to gain judicial relief.

# FORM I-589 (PAGE 6)

OMB No. 1115-0086

**PART B.    INFORMATION ABOUT YOUR APPLICATION Continued**

2.  Have you or your family members ever been accused, charged, arrested, detained, interrogated, convicted and sentenced, or imprisoned in any country other than the United States?

☒ No    ☐ Yes  If "Yes," explain the circumstances and reasons for the action.

3. A.  Have you or your family members ever belonged to or been associated with any organizations or groups in your home country, such as, but not limited to, a political party, student group, labor union, religious organization, military or paramilitary group, civil patrol, guerrilla organization, ethnic group, human rights group, or the press or media?

☐ No    ☒ Yes  If "Yes," describe for each person the level of participation, any leadership or other positions held, and the length of time you or your family members were involved in each organization or activity.

I was a member of Students United for Free Speech from 1983 to 1986. I was a member of the Legal Committee for Redress from 1998 until I left Guatemala in 2002.

B.  Do you or your family members continue to participate in any way in these organizations or groups?

☒ No    ☐ Yes  If "Yes," describe for each person, your or your family members' current level of participation, any leadership or other positions currently held, and the length of time you or your family members have been involved in each organization or group.

4.  Are you afraid of being subjected to torture in your home country or any other country to which you may be returned?

☐ No    ☒ Yes  If "Yes," explain why you are afraid and describe the nature of the torture you fear, by whom, and why it would be inflicted.

Other human rights activists, including a former clerk at the office where I work, have been questioned and tortured by members of the Guatemalan police and military.

Form I-589 (Rev. 10/18/01)N Page 6

# FORM I-589 (PAGE 7)

OMB No. 1115-0086

## PART C.    ADDITIONAL INFORMATION ABOUT YOUR APPLICATION

*(Use Supplement B Form I-589 or attach additional sheets of paper as needed to complete your responses to the questions contained in Part C.)*

1.  Have you, your spouse, your child(ren), your parents, or your siblings ever applied to the United States Government for refugee status, asylum, or withholding of removal?    ☒ No  ☐  Yes

    If "Yes" explain the decision and what happened to any status you, your spouse, your child(ren), your parents, or your siblings received as a result of that decision.  Please indicate whether or not you were included in a parent or spouse's application.  If so, please include your parent or spouse's A- number in your response.   If you have been denied asylum by an Immigration Judge or the Board of Immigration Appeals, please describe any change(s) in conditions in your country or your own personal circumstances since the date of the denial that may affect your eligibility for asylum.

2.  A.  After leaving the country from which you are claiming asylum, did you or your spouse or child(ren), who are now in the United States, travel through or reside in any other country before entering the United States?    ☒ No  ☐ Yes

    B.  Have you, your spouse, your child(ren), or other family members such as your parents or siblings ever applied for or received any lawful status in any country other than the one from which you are now claiming asylum?    ☒ No  ☐ Yes

    If "Yes" to either or both questions (2A and/or 2B), provide for each person the following: the name of each country and the length of stay; the person's status while there; the reasons for leaving; whether the person is entitled to return for lawful residence purposes; and whether the person applied for refugee status or for asylum while there, and, if not, why he or she did not do so.

3.  Have you, your spouse, or child(ren) ever ordered, incited, assisted, or otherwise participated in causing harm or suffering to any person because of his or her race, religion, nationality, membership in a particular social group or belief in a particular political opinion?

    ☒ No  ☐ Yes  If "Yes," describe in detail each such incident and your own or your spouse's or child(ren)'s involvement.

# FORM I-589 (PAGE 8)

OMB No. 1115-0086

**PART C. ADDITIONAL INFORMATION ABOUT YOUR APPLICATION Continued**

4. After you left the country where you were harmed or fear harm, did you return to that country?

    ☒ No ☐ Yes If "Yes," describe in detail the circumstances of your visit (for example, the date(s) of the trip(s), the purpose(s) of the trip(s), and the length of time you remained in that country for the visit(s)).

5. Are you filing the application more than one year after your last arrival in the United States?

    ☒ No ☐ Yes If "Yes," explain why you did not file within the first year after you arrived. You should be prepared to explain at your interview or hearing why you did not file your asylum application within the first year after you arrived. For guidance in answering this question, see Instructions, Part 1: Filing Instructions, Section V. "Completing the Form," Part C.

6. Have you or any member of your family included in the application ever committed any crime and/or been arrested, charged, convicted and sentenced for any crimes in the United States?

    ☒ No ☐ Yes If "Yes," for each instance, specify in your response what occurred and the circumstances; dates; length of sentence received; location; the duration of the detention or imprisonment; the reason(s) for the detention or conviction; any formal charges that were lodged against you or your relatives included in your application; the reason(s) for release. Attach documents referring to these incidents, if they are available, or an explanation of why documents are not available.

Form I-589 (Rev. 10/18/01)N Page 8

# FORM I-589 (PAGE 9)

OMB No. 1115-0086

## PART D.    YOUR SIGNATURE

*After reading the information regarding penalties in the instructions, complete and sign below. If someone helped you prepare this application, he or she must complete Part E.*

I certify, under penalty of perjury under the laws of the United States of America, that this application and the evidence submitted with it are all true and correct. Title 18, United States Code, Section 1546, provides in part: "Whoever knowingly makes under oath, or as permitted under penalty of perjury under Section 1746 of Title 28, United States Code, knowingly subscribes as true, any false statement with respect to a material fact in any application, affidavit, or knowingly presents any such application, affidavit, or other document required by the immigration laws or regulations prescribed thereunder, or knowingly presents any such application, affidavit, or other document containing any such false statement or which fails to contain any reasonable basis in law or fact - shall be fined in accordance with this title or imprisoned not more than five years, or both." I authorize the release of any information from my record which the Immigration and Naturalization Service needs to determine eligibility for the benefit I am seeking.

Staple your photograph here or the photograph of the family member to be included on the extra copy of the application submitted for that person.

**WARNING:** Applicants who are in the United States illegally are subject to removal if their asylum or withholding claims are not granted by an Asylum Officer or an Immigration Judge. Any information provided in completing this application may be used as a basis for the institution of, or as evidence in, removal proceedings even if the application is later withdrawn. Applicants determined to have knowingly made a frivolous application for asylum will be permanently ineligible for any benefits under the Immigration and Nationality Act. See 208(d)(6) of the Act and 8 CFR 208.20.

| Print Complete Name | Write your name in your native alphabet |
|---|---|
| Luiz Manuel Romero | n/a |

Did your spouse, parent, or child(ren) assist you in completing this application?    ☒ No  ☐ Yes *(If "Yes," list the name and relationship.)*

_____   _____        _____   _____
*(Name)*                              *(Relationship)*                                      *(Name)*                         *(Relationship)*

Did someone other than your spouse, parent, or child(ren) prepare this application?    ☒ No  ☐ Yes *(If "Yes," complete Part E)*

Asylum applicants may be represented by counsel. Have you been provided with a list of persons who may be available to assist you, at little or no cost, with your asylum claim?    ☐ No  ☒ Yes

Signature of Applicant *(The person in Part A. I.)*

[ *Luiz Manuel Romero* ]                                        December 12, 2002
Sign your name so it all appears within the brackets                              Date *(Mo/Day/Yr)*

## PART E.    DECLARATION OF PERSON PREPARING FORM IF OTHER THAN APPLICANT, SPOUSE, PARENT OR CHILD

I declare that I have prepared this application at the request of the person named in Part D, that the responses provided are based on all information of which I have knowledge, or which was provided to me by the applicant and that the completed application was read to the applicant in his or her native language or a language he or she understands for verification before he or she signed the application in my presence. I am aware that the knowing placement of false information on the Form I-589 may also subject me to civil penalties under 8 U.S.C. 1324(c).

| Signature of Preparer | | Print Complete Name | | |
|---|---|---|---|---|
| Daytime Telephone Number (     ) | | Address of Preparer: Street Number and Name | | |
| Apt. No. | City | | State | ZIP Code |

## PART F.    TO BE COMPLETED AT INTERVIEW OR HEARING

*You will be asked to complete this Part when you appear before an Asylum Officer of the Immigration and Naturalization Service (INS), or an Immigration Judge of the Executive Office for Immigration Review (EOIR) for examination.*

I swear (affirm) that I know the contents of this application that I am signing, including the attached documents and supplements, that they are all true to the best of my knowledge taking into account correction(s) numbered _____ to _____ that were made by me or at my request.

Signed and sworn to before me by the above named applicant on:

_____                    _____
Signature of Applicant                                          Date *(Mo/Day/Yr)*

_____                    _____
Write Your Name in Your Native Alphabet                    Signature of Asylum Officer or Immigration Judge

Form I-589 (Rev. 10/18/01)N Page 9

## FORM I-589 (PAGE 10)

OMB No. 1115-0086

SUPPLEMENT A FORM I-589

| A # *(If available)* | Date |
|---|---|
| Applicant's Name | Applicant's Signature |

**LIST ALL OF YOUR CHILDREN, REGARDLESS OF AGE OR MARITAL STATUS.**
*(Use this form and attach additional pages and documentation as needed to your application if you have more than four (4) children.)*

| 1. Alien Registration Number (A#)*(If any)* | 2. Passport/ID Card No. *(If any)* | 3. Marital Status *(Married, Single, Divorced, Widowed)* | 4. Social Security No. *(If any)* |
|---|---|---|---|
| 5. Complete Last Name | 6. First Name | 7. Middle Name | 8. Date of Birth *(Mo/Day/Yr)* |
| 9. City and Country of Birth | 10. Nationality *(Citizenship)* | 11. Race, Ethnic or Tribal Group | 12. Sex ☐ Male ☐ Female |

13. Is this child in the U.S.? ☐ Yes *(Complete blocks 14 to 21.)* ☐ No *(Specify Location)*

| 14. Place of last entry in the U.S.? | 15. Date of last entry in the U.S.? *(Mo/Day/Yr)* | 16. I-94 No. *(If any)* | 17. Status when last admitted *(Visa type, if any)* |
|---|---|---|---|
| 18. What is your child's current status? | 19. What is the expiration date of his/her authorized stay, if any? *(Mo/Day/Yr)* | 20. Is your child in immigration court proceedings? ☐ Yes ☐ No | |

21. If in the U.S., is this child to be included in this application? *(Check the appropriate box.)*
 ☐ Yes *(Attach one (1) photograph of your child in the upper right hand corner of page 9 on the extra copy of the application submitted for this person.)*
 ☐ No

| 1. Alien Registration Number (A#)*(If any)* | 2. Passport/ID Card No. *(If any)* | 3. Marital Status *(Married, Single, Divorced, Widowed)* | 4. Social Security No. *(If any)* |
|---|---|---|---|
| 5. Complete Last Name | 6. First Name | 7. Middle Name | 8. Date of Birth *(Mo/Day/Yr)* |
| 9. City and Country of Birth | 10. Nationality *(Citizenship)* | 11. Race, Ethnic or Tribal Group | 12. Sex ☐ Male ☐ Female |

13. Is this child in the U.S.? ☐ Yes *(Complete blocks 14 to 21.)* ☐ No *(Specify Location)*

| 14. Place of last entry in the U.S.? | 15. Date of last entry in the U.S.? *(Mo/Day/Yr)* | 16. I-94 No. *(If any)* | 17. Status when last admitted *(Visa type, if any)* |
|---|---|---|---|
| 18. What is your child's current status? | 19. What is the expiration date of his/her authorized stay, if any? *(Mo/Day/Yr)* | 20. Is your child in immigration court proceedings? ☐ Yes ☐ No | |

21. If in the U.S., is this child to be included in this application? *(Check the appropriate box.)*
 ☐ Yes *(Attach one (1) photograph of your child in the upper right hand corner of page 9 on the extra copy of the application submitted for this person.)*
 ☐ No

# FORM I-589 (PAGE 11)

OMB No. 1115-0086
**SUPPLEMENT B FORM I-589**

**ADDITIONAL INFORMATION ABOUT YOUR CLAIM TO ASYLUM.**

| A # *(If available)* | Date |
|---|---|
| Applicant's Name | Applicant's Signature |

*Use this as a continuation page for any information requested.  Please copy and complete as needed.*

**PART** _____

**QUESTION** _____

# 22

# GROUNDS OF INADMISSIBILITY

## Sorry, You're Not Welcome Here

The U.S. government has decided that people with certain histories or conditions are a risk to others and therefore should not be allowed to enter the country. These people are called inadmissible. Inadmissibility creates problems in green card applications. This chapter explains the conditions that make a person inadmissible—and whether there is any way around the ban of inadmissibility.

## A. INADMISSIBILITY DEFINED

There are many reasons why the U.S. government considers that a person may not be welcome in the United States. Each of these reasons represents a different category of inadmissibility. The list includes affliction with various physical and mental disorders, commission of crimes and participation in terrorist or subversive activity.

You may be judged inadmissible any time after you have filed an application for a green card, nonimmigrant visa or status. Even a permanent resident who departs the United States for more than 180 days may be found inadmissible on her return.

If you are found inadmissible, your immigration application will be denied. The notice of denial will be issued in the same manner as denials for any other reason. Even if you manage to hide your inadmissibility long enough to receive a green card or visa and be admitted into the U.S., if the problem is discovered later, you can be removed or deported.

## B. THE POSSIBILITY OF WAIVING INADMISSIBILITY

Just because you fall into one of the categories of inadmissibility does not mean you are absolutely barred from getting a green card or otherwise entering the United States. Some grounds of inadmissibility may be legally excused or waived. Others may not. Below is a chart summarizing all the grounds of inadmissibility, whether or not a waiver is available, and the special conditions you must meet to get a waiver. For more detail, see I.N.A. §212, 8 U.S.C. §1182.

## INADMISSIBILITY

| GROUND OF INADMISSIBILITY | WAIVER AVAILABLE | CONDITIONS OF WAIVER |
|---|---|---|
| **Health Problems** | | |
| People with communicable diseases. The most common diseases are tuberculosis and HIV (AIDS). | Yes | A waiver is available to an individual who is the spouse or the unmarried son or daughter or the unmarried minor lawfully adopted child of a U.S. citizen or permanent resident, or of an alien who has been issued an immigrant visa; or to an individual who has a son or daughter who is a U.S. citizen, or a permanent resident, or an alien issued an immigrant visa, upon compliance with BCIS's terms and regulations. |
| People with physical or mental disorders which threaten the property, welfare and safety of themselves or others. | Yes | Special conditions required by BCIS, at its discretion. |
| Drug abusers or addicts. | No | |
| People who fail to show that they have been vaccinated against certain vaccine-preventable diseases. | Yes | The applicant must show either that he or she subsequently received the vaccine; that the vaccine is medically inappropriate as certified by a civil surgeon; or that having the vaccine administered is contrary to the applicant's religious beliefs or moral convictions. |
| **Criminal and Related Violations** | | |
| People who have committed crimes involving moral turpitude. | Yes | Waivers are not available for commission of crimes such as attempted murder or conspiracy to commit murder or murder, torture or drug crimes, or for people previously admitted as permanent residents, if they have been convicted of aggravated felony since such admission or if they have less than seven years of lawful continuous residence before deportation proceedings are initiated aginst them. Waivers for all other offenses are available only if the applicant is a spouse, parent or child of a U.S. citizen or green cardholder; or the only criminal activity was prostitution; or the actions occurred more than 15 years before the application for a visa or green card is filed and the alien shows that he or she is rehabilitated and is not a threat to U.S. security. |
| People with two or more criminal convictions. | Yes | |
| Prostitutes or procurers of prostitutes. | Yes | |
| Diplomats or others involved in serious criminal activity who have received immunity from prosecution. | Yes | |
| Drug offenders. | No | However, there may be an exception for a first and only offense or for juvenile offenders. There's also a waiver for simple possession of less than 30 grams of marijuana. |
| Drug traffickers. | No | |
| Immediate family members of drug traffickers who knowingly benefited from their illicit money within the last five years. | No | But note that the problem "washes out" after five years. |

## INADMISSIBILITY

| GROUND OF INADMISSIBILITY | WAIVER AVAILABLE | CONDITIONS OF WAIVER |
| --- | --- | --- |
| **National Security and Related Violations** | | |
| Spies, governmental saboteurs, violators of export or technology transfer laws. | No | |
| People intending to overthrow the U.S. government. | No | |
| Terrorists and members or representatives of foreign terrorist organizations. | No | |
| People whose entry would have adverse consequences for U.S. foreign policy, unless the applicant is an official of a foreign government, or the applicant's activities or beliefs would normally be lawful in the U.S., under the constitution. | No | |
| Members of totalitarian parties. | Yes | An exception is made if the membership was involuntary, or is or was when the applicant was under 16 years old, by operation of law, or for purposes of obtaining employment, food rations or other "essentials" of living. An exception is also possible for past membership if the membership ended at least two years prior to the application (five years if the party in control of a foreign state is considered a totalitarian dictatorship). If neither applies, a waiver is available for an immigrant who is the parent, spouse, son, daughter, brother or sister of a U.S. citizen, or a spouse, son or daughter of a permanent resident. |
| **Nazis** | No | |
| **Economic Grounds** | No | |
| Any person who, in the opinion of a BCIS, border, or consular official, is likely to become a "public charge," that is, receive public assistance or welfare in the United States. The official can consider factors such as the person's age, health, family and work history and previous use of public benefits | No | However, the applicant may cure the ground of inadmissibility by overcoming the reasons for it or obtaining an Affidavit of Support from a family member or friend. |
| Family-sponsored immigrants and employment-sponsored immigrants where a family member is the employment sponsor (or such a family member owns 5% of the petitioning business) whose sponsor has not executed an Affidavit of Support (Form I-864). | No | But an applicant may cure the ground of inadmissibility by subsequently satisfying affidavit of support requirements. |
| Nonimmigrant public benefit recipients (where the individual came as nonimmigrant and applied for benefits when he or she was not eligible or through fraud). Five-year bar to admissibility. | No | But ground of inadmissibility expires after five years. |

## INADMISSIBILITY

| GROUNDS OF INADMISSIBILITY | WAIVER AVAILABLE | CONDITIONS OF WAIVER |
| --- | --- | --- |
| **Labor Certifications & Employment Qualifications** | No | |
| People without approved labor certifications, if one is required in the category under which the green card application is made. | No | |
| Graduates of unaccredited medical schools, whether inside or outside of the U.S., immigrating to the U.S. in a Second or Third Preference category based on their profession, who have not both passed the foreign medical graduates exam and shown proficiency in English. (Physicians qualifying as special immigrants who have been practicing medicine in the U.S. with a license since January 9, 1978, are not subject to this exclusion.) | No | |
| Uncertified foreign healthcare workers seeking entry based on clinical employment in their field (but not including physicians). | No | But applicant may show qualifications by submitting a certificate from the Commission on Graduates of Foreign Nursing Schools or the equivalent. |
| **Immigration Violators** | | |
| People who entered in the U.S. without inspection by the U.S. border authorities. | Yes | Available for certain battered women and children who came to the U.S. escaping such battery or who qualify as self-petitioners. Also available for individuals who had visa petitions or labor certifications on file before January 14, 1998 or before April 30, 2001 if they were in the U.S. on December 21, 2000 ($1,000 penalty required for latter waiver). Does **not** apply to applicants outside of the U.S. |
| People who were deported after a hearing and seek admission within ten years. | Yes | Discretionary with BCIS. |
| People who have failed to attend removal (deportation) proceedings (unless they had reasonable cause for doing so). Five-year bar to reentry. | Yes | Discretionary with BCIS. |
| People who have been summarily excluded from the U.S. and again attempt to enter within five years. | Yes | Advance permission to apply for readmission. Discretionary with BCIS. |
| People who made misrepresentations during the immigration process. | Yes | The applicant must be the spouse or child of a U.S. citizen or green cardholder. A waiver will be granted if the refusal of admission would cause extreme hardship to that relative. Discretionary with BCIS. |
| People who made a false claim to U.S. citizenship. | No | |
| Individuals subject to a final removal (deportation) order under the Immigration and Naturalization Act §274C (Civil Document Fraud Proceedings). | Yes | Available to permanent residents who voluntarily left the U.S., and for those applying for permanent residence as immediate relatives or other family-based petitions if the fraud was committed solely to assist the person's spouse or child and provided that no fine was imposed as part of the previous civil proceeding. |

## INADMISSIBILITY

| GROUND OF INADMISSIBILITY | WAIVER AVAILABLE | CONDITIONS OF WAIVER |
| --- | --- | --- |
| Student visa abusers (person who improperly obtains F-1 status to attend a public elementary school or adult education program, or transfers from a private to a public program except as permitted). Five-year bar to admissibility. | No | |
| Certain individuals twice removed (deported) or removed after aggravated felony. Twenty-year bar to admissibility for those twice deported. | Yes | Discretionary with BCIS (advance permission to apply for readmission). |
| Individuals unlawfully present (time counted only after April 1, 1997 and after the age of 18). Presence for 180–364 days results in three-year bar to admissibility. Presence for 365 or more days creates ten-year bar to admissibility. Bars kick in only when the individual departs the U.S. and seeks reentry. | Yes | A waiver is provided for an immigrant who has a U.S. citizen or permanent resident spouse or parent to whom refusal of the application would cause extreme hardship. There is also a complex body of law concerning when a person's presence will be considered "lawful," for example, if one has certain applications awaiting decisions by the BCIS or is protected by battered spouse/child provisions of the immigration laws. |
| Individuals unlawfully present after previous immigration violations. (Applies to persons who were in the U.S. unlawfully for an aggregate period over one year, who subsequently reenter without being properly admitted. Also applies to anyone ordered removed who subsequently attempts entry without admission.) | No | A permanent ground of inadmissibility. However, after being gone for ten years an applicant can apply for permission to reapply for admission. |
| Stowaways. | No | |
| Smugglers of illegal aliens. | Yes | Waivable if the applicant was smuggling in people who were immediate family members at the time, and either is a permanent resident or is immigrating under a family-based visa petition as an Immediate Relative; the unmarried son or daughter of a U.S. citizen or permanent resident; or the spouse of a U.S. permanent resident. |

### Document Violations

| | | |
| --- | --- | --- |
| People without required current passports or visas. | No | Except limited circumstance waivers. Under new "summary removal" procedures, border officials may quickly deport people for five years who arrive without proper documents or make misrepresentations during the inspection process. |

### Draft Evasion and Ineligibility for Citizenship

| | | |
| --- | --- | --- |
| People who are permanently ineligible for citizenship. | No | |
| People who are draft evaders, unless they were U.S. citizens at the time of evasion or desertion. | No | |

### Miscellaneous Grounds

| | | |
| --- | --- | --- |
| Practicing polygamists. | No | |
| Guardians accompanying excludable aliens. | No | |
| International child abductors. (The exclusion does not apply if the applicant is a national of a country that signed the Hague Convention on International Child Abduction.) | No | |
| Unlawful voters (voting in violation of any federal, state or local law or regulation). | No | |
| Former U.S. citizens who renounced citizenship to avoid taxation. | No | |

## C. REVERSING AN INADMISSIBILITY FINDING

There are four ways to overcome a finding of inadmissibility. Each of them is discussed in some detail below.

- In the case of physical or mental illness only, you may be able to correct the condition. Some criminal grounds of inadmissibility can be removed by vacating or expunging the underlying criminal conviction.
- You can prove that you really don't fall into the category of inadmissibility the BCIS believes you do.
- You can prove that the accusations of inadmissibility against you are false.
- You can apply for a waiver of inadmissibility.

## 1. Correcting grounds of inadmissibility

If you have had a physical or mental illness that is a ground of inadmissibility and you have been cured of the condition by the time you submit your green card application, you will no longer be considered inadmissible for that reason. If the condition is not cured by the time you apply, with certain illnesses you can still get a waiver of inadmissibility.

## 2. Proving that inadmissibility does not apply

Proving that inadmissibility does not apply in your case is a method used mainly to overcome criminal and ideological grounds of inadmissibility. When dealing with criminal grounds of inadmissibility, it is very important to consider both the type of crime committed and the nature of the punishment to see whether your criminal activity really constitutes a ground of inadmissibility.

For example, with some criminal activity, only actual convictions are grounds of inadmissibility. If you have been charged with a crime and the charges were then dropped, you may not be inadmissible.

Another example involves crimes of moral turpitude. Crimes of moral turpitude are those showing dishonesty or basically immoral conduct. Committing an act that is considered a crime of moral turpitude can make you inadmissible, even if you have not been convicted.

Crimes with no element of moral turpitude, however, are often not considered grounds of inadmissibility. Laws differ from state to state on which crimes are considered to involve moral turpitude and which are not.

Other factors that may work to your benefit are:

- expungement laws that remove the crime from your record
- the length of the prison terms
- how long ago the crime was committed
- the number of convictions in your background
- conditions of plea bargaining, and
- available pardons.

Sometimes, a conviction can be erased or vacated if you can show it was unlawfully obtained or you were not advised of its immigration consequences.

Proving that a criminal ground of inadmissibility does not apply in your case is a complicated business. You need to have a firm grasp not only of immigration law, but also the technicalities of criminal law. If you have a criminal problem in your past, you may be able to get a green card, but not without the help of an experienced immigration lawyer. (See Chapter 31.)

## 3. Proving inadmissibility is incorrect

When your green card or nonimmigrant visa application is denied because you are found inadmissible, you can try to prove that the finding of inadmissibility is incorrect. For example, if a BCIS medical examination shows that you have certain medical problems, you can present reports from other doctors stating that the first diagnosis was wrong and that you are free of the problem condition. If you are accused of lying on a visa application, you can present evidence proving you told the truth, or that any false statements were made unintentionally.

## 4. Applying for a waiver

In many circumstances, you may be able to get a waiver of inadmissibility. By obtaining a waiver, you don't eliminate or disprove the ground of inadmissibility. Instead you ask the BCIS to overlook the problem and give you a green card or visa anyway.

All green card and visa application forms ask questions designed to find out if any grounds of inadmissibility apply in your case. When the answers to the questions on these forms clearly show that you are inadmissible, you may be authorized to begin applying for a waiver immediately on filing your application. In most cases, however, the Consulate or BCIS office insists on having your final visa interview before ruling that you are inadmissible. If the BCIS office or Consulate handling your case decides to wait until your final interview before finding you inadmissible, it will delay your ability to file for a waiver. This may delay your getting a green card or visa; waivers can take many months to process.

Once it is determined that a waiver is necessary, you will need to complete Form I-601 and pay a $195 filing fee. Note that if you file this with a U.S. Consulate abroad, you will have to wait for the Consulate to send your application to a BCIS office. The Consulate cannot approve the waiver.

Once again, there are many technical factors that control whether or not a waiver of inadmissibility is granted. If you want to get one approved, you stand the best chance of success by hiring a good immigration lawyer. (See Chapter 31.)

## D. NEW GROUNDS OF INADMISSIBILITY

The 1996 Immigration Reform law made many changes to the Immigration Code, most of them restrictive. Although it's been a few years since their passage, these continue to be among the most troublesome of the grounds of inadmissibility for many immigrants. Some of the grounds which have the most significant impact are summarized here.

### 1. Affidavit of support for family-based petitions

All family-based immigrants seeking permanent residence—and employment-based immigrants where the applicant's relatives submitted the visa petition or own at least 5% of the petitioning company—must now include an Affidavit of Support, Form I-864. (See Chapter 4, Sections A and B.) This form helps satisfy the requirement that an immigrant show he or she is not likely to become a public charge. Note that this form is not required for other employment-based petitions or nonimmigrant visas.

There are, however, limited exceptions to this requirement. If the immigrant will qualify for automatic U.S. citizenship upon becoming a permanent resident (discussed in Chapter 11), the I-864 is not necessary. Also, if the beneficiary has already worked in the U.S. for 40 or more work quarters as defined by Social Security (about ten years), Form I-864 is not required. Moreover, the beneficiary can count time worked by a parent while the beneficiary was under the age of 18 toward these 40 quarters.

The requirements for this Affidavit of Support are very different from those of its predecessor, Form I-134. The government can rely on the newer form to hold the sponsor responsible if the immigrant receives public benefits. And it is also enforceable by the immigrant-family member against the sponsor for support. Finally, it requires that the sponsor show that he or she has at least 125% of income for a similar family size, according to the federal Poverty Guidelines level.

Family-based immigrants who file Adjustment of Status or immigrant visa applications are required to have Form I-864 filed by the person who is sponsoring their immigrant petition. However, another person—a joint sponsor—may add income to the sponsor's if he or she meets the 125% income requirement for the household and is:

- willing to be jointly liable
- a U.S. legal permanent resident or citizen
- over 18 years old, and
- living in the United States.

The joint sponsor files a separate Affidavit of Support. Other household members may join their income to that of the primary sponsor to help reach the 125% level, but only if they have been living with the sponsor for six months and they agree to be jointly liable by filing Form I-864A, Contract Between Sponsor and Household Member. Personal assets of the sponsor or the immigrant—such as property, bank account deposits and personal property such as automobiles—may also be used to supplement the sponsor's income if the primary sponsor's actual income does not add up to 125% of the federal Poverty Guidelines income levels.

The requirements and paperwork burden of the Affidavit are complicated and substantial; most of the requirements are spelled out on the forms. If you have questions about your eligibility or the scope of your legal responsibility, consult an experienced immigration attorney. (See Chapter 31.)

### 2. Summary exclusion

Another law which has a drastic impact on individuals requesting to enter the United States is the summary exclusion law. This law empowers an inspector at the airport to exclude and deport you at your entry to the U.S. if:

- the inspector thinks you are making a misrepresentation about practically anything connected to your right to enter the U.S.—such as your purpose in coming, intent to return, prior immigration history or use of false documents, or
- you do not have the proper documentation to support your entry to the U.S. in the category you are requesting.

If the inspector excludes you, you may not request entry for five years, unless a special waiver is granted. For this reason, it is extremely important to understand the terms of your requested status and not make any misrepresentations.

If the inspector looks likely to summarily exclude you, you may request withdrawing your application to enter the U.S. to prevent having the five-year deportation order on your record. The inspector may allow you to do this in some cases.

### 3. Unlawful presence and the overstay bars

A new ground of inadmissibility applies to people who were unlawfully present in the United States for six months after April 1, 1997, who subsequently left and who now seek admission through Adjustment of Status or by applying for an immigrant or nonimmigrant visa. Such people are subject to a three-year waiting period; the period is ten years if they were unlawfully present for one year after April 1, 1997. (See Chapter 8.)

## 4. Bars to adjusting status

The rules concerning Adjustment of Status—or getting your green card in the U.S.—are somewhat complicated. In general, if you entered the U.S. properly—by being inspected by a border official—and maintained your nonimmigrant status, you can probably get your green card without leaving the United States. Most people who marry U.S. citizens can adjust their status even if they have fallen out of status or worked without authorization, as long as they did not enter without being properly inspected, as a crewman or stowaway. Those who marry U.S. citizens and who entered without inspection or as crewmen or stowaways need to use the grandfather clause. (See Chapter 8.)

Unfortunately, the grandfather clause only helps a few people who happened to be in the United States when certain laws were changed (in particular, a law known as §245(i)). Under the old laws, practically everyone had the right to stay in the United States to adjust their status, simply by paying a $1,000 penalty fee. But under the newer laws, paying this fee is no longer an option.

That means that many people who are just becoming eligible for green cards are in a trap. If they stay in the United States, the fact that they entered illegally or committed certain other violations means that they're not allowed to adjust their status to permanent resident within the United States. But if they leave the United States and attempt to apply for their green card through an overseas consulate, they may well face a three- or ten-year bar to returning to the United States, as punishment for their illegal stay.

If you believe you're in this trap, consult a lawyer to make sure, and to see if you might qualify for a waiver of the three- or ten-year bar. All refugees or political asylees can stay in the U.S. to adjust status. ■

# 23

# **VETERANS AND ENLISTEES**

## Green Card for Sinbad the Sailor

I have been a cook on the U.S. Navy ship *J.F. Kennedy* since 1985. I heard that the law may give me the right to get a green card. Is this true?

The Armed Forces Immigration Adjustment Act of 1991 was enacted to recognize "the patriotism and valor of aliens who, by virtue of their military service, have clearly demonstrated a commitment to support and defend the Constitution and laws of the United States."

This Act favors aliens who entered military service under the United States flag by special agreements between the U.S. and the Philippines, Micronesia, the Marshall Islands and Palau. Most of those who enlisted under this executive agreement are in the U.S. Navy and are from the Philippines.

## A. WHO QUALIFIES

In general, the law allows two classes of alien military personnel to get permanent residence—and then gives green cards under the classification of Special Immigrant.

The spouse and minor children under 21 years of age who are joining or accompanying the veteran or enlistee are also entitled to immigrant visas.

### 1. Veterans

An alien veteran of the U.S. Armed Forces can apply for permanent residence if he or she:
- has served honorably
- has served on active duty
- has served after October 15, 1978
- is recommended for a Special Immigrant visa by the U.S. Armed Forces or Navy officer under whom he or she serves
- originally enlisted outside the United States
- has served for an aggregate of 12 years, and
- was honorably discharged when separated from the service.

### 2. Enlistees

An alien enlistee in the U.S. Armed Forces can apply for permanent residence if he or she:
- originally enlisted outside the United States for six years
- is on active duty when applying for Adjustment of Status under this law, and
- has re-enlisted for another six years, giving a total of 12 years active duty service, and

- is recommended for a Special Immigrant visa by the U.S. Armed Forces or Navy officer under whom he or she serves.

---

**A BREAK FOR ILLEGAL WORKERS**

Because of this special law for alien members of the U.S. Armed Forces, the Act allows the applicant—and his or her spouse and children—to get permanent residence even if they may have worked illegally in the United States.

---

## B. HOW TO FILE

The following forms must be completed and filed, along with a filing fee of $130 for the application and $50 for fingerprints in money order or certified check made payable to the BCIS:
- Form I-360, Petition for Amerasian, Widow or Special Immigrant. (See sample at the end of Chapter 13.)
- Form N-426, Request for Certification for Military or Naval Service
- Form G-325A/G-325B, Biographic Information
- certification of past active duty status of 12 years for the veteran or certified proof of reenlistment after six years of active duty service for the enlistee, issued by an authorized Armed Forces official, and
- birth certificate of the applicant to show that he or she is a national of the country which has an agreement with the United States allowing the enlistment of its nationals in the U.S. Armed Forces.

These papers have to be filed with either:
- the BCIS office having jurisdiction over the veteran or enlistee's current residence or intended place of residence in the United States, or
- with the overseas BCIS office having jurisdiction over the residence abroad.

If the veteran is in the U.S., he may apply directly for Adjustment of Status (see Chapter 8) and so may the spouse and children under 21 years of age. Form I-360 and accompanying materials should be included with the rest of the Adjustment of Status application.

If the spouse and children are outside the United States, the veteran or enlistee may file Form I-824, Application for Action on an Approved Application or Petition, to be sent to the U.S. Consulate where the spouse and children will apply for immigrant visas as derivative relatives of a Special Immigrant.

## C. FAILING TO SERVE SIX YEARS

The BCIS will automatically revoke the petition and bar the enlistee from getting a green card if he or she:

- fails to complete the period of reenlistment, or
- receives other than an honorable discharge.

The enlistee's spouse and children will also be barred from getting green cards. If any of them already have green cards, the BCIS will begin proceedings to have them taken away.

## D. BECOMING A U.S. CITIZEN

When the Adjustment of Status is granted, the BCIS should remind the veteran or enlistee that he or she is eligible to apply for citizenship immediately because of active service.

Those who want to be American citizens should obtain Form N-400 Application for Naturalization and file it as soon as possible. The BCIS will speed up the interview schedule for members of the military.

But if the alien war veteran has honorably and actively served the U.S. military in a time of war or conflict, he or she is exempt from all green card requirements and qualifies for immediate citizenship. This special benefit depends, however, on the war or conflict in which the veteran fought under the U.S. Armed Forces. It includes:

- World War I
- World War II, specifically between September 1, 1939, and December 31, 1946. A special provision was signed into law extending anew the Filipino war veterans' rights to U.S. citizenship. This special provision allows Filipino war veterans to file applications for citizenship until February 3, 2001.
- the Korean War, specifically between June 25, 1950, and July 1, 1955
- the Vietnam War, specifically between February 28, 1961, and October 15, 1978
- the Persian Gulf Conflict, specifically between August 2, 1990, and April 11, 1991, and
- the "war against terrorists" that began on September 11, 2001 and will end on a date to be determined by the U.S. President.

To file for naturalization, you must file the following forms and documents with the BCIS together with a $260 filing fee plus $50 for fingerprints:

- Form N-400, Application for Citizenship
- Form N-426, Request for Certification for Military or Naval Service
- Form G-325A/G-325B, Biographic Information, and
- two photographs. ■

# 24

## GETTING AMNESTY

## Forgetting the Past

One of the more important parts of the law that the U.S. Congress passed in 1986 was a section which "forgave" some of those who came to the United States illegally by granting them permanent residence. The law—the Immigration Reform and Control Act (IRCA)—was commonly known as the Amnesty Law. Applicants had to prove they had been physically in the United States as of January 1, 1982.

Most, but not all of the 1986 Amnesty applicants have had their cases decided, so this chapter does not cover this type of amnesty in detail.

However, in 1997, a new type of amnesty law was passed by Congress, known as "NACARA," discussed below.

**If you participated in one of the Amnesty class action lawsuits against the BCIS, you may be eligible for a green card.** In December 2000, Congress tried to help close the 1986 Amnesty cases once and for all by missing the "LIFE Act," making certain applicants eligible for permanent residence. If your case remains undecided, or if you were a member of the "CSS," "LULAC" or "Zambrano" class, see a lawyer immediately. You'll still need to prove that you were eligible for Amnesty and are not inadmissible. The application deadline is June 4, 2003.

In addition, class members of the Proyecto San Pablo litigation (which obtained a right to amnesty for people formerly denied because they had been deported between January 1, 1982, and the date of filing their application) can apply for their case to be reopened for a decision. However, the deadline is one year from the date they receive a notice from the BCIS advising them of this opportunity. Again, see an attorney if you think you might qualify—even if you haven't received a notice from the BCIS.

## A. THE NICARAGUAN ADJUSTMENT AND CENTRAL AMERICAN RELIEF ACT

While not exactly an amnesty program, Congress passed legislation in December of 1997 called the Nicaraguan Adjustment and Central American Relief Act (NACARA). The purpose of this law was to provide permanent resident status to Nicaraguans, Cubans, certain nationals of Guatemala, El Salvador and the former Soviet Bloc countries. The deadlines to apply have all passed.

### 1. Nicaraguans and Cubans

An individual who is a national of Cuba or Nicaragua must have been physically present continuously in the United States starting December 1, 1995, and cannot have been outside the country more than a total of 180 days. The spouse of an individual granted permanent residence under this procedure also qualifies for permanent residence, as do their unmarried children under 21 years old, even if they do not meet the requirements themselves.

An unmarried child over 21 years old may also qualify for permanent residence if the parent was granted a green card under this part of the law, but only if the child was continuously present in the United States beginning on or before December 1, 1995.

The applicants must also show that they are otherwise admissible to the United States; in other words, that none of the grounds of inadmissibility apply to them—or if they could be excluded based on a criminal conviction, that they have applied for and been granted a waiver (see Chapter 22).

**Note:** The law allows these people to become permanent residents through this procedure even if they had been ordered removed from the United States, were ordered excluded or failed to depart when they were told to. They must only meet the requirements described below and have filed their application before April 1, 2000.

Certain grounds of inadmissibility which apply to most green card applicants will not apply to NACARA applicants, including:

- being a public charge
- the need for labor certification
- being present in the United States without having been admitted or paroled
- the requirement that the person entered the U.S. with a valid visa or other documents
- being lawfully present (the three- and ten-year bars resulting from six or twelve months of unlawful presence after April 1, 1997), and
- having reentered after a prior order of deportation or removal.

### a. Proving continuous physical presence

Although the law requires proof of "continuous physical presence" since December 1, 1995, it allows a person to take advantage of the NACARA program even if they have been outside the United States for as many as 180 days between December 1, 1995, and the date of the application. In addition, if you must leave the United States before your application has been approved, you must get permission before leaving by requesting Advance Parole. It is best that you consult with a lawyer if you are having difficulty or have questions about getting Advance Parole.

To prove you were here before December 2, 1995, you can show:

- an earlier asylum application on file with the INS (now called the BCIS)
- an order to appear for a deportation hearing or at an immigration court before December 2, 1995, and that the date of your entry into the United States was accepted as valid by the hearing officer or immigration judge
- an earlier application for adjustment of status or employment authorization
- proof of employment or business ownership or payment of Social Security taxes.
- tax documents—such as W-2 forms, wage statements, rental agreements or utility bills— that show you were in the United States.
- an earlier application for immigration benefits
- a passport stamp, or
- any other evidence that you can think of to prove you were in the United States before December 2, 1995.

Once again, common sense should help you here. The law does not say how you must support your claim that you did not leave the United States. State or local government documents with your name and date on them may be enough. A college transcript or an employment record may show that an applicant attended school or worked in the United States throughout the entire post–December 1, 1995, period. If you were actually here according to the requirements of the statute, the law will not require that you prove that you were here for every single day since December 2, 1995, but there should be no significant chronological gaps in the documentation, either. Generally, a gap of three months or less in documentation is not considered significant. Furthermore, if you are relying on documents in the INS or BCIS files, then all you will need to do is list those.

## b. When and how to apply

The application period for NACARA benefits ended March 31, 2000. Each applicant must have filed Form I-485 along with the required filing fee (at that time, $220 for applicants

14 years or older and $160 for an applicant under 14 years of age) and the supporting documents described below. In Part 2 of the form (Application Type), NACARA applicants should have checked box "h" and written "NACARA— Principal" or "NACARA—Dependent" next to that box. Each application must also have included:

- a birth certificate or other record of birth
- two photographs
- a completed Biographic Information sheet (Form G-325A) if the applicant is between 14 and 79 years of age
- a medical examination report
- If the applicant is 14 years old or older, a local police clearance from each jurisdiction where the alien has resided for six months or longer since arriving in the United States
- a copy of the applicant's Arrival-Departure Record (Form I-94) or other evidence of inspection and admission or parole into the United States
- one or more of the documents described in Section a above to prove continuous physical presence in the United States, and
- a statement outlining all departures from and arrivals in the United States since December 1, 1995.

Finally, if the person applied as the spouse or unmarried child of another NACARA beneficiary, the applicant must have submitted evidence of the relationship (for example, a marriage certificate).

## c. Applicants in removal proceedings

An immigration judge cannot order an eligible applicant deported while he or she has a pending NACARA application on file.

## 2. Guatemalans, El Salvadorans and certain Eastern Europeans

The NACARA law also contains provisions that allow certain Guatemalans, Salvadorans and nationals of former Soviet Bloc countries to apply for suspension of deportation (now called "cancellation of removal") under the more liberal rules that existed before the 1996 immigration law changes.

### a. Special cancellation of removal

In addition to providing special relief for Nicaraguans and Cubans, NACARA allowed certain Guatemalans, El Salvadorans and Eastern Europeans to become permanent residents upon showing good moral character and extreme hardship to the applicant or a qualifying family member, as well as the characteristics described below. In short, the law allows people from these countries who meet the requirements to apply for permanent residence regardless of whether they are in removal proceedings.

### b. Qualifications

The following groups of people may still qualify for permanent residence under the old suspension rules.

**Salvadoran ABC (American Baptist Church) or TPS (Temporary Protected Status) Registrants Present Since 1990.** Salvadoran nationals who entered the U.S. on or before September 19, 1990, and who have registered for ABC benefits under that class action lawsuit or for Temporary Protected Status (TPS) on or before October 31, 1991. (Under the requirements of the ABC settlement an El Salvadoran was required to submit an asylum application on or before February 16, 1996.)

**Guatemalan ABC Registrants.** Guatemalan nationals who entered the U.S. on or before October 1, 1990, and who registered for ABC benefits on or before December 31, 1991. (Under the requirements of the ABC settlement a Guatemalan was required to submit an asylum application on or before January 3, 1995.)

**Salvadoran or Guatemalan Asylum Applicants.** Salvadorans or Guatemalans who applied for asylum on or before April 1, 1990.

**Nationals of East Bloc Countries.** Individuals who entered the U.S. before December 31, 1990, who filed an application for asylum on or before December 31, 1991, and who were at the time of filing a national of the Soviet Union, Russia, any Republic of the former Soviet Union, Estonia, Latvia, Lithuania, Poland, Czechoslovakia, Romania, Hungary, Bulgaria, Albania, East Germany, Yugoslavia or any state of the former Yugoslavia.

### c. Spouses and children

Spouses and children of an individual who is granted cancellation or suspension under the provisions described above also qualify for permanent residence under NACARA. Unmarried children who are over 21 years old whose parent was granted suspension or cancellation must have entered the U.S. before October 1, 1990, to qualify on the basis of a grant of cancellation of removal to their parents.

## B. Preparing the Application for Cancellation of Removal

All applicants who have not yet filed for NACARA benefits with the BCIS will be required to use Form I-881 (Application for Suspension of Deportation or Special Rule Cancellation of Removal). The fee is $215 per person, with a $430 limit per family, if all members file applications at the same time. (A family is defined as a husband, a wife and unmarried children under 21.)

Applications submitted to the Immigration Court (because the person was in removal proceedings) will be charged a single $100 fee for adjudication by the Immigration Court (a single fee of $100 will be charged whenever applications are filed by one or more people in the same family in the same proceedings).

The $100 fee will not be required if the Form I-881 is later referred to the Immigration Court by the INS because it denied the request.

Every applicant over the age of 14 is required to pay $50 for fingerprinting. Applicants may file a fee waiver—however these requests in the past have caused significant delays in processing.

**Note:** An applicant who used Form EOIR-40 (Application for Suspension of Deportation) before June 21, 1999, may apply for NACARA benefits by filling out the first page of Form I-881 and attaching their completed Form EOIR-40 along with any supporting documents. The application must be filed at the regional BCIS Service Center indicated on the Form.

### 1. Proving your case

Aliens who meet the requirements as ABC class members (see Section A2b, above) should not have to prove again that they are eligible for NACARA status because of extreme hardship (although all other aliens filing under NACARA will need to show evidence of extreme hardship). For these people, it is up to the BCIS to show why extreme hardship has not been presented. Still, it is strongly recommended that every applicant prepare evidence of the hardships they or their family members would face if deported. Remember that the problems that deportation alone would cause are not enough to establish hardship.

You should prepare as much of the following information as possible:

- The age of the people in the application or immediate family members who may be U.S. citizens or permanent residents, both at the time of entry to the United States and at the time of application for the benefit
- The age, number and immigration status of the people who face the possibility of deportation (it is helpful to show how the limited ability of any children to speak the native language and adjust to life in the country might make things more difficult for them)
- The health condition of the persons who might be required to leave the U.S., including the children, spouse or parents, and the availability of any required medical treatment in the country to which the alien would be returned
- The possibility of obtaining employment in the country to which the people would be returned
- The length of residence in the United States
- The existence of other family members who are or will be legally residing in the United States
- The financial impact of the alien's departure
- The impact of a disruption of educational opportunities
- The psychological impact of being forced to leave the United States
- The current political and economic conditions in the country to which the person would be returned
- The lack of family and other ties to the country to which the people would be returned
- Contributions to and ties to a community in the United States, including the degree of integration into society
- Immigration history, including authorized residence in the United States, and
- The availability of other means of adjusting to permanent resident status.

## C. IF YOU ARE NOT IN REMOVAL PROCEEDINGS

Aliens with asylum claims pending before the BCIS will have their petitions decided by the asylum office. If they are denied relief, the BCIS will probably begin removal proceedings. Then, they will be allowed to make their case before an immigration judge. If an alien's claim was already before an immigration judge, but has been "administra-

tively closed" or "continued" to allow the person to file under NACARA, the person can elect to have their case initially determined by an asylum officer. If the asylum office rejects their claim, it can be renewed before the immigration court.

 **WARNING**

It is important that you not go to the BCIS before making sure that you qualify for this relief, because if you are not part of the group of persons intended to receive this benefit you could, in effect, cause your own deportation. See an immigration attorney if you have any questions about this issue.

## D. IF YOU ARE IN REMOVAL PROCEEDINGS

Most people who are in removal proceedings will have their claims for adjustment of status under NACARA heard by an immigration judge. However, some people may file their applications for NACARA with the BCIS, which could be a better strategy because it allows the applicant to renew the application before an immigration judge if the BCIS rejects it. People who can file before the BCIS include:

- registered ABC class members whose proceedings before the Immigration Court or the Board of Immigration Appeals were administratively closed or who filed and were granted motions to reopen
- qualified family member of an individual who has a NACARA application pending with the INS, or a person who has been granted relief under NACARA.

People in the second group may ask the court to close the proceedings before the Immigration Court in order to apply with the BCIS.

 **CONSULT AN EXPERT**

Due to the complexity of the NACARA application procedures, it is probably best to seek advice from an experienced attorney or other individual to represent you. (See Chapter 31.) Many volunteer and nonprofit organizations are also active in offering assistance with NACARA applications.

**If You Have an "Aggravated" Felony Conviction**

Anyone who has been convicted of an "aggravated felony" should not apply for NACARA benefits without first seeing an attorney. The attorney can help you try to vacate the judgment or decide whether he can argue that the felony you were convicted of was not actually an "aggravated" crime. The definition of "aggravated" is very complex and arguments to attack the conviction generally should be made by an experienced lawyer.

**NACARA Is Not the Only Way**

Any person not legally in the U.S. who is fighting their removal from the United States and does not qualify for NACARA—because they did not register for ABC benefits or file for asylum—may still be able to remain in the U.S. For example, if they have been in the United States for ten years, and were caught in August 1999, they would be able to argue that they are eligible to apply for cancellation of removal under the current law, assuming that they meet the requirements of exceptional and extremely unusual hardship to the alien's spouse, parent or child, who is a U.S. citizen or an alien lawfully admitted for permanent residence. The same is true for Guatemalans, El Salvadorans or Eastern Europeans with criminal or fraud convictions. They can win permanent residence if they can prove they have been in the U.S. for ten years and that their removal would cause them or their U.S. or lawful permanent resident spouse and/or children exceptional and extremely unusual hardship.

■

# 25

# REGISTRY: FOR THOSE IN THE U.S. SINCE 1972

## Green Cards for Old-Timers

My husband and I have been here since 1968 on a diplomatic visa and have since left government service. When the amnesty came in 1986, I applied for a green card but my husband did not want to because he was afraid that the immigration authorities would still go after him and deport him. Now it is too late for him to apply for amnesty.

Although I have already petitioned for him, his Priority Date is far off and it may take several years before he gets his green card. He would like to visit his aging parents. If he leaves without a green card, he may not be given a tourist visa to come back here. Does he have any recourse?

If you are one of the few people who, for one reason or another, did not take advantage of amnesty, and if you have been living continuously in the United States since January 1, 1972, you have one final avenue available to get a green card. It is called Registry.

Congress has been talking about moving the January 1, 1972 eligibility date forward. Keep your eye on Nolo's website for updates.

## A. How You Got Here Is Irrelevant

You can apply for Registry no matter how you entered the United States and no matter what your current immigration status. For example, it doesn't matter that you crossed the border from Mexico, or that you came as a tourist for the World's Fair and stayed longer than your visa allowed, or that you were a transit passenger on your way to London. You won't be barred from registering if you cannot find your passport showing your date of entry, or if the BCIS cannot find its own records of your entry.

Although you normally would be denied a green card if you entered the U.S. without inspection by a border official, or if you were transit passengers or stowaways, this applica-

tion is special. In a sense, you are being rewarded for having been able to stay for so long without getting in trouble with the U.S. government.

## B. Short Absences Allowed

If you went for a short trip across the Mexican border or took a month's vacation in your home country, your departure will probably not be considered an interruption of your continuous residence in the United States.

Such absence must be "brief, casual and innocent." This means that you must have done nothing either before or during your absence to show that you intended to abandon your residence in the United States.

Of course, if you quit your job, gave up the lease on your apartment, were feted at good-bye parties, stopped paying your bills and left the United States with all your belongings, your departure is no longer casual or innocent, however brief it may have been. If there is enough evidence that you intended to leave permanently, the BCIS is likely to deny your Registry application because you interrupted your continuous residence in the United States.

 **Medical Personnel Beware**

Foreign medical graduates who have come to the United States on a J-1 visa and who must fulfill the two-year home country residence requirement, and other foreign medical graduates, may encounter resistance from the BCIS in applying for Registry. If you are in this situation, seek legal counsel before proceeding. (See Chapter 31.)

## C. How to File

There is no immigration form specifically for Registry. To file, you must complete Form I-485, Adjustment of Status (as explained in detail in Chapter 8).

## D. Additional Documentation Required

Registry is basically a paper chase. Simply saying that you have lived in the United States since January 1, 1972—without providing any documents to substantiate your testimony and those of your witnesses—is useless. To prove your continuous residence in the United States, you must submit as many of the following documents as possible:

- your passport and Form I-94, which shows your date of arrival into the United States
- any certificate issued by the government showing birth, death or marriage of any member of your immediate family in the United States
- any government-issued license, such as a driver's license, business license, fishing license, car license or professional license
- lease to your apartment and business, rent receipts, or, if you owned your own home, title to your home, mortgage contract and deed of sale
- bills showing use of gas and electricity, telephone bills and fuel oil bills for each of your home addresses during the years you have been living in the United States
- bank statements, bank book, deposit box agreement or credit union savings account
- pay stubs, job identification card, union membership, W-2 forms, letters of recommendation from previous employers, daily attendance sheets and job memos addressed to you
- subscriptions to magazines and newspapers from health or private clubs, or similar proof of membership in a church or social organization that are in your name and mailed to your address
- any photos showing you at events that indicate precise dates, such as marriage or religious ceremonies, with invitations showing when and where they occurred
- medical and dental records
- credit card statements or statements from credit institutions showing payment of long-standing debts, such as car loans, student loans and vacation loans
- letters addressed to you with clear postmarks, and
- written statements from relatives, friends, employers, a pastor or a priest, a school officer or a police precinct attesting to the fact that you have lived continuously in the United States since January 1, 1972.

## E. APPROVAL OF REGISTRY

If you have concrete evidence that you have been living in the United States all these years, the BCIS will grant your application. You will be registered in the BCIS records as having entered the United States as a permanent resident as of January 1, 1972.

If you are unable to convince the BCIS of your long stay, and if the BCIS decides to start removal proceedings against you, you may wish to avail yourself of Cancellation of Removal relief. (See Chapter 26.) ■

# 26

# CANCELLATION OF REMOVAL

## Do Ten Illegal Years Equal One Green Card?

I arrived in the United States more than ten years ago. I fell in love with an American citizen and we were scheduled to get married when he died in a car accident. Eight months later, I gave birth to our son. I am managing to bring him up alone, although his father's parents help me with some financial support. My son is their only grandson, so they dote on him. I set up my own dry cleaning shop with the life insurance money I received as my late fiancé's beneficiary. I heard that after being in the United States for ten years, I could get a green card. How do I go about it?

Immigration law does provide a green card as a form of relief to a person who has been in the United States for more than ten years, but the process is long and arduous. This relief is called Cancellation of Removal; it was formerly called Suspension of Deportation. When granted, an alien immediately becomes a lawful permanent resident—and receives a green card soon after the court hearing.

This area of immigration law has changed drastically in recent years. The rules controlling who qualifies have become tougher since Congress passed changes in 1996. Some people can still qualify under the former, more flexible rules; others will only qualify if they meet the more restrictive rules passed more recently.

## A. CANCELLATION OF REMOVAL PROCEEDINGS

You cannot file an application to begin Cancellation of Removal with the BCIS directly, as you can other immigration applications. This process is available only when an alien is in immigration court, under removal proceedings. The only exception to this rule is for people who qualify for benefits under the Nicaraguan Adjustment and Central American Relief Act. (See Chapter 24.) Being in removal proceedings means that the BCIS has learned of your illegal status and has served you with a summons called a Notice to Appear, (which used to be called an Order to Show Cause). The notice is a formal order giving you the time, date and place to appear for a hearing on whether or not you should be deported by the U.S. government.

If the BCIS has not started a removal proceeding against you, you cannot file an application for Cancellation of Removal, except in the rare circumstance mentioned above. If there is no removal proceeding against you, you must turn yourself in to the BCIS—and it may then start removal proceedings against you. But you should not do this before consulting an experienced immigration attorney to be sure

you qualify for relief before turning yourself into the BCIS; and to assess the chances that the agency is likely to cooperate with you. More often, they just let your application sit in their files for years and years, perhaps waiting for the laws to turn against you.

Assuming that you have actually been in the United States for ten years, that you are of good moral character and that your deportation would cause hardship to your U.S. citizen and permanent resident family members, there is a chance that your application for Cancellation of Removal will be granted. If you were present in the United States for only seven years but the BCIS issued your Order to Show Cause after you accumulated those seven years, you may qualify for the old Suspension of Deportation which didn't require you to show hardship to your relatives.

 **CONSULT AN EXPERT**

It is very risky to ask to be placed in removal proceedings solely to request cancellation, because this relief is difficult to have granted. If you are contemplating turning yourself in to the BCIS, discuss your situation first with an immigration attorney who specializes in cancellation issues, an immigration law clinic or a group that specializes in counseling on immigration matters. (See Chapter 31.)

## B. WHO IS NOT ELIGIBLE FOR CANCELLATION

A number of aliens cannot apply for a Cancellation of Removal proceedings. They include:
- aliens who entered the United States as crewmen after June 30, 1964
- J-1 visa holders who have not fulfilled a two-year home country residency requirement if they are required to do so, and those who came to the U.S. to receive graduate medical education or training
- those who belong to certain categories of inadmissible aliens, including those who the U.S. government believes are coming to the U.S. to engage in espionage, unlawful activities to overturn the U.S. government, terrorist activities and those who have been members of totalitarian or some communist parties
- aliens who are deportable for offenses including national security, espionage, terrorism and foreign policy

- aliens who have participated in persecuting others
- certain people previously given relief from removal or deportation
- those who have been convicted of certain crimes involving morally bad conduct or illegal drugs
- those convicted of a crime involving morally bad conduct in the five years after being admitted to the U.S. if the crime may be punished by a sentence of one year or more
- those who have been convicted of certain offenses involving failure to comply with alien registration or change of address requirements, or who have been convicted of certain offenses involving document fraud
- those convicted of an aggravated felony. This includes murder, rape, sexual abuse of a minor, illegal trafficking in drugs or firearms, money laundering, crimes of violence, theft or burglary—or other offenses with possible prison terms of one year or more. If you have been convicted of a crime, get advice from an experienced attorney to see if you can clear your criminal record.

## C. Presenting a Convincing Case

If you decide that your best approach is to file for Cancellation of Removal, know in advance that you will have some difficult times ahead. Your first task will be to explain your situation to a lawyer—and convince him or her that you are eligible. In making your case, you must have strong evidence of several things. Before you consult with a lawyer, try to collect as many of the following documents as possible.

### 1. Proof of good moral character

You must show that you've been a person of good moral character for at least the last ten years. You may be able to secure a Certificate of Good Conduct from your local police station. This certificate will attest that, according to computer records, you have never been in trouble with the police. Although the BCIS will also send your fingerprints to the Federal Bureau of Investigation in Washington, D.C., submitting your own record from the local police will help prove to the court that you are a person of good moral character. You can also submit declarations from relatives, friends and community members verifying that you have participated in religious institutions, volunteered at schools or other civic places, or in any other way demonstrated that you are a good person.

If you have committed any serious crime during the ten years you were in the United States, the immigration judge may find that you lack good moral character. Ten years must pass from the time you committed the crime until the time you can apply for a suspension of deportation. However, committing certain serious crimes will make you ineligible forever.

### 2. Proof you stayed in the U.S. ten years

You must show also that you have lived in the United States continuously for at least ten years. A copy of your passport and the I-94 Record of Arrival and Departure which was attached to your passport when you first arrived in the United States are the best proof of this.

In addition, copies of your apartment lease, bank statements and copies of your income tax returns are good evidence that you have been in the United States for ten years. School and medical records, subscriptions and memberships and statements from friends, landlords or coworkers are also useful.

---

#### What Does "Continuous Physical Presence" Mean?

The court will consider that you have been continuously present in the U.S. even if you departed from the country—as long as your absences did not exceed more than 90 days per trip or 180 days total. There are exceptions for individuals who served honorably in the Armed Forces for at least two years. Also, the time that can be used toward the ten-year presence period will be cut short if the person commits an act that makes him or her deportable or inadmissible, or at the time the BCIS issues a Notice to Appear at Removal Proceedings.

---

### 3. Proof of hardship

You must convince the court that if you are deported from the United States, it would cause exceptional and extremely unusual hardship to your spouse, child or parent who is a U.S. citizen or a permanent resident. (The law in effect before 1996 allowed an individual to qualify by showing extreme hardship to himself or herself as well as to one of those family members, but this no longer works.)

Of course, if your spouse, parent or your adult child (21 or over) is an American citizen, you qualify as a candidate for an immigrant visa as an Immediate Relative or as a

Family Preference beneficiary (see Chapter 4). The relief of Cancellation of Removal is often a delaying tactic which your lawyer will resort to when, for some reason, you cannot immediately obtain your green card through any one of those Immediate Relatives.

Because the relief of Cancellation of Removal depends almost completely on the discretion of the judge, you can only hope for a judge who is compassionate and humane. You and your lawyer must convince the judge that leaving the United States and returning to your own country would cause exceptional and extremely unusual hardship for your family members due to any combination of personal, economic, socio-cultural and psychological reasons.

**Personal reasons.** The immigration court will need the birth certificate of your child, your marriage certificate and your own birth certificate if your parents are U.S. citizens or permanent residents who will suffer hardship should you leave the United States.

For starters, your relatives should be prepared to testify in court about how much you mean to them, how much they depend on you and how empty life would be for them if you were not allowed to remain in the United States. However, this sort of testimony is not enough by itself, since nearly every family would face similar pain. But the judge wants to see that the hardship your family would face is "exceptional and extremely unusual."

If your American children are under 14, the judge would normally not ask to hear their testimony. However, the testimony of such young children, detailing their affection for you and the hardships they would endure if they accompanied you to your native country—problems with language, problems being uprooted from friend and schools—could strengthen your case.

Although testimony by your young children that, as Americans, they would rather stay in the United States with their grandparents or with a foster family than leave for a country they don't know could be hurtful for you to hear, such testimony would be further evidence that your deportation would cause them hardship.

Proof that any illness for which you or a family member is being treated in the United States, and evidence that the same treatment or medicine is either lacking or too expensive in your own country should also be given to the judge, supported by letters from doctors and pharmacists in the United States and the foreign country.

Provided they are either U.S. citizens or permanent residents, more distant relatives—including the grandparents or the biological parent of your child, their aunts, uncles or cousins, or your own brothers and sisters—may all testify that your departure would also be an extreme hardship to them and to the family in general.

If you have a boyfriend or girlfriend who is married to somebody else, it is not recommended that he or she testify either on your behalf, or on behalf of the child he or she had with you. Although adultery has been repealed from immigration law as proof of the lack of good moral character, many judges will not look with favor upon such situations.

**Economic reasons.** Although you are probably earning much more in the United States than you would earn in your own country, economic reasons are the least persuasive arguments against deportation. Economic hardship by itself has never been considered by the immigration court as sufficient reason to cancel deportation.

If you are receiving welfare, government subsidies or any form of public assistance, you may have an even more difficult time receiving mercy from the judge. A judge is unlikely to grant you permission to stay in the United States permanently if you may be seen as a burden to the government.

Proof of regular and continuous employment is very important. Letters from your employers, past and present, detailing your employment history and your value as an employee; your most current pay stubs; and evidence of your work product, in the form of photos or newspaper articles are all useful in demonstrating your contribution to the economic life of the nation.

You should have filed income tax returns for the past ten years, so submit copies as proof. This will show that, except for your illegal immigration status, you have been law-abiding. If you have not filed any tax returns because you do not have a Social Security number or because you have always been paid in cash, you should consult a tax expert at once. You may have to pay back taxes.

If you are in business for yourself, submit a financial statement from an accountant to the court, along with incorporation papers showing you as the major or only stockholder; photos of your business in operation; a letter from your bank giving your account history and the average balance of your business account; and any savings, stocks and bonds certificates. Letters from your business partners and testimony in court explaining how the business would be affected if you were forced to leave it should also be presented during the hearing.

If you have invested in real estate, present proof of ownership, mortgage papers and a letter from a real estate broker concerning how much your property would be worth if sold in the present market and how much financial loss this would cause you.

Obtain a copy of your credit history from any of the national companies such as Experian, whose credit reports are consulted by banks. This will prove that you have no judgments pending from creditors.

**Socio-cultural reasons.** Convince the court that you are in good standing in your community. Present letters from your church, temple or mosque about your active membership, from your block or village association, from the Parent-Teachers' Association, from volunteer organizations and from people you have cared for or helped. All are important to show that your life in the United States has been intimately entwined with American society and that you have been a useful member of your community.

Letters from the union supervisor or from your co-workers explaining the kind of person you are and how valuable you are to them personally and in terms of work, are also persuasive documents to present to the judge.

The judge will want to know whether you have any other forms of relief from deportation, any pending petitions submitted on your behalf by a relative or an employer and why it is advantageous for the U.S. government to grant you permanent residence through an immediate Cancellation of Removal instead of waiting for the Priority Date of any other immigration petition that may be pending.

**Psychological reasons.** You will have to acquaint the judge with the social, cultural and political situation in your country and how your family may be subjected to prejudice, bigotry or ostracism.

If you have a child born outside of marriage, or who is of a different race or is physically handicapped, provide evidence of how such children are treated in your country. Explain how going back to your country would affect your emotional and psychological health, thereby affecting your U.S. citizen and permanent resident family members. Also explain how going back would directly affect the emotional or psychological health of any relative who is an American citizen or a permanent resident. Testimony from an expert witness, such as a psychiatrist or a psychologist, would bolster your case.

If you have a child who is a U.S. citizen, explain that his or her inability to speak the language of your native country and removing him or her from relatives, friends, classmates and school could cause great psychological shock for the child.

## D. How to File

You and your lawyer must submit the following documents to the immigration judge, along with a filing fee of $100:

- Form EOIR-42A (Application for Cancellation of Removal for Permanent Residents), or
- Form EOIR-42B (Application for Cancellation of Removal and Adjustment of Status for Certain Nonpermanent Residents)
- Form I-765, Application for Employment Authorization, with an additional filing fee of $120 (see the sample at the end of Chapter 8)

- Form G-325A, Biographic Information
- two color photographs taken within 30 days of submitting the application, and
- a $50 fingerprinting fee.

The immigration judge will set a hearing date for your case—time enough for you and your lawyer to prepare and for the BCIS to investigate your case, if it warrants an investigation. In the meantime, the BCIS should issue you a work permit within 60 days from the date you filed the application for Cancellation of Removal. Be sure that BCIS has your correct address.

The hearing may not finish the first day. In fact, it may be postponed one or more times because the immigration court devotes only a few hours at a time to each case on its calendar. Unless you are being detained at the immigration jail, or your lawyer is particularly insistent, your case may take one or two years before it is fully heard and a decision is reached.

## E. APPROVING YOUR APPLICATION

If the immigration judge approves your application for Cancellation of Removal, you will be granted permanent residence that day if there are still visa numbers available for the current year.

Because you have shown that you have lived a productive and useful life in the United States all those years that you were living illegally, and that your deportation would be extremely hard for your American or lawful permanent spouse, child or parents, the U.S. government wants you to remain in the United States legally.

---

### WINNING IS NOT ENOUGH

Even if an immigration judge decides to cancel your removal order, you could face a problem. Only 4,000 people each year are granted formal cancellation of removal. Immigration judges have the power to grant "conditional" or temporary cancellation of removal orders until the person becomes eligible. The removal proceedings will not be formally ended, and permanent residence will not be formally granted, until their waiting number is reached.

---

## F. ADDITIONAL FORMS OF CANCELLATION OF REMOVAL

There are two additional forms of cancellation of removal. One is for permanent residents (green cardholders) who have become deportable or removable. The other is for people who have been subjected to extreme cruelty or battery by a spouse or parent who is a U.S. citizen or permanent resident while in the United States.

### 1. Permanent residents

An immigration judge may cancel the removal of, and grant a green card to, a permanent resident if the person:

- has five years as a permanent resident
- has lived continuously in the U.S. for at least seven years after having been admitted in any status, and
- has not been convicted of an aggravated felony.

This relief will serve as a waiver of removal for many permanent residents who commit acts which make them deportable. See a lawyer for help with this.

### 2. Abused spouse or child

An abused spouse or child of a U.S. citizen or permanent resident may apply for Cancellation of Removal under different rules.

In this case the applicant must show that he or she:

- suffered physical abuse or extreme mental cruelty in the U.S. at the hands of a permanent resident or U.S. citizen who is or was their parent or spouse—or the applicant is the parent of such an abused child
- has been physically present in the U.S. for a continuous period of at least three years at the time of the application
- has had good moral character for at least the three-year period, and
- is not inadmissible due to a conviction for a crime involving moral turpitude or drugs, not inadmissible on national security or terrorism grounds or other specified grounds, and has not been convicted of an aggravated felony.

The applicant must also show that the removal would result in extreme hardship to the applicant, the alien's child or to the alien's parent if the applicant is a child. Congress added this provision so that spouses and children who are victims of abuse by their petitioning relative would have a way to obtain status if they left the household of the abuser.

# 27

●●●●●●●●●●●●●●

# PRIVATE BILLS

## It's Not What You Know, It's Who You Know

I have heard from a neighbor that his grandfather became a permanent resident by means of a private bill passed by the U.S. Congress. Could I get a green card the same way since I personally know our Congressman?

Just knowing the Congressman will not be enough. You must have very special circumstances—and very strong political ties—to get a private bill passed.

You should think of a private bill where the law is against you, but your case has strong humanitarian factors. Private bills succeed when an injustice can only be corrected by a special act of the U.S. Congress.

## A. What Is a Private Bill?

A private bill is the last resort of a desperate alien facing deportation—a special urging by high-level American politicians to allow you to stay in the U.S. legally. Currently, very few private bills are filed on behalf of aliens. Only about 100 private bills have been successful during each of the past several years.

## B. How a Private Bill Is Passed

A private bill must be sponsored by one or more members of the House of Representatives and one or more members of the Senate who urge that one individual should be given special consideration in being allowed to become a permanent resident or to get citizenship.

Like a law, a private bill has to be introduced in both houses of Congress. It then has to be recommended favorably by the Judiciary Committee to which it has been assigned in both houses, after having been favorably reported by the Subcommittee on Immigration of both houses.

Both houses of Congress must approve the bill during a regular session. The President of the United States must then sign it into law.

Thus, if you are an alien facing deportation, you will have to go through the eye of a needle before getting your private bill passed by Congress and signed by the President. In short, hiring the best immigration lawyer in town will give you a better chance to obtain a green card than will the private bill route. ■

# 28

●●●●●●●●●●●●●●●

# INSIDE THE
# IMMIGRATION BUREAUCRACY

## The Land of Oz

When you submitted an application to the Bureau of Citizenship and Immigration Services (BCIS, formerly called the INS), a worker there told you that you would receive an official reply to it within a month. But five weeks pass, then six—and still no letter arrives. You would like to find out why your application is delayed, but each time you contact the BCIS office, you are simply told to be patient and wait—that your paperwork is "being processed."

The BCIS is a branch of the Department of Homeland Security. Its emphasis is more on enforcing the law and less on delivering services. Furthermore, the people working in the BCIS reflect the workforce of any other government bureaucracy. These workers can generally be divided into two kinds: those who are earnest and conscientious in doing their jobs and those who are at their posts in body but not in spirit. You take the luck of the draw as to which kind of bureaucrat will be handling your application or answering your questions.

But there are a number of things you can do to be sure that your dealings with the BCIS move as smoothly and efficiently as possible. Those options are explained in this chapter.

## A. Finding Out About Office Procedures

Although the BCIS is governed by law (the Immigration and Nationality Act, Code of Federal Regulations and Operational Instructions), how the controlling rules and laws are applied depends upon BCIS office workers who have their own cultural and social biases.

For example, you may be confronted with an immigration officer whose cultural background is anti-immigrant, and who detests dealing on a daily basis with people who do not speak English, who speak with an accent, or who look, dress or even smell differently from what he or she thinks of as "ordinary" Americans. This bias may make the worker grumpy, officious, intimidating, unhelpful, unreasonable, discourteous or downright infuriating.

Because the BCIS is not very phone-accessible, and the people at its national information line aren't well-informed about local office procedures, you may learn the particular idiosyncrasies of your local BCIS office only by making a personal visit.

## B. Where to Go

Whenever a situation arises where you feel an immigration officer is being unreasonable, go up the chain of command and appeal to the worker's supervisor. Insist on speaking with the supervisor personally. If that's not possible, try to obtain the supervisor's telephone number to call and explain what happened—or write a detailed letter of explanation. Be clear on what action was taken by the worker and what you want the supervising officer to do.

Because the DHS is a bureaucracy with many departments and branches, it is easy to get mixed up in a game of finger-pointing in which each person with whom you speak claims that the problem is not his or her fault.

The most important bit of knowledge you can learn is the exact section where your application is pending or where you are directing your inquiry.

- **The BCIS District Office** is open to the public for forms and information and also handles some (but not all) green card applications. Most states have at least one.
- **The BCIS Regional Service Center** is a processing facility that has you cannot normally visit, but to which you may be required to send your visa petition or green card application, depending on your eligibility category. There are four service centers nationwide. You can check on the status of applications that you've filed with the service centers by telephone (see the phone number on your receipt notice) or online at https://egov.immigration.gov/graphics/cris/jsps/caseStat.jsp.
- **The Records and Information Section** takes care of all the immigration forms and records and creates, consolidates, searches and sends files to the units or districts that request them.
- **The Examinations and Adjudication Section** makes the decisions on all petitions and applications for immigrant or nonimmigrant status, conducts the interviews prior to such decisions and refers cases to the investigation unit when they warrant further inquiry.
- **The Bureau of Immigration and Customs Enforcement** is the enforcement arm of the DHS. Its investigators check on whether both employers and employees have complied with the immigration laws. They do surveillance, make arrests and issue orders to show up for deportation or exclusion hearings before the Immigration Court.
- **The Detention Section** is in charge of detaining all aliens caught by the Investigations Section or apprehended at the airport or the border.

- **The Naturalization Section** is responsible for deciding which aliens are eligible for citizenship and who qualifies as a citizen of the United States.
- **The Litigation Section** is the legal arm of the DHS and represents the government during hearings involving an alien before the Immigration Court and the federal and state courts. It also counsels the other sections of the DHS on legal matters.
- **The Immigration Court** (also called the Executive Office of Immigration Review), which was part of the INS until 1987, is now a separate bureaucracy, totally outside the control of the district director.

 **CONSULT AN EXPERT**

Note that if you are under removal proceedings in court, it may be risky to proceed on your own. Consult an experienced immigration attorney for advice. (See Chapter 31.)

## C. REPORTING WRONGDOING

Sometimes, a BCIS worker's actions may be truly reprehensible, involving gross incompetence, immoral conduct or unlawful behavior—for instance asking for a bribe, either before or after doing what the worker is supposed to do. In such cases, report the misdeed both to the district director of the BCIS office (see Appendix 1 at the back of this book for addresses) and to:

> Office of the Inspector General
> U.S. Department of Justice
> Investigations Division
> 950 Pennsylvania Avenue, NW Room 4706
> Washington, DC 20530

Your letter should specify the name of the BCIS worker, if known. If you did not ask for the name or the BCIS worker refused to answer, describe him or her. You also should indicate the time, date and manner of misconduct and the names of any witnesses.

Although your complaint may lead to an investigation where you may be asked to repeat your facts in front of an investigator or an administrative judge, do not be afraid or unwilling to get involved. The officer's abusive behavior is not likely to stop and many more people are likely to be injured by it unless you take action.

 **CONSULT AN EXPERT**

It is wise in this situation to consult an experienced immigration attorney for advice before proceeding—especially if your legal status is unresolved. (See Chapter 31.)

## SAMPLE LETTER

Office of the Inspector General
U.S. Department of Justice
Investigations Division
950 Pennsylvania Avenue, NW Room 4706
Washington, DC 20530

April 15, 200_

Dear Investigating Officer:

This is a complaint against a male BCIS officer who refused to give me his name. He is Caucasian, medium built, with gray hair and wears eyeglasses.

I spoke with this officer on Tuesday, April 5, 200_, at 10:00 a.m. on the 8th floor of the Adjudications Section of the BCIS in New York. He demanded a hundred extra dollars in cash before approving my request for Advance Parole.

When I refused to pay the additional money, he said that although all my paperwork was in order, he would have to deny the request since I wasn't willing to "pay what it took to get the wheels in motion."

Alfred Beiz, a paralegal at the law firm of Dias & Associates, was standing in line behind me, waiting to file some papers, and overheard the officer's remarks. Mr. Beiz is willing to file an affidavit swearing to the conversation he heard.

I request that you promptly investigate my charge against this officer, and inform me about what action is taken.

Thank you for your attention.

With my best regards,
*Ali Mufti*
Ali Mufti

## D. Filing an Application

Take all applications and other immigration papers to the Post Office and send them by registered mail with return receipt requested. Keep copies for your files.

Documents received at your local BCIS office, regional office or special office set up for a definite purpose such as political asylum will be processed by the clerical staff. They will first examine your papers to see if everything has been filled out properly. Your papers will likely be returned to you if you:

- did not enter your full name, including middle name
- did not sign your application or other papers requiring a signature
- signed a name different from that shown on your attached birth certificate
- did not enclose the correct filing fee
- left some questions unanswered, or
- forgot to include some documents.

When your papers are returned, there should be a letter included with them, telling you what information was incorrect or missing. You will usually have a chance to make things right by simply correcting what was wrong and sending back your documents and check or money order to cover the fees.

When your form is properly answered and your documents are in order, the BCIS will accept your submission and will send you a receipt notice telling you the minimum time you'll have to wait for a decision.

If your application needs to be submitted in person—such as an application for Employment Authorization or Advance Parole—the BCIS worker to whom you are assigned will tell you whether or not your application is properly answered and documented. You will have the opportunity to correct your answers right then and there. The BCIS worker will then direct you to pay the filing fee to the cashier, who will give you a receipt. Be sure to keep the receipt in case you need to use it as proof of filing.

### 1. Your Alien Number

There are two kinds of numbers by which the DHS identifies every person who comes in contact with it. The first one, an A followed by 8 numbers—for example: A93 465 345—is given to those who apply for Adjustment of Status to become permanent residents (see Chapter 8) or who have a removal case. It's called an Alien Registration Number or A Number.

The second type of number the BCIS assigns starts with the initials of your district or of the Regional Service Center followed by ten numbers—for example: WAC 1122334455 or EAC 9512345678—and is given to applications submitted there, to track them through processing.

Once your immigration papers are accepted by the BCIS, its computer system verifies whether you have ever been assigned an alien number or whether the alien number you wrote on your application is the right one for you.

The clerk then checks the computer files, looking for all the names you may have used, your date and place of birth and your parents' names. The clerk will confirm the alien number you wrote on your application, or if you have other alien numbers previously assigned, will note them on your application so that all your files can be consolidated under one alien number. If you do not have a previous alien number, the clerk will give your file a new one.

Keep a record of your immigration case number, because any time you have a question to pose to the BCIS, it will ask you first for your number. If you have the number handy, you are likely to get a quicker response.

### 2. Looking at your file

If you need to see your immigration records, or to have a copy of a document you submitted, you can do so by filing form G-639, Freedom of Information/Privacy Act Request. Request a current form from the nearest BCIS office or download it from the BCIS website (www.bcis.gov). Mark your envelope "Freedom of Information Request." Send it to your local BCIS office (see Appendix I for the address).

Although the BCIS has promised that it will answer a Freedom of Information/Privacy Act Request within ten days, it may not be able to live up to its promise. If you have not heard from the BCIS within two weeks after requesting to see your file, let them know that you are aware that it has a mandate to respond to these requests within ten days. Go to the Records Section and speak with the supervisor—armed with copies of your application and your receipt.

## SOMETIMES, THEY SURPRISE YOU

While it's important to make your dissatisfaction known about a BCIS officer's bad or abusive behavior, the contrary should also be true. If you are served by a BCIS worker who goes the extra mile to be helpful, by all means, write to the District and Central Offices of the BCIS and let them know that there is an outstanding worker in their midst.

It may encourage more workers to deliver superlative service to the public.

## E. SPEEDING UP PROCESSING IN EMERGENCIES

An emergency may arise where you need an action expedited or your immigration papers approved very quickly. For example, your alien wife may still be abroad because your petition for her is not yet approved, when she is stricken with a rare disease for which the only treatment is found in the United States.

Normally, the BCIS is loath to bend its rules and act outside the standard operating procedures. But if your case truly deserves an exception from the general rule, and you approach the right BCIS worker in the right way, you may get a satisfactory resolution because there is a humanitarian reason to grant your request. It enables the BCIS to show its human side.

But it is sometimes difficult to locate that human side.

First of all, be resigned to the fact that there are two kinds of BCIS workers: one makes a decision strictly according to the letter of the law and the other exercises discretion when appropriate and makes a decision according to the spirit of the law.

You may get the best help if you write a letter explaining your situation, attaching documents to substantiate why immediate action is necessary.

As mentioned earlier, when the BCIS worker fails to respond to your inquiry or denies your request, go up the chain of command and speak with the supervisor.

If you are unable to speak with the supervisor, or he or she is unable or unwilling to solve your problem, go to the second line supervisor. If you do not know the second line supervisor, you may have to go to the very top—the district director for services of the BCIS office.

Again, there are two kinds of district directors for services. One always refers cases to subordinates and will never interfere with any decision; the other has the wisdom to discern which cases deserve direct involvement and which do not.

If your case is assigned to the compassionate kind of district director, you are lucky.

If you get the nitpicky or mean-spirited kind of district director, you are better off trying to get help from the immediate or second-line supervisor because one of them will be more likely to give your request a hearing.

If your request for immediate action is still denied unjustly, you may have to hire a lawyer to file a case of mandamus in the federal district court to force the BCIS to act on your request.

## SAMPLE LETTER

Leona Burgett
District Director for Services
BCIS Office
Anytown, Anystate   12345

August 12, 200_

Dear Ms. Burgett:

My file number is A 12345678 and I have an Adjustment of Status application pending in your office.

I received a letter from my mother with a certification from the hospital that my father suffered a heart attack and prognosis is dim. I filed for Advance Parole two days ago, but my application was denied. The BCIS worker said he believed that the certification from the hospital was fraudulently obtained and did not accept my mother's letter because it was not translated into English.

Yesterday, I returned with a translation of the letter and my affidavit explaining that in our remote hometown, the most modern equipment available is a manual typewriter, on which some letters may be crooked or spaces may be skipped. The BCIS worker said that my Advance Parole will still be denied regardless of my explanations that my father is truly very ill.

I am married to an American citizen and have been law-abiding—except for overstaying in this country for the last seven years.

Please help me with my Advance Parole request.

Sincerely,
*Max Haxsim*
Max Haxsim

# 29

## IMMIGRATION FORMS: GETTING STARTED

### Paper, Paper, Everywhere

My father was recently naturalized as a U.S. citizen and would like to petition for me. But the civil registry office which records births and deaths in our town burned down during the war. What do I do now?

I was divorced in Algeria and the divorce decree is in Arabic. Can I submit it with my father's petition for me now that I am an unmarried daughter of a lawful permanent resident?

The most important part of obtaining a green card is the paperwork. The key to getting one is to pay very close attention to the immigration forms and other documents you submit as evidence to the U.S. government.

## A. GIVING FALSE ANSWERS

There is one primary rule to keep in mind while answering the questions on the immigration forms: Honesty Is the Best Policy.

If you have been previously married, acknowledge this and provide the documents to prove that your previous marriage ended by divorce, annulment or the death of your spouse.

If you have children by a previous marriage, or you have had any children while you were unmarried, list all of them on the immigration form, together with their correct names and dates of birth as shown on their birth certificates.

If the immigration form requests such information, be sure to list all your brothers and sisters, whether they are full-blood siblings, half-brothers or half-sisters, stepbrothers or stepsisters.

Once you submit the immigration forms, it is very difficult to change your answers. If you attempt later changes, you run the risk of having your petition denied.

**EXAMPLE:** Suppose you never told your American husband that you had an illegitimate child. For this reason, you do not mention this child in your immigration papers. Later on, you decide to reveal the truth to your husband. If you want to petition for an immigrant visa for the child you left behind in your country, you will have a hard time convincing the BCIS that you had a child prior to your marriage.

### 1. Criminal penalties

Aside from the complications of trying to convince the U.S. officials that an omission was an honest mistake, you also run the risk of being prosecuted for obtaining entry by a "willfully false or misleading representation or willful concealment of a material fact." In simple terms, you could be accused of lying on the immigration forms. Or you may be accused of filing documents which do not belong to you.

If you are found guilty of committing these offenses, you may be imprisoned for as long as five years or fined as much as $10,000, or receive both forms of punishment. If you received your green card by a fraudulent marriage, the punishment is more severe. (See Chapter 7, Section A.)

### 2. Civil penalties

There are also civil penalties for those who "forge, counterfeit, alter or falsely make any document" to satisfy a requirement of immigration law.

If you are found guilty, you can be fined $250 to $5,000 for each fraudulent document which you have in your possession or have already submitted to the BCIS. In addition, if you are an alien, you may also be excluded from entering the United States or, if you are already there, you may be removed or deported.

## B. CHECKING FOR CURRENT FORMS AND FEES

The law and the rules on immigration procedures change frequently. Using old, outdated forms may cause your immigration petition to be delayed or, worse—denied. And if your immigration papers are filed with the wrong fee, they will be returned; this will further delay your legal entry as an immigrant.

Therefore, before mailing any immigration applications, take the time to request the most recent forms and to double-check the filing fees with the local INS office or with an American Consulate in your country of residence, whichever is most convenient. If you have access to the Internet, you can check fees and request forms—or download most of them—from the BCIS website at www.bcis.gov.

## C. TIPS FOR FILLING OUT FORMS

A number of immigration forms ask for the same kinds of identifying information—your name, address, identification numbers. While the answers may often seem obvious, the BCIS requires that they be phrased in specific ways.

## 1. Your family name

When an immigration form asks you to fill in your name, write the complete name that you were given on your birth certificate or the name written in your passport, whichever document is required. Add your full middle name (if you have one), even if the form asks only for your middle initial. The BCIS asks all applicants to add this for security check purposes, and may delay your application if you don't. If the name on your birth certificate is not your name at present, explain the difference in a letter and submit the corresponding documents that show the change.

> EXAMPLE: If you are a woman named Jane who is using the surname of your husband, John Smith, as your family name, write your husband's surname—that is, Jane Smith.
>
> On the space that says "other names used," write your maiden name and any other names you have used—that is, Jane Doe.
>
> If you were married previously, write your previous married name on that space. Attach your marriage certificate or divorce decree.

## 2. Your address

Your address, as far as the BCIS is concerned, is the place where you receive mail. The post office is very important in your immigration relationship because everything from the BCIS will come by mail—notice of approval of petition, notice of incomplete submission, notice of interview, notice of proceedings and your green card.

If the mail carrier does not deliver mail in your locality, rent a post office box. However, some BCIS forms ask not only for your mailing address but also for your actual address. In that case, write the exact address or location of your home or c/o—meaning "in care of"—the person you are living with.

## 3. Your Social Security and Alien Registration numbers

The Social Security number requested on immigration forms is issued by the United States government, not by your country's own Social Security administration. An alien registration number is issued by the BCIS (or, formerly, the INS). If you have not been assigned one or both of these numbers, write "none" in the space provided on the immigration forms.

---

### ANSWER EVERY QUESTION

Answer all questions and do not leave a line on the form blank unless it clearly directs you to do otherwise. If the question being posed does not apply to you, write "not applicable" or if you do not have a number or document, write "none." If you do not know the answer, write "not known." If you fail to answer all questions, processing your forms is likely to be delayed while the BCIS sends them back and asks for more complete information.

---

## D. WHEN ADDITIONAL PROOF IS REQUIRED

The BCIS requires specific proof to be submitted along with the answers on some of its forms, because you are entitled to a green card only when you can prove by convincing documentation that you meet specific qualifications. You can go a long way toward eliminating delays and confusion if you take the time to be sure your additional proof is accurate and complete.

## 1. Proving a family relationship

As requested on the immigration forms, you must provide documents to prove that a relationship permits you to apply as a family-based immigrant. (See Chapter 4, Sections A and B.) If you do not submit the right documents, or if you fail to fill them out correctly, they will be returned and the whole process will be delayed.

**You must have the official documents.** To prove a family relationship, you must have the original birth certificate, marriage certificate or death certificate issued by the civil registry of your country with the official government seal, stamp or ribbon attached, depending on how official documents are marked in your country. Nongovernmental documents, such as church or hospital certificates, are usually not sufficient.

Use your fingers to verify the indentation of the government seal that is embossed or pressed into the paper. The BCIS will often assume that a document without such a seal is fraudulent.

If you have lost the documents, you can request certified copies from your government for an additional charge. Be sure these copies also have the official government seal.

The BCIS has to check carefully the documents it receives. Some unscrupulous people present counterfeit documents to show relationships which do not exist, such as father and son, brother and sister, or to show educational attainment, such as school transcripts or diplomas, which have not been earned.

---

### DO NOT SEND YOUR ORIGINALS

Make a copy of your original document—and take or send the copy to the BCIS. Things often get lost in the mail. And added to that, the BCIS offices are busy places crowded with many people and even more documents, so things can get lost there, too. The BCIS often makes no effort to return originals to you, and takes no responsibility if they are lost. Keep the originals of your documents in a safe place—one that's fireproof if possible. Then show it to the BCIS officer at your interview.

---

**If you don't have the official document.** Sometimes, you cannot get your original documents because of war, destruction of the civil registry, your government's prohibition on emigration or simple oversight or ignorance.

In such cases, family relationships such as parent-child, brother-sister, husband-wife, can be proved by what is called secondary evidence—a combination of documents that may not come from the civil registry, but which nevertheless prove a relationship.

- Church records, for example, can sometimes be submitted. A baptismal certificate will show the parents' names and the date and place of birth of the child.
- Annotations in a family Bible, old letters, school records or data from a relevant government census are other types of secondary evidence.
- The BCIS will also accept the sworn statements, or affidavits, of two people who have witnessed your birth, your marriage, the death of a spouse or whatever event you need to prove. The statement should include the witnesses' names and addresses, their relationship to you or your family and why and how they know about the alleged event. The strongest evidence is from witnesses who were present at the event you need to prove.

For example, if you never had a birth certificate or you could not obtain a copy, an affidavit written by your sister could read as written below.

**Sample affidavit**

---

My name is Jane Doe and I am the older sister of John Doe.

I live at 123 Middle Abbey Street, Dublin, Ireland.

I was 7 years old when my brother, John Doe, was born to our mother, Carolyn Doe, on July 4, 1930, at our home in Cork, Ireland.

This affidavit is submitted because the civil registry in Cork was burned in 1932 and my brother's birth certificate was lost when the family moved to Dublin in the same year.

Signature: _____

Signed and sworn to before me on March 1, 200_

Notary

---

The witnesses have to swear to the truth of their statements before a notary public—a person who is authorized by the state to verify signatures. You can find a notary by looking in the telephone book, although most banks have one on staff. Most notaries will charge for their services, so it may be worthwhile to shop around for the one with the most reasonable charge. If required by the U.S. Embassy in your country, the affidavits must be sworn to before the American consular official, who will also charge a slight fee for the service.

You may need to submit your own affidavit stating why you cannot submit the original documents and what efforts you have made to try to obtain them.

The BCIS may further investigate your family relationship, or request that you and your relative undergo blood tests or give additional testimony. An investigation may even be conducted in the neighborhood in which you lived in your native country.

Before it confers an immigration benefit, the U.S. government must be certain that the person immigrating into the United States is truly the child, brother, sister, husband or wife—and not the niece, nephew, aunt, uncle, cousin or friend—of the American citizen or permanent resident petitioner.

## DOCUMENTS IN LANGUAGES OTHER THAN ENGLISH

If the documents you are submitting are not in English, have them translated accurately. An English summary of the document is not enough—although you do not have to hire a professional translator to do the job. Somebody who has competent knowledge of both English and the language in which the documents are written should be able to do the translation.

The translator must attach the following statement to the translated document and sign and date it:

*I hereby certify that I am competent to translate this document from (the foreign language) to English and that this translation is accurate and complete to the best of my knowledge and ability.*

## 2. Proving an INS or BCIS approval

In some situations, you may have an application or petition which has been approved by the INS or BCIS, but need further action because:

• You lost the approval notice or you need a duplicate

• The U.S. Embassy or Consulate which originally received the approval notice closed down or you simply could not go to your home country and another U.S. Consulate is willing to process your immigration visa and needs to be officially notified, or

• You need the BCIS to notify the U.S. Consulate in your country that you became a green cardholder in the United States so that your spouse and children can receive visas to join you.

In any of these circumstances, you must file Form I-824, Application for Action on an Approved Application or Petition, with the BCIS office which approved the original application or petition. You'll find a copy in the Appendix. The filing fee is $140.

If you have a copy of the approval, make a copy of that and send or bring it to the BCIS office to help in locating your case.

## 3. Proving citizenship

An American citizen has the right to bestow permanent resident status on a spouse, parent, child, brother, sister, fiancée or fiancé, and upon a widow or widower. But the BCIS must first see documents proving the U.S. citizenship of this person.

The following are accepted as proof:

• a birth certificate showing the place of birth to be any of the 50 states of the United States, Puerto Rico, the U.S. Virgin Islands or Guam

• a valid U.S. passport issued for a full five or ten years

• a baptismal certificate with the seal of the church showing the place of birth and date of baptism, which must have occurred within two months after birth, if the birth certificate cannot be obtained

• affidavits of two American citizens who have personal knowledge of the petitioner's birth in the United States, if neither the birth nor the baptismal certificate can be obtained

- the certificate of naturalization from someone who has become a citizen by naturalization and who files a petition for a relative within 90 days of the date of naturalization
- Department of State Form FS-240, Report of Birth Abroad of a Citizen of the United States, which proves American citizenship for someone born abroad, and
- the certificate of citizenship issued by the INS or BCIS, which is also adequate proof that one is an American citizen born abroad.

## 4. Proving lawful permanent residence

As a green cardholder, you have the right to petition for your spouse and unmarried children by submitting proof that you are a permanent resident. Although the BCIS has your file and alien registration number in its records, you must still present your green card, or submit a copy of it if you are sending your immigration papers by mail.

The official name of your green card is Alien Registration Receipt Card Form I-551. Only the Form I-551 will be recognized as proof of lawful permanent residence.

If your green card is lost or not available, your passport—bearing the BCIS rubber stamp showing lawful admission for permanent residence and your alien registration number—is acceptable proof of your permanent resident status.

## E. SUBMITTING PHOTOGRAPHS FOR IDENTIFICATION

Because good, accurate photographs are essential to ensure that a person is correctly represented for immigration purposes, the BCIS has imposed a number of strict specifications for the photographs and the poses it will accept.

While it is not essential to hire a professional photographer to take your BCIS photos, it may be tough to comply with the picky requirements for size, lighting and clarity. If you or a friend attempt to take the photos on your own, be sure to take a couple rolls of film—and to read the requirements first.

You must have at least two clear photographs of the head, from left cheek to right ear, that meet the specifications described below.

## 1. The photographs

The overall size of the picture, including the background, must be at least 40 mm ($1^9/_{16}$ inches) high and 35 mm ($1^3/_8$ inch) wide.

The photographs must be in color—with no shadows, marks or discolorations on them. The background must be white or off-white; it is not acceptable to be photographed against a patterned or colored background. There must be good lighting; the photo must not appear too light or too dark. And the final image must be original, not retouched in any way.

Pay special attention to the contrast between the image and the background. Photos for very light-skinned people should be slightly under-exposed; photos for very dark-skinned people should be slightly over-exposed.

Polaroid Hybrid #5 is an acceptable type of film to use; SX-70 or any other instant processing film is not acceptable. The photo must have a glossy or matte finish.

## 2. The image

The image on the photo—total size of the head—must be 30 mm ($1^3/_{16}$ inches) from the neck just below the chin and 26 mm (1 inch) from the right ear to the left cheek. The image cannot be larger than 32 mm by 28 mm—that is, $1^1/_4$ inch by $1^1/_{16}$ inch.

At least three-quarters of the person's face should be pictured—including the right ear and left eye. Be sure that no jewelry or hats are worn—and that the hair is brushed away so that the right ear is completely visible.

---

**BEFORE YOU PUT ANYTHING IN THE MAIL**

It is usually best to file the immigration papers personally in case there are questions about your answers or your documents. However, some immigration offices may only allow you to file by mail. Before mailing any immigration documents, make copies for your own records.

Submit most papers using certified mail, return receipt requested. This way, you will get confirmation that your papers were received.

**Sample Form M-378**

# U. S. IMMIGRATION & NATURALIZATION SERVICE

## COLOR   PHOTOGRAPH
## SPECIFICATIONS

IDEAL PHOTOGRAPH
◄

IMAGE MUST FIT INSIDE THIS
BOX ►

THE PICTURE AT LEFT IS IDEAL SIZE, COLOR,
BACKGROUND, AND POSE.  THE IMAGE SHOULD
BE 30MM (1 3/16IN) FROM THE HAIR TO
JUST BELOW THE CHIN, AND 26MM (1 IN)
FROM LEFT CHEEK TO RIGHT EAR.  THE IMAGE
MUST FIT IN THE BOX AT RIGHT.

**THE PHOTOGRAPH**
* THE OVERALL SIZE OF THE PICTURE, INCLUDING THE
BACKGROUND, MUST BE AT LEAST 40MM (1 9/16 INCHES)
IN HEIGHT BY 35MM (1 3/8IN) IN WIDTH.

* PHOTOS MUST BE FREE OF SHADOWS AND CONTAIN NO MARKS,
SPLOTCHES, OR DISCOLORATIONS.

* PHOTOS SHOULD BE HIGH QUALITY, WITH GOOD BACK
LIGHTING OR WRAP AROUND LIGHTING, AND MUST HAVE
A WHITE OR OFF-WHITE BACKGROUND.

* PHOTOS MUST BE A GLOSSY OR MATTE FINISH AND
UN-RETOUCHED.

* POLAROID FILM HYBRID #5 IS ACCEPTABLE; HOWEVER SX-70
TYPE FILM OR ANY OTHER INSTANT PROCESSING TYPE FILM IS
UNACCEPTABLE.  NON-PEEL APART FILMS ARE EASILY RECOGNIZED
BECAUSE THE BACK OF THE FILM IS BLACK.  ACCEPTABLE INSTANT
COLOR FILM HAS A GRAY-TONED BACKING.

**THE IMAGE OF THE PERSON**
* THE DIMENSIONS OF THE IMAGE SHOULD BE 30MM (1 3/16
INCHES) FROM THE HAIR TO THE NECK JUST BELOW THE CHIN,
AND 26MM (1 INCH) FROM THE RIGHT EAR TO THE LEFT CHEEK.
IMAGE CANNOT EXCEED 32MM BY 28MM (1 1/4IN X 1 1/16IN).

* IF THE IMAGE AREA ON THE PHOTOGRAPH IS TOO LARGE
OR TOO SMALL, THE PHOTO CANNOT BE USED.

* PHOTOGRAPHS MUST SHOW THE ENTIRE FACE OF THE PERSON
IN A 3/4 VIEW SHOWING THE RIGHT EAR AND LEFT EYE.

* FACIAL FEATURES **MUST BE IDENTIFIABLE.**

* CONTRAST BETWEEN THE IMAGE AND BACKGROUND IS
ESSENTIAL.  PHOTOS FOR VERY LIGHT SKINNED PEOPLE
SHOULD BE SLIGHTLY UNDER-EXPOSED.  PHOTOS FOR VERY
DARK SKINNED PEOPLE SHOULD BE SLIGHTLY OVER-EXPOSED.

## SAMPLES OF UNACCEPTABLE PHOTOGRAPHS

INCORRECT POSE               IMAGE TOO LARGE               IMAGE TOO SMALL               IMAGE TOO DARK
                                                                                          UNDER-EXPOSED

IMAGE TOO LIGHT               DARK BACKGROUND               OVER-EXPOSED               SHADOWS ON PIC

Immigration & Naturalization Service
Form M-378 (6-92)

## F.  FINGERPRINTING REQUIREMENTS

The BCIS requires fingerprinting to accompany a variety of applications, including permanent residence, asylum and naturalization, among others. Recently, the BCIS has stopped using outside organizations to take fingerprints and, in most cases, requires fingerprinting at a BCIS-authorized site.

Fingerprints are generally reviewed by the FBI to determine an applicant's actual identity and to determine if they have a criminal background that would make them inadmissible. The BCIS will also check to see whether you've submitted previous applications under a different name.

### 1.  General rules

If the application you are filing requires fingerprinting, you should include a $50 check or money order made out to the BCIS for the cost of fingerprinting. This is in addition to any fees for the application itself. The BCIS has 90 days to contact you by letter, telling you when you should go to a BCIS-authorized site for fingerprinting. You will be given directions and a specific week within which you must appear at the fingerprinting site. If you cannot make it during that time, you can ask to be rescheduled. At some locations, the BCIS is also developing mobile fingerprinting vans that will make it easier for people who live outside major urban areas to comply with the fingerprinting requirements.

If you live abroad and are filing your application outside the United States, you may be fingerprinted at a U.S. Consulate or military installation. The fee is $85.

### 2.  Political Asylum seekers

All applicants for political asylum (Form I-589) are exempt from the $50 fee. After filing their forms with the BCIS, applicants in the United States will receive a letter with the time and place of their fingerprinting appointment (see Section 1, above).

### 3.  Adoptions

BCIS regulations require that prospective adoptive parents and every adult who lives in the house (18 years old and over) provide fingerprints for FBI criminal background checks. They are used to decide if the prospective adoptive parents and the home environment are suitable for an orphan. Prospective adoptive parents residing in the United States must submit $50 for each prospective parent and each adult member of the household, in addition to the Orphan Petition or Advance Processing Application filing fee.

For example, married prospective adoptive parents with two additional adult members of the household must submit $200 ($50 x 4) along with the $460 filing fee for a total check or money order of $660. The prospective parents must advise the BCIS of all adult members of the household at the time of filing the orphan petition or application for advance processing. If they are not all listed, the processing of the application can be delayed.

After receiving an Orphan Petition or Advance Processing Application, the BCIS will send appointment letters with the date and location for all prospective adoptive parents and additional adult members of the household to be fingerprinted. Prospective adoptive parents residing abroad, and any adult members of their household may need to be fingerprinted at a U.S. Consulate or military installation abroad. The overseas fingerprint fee is $85.

## G.  SUBMITTING A COPY OF EACH DOCUMENT

The BCIS requires you to submit a copy of all original or other documents needed to establish the relationship on the basis of which you are claiming your green card.

You must write or type the following statement on the back of each photocopy:

> Copies of documents submitted are exact photocopies of unaltered original documents and I understand that I may be required to submit original documents to an Immigration or Consular official at a later date.

Include your signature and date of signature. There is no need to have your signature verified by a notary public.

If you submit the original document or certified copies of it instead of the photocopies as instructed, you may have a difficult time getting your original documents back. The BCIS bureaucracy is not equipped to make copies of your documents for you.

## IF THERE IS A PROBLEM...

Never, never try to explain your problem to the answering operator or the receptionist.

Bureaucrats in every country are programmed to answer your initial inquiry with the same response: "I do not know what you're talking about." Worse yet, they may give you wrong advice.

Speak only to the director of the agency, the supervisor of the operator, or the person in charge of the section. A higher-level officer is usually more knowledgeable and will be able to answer your questions, and if not, will be able to refer you to the appropriate person.

## H. KEEPING YOUR OWN FILE

For your own records, make copies of everything that you submit to the U.S. government, including the immigration forms and the supporting documents. Also make a copy of the receipt the BCIS issues to you after you pay the filing fee.

After you have made copies and mailed your immigration papers (certified mail, return receipt requested), or after you have personally submitted them to the BCIS, keep your own copies and original documents in a safe place. You will need them again when you are called to receive your immigrant visa at the American Embassy or when you attend your personal interview for your green card at the BCIS .

Also, like any other bureaucracy, the BCIS does sometimes misplace files. It will save you a lot of headache and heartache if you can show that you have already filed the application with the BCIS by presenting a copy of the documents filed, the receipt from the BCIS and your certified check or money order. ■

# 30

**KEEPING, RENEWING AND REPLACING YOUR GREEN CARD**

When Your Green Card Is Lost,
Stolen or Canceled

Now that you have finally obtained that plastic card giving you the right to stay and work in the United States without any hassle, and to leave and return without applying for a visa, make sure you don't you lose the card—or your right to it.

If all goes as it should, your green card will give you the right to live in the United States for as long as you want to. However, you need to protect this right by taking such measures as telling the BCIS when you move, not spending too long outside the United States and not becoming inadmissible or deportable. You should also make sure to renew your green card on time and replace it if it's lost.

⚠ **Think about applying for U.S. citizenship.**
After a certain number of years with a green card (usually five, but less for some people), you can apply for U.S. citizenship. This is a much more secure status—you'll be able to travel for longer periods of time, are safe from deportation and will gain the right to vote. For complete instructions, see *Becoming a U.S. Citizen; A Guide to the Law, Exam & Interview*, by Ilona Bray (Nolo).

## A. Renewing or Replacing Your Green Card

Whether your green card is lost or expires and needs to be renewed, the Bureau of Citizenship and Immigration Services (BCIS) requires that you file Form I-90, Application by Lawful Permanent Resident for New Alien Registration Receipt Card. (See the sample at the end of this chapter.)

The filing fee is $130. For most cases, you'll mail your check and two photographs (see Chapter 29, Section E, for guidance), together with the Form I-90 to the Service Center nearest your place of residence. (See the BCIS website for contact details.) However, if your card was lost, damaged or destroyed, you'll need to take your application in person to the BCIS District Office nearest you.

You can also use Form I-90 to get a new green card when:

- your name has been changed, due to marriage or divorce, in which case you must include a copy of your marriage or divorce certificate and your old card
- you turn 14 years of age; the BCIS requires that you change your green card for a new one

- you receive an incorrect card with an erroneous name, birthdate, photo or date of entry
- you never received your green card, or
- your green card is blue, Form I-151; these old cards were issued during the 1960s and 1970s and expired on August 2, 1996, because of their lack of security features, giving opportunities for fraud.

You must swear that all the answers you give when applying for a green card are correct. If you knowingly falsify or conceal a material fact, or use any false document in submitting the application, you may be fined up to $10,000, imprisoned for up to five years, or both.

You should receive your new green card (Form I-551) within 30 to 45 days after the BCIS receives your paperwork and filing fee.

## B. When the Immigration Authorities Can Take Your Card Away

As a green cardholder, you are expected to be law-abiding. Because you were not born with the right to stay in the United States and have not yet been naturalized, the immigration laws put certain restrictions on you which do not apply to American citizens.

### 1. Failing to report a change of address

The immigration law provides that an alien who fails to give written notice to the BCIS of a change of address can be deported or removed. Not only that, the alien could be charged with a misdemeanor and if found guilty, fined up to $200, imprisoned up to 30 days, or both.

The alien would have to convince the immigration judge during removal hearings that failure to notify the BCIS of an address change was reasonably excusable or was not willful.

Therefore, to avoid any possible problem whenever you move to a new address, mail Form AR-11 (available in Appendix 2, at BCIS offices or on the BCIS website at www.bcis.gov) to:

Department of Justice
Department of Citizenship and Immigration Services
Change of Address
P.O. Box 7134
London, KY 40742-7134

### 2. Failing to maintain a residence in the U.S.

You became a permanent resident presumably because you intend to live in the United States. If you live outside the United States for more than 12 months, it will appear to the immigration authorities that you do not intend to reside in America.

It is wise to be gone for no more than six months. This will decrease your risk of losing your green card and help ensure that your admission at the airport or other port of entry is as free of trouble as possible.

Otherwise, when you return after your year abroad, the border officials may put you under removal proceedings to determine whether you have lost the right to live in the United States as a permanent resident. Your green card may be taken away.

But you can do something to help avoid such a situation. If you know in advance that you may not be able to return to the United States within a year's time, you can apply for a reentry permit by mailing the following to the BCIS Nebraska Service Center (get the address from the BCIS website) at least 30 days before you intend to depart, along with a filing fee of $110:

- Form I-131, Application for Issuance of Permit to Reenter the United States (see the sample at the end of this chapter)
- a copy of your green card (front and back), and
- two photographs (see Chapter 29, Section E for details).

The BCIS will mail a reentry permit to the address in the United States you have indicated on your application.

You can protect your right to your green card. The best way to do this is to understand what you might do that could lead the authorities to decide that you have lost or abandoned your permanent residence status. In determining this, they look at your intentions about your permanent residence when you leave the United States. If your intent is to be gone temporarily, then legally, you should be able to maintain your status.

Since the U.S. government cannot know your real intent, it will look at things such as:

- your purpose in leaving
- whether your purpose is consistent with a temporary absence
- whether you still have a job, home or family in the United States, and
- the duration of your trip.

Getting a reentry permit before you leave is good evidence that you intend to return to the United States to continue living. It also means that the authorities cannot rely solely on the length of your absence to determine that you have lost your permanent residence status. However, since they can still look at other facts in your life, you should maintain as many ties to the United States as possible—even if you get a reentry permit.

If you have to go abroad before you receive the permit, you can request that the permit be delivered to your address overseas or, if the mail in your country is not reliable, through the United States Embassy or Consulate in your country.

However, you must be physically present in the United States when you file the application. If you have been outside of the U.S. for four out of the past five years, the permit will only be issued for one year. And if you have been out of the U.S. for that amount of time, you can also expect to receive intense questions at the airport about whether you have maintained your legal residence in the United States.

If a reentry permit is issued, it is good for two years.

## 3. Explaining your failure to reenter the U.S.

If you stay longer than the two years allowed by the reentry permit or if you stay longer than one year without applying for the reentry permit, you will jeopardize your immigration status.

Upon arriving at the port of entry, the officials will question you on your right to return as a green card holder. Therefore, you must be ready to present proof of why you did not return to the United States within the time expected.

**Illness.** A permissible delay could be due to your own serious illness or to that of a close relative, especially if the illness started after you left. Convincing evidence of the illness would be copies of a doctor's written diagnosis, medical bills, prescriptions and letters to you from friends.

**Death.** A death in the family could be another reason for delay. Bring with you copies of the death certificate, letters from the court or lawyer on settlement of the estate, life insurance letters concerning distribution of the insurance proceeds and a court order dividing property of the deceased.

**Business reasons.** Setting up or closing down a business enterprise could also be a valid reason for delay. Be ready to show bank statements, a contract of sale, invoices, letters from the bank and letters from your business partners, your lawyer and your accountant.

In other words, if you are detained at the airport for a more thorough questioning, you must be ready to convince the officer that you had a very good reason for not returning to the United States when expected. If the immigration officer is still not convinced, you will have another chance to explain your case before the immigration judge at your hearing.

Insist on your right to a hearing. Too often, the officer applies the third degree and the scared green card holder signs away his or her green card on Form I-407, Application for Abandonment of Residence. Once you sign this form, it is very difficult to get a second chance to explain your side before the immigration court. Your status will most likely automatically revert to that of a nonimmigrant—and you will have to repeat the process of getting a green card all over again.

However, if you were coerced or forced to sign the Form 407, contact an immigration attorney who may be able to help you fight to keep your green card. (See Chapter 31.)

## 4. Becoming inadmissible

Grounds of inadmissibility are conditions which the immigration authorities can legally use to keep you from entering the United States. You had to prove that you weren't inadmissible (that is, hadn't committed any crimes, didn't have any serious illnesses and weren't likely to need public assistance) in order to get your green card. But these same grounds apply to you every time you leave the United States and try to return. Even with your green card, you could be refused reentry. If one of these grounds applies to you, however, you may be able to get it waived. (See Chapter 22.)

## 5. Becoming removable

In addition to the grounds of inadmissibility described above, the immigration laws list grounds of removability. These are actions or circumstances that can cause you to lose your right to the green card and be placed in removal proceedings in the United States. If you lose, you could be deported back to the country you came from.

The grounds of removability are too complex to explain in detail here. We have already discussed one of them, namely your obligation to report your changes of address to the BCIS. In general, however, you need to make sure not to violate any immigration or criminal laws and not to get involved with any organizations that the U.S. government believes to be terrorist.

## APPLICATION TO REPLACE ALIEN REGISTRATION CARD, SAMPLE FORM I-90

**U.S. Department of Justice**
Immigration and Naturalization Service

OMB #1115-0004

### Application to Replace Permanent Resident Card

## START HERE - Please Type or Print

### Part 1. Information about you.

| Family Name | Cosmin | Given Name | Mihaita | Middle Initial | |
|---|---|---|---|---|---|

**U.S. Mailing Address - C/O**
Ravin Cosmin

| Street Number and Name | 8383 Kew Gardens | Apt. # | 4001 |
|---|---|---|---|

| City | Queens |
|---|---|

| State | New York | ZIP Code | 11415 |
|---|---|---|---|

| Date of Birth (Month/Day/Year) | October 2, 1949 | Country of Birth | Romania |
|---|---|---|---|

| Social Security # | 112-64-5793 | A # | A24-070-502 |
|---|---|---|---|

### Part 2. Application type.

**1. My status is:** (check one)
- a. ☑ Permanent Resident - (Not a Commuter)
- b. ☐ Permanent Resident - (Commuter)
- c. ☐ Conditional Permanent Resident

**2. Reason for application:** (check one)

**I am a Permanent Resident or Conditional Permanent Resident and:**
- a. ☑ my card was lost, stolen or destroyed. I have attached a copy of an identity document.
- b. ☐ my authorized card was never received. I have attached a copy of an identity document.
- c. ☐ my card is mutilated. I have attached the mutilated card.
- d. ☐ my card was issued with incorrect information because of INS administrative error. I have attached the incorrect card and evidence of the correct information.
- e. ☐ my name or other biographic information has changed since the card was issued. I have attached my present card and evidence of the new information.

**I am a Permanent Resident and:**
- f. ☐ my present card has an expiration date and it is expiring.
- g. ☐ I have reached my 14th birthday since my card was issued. I have attached my present card.
- h. 1. ☐ I have taken up Commuter status. I have attached my present card and evidence of my foreign residence.
- h. 2. ☐ I was a Commuter and am now taking up residence in the U.S. I have attached my present card and evidence of my residence in the U.S.
- i. ☐ my status has been automatically converted to permanent resident. I have attached my Temporary Status Document.
- j. ☐ I have an old edition of the card.

### Part 3. Processing information.

| Mother's First Name | Silvia | Father's First Name | Claidus |
|---|---|---|---|

| City of Residence where you applied for an Immigrant Visa or Adjustment of Status | Bucharest, Romania | Consulate where Immigrant Visa was issued or INS office where status was Adjusted | U.S. Consulate, Bucharest |
|---|---|---|---|

| City/Town/Village of Birth | Bucharest | Date of Admission as an immigrant or Adjustment of Status | October 31, 1998 |
|---|---|---|---|

**Continued on back.**

**FOR INS USE ONLY**

| Returned | Receipt |
|---|---|

Resubmitted

Reloc Sent

Reloc Rec'd

☐ Applicant Interviewed

Status as _____ Verified by _____

Class _____ Initials _____

FD-258 forwarded on _____

I-89 forwarded on _____

I-551 seen and returned _____ (Initials)

Photocopy of I-551 verified _____ (Initials)

_____
Name                    Date

Sticker # _____
              (ten-digit number)

**Action Block**

**To Be Completed by Attorney or Representative, if any**
☐ Fill in box if G-28 is attached to represent the applicant

VOLAG#

ATTY State License #

Form I-90 (Rev. 06/05/02)Y

## SAMPLE FORM I-90 (PAGE 2)

### Part 3. Processing information (continued):

If you entered the U.S. with an Immigrant Visa, also complete the following:

Destination in U.S. at
time of Admission          New York, New York

Port of Entry where
Admitted to U.S.          JFK Airport

Are you in deportation or exclusion proceedings?          ☑ No  ☐ Yes

Since you were granted permanent residence, have you ever filed Form I-407, Abandonment by Alien of Status as Lawful Permanent Resident, or
otherwise been judged to have abandoned your status?          ☑ No  ☐ Yes

If you answer yes to any of the above questions, explain in detail on a separate piece of paper.

### Part 4. Signature. *(Read the information on penalties in the instructions before completing this section. You must file this application while in the United States.*

I certify, under penalty of perjury under the laws of the United States of America, that this application and the evidence submitted with it is all true and correct. I authorize the release of any information from my records that the Immigration and Naturalization Service needs to determine eligibility for the benefit I am seeking.

| Signature | Date | Daytime Phone Number |
|---|---|---|
| *Mihaita Cosmin* | January 6, 2003 | 718-675-4892 |

*Please Note: If you do not completely fill out this form or fail to submit required documents listed in the instructions, you cannot be found eligible for the requested document and this application may be denied.*

### Part 5. Signature of person preparing form, if other than above. *(Sign below)*

*I declare that I prepared this application at the request of the above person and it is based on all information of which I have knowledge.*

| Signature | Print Your Name | Date | Daytime Phone Number |
|---|---|---|---|
| | | | |

Name and Address of Business/Organization (if applicable)

# APPLICATION FOR TRAVEL DOCUMENT, SAMPLE FORM I-131

**U.S. Department of Justice**
Immigration and Naturalization Service

OMB #1115-0005
Application for Travel Document

## START HERE - Please Type or Print

## Part 1.  Information about you.

| Family Name | Cosmin | Given Name | Mihaita | Middle Initial | |
|---|---|---|---|---|---|

Address - C/O

Ravin Cosmin

| Street Number and Name | 8383 Kew Gardens | Apt. # | 4001 |
|---|---|---|---|

| City | Queens | State or Province | |
|---|---|---|---|

| Country | New York | ZIP/Postal Code | 11415 |
|---|---|---|---|

| Date of Birth (Month/Day/Year) | October 2, 1949 | Country of Birth | Romania |
|---|---|---|---|

| Social Security # | 112-64-5793 | A # | A24-070-502 |
|---|---|---|---|

## Part 2.  Application Type (check one).

a.  ☑ I am a permanent resident or conditional resident of the United States and I am applying for a Reentry Permit.

b.  ☐ I now hold U.S. refugee or asylee status and I am applying for a Refugee Travel Document.

c.  ☐ I am a permanent resident as a direct result of refugee or asylee status, and am applying for a Refugee Travel Document.

d.  ☐ I am applying for an Advance Parole to allow me to return to the U.S. after temporary foreign travel.

e.  ☐ I am outside the U.S. and am applying for an Advance Parole.

f.  ☐ I am applying for an Advance Parole for another person who is outside the U.S.  *Give the following information about that person:*

| Family Name | | Given Name | | Middle Initial | |
|---|---|---|---|---|---|

| Date of Birth (Month/Day/Year) | | Country of Birth | |
|---|---|---|---|

Foreign Address - C/O

| Street Number and Name | | Apt. # | |
|---|---|---|---|

| City | | State or Province | |
|---|---|---|---|

| Country | | ZIP/Postal Code | |
|---|---|---|---|

## Part 3.  Processing Information.

| Date of intended departure (Month/Day/Year) | December 15, 2003 | Expected length of trip. | 1 year |
|---|---|---|---|

Are you, or any person included in this application, now in exclusion or deportation proceedings?

☑ No     ☐ Yes, at (give office name) _____

*If applying for an Advance Parole Document, skip to Part 7.*

Have you ever before been issued a Reentry Permit or Refugee Travel Document?

☐ No     ☐ Yes (give the following for the last document issued to you)

| | Date Issued | Disposition (attached, lost, etc.) |
|---|---|---|

Form I-131 (Rev. 12/10/91) N          *Continued on back.*

### FOR INS USE ONLY

| Returned | Receipt |
|---|---|
| | |

Resubmitted

Reloc Sent

Reloc Rec'd

☐ Applicant Interviewed on

**Document Issued**
☐ Reentry Permit
☐ Refugee Travel Document
☐ Single Advance Parole
☐ Multiple Advance Parole
Validity to _____

**If Reentry Permit or Refugee Travel Document**
☐ Mail to Address in Part 2
☐ Mail to American Consulate
☐ Mail to INS overseas office
AT

**Remarks:**
☐ Document Hand Delivered
On _____  By _____

**Action Block**

**To Be Completed by Attorney or Representative, if any**
☐ Fill in box if G-28 is attached to represent the applicant

VOLAG#

ATTY State License #

## Sample Form I-131 (page 2)

### Part 3. Processing Information. (continued)

Where do you want this travel document sent? (check one)

a. ☑ Address in Part 2, above
b. ☐ American Consulate at (give City and Country, below)
c. ☐ INS overseas office at (give City and Country, below)

City                                    Country

If you checked b. or c., above, give your overseas address:

### Part 4. Information about the Proposed Travel.

| Purpose of trip. *If you need more room, continue on a separate sheet of paper.* | List the countries you intend to visit. |
|---|---|
| To attend the settlement of the estate of my deceased brother | Romania |

### Part 5. Complete only if applying for a Reentry Permit.

Since becoming a Permanent Resident (or during the past five years, whichever is less) how much total time have you spent outside the United States?

☑ less than 6 months   ☐ 2 to 3 years
☐ 6 months to 1 year   ☐ 3 to 4 years
☐ 1 to 2 years   ☐ more than 4 years

Since you became a Permanent Resident, have you ever filed a federal income tax return as a nonresident, or failed to file a federal return because you considered yourself to be a nonresident? (if yes, give details on a separate sheet of paper).     ☐ Yes   ☑ No

### Part 6. Complete only if applying for a Refugee Travel Document.

Country from which you are a refugee or asylee:

If you answer yes to any of the following questions, explain on a separate sheet of paper.

Do you plan to travel to the above-named country?     ☐ Yes     ☐ No

Since you were accorded Refugee/Asylee status, have you ever: returned to the above-named country; applied for an/or obtained a national passport, passport renewal, or entry permit into this country; or applied for an/or received any benefit from such country (for example, health insurance benefits)?     ☐ Yes     ☐ No

Since being accorded Refugee/Asylee status, have you, by any legal procedure or voluntary act, re-acquired the nationality of the above-named country, acquired a new nationality, or been granted refugee or asylee status in any other country?     ☐ Yes     ☐ No

### Part 7. Complete only if applying for an Advance Parole.

On a separate sheet of paper, please explain how you qualify for an Advance Parole and what circumstances warrant issuance of Advance Parole. Include copies of any documents you wish considered. (See instructions.)

For how may trips do you intend to use this document?     ☐ 1 trip     ☐ More than 1 trip
If outside the U.S., at right give the U.S. Consulate or INS office you wish notified if this application is approved.

### Part 8. Signature.

*Read the information on penalties in the instructions before completing this section. You must file this application while in the United States if filing for a reentry permit or refugee travel document.*

I certify under penalty of perjury under the laws of the United States of America that this petition, and the evidence submitted with it, is all true and correct. I authorize the release of any information from my records which the Immigration and Naturalization Service needs to determine eligibility for the benefit I am seeking.

| Signature | Date | Daytime Telephone # |
|---|---|---|
| *Mihaita Cosmin* | November 4, 2003 | ( 718 ) 675-4892 |

**Please Note:** If you do not completely fill out this form, or fail to submit required documents listed in the instructions, you may not be found eligible for the requested document and this application will have to be denied.

### Part 9. Signature of person preparing form if other than above. (sign below)

I declare that I prepared this application at the request of the above person and it is based on all information of which I have knowledge.

| Signature | Print Your Name | Date |
|---|---|---|
| | | |

Firm Name and Address                    Daytime Telephone #   ( )

●●●●●●●●●●●●●●

# How to Find and Work With a Lawyer

If It Is Possible, As Far As It Depends on You,
Live at Peace With Everyone.
Romans 12:18

As a rule, in your daily life, be a peacemaker by honest dealing, truthful communications, mutually acceptable compromises and, when necessary, seeking legal information from reliable sources so that you know your rights and your options.

Although this book's philosophy is to help you understand the immigration law and procedures, your situation may be too complicated for you to handle on your own—such as Labor Certification. Or you may be unable to get the BCIS to respond to a request for action on your application. It may become necessary to hire a lawyer or other immigration professional for help. This chapter gives you valuable tips on where to find help—and what to do once you find that help.

## A. WHERE TO LOOK FOR A LAWYER

A bad lawyer is worse than a thief. Good lawyers are worth their weight in gold. Look carefully to find a good, competent, honest lawyer who will help you with your immigration problems without charging you a hefty fee up front and a huge hourly fee as your case proceeds.

You can go a long way toward ensuring that you get the best lawyer possible by spending some time and effort before you hire him or her. There are a number of good places to begin your search.

### 1. Immigration groups

Organizations that specialize in helping people with immigration problems may be able to answer your questions, to represent you in your case or to refer you to an experienced immigration lawyer if the group does not take on individual cases. Ask your local BCIS office or church, mosque or temple for referrals. Also see the Department of Justice's Web list, at www.usdoj.gov/eoir/statspub/recognitionaccreditationroster.pdf.

### 2. Friends and relatives

Ask your friends and relatives about their own experiences with their immigration lawyers—whether they were satisfied with the representation, with the competency, with the fees charged and with their personal rapport with their attorney. Never choose a lawyer simply because he or she was the relative or classmate or friend of your brother or sister or best friend, without having an idea of the lawyer's competency or track record.

### 3. Embassies or consulates

Your own embassy or consulate may have a list of immigration lawyers to recommend to you. Normally, your country's consular officers have your interests at heart and would not recommend a lawyer who is incompetent, a rogue or a cheat.

### 4. Ads in ethnic newspapers

Your own ethnic newspapers and journals usually have an array of immigration lawyers offering their services directly through advertisements. But beware—anyone can buy ad space. Be sure to investigate the lawyer's reputation on your own. Ask your friends. Check with the local bar association or with immigration support groups in the area.

### 5. Lawyer referral groups

Although the local bar association and other lawyer groups may offer referral services, there is little or no screening of lawyers listed in these services. The only qualification may be that no malpractice case has been filed against the lawyer.

The American Immigration Lawyers Association, 1400 I Street NW, Suite 1200; Washington DC 20005; telephone: 202-216-2400; Fax: 202-371-9449; website: www.aila.org, has a list of its members in each state and in some other countries. The lawyers it lists are usually competent and knowledgeable.

---

**BEWARE OF THE BAD GUYS**

Non-attorney practitioners, visa consultants, immigration pseudo-experts, travel agents, people posing as attorneys and nonprofit organizations not authorized by the Bureau of Citizenship and Immigration Services (BCIS) to represent aliens before the BCIS—all of them litter the immigration marketplace.

Some of them provide good advice. But for the most part, be wary of the—especially if they promise you a green card without any hassle for a certain amount of money. Aside from the fact that it is unlawful to practice law without being admitted by the state bar association, there is no way you can check on these individuals' expertise and nowhere to complain if their services are poor.

Report any wrongdoers to the attorney general's office in your state so that they will be forced to stop victimizing unsuspecting aliens.

## B. DECIDING ON A PARTICULAR LAWYER

Once you have a referral to a lawyer—or even better, several referrals—contact each and see whether he or she meets your needs.

A law firm may have a good reputation on immigration practice, but the lawyer assigned to handle your case is the lawyer responsible for the success or failure of your case. Base your decision about whether to hire an individual on the rapport you feel with him or her—not just on a law firm's reputation.

### 1. The initial interview

Start by asking for an appointment. The office may try to screen you by asking you to first discuss your immigration problem over the phone because the lawyer may not handle cases such as yours.

When you do find a lawyer who agrees to meet with you, go to the meeting with the thought in mind that you are interviewing him or her—not the other way around. It will be you who decides whether or not you want to hire that particular lawyer to handle your case.

Rely on your instincts when you first interview the lawyer. Does he or she seem competent, knowledgeable, fair, efficient, courteous and personable? You should be comfortable with the representation. It would be unfortunate and unwise for you to feel uneasy every time you are in contact with your lawyer while paying him or her your hard-earned money.

### 2. Consultation fees

Some lawyers may not charge you an initial consultation fee, but most immigration lawyers charge between $50 to $150 depending on the city where you live, the expertise of the lawyer and how long the interview lasts. When you ask for an appointment, also ask whether a consultation fee is charged and how much it is. And if you do not know, ask how long the lawyer has been in immigration law practice and how many cases like yours the attorney has handled.

If you take a few minutes to get organized before you go to the lawyer, 30 minutes to an hour should be enough time to explain your situation and get at least a basic opinion of what the lawyer can do for you and what that help is likely to cost. Bring with you:

- your passport
- Form I-94 (see Chapter 2, Section C2)
- a copy of any immigration forms you may have filled out and received from the INS or BCIS, and

- documents you may need to prove family relationships, such as husband and wife or parent and child. (See Chapter 29, Section D1.)

### 3. Dealing with paralegals and assistants

Because the practice of immigration law usually involves filling out a great number of forms, the lawyer may hire a paralegal or secretary who interviews you to get many of the answers needed to complete your paperwork.

The paralegal or secretary becomes your contact person. At the initial interview, ask permission to interview the paralegal who will be working on your case, too, so that you have an idea of how comfortable you will be in dealing with the assistant. Ask whether he or she is supervised and whether he or she normally gives the forms to the lawyer for review before submitting them to the U.S. government.

## C. PAYING THE LAWYER

Some organizations specializing in immigration may take your case *pro bono*, meaning they will provide a lawyer to handle your case without asking for any money or for only a small amount to cover expenses. However, due to limited resources and great demand, they may not be able to accept your immigration case and may only be able to tell you what your legal options are and advise you about whether you seem to have a strong case. These groups may refer you to a list of attorneys they feel would be representing you in the same spirit of service as they do and whose fees would be reasonable.

### 1. Types of fee arrangements

Most lawyers are guided by the principle that Time is Money. Many will charge for their work based on quarter-hours, so that if you call and spend ten minutes on the telephone, you will be charged for a minimum of 15 minutes of work. Unless you are completely satisfied that your lawyer is honest, you may be opening yourself up to paying into a bottomless money pit in legal fees when you agree to pay the lawyer according to an hourly charge.

If you agree to the per hour billing rate—usually unwise unless you are in a deportation or exclusion proceeding due to grave criminal conduct or some other complicated case—request a schedule of legal work to be done and a maximum you will pay for each task. This is called a flat fee.

If the case is simple, as usually is the case with an immigration petition for relatives, you may be charged a flat fee, from several hundred to a few thousand dollars. And if the lawyer agrees, you can pay the fee in installments during the period it takes to process your immigration papers.

## 2. Get it in writing

Most disagreements between lawyers and clients involve fees, so be sure to get all the details involving money in writing—either the per hour billing rate or flat maximum fee—how often you will be billed and how the attorney will handle any funds you may have deposited in advance to cover expenses.

## D. Managing the Lawyer

A great many complaints against lawyers have to do with their failure to communicate with their clients. Your lawyer may be the one with the legal expertise, but the rights that are being pursued are yours—and you are the most important person involved in your case. You have the right to demand that your lawyer be reasonably available to answer your questions and to keep you posted on your case.

You may need to put some energy into managing your lawyer.

## 1. Carefully check every statement

Each statement or bill should list costs that the lawyer has paid or that you are expected to pay. If any one lacks sufficient detail for you to verify that it complies with your written fee agreement, call your lawyer and politely demand that a new, more detailed version be sent before you pay it. Don't feel as though you're being too pushy by demanding more detail: The laws in many states actually require thorough detail in lawyers' billing statements.

## 2. Educate yourself

By learning the most you can about immigration laws and what to expect during the procedure, you'll be able to monitor your lawyer's work and may even be able to do some legwork, make a suggestion or provide information that will move your case along faster.

Unfortunately, the BCIS and State Department are bureaucracies and oftentimes, a case is simply held up until the slow-grinding wheels of procedure get through it. However, if an immigration application is proceeding much more slowly than your lawyer initially told you it would, then ask your lawyer to contact the appropriate office and find out the reason for the delay.

## 3. Keep your own calendar

Note when papers and appearances are due in court. If you rely on your lawyer to keep your case on schedule, you may be unpleasantly surprised to find that an important dead-line has been missed. And your immigration status may be put in jeopardy. Call or write to your lawyer at least a week before any important deadline in your case to inquire about plans to meet it.

## 4. Maintain your own file

Never give away original documents connected with your case; keep the originals for your own files and give only copies to your lawyer. The BCIS will accept copies of the original documents. Also, ask for a copy of every letter and application your lawyer sends to the BCIS. By having a well-organized file of your own, you'll be able to discuss your case with your lawyer intelligently and efficiently—even over the telephone.

Being well-informed will help keep your lawyer's effectiveness up and your costs down, especially if your lawyer is working on an hourly basis, in which case telephone consultations are less expensive than office visits.

Also, your lawyer cannot hold your immigration files ransom in case you decide to change legal counsel, because you have copies of everything the office file has on your case.

In any event, you have a right to promptly receive a copy of your file. The attorney may ask you to sign or produce a written authorization and transfer request.

## E. Firing a Lawyer

Change lawyers if you feel that's necessary. If the relationship between you and the lawyer you chose doesn't seem to be working out, or if you feel that your case isn't progressing as it should, think about asking another lawyer to take over.

If you get upset every time you talk to your lawyer because he or she does not seem to understand what you are saying about your case, or will not take the time to listen, you will save yourself both money and mental anguish if you look for someone else to represent you.

But be clear with the first lawyer that you are taking your business elsewhere, and immediately put your decision in writing. You could end up receiving bills from both lawyers—both of whom will claim they handled the lion's share of your case. Before you pay anything, be sure that the total amount of the bills does not amount to more than you agreed to pay. Do not be embarrassed to negotiate with your lawyer. If you have a contingency fee arrangement, it is up to your new lawyer and former lawyer to work out how to split the fee.

## What to do about Bad Legal Advice

Take prompt action against any behavior by a lawyer that appears to be deceptive, unethical or otherwise illegal. A call to the local bar association, listed in the telephone directory under Attorneys, should provide you with guidance on what types of lawyer behavior are prohibited and how to file a complaint.

Still, in most states, groups that regulate attorneys are biased toward lawyers. Unless the lawyer's conduct is plainly dishonest or he or she has abandoned your case, you will probably not get much satisfaction. However, sometimes the threat of filing a complaint can move your lawyer into action. And if worst comes to worst, filing a formal complaint will create a document that you'll need should you end up later filing a lawsuit against a lawyer for malpractice.

■

# RESPONSIBILITIES OF THE NEW IMMIGRANT

## E Pluribus Unum: One Out of Many

This nation is a pluralistic and open society, unique and different from all other countries in the modern world. Its diversity, democracy and free market economy have produced the most powerful nation of our times.

As a newcomer to the United States, try to keep the best of your old country—traditions of family unity, respect for elders, care of the young, high priority for education, fidelity to a form of worship. You should also strive to adapt yourself to the best that your new country offers—the freedom to be what you want to be and the opportunities for economic and educational betterment.

It is vital never to lose your moral perspective in pursuit of the dollar. The new society may differ from your old country, but it still deserves every effort you can make to understand, to improve—and to serve it and its people.

How unfortunate it is when the newcomer views the native only as an economic unit that will contribute to a cash register. How regrettable it is when the native views the newcomer as an intruder, a carpetbagger, one who takes food from the table. It is very sad that we look at each other as enemies, to be viewed with suspicion, anger and disrespect.

As the new immigrant, you can do better than this.

You can begin by going back to living by The Golden Rule: Do to others what you would want them to do to you. After all, we are all one community, one nation. What we do today affects everyone around us, more than we will ever know. In the final analysis, what we do to our neighbor, we do to ourselves.

The motto of the United States of America says it all: *E pluribus unum.* We are one out of many. ■

# BCIS AND DOL OFFICES

**Note:** This list shows the main address for each BCIS office and sub-office in the United States. However, for many BCIS offices, in particular the service centers, you also need a post office box number for each type of application. Check these on the BCIS website at www.immigration.gov/graphics/fieldoffices/index.htm

## BCIS CENTRAL OFFICE

**Bureau of Citizenship & Immigration Services**
425 Eye St. NW
Washington, DC 20536
202-514-4316
Information: 800-375-5283
Form Requests: 800-870-3676

## BCIS REGIONAL SERVICE CENTERS

**California Service Center**
BCIS California Service Center
P.O. Box 30111
Laguna Niguel, CA 92677-0111
Telephone: 949-831-8427

**Nebraska Service Center**
BCIS Nebraska Service Center
850 S Street
P.O. Box [xxxx]
Lincoln, NE 68508

**Texas Service Center**
BCIS Texas Service Center
P.O. Box 851488
Dallas, TX 75185-1488
Telephone: 214-381-1423

**Vermont Service Center**
BCIS Vermont Service Center
75 Lower Weldon St.
St. Albans, VT 05479-0001
Telephone: 802-527-4913

## BCIS DISTRICT AND SUB-OFFICES

### ALABAMA
BCIS Atlanta District Office
Martin Luther King Jr. Federal Building
77 Forsyth Street SW
Atlanta, GA 30303

### ALASKA
BCIS Anchorage District Office
620 East 10th Avenue, Suite 102
Anchorage, AK 99501

### ARIZONA
BCIS Tucson Sub-Office
6431 South Country Club Road
Tucson, AZ 85706-5907

BCIS Phoenix District Office
2035 North Central Avenue
Phoenix, AZ 85004

### ARKANSAS
BCIS New Orleans District Office
701 Loyola Avenue
New Orleans, LA 70113

INS Fort Smith Sub-Office
4991 Old Greenwood Road
Fort Smith, AR 72903

### CALIFORNIA
BCIS Fresno Sub-Office
865 Fulton Mall
Fresno, CA 93721

BCIS Los Angeles District Office
300 North Los Angeles Street, Room 1001
Los Angeles, CA 90012

BCIS Sacramento Sub-Office
650 Capitol Mall
Sacramento, CA 95814

BCIS San Diego District Office
880 Front Street, Suite 1234
San Diego, CA 92101

BCIS San Francisco District Office
630 Sansome Street
San Francisco, CA 94111

BCIS San Jose Sub-Office
1887 Monterey Road
San Jose, CA 95112

BCIS Santa Ana Sub-Office
34 Civic Center Plaza
Federal Building
Santa Ana, CA 92701

### COLORADO
BCIS Denver District Office
4730 Paris Street
Denver, CO 80239

### CONNECTICUT
BCIS Boston District Office
John F. Kennedy Federal Building
Government Center
Boston, MA 02203

BCIS Hartford Sub-Office
450 Main Street, 4th Floor
Hartford, CT 06103-3060

### DELAWARE
BCIS Philadelphia District Office
1600 Callowhill Street
Philadelphia, PA 19130

BCIS Dover Satellite Office
1305 McD Drive
Dover, DE 19901

### DISTRICT OF COLUMBIA
BCIS Washington District Office
4420 N. Fairfax Drive
Arlington, VA 22203

### FLORIDA
BCIS Miami District Office
7880 Biscayne Boulevard
Miami, FL 33138

BCIS Jacksonville Sub-Office
4121 Southpoint Boulevard
Jacksonville, FL 32216

BCIS Orlando Sub-Office
9403 Tradeport Drive
Orlando, FL 32827

BCIS Tampa Sub-Office
5524 West Cypress Street
Tampa, FL 33607-1708

BCIS West Palm Beach Satellite Office
301 Broadway
Riviera Beach, FL 33401

### GEORGIA
BCIS Atlanta District Office
Martin Luther King Jr. Federal Building
77 Forsyth Street SW
Atlanta, GA 30303

### GUAM
BCIS Honolulu District Office
595 Ala Moana Boulevard
Honolulu, HI 96813

### HAWAII
BCIS Honolulu District Office
595 Ala Moana Boulevard
Honolulu, HI 96813

### IDAHO
BCIS Helena District Office
2800 Skyway Drive
Helena, MT 59602

BCIS Boise Sub-Office
1185 South Vinnell Way
Boise, ID 83709

### ILLINOIS
BCIS Chicago District Office
10 West Jackson Boulevard
Chicago, IL 60604

Chicago BCIS Adjudications Office
230 S. Dearborn, 23rd floor
Chicago, IL 60604

Chicago BCIS Citizenship Office
539 S. LaSalle
Chicago, IL 60605

### INDIANA
BCIS Chicago District Office
10 West Jackson Boulevard
Chicago, IL 60604

Indianapolis Sub-Office
950 N. Meridian St., Room 400
Indianapolis, IN 46204

### IOWA
BCIS Omaha District Office
3736 South 132nd Street
Omaha, NE 68144

### KANSAS
BCIS Kansas City District Office
9747 Northwest Conant Avenue
Kansas City, MO 64153

BCIS Wichita Satellite Office
271 West 3rd Street North,
Suite 1050
Wichita, KS 67202-1212

**KENTUCKY**
BCIS New Orleans District
701 Loyola Avenue
New Orleans, LA 70113

BCIS Louisville Sub-Office
Gene Snyder U.S. Courthouse
and Customhouse
Room 390
601 West Broadway
Louisville, KY 40202

**LOUISIANA**
BCIS New Orleans District
701 Loyola Avenue
New Orleans, LA 70113

**MAINE**
BCIS Portland District Office
176 Gannett Drive
South Portland, ME 04106

**MARYLAND**
BCIS Baltimore District Office
Fallon Federal Building
31 Hopkins Plaza
Baltimore, MD 21201

**MASSACHUSETTS**
BCIS Boston District Office
John F. Kennedy Federal Building
Government Center
Boston, MA 02203

**MICHIGAN**
BCIS Detroit District Office
333 Mt. Elliot
Detroit, MI 48207

**MINNESOTA**
BCIS St. Paul District Office
2901 Metro Drive, Suite 100
Bloomington, MN 55425

**MISSISSIPPI**
BCIS New Orleans District Office
701 Loyola Avenue
New Orleans, LA 70113

BCIS Jackson Sub-Office
100 West Capitol Street
Jackson, MS 36269

**MISSOURI**
BCIS Kansas City District Office
9747 Northwest Conant Avenue
Kansas City, MO 64153

**MONTANA**
BCIS Helena District Office
2800 Skyway Drive
Helena, MT 59602

**NEBRASKA**
BCIS Omaha District Office
3736 South 132nd Street
Omaha, NE 68144

**NEVADA**
BCIS Phoenix District Office
2035 North Central Avenue
Phoenix, AZ 85004

BCIS Las Vegas Sub-Office
3373 Pepper Lane
Las Vegas, NV 89120-2739

BCIS Reno Sub-Office
1351 Corporate Boulevard
Reno, NV 89502

**NEW HAMPSHIRE**
BCIS Boston District Office
John F. Kennedy Federal Building
Government Center
Boston, MA 02203

BCIS Manchester Satellite Office
803 Canal Street
Manchester, NH 03101

**NEW JERSEY**
BCIS Newark District Office
Peter Rodino, Jr. Federal Building
970 Broad Street
Newark, NJ 07102

BCIS Cherry Hill Sub-Office
1886 Greentree Road
Cherry Hill, NJ 08003

**NEW MEXICO**
BCIS El Paso District Office
1545 Hawkins Boulevard, Suite 167
El Paso, TX 79925

BCIS Albuquerque Sub-Office
1720 Randolph Road SE
Albuquerque, NM 87106

**NEW YORK**
BCIS Buffalo District Office
Federal Center
130 Delaware Avenue
Buffalo, NY 14202

BCIS New York City District
Office
26 Federal Plaza
New York City, NY 10278

BCIS Albany Sub-Office
1086 Troy-Schenectady Road
Latham, NY 12110

**NORTH CAROLINA**
BCIS Atlanta District Office
Martin Luther King Jr. Federal
Building
77 Forsyth Street SW
Atlanta, GA 30303

BCIS Charlotte Sub-Office
210 E. Woodlawn Road
Building 6, Suite 138 (Woodlawn
Green Office Complex)
Charlotte, NC 28217

**NORTH DAKOTA**
BCIS St. Paul District Office
2901 Metro Drive, Suite 100
Bloomington, MN 55425

**OHIO**
BCIS Cleveland District Office
A.J.C. Federal Building
1240 East Ninth Street, Room 1917
Cleveland, OH 44199

BCIS Cincinnati Sub-Office
J.W. Peck Federal Building
550 Main Street, Room 4001
Cincinnati, OH 45202

**OKLAHOMA**
BCIS Dallas District Office
8101 North Stemmons Freeway
Dallas, TX 75247

BCIS Oklahoma City Sub-Office
4149 Highline Boulevard, Suite #300
Oklahoma City, OK 73108-2081

**OREGON**
BCIS Portland, Oregon District
Office
511 NW Broadway
Portland, OR 97209

**PENNSYLVANIA**
BCIS Philadelphia District Office
1600 Callowhill Street
Philadelphia, PA 19130

BCIS Pittsburgh Sub-Office
1000 Liberty Avenue, Federal
Building, Room 314
Pittsburgh, PA 15222-4181

**PUERTO RICO**
BCIS San Juan District Office
San Patricio Office Center
7 Tabonuco Street, Suite 100
Guaynabo, Puerto Rico 00968

BCIS Charlotte Amalie Sub Office
Nisky Center, Suite 1A First Floor
South
Charlotte Amalie, St. Thomas
U.S. Virgin Islands 00802

BCIS San Croix Sub-Office
Sunny Isle Shopping Center
Christiansted, St. Croix
U.S. Virgin Islands 00820

**RHODE ISLAND**
BCIS Boston District Office
John F. Kennedy Federal Building
Government Center
Boston, MA 02203

BCIS Providence Sub-Office
200 Dyer Street
Providence, RI 02903

**SOUTH CAROLINA**
BCIS Atlanta District Office
Martin Luther King Jr. Federal
Building
77 Forsyth Street SW
Atlanta, GA 30303

BCIS Charleston Satellite Office
170 Meeting Street, Fifth Floor
Charleston, SC 29401

**SOUTH DAKOTA**
BCIS St. Paul District Office
2901 Metro Drive, Suite 100
Bloomington, MN 55425

**TENNESSEE**
BCIS New Orleans District Office
701 Loyola Avenue
New Orleans, LA 70113

BCIS Memphis Sub-Office
Suite 100
1341 Sycamore View Road
Memphis, TN 38134

**TEXAS**
BCIS Dallas District Office
8101 North Stemmons Freeway
Dallas, TX 75247

BCIS El Paso District Office
1545 Hawkins Boulevard, Suite 167
El Paso, TX 79925

BCIS Harlingen District Office
2102 Teege Avenue
Harlingen, TX 78550

Houston BCIS District Office
126 Northpoint
Houston, TX 77060

BCIS San Antonio District Office
8940 Fourwinds Drive
San Antonio, TX 78239

**UTAH**
BCIS Denver District Office
4730 Paris Street
Denver, CO 80239

BCIS Salt Lake City Sub-Office
5272 South College Drive, #100
Murray, UT 84123

**VERMONT**
BCIS Portland District Office
176 Gannett Drive
South Portland, ME 04106

BCIS St. Albans Sub-Office
64 Gricebrook Road
St. Albans, VT 05478

**VIRGIN ISLANDS**
BCIS San Juan District Office
San Patricio Office Center
7 Tabonuco Street, Suite 100
Guaynabo, Puerto Rico 00968

BCIS Charlotte Amalie Sub-Office
Nisky Center, Suite 1A First Floor
South
Charlotte Amalie, St. Thomas
U.S. Virgin Islands 00802

San Croix Sub-Office
Sunny Isle Shopping Center
Christiansted, St. Croix
U.S. Virgin Islands 00820

**VIRGINIA**
BCIS Washington District Office
4420 N. Fairfax Drive
Arlington, VA 22203

BCIS Norfolk Sub-Office
5280 Henneman Drive
Norfolk, VA 23513

**WASHINGTON**
BCIS Seattle District Office
815 Airport Way South
Seattle, WA 98134

BCIS Spokane Sub-Office
U.S. Courthouse
920 W. Riverside Room 691
Spokane, WA 99201

BCIS Yakima Sub-Office
417 E. Chestnut
Yakima, WA 98901

**WEST VIRGINIA**
BCIS Philadelphia District Office
1600 Callowhill Street
Philadelphia, PA 19130

BCIS West Virginia Satellite Office
210 Kanawha Boulevard West
Charleston, WV 25302

BCIS Pittsburgh Sub-Office
1000 Liberty Avenue, Federal
Building, Room 314
Pittsburgh, PA 15222-4181

**WISCONSIN**
BCIS Chicago District Office
10 West Jackson Boulevard
Chicago, IL 60604

BCIS Milwaukee Sub-Office
310 E. Knapp Street
Milwaukee, WI 53202

**WYOMING**
BCIS Denver District Office
4730 Paris Street
Denver, CO 80239

## REGIONAL DEPARTMENT OF LABOR OFFICES

| REGION | STATES | REGION | STATES |
| --- | --- | --- | --- |
| **Atlanta**<br>Atlanta Federal Center<br>Room 6M12<br>61 Forsyth Street, SW<br>Atlanta, GA 30303<br>Tel: 404-562-2086 | Alabama, Florida, Georgia, Kentucky, Mississippi, North Carolina, South Carolina, Tennessee | **Kansas City**<br>110 Main St., Suite 1050<br>City Center Square<br>Kansas City, MO 64105<br>Tel: 816-502-9000; 9002 | Iowa, Kansas, Missouri, Nebraska |
| **Boston**<br>JFK Federal Building<br>Room E-350<br>Boston, MA 02203<br>Tel: 617-565-3929; 2205 | Connecticut, Maine, Massachusetts, New Hampshire, Rhode Island, Vermont | **New York**<br>201 Varick Street<br>Room 755 N<br>New York, NY 10014<br>Tel: 212-337-2184;<br>2193; 2185 | New York, New Jersey, Puerto Rico, Virgin Islands |
| **Chicago**<br>230 South Dearborn St.<br>6th Floor<br>Chicago, IL 60604<br>Tel: 312-353-2595; 1059 | Ilinois, Indiana, Michigan, Minnesota, Ohio, Wisconsin | **Philadelphia**<br>The Curtis Center<br>170 S. Independence<br>Mall West<br>Philadelphia, PA 19106<br>Tel: 215-861-5250; 5262 | Delaware, District of Columbia, Maryland, Pennsylvania, Virginia, West Virginia |
| **Dallas**<br>525 Griffin Street<br>Room 317<br>Dallas, TX 75202<br>Tel: 214-767-8263 | Arkansas, Louisiana, New Mexico, Oklahoma, Texas | **San Francisco**<br>P.O. Box 193767<br>71 Stevenson St., Suite 830<br>San Francisco, CA 94119-3767<br>Tel: 415-975-4660 | Arizona, California, Guam, Hawaii, Nevada |
| **Denver**<br>1999 Broadway<br>Suite 1780<br>P.O. Box 46550<br>Denver, CO 80202-5716<br>Tel: 303-844-1651 | Colorado, Montana, North Dakota, South Dakota, Utah, Wyoming | **Seattle**<br>1111 Third Avenue<br>Suite 815<br>Seattle, WA 98101-3212<br>Tel: 206-553-5297 x 8011<br>553-7607 x 8013 | Alaska, Idaho, Oregon, Washington |

Note: Immigration forms change often, and you are required to use the most up-to-date form. Also, many of the forms come with instructions, which space does not always allow us to include in this book. To get the most complete, up-to-date forms, visit the BCIS website at www.bcis.gov, or call their automated forms line at 800-870-3676.

# FORMS

| | |
|---|---|
| Form AR-11 | Alien's Change of Address Card |
| Form OF-169 | Instructions for Immigrant Visa Applicants |
| Form DS-230 (Parts I & II) | Application for Immigrant Visa and Alien Registration |
| Form ETA 750 Part A | Application for Alien Employment Certification |
| Form ETA 750 Part B | Statement of Qualifications of Alien |
| Form G-325A | Biographic Information |
| Form I-90 | Application to Replace Permanent Resident Card |
| Form I-102 | Application for Replacement/Initial Nonimmigrant Arrival-Departure Document |
| Form I-129F | Petition for Alien Fiancé(e) |
| Form I-130 | Petition for Alien Relative |
| Form I-131 | Application for Travel Document |
| Form I-134 | Affidavit of Support |
| Form I-140 | Immigrant Petition for Alien Worker |
| Form I-360 | Petition for Amerasian, Widow(er) or Special Immigrant |
| Form I-485 | Application to Register Permanent Residence or Adjust Status |
| Form I-485 Supp. A | Supplement A to Form I-485 |
| Form I-526 | Immigrant Petition by Alien Entrepreneur |
| Form I-539 | Application to Extend/Change Nonimmigrant Status |
| Form I-589 | Application for Asylum and for Withholding of Removal |
| Form I-600 | Petition to Classify Orphan as an Immediate Relative |
| Form I-600A | Application for Advance Processing of Orphan Petition |
| Form I-751 | Petition to Remove the Conditions on Residence |
| Form I-765 | Application for Employment Authorization |

# FORMS (CONTINUED)

OMB No. 1115-0003; Exp. 10/31/04

**Department of Justice**
Immigration and Naturalization Service

# Alien's Change of Address Card

| NAME (Last in CAPS) | (First) | (Middle) | I AM IN THE UNITED STATES AS: |
|---|---|---|---|

☐ Visitor ☐ Permanent Resident
☐ Student ☐ Other . . . . . . . .　(Specify)

| COUNTRY OF CITIZENSHIP | DATE OF BIRTH | **A** | COPY NUMBER FROM ALIEN CARD |
|---|---|---|---|

| PRESENT ADDRESS | (Street or Rural Route) | (City or Post Office) | (State) | (ZIP Code) |
|---|---|---|---|---|

(IF ABOVE ADDRESS IS TEMPORARY) I expect to remain there _____ years _____ months

| LAST ADDRESS | (Street or Rural Route) | (City or Post Office) | (State) | (ZIP Code) |
|---|---|---|---|---|

I WORK FOR OR ATTEND SCHOOL AT: (Employer's Name or Name of School)

| (Street Address or Rural Route) | (City or Post Office) | (State) | (ZIP Code) |
|---|---|---|---|

| PORT OF ENTRY INTO U.S. | DATE OF ENTRY INTO U.S. | IF NOT A PERMANENT RESIDENT, MY STAY IN THE U.S. EXPIRES ON: (Date) |
|---|---|---|
| SIGNATURE | DATE | |

AR-11 (Rev. 11/07/02)Y

## ALIEN'S CHANGE OF ADDRESS CARD

This card is to be used by all aliens to report change of address within 10 days of such change.

The collection of this information is required by Section 265 of the I&N Act (8 U.S.C. 1305). The data used by the Immigration and Naturalization Service for statistical and record purposes and may be furnished to federal, state, local and foreign law enforcement officials. Failure to report is punishable by fine or imprisonment and/or deportation.

This card is not evidence of identity, age, or status claimed.

**Public Reporting Burden.** Under the Paperwork Reduction Act, an agency may not conduct or sponsor an information collection and a person is not required to respond to an information collection unless it displays a currently valid OMB control number. We try to create forms and instructions that are accurate, can be easily understood, and which impose the least possible burden on you to provide us with information. Often this is difficult because some immigration laws are very complex. This collection of information is estimated to average 5 minutes per response, including the time for reviewing instructions, searching existing data sources, gathering and maintaining the data needed, and completing and reviewing the collection of information. Send comments regarding this burden estimate or any other aspect of this collection of information, including for reducing this burden to: Immigration and Naturalization Service, 425 I Street, N.W., Room 4034, Washington, DC 20536; OMB No. 1115-0003. *Do not mail your completed form to this address.* **MAIL YOUR FORM TO THE ADDRESSES SHOWN BELOW:**

For regular US Postal Service:

U.S. DEPARTMENT OF JUSTICE
Immigration and Naturalization Service
Change of Address
P.O. Box 7134
London, KY 40742-7134

For overnight mailings, **only**:

U.S. DEPARTMENT OF JUSTICE
Immigration and Naturalization Service
Change of Address
1084-I South Laurel Road
London, KY 40744

# INSTRUCTIONS FOR IMMIGRANT VISA APPLICANTS

This office has received evidence entitling you to immigrant visa status. While no assurance can be given regarding the date of your visa interview appointment, you should now prepare for that appointment by taking the following three steps:

**FIRST:** Complete and send immediately to the consular office processing your case the enclosed Form OF-230 Part I, APPLICA TION FOR IMMIGRANT VISA AND ALIEN REGISTRATION (Biographic Data). The consular office cannot process your case until this form is received.

**SECOND:** Obtain the following documents on this checklist which pertain to you. As you obtain each document, check the box before each item. Do NOT send them to the consular office.

☐**1. PASSPORTS:** A Passport must be valid for travel to the United States and must have at least six months validity beyond the issuance date of the visa. Children may be included on a parent's passport, but if over the age of 16, they must have their photographs attached to the passport.

☐**2. BIRTH CERTIFICATES:** One certified copy of the birth certificate of each person named in the application is required. Birth records must be presented for all unmarried children under age 21, even if they do not wish to immigrate at this time. (If children are deceased, so state giving year of death.) The certificate must state the date and place of birth and the names of both parents. The certificate must also indicate that it is an extract from official records. If you, or any children were adopted, you must submit a certified copy of the final adoption decree. Photostatic copies are acceptable provided the original is offered for inspection by the consular officer.

   **UNOBTAINABLE BIRTH CERTIFICATE:** In rare cases, it may be impossible to obtain a birth certificate because records have been destroyed or the government will not issue one. In such cases, you should obtain a statement to that effect from the civil registrar's office and proceed to obtain secondary evidence of birth. A baptismal certificate may be submitted for consideration provided it contains the date and place of the applicant's birth and information concerning parentage and provided the baptism took place shortly after birth. Should a baptismal certificate be unobtainable, a close relative, preferably the applicant's mother, should prepare a notarized statement giving the place and date of the applicant's birth, the names of both parents, and the maiden name of the mother. The statement must be executed before an official authorized to administer oaths or affirmations. In such cases, please bring any secondary evidence you might have concerning your birth.

☐**3. POLICE CERTIFICATES:** Each visa applicant aged 16 years or over is required to submit a police certificate from the police authorities of each locality of the country of the applicant's nationality or current residence where the applicant has resided for at least six months since attaining the age of sixteen. Police certificates are also required from all other countries where the applicant has resided for at least one year. A police certificate must also be obtained from the police authorities of any place where the applicant has been arrested for any reason, regardless of how long he or she lived there. Police certificates must cover the entire period of the applicant's residence in any area. A certificate issued by the police authorities where you now reside must be of recent date when presented to the consular officer. The term "police certificate" as used in this paragraph means a certification by appropri    ate police authorities stating what their records show concerning each applicant, including all arrests, the reasons for the arrests, and the disposition of each case of which there is a record.

Police certificates from certain countries are considered unobtainable. See the attached list on form DSL-1083. If specific questions arise regarding police certificates, please consult the consular office.

☐**4. COURT AND PRISON RECORDS:** Persons who have been convicted of a crime must obtain a certified copy of each court record and of any prison record, regardless of the fact that they may have benefited subsequently from an amnesty, pardon, or other act of clemency.

☐**5. MILITARY RECORDS:** A certified copy of any military record, if applicable and obtainable, is required.

☐**6. PHOTOGRAPHS:** Two (2) color photographs with white background on glossy paper, unretouched, and unmounted are required. The photograph must be a three-quarter frontal portrait with the right side of the face and right ear visible. The dimensions of the facial image must measure about one inch (30 mm) from chin to top of hair. No head covering or dark glasses should be worn.

☐**7. EVIDENCE OF SUPPORT:** Form I-864, a contractual affidavit of support, must be submitted for most family-based applicants and employment-based applicants when a relative is the petitioner or has ownership interest in the petitioning business. The enclosed information sheet provides guidance for preparing the I-864. Other applicants must show evidence that they are not likely to become public charges while in the United States.

**8. MARRIAGE CERTIFICATES:** Married persons are required to present a certified copy of their marriage certificate. Proof of the termination of any previous marriage must also be submitted (e.g., death certificate of spouse, final decrees of divorce or annulment).

**9. ORIGINAL DOCUMENTS:** If you are the beneficiary of a family-based immigrant visa petition, you must be prepared to present the **originals** of all civil documents which establish your claimed relationship to the petitioner.

**10. TRANSLATIONS:** All documents not in English, or in the official language of the country in which application for a visa is being made, must be accompanied by certified English translations. Translations must be certified by a competent translator and sworn to before a Notary Public. ( <u>All</u> documents in Japanese must be translated.)

ONLY ONE COPY OF EACH DOCUMENT, EXCEPT PHOTOGRAPHS, MUST BE SUBMITTED WITH THE VISA APPLICATION. YOU ARE ADVISED, HOWEVER, TO OBTAIN THE NECESSARY DOCUMENTS IN DUPLICATE, AS THIS WILL ENABLE YOU TO PROVIDE IDENTICAL COPIES IN THE EVENT THE FIRST SET IS LOST OR DAMAGED.

**PLEASE READ THE FOLLOWING CAREFULLY**

**THIRD:** As soon as you have obtained all of the documents that apply to your case, carefully read the statement at the bottom of this page, sign and date it, and send the form to the consular office processing your case. You will not be scheduled for an appointment until you sign and return the checklist.

After this form has been sent to the consular office, you will be scheduled for a visa interview at the earliest possible date. It is not possible to predict when this will be since it depends upon when the priority date for your visa category and country becomes current. You will receive an appointment letter along with instructions for a medical examination approximately one month before your scheduled interview with a consular officer. You may not receive any further correspondence from the consular office until the appointment is scheduled.

The total fee for an immigrant visa is U.S. $325, or the local currency equivalent. Each applicant must be prepared to pay this fee on the appointment date.

You need not check with the consular office unless you have to report a CHANGE OF ADDRESS or change in your situation such as marriage, death of petitioner, or birth of children. Please do not send any documents to the consular office unless you are specifically requested to do so.

Enclosures:
1. Optional Form 230 Part I, Application for Immigrant Visa and Alien Registration - Biographic Data
2. Form DSL-1083, Immigrant Visa Supplemental Information Sheet
3. Form I-864, Affidavit of Support and Checklist

## APPLICANT'S STATEMENT

I have in my possession and am prepared to present all the documents listed in items 1 through 10 which apply to my case, as indicated by the check mark I have placed in the appropriate boxes. I fully realize that no advance assurance can be given when or whether a visa will actually be issued to me and I also understand that I should NOT give up my job, dispose of property, or make any final travel arrangements until a visa is actually issued to me. When it is possible for me to receive an appointment to make formal visa application, I intend to apply: (check appropriate boxes)

☐1. Alone

☐2. Together with my spouse (Print first name: _____ )

☐3. Together with my spouse and the following minor children: (Print first names of each

child

who will accompany you)

_____

_____          DATE: _____

_____          CASE NUMBER: _____

_____          SIGNATURE: _____

_____          PRINT NAME : _____

_____          CURRENT ADDRESS: _____

_____          _____

U.S. Department of State
# APPLICATION FOR IMMIGRANT VISA AND ALIEN REGISTRATION

OMB APPROVAL NO. 1405-0015
EXPIRES: 05/31/2004
ESTIMATED BURDEN: 1 HOUR*
(See Page 2)

## PART I - BIOGRAPHIC DATA

**INSTRUCTIONS:** Complete one copy of this form for yourself and each member of your family, regardless of age, who will immigrate with you. Please print or type your answers to all questions. Mark questions that are Not Applicable with "N/A". If there is insufficient room on the form, answer on a separate sheet using the same numbers that appear on the form. Attach any additional sheets to this form.

**WARNING:** Any false statement or concealment of a material fact may result in your permanent exclusion from the United States.

This form (DS-230 PART I) is the first of two parts. This part, together with Form DS-230 PART II, constitutes the complete Application for Immigrant Visa and Alien Registration.

| 1. Family Name | First Name | Middle Name |
|---|---|---|

2. Other Names Used or Aliases *(If married woman, give maiden name)*

3. Full Name in Native Alphabet *(If Roman letters not used)*

| 4. Date of Birth *(mm-dd-yyyy)* | 5. Age | 6. Place of Birth |
|---|---|---|
| | | (City or town)    *(Province)*    *(Country)* |

7. Nationality *(If dual national, give both)*

8. Gender
☐ Male
☐ Female

9. Marital Status
☐ Single *(Never married)*   ☐ Married   ☐ Widowed   ☐ Divorced   ☐ Separated
Including my present marriage, I have been married _____ times.

10. Permanent address in the United States where you intend to live, if known *(street address including zip code)*. Include the name of a person who currently lives there.

Telephone number:

11. Address in the United States where you want your Permanent Resident Card *(Green Card)* mailed, if different from address in item #10 *(include the name of a person who currently lives there)*.

Telephone number:

12. Your Present Occupation

13. Present Address *(Street Address) (City or Town) (Province) (Country)*

Telephone number:  Home                    Office

14. Name of Spouse *(Maiden or family name)*                First Name                Middle Name

Date *(mm-dd-yyyy)* and place of birth of spouse:

Address of spouse *(If different from your own)*:

Spouse's occupation:                    Date of marriage *(mm-dd-yyyy)*:

| 15. Father's Family Name | First Name | Middle Name |
|---|---|---|

| 16. Father's Date of Birth *(mm-dd-yyyy)* | Place of Birth | Current Address | If deceased, give year of death |
|---|---|---|---|

| 17. Mother's Family Name at Birth | First Name | Middle Name |
|---|---|---|

| 18. Mother's Date of Birth *(mm-dd-yyyy)* | Place of Birth | Current Address | If deceased, give year of death |
|---|---|---|---|

19. List Names, Dates and Places of Birth, and Addresses of ALL Children.

| NAME | DATE (mm-dd-yyyy) | PLACE OF BIRTH | ADDRESS (If different from your own) |
|------|-------------------|----------------|--------------------------------------|
| | | | |
| | | | |
| | | | |
| | | | |
| | | | |
| | | | |
| | | | |
| | | | |

20. List below all places you have lived for at least six months since reaching the age of 16, including places in your country of nationality. Begin with your present residence.

| CITY OR TOWN | PROVINCE | COUNTRY | FROM/TO (mm-yyyy) |
|--------------|----------|---------|-------------------|
| | | | |
| | | | |
| | | | |
| | | | |
| | | | |
| | | | |
| | | | |

21a. Person(s) named in 14 and 19 who will accompany you to the United States now.

21b. Person(s) named in 14 and 19 who will follow you to the United States at a later date.

22. List below all employment for the last ten years.

| EMPLOYER | LOCATION | JOB TITLE | FROM/TO (mm-yyyy) |
|----------|----------|-----------|-------------------|
| | | | |
| | | | |
| | | | |
| | | | |
| | | | |

In what occupation do you intend to work in the United States? _____

23. List below all educational institutions attended.

| SCHOOL AND LOCATION | FROM/TO (mm-yyyy) | COURSE OF STUDY | DEGREE OR DIPLOMA |
|---------------------|-------------------|-----------------|-------------------|
| | | | |
| | | | |
| | | | |
| | | | |

Languages spoken or read: _____

Professional associations to which you belong: _____

24. Previous Military Service ☐ Yes ☐ No

Branch: _____ Dates (mm-dd-yyyy) of Service: _____

Rank/Position: _____ Military Speciality/Occupation: _____

25. List dates of all previous visits to or residence in the United States. (If never, write "never") Give type of visa status, if known. Give INS "A" number if any.

| FROM/TO (mm-yyyy) | LOCATION | TYPE OF VISA | "A" NO. (If known) |
|-------------------|----------|--------------|--------------------|
| | | | |
| | | | |
| | | | |

| SIGNATURE OF APPLICANT | DATE (mm-dd-yyyy) |
|------------------------|-------------------|
| | |

**Privacy Act and Paperwork Reduction Act Statements**

The information asked for on this form is requested pursuant to Section 222 of the Immigration and Nationality Act. The U.S. Department of State uses the facts you provide on this form primarily to determine your classification and eligibility for a U.S. immigrant visa. Individuals who fail to submit this form or who do not provide all the requested information may be denied a U.S. immigrant visa. If you are issued an immigrant visa and are subsequently admitted to the United States as an immigrant, the Immigration and Naturalization Service will use the information on this form to issue you a Permanent Resident Card, and, if you so indicate, the Social Security Administration will use the information to issue you a social security number and card.

*Public reporting burden for this collection of information is estimated to average 1 hour per response, including time required for searching existing data sources, gathering the necessary data, providing the information required, and reviewing the final collection. In accordance with 5 CFR 1320 5(b), persons are not required to respond to the collection of this information unless this form displays a currently valid OMB control number. Send comments on the accuracy of this estimate of the burden and recommendations for reducing it to: U.S. Department of State (A/RPS/DIR) Washington, D.C. 20520.

U.S. Department of State
# APPLICATION FOR IMMIGRANT VISA AND ALIEN REGISTRATION

OMB APPROVAL NO. 1405-0015
EXPIRES: 05/31/2004
ESTIMATED BURDEN: 1 HOUR*

## PART II - SWORN STATEMENT

INSTRUCTIONS: Complete one copy of this form for yourself and each member of your family, regardless of age, who will immigrate with you. Please print or type your answers to all questions. Mark questions that are Not Applicable with "N/A". If there is insufficient room on the form, answer on a separate sheet using the same numbers that appear on the form. Attach any additional sheets to this form. The fee should be paid in United States dollars or local currency equivalent, or by bank draft.

WARNING: Any false statement or concealment of a material fact may result in your permanent exclusion from the United States. Even if you are issued an immigrant visa and are subsequently admitted to the United States, providing false information on this form could be grounds for your prosecution and/or deportation.

This form (DS-230 PART II), together with Form DS-230 PART I, constitutes the complete Application for Immigrant Visa and Alien Registration.

26. Family Name                    First Name                    Middle Name

27. Other Names Used or Aliases *(If married woman, give maiden name)*

28. Full Name in Native Alphabet *(If Roman letters not used)*

29. Name and Address of Petitioner

Telephone number:

30. United States laws governing the issuance of visas require each applicant to state whether or not he or she is a member of any class of individuals excluded from admission into the United States. The excludable classes are described below in general terms. You should read carefully the following list and answer YES or NO to each category. The answers you give will assist the consular officer to reach a decision on your eligibility to receive a visa.

**EXCEPT AS OTHERWISE PROVIDED BY LAW, ALIENS WITHIN THE FOLLOWING CLASSIFICATIONS ARE INELIGIBLE TO RECEIVE A VISA. DO ANY OF THE FOLLOWING CLASSES APPLY TO YOU?**

a. An alien who has a communicable disease of public health significance; who has failed to present documentation of having received vaccinations in accordance with U.S. law; who has or has had a physical or mental disorder that poses or is likely to pose a threat to the safety ☐ Yes ☐ No

b. An alien convicted of, or who admits having committed, a crime involving moral turpitude or violation of any law relating to a controlled substance or who is the spouse, son or daughter of such a trafficker who knowingly has benefited from the trafficking activities in the past five years; who has been convicted of 2 or more offenses for which the aggregate sentences were 5 years or more; who is coming to the United States to engage in prostitution or commercialized vice or who has engaged in prostitution or procuring within the past 10 years; who is or has been an illicit trafficker in any controlled substance; who has committed a serious criminal offense in the United States and who has asserted immunity from prosecution; who, while serving as a foreign government official and within the previous 24-month period, was responsible for or directly carried out particularly severe violations of religious freedom; or whom the President has identified as a person who plays a significant role in a severe form of trafficking in persons, who otherwise has knowingly aided, abetted, assisted or colluded with such a trafficker in severe forms of trafficking in persons, or who is the spouse, son or daughter of such a trafficker who knowingly has benefited from the trafficking activities within the past five years. ☐ Yes ☐ No

c. An alien who seeks to enter the United States to engage in espionage, sabotage, export control violations, terrorist activities, the overthrow of the Government of the United States or other unlawful activity; who is a member of or affiliated with the Communist or other totalitarian party; who participated in Nazi persecutions or genocide; who has engaged in genocide; or who is a member or representative of a terrorist organization as currently designated by the U.S. Secretary of State. ☐ Yes ☐ No

d. An alien who is likely to become a public charge. ☐ Yes ☐ No

e. An alien who seeks to enter for the purpose of performing skilled or unskilled labor who has not been certified by the Secretary of Labor; who is a graduate of a foreign medical school seeking to perform medical services who has not passed the NBME exam or its equivalent; or who is a health care worker seeking to perform such work without a certificate from the CGFNS or from an equivalent approved independent credentialing organization. ☐ Yes ☐ No

f. An alien who failed to attend a hearing on deportation or inadmissibility within the last 5 years; who seeks or has sought a visa, entry into the United States, or any immigration benefit by fraud or misrepresentation; who knowingly assisted any other alien to enter or try to enter the United States in violation of law; who, after November 30, 1996, attended in student (F) visa status a U.S. public elementary school or who attended a U.S. public secondary school without reimbursing the school; or who is subject to a civil penalty under INA 274C. ☐ Yes ☐ No

### Privacy Act and Paperwork Reduction Act Statements

g. An alien who is permanently ineligible for U.S. citizenship; or who departed the United States to evade military service in time of war. ☐ Yes ☐ No

h. An alien who was previously ordered removed within the last 5 years or ordered removed a second time within the last 20 years; who was previously unlawfully present and ordered removed within the last 10 years or ordered removed a second time within the last 20 years; who was convicted of an aggravated felony and ordered removed; who was previously unlawfully present in the United States for more than 180 days but less than one year who voluntarily departed within the last 3 years; or who was unlawfully present for more than one year or an aggregate of one year within the last 10 years. ☐ Yes ☐ No

i. An alien who is coming to the United States to practice polygamy; who withholds custody of a U.S. citizen child outside the United States from a person granted legal custody by a U.S. court or intentionally assists another person to do so; who has voted in the United States in ☐ Yes ☐ No

j. An alien who is a former exchange visitor who has not fulfilled the 2-year foreign residence requirement. ☐ Yes ☐ No

k. An alien determined by the Attorney General to have knowingly made a frivolous application for asylum. ☐ Yes ☐ No

l. An alien who has ordered, carried out or materially assisted in extrajudicial and political killings and other acts of violence against the Haitian people; who has directly or indirectly assisted or supported any of the groups in Colombia known as FARC, ELN, or AUC; who through abuse of a governmental or political position has converted for personal gain, confiscated or expropriated property in Cuba, a claim to which is owned by a national of the United States, has trafficked in such property or has been complicit in such conversion, has committed similar acts in another country, or is the spouse, minor child or agent of an alien who has committed such acts; who has been directly involved in the establishment or enforcement of population controls forcing a woman to undergo an abortion against her free choice or a man or a woman to undergo sterilization against his or her free choice; or who has disclosed or trafficked in confidential U.S. business information obtained in connection with U.S. participation in the Chemical Weapons Convention or is the spouse, minor child or agent of such a person. ☐ Yes ☐ No

31. Have you ever been charged, arrested or convicted of any offense or crime?
*(If answer is Yes, please explain)* ☐ Yes ☐ No

32. Have you ever been refused admission to the United States at a port-of-entry?
*(If answer is Yes, please explain)* ☐ Yes ☐ No

33a. Have you ever applied for a Social Security Number (SSN)?

☐ Yes    Give the number _____ ☐ No

Do you want the Social Security Administration to assign you an SSN (and issue a card) or issue you a new card (if you have an SSN)? You must answer "Yes" to this question and to the "Consent To Disclosure" in order to receive an SSN and/or card.

☐ Yes ☐ No

33b. CONSENT TO DISCLOSURE: I authorize disclosure of information from this form to the Immigration and Naturalization Service (INS), the Social Security Administration (SSA), such other U.S. Government agencies as may be required for the purpose of assigning me an SSN and issuing me a Social Security card, and I authorize the SSA to share my SSN with the INS.

☐ Yes ☐ No

The applicant's response does not limit or restrict the Government's ability to obtain his or her SSN, or other information on this form, for enforcement or other purposes as authorized by law.

34. WERE YOU ASSISTED IN COMPLETING THIS APPLICATION? ☐ Yes ☐ No
(If answer is Yes, give name and address of person assisting you, indicating whether relative, friend, travel agent, attorney, or other)

**DO NOT WRITE BELOW THE FOLLOWING LINE**
**The consular officer will assist you in answering item 35.**
**DO NOT SIGN this form until instructed to do so by the consular officer**

35. I claim to be:

☐ A Family-Sponsored Immigrant
☐ An Employment-Based Immigrant
☐ A Diversity Immigrant
☐ A Special Category *(Specify)* _____
(Returning resident, Hong Kong, Tibetan, Private Legislation, etc.)

☐ I derive foreign state chargeability under Sec. 202(b) through my _____

☐ Preference: _____
☐ Numerical limitation: _____
*(foreign state)*

I understand that I am required to surrender my visa to the United States Immigration Officer at the place where I apply to enter the United States, and that the possession of a visa does not entitle me to enter the United States if at that time I am found to be inadmissible under the immigration laws.

I understand that any willfully false or misleading statement or willful concealment of a material fact made by me herein may subject me to permanent exclusion from the United States and, if I am admitted to the United States, may subject me to criminal prosecution and/or deportation.

I, the undersigned applicant for a United States immigrant visa, do solemnly swear (or affirm) that all statements which appear in this application, consisting of Form DS-230 Part I and Part II combined, have been made by me, including the answers to items 1 through 35 inclusive, and that they are true and complete to the best of my knowledge and belief. I do further swear (or affirm) that, if admitted into the United States, I will not engage in activities which would be prejudicial to the public interest, or endanger the welfare, safety, or security of the United States; in activities which would be prohibited by the laws of the United States relating to espionage, sabotage, public disorder, or in other activities subversive to the national security; in any activity a purpose of which is the opposition to or the control, or overthrow of, the Government of the United States, by force, violence, or other unconstitutional means.

I understand that completion of this form by persons required by law to register with the Selective Service System (males 18 through 25 years of age) constitutes such registration in accordance with the Military Selective Service Act.

I understand all the foregoing statements, having asked for and obtained an explanation on every point which was not clear to me.

_____
Signature of Applicant

Subscribed and sworn to before me this _____ day of _____ _____ at: _____

_____
Consular Officer

U.S. DEPARTMENT OF LABOR
Employment and Training Administration

## APPLICATION
## FOR
## ALIEN EMPLOYMENT CERTIFICATION

**IMPORTANT: READ CAREFULLY BEFORE COMPLETING THIS FORM**

*PRINT legibly in ink or use a typewriter. If you need more space to answer questions on this form, use a separate sheet. Identify each answer with the number of the corresponding question. SIGN AND DATE each sheet in original signature.*

*To knowingly furnish any false information in the preparation of this form and any supplement thereto or to aid, abet, or counsel another to do so is a felony punishable by $10,000 fine or 5 years in the penitentiary, or both (18 U.S.C. 1001).*

### PART A. OFFER OF EMPLOYMENT

1. Name of Alien *(Family name in capital letters, First, Middle, Maiden)*

2. Present Address of Alien *(Number, Street, City and Town, State, ZIP Code or Province, Country)*

3. Type of Visa *(If in U.S.)*

The following information is submitted as evidence of an offer of employment.

4. Name of Employer *(Full name of organization)*

5. Telephone *(Area Code and Number)*

6. Address *(Number, Street, City or Town, County, State, ZIP Code)*

7. Address Where Alien Will Work *(if different from item 6)*

8. Nature of Employer's Business Activity

9. Name of Job Title

10. Total Hours Per Week
   a. Basic
   b. Overtime

11. Work Schedule *(Hourly)*
   a.m.
   p.m.

12. Rate of Pay
   a. Basic  $ per ............
   b. Overtime  $ per hour

13. Describe Fully the Job to be Performed *(Duties)*

14. State in detail the MINIMUM education, training, and experience for a worker to perform satisfactorily the job duties described in Item 13 above.

15. Other Special Requirements

| EDU-CATION *(Enter number of years)* | Grade School | High School | College | College Degree Required *(specify)* |
| --- | --- | --- | --- | --- |
| | | | | Major Field of Study |

| TRAIN-ING | No. Yrs. | No. Mos. | Type of Training |
| --- | --- | --- | --- |
| | | | |

| EXPERI-ENCE | Job Offered | | Related Occupation | | Related Occupation *(specify)* |
| --- | --- | --- | --- | --- | --- |
| | Number | | | | |
| | Yrs. | Mos. | Yrs. | Mos. | |

16. Occupational Title of Person Who Will Be Alien's Immediate Supervisor ➤ ➤

17. Number of Employees Alien will Supervise ➤

◀ ENDORSEMENTS *(Make no entry in section - for government use only)*

| Date Forms Received | |
| --- | --- |
| L.O. | S.O. |
| R.O. | N.O. |
| Ind. Code | Occ. Code |
| Occ. Title | |

*Replaces MA 7-50A, B and C (Apr. 1970 edition) which is obsolete.*

ETA 750 (Oct. 1979)

| 18. COMPLETE ITEMS ONLY IF JOB IS TEMPORARY | | | 19. IF JOB IS UNIONIZED *(Complete)* | |
|---|---|---|---|---|
| a. No. of Openings To Be Filled By Aliens Under Job Offer | b. Exact Dates You Expect To Employ Alien | | a. Number of Local | b. Name of Local |
| | From | To | | |
| | | | | c. City and State |

| 20. STATEMENT FOR LIVE-AT-WORK JOB OFFERS *(Complete for Private Household Job ONLY)* | | | | | | |
|---|---|---|---|---|---|---|
| a. Description of Residence | | b. No. Persons Residing at Place of Employment | | | | c. Will free board and private room not shared with anyone be provided? *("X" one)* |
| *("X" one)* ☐ House ☐ Apartment | Number of Rooms | Adults | | Children | Ages | ☐ YES ☐ NO |
| | | BOYS | | | | |
| | | GIRLS | | | | |

**21. DESCRIBE EFFORTS TO RECRUIT U.S. WORKERS AND THE RESULTS.** *(Specify Sources of Recruitment by Name)*

**22.** Applications require various types of documentation. Please read PART II of the instructions to assure that appropriate supporting documentation is included with your application.

## 23. EMPLOYER CERTIFICATIONS

*By virtue of my signature below, I HEREBY CERTIFY the following conditions of employment.*

a. I have enough funds available to pay the wage or salary offered the alien.

b. The wage offered equals or exceeds the prevailing wage and I guarantee that, if a labor certification is granted, the wage paid to the alien when the alien begins work will equal or exceed the prevailing wage which is applicable at the time the alien begins work.

c. The wage offered is not based on commissions, bonuses, or other incentives, unless I guarantee a wage paid on a weekly, bi-weekly or monthly basis.

d. I will be able to place the alien on the payroll on or before the date of the alien's proposed entrance into the United States.

e. The job opportunity does not involve unlawful discrimination by race, creed, color, national origin, age, sex, religion, handicap, or citizenship.

f. The job opportunity is not:

    (1) Vacant because the former occupant is on strike or is being locked out in the course of a labor dispute involving a work stoppage.

    (2) At issue in a labor dispute involving a work stoppage.

g. The job opportunity's terms, conditions and occupational environment are not contrary to Federal, State or local law.

h. The job opportunity has been and is clearly open to any qualified U.S. worker.

## 24. DECLARATIONS

DECLARATION OF EMPLOYER ➤ *Pursuant to 28 U.S.C. 1746, I declare under penalty of perjury the foregoing is true and correct.*

| SIGNATURE | DATE |
|---|---|
| | |

| NAME *(Type or Print)* | TITLE |
|---|---|
| | |

AUTHORIZATION OF AGENT OF EMPLOYER ➤ *I HEREBY DESIGNATE the agent below to represent me for the purposes of labor certification and I TAKE FULL RESPONSIBILITY for accuracy of any representations made by my agent.*

| SIGNATURE OF EMPLOYER | DATE |
|---|---|
| | |

| NAME OF AGENT *(Type or Print)* | ADDRESS OF AGENT *(Number, Street, City, State, ZIP Code)* |
|---|---|
| | |

## PART B. STATEMENT OF QUALIFICATIONS OF ALIEN

**FOR ADVICE CONCERNING REQUIREMENTS FOR ALIEN EMPLOYMENT CERTIFICATION:** *If alien is in the U.S., contact nearest office of Immigration and Naturalization Service. If alien is outside U.S., contact nearest U.S. Consulate.*

**IMPORTANT: READ ATTACHED INSTRUCTIONS BEFORE COMPLETING THIS FORM.**

*Print legibly in ink or use a typewriter. If you need more space to fully answer any questions on this form, use a separate sheet. Identify each answer with the number of the corresponding question. Sign and date each sheet.*

| 1. Name of Alien *(Family name in capital letters)* | First name | Middle name | Maiden name |
|---|---|---|---|
| | | | |

| 2. Present Address *(No., Street, City or Town, State or Province and ZIP Code* | Country | 3. Type of Visa *(If in U.S.)* |
|---|---|---|
| | | |

| 4. Alien's Birthdate *(Month, Day, Year)* | 5. Birthplace *(City or Town, State or Province)* | Country | 6. Present Nationality or Citizenship *(Country)* |
|---|---|---|---|
| | | | |

**7. Address in United States Where Alien Will Reside**

| 8. Name and Address of Prospective Employer if Alien has Job offer in U.S. | 9. Occupation in which Alien is Seeking Work |
|---|---|
| | |

10. "X" the appropriate box below and furnish the information required for the box marked

a. ☐ Alien will apply for a visa abroad at the American Consulate in ———————▶  City in Foreign Country / Foreign Country

b. ☐ Alien is in the United States and will apply for adjustment of status to that of a lawful permanent resident in the office of the Immigration and Naturalization Service at ———————▶  City / State

| 11. Names and Addresses of Schools, Colleges and Universities Attended *(Include trade or vocational training facilities)* | Field of Study | FROM Month | FROM Year | TO Month | TO Year | Degrees or Certificates Received |
|---|---|---|---|---|---|---|
| | | | | | | |
| | | | | | | |
| | | | | | | |
| | | | | | | |
| | | | | | | |

### SPECIAL QUALIFICATIONS AND SKILLS

12. Additional Qualifications and Skills Alien Possesses and Proficiency in the use of Tools, Machines or Equipment Which Would Help Establish if Alien Meets Requirements for Occupation in Item 9.

13. List Licenses *(Professional, journeyman, etc.)*

14. List Documents Attached Which are Submitted as Evidence that Alien Possesses the Education, Training, Experience, and Abilities Represented

| Endorsements | DATE REC. DOL |
|---|---|
| | O.T. & C. |
| *(Make no entry in this section — FOR Government Agency USE ONLY)* | |

*(Items continued on next page)*

**15. WORK EXPERIENCE.** *List all jobs held during past three (3) years. Also, list any other jobs related to the occupation for which the alien is seeking certification as·indicated in item 9.*

**a. NAME AND ADDRESS OF EMPLOYER**

| NAME OF JOB | DATE STARTED Month | Year | DATE LEFT Month | Year | KIND OF BUSINESS |
|---|---|---|---|---|---|

| DESCRIBE IN DETAILS THE DUTIES PERFORMED, INCLUDING THE USE OF TOOLS, MACHINES, OR EQUIPMENT | NO. OF HOURS PER WEEK |
|---|---|

--------------------------------

--------------------------------

--------------------------------

**b. NAME AND ADDRESS OF EMPLOYER**

| NAME OF JOB | DATE STARTED Month | Year | DATE LEFT Month | Year | KIND OF BUSINESS |
|---|---|---|---|---|---|

| DESCRIBE IN DETAIL THE DUTIES PERFORMED, INCLUDING THE USE OF TOOLS, MACHINES, OR EQUIPMENT | NO. OF HOURS PER WEEK |
|---|---|

--------------------------------

--------------------------------

--------------------------------

**c. NAME AND ADDRESS OF EMPLOYER**

| NAME OF JOB | DATE STARTED Month | Year | DATE LEFT Month | Year | KIND OF BUSINESS |
|---|---|---|---|---|---|

| DESCRIBE IN DETAIL THE DUTIES PERFORMED, INCLUDING THE USE OF TOOLS, MACHINES, OR EQUIPMENT | NO. OF HOURS PER WEEK |
|---|---|

--------------------------------

--------------------------------

--------------------------------

## 16. DECLARATIONS

**DECLARATION OF ➤ ➤ ALIEN**   *Pursuant to 28 U.S.C. 1746, I declare under penalty of perjury the foregoing is true and correct.*

| SIGNATURE OF ALIEN | DATE |
|---|---|

**AUTHORIZATION OF ➤ ➤ AGENT OF ALIEN**   *I hereby designate the agent below to represent me for the purposes of labor certification and I take full responsibility for accuracy of any representations made by my agent.*

| SIGNATURE OF ALIEN | DATE |
|---|---|

| NAME OF AGENT *(Type or print)* | ADDRESS OF AGENT *(No., Street, City, State, ZIP Code)* |
|---|---|

OMB No. 1115-0066
# BIOGRAPHIC INFORMATION

| (Family name) | (First name) | (Middle name) | ☐ MALE ☐ FEMALE | BIRTHDATE (Mo.-Day-Yr.) | NATIONALITY | FILE NUMBER A- |
|---|---|---|---|---|---|---|

| ALL OTHER NAMES USED (Including names by previous marriages) | CITY AND COUNTRY OF BIRTH | SOCIAL SECURITY NO. (If any) |
|---|---|---|

|  | FAMILY NAME | FIRST NAME | DATE, CITY AND COUNTRY OF BIRTH (If known) | CITY AND COUNTRY OF RESIDENCE. |
|---|---|---|---|---|
| FATHER |  |  |  |  |
| MOTHER (Maiden name) |  |  |  |  |

| HUSBAND (If none, so state) OR WIFE | FAMILY NAME (For wife, give maiden name) | FIRST NAME | BIRTHDATE | CITY & COUNTRY OF BIRTH | DATE OF MARRIAGE | PLACE OF MARRIAGE |
|---|---|---|---|---|---|---|

FORMER HUSBANDS OR WIVES (if none, so state)

| FAMILY NAME (For wife, give maiden name) | FIRST NAME | BIRTHDATE | DATE & PLACE OF MARRIAGE | DATE AND PLACE OF TERMINATION OF MARRIAGE |
|---|---|---|---|---|
|  |  |  |  |  |
|  |  |  |  |  |

APPLICANT'S RESIDENCE LAST FIVE YEARS. LIST PRESENT ADDRESS FIRST

| STREET AND NUMBER | CITY | PROVINCE OR STATE | COUNTRY | FROM MONTH | YEAR | TO MONTH | YEAR |
|---|---|---|---|---|---|---|---|
|  |  |  |  |  |  | PRESENT TIME |  |
|  |  |  |  |  |  |  |  |
|  |  |  |  |  |  |  |  |
|  |  |  |  |  |  |  |  |
|  |  |  |  |  |  |  |  |
|  |  |  |  |  |  |  |  |

APPLICANT'S LAST ADDRESS OUTSIDE THE UNITED STATES OF MORE THAN ONE YEAR

| STREET AND NUMBER | CITY | PROVINCE OR STATE | COUNTRY | FROM MONTH | YEAR | TO MONTH | YEAR |
|---|---|---|---|---|---|---|---|
|  |  |  |  |  |  |  |  |

APPLICANT'S EMPLOYMENT LAST FIVE YEARS. (IF NONE, SO STATE) LIST PRESENT EMPLOYMENT FIRST

| FULL NAME AND ADDRESS OF EMPLOYER | OCCUPATION (SPECIFY) | FROM MONTH | YEAR | TO MONTH | YEAR |
|---|---|---|---|---|---|
|  |  |  |  | PRESENT TIME |  |
|  |  |  |  |  |  |
|  |  |  |  |  |  |
|  |  |  |  |  |  |
|  |  |  |  |  |  |

| Show below last occupation abroad if not shown above. (Include all information requested above.) |
|---|
|  |

| THIS FORM IS SUBMITTED IN CONNECTION WITH APPLICATION FOR: ☐ NATURALIZATION ☐ STATUS AS PERMANENT RESIDENT ☐ OTHER (SPECIFY): | SIGNATURE OF APPLICANT | DATE |
|---|---|---|
| **Submit all four pages of this form.** | If your native alphabet is other than roman letters, write your name in your native alphabet here: | |

PENALTIES: SEVERE PENALTIES ARE PROVIDED BY LAW FOR KNOWINGLY AND WILLFULLY FALSIFYING OR CONCEALING A MATERIAL FACT.

# APPLICANT: BE SURE TO PUT YOUR NAME AND ALIEN REGISTRATION NUMBER IN THE BOX OUTLINED BY HEAVY BORDER BELOW.

| COMPLETE THIS BOX (Family name) | (Given name) | (Middle name) | (Alien registration number) |
|---|---|---|---|
|  |  |  |  |

**(1) Ident.**

Form G-325A (Rev. 09/11/00) Y

# Application to Replace Permanent Resident Card

## INSTRUCTIONS

### Purpose of This Form.

This form is for permanent residents and conditional residents to apply to the Immigration and Naturalization Service (INS) for replacement of permanent resident cards. If you are a conditional resident and your status is expiring, use Form I-751 to apply for the removal of conditions.

### Who May File.

If you are a permanent resident or conditional resident, file this application:

- to replace a lost, stolen or destroyed card;
- to update a card after change of name or other biographic data;
- to replace a card that is mutilated;
- to replace a card that is incorrect on account of INS error; or
- to replace a card that was never received.

If you are a permanent resident, you must also file this application:

- to replace a card that has an expiration date on it and is expiring; or
- within 30 days of your 14th birthday, to replace a card issued before your 14th birthday; or
- if you have been a lawful permanent resident in the U.S. and are now taking up Commuter status while actually residing outside the U.S.; or
- if you have been in resident Commuter status and are now taking up actual residence in the U.S; or
- if your status has been automatically converted to permanent resident; or
- when you have an older edition of the card and must replace it with the current type of card.

### General Filing Instructions.

Please answer all questions by typing or clearly printing in black ink. Indicate that an item is not applicable with "N/A." If an answer is "none," write "none." If you need extra space to answer any item, attach a sheet of paper with your name and your alien registration number (A#), and indicate the number of the item to which the answer refers. You must file your application with the required Initial Evidence. Every application must be properly signed and accompanied by the appropriate fee (see "Fee" on page 2). If you are under 14 years of age, your parent or guardian may sign the application on your behalf.

**Translations.** Any foreign language document must be accompanied by a full English translation that the translator has certified as complete and correct, and by the translator's certification that he or she is competent to translate the foreign language into English.

**Copies.** If these instructions state that a copy of a document may be filed with this application, and you choose to send us the original, we may keep that original for our records.

### Initial Evidence.

You must file your application with:

- Your Prior Card or other Evidence of Identity. You must submit your original permanent resident card with your application unless it has been lost, stolen, destroyed or you never received it. If your card has an expiration date on it, and it is expiring, you will be required to present your card at the time of the in-person appearance, and may be required to submit the card with the application at that time. If you have been automatically converted to permanent resident status, you must attach your original temporary status document.

  If these instructions do not require that you submit your original permanent resident card, submit a copy if you have one. If you do not have a copy and are at least 18 years old, you must file your application with a copy of an identity document, such as a driver's license, passport or a copy of another document containing your name, date of birth, photograph and signature.

- **Photos.** You must submit 2 identical natural color photographs of yourself taken within 30 days of this application. The photos must have a white background, be unmounted, printed on thin paper and be glossy and unretouched. The photo should show a three-quarter frontal profile showing the right side of your face, with your right ear visible and with your head bare (unless you are wearing a headdress as required by a religious order of which you are a member). The photos should be no larger than 2 X 2 inches, with the distance from the top of the head to just below the chin about 1 and 1/4 inches. Lightly print your A# on the back of each photo with a pencil.

- **Fingerprints.** If you are filing this application to register as a result of turning 14 years of age, you must be fingerprinted. After filing this application, INS will notify you in writing of the time and location where you must go to be fingerprinted. Failure to appear to be fingerprinted may result in a denial of your application.

- **Correction or change in biographic data.** If you are applying to replace a card because of a name change, you must submit a copy of a court order or marriage certificate reflecting the new name. To replace a card because of a change in any other biographic data, you must submit copies of documentation to prove that the new data is correct. A replacement application based on administrative INS error must also include an explanation.

**Where to File.**

Unless otherwise instructed, file this application in person at the local INS office having jurisdiction over where you live. When you file in person you will have to complete the signature and fingerprint blocks of a Form I-89, Data Collection Form at an INS office when you file this application. If you are instructed to mail this application to INS, you will be instructed when to appear to complete the I-89. Appearance requirements may be waived in cases of confinement due to advanced age or physical infirmity.

If you are outside the United States, contact the nearest American Consulate, INS office or Port of Entry, before submitting this application.

**Fee.**

The fee for this application is $130.00. If you must be fingerprinted in connection with this application (see instruction on Fingerprints), the fee for fingerprinting is $50.00. You may submit one check or money order for both the application and fingerprinting fees, for a total of $180.00. Fees must be submitted in the exact amount. Fees cannot be refunded. **DO NOT MAIL CASH.**

All checks and money orders must be drawn on a bank or other institution located in the United States and must be payable in United States currency. The check or money order should be made payable to the Immigration and Naturalization Service, except that:

- If you live in Guam and are filing this application in Guam, make your check or money order payable to the "Treasurer, Guam."

- If you live in the U.S. Virgin Islands and are filing this application in the U.S. Virgin Islands, make your check or money order payable to the "Commissioner of Finance of the Virgin Islands."

Checks are accepted subject to collection. An uncollected check in payment of an application fee will render the application and any document issued invalid. A charge of $30.00 will be imposed if a check in payment of a fee is not honored by the bank on which it is drawn.

**Evidence of Registration.**

A pending application for a replacement permanent resident card is temporary evidence of registration.

**Processing Information.**

*Acceptance.* Any application that is not signed or is not accompanied by the correct fee will be rejected with a notice that the application is deficient. You may correct the deficiency and resubmit the application. However, an application is not considered properly filed until it is accepted by INS.

*Initial processing.* Once the application has been accepted, it will be checked for completeness, including submission of the required initial evidence. If you do not completely fill out the form, you will not establish a basis for eligibility and we may deny your application.

*Requests for more information or interview.* We may request more information or evidence or we may request that you appear at an INS office for an interview. We may also request that you submit the originals of any copy. We will return these originals when they are no longer required.

*Decision.* You will be notified in writing of the decision on your application. If your application is approved and you have completed the required Form I-89, Data Collection Card, your card will be manufactured and sent to you.

**Penalties.**

If you knowingly and willfully falsify or conceal a material fact or submit a false document with this request, we will deny the benefit you are filing for and may deny any other immigration benefit. In addition, you will face severe penalties provided by law and may be subject to criminal prosecution.

**Privacy Act Notice.**

We ask for the information on this form, and associated evidence, to determine if you have established eligibility for the immigration benefit you are seeking. Our legal right to ask for this information is in 8 USC 1302 and 1304. We may provide this information to other government agencies. Failure to provide this information and any requested evidence may delay a final decision or result in denial of your request.

**Paperwork Reduction Act Notice.**

A person is not required to respond to a collection of information unless it displays a currently valid OMB control number. We try to create forms and instructions that are accurate, can be easily understood and that impose the least possible burden on you to provide us with information. Often this is difficult because some immigration laws are very complex. The estimated average time to complete and file this application is computed as follows: (1) 10 minutes to learn about the law and form; (2) 10 minutes to complete the form; and (3) 35 minutes to assemble and file the application, including the required in person filing; for a total estimated average of 55 minutes per application. If you have comments regarding the accuracy of this estimate, or suggestions for making this form simpler, you can write to the Immigration and Naturalization Service, HQPDI, 425 I Street N.W., Room 4034; Washington, DC 20536; OMB No. 1115-0004. **DO NOT MAIL YOUR COMPLETED APPLICATION TO THIS ADDRESS.**

# Application to Replace Permanent Resident Card

## START HERE - Please Type or Print

### Part 1. Information about you.

| Family Name | Given Name | Middle Initial |
|---|---|---|

**U.S. Mailing Address - C/O**

| Street Number and Name | Apt. # |
|---|---|

| City |
|---|

| State | ZIP Code |
|---|---|

| Date of Birth (Month/Day/Year) | Country of Birth |
|---|---|

| Social Security # | A # |
|---|---|

### Part 2. Application type.

**1. My status is:** (check one)

- a. ☐ Permanent Resident - (Not a Commuter)
- b. ☐ Permanent Resident - (Commuter)
- c. ☐ Conditional Permanent Resident

**2. Reason for application:** (check one)

**I am a Permanent Resident or Conditional Permanent Resident and:**

- a. ☐ my card was lost, stolen or destroyed. I have attached a copy of an identity document.
- b. ☐ my authorized card was never received. I have attached a copy of an identity document.
- c. ☐ my card is mutilated. I have attached the mutilated card.
- d. ☐ my card was issued with incorrect information because of INS administrative error. I have attached the incorrect card and evidence of the correct information.
- e. ☐ my name or other biographic information has changed since the card was issued. I have attached my present card and evidence of the new information.

**I am a Permanent Resident and:**

- f. ☐ my present card has an expiration date and it is expiring.
- g. ☐ I have reached my 14th birthday since my card was issued. I have attached my present card.
- h. 1. ☐ I have taken up Commuter status. I have attached my present card and evidence of my foreign residence.
- h. 2. ☐ I was a Commuter and am now taking up residence in the U.S. I have attached my present card and evidence of my residence in the U.S.
- i. ☐ my status has been automatically converted to permanent resident. I have attached my Temporary Status Document.
- j. ☐ I have an old edition of the card.

### Part 3. Processing information.

| Mother's First Name | Father's First Name |
|---|---|

| City of Residence where you applied for an Immigrant Visa or Adjustment of Status | Consulate where Immigrant Visa was issued or INS office where status was Adjusted |
|---|---|

| City/Town/Village of Birth | Date of Admission as an immigrant or Adjustment of Status |
|---|---|

**Continued on back.**

---

### FOR INS USE ONLY

| Returned | Receipt |
|---|---|
| | |
| Resubmitted | |
| | |
| Reloc Sent | |
| | |
| Reloc Rec'd | |
| | |
| ☐ Applicant Interviewed | |

Status as _____ Verified by _____

Class _____ Initials _____

FD-258 forwarded on _____

I-89 forwarded on _____

I-551 seen and returned _____ (Initials)

Photocopy of I-551 verified _____ (Initials)

_____ _____
Name         Date

Sticker # _____ (ten-digit number)

**Action Block**

**To Be Completed by Attorney or Representative, if any**

☐ Fill in box if G-28 is attached to represent the applicant

VOLAG#

ATTY State License #

---

Form I-90 (Rev. 06/05/02)Y

## Part 3. Processing information (continued):

If you entered the U.S. with an Immigrant Visa, also complete the following:

Destination in U.S. at
time of Admission

Port of Entry where
Admitted to U.S.

Are you in deportation or exclusion proceedings?  ☐ No  ☐ Yes

Since you were granted permanent residence, have you ever filed Form I-407, Abandonment by Alien of Status as Lawful Permanent Resident, or otherwise been judged to have abandoned your status?  ☐ No  ☐ Yes

If you answer yes to any of the above questions, explain in detail on a separate piece of paper.

## Part 4. Signature. *(Read the information on penalties in the instructions before completing this section. You must file this application while in the United States.*

I certify, under penalty of perjury under the laws of the United States of America, that this application and the evidence submitted with it is all true and correct. I authorize the release of any information from my records that the Immigration and Naturalization Service needs to determine eligibility for the benefit I am seeking.

Signature                                              Date                          Daytime Phone Number

*Please Note:  If you do not completely fill out this form or fail to submit required documents listed in the instructions, you cannot be found eligible for the requested document and this application may be denied.*

## Part 5.  Signature of person preparing form, if other than above. *(Sign below)*

*I declare that I prepared this application at the request of the above person and it is based on all information of which I have knowledge.*

**Signature**                    **Print Your Name**                **Date**              **Daytime Phone Number**

Name and Address of Business/Organization (if applicable)

## Purpose of This Form.

This form is used by a nonimmigrant to apply to the Bureau of Citizenship and Immigration Services (BCIS) for a new or replacement:

- Form I-94, Nonimmigrant Arrival-Departure Record (includes also Form I-94W, Nonimmigrant Visa Waiver Arrival-Departure Record); or
- Form I-95, Crewman Landing Permit.

(The BCIS is comprised of offices of the former Immigration and Naturalization Service.)

## Who May File?

If you are a nonimmigrant in the United States, file this application to:

- Replace your lost or stolen Form I-94 or Form I-95; or
- Replace your mutilated Form I-94 or Form I-95; or
- Receive an initial Form I-94 if you were not issued one when you entered as a nonimmigrant, and you are filing this form with an application for extension of stay or change of status; or
- Receive a corrected Form I-94 or Form I-95 if you were issued one with incorrect information when you entered as a nonimmigrant; or
- Receive an initial Form I-94 if you were not issued a Form I-94 when you were originally admitted into the U. S. due to your military membership as described below:

  -- nonimmigrant member of the U.S. armed forces; or
  -- nonimmigrant member of the North Atlantic Treaty Organization (NATO) armed forces; or
  -- nonimmigrant member of the Partnership for Peace military program under the Status of Forces Agreement (SOFA).

## General Filing Instructions.

Please answer all questions by typing or printing clearly in black ink. If you need extra space to answer any item, attach a sheet of paper with your name and your alien registration number (A#), if any, and indicate the number of the item to which the answer refers. You must file your application with the required initial evidence. Every application must be properly signed and filed with the correct fee. If you are under 14 years of age, your parent or guardian may sign the application.

## Initial Evidence.

*Lost or Stolen Form.* If you are applying to replace a lost or stolen Form I-94 or Form I-95, submit a copy of the original or submit a copy of the biographic page from your passport and a copy of the page indicating admission as claimed, or other evidence of your admission. If you are unable to submit this evidence, submit a full explanation of why you cannot give any of the above evidence, along with a copy of evidence of your identity and copies of any evidence in your possession to substantiate your claim. If your card was stolen, submit a copy of the police report relating to the theft.

*Mutilated Form.* If you are applying to replace a mutilated Form I-94 or I-95, attach the original form.

*First Form I-94.* If you were not issued a Form I-94 at admission and have not since been issued a Form I-94, but now require a Form I-94 for another application you are filing, submit a copy of any evidence in your possession to substantiate your claimed admission.

*Nonimmigrant Military Member.* If you are filing as a nonimmigrant military member in the U.S. armed forces, NATO or the Partnership for Peace program and you are requesting an initial Form I-94, contact your foreign commander or his or her designee in the United States for filing information.

*Document With Incorrect Information.* If you want the BCIS to correct inaccurate information on your Form I-94, attach the Form I-94 to your Form I-102 application. If you check box **"g"** on **Part 2, Application Type**, attach a statement dated and signed by you, citing specifically what information on your Form I-94 or Form I-95 copy requires correction. You must also attach evidence verifying that the corrected information is valid.

*Translations.* Any foreign language document must be accompanied by a full English translation that a translator has certified as complete and correct. The translator must also certify that he or she is competent to translate the foreign language into English.

*Copies.* If these instructions state that a copy of a document may be filed with this application, and you choose to send us the original, we may keep that original for our records.

## Where to File.

To request BCIS to correct inaccurate information on your Form I-94 or Form I-95, submit your application at the local BCIS office having jurisdiction over where you are temporarily located. Contact the local BCIS office for specific information on how to file the application.

If you are filing to replace a Form I-95, file this application at the local BCIS office having jurisdiction over where you are temporarily located.

If you were not issued a Form I-94 at admission or are filing this application with an application for extension of stay or change of status, file this application where you are filing the accompanying extension of stay or change of status application.

If you are a nonimmigrant member of the U.S. armed forces, file this application at the local BCIS office having jurisdiction over the area where you are temporarily located.

If you are in a NATO or Partnership for Peace military program under SOFA, and are seeking an initial Form I-94, submit this application through your foreign commander or his or her designee to NATO/Headquarters of the Supreme Allied Commander, Atlantic (SACLANT).

In all other instances, file your application as follows:

If you are in Connecticut, Delaware, District of Columbia, Maine, Maryland, Massachusetts, New Hampshire, New Jersey, New York, Pennsylvania, Puerto Rico, Rhode Island, Vermont, the Virgin Islands, Virginia or West Virginia, mail this application to: **BCIS Vermont Service Center, 75 Lower Welden Street, St. Albans, VT 05479-0001.**

If you are in Alabama, Arkansas, Florida, Georgia, Kentucky, Louisiana, Mississippi, New Mexico, North Carolina, Oklahoma, South Carolina, Tennessee or Texas, mail this application to: **BCIS Texas Service Center, P.O. Box 851182, Mesquite, TX 75185-1182.**

If you are in Arizona, California, Guam, Hawaii or Nevada, mail this application to: **BCIS California Service Center, P.O. Box 10102, Laguna Niguel, CA. 92607-0040.**

If you are elsewhere in the United States, mail this application to: **BCIS Nebraska Service Center, P.O. Box 87102, Lincoln, NE 68501-7102.**

### Fee.

The fee for this application is **$100.00**. The fee must be submitted in the exact amount. It cannot be refunded. **DO NOT MAIL CASH.**

All checks and money orders must be drawn on a bank or other institution located in the United States and must be payable in United States currency. The check or money order should be made payable to the "Bureau of Citizenship and Immigration Services," except that:

- if you are in Guam and are filing this application in Guam, make your check or money order payable to the "Treasurer, Guam."

- if you are in the U.S. Virgin Islands and are filing this application in the U.S. Virgin Islands, make your check or money order payable to the "Commissioner of Finance of the Virgin Islands."

Checks are accepted subject to collection. An uncollected check will render the application and any document issued invalid. A charge of $30.00 will be imposed if a check in payment of a fee is not honored by the bank on which it is drawn.

You do **not** need to pay the fee to request the BCIS to correct your Form I-94 or Form I-95 copy if the error(s) on your document was made by BCIS, through no fault of you own. If, however, the error(s) was made because of information you provided or failed to provide to the BCIS or the U.S. Department of State, you must pay the fee.

You do not need to pay the fee if you are nonimmigrant military member in the U.S. armed forces or you are participating in a NATO or Partnership for Peace military program under the SOFA and you are requesting an initial or replacement Form I-94.

### Processing Information.

*Acceptance.* Any application that is not signed or is not accompanied by the proper fee, if required, will be rejected with a notice that the application is deficient. You may correct the deficiency and resubmit the application. However, an application is not considered properly filed until it is accepted by the BCIS.

*Initial processing.* Once the application has been accepted, it will be checked for completeness, including submission of the required initial evidence. If you do not completely fill out the form or file it without required initial evidence, you will not establish a basis for eligibility and we may deny your application.

*Decision.* You will be notified in writing of the decision on your application. If the application is approved, a new Form I-94 or Form I-95 will be issued to you.

### Penalties.

If you knowingly and willfully falsify or conceal a material fact or submit a false document with this request, we will deny the benefit you are seeking and may deny any other immigration benefit. In addition, you will face severe penalties provided by law, and you may be subject to criminal prosecution and/or removal from the United States.

### Privacy Act Notice.

We ask for the information on this form and associated evidence to determine if you have established eligibility for the immigration benefit you are seeking. We may provide this information to other government agencies. Failure to provide this information and any requested evidence may delay a final decision or result in denial of your request.

### Information and BCIS Forms.

For information on immigration laws, regulations and procedures and to order BCIS forms, call our **National Customer Service Center** toll-free at **1-800-375-5283** or visit our internet web site at **www.bcis.gov**.

### Paperwork Reduction Act Notice.

We try to create forms and instructions that are accurate, can be easily understood and that impose the least possible burden on you to provide us with information. Often this is difficult because some immigration laws are very complex. The estimated average time to complete and file this application is as follows: (1) 5 minutes to learn about the law and form; (2) 5 minutes to complete the form; (3) 15 minutes to assemble and file the application -- for a total estimated average of 25 minutes per application. If you have comments regarding the accuracy of this estimate or suggestions for making this form simpler, you may write to: Bureau of Citizenship and Immigration Services, HQRFS, 425 I Street, N.W., Room 4034, Washington, DC 20536; OMB No. 1615-0079. **DO NOT MAIL YOUR COMPLETED APPLICATION TO THIS ADDRESS.**

**U.S. Department of Homeland Security**
Bureau of Citizehsip and Immigration Services

# I-102, Application for Replacement/Initial Nonimmigrant Arrival - Departure Document

**START HERE - Please Type or Print**

## Part 1. Information about you.

| FOR BCIS USE ONLY | |
| --- | --- |
| Returned | Receipt |
| Date | |
| Date | |
| Resubmitted | |
| Date | |
| Date | |
| Reloc Sent | |
| Date | |
| Date | |
| Reloc Rec'd | |
| Date | |
| Date | |

Family Name | Given Name | Middle Name

**Address** - In care of -

Street Number and Name | Apt./Suite #

City | State or Province | Zip/Postal Code | Country

Date of Birth *(mm/dd/yyyy)* | Country of Birth

Social Security # *(if any)* | A # *(if any)*

Date of Last Admission *(mm/dd/yyyy)* | Expires on *(mm/dd/yyyy)*

Current Nonimmigrant Status | I-94, Arrival/Departure Document #

## Part 2. Application type. (check one)

a. ☐ I am applying to replace my lost or stolen Form I-94 (I-94W).

b. ☐ I am applying to replace my lost or stolen Form I-95.

c. ☐ I am applying to replace Form I-94 because it is mutilated. I have attached my original I-94.

d. ☐ I am applying to replace Form I-95 because it is mutilated. I have attached my original I-95.

e. ☐ I was not issued a Form I-94 when I entered as a nonimmigrant, and I am filing this application together with an application for an extension of stay/change of status.

f. ☐ I was not issued a Form I-94 when I entered as a nonimmigrant member of the military and I am filing this application for an initial Form I-94.

g. ☐ I was issued a Form I-94 or Form I-95 with incorrect information, and I am requesting the BCIS to correct the document.

☐ Applicant Interviewed on _____

**New I-94 #**

**Action Block**

## Part 3. Processing information.

Are you filing this application with any other petition or application?

☐ No ☐ Yes - Form #

Are you now in removal proceedings?

☐ No ☐ Yes (Attach an explanation on a separate sheet of paper.)

**If you are unable to provide the original of your Form I-94, give the following information:**

Class of Admission: | Place of Admission:

Your name exactly as it appears on Form I-94 or I-95, if known

**To Be Completed By**
*Attorney or Representative*, if any.

☐ Fill in box if G-28 is attached to represent the applicant.

ATTY State License #

## Part 4. Signature. *Read the information on penalties in the instructions before completing this section. You must file this application while in the United States.*

I certify, under penalty of perjury under the laws of the United States of America, that this application and the evidence submitted with it is all true and correct. I authorize the release of any information from my records which the Bureau of Citizenship and Immigration Services needs to determine eligibility for the benefit I am seeking.

*Signature* | **Daytime Telephone Number** *(with area code)* | **Date** (mm/dd/yyyy)

## Part 5. Signature of person preparing form, if other than above. (Sign below)

I declare that I prepared this application at the request of the above person and it is based on all information of which I have knowledge.

*Signature* | Print or Type Your Name | Fax Number *(if any)* | Date *(MM/DD/YYYY)*

Firm Name and Address | Daytime Telephone Number *(with area code)*

> Read the instructions carefully. If you do not follow the instructions, we may have to return your petition, which may delay final action.

## 1. Who may file?

A. You are a United States citizen, and

B. You and your fiancé(e) intend to marry within 90 days of your fiancé(e) entering the United States, and are both free to marry, and have met in person within two years before your filing of this petition unless:

   1) The requirement to meet your fiancé(e) in person would violate strict and long-established customs of your or your fiancé(e)'s foreign culture or social pratice; or

   2) It is established that the requirement to personally meet your fiancé(e) would result in extreme hardship to you.

   **OR**

C. You wish to have your alien spouse or child enter as a nonimmigrant. See question 12.

   **NOTE**: Unmarried children of your fiancé(e) or spouse who are under 21 years of age and are listed on this form will be eligible to apply to accompany your fiancé(e) or spouse.

## 2. General Filing Instructions.

A. Type or print legibly in ink.

B. If extra space is needed to complete any item, attach a continuation sheet, indicate the item number, and date and sign each sheet.

C. Answer all questions fully and accurately. If any item does not not apply, please write "N/A."

D. Translations. Any foreign language document must be accompanied by a full English translation, which the translator has certified as complete and correct, and by the translator's certification that he or she is competent to translate the foreign language into English.

E. Copies. If these instructions state that a copy of a document may be filed with this petition and you choose to send us the original, INS will keep that original for our records. If INS requires the original, we will request it.

## 3. What documents do you need to show you are a United States citizen?

A. If you were born in the United States, give INS a copy, front and back, of your birth certificate.

B. If you were naturalized, give INS a copy, front and back, of your original Certificate of Naturalization.

C. If you were born outside the United States, and you are a U.S. citizen through your parents, give INS:

   1) your original Certificate of Citizenship, or

   2) your Form FS-240 (Report of Birth Abroad of a United States Citizen).

D. In place of any of the above, you may give INS a copy of your valid, unexpired U.S. passport that was issued for at least 5 years. You must submit copies of all pages in the passport.

E. If you do not have any of the above and were born in the United States, see instruction under 4 below. "What if a document is not available?".

## 4. What if a document is not available?

If the documents needed above are not available, you can give INS the following instead. However, INS may request, in writing, that you obtain a statement from the appropriate civil authority certifying that the needed document is not available. Any evidence submitted must contain enough information, such as a birth date, to establish the event you are trying to prove.

A. Baptismal certificate. A copy, front and back, of the certificate under the seal of the church showing where the baptism dedication or comparable rite occurred, as well as the date and place of the child's birth, date of baptism and names of the child's parents. The baptism must have occurred within two (2) months after the birth of the child.

B. School record. A letter from the school authority (preferably from the first school attended), showing the date of admission to the school, child's date or age at that time, place of birth, and the names of the parents.

C. Census record. State or federal census record showing the name(s), date(s) and place(s) of birth or age(s) of the person(s) listed.

D. Affidavits. Written statements sworn to, or affirmed by, two persons who were living at the time and who have personal knowledge of the event. For example, a birth, marriage, or death. These persons may be relatives and do not have to be citizens of the United States. Each affidavit should contain the person's full name and address, date and place of birth, and relationship to you and must fully describe the event and explain how he or she acquired knowledge of the event.

## 5. What documents do you need to prove you can legally marry?

A. Copies of evidence that you and your fiancé(e) have personally met within the last two years, or if you have never met within the last two years, provide a detailed explanation and evidence of the extreme hardship or customary, cultural or social practices which have prohibited your meeting; and

B. Original statements from you and your fiancé(e) whom you plan to marry within 90 days of his/her admission, and copies of any evidence you wish to submit to establish your mutual intent.

C. If either of you is of an age that requires special consent or permission for you to marry in the jurisdiction in which your marriage will occur, give proof of that consent or permission.

D. If either you or your fiancé(e) were married before, give copies of documents showing that each prior marriage was legally terminated; and

## 6. What other documents do you need?

A. Give INS one color photo of you and one of your fiancé(e), taken within 30 days of the date of this petition. These photos must have a white background. They must be glossy, un-retouched and not mounted. The dimension of the facial image should be about one inch from your chin to the top of your hair in 3/4 frontal view, showing the right side of your face with your right ear visible. Using pencil or felt pen, lightly print name (and Alien Registration Number, if known) on the back of each photograph.

B. Give a completed and signed Form G-325A (Biographic Information) for you and one for your fiancé(e). Except for name and signature, you do not have to repeat on the Biographic Information forms the information given on your I-129F.

C. If either you or the person you are filing for is using a name other than that shown on the relevant documents, you must give INS copies of the legal documents that made the change, such as a marriage certificate, adoption decree or court order.

## 7. How should you prepare this form?

A. Type or print legibly in ink.

B. If extra space is needed to complete any item, attach a continuation sheet, indicate the item number, and sign each sheet.

C. Answer all questions fully and accurately. If any item does not apply, please write "N/A."

## 8. Where should you file this form?

A. If you are filing for your fiance(e), file this application according to your place of residence, as listed below:

If you live in Connecticut, Delaware, District of Columbia, Maine, Maryland, Massachusetts, New Hampshire, New Jersey, New York, Pennsylvania, Puerto Rico, Rhode Island, Vermont, U.S. Virgin Islands, Virginia or West Virginia, mail this petition to: **USINS Vermont Service Center, 75 Lower Welden Street, St. Albans, VT 05479-0001**

If you live in Alabama, Arkansas, Florida, George, Kentucky, Louisiana, Mississippi, New Mexico, North Carolina, Oklahoma, South Carolina, Tennessee or Texas, mail this petition to: **USINS Texas Service Center, P.O. Box 850965, Mesquite, TX 75185-0965**

If you live in Arizona, California, Guam, Hawaii or Nevada, mail this petitition to: **USINS California Service Center, P.O. Box 10130, Laguna Niguel, CA 92607-1013.**

If you live in Alaska, Colorado, Idaho, Illinois, Indiana, Iowa, Kansas, Michigan, Minnesota, Missouri, Montana, Nebraska, North Dakota, Ohio, Oregon, South Dakota, Utah, Washington, Wisconsin or Wyoming, mail the petition to: **USINS Nebraska Service Center, P.O. Box 87130, Lincoln, NE 68501-7130.**

If you live outside the U.S., you may mail your petition to the INS Service Center, listed above, which has jurisdiction over the last place you lived in the U.S., or you may file it at the INS overseas office which has jurisdiction over where you now live. You may inquire at a U.S. consulate for the address of the appropriate INS overseas office.

B. If you are filing for your spouse, mail your application to: **USINS, P.O. Box 7218, Chicago, IL 60680-7218**

## 9. What is the fee?

You must pay $110.00 to file this form. **The fee will not be refunded, whether the petition is approved or not.** DO NOT MAIL CASH. All checks or money orders, whether U.S. or foreign, must be payable in U.S. currency at a financial institution in the United States. When a check is drawn on the account of a person other than yourself, write your name on the face of the check. If the check is not honored, INS will charge you $30.00.

Pay by check or money in the exact amount. Make the check or money order payable to "Immigration and Naturalization Service," unless:

A. If you live in Guam and are filing your petition in Guam, make the check or money order payable to "Treassurer, Guam" or

B. If you live in the U.S. Virgin Island and are filing your petition in the U.S. Virgin Islands make the check or money order payable to "Commissioner of Finance of the Virgin Islands."

## 10. How does your alien fiancé(e) get his or her permanent resident status?

Your alien fiancé(e) may apply for conditional permanent resident status after you have entered into a valid marriage to each other within 90 days of your fiancé(e)'s entry into the United States. Your alien spouse should then apply promptly to the Immigration and Naturalization Service for adjustment of status to conditional permanent resident, using Form I-485.

## 11. How does your conditional permanent resident spouse become a lawful permanent resident without conditions?

Both you and your conditional permanent resident spouse are required to file a petition, Form I-751, Joint Petition to Remove the Conditional Basis of Alien's Permanent Resident Status, during the 90-day period immediately before the second anniversary of the date your alien spouse was granted conditional permanent residence. Children who were admitted as conditional permanent residents with your spouse may be included in the joint petition to remove conditions.

The rights, privileges, responsibilities and duties that apply to all other permanent residents apply equally to a conditional permanent resident to file petitions in behalf of qualifying relatives, or to reside permanently in the United States as an immigrant in accordance with the immigration laws.

---

### NOTICE

**Failure to file Form I-751, Joint Petition to Remove the Conditional Basis of Alien's Permanent Residence Status, will result in termination of permanent residence status and initiation of removal or deportation proceedings.**

---

## 12. How do I use this form for my spouse or child seeking entry using a K-3/K-4 visa?

This form may be used to obtain a K-3/K-4 visa for your alien spouse or child. Fill out the form as directed, except assume that "fiance" or "fiancee" means "spouse." In addition, omit questions B.18 and B.19 by entering "N/A." Note that this form is only necessary to facilitate the entry of your spouse or child as a NONIMMIGRANT.

You must submit the documents required in questions 3, 4 and 6 of the instructions, but may omit the documents required in question 5. In addition, citizens petitioning for K-3 visas for their alien spouses must also include evidence that they have filed Form I-130 on behalf of the alien spouse listed on this form, and a marriage certificate evidencing the legal marriage between the citizen and alien.

The LIFE Act requires applicants to apply for a K-3/K-4 visa in the country where their marriage to the U.S. citizen petitioner took place. Petitioners should be sure to identify the appropriate consulate, in the same country in which they married the alien for whom they are petitioning, in block 20, to avoid lengthy delays. In the event the petitioner and alien were married in the United States they should list the country of the alien's current residence. See State Department regulations at 21 CFR 41.81.

## 13. Processing Information.

Any petition that is not signed or accompanied by the correct fee will be rejected with a notice that it is deficient. You may correct the deficiency and resubmit the petition. However, a petition is not considered properly filed until accepted by INS. Once the petition has been accepted, it will be checked for completeness, including submission of the required evidence. If you do not completely fill out the form or file it without required initial evidence, you will not establish a basis for eligibility and we may deny your petition.

We may request more information or evidence or we may request that you appear at an INS office for an interview.

## 14. What are the penalties for committing marriage fraud or submitting false information or both?

Title 18, United States Code, Section 100 states that whoever willfully and knowingly falsifies a material fact, makes a false statement, or makes use of a false document will be fined up to $10,000 or imprisoned up to five years, or both.

Title 8, United States Code, Section 1325 states that any individual who knowingly enters into a marriage contract for the purpose of evading any provision of the immigration laws shall be imprisoned for not more than five years, or fined not more than $250,000, or both.

## 15. What is our authority for collecting this information?

We request the information on this form to carry out the immigration laws contained in Title 8, United States Code 1184(d). We need this information to determine whether a person is eligible for immigration benefits. The information you provide may also be disclosed to other federal, state, local and foreign law enforcement and regulatory agencies during the course of the investigation required by INS. You do not have to give this information. However, if you refuse to give some or all of it, your petition may be denied.

## 16. What is the Reporting Burden?

Under the Paperwork Reduction Act, a person is not required to respond to a collection of information unless it displays a currently valid OMB control number. We try to create forms and instructions that are accurate, can be easily understood and that impose the least possible burden on you to provide us with information. Often this is difficult because some immigration laws are very complex. The estimated time to file this application is 30 minutes per application.

If you have any comments regarding the accuracy of this estimate, or suggestions for making this form simpler, you can write to the Immigration and Naturalization Service, HQPDI, 425 I Street, N.W., Room 4034, Washington, DC 20536, OMB No. 1115-0071. **DO NOT MAIL YOUR COMPLETED APPLICATION TO THIS ADDRESS.**

---

**It is not possible to cover all the conditions for eligibility or to give instructions for every situation. If you have carefully read all the instructions and still have questions, please contact the INS National Customer Service Center at 1-800-375-5283 or visit our internet website at *www.ins.usdoj.gov.***

**U.S. Department of Justice**
Immigration and Naturalization Service

OMB No. 1115-0071

# Petition for Alien Fiancé(e)

| DO NOT WRITE IN THIS BLOCK | | |
|---|---|---|
| Case ID# | Action Stamp | Fee Stamp |
| A# | | |
| G-28 or Volag # | | |
| The petition is approved for status under Section 101(a)(15)(k). It is valid for four months from date of action. | | AMCON: _____ □ Personal Interview □ Previously Forwarded □ Document Check □ Field Investigations |
| Remarks: | | |

## A.  Information about you.

**1. Name** (Family name in CAPS)    (First)    (Middle)

**2. Address** (Number and Street)    (Apartment Number)

(Town or City)    (State/Country)    (Zip/Postal Code)

**3. Place of Birth** (Town or City)    (State/Country)

**4. Date of Birth** (Mo/Day/Yr)

**5. Sex**  ☑ Male  ☑ Female

**6. Marital Status**  □ Married  □ Single  □ Widowed  □ Divorced

**7. Other Names Used** (including maiden name)

**8. Social Security Number** (if any)    **9. Alien Registration Number** (if any)

**10. Names of Prior Husband/Wives**    **11. Date(s) Marriages(s)**

**12. If you are a U.S. citizen, complete the following:**
My citizenship was acquired through (check one)

□ Birth in the U.S.    □ Naturalization

Give number of certificate, date and place it was issued

□ Parents
Have you obtained a certificate of citizenship in your own name?
□ Yes  □ No
If "Yes," give number of certificate, date and place it was issued.

**13. Have you ever filed for this or any other alien fiancé(e) before?**  □ Yes  □ No
If you checked "yes," give name of alien, place and date of filing, and result.

## B.  Information about your alien fiancé(e).

**1. Name** (Family name in CAPS)    (First)    (Middle)

**2. Address** (Number and Street)    (Apartment Number)

(Town or City)    (State/Country)    (Zip/Postal Code)

**3. Place of Birth** (Town or City)    (State/Country)

**4. Date of Birth** (Mo/Day/Yr)

**5. Sex**  □ Male  □ Female

**6. Marital Status**  □ Married  □ Single  □ Widowed  □ Divorced

**7. Other Names Used** (including maiden name)

**8. Social Security Number** (if any)    **9. Alien Registration Number** (if any)

**10. Names of Prior Husbands/Wives**    **11. Date(s) Marriages(s)**

**12. Has your fiancé(e) ever been in the U.S.?**
□ Yes  □ No

**13. If your fiancé(e) is currently in the U.S., complete the following:**
**He or she last arrived as a** (visitor, student, exchange alien, crewman, stowaway, temporary worker, without inspection, etc.)

**Arrival/Departure Record (I-94)**    **Date arrived** (Month/Day/Year)

**Date authorized stay expired, or will expire, as shown on Form I-94**

| INITIAL | RESUBMITTED | RELOCATED | | COMPLETED | | |
|---|---|---|---|---|---|---|
| | | Rec'd | Sent | Approved | Denied | Returned |
| | | | | | | |

Form I-129F (Rev.11/20/01) Y  Page 1

## B. Information about your alien fiancé(e)     (Continued)

**14. List all children of your alien fiancé(e)** (if any)

(Name) (Date of Birth) (Country of Birth) (Present Address)

**15. Address in the United States where your fiancé(e) intends to live**
(Number and Street) (Town or City) (State)

**16. Your fiancé(e)'s address abroad**
(Number and Street) (Town or City) (Province) (Country) (Phone Number)

**17. If your fiancé(e)'s native alphabet uses other than Roman letters, write his or her name and address abroad in the native alphabet:**
(Name) (Number and Street) (Town or City) (Province) (Country)

**18. Is your fiancé(e) related to you?**  ☐ Yes  ☐ No
If you are related, state the nature and degree of relationship, e.g., third cousin or maternal uncle, etc.

**19. Has your fiancé(e) met and seen you?**  ☐ Yes  ☐ No
Describe the circumstances under which you met.  If you have not personally met each ether, explain how the relationship was established, and explain in detail any reasons you may have for requesting that the requirement that you and your fiancé(e) must have met should not apply to you.

**20. Your fiancé(e) will apply for a visa abroad at the American Consulate in**
(City) (Country)

(Designation of a consulate outside the country of your fiancé(e)'s last residence does not guarantee acceptance for processing by that consulate. Acceptance is at the discretion of the designated consulate.)

## C. Other information

**If you are serving overseas in the Armed Forces of the United States, please answer the following:**

I presently reside or am stationed overseas and my current mailing address is

I plan to return to the United States on or about

**Penalties:  You may, by law, be imprisoned for not more than five years, or fined $250,000, or both, for entering into a marriage contract for the purpose of evading any provision of the immigration laws and you may be fined up to $10,000 or imprisoned up to five years, or both, for knowingly and willfully falsifying or concealing a material fact or using any false document in submitting this petition.**

**Your Certification:**
**I am legally able to and intend to marry my alien fiancé(e) within 90 days of his or her arrival in the United States.  I certify, under penalty of perjury under the laws of the United States of America, that the foregoing is true and correct.  Furthermore, I authorize the release of any information from my records which the Immigration and Naturalizaton Service needs to determine eligibility for the benefit that I am seeking.**

Signature _____  (Date)_____  (Phone Number)_____

**Signature of Person Preparing Form, If Other Than Above:**
I declare that I prepared this document at the request of the person above and that it is based on all information of which I have any knowledge.

Print Name _____  (Address) _____  (Signature) _____  (Date)_____

**G-28 ID**  _____  **Volag**  _____

# Instructions

> Read the instructions carefully. If you do not follow the instructions, we may have to return your petition, which may delay final action.

## 1. Who may file?

A citizen or lawful permanent resident of the United States may file this form with the Immigration and Naturalization Service (INS) to establish the relationship to certain alien relatives who wish to immigrate to the United States. You must file a separate form for each eligible relative.

## 2. For whom may you file?

A. If you are a citizen, you may file this form for:

1) your husband, wife or unmarried child under 21 years old.
2) your unmarried son or daughter over 21, or married son or daughter of any age.
3) your brother or sister if you are at least 21 years old.
4) your parent if you are at least 21 years old.

B. If you are a lawful permanent resident, you may file this form for:

1) your husband or wife.
2) your unmarried child under 21 years of age.
3) your unmarried son or daughter over 21 years of age.

**NOTE:** If your relative qualifies under paragraph A(2) or A(3) above, separate petitions are not required for his or her husband or wife or unmarried children under 21 years of age. If your relative qualifies under paragraph B(2) or B(3) above, separate petitions are not required for his or her unmarried children under 21 years of age. These persons will be able to apply for the same category of immigrant visa as your relative.

## 3. For whom may you not file?

You may not file for a person in the following categories.

A. An adoptive parent or adopted child, if the adoption took place after the child's 16th birthday, or if the child has not been in the legal custody and living with the parent(s) for at least two years.

B. A natural parent, if the United States citizen son or daughter gained permanent residence through adoption.

C. A stepparent or stepchild, if the marriage that created the relationship took place after the child's 18th birthday.

D. A husband or wife, if you were not both physically present at the marriage ceremony, and the marriage was not consummated.

E. A husband or wife, if you gained lawful permanent resident status by virtue of a prior marriage to a United States citizen or lawful permanent resident unless:

1) a period of five years has elapsed since you became a lawful permanent resident; or

2) you can establish by clear and covincing evidence that the prior marriage (through which you gained your immigrant status) was not entered into for the purpose of evading any provision of the immigration laws; or

3) your prior marriage (through which you gained your immigrant status) was terminated by the death of your former spouse.

F. A husband or wife, if he, or she was in exclusion, removal, rescission or judicial proceedings regarding his or her right to remain in the United States when the marriage took place, unless such spouse has resided outside the United States for a two-year period after the date of the marriage.

G. A husband or wife, if the Attorney General has determined that such an alien has attempted or conspired to enter into a marriage for the purpose of evading the immigration laws.

H. A grandparent, grandchild, nephew, niece, uncle, aunt, cousin or in-law.

## 4. What are the general filing instructions?

A. Type or print legibly in black or dark blue ink.

B. If extra space is needed to complete any item, attach a continuation sheet, indicate the item number, and date and sign each sheet.

C. Answer all questions fully and accurately. If any item does not apply, please write "N/A."

D. **Translations.** Any foreign language document must be accompanied by a full English translation, which the translator has certified as complete and correct, and by the translator's certification that he or she is competent to translate the foreign language into English.

E. **Copies.** If these instructions state that a copy of a document may be filed with this petition and you choose to send us the original, INS will keep that original for our records. If INS requires the original, it will be requested.

## 5. What documents do you need to show that you are a United States citizen?

A. If you were born in the United States, a copy of your birth certificate, issued by the civil registrar, vital statistics office, or other civil authority. If a birth certificate is not available, see the section below titled "What if a document is not avaliable?"

**B.** A copy of your naturalization certificate or certificate of citizenship issued by INS.

**C.** A copy of Form FS-240, Report of Birth Abroad of a Citizen of the United States, issued by an American embassy or

**D.** A copy of your unexpired U.S. passport; or

**E.** An original statement from a U.S. consular officer verifying that you are a U.S. citizen with a valid passport.

**F.** If you do not have any of the above documents and you were born in the United States, see instruction under 9 below, "What if a document is not available?"

## 6. What documents do you need to show that you are a permanent resident?

If you are a permanent resident, you must file your petition with a copy of the front and back of your permanent resident card. If you have not yet received your card, submit copies of your passport biographic page and the page showing admission as a permanent resident, or other evidence of permanent resident status issued by INS.

## 7. What documents do you need to prove a family relationship?

You have to prove that there is a family relationship between you and your relative. If you are filing for:

**A. A husband or wife,** give INS the following documentation:
1) a copy of your marriage certificate.

2) if either you or your spouse were previously marrried, submit copies of documents showing that all prior marriages were legally terminated.

3) a color photo of you and one of your husband or wife, taken within 30 days of the date of this petition. The photos must have a white background and be glossy, unretouched and not mounted. The dimensions of the facial image should be about 1 inch from the chin to top of the hair, in a 3/4 frontal view, showing the right side of the face with the right ear visible. Using pencil or felt pen, lightly print the name (and Alien Registration Number, if known) on the back of each photograph.

4) a completed and signed G-325A (Biographic Information Form) for you and one for your husband or wife. Except for name and signature, you do not have to repeat on the G-325A the information given on your I-130 petition.

**B. A child and you are the mother:** give a copy of the child's birth certificate showing your name and the name of your child.

**C. A child and you are the father:** give a copy of the child's birth certificate showing both parents' names and your marriage certificate.

**D. A child born out of wedlock and you are the father:** if the child was not legitimated before reaching 18 years old, you must file your petition with copies of evidence that a bona fide parent-child relationship existed between the father and the child before the child reached 21 years. This may include evidence that the father lived with the child, supported him or her, or otherwise showed continuing parental interest in the child's welfare.

**E. A brother or sister:** give a copy of your birth certificate and a copy of your brother's or sister's birth certificate showing that you have at least one common parent. If you and your brother or sister have a common father but different mothers, submit copies of the marriage certificates of the father to each mother and copies of documents showing that any prior marriages of either your father or mothers were legally terminated. If you and your brother or sister are related through adoption or through a stepparent, or if you have a common father and either of you were not legitimated before your 18th birthday, see also H and I below.

**F. A mother:** give a copy of your birth certificate showing your name and your mother's name.

**G. A father:** give a copy of your birth certificate showing the names of both parents. Also give a copy of your parents' marriage certificate establishing that your father was married to your mother before you were born, and copies of documents showing that any prior marriages of either your father or mother were legally terminated. If you are filing for a stepparent or adoptive parent, or if you are filing for your father and were not legitimated before your 18th birthday, also see D, H and I.

**H. Stepparent/stepchild:** if your petition is based on a stepparent-stepchild relationship, you must file your petition with a copy of the marriage certificate of the stepparent to the child's natural parent showing that the marriage occurred before the child's 18th birthday, and copies of documents showing that any prior marriages were legally terminated.

**I. Adoptive parent or adopted child:** if you and the person you are filing for are related by adoption, you must submit a copy of the adoption decree(s) showing that the adoption took place before the child became 16 years old. If you adopted the sibling of a child you already adopted, you must submit a copy of the adoption decree(s) showing that the adoption of the sibling occured before that child's 18th birthday. In either case, you must also submit copies of evidence that each child was in the legal custody of and resided with the parent(s) who adopted him or her for at least two years before or after the adoption. Legal custody may only be granted by a court or recognized government entity and is usually granted at the time the adoption is finalized. However, if legal custody is granted by a court or recognized government agency prior to the adoption, that time may be counted toward fulfilling the two-year legal custody requirement.

## 8. What if your name has changed?

If either you or the person you are filing for is using a name other than that shown on the relevant documents, you must file your petition with copies of the legal documents that effected the change, such as a marriage certificate, adoption decree or court order.

## 9. What if a document is not available?

If the documents needed are not available, give INS a statement from the appropriate civil authority certifying that the document or documents are not available. In such situation, you may submit secondary evidence, including:

**A. Church record:** a copy of a document bearing the seal of the church, showing the baptism, dedication or comparable rite occurred within two months after birth, and showing the date and place of the child's birth, date of the religious ceremony and the names of the child's parents.

**B. School record:** a letter from the authority (preferably the first school attended) showing the date of admission to the school, child's date of birth or age at that time, the place of birth, and the names of the parents.

**C. Census record:** state or federal census record showing the names, place of birth, date of birth or the age of the person listed.

**D. Affidavits:** written statements sworn to or affirmed by two persons who were living at the time and who have personal knowledge of the event you are trying to prove. For example, the date and place of birth, marriage or death. The person making the affidavit does not have to be a citizen of the United States. Each affidavit should contain the following information regarding the person making the affidavit: his or her full name, address, date and place of birth and his or her relationship to you, if any, full information concerning the event, and complete details explaining how the person acquired knowledge of the event.

## 10. Where should you file this form?

If you reside in the U.S., file this form at the INS service Center having jurisdiction over your place of residence.

If you live in Connecticut, Delaware, District of Columbia, Maine, Maryland, Massachusetts, New Hampshire, New Jersey, New York, Pennsylvania, Puerto Rico, Rhode Island, Vermont, Virgin Islands, Virginia or West Virginia, mail this petition to: **USINS Vermont Service Center, 75 Lower Welden Street, St. Albans, VT 05479-0001.**

**NOTE:** If the I-130 petition is being filed concurrently with Form I-485, Application to Register Permanent Residence or to Adjust Status, submit both forms at the local INS office having jurisdiction over the place where the I-485 applicant resides. Applicants who reside in the jurisdiction of the Baltimore, MD, District Office should submit the I-130 petition and the Form I-485 concurrently to the **USINS Vermont Service Center, 75 Lower Welden Street, St. Albans, VT 05479-0001.**

If you live in Alaska, Colorado, Idaho, Illinois, Indiana, Iowa, Kansas, Michigan, Minnesota, Missouri, Montana, Nebraska, North Dakota, Ohio, Oregon, South Dakota, Utah, Washington, Wisconsin or Wyoming, mail this petition to: **USINS Nebraska Service Center, P.O. Box 87130, Lincoln, NE 68501-7130.**

If you live in Alabama, Arkansas, Florida, Georgia, Kentucky, Louisiana, Mississippi, New Mexico, North Carolina, Oklahoma, South Carolina, Tennessee or Texas, mail this petition to: **USINS Texas Service Center, P.O. Box 850919, Mesquite,TX 75185-0919.**

If you live in Arizona, California, Guam, Hawaii or Nevada, mail this petition to: **USINS California Service Center, P.O. Box 10130, Laguna Niguel, CA 92607-0130.**

**Petitioners residing abroad:** If you live outside the United States, you may file your relative petition at the INS office overseas or the U.S. consulate or embassy having jurisdiction over the area where you live. For further information, contact the nearest American consulate or embassy.

## 11. What is the fee?

You must pay $130.00 to file this form. **The fee will not be refunded, whether the petition is approved or not. DO NOT MAIL CASH.** All checks or money orders, whether U.S. or foreign, must be payable in U.S. currency at a financial institution in the United States. When a check is drawn on the account of a person other than yourself, write your name on the face of the check. If the check is not honored, INS will charge you $30.00.

Pay by check or money order in the exact amount. Make the check or money order payable to Immigration and Naturalization Service, unless:

**A.** you live in Guam, and are filing your petition there, make the check or money order payable to the "Treasurer, Guam" or

**B.** you live in the U.S. Virgin Islands, and you are filing your petition there, make your check or money order payable to the "Commissioner of Finance of the Virgin Islands."

## 12. When will a visa become available?

When a petition is approved for the husband, wife, parent or unmarried minor child of a United States citizen, these relatives do not have to wait for a visa number because they are not subject to the immigrant visa limit.

However, for a child to qualify for the immediate relative category, all processing must be completed and the child must enter the United States before his or her 21st birthday.

For all other alien relatives, there are only a limited number of immigrant visas each year. The visas are issued in the order in which the petitions are properly filed and accepted by INS. To be considered properly filed, a petition must be fully completed and signed, and the fee must be paid.

For a monthly report on the dates when immigrant visas are available, call the **U.S. Department of State** at **(202) 647-0508**.

## 13. Notice to persons filing for spouses, if married less than two years.

Pursuant to section 216 of the Immigration and Nationality Act, your alien spouse may be granted conditional permanent resident status in the United States as of the date he or she is admitted or adjusted to conditional status by an INS Officer. Both you and your conditional resident spouse are required to file Form I-751, Joint Petition to Remove Conditional Basis of Alien's Permanent Resident Status, during the 90-day period immediately before the second anniversary of the date your alein spouse was granted conditional permanent resident status.

Otherwise, the rights, privileges, responsibilites and duties that apply to all other permanent residents apply equally to a conditional permanent resident. A conditional permanent resident is not limited to the right to apply for naturalization, to file petitions on behalf of qualifying relatives or to reside permanently in the United States as an immigrant in accordance with our nation's immigration laws.

**NOTE**: Failure to file the Form I-751 joint petition to remove the conditional basis of the alien spouse's permanent resident status will result in the termination of his or her permanent resident status and initiation of removal proceedings.

## 14. What are the penalties for committing marriage fraud or submitting false information or both?

Title 8, United States Code, Section 1325, states that any individual who knowingly enters into a marriage contract for the purpose of evading any provision of the immigration laws shall be imprisoned for not more than five years, or fined not more than $250,000, or both.

Title 18, United States Code, Section 1001, states that whoever willfully and knowingly falsifies a material fact, makes a false statement, or makes use of a false document will be fined up to $10,000, imprisoned for up to five years, or both.

## 15. What is our authority for collecting this information?

We request the information on the form to carry out the immigration laws contained in Title 8, United States Code, Section 1154(a). We need this information to determine whether a person is eligible for immigration benefits. The information you provide may also be disclosed to other Federal, state, local and foreign law enforcement and regulatory agencies during the course of the investigation required by INS. You do not have to give this information. However, if you refuse to give some or all of it, your petition may be denied.

## 16. Paperwork Reduction Act Notice.

A person is not required to respond to a collection of information unless it displays a currently valid OMB control number. Public reporting burden for this collection of information is estimated to average 30 minutes per response, including the time for reviewing instructions, searching existing data sources, gathering and maintaining the data needed, and completing and reviewing the collection of information. Send comments regarding this burden estimate or any other aspect of this collection of information, including suggestions for reducing this burden to: U.S. Department of Justice, Immigration and Naturalization Service, Room 4034, Washington, D.C. 20536; OMB No.1115-0054. **DO NOT MAIL YOUR COMPLETED APPLICATION TO THIS ADDRESS.**

---

**Checklist.**

- Did you answer each question on the Form I-130 petition?
- Did you sign the petition?
- Did you enclose the correct filing fee for each petition?
- Did you submit proof of your U.S. citizenship or lawful permanent residence?
- Did you submit other required supporting evidence?

**If you are filing for your husband or wife, did you include:**
- your photograph?
- his or her photograph?
- your completed Form G-325A?
- his or her Form G-325A?

---

**Information and Forms:** For information on immigration laws, regulations and procedures or to order INS forms, call our National Customer Service Center at 1-800-375-5283 or visit the INS website at _www.ins.usdoj.gov._

## DO NOT WRITE IN THIS BLOCK - FOR EXAMINING OFFICE ONLY

| A# | Action Stamp | Fee Stamp |
|---|---|---|

**Section of Law/Visa Category**
- [ ] 201(b) Spouse - IR-1/CR-1
- [ ] 201(b) Child - IR-2/CR-2
- [ ] 201(b) Parent - IR-5
- [ ] 203(a)(1) Unm. S or D - F1-1
- [ ] 203(a)(2)(A)Spouse - F2-1
- [ ] 203(a)(2)(A) Child - F2-2
- [ ] 203(a)(2)(B) Unm. S or D - F2-4
- [ ] 203(a)(3) Married S or D - F3-1
- [ ] 203(a)(4) Brother/Sister - F4-1

Petition was filed on: _____ (priority date)
- [ ] Personal Interview
- [ ] Pet. [ ] Ben. " A" File Reviewed
- [ ] Field Investigation
- [ ] 203(a)(2)(A) Resolved
- [ ] Previously Forwarded
- [ ] I-485 Filed Simultaneously
- [ ] 204(g) Resolved
- [ ] 203(g) Resolved

Remarks:

## A. Relationship    You are the petitioner;  your relative is the beneficiary.

**1. I am filing this petition for my:**
- [ ] Husband/Wife
- [ ] Parent
- [ ] Brother/Sister
- [ ] Child

**2. Are you related by adoption?**
- [ ] Yes
- [ ] No

**3. Did you gain permanent residence through adoption?**
- [ ] Yes
- [ ] No

## B. Information about you

**1. Name** (Family name in CAPS)    (First)    (Middle)

**2. Address** (Number and Street)    (Apt.No.)

(Town or City)    (State/Country)    (Zip/Postal Code)

**3. Place of Birth** (Town or City)    (State/Country)

**4. Date of Birth** (Month/Day/Year)

**5. Gender**
- [ ] Male
- [ ] Female

**6. Marital Status**
- [ ] Married
- [ ] Widowed
- [ ] Single
- [ ] Divorced

**7. Other Names Used** (including maiden name)

**8. Date and Place of Present Marriage** (if married)

**9. Social Security Number** (if any)    **10. Alien Registration Number**

**11. Name(s) of Prior Husband(s)/Wive(s)**    **12. Date(s) Marriage(s) Ended**

**13. If you are a U.S. citizen, complete the following:**
My citizenship was acquired through (check one):
- [ ] Birth in the U.S.
- [ ] Naturalization. Give certificate number and date and place of issuance.

_____

- [ ] Parents. Have you obtained a certificate of citizenship in your own name?
  - [ ] Yes. Give certificate number, date and place of issuance.  [ ] No

**14a. If you are a lawful permanent resident alien, complete the following:** Date and place of admission for, or adjustment to, lawful permanent residence and class of admission.

**14b. Did you gain permanent resident status through marriage to a United States citizen or lawful permanent resident?**
- [ ] Yes
- [ ] No

## C. Information about your relative

**1. Name** (Family name in CAPS)    (First)    (Middle)

**2. Address** (Number and Street)    (Apt. No.)

(Town or City)    (State/Country)    (Zip/Postal Code)

**3. Place of Birth** (Town or City)    (State/Country)

**4. Date of Birth** (Month/Day/Year)

**5. Gender**
- [ ] Male
- [ ] Female

**6. Marital Status**
- [ ] Married
- [ ] Widowed
- [ ] Single
- [ ] Divorced

**7. Other Names Used** (including maiden name)

**8. Date and Place of Present Marriage** (if married)

**9. Social Security Number** (if any)    **10. Alien Registration Number**

**11. Name(s) of Prior Husband(s)/Wive(s)**    **12. Date(s) Marriage(s) Ended**

**13. Has your relative ever been in the U.S.?**  [ ] Yes  [ ] No

**14. If your relative is currently in the U.S., complete the following:**
He or she arrived as a::
(visitor, student, stowaway, without inspection, etc.)

Arrival/Departure Record (I-94)    Date arrived (Month/Day/Year)

| | | ▬ | | | | | | | |

Date authorized stay expired, or will expire, as shown on Form I-94 or I-95

**15. Name and address of present employer** (if any)

Date this employment began (Month/Day/Year)

**16. Has your relative ever been under immigration proceedings?**
- [ ] No  [ ] Yes  Where _____  When _____
- [ ] Removal  [ ] Exclusion/Deportation  [ ] Recission  [ ] Judicial Proceedings

INITIAL RECEIPT _____ RESUBMITTED _____ RELOCATED: Rec'd _____ Sent _____ COMPLETED: Appv'd _____ Denied _____ Ret'd _____

## C. Information about your alien relative (continued)

**17. List husband/wife and all children of your relative.**

| (Name) | (Relationship) | (Date of Birth) | (Country of Birth) |
|---|---|---|---|
| | | | |
| | | | |
| | | | |
| | | | |

**18. Address in the United States where your relative intends to live.**

(Street Address)      (Town or City)      (State)

**19. Your relative's address abroad.** (Include street, city, province and country)

Phone Number (if any)

**20. If your relative's native alphabet is other than Roman letters, write his or her name and foreign address in the native alphabet.**

(Name)      Address (Include street, city, province and country):

**21. If filing for your husband/wife, give last address at which you lived together.** (Include street, city, province, if any, and country):

From: (Month) (Year)    To: (Month) (Year)

**22. Complete the information below if your relative is in the United States and will apply for adjustment of status**

Your relative is in the United States and will apply for adjustment of status to that of a lawful permanent resident at the office of the Immigration and Naturalization Service in _____. If your relative is not eligible for adjustment of status, he or she

(City)      (State)

will apply for a visa abroad at the American consular post in _____

(City)      (Country)

NOTE: Designation of an American embassy or consulate outside the country of your relative's last residence does not guarantee acceptance for processing by that post. Acceptance is at the discretion of the designated embassy or consulate.

## D. Other information

**1. If separate petitions are also being submitted for other relatives, give names of each and relationship.**

**2. Have you ever filed a petition for this or any other alien before?** ☐ Yes ☐ No

If "Yes," give name, place and date of filing and result.

**WARNING:** INS investigates claimed relationships and verifies the validity of documents. INS seeks criminal prosecutions when family relationships are falsified to obtain visas.

**PENALTIES:** By law, you may be imprisoned for not more than five years or fined $250,000, or both, for entering into a marriage contract for the purpose of evading any provision of the immigration laws. In addition, you may be fined up to $10,000 and imprisoned for up to five years, or both, for knowingly and willfully falsifying or concealing a material fact or using any false document in submitting this petition.

**YOUR CERTIFICATION:** I certify, under penalty of perjury under the laws of the United States of America, that the foregoing is true and correct. Furthermore, I authorize the release of any information from my records which the Immigration and Naturalization Service needs to determine eligibility for the benefit that I am seeking.

## E. Signature of petitioner.

Date      Phone Number

## F. Signature of person preparing this form, if other than the petitioner.

I declare that I prepared this document at the request of the person above and that it is based on all information of which I have any knowledge.

Print Name _____ Signature _____ Date _____

Address _____ G-28 ID or VOLAG Number, if any. _____

## INSTRUCTIONS

**Purpose of This Form.**
This form is used to apply for an INS travel document, reentry permit, refugee travel document, or advance parole document. Each applicant must file a separate application.

**Who May File.**
*Reentry permit.* If you are in the United States as a permanent resident or conditional resident, you may apply for a reentry permit. A reentry permit allows a permanent resident or conditional resident to apply for admission to the U.S. during the permit's validity without having to obtain a returning resident visa from an American Consulate. A reentry permit is not required for return from a trip of less than one year's duration.

Possession of a reentry permit does not relieve you of any of the requirements of the immigration laws except the necessity to obtain a visa from an American consulate. For the purpose of later naturalization, absence from the United States for 1 year or more will normally break the continuity of any required period of continuous residence in the United States and you will need to file an application to preserve residence for naturalization purposes. Inquire at your local INS office for further information.

*Refugee travel document.* If you are in the United States in a valid refugee or asylee status, or obtained permanent residence as a direct result of refugee or asylee status in the U.S. you may apply for a refugee travel document. A refugee travel document is a document issued by the Service in implementation of Article 28 of the U.N. Convention of July 28, 1951. You must have a refugee travel document to return to the United States after temporary travel abroad unless you are traveling to Canada to apply for a U.S. immigrant visa (see advance parole document below).

*Advance parole document.* If you are outside the United States and must travel to the United States temporarily for emergent business or personal reasons, you may apply for an advance parole document to be paroled into the U.S. on humanitarian grounds if you cannot obtain the necessary visa and any required waiver of excludability. Parole cannot be used to circumvent normal visa issuing procedures, and is not a means to bypass delays in visa issuance. Parole is an extraordinary measure, sparingly used to bring an otherwise inadmissible alien into the U.S. for a temporary period of time due to a very compelling emergency.

Another person who is in the U.S. may file this application in your behalf. He or she should complete Part 1 with information about himself or herself.

*If you are in the United States* you may apply for an Advance Parole document if you:
- have an adjustment of status application pending which is only being held in abeyance because a visa number is not immediately available and you seek to travel abroad for bona fide business or emergent personal reasons;
- have an adjustment of status application pending for any other reason and you seek to travel abroad for emergent personal or bona fide business reasons;
- hold refugee or asylum status and intend to depart temporarily to apply for a U.S. immigrant visa in Canada; or
- seek to travel abroad temporarily for emergent personal or bona fide business reasons.

An advance parole document is issued solely to authorize the temporary parole of an individual into the United States. It may be accepted by a transportation company in lieu of a visa as authorization for the holder to travel to the United States. It is not issued to serve in lieu of any required passport.

**Additional Processing Criteria.**
*Reentry Permit or Refugee Travel Document.* A reentry permit or refugee travel document may not be issued to you if:

- you have already been issued such a document and it is still valid, unless the prior document has been returned to the Service or you can demonstrate it was lost; or
- due to national security, diplomatic or public safety reasons the government has published a notice in the Federal Register precluding issuance of such a document for travel to the area you intend to go to.

In addition, a reentry permit may not be issued if you have been a permanent resident for more than 5 years and have been outside the U.S. for more than 4 of the last 5 years, unless you are a crewman regularly serving abroad an aircraft or vessel of American registry and the travel is in connection with your duties as a crewman, or your travel is on the orders of the United States government, other than exclusion or deportation order.)

*Advance Parole.* An advance parole may not be issued to a person who is in deportation proceedings, is the beneficiary of a private bill, or is subject to the 2 year foreign residence requirement due to having held J-1 nonimmigrant status.

**General Filing Instructions.**
Please answer all questions by typing or clearly printing in black ink. Indicate that an item is not applicable with "N/A". If an answer is "none," please so state. If you need extra space to answer any item, attach a sheet of paper with your name and your A#, if any, and indicate the number of the item. Every application must be properly signed and filed with the correct fee. You must file your application with the required Initial Evidence. If you are under 14 years of age, your parent or guardian may sign the application in your behalf.

A reentry permit or refugee travel document may be sent to a U.S. Consulate or INS office overseas for you to pick up if you request it when you file your application. However, you must be in the U.S. when you file the application.

**Initial Evidence.**
*Evidence of eligibility. If you are a permanent resident or conditional resident,* you must attach:
- a copy of your alien registration receipt card; or
- if you have not yet received your alien registration receipt card, a copy of the biographic page and the page indicating initial admission as a permanent resident of your passport, or other evidence that you are a permanent resident; or
- a copy of the approval notice of a separate application for replacement of your alien registration receipt card or temporary evidence of permanent resident status.

*If you are a refugee or asylee applying for a refugee travel document,* you must attach a copy of the document issued to you by the Service showing your refugee or asylee status and indicating the expiration of such status.

*If you are in the U.S. and are applying for an advance parole document for yourself* you must attach a copy of any document for yourself issued by the Service showing any present status in the United States, and an explanation or other evidence demonstrating the circumstances that warrant issuance of advance parole. If you are basing your eligibility for advance parole on your separate application for adjustment of status, you must also attach a copy of the filing receipt for that application. If you are traveling to Canada to apply for an immigrant visa, you must also attach a copy of the consular appointment.

*If the person to be paroled is outside the U.S., you must also submit:*
- a statement of how, and by whom, medical care, housing, transportation, and other expenses and subsistence need will be met;
- an Affidavit of Support (Form I-134), with evidence of the sponsor's occupation and ability to provide necessary support;

- a statement of why a U.S. visa cannot be obtained, including when and where attempts were made to obtain a visa;
- a statement of why a waiver of excludability cannot be obtained to allow issuance of a visa, including when and where attempts were made to obtain a waiver, and a copy of any written decision;
- a copy of any decision on an immigrant petition filed for the person, and evidence regarding any pending immigrant petition; and
- a complete description of the emergent reasons why parole should be authorized and copies of any evidence you wish considered, and indicating the length of time for which parole is requested.

**Photographs.** You must submit 2 identical natural color photographs of yourself taken within 30 days of this application. The photos must have a white background, be unmounted, printed on thin paper, and be glossy and unretouched. They should show a three-quarter frontal profile showing the right side of your face, with your right ear visible and with your head bare (unless you are wearing a headdress as required by a religious order of which you are a member). The photos should be no larger than 2 X 2 inches, with the distance from the top of the head to just below the chin about 1 and 1/4 inches. Lightly print your A# on the back of each photo with a pencil. (If you are applying for an advance parole and are outside the U.S., keep these photographs. You will be instructed as to where to submit them if parole is approved. If you are applying for parole for another person, the required photographs are of the person to be paroled.)

**Copies.** If these instructions state that a copy of a document may be filed with this application and you choose to send us the original, we may keep that original for our records.

**Where to File.**
**Reentry Permit or Refugee Travel Document.** Mail your application to: USINS, Northern Service Center, 100 Centennial Mall North, Room B-26, Lincoln, NE 68508.

**Advance Parole.** If the person being filed for is in the United States, file the application at the INS office with jurisdiction over the area in which you live. If he or she is not in the United States, mail it to: USINS, Office of International Affairs and Parole, 425 I Street N.W., Room 1203, Washington, DC 20536.

**Effect of Travel Before the Travel Document is Issued.**
Departure from the United States before a decision is made on an application for a reentry permit or refugee travel document does not affect the application. Departure from the United States or application for admission to the United States before a decision is made on an application for an advance parole document shall be deemed an abandonment of the application.

**Fee.**
The fee for this application is $65.00. The fee must be submitted in the exact amount. It cannot be refunded. DO NOT MAIL CASH. All checks and money orders must be drawn on a bank or other institution located in the United States and must be payable in United States currency. The check or money order should be made payable to the Immigration and Naturalization Service, except that:
- If you live in Guam, and are filing this application in Guam, make your check or money order payable to the "Treasurer, Guam."
- If you live in the Virgin Islands, and are filing this application in the Virgin Islands, make your check or money order payable to the "Commissioner of Finance of the Virgin Islands."

Checks are accepted subject to collection. An uncollected check will render the application and any document issued invalid. A charge of $5.00 will be imposed if a check in payment of a fee is not honored by the bank on which it is drawn.

**Processing Information.**
*Acceptance.* Any application that is not signed or is not accompanied by the correct fee will be rejected with a notice that the application is deficient. You may correct the deficiency and resubmit the application. However, an application is not considered properly filed until it is accepted by the Service.

*Initial processing.* Once the application has been accepted, it will be checked for completeness, including submission of the required initial evidence. If you do not completely fill out the form, or file it without required initial evidence, you will not establish a basis for eligibility, and we may deny your application.

*Requests for more information or interview.* We may request more information or evidence or we may request that you appear at an INS office for an interview. We may also request that you submit the originals of any copy. We will return these originals when they are no longer required.

*Decision.* You will be advised of the decision on your application. If it is approved, the document will be issued.

*Invalidation.* Any travel document obtained by making a material false representation or concealment in this application will be invalid. A document will also be invalid if you are ordered excluded or deported. In addition, a refugee travel document will be invalid if the U.N. Convention of July 28, 1951, shall cease to apply or shall not apply to you as provided in Article 1C, D, E, or F of the Convention.

**Effect of Claim to Nonresident Alien Status for Federal Income Tax Purposes.**
An alien who has actually established residence in the United States after having been admitted as an immigrant or after having adjusted status to that of an immigrant, and who is considering the filing of a nonresident alien tax return or the non-filing of a tax return on the ground that he/she is a nonresident alien, should consider carefully the consequences under the immigration and naturalization laws if he/she does so.

If you take such action, you may be regarded as having abandoned residence in the United States and as having lost immigrant status under the immigration and naturalization laws. As a consequence, you may be ineligible for a visa or other document for which lawful permanent resident aliens are eligible; you may be inadmissible to the United States if you seek admission as a returning resident; and you may become ineligible for naturalization on the basis of your original entry or adjustment as an immigrant.

**Penalties.**
If you knowingly and willfully falsify or conceal a material fact or submit a false document with this request, we will deny the benefit you are filing for, and may deny any other immigration benefit. In addition, you will face severe penalties provided by law, and may be subject to criminal prosecution.

**Privacy Act Notice.**
We ask for the information on this form, and associated evidence, to determine if you have established eligibility for the immigration benefit you are filing for. Our legal right to ask for this information is in 8 USC 1203 and 1225. We may provide this information to other government agencies. Failure to provide this information, and any requested evidence, may delay a final decision or result in denial of your request.

**Paperwork Reduction Act Notice.**
We try to create forms and instructions that are accurate, can be easily understood, and which impose the least possible burden on you to provide us with information. Often this is difficult because some immigration laws are very complex. The estimated average time to complete and file this application is as follows: (1) 10 minutes to learn about the law and form; (2) 10 minutes to complete the form; and (3) 35 minutes to assemble and file the application, for a total estimated average of 55 minutes per application. If you have comments regarding the accuracy of this estimate, or suggestions for making this form simpler, you can write to both the Immigration and Naturalization Service, 425 I Street, N.W., Room 5304, Washington, D.C. 20536; and the Office of Management and Budget, Paperwork Reduction Project, OMB No. 1115-0005, Washington, D.C. 20503.

## START HERE - Please Type or Print

### Part 1.  Information about you.

| Family Name | Given Name | Middle Initial |
|---|---|---|

**Address - C/O**

| Street Number and Name | | Apt. # |
|---|---|---|
| City | State or Province | |
| Country | ZIP/Postal Code | |

| Date of Birth (Month/Day/Year) | Country of Birth |
|---|---|
| Social Security # | A # |

### Part 2.  Application Type (check one).

**a.** ☐  I am a permanent resident or conditional resident of the United States and I am applying for a Reentry Permit.

**b.** ☐  I now hold U.S. refugee or asylee status and I am applying for a Refugee Travel Document.

**c.** ☐  I am a permanent resident as a direct result of refugee or asylee status, and am applying for a Refugee Travel Document.

**d.** ☐  I am applying for an Advance Parole to allow me to return to the U.S. after temporary foreign travel.

**e.** ☐  I am outside the U.S. and am applying for an Advance Parole.

**f.** ☐  I am applying for an Advance Parole for another person who is outside the U.S.  *Give the following information about that person:*

| Family Name | Given Name | Middle Initial |
|---|---|---|
| Date of Birth (Month/Day/Year) | Country of Birth | |

**Foreign Address - C/O**

| Street Number and Name | | Apt. # |
|---|---|---|
| City | State or Province | |
| Country | ZIP/Postal Code | |

### Part 3.  Processing Information.

| Date of Intended departure (Month/Day/Year) | Expected length of trip. |
|---|---|

Are you, or any person included in this application, now in exclusion or deportation proceedings?
☐ No    ☐ Yes, at (give office name) _____

*If applying for an Advance Parole Document, skip to Part 7.*

Have you ever before been issued a Reentry Permit or Refugee Travel Document?
☐ No    ☐ Yes (give the following for the last document issued to you)

| Date Issued | Disposition (attached, lost, etc.) |
|---|---|

Form I-131 (Rev. 12/10/91) N                *Continued on back.*

**FOR INS USE ONLY**

| Returned | Receipt |
|---|---|
| _____ | |
| _____ | |
| **Resubmitted** | |
| _____ | |
| _____ | |
| **Reloc Sent** | |
| _____ | |
| _____ | |
| **Reloc Rec'd** | |
| _____ | |
| _____ | |

☐ Applicant Interviewed on

**Document Issued**
☐ Reentry Permit
☐ Refugee Travel Document
☐ Single Advance Parole
☐ Multiple Advance Parole
Validity to _____

**If Reentry Permit or Refugee Travel Document**
☐ Mail to Address in Part 2
☐ Mail to American Consulate
☐ Mail to INS overseas office
AT

**Remarks:**
☐ Document Hand Delivered
On _____ By _____

**Action Block**

**To Be Completed by**
*Attorney or Representative, if any*
☐ Fill in box if G-28 is attached to represent the applicant
VOLAG#

ATTY State License #

## Part 3. Processing Information. (continued)

Where do you want this travel document sent? (check one)

a. ☐ Address in Part 2, above

b. ☐ American Consulate at (give City and Country, below)

c. ☐ INS overseas office at (give City and Country, below)

City              Country

If you checked b. or c., above, give your overseas address:

## Part 4. Information about the Proposed Travel.

| Purpose of trip. *If you need more room, continue on a separate sheet of paper.* | List the countries you intend to visit. |
|---|---|
| | |

## Part 5. Complete only if applying for a Reentry Permit.

| | |
|---|---|
| Since becoming a Permanent Resident (or during the past five years, whichever is less) how much total time have you spent outside the United States? | ☐ less than 6 months    ☐ 2 to 3 years<br>☐ 6 months to 1 year    ☐ 3 to 4 years<br>☐ 1 to 2 years    ☐ more than 4 years |
| Since you became a Permanent Resident, have you ever filed a federal income tax return as a nonresident, or failed to file a federal return because you considered yourself to be a nonresident? (if yes, give details on a separate sheet of paper). | ☐ Yes      ☐ No |

## Part 6. Complete only if applying for a Refugee Travel Document.

Country from which you are a refugee or asylee:

If you answer yes to any of the following questions, explain on a separate sheet of paper.

| | |
|---|---|
| Do you plan to travel to the above-named country? | ☐ Yes      ☐ No |
| Since you were accorded Refugee/Asylee status, have you ever: returned to the above-named country; applied for an/or obtained a national passport, passport renewal, or entry permit into this country; or applied for an/or received any benefit from such country (for example, health insurance benefits)? | ☐ Yes      ☐ No |
| Since being accorded Refugee/Asylee status, have you, by any legal procedure or voluntary act, re-acquired the nationality of the above-named country, acquired a new nationality, or been granted refugee or asylee status in any other country? | ☐ Yes      ☐ No |

## Part 7. Complete only if applying for an Advance Parole.

*On a separate sheet of paper, please explain how you qualify for an Advance Parole and what circumstances warrant issuance of Advance Parole. Include copies of any documents you wish considered. (See instructions.)*

For how may trips do you intend to use this document?      ☐ 1 trip      ☐ More than 1 trip
*If outside the U.S., at right give the U.S. Consulate or INS office you wish notified if this application is approved.*

## Part 8. Signature.
Read the information on penalties in the instructions before completing this section. You must file this application while in the United States if filing for a reentry permit or refugee travel document.

I certify under penalty of perjury under the laws of the United States of America that this petition, and the evidence submitted with it, is all true and correct. I authorize the release of any information from my records which the Immigration and Naturalization Service needs to determine eligibility for the benefit I am seeking.

Signature            Date            Daytime Telephone #
(    )

**Please Note:** *If you do not completely fill out this form, or fail to submit required documents listed in the instructions, you may not be found eligible for the requested document and this application will have to be denied.*

## Part 9. Signature of person preparing form if other than above. (sign below)

I declare that I prepared this application at the request of the above person and it is based on all information of which I have knowledge.

Signature            Print Your Name            Date

Firm Name            Daytime Telephone #
and Address            (    )

*(Answer All Items: Fill in with Typewriter or Print in Block Letters in Ink.)*

I, _____ residing at _____
(Name)      (Street and Number)

_____
(City)    (State)    (Zip Code if in U.S.)    (Country)

**BEING DULY SWORN DEPOSE AND SAY:**

1. I was born on _____ at _____
(Date)    (City)    (Country)

If you are **not** a native born United States citizen, answer the following as appropriate:
   a. If a United States citizen through naturalization, give certificate of naturalization number _____
   b. If a United States citizen through parent(s) or marriage, give citizenship certificate number _____
   c. If United States citizenship was derived by some other method, attach a statement of explanation.
   d. If a lawfully admitted permanent resident of the United States, give "A" number _____

2. That I am _____ years of age and have resided in the United States since (date) _____

3. That this affidavit is executed in behalf of the following person:

| Name | | Gender | Age |
|---|---|---|---|
| Citizen of (Country) | Marital Status | Relationship to Sponsor | |
| Presently resides at (Street and Number) | (City) | (State) | (Country) |

Name of spouse and children accompanying or following to join person:

| Spouse | Gender | Age | Child | | Gender | Age |
|---|---|---|---|---|---|---|
| Child | Gender | Age | Child | | Gender | Age |
| Child | Gender | Age | Child | | Gender | Age |

4. That this affidavit is made by me for the purpose of assuring the United States Government that the person(s) named in item 3 will not become a public charge in the United States.

5. That I am willing and able to receive, maintain and support the person(s) named in item 3. That I am ready and willing to deposit a bond, if necessary, to guarantee that such person(s) will not become a public charge during his or her stay in the United States, or to guarantee that the above named person(s) will maintain his or her nonimmigrant status, if admitted temporarily and will depart prior to the expiration of his or her authorized stay in the United States.

6. That I understand this affidavit will be binding upon me for a period of three (3) years after entry of the person(s) named in item 3 and that the information and documentation provided by me may be made available to the Secretary of Health and Human Services and the Secretary of Agriculture, who may make it available to a public assistance agency.

7. That I am employed as, or engaged in the business of _____ with _____
(Type of Business)    (Name of concern)

at _____
(Street and Number)    (City)    (State)    (Zip Code)

I derive an annual income of *(if self-employed, I have attached a copy of my last income tax return or report of commercial rating concern which I certify to be true and correct to the best of my knowledge and belief. See instructions for nature of evidence of net worth to be submitted.)*    $ _____

I have on deposit in savings banks in the United States    $ _____

I have other personal property, the reasonable value of which is    $ _____

OVER

I have stocks and bonds with the following market value, as indicated on the attached list,
which I certify to be true and correct to the best of my knowledge and belief.   $ _____

I have life insurance in the sum of   $ _____

With a cash surrender value of   $ _____

I own real estate valued at   $ _____

  With mortgage(s) or other encumbrance(s) thereon amounting to $ _____

  Which is located at _____
         (Street and Number)         (City)         (State)         (Zip Code)

8. That the following persons are dependent upon me for support: *(Place an "x" in the appropriate column to indicate whether the person named is wholly or partially dependent upon you for support.)*

| Name of Person | Wholly Dependent | Partially Dependent | Age | Relationship to Me |
|---|---|---|---|---|
|  |  |  |  |  |
|  |  |  |  |  |
|  |  |  |  |  |

9. That I have previously submitted affidavit(s) of support for the following person(s). If none, state *"None."*

           Name                                                    Date submitted

_____

_____

10. That I have submitted visa petition(s) to the Immigration and Naturalization Service on behalf of the following person(s). If none, state none.

           Name                           Relationship           Date submitted

_____

_____

11. *(Complete this block only if the person named in the item 3 will be in the United States temporarily.)*
  That I ☐ intend ☐ do not intend, to make specific contributions to the support of the person named in item 3. *(If you check "intend," indicate the exact nature and duration of the contributions. For example, if you intend to furnish room and board, state for how long and, if money, state the amount in United States dollars and state whether it is to be given in a lump sum, weekly or monthly, or for how long.)*

_____

_____

_____

## Oath or Affirmation of Sponsor

*I acknowledge at that I have read Part III of the Instructions, Sponsor and Alien Liability, and am aware of my responsibilities as an immigrant sponsor under the Social Security Act, as amended, and the Food Stamp Act, as amended.*

**I swear (affirm) that I know the contents of this affidavit signed by me and the statements are true and correct.**

**Signature of sponsor** _____

**Subscribed and sworn to (affirmed) before me this** _____ **day of** _____, _____

**at** _____ . **My commission expires on** _____

*Signature of Officer Administering Oath* _____ **Title** _____

**If affidavit prepared by other than sponsor, please complete the following: I declare that this document was prepared by me at the request of the sponsor and is based on all information of which I have knowledge.**

_____    _____    _____
    **(Signature)**                      **(Address)**                      **(Date)**

**U.S. Department of Justice**
Immigration and Naturalization Service

# Affidavit of Support

## INSTRUCTIONS

**I. EXECUTION OF AFFIDAVIT.** A separate affidavit must be submitted for each person. You must sign the affidavit in your full, true and correct name and affirm or make it under oath. If you are **in the United States,** the affidavit may be sworn to or affirmed before an immigration officer without the payment of fee, or before a notary public or other officer authorized to administer oaths for general purposes, in which case the official seal or certificate of authority to administer oaths must be affixed. If you are **outside the United States** the affidavit must be sworn to or affirmed before a United States consular or immigration officer.

**II. SUPPORTING EVIDENCE.** The deponent must submit, in duplicate, evidence of income and resources, as appropriate:

A . Statement from an officer of the bank or other financial institution in which you have deposits giving the following details regarding your account:

1. Date account opened
2. Total amount deposited for the past year
3. Present balance

B. Statement of your employer on business stationery, showing:

1. Date and nature of employment
2. Salary paid
3. Whether position is temporary or permanent

C. If self-employed:

1. Copy of last income tax return filed, or
2. Report of commercial rating concern

D. List containing serial numbers and denominations of bonds and name of record owner(s).

**III. SPONSOR AND ALIEN LIABILITY.** Effective October 1, 1980, amendments to section 1614(f) of the Social Security Act and Part A of Title XVI of the Social Security Act establish certain requirements for determining the eligibility of aliens who apply for the first time for Supplemental Security Income (SSI) benefits. Effective October 1, 1981, amendments to section 415 of the Social Security Act establish similar requirements for determining the eligibility of aliens who apply for the first time for Aid to Families with Dependent Children (AFDC) benefits. Effective December 22, 1981, amendments to the Food Stamp Act of 1977 affect the eligibility of alien participation in the Food Stamp Program. These amendments require that the income and resources of any person, who as the sponsor of an alien's entry into the United States, executes an affidavit of support or similar agreement on behalf of the alien, and the income and resources of the sponsor's spouse *(if living with the sponsor)* shall be deemed to be the income and resources of the alien under formulas for determining eligibility for SSI, AFDC and Food Stamp benefits during the three years following the alien's entry into the United States.

An alien applying for SSI must make available to the Social Security Administration documentation concerning his or her income and resources and those of the sponsor, including information that was provided in support of the application for an immigrant visa or adjustment of status. An alien applying for AFDC or Food Stamps must make similar information available to the State public assistance agency. The Secretary of Health and Human Services and the Secretary of Agriculture are authorized to obtain copies of any such documentation submitted to INS or the Department of State and to release such documentation to a State public assistance agency.

Sections 1621(e) and 415(d) of the Social Security Act and subsection 5(i) of the Food Stamp Act also provide that an alien and his or her sponsor shall be jointly and severably liable to repay any SSI, AFDC or Food Stamp benefits that are incorrectly paid because of misinformation provided by a sponsor or because of a sponsor's failure to provide information. Incorrect payments that are not repaid will be withheld from any subsequent payments for which the alien or sponsor are otherwise eligible under the Social Security Act or Food Stamp Act, except that the sponsor was without fault or where good cause existed.

These provisions do not apply to the SSI, AFDC or Food Stamp eligibility of aliens admitted as refugees, granted political asylum by the Attorney General, or Cuban/ Haitian entrants as defined in section 501(e) of P.L. 96-422 and of dependent children of the sponsor or sponsor's spouse. The provisions also do not apply to the SSI or Food Stamp eligibility of an alien who becomes blind or disabled after admission to the United States for permanent residency.

**IV. AUTHORITY/ USE/ PENALTIES.** Authority for the collection of the information requested on this form is contained in 8 U.S.C. 1182(a)(15),1184(a) and 1258. The information will be used principally by the Service, or by any consular officer to whom it may be furnished, to support an alien's application for benefits under the Immigration and Nationality Act and specifically the assertion that he or she has adequate means of financial support and will not become a public charge. Submission of the information is voluntary. It may also, as a matter of routine use, be disclosed to other federal, state, local and foreign law enforcement and regulatory agencies, including the Department of Health and Human Services, Department of Agriculture, Department of State, Department of Defense and any component thereof (if the deponent has served or is serving in the armed forces of the United States), Central Intelligence Agency, and individuals and organizations during the course of any investigation to elicit further information required to carry out Service functions. Failure to provide the information may result in the denial of the alien's application for a visa or his or her exclusion from the United States.

## Purpose of This Form.

This form is used to petition to the Bureau of Citizenship and Immigration Services (BCIS) for an immigrant visa based on employment. The BCIS is comprised of offices of the former Immigration and Naturalization Service.

## Who May File.

**A U.S. employer may file this petition for:**

- An outstanding professor or researcher, with at least three years of experience in teaching or research in the academic area, who is recognized internationally as outstanding:

  -- in a tenured or tenure-track position at a university or institution of higher education to teach in the academic area; or

  -- in a comparable position at a university or institution of higher education to conduct research in the area; or

  -- in a comparable position to conduct research for a private employer that employs at least three persons in full-time research activities and which achieved documented accomplishments in an academic field.

- An alien who, in the three years preceding the filing of this petition, has been employed for at least one year by a firm or corporation or other legal entity and who seeks to enter the United States to continue to render services to the same employer, or to a subsidiary or affiliate, in a capacity that is managerial or executive.

- A member of the professions holding an advanced degree or an alien with exceptional ability in the sciences, arts, or business who will substantially benefit the national economy, cultural or educational interests, or welfare of the United States.

- A skilled worker (requiring at least two years of specialized training or experience in the skill) to perform labor for which qualified workers are not available in the United States.

- A member of the professions with a baccalaureate degree.

- An unskilled worker (requiring less than two years of specialized training or experience) to perform labor for which qualified workers are not available in the United States.

In addition, a person may file this petition on his or her own behalf if he or she:

- has extraordinary ability in the sciences, arts, education, business, or athletics demonstrated by sustained national or international acclaim, whose achievements have been recognized in the field; or

- is a member of the profession holding an advanced degree or is claiming exceptional ability in the sciences, arts, or business, and is seeking an exemption of the requirement of a job offer in the national interest (NIW).

## General Filing Instructions.

Please answer all questions by typing or clearly printing in black ink. Indicate that an item is not applicable with "N/A." If an answer to a question is "none," write "none." If you need extra space to answer any item, attach a sheet of paper with your name and your A#, if any, and indicate the number of the item to which the answer refers. You must file your petition with the required initial evidence. Your petition must be properly signed and filed with the correct fee.

## Initial Evidence.

*If you are filing for an alien of extraordinary ability in the sciences, arts, education, business, or athletics,* you must file your petition with evidence that the alien has sustained national or international acclaim and that the achievements have been recognized in the field experience.

- Evidence of a one-time achievement (i.e., a major, internationally recognized award); or

- At least three of the following:
  -- receipt of lesser nationally or internationally recognized prizes or awards for excellence in the field of endeavor,

  -- membership in associations in the field which require outstanding achievements as judged by recognized national or international experts,

  -- published material about the alien in professional or major trade publications or other major media,

  -- participation on a panel or individually as a judge of the work of others in the field or an allied field,

  -- original scientific, scholarly, artistic, athletic, or business-related contributions of major significance in the field,

  -- authorship of scholarly articles in the field, in professional or major trade publications or other major media,

  -- display of the alien's work at artistic exhibitions or showcases,

  -- evidence that the alien has performed in a leading or critical role for organizations or establishments that have distinguished reputations,

  -- evidence that the alien has commanded a high salary or other high remuneration for services,

  -- evidence of commercial successes in the performing arts, as shown by box office receipts or record, cassette, compact disk, or video sales.

- If the above standards do not readily apply to the alien's occupation, you may submit comparable evidence to establish the alien's eligibility; and

- Evidence that the alien is coming to the United States to continue work in the area of expertise. Such evidence may include letter(s) from prospective employer(s), evidence of prearranged commitments such as contracts, or a statement from the alien detailing plans on how he or she intends to continue work in the United States.

*A U.S. employer filing for an outstanding professor or researcher* must file the petition with:

- Evidence that the professor or researcher is recognized internationally as outstanding in the academic field specified in the petition. Such evidence shall consist of at least two of the following:

    -- receipt of major prizes or awards for outstanding achievement in the academic field,

    -- membership in associations in the academic field, which require outstanding achievements of their members,

    -- published material in professional publications written by others about the alien's work in the academic field,

    -- participation on a panel, or individually, as the judge of the work of others in the same or an allied academic field,

    -- original scientific or scholarly research contributions to the academic field, or

    -- authorship of scholarly books or articles, in scholarly journals with international circulation, in the academic field.

- Evidence the beneficiary has at least three years of experience in teaching and/or research in the academic field; and

- If you are a university or other institution of higher education, a letter indicating that you intend to employ the beneficiary in a tenured or tenure-track position as a teacher or in a permanent position as a researcher in the academic field; or

- If you are a private employer, a letter indicating that you intend to employ the beneficiary in a permanent research position in the academic field, and evidence that you employ at least three full-time researchers and have achieved documented accomplishments in the field.

*A U.S. employer filing for a multinational executive or manager* must file the petition with a statement which demonstrates that:

- If the worker is now employed outside the United States, that he or she has been employed outside the United States for at least one year in the past three years in an executive or managerial capacity by the petitioner or by its parent, branch, subsidiary or affiliate; or, if the worker is already employed in the United States, that he or she was employed outside the United States for at least one year in the three years preceding admission as a nonimmigrant in an executive or managerial capacity by the petitioner or by its parent, branch, subsidiary or affiliate;

- The prospective employer in the United States is the same employer or a subsidiary or affiliate of the firm or corporation or other legal entity by which the alien was employed abroad;

- The prospective United States employer has been doing business for at least one year; and

- The alien is to be employed in the United States in a managerial or executive capacity. A description of the duties to be performed should be included.

*A U.S. employer filing for a member of the professions with an advanced degree or a person with exceptional ability in the sciences, arts or business* must file the petition with:

- A labor certification (see **GENERAL EVIDENCE**), or a request for a waiver of a job offer because the employment is deemed to be in the national interest, with documentation provided to show that the beneficiary's presence in the United States would be in the national interest; and either:

    -- An official academic record showing that the alien has a U.S. advanced degree or an equivalent foreign degree, or an official academic record showing that the alien has a U.S. baccalaureate degree or an equivalent foreign degree and letters from current or former employers showing that the alien has at least five years of progressive post-baccalaureate experience in the specialty; or

    -- At least three of the following:

        - an official academic record showing that the alien has a degree, diploma, certificate, or similar award from an institution of learning relating to the area of exceptional ability;

        - letters from current or former employers showing that the alien has at least ten years of full-time experience in the occupation for which he or she is being sought;

        - a license to practice the profession or certification for a particular profession or occupation;

        - evidence that the alien has commanded a salary, or other remuneration for services, which demonstrates exceptional ability;

        - evidence of membership in professional associations; or

        - evidence of recognition for achievements and significant contributions to the industry or field by peers, governmental entities, or professional or business organizations.

- If the above standards do not readily apply to the alien's occupation, you may submit comparable evidence to establish the alien's eligibility.

*A U.S. employer filing for a skilled worker* must file the petition with:

- A labor certification (see **GENERAL EVIDENCE**);

- Evidence that the alien meets the educational, training, or experience and any other requirements of the labor certification (the minimum requirement is two years of training or experience).

*A U.S. employer filing for a professional* must file the petition with:

- A labor certification (see **GENERAL EVIDENCE**);

- Evidence that the alien holds a U.S. baccalaureate degree or equivalent foreign degree; and

- Evidence that a baccalaureate degree is required for entry into the occupation.

*A U.S. employer filing for an unskilled worker* must file the petition with:

- A labor certification (see **GENERAL EVIDENCE**); and

- Evidence that the beneficiary meets any education, training, or experience requirements required in the labor certification.

## General Evidence.

*Labor certification.* Petitions for certain classifications must be filed with a certification from the U.S. Department of Labor or with documentation to establish that the alien qualifies for one of the shortage occupations in the Department of Labor's Labor Market Information Pilot Program or for an occupation in Group I or II of the Department of Labor's Schedule A.

A certification establishes that there are not sufficient workers who are able, willing, qualified, and available at the time and place where the alien is to be employed and that employment of the alien, if qualified, will not adversely affect the wages and working conditions of similarly employed U.S. workers. Application for certification is made on Form ETA-750 and is filed at the local office of the State Employment Service. If the alien is in a shortage occupation, or for a Schedule A/Group I or II occupation, you may file a fully completed, uncertified Form ETA-750 in duplicate with your petition for determination by the BCIS that the alien belongs to the shortage occupation.

*Ability to pay wage.* Petitions which require job offers must be accompanied by evidence that the prospective U.S. employer has the ability to pay the proffered wage. Such evidence shall be in the form of copies of annual reports, federal tax returns, or audited financial statements.

In a case where the prospective U.S. employer employs 100 or more workers, a statement from a financial officer of the organization which establishes ability to pay the wage may be submitted. In appropriate cases, additional evidence, such as profit/loss statements, bank account records, or personnel records, may be submitted.

*Translations.* Any foreign language document must be accompanied by a full English translation, which the translator has certified as complete and correct, and by the translator's certification that he or she is competent to translate the foreign language into English.

*Copies.* If these instructions state that a copy of a document may be filed with this petition and you choose to send us the original, we may keep that original for our records. Copies may be submitted of all documentation with the exception of the Labor Certification which **must** be submitted in the original.

## Where to File.

File this petition at the BCIS service center with jurisdiction over the place where the alien will be employed.

If the alien's employment will be in Alabama, Arkansas, Florida, Georgia, Kentucky, Louisiana, Mississippi, New Mexico, North Carolina, South Carolina, Oklahoma, Tennessee, or Texas, mail the petition to:

> **USBCIS Texas Service Center**
> **P.O. Box 852135**
> **Mesquite, TX 75185-2135**

If the alien's employment will be in Connecticut, Delaware, District of Columbia, Maine, Maryland, Massachusetts, New Hampshire, New Jersey, New York, Pennsylvania, Puerto Rico, Rhode Island, Vermont, the U.S. Virgin Islands, Virginia or West Virginia, mail the petition to:

> **USBCIS Vermont Service Center**
> **75 Lower Welden Street**
> **St. Albans, VT 05479-0001**

If the alien's employment will be in Arizona, California, Guam, Hawaii or Nevada, mail the petition to:

> **USBCIS California Service Center**
> **P.O. Box 10140**
> **Laguna Niguel, CA 92607-1014**

If the alien's employment will be in Alaska, Colorado, Idaho, Illinois, Indiana, Iowa, Kansas, Michigan, Minnesota, Missouri, Montana, Nebraska, North Dakota, Ohio, Oregon, South Dakota, Utah, Washington, Wisconsin or Wyoming, mail the petition to:

> **USBCIS Nebraska Service Center**
> **P.O. Box 87140**
> **Lincoln, NE 68501-7140**

## Fee.

The fee for this petition is **$135.00**. The fee must be submitted in the exact amount. It cannot be refunded. **DO NOT MAIL CASH.** All checks and money orders must be drawn on a bank or other financial institution located in the United States and must be payable in United States currency. The check or money order should be made payable to the Bureau of Citizenship and Immigration Services, except:

- If you live in Guam and are filing this petition in Guam, make your check or money order payable to the "Treasurer, Guam."

- If you live in the U.S. Virgin Islands and are filing this petition in the U.S. Virgin Islands, make your check or money order payable to the "Commissioner of Finance of the Virgin Islands."

Checks are accepted subject to collection. An uncollected check will render the petition and any document issued invalid. A charge of $30.00 will be imposed if a check in payment of a fee is not honored by the bank on which it is drawn.

## Processing Information.

*Acceptance.* Any petition that is not signed or is not accompanied by the correct fee will be rejected with a notice that it is deficient. You may correct the deficiency and resubmit the petition. However, a petition is not considered properly filed until accepted by the BCIS. A priority date will not be assigned until the petition is properly filed.

*Initial processing.* Once the petition has been accepted, it will be checked for completeness, including submission of the required initial evidence. If you do not completely fill out the form, or file it without the required initial evidence, you will not establish a basis for eligibility, and we may deny your petition.

*Requests for more information or interview.* We may request more information or evidence, or we may request that you appear at a BCIS office for an interview. We may also request that you submit the originals of any copy. We will return these originals when they are no longer required.

*Decision.* If you have established eligibility for the benefit requested, your petition will be approved. If you have not established eligibility, your petition will be denied. You will be notified in writing of the decision on your petition.

*Meaning of petition approval.* Approval of a petition means you have established that the person you are filling for is eligible for the requested classification.

This is the first step towards permanent residence. However, this does not in itself grant permanent residence or employment authorization. You will be given information about the requirements for the person to receive an immigrant visa or to adjust status after your petition is approved.

## Instructions for Industry and Occupation Codes.

*NAICS Code.* The North American Industry Classification System (NAICS) code can be obtained from the U.S. Department of Commerce, U.S. Census Bureau at (www.census.gov/epcd/www/naics.html). Enter the code from left to right, one digit in each of the six boxes. If you use a code which is less than six digits, enter the code left to right and then add zeros in the remaining unoccupied boxes.

The code sequence 33466 would be entered as:

| 3 | 3 | 4 | 6 | 6 | 0 |
|---|---|---|---|---|---|

The code sequence 5133 would be entered as:

| 5 | 1 | 3 | 3 | 0 | 0 |
|---|---|---|---|---|---|

*SOC Code.* The Standard Occupational Classification (SOC) System codes can be obtained from the Department of Labor, U.S. Bureau of Labor Statistics (http://stats.bls.gov/soc/socguide.htm). Enter the code from left to right, one digit in each of the six boxes. If you use a code which is less than six digits, enter the code left to right and then add zeros in the remaining unoccupied boxes.

The code sequence 19-1021 would be entered as:

| 1 | 9 | — | 1 | 0 | 2 | 1 |
|---|---|---|---|---|---|---|

The code sequence 15-100 would be entered as:

| 1 | 5 | — | 1 | 0 | 0 | 0 |
|---|---|---|---|---|---|---|

## Penalties.

If you knowingly and willfully falsify or conceal a material fact or submit a false document with this petition, we will deny the benefit your are seeking and may deny any other immigration benefit. In addition, you will face severe penalties provided by law and may be subject to criminal prosecution.

## Privacy Act Notice.

We ask for the information on this form and associated evidence to determine if you have established eligibility for the immigration benefit you are seeking. Our legal right to ask for this information is in 8 U.S.C. 1154. We may provide this information to other government agencies. Failure to provide this information and any requested evidence may delay a final decision or result in denial of your request.

## Information and BCIS Forms.

For information on immigration laws, regulations and procedures and to order BCIS forms, call our National Customer Service Center at **1-800-375-5283** or visit our internet website at **www. bcis.gov.**

## Paperwork Reduction Act Notice.

An agency may not conduct or sponsor an information collection and a person is not required to respond to a collection of information unless it displays a currently valid OMB control number. We try to create forms and instructions that are accurate, can easily be understood, and which impose the least possible burden on you to provide us with information. Often this is difficult because some immigration laws are very complex. The estimate average time to complete and file this application is as follows: (1) 20 minutes to learn about the law and form; (2) 15 minutes to complete the form; and (3) 25 minutes to assemble and file the petition; for a total estimated average of 1 hour per petition. If you have comments regarding the accuracy of this estimate, or suggestions for making this form simpler, you can write to the Bureau of Citizenship and Immigration Services, HQRFS, 425 I Street, N.W., Room 4034, Washington, D.C. 20536; OMB No. 1615-0015. **DO NOT MAIL YOUR COMPLETED PETITION TO THIS ADDRESS.**

U.S. Department of Homeland Security
Bureau of Citizenship and Immigration Services

OMB No. 1615-0015; Exp. 8-31-04

# I-140, Immigrant Petition for Alien Worker

## START HERE - Please Type or Print.

### Part 1.   Information about the person or organization filing this petition.

If an individual is filing, use the top name line. Organizations should use the second line.

Family Name (Last Name)   Given Name (First Name)   Full Middle Name

Company or Organization Name

Address:  (Street Number and Name)   Suite #

Attn:

City   State/Province

Country   Zip/Postal Code

IRS Tax #   Social Security # *(if any)*   E-Mail Address *(if any)*

### Part 2.   Petition type.

**This petition is being filed for:** *(Check one)*

a. ☐ An alien of extraordinary ability.

b. ☐ An outstanding professor or researcher.

c. ☐ A multinational executive or manager.

d. ☐ A member of the professions holding an advanced degree or an alien of exceptional ability (who is **NOT** seeking a National Interest Waiver).

e. ☐ A skilled worker (requiring at least two years of specialized training or experience) or professional.

f. ☐ Item F- no longer available.

g. ☐ Any other worker (requiring less than two years of training or experience).

h. ☐ An alien applying for a National Interest Waiver (who **IS** a member of the professions holding an advanced degree or an alien of exceptional ability).

### Part 3.   Information about the person you are filing for.

Family Name (Last Name)   Given Name (First Name)   Full Middle Name

Address:  (Street Number and Name)   Apt. #

C/O:  (In Care Of)

City   State/Province

Country   Zip/Postal Code   E-Mail Address *(if any)*

Daytime Phone # *(with area/country code)*   Date of Birth *(mm/dd/yyyy)*

City/Town/Village of Birth   State/Province of Birth   Country of Birth

Country of Nationality/Citizenship   A # *(if any)*   Social Security # *(if any)*

**IF IN THE U.S.**

Date of Arrival *(mm/dd/yyyy)*   I-94 # *(Arrival/Departure Document)*

Current Nonimmigrant Status   Date Status Expires *(mm/dd/yyyy)*

### FOR BCIS USE ONLY

| Returned | Receipt |
|---|---|
| Date | |
| Date | |
| Resubmitted | |
| Date | |
| Date | |
| Reloc Sent | |
| Date | |
| Date | |
| Reloc Rec'd | |
| Date | |
| Date | |

**Classification:**

☐ 203(b)(1)(A) Alien of Extraordinary

☐ 203(b)(1)(B) Outstanding Professor or Researcher

☐ 203(b)(1)(C) Multi-national executive or manager

☐ 203(b)(2) Member of professions w/adv. degree or exceptional ability

☐ 203(b)(3)(A)(i) Skilled Worker

☐ 203(b)(3)(A)(ii) Professional

☐ 203(b)(3)(A)(iii) Other worker

**Certification:**

☐ National Interest Waiver (NIW)

☐ Schedule A, Group I

☐ Schedule A, Group II

| Priority Date | Consulate |
|---|---|

**Remarks**

**Action Block**

**To Be Completed By**
*Attorney or Representative*, if any.

☐ Fill in box if G-28 is attached to represent the applicant.

ATTY State License #

Form I-140 (Rev.  05/120/03)N (Prior versions may be used unitl 09/30/03)

## Part 4.  Processing Information.

**1.** Please complete the following for the person named in Part 3: *(Check one)*

☐ Alien will apply for a visa abroad at the American Embassy or Consulate at:

City

Foreign Country

☐ Alien is in the United States and will apply for adjustment of status to that of lawful permanent resident.
Alien's country of current residence or, if now in the U.S., last permanent residence abroad

**2.** If you provided a U.S. address in Part 3, print the person's foreign address:

**3.** If the person's native alphabet is other than Roman letters, write the person's foreign name and address in the native alphabet:

**4.** Are you filing any other petitions or applications with this one?    ☐ No    ☐ Yes-attach an explanation

**5.** Is the person you are filing for in removal proceedings?    ☐ No    ☐ Yes-attach an explanation

**6.** Has any immigrant visa petition ever been filed by or on behalf of this person?    ☐ No    ☐ Yes-attach an explanation

If you answered yes to any of these questions, please provide the case number, office location, date of decision and disposition of the decision on a separate sheet(s) of paper.

## Part 5.  Additional information about the petitioner.

**1.** Type of petitioner *(Check one)*.

☐ Employer    ☐ Self    ☐ Other (Explain, e.g., Permanent Resident, U.S. Citzen or any other person filing on behalf of the alien.)

**2.** If a company, give the following:

Type of Business

Date Established *(mm/dd/yyyy)*

Current Number of Employees

Gross Annual Income

Net Annual Income

NAICS Code

**3.** If an individual, give the following:

Occupation

Annual Income

## Part 6.  Basic information about the proposed employment.

**1.** Job Title

**2.** SOC Code

**3.** Nontechnical Description of Job

**4.** Address where the person will work if different from address in Part 1.

**5.** Is this a full-time position?

☐ Yes    ☐ No

**6.** If the answer to Number 5 is "No," how many hours per week for the position?

**7.** Is this a permanent position?

☐ Yes    ☐ No

**8.** Is this a new position?

☐ Yes    ☐ No

**9.** Wages per week

$

## Part 7.  Information on spouse and all children of the person for whom you are filing.

**List husband/wife and all children related to the individual for whom the petition is being filed.** Provide an attachment of additional family members, if needed.

| Name *(First/Middle/Last)* | Relationship | Date of Birth *(mm/dd/yyyy)* | Country of Birth |
|---|---|---|---|
|  |  |  |  |
|  |  |  |  |
|  |  |  |  |
|  |  |  |  |
|  |  |  |  |
|  |  |  |  |

## Part 8.  Signature.  *Read the information on penalties in the instructions before completing this section.  If someone helped you prepare this petition, he or she must complete Part 9.*

I certify, under penalty of perjury under the laws of the United States of America, that this petition and the evidence submitted with it are all true and correct.  I authorize the release of any information from my records that the Bureau of Citizenship Immigration Services needs to determine eligibility for the benefit I am seeking.

**Petitioner's Signature**   **Daytime Phone Number** *(Area/Country Code)*   **E-mail Address**

**Print Name**   **Date** *(mm/dd/yyyy)*

**Please Note:**  *If you do not completely fill out this form or fail to submit required documents listed in the instructions, you may not  be found eligible for the requested benefit and this petition may be denied.*

## Part 9.  Signature of person preparing form, if other than above.   *(Sign below)*

I declare that I prepared this petition at the request of the above person and it is based on all information of which I have knowledge.

**Attorney or Representative:** In the event of a Request for Evidence (RFE) may the BCIS contact you by Fax or E-mail?  ☐ Yes   ☐ No

**Signature**   **Print Name**   **Date** *(mm/dd/yyyy)*

**Firm Name and Address**

**Daytime Phone Number** *(Area/Country Code)*   **Fax Number** *(Area/Country Code)*   **E-mail Address**

OMB No. 1115-0117

**U.S. Department of Justice**
Immigration and Naturalization Service

# Petition for Amerasian, Widow(er), or Special Immigrant

# INSTRUCTIONS

## Purpose of This Form.

This petition is used to classify an alien as:

- an Amenasian;
- a Widow or Widower,
- a Battered or Abused Spouse or Chid of a U.S. Citizen or Lawful Permanent Resident
- a Special Immigrant (Religious Worker; Panama Canal Company Employee, Canal Zone Government Employee, U.S. Government in the Canal Zone Employee; Physician; International Organization Employee or Family Member, Juvenile Court Dependent or Armed Forces Member).

## Initial Evidence Requirements.

If these instructions state that a copy of a document may be filed with this petition, and you choose to send us the original, we may keep that original for our records. Any foreign language document must be accompanied by an English translation certified by the translator that he/she is competent to translate the foreign language into English and that the translation is accurate.

*Amerasian.* Any person who is 18 or older, an emancipated minor, or a U.S. corporation may file this petition for an alien who was born in Korea, Vietnam, Laos, Kampuchea, or Thailand after December 31, 1950, and before October 22, 1982, and was fathered by a U.S. citizen.

The petition must be filed with:

- copies of evidence showing that the person this petition is for was born in one of the above countries between those dates. If he/she was born in Vietnam, you must also submit a copy of his/her Vietnamese I.D. card, or an affidavit explaining why it is not available;
- copies of evidence establishing the parentage of the person, and of evidence establishing that the biological father was a U.S. citizen. Examples of documents that may be submitted are birth or baptismal records or other religious documents; local civil records; an affidavit, correspondence or evidence of financial support from the father; photographs of the father (especially with the child); or, absent other documents, affidavits from knowledgeable witnesses which detail the parentage of the child and how they know such facts;
- a photograph of the person;
- if the person is married, submit a copy of the marriage certificate, and proof of the termination of any prior marriages; and
- if the person is under 18 years old, submit a written statement from his/her mother or legal guardian which:

  - irrevocably releases him/her for emigration and authorizes the placement agencies to make necessary decisions for his/her immediate care until a sponsor receives custody;
  - shows an understanding of the effects of the release, and states whether any money was paid or coercion used prior to obtaining the release; and
  - includes the full name, date and place of birth, and present or permanent address of the mother or guardian, and with the signature of the mother or guardian on the release authenticated by a local registrar, court of minors, or a U.S. immigration or consular officer.

The following sponsorship documents are also required. You may file these documents with the petition, or wait until we review the petition and request them. However, not filing

them with the petition will add to the overall processing time.

- An Affidavit of Financial Support executed by the sponsor, with the evidence of financial ability required by that form. Please note that the original sponsor remains financially responsible for the Amerasian if any subsequent sponsor fails in this area;
- Copies of evidence showing that the sponsor is at least 21 years old and is a U.S. citizen or permanent resident;
- Fingerprints of the sponsor on Form FD-258; and
- If this petition is for a person under 18 years old, the following documents issued by a placement agency must be submitted:

  - a copy of the private, public or state agency's license to place children in the U.S., proof of the agency's recent experience in the intercountry placement of children and of the agency's financial ability to arrange the placement;
  - a favorable home study of the sponsor conducted by a legally authorized agency;
  - a pre-placement report from the agency, including information regarding any family separation or dislocation abroad that would result from the placement;
  - a written description of the orientation given to the sponsor and to the parent or guardian on the legal and cultural aspects of the placement;
  - a statement from the agency showing that the sponsor has been given a report on the pre-placement screening and evaluation of the child; and
  - a written plan from the agency to provide follow-up services, including mediation and counseling, and describing the contingency plans to place the person this petition is for in another suitable home if the initial placement fails.

*Widow/Widower of a United States Citizen.* You may file this petition for yourself if:

- you were married for at least two years to a U.S. citizen who is now deceased and who was a U.S. citizen at the time of death;
- your citizen spouse's death was less than two years ago;
- you were not legally separated from your citizen spouse at the time of death; and
- you have not remarried.

The petition must be filed with:

- a copy of your marriage certificate to the U.S. citizen and proof of termination of any pnor marriages of either of you;
- copies of evidence that your spouse was a U.S. citizen, such as a birth certificate if born in the U.S., Naturalization Certificate or Certificate of Citizenship issued by this Service, Form FS-240, Report of Birth Abroad of a Citizen of the United States; or a U.S. passport which was valid at the time of the citizen's death; and
- a copy of the death certificate of your U.S. citizen spouse.

***Self-Petitioning Battered or Abused Spouse or Child of a U.S. Citizen or Lawful Permanent Resident.*** You may self-petition for immediate relative or family-sponsored immigrant classification if you:

- are now the spouse or child of an abusive U.S. citizen or lawful permanent resident;
- are eligible for immigrant classification based on that relationship;
- are now residing in the United States;
- have resided in the United States with the U.S. citizen or lawful permanent resident abuser in the past;
- have been battered by, or have been the subject of extreme cruelty perpetrated by:
  -- your U.S. citizen or lawful permanent resident spouse during the marriage; or are the parent of a child who has been battered by or has been the subject of extreme cruelty perpetrated by, your abusive citizen or lawful permanent resident spouse during your marriage; or
  -- your citizen or lawful permanent resident parent while residing with that parent;
- are a person of good moral character;
- are a person whose removal or deportation would result in extreme hardship to yourself, or to your child if you are a spouse; and if you
- are a spouse who entered into the marriage to the citizen or lawful permanent resident abuser in good faith.

**NOTE:** Divorce or other legal termination of the marriage to the abuser AFTER the self-petition is properly filed with INS will not be the sole basis for denial or revocation of an approved self-petition. If you remarry before you become a lawful permanent resident, however, your self-petition will be denied or the approval revoked.

Your self-petition may be filed with any credible relevant evidence of eligibility. The determination of what evidence is credible and the weight to be given that evidence is within the sole discretion of INS; therefore, you are encouraged to provide the following documentation:

- evidence of the abuser's U.S. citizenship or lawful permanent resident status;
- marriage and divorce decrees, birth certificates, or other evidence of your legal relationship to the abuser;
- one or more documents showing that you and the abuser have resided together in the United States in the past, such as employment records, utility receipts, school records, hospital or medical records, birth certificates of children, deeds, mortgages, rental records, insurance policies, or affidavits;
- one or more documents showing that you are now residing in the United States, such as the documents listed above;
- evidence of the abuse, such as reports and affidavits from police, judges and other court officials, medical personnel, school officials, clergy, social workers, and other social service agency personnel. If you have an order of protection or have taken other legal steps to end the abuse, you should submit copies of those court documents;

- if you are more than 14 years of age, your affidavit of good moral character accompanied by a local police clearance, state-issued criminal background check, or similar report from each locality or state in the United States or abroad in which you have resided for six or more months during the three (3) year period immediately preceding the filing of your sellf-petition;
- affidavits, birth certificates of children, medical reports and other relevant credible evidence of the extreme hardship that would result if you were to be removed or deported; and
- if you are a spouse, proof that one spouse has been listed as the other's spouse on insurance policies, property leases, income tax forms, or bank accounts; and testimony or other evidence regarding your courtship, wedding ceremony, shared residence and experiences showing that your marriage was entered in good faith.

***Special Immigrant Juvenile.*** Any person, including the alien, may file this petition for an alien who:
- is unmarried and less than 21 years old;
- has been declared dependent upon a juvenile court in the United States or who such a court has legally committed to, or placed under the custody of, an agency or department of a state and who has been found eligible for long-term foster care; and
- has been the subject of administrative or judicial proceedings in which it was determined that it would not be in the juvenile's best interests to be returned to the juvenile's or his/her parent's country of nationality or last habitual residence.

**NOTE:** After a special immigrant juvenile becomes a permanent resident, his or her parent(s) may not receive any immigration benefit based on the relationship to the juvenile.

The petition must be filed with:
- a copy of the juvenile's birth certificate or other evidence of his or her age;
- copies of the court or administrative document(s) upon which the claim to eligibility is based.

***Special Immigrant Religious Worker.*** Any person, including the alien, may file this petition for an alien who for the past two (2) years has been a member of a religious denomination which has a bona fide nonprofit, religious organization in the U.S; and who has been carrying on the vocation, professional work, or other work described below, continuously for the past two (2) years; and seeks to enter the U.S. to work solely:
- as a minister of that denomination; or
- in a professional capacity in a religious vocation or occupation for that organization; or
- in a religious vocation or occupation for the organization or its nonprofit affiliate.

**NOTE:** A petition for a special immigrant for a person who is not a minister may only be filed until October 1, 2000.

The petition must be filed with:
- a letter from the authorized official of the religious organization establishing that the proposed services and alien qualify as above;
- a letter from the authorized official of the religious organization attesting to the alien's membership in the religious denomination and explaining, in detail, the person's religious work and all employment during the past two (2) years and the proposed employment; and
- evidence establishing that the religious organization, and any affiliate which will employ the person, is a bona fide nonprofit religious organization in the U.S. and is exempt from taxation under section 501(c)(3) of the Internal Revenue Code of 1986.

**Special immigrant based on employment with the Panama Canal Company, Canal Zone Government or U.S. government in the Canal Zone.** Any person may file this petition for an alien who, at the time the Panama Canal Treaty of 1977 entered into force, either:
- was resident in the Canal Zone and had been employed by the Panama Canal Company or Canal Zone Government for at least one (1) year, or
- was a Panamanian national and either honorably retired from U.S. Government employment in the Canal Zone with a total of 15 or more years of faithful service or so employed for 15 years and since honorably retired; or
- was an employee of the Panama Canal Company or Canal Zone government, had performed faithful service for five (5) years or more as an employee, and whose personal safety, or the personal safety of his/her spouse or child, is in danger as a direct result of the special nature of his/her employment and as a direct result of the Treaty.

The petition must be filed with:
- a letter from the Panama Canal Company, Canal Zone government or U.S. government agency employing the person in the Canal Zone, indicating the length and circumstances of employment and any retirement or termination; and
- copies of evidence to establish any claim of danger to personal safety.

**Special Immigrant Physician.** Any person may file this petition for an alien who:
- graduated from a medical school or qualified to practice medicine in a foreign state;
- was fully and permanently licensed to practice medicine in a State of the U.S. on January 9, 1978, and was practicing medicine in a State on that date;
- entered the U.S. as an "H" or "J" nonimmigrant before January 9, 1978; and
- has been continuously present in the U.S. and continuously engaged in the practice or study of medicine since the date of such entry.

The petition must be filed with:
- letters from the person's employers, detailing his/her employment since January 8, 1978, including the current employment; and
- copies of relevant documents that demonstrate that the person filed for meets all the above criteria.

**Special Immigrant International Organization Employee or family member.** Certain long-term "G" and "N" nonimmigrant employees of a qualifying international organization entitled to enjoy privileges, exemptions and immunities under the International Organizations Immunities Act, and certain relatives of such an employee, may be eligible to apply for classification as a Special Immigrant. To determine eligibility, contact the qualifying international organization or your local INS office.
The petition must be filed with:
- a letter from the international organization demonstrating that it is a qualifying organization and explaining the circumstances of qualifying employment and the immigration status held by the person the petition is for, and
- copies of evidence documenting the relationship between the person this petition is for and the employee.

**Armed Forces Member.** You may file this petition for yourself, if:
- you have served honorably on active duty in the Armed Forces of the United States after October 15, 1978;
- you originally lawfully enlisted outside the United States under a treaty or agreement in effect on October 1, 1991, for a period or periods aggregating:
  - twelve (12) years, and were never separated from such service except under honorable conditions; or
  - six years, are now on active duty, and have reenlisted to incur a total active duty service obligation of at least 12 years;
- you are a national of an independent state which maintains a treaty or agreement allowing nationals of that state to enlist in the United States Armed Forces each year; and
- the executive department under which you have served or are serving has recommended you for this

The petition must be filed with:
- certified proof issued by the authorizing official of the executive department in which you are serving or have served which certifies that you have the required honorable active duty service and/or commitment; and
- your birth certificate.

**General Filing Instructions.**
Please answer all questions by typing or clearly printing in black ink only. Indicate that an item is not applicable with "N/A." If an answer is "none," please so state. If you need extra space to answer any item, attach a sheet of paper with your name and your alien registration number (A#), if any, and indicate the number of the item the answer refers to. Every petition must be properly signed, and accompanied by the proper fee. If you are under 14 years of age, your parent or guardian may sign the petition.

**Where to File.**
If you are filing for a Special Immigrant Juvenile, file the petition at the local INS office having jurisdiction over the place he/she lives.

If you are filing for Amerasian classification and the person you are filing for is outside the United States, you may file this petition at the INS office that has jurisdiction over the place he/she lives or the office that has jurisdiction over the place he/she will live.

If you are in the United States and filing as a Widow/Widower you may file this petition together with your application for adjustment of status.

If this petition is for an Amerasian, a Widow/Widower, or a Special Immigrant Armed Forces member, and that person lives outside the United States, you may file this petition at the INS office overseas or the U.S. consulate or embassy abroad having jurisdiction over the area in which he or she lives.

In all other instances (except for a self-petitioning battered or abused spouse or child described below), file this petition at an INS Service Center, as follows:

If you live in Connecticut, Delaware, District of Columbia, Maine, Maryland, Massachusetts, New Hampshire, New Jersey, New York, Pennsylvania, Puerto Rico, Rhode Island, Vermont, Virgin Islands, Virginia, or West Virginia, mail this petition to USINS, Vermont Service Center, 75 Lower Welden Street, St. Albans, VT 05479-0001.

If you live in Alabama, Arkansas, Florida, Georgia, Kentucky, Louisiana, Mississippi, New Mexico, North Carolina, Oklahoma, South Carolina, Tennessee, or Texas, mail this petition to USINS, Texas Service Center, P.O. Box 152122, Dept A, Irving, TX 75015-2122.

If you live in Arizona, California, Guam, Hawaii, or Nevada, mail this petition to USINS, California Service Center, P.O. Box 10360, Laguna Niguel, CA 92607-0360

If you live elsewhere in the U.S., mail this petition to USINS, Nebraska Service Center, 850 S Street, Lincoln, NE 68501-2521

If you are a self petitioning battered spouse or abused spouse or child, mail your completed Form I-360 with supporting documents and correct fee to the Vermont Service Center at the following address:

> USINS
> Vermont Service Center
> 75 Lower Welden Street,
> St. Albans, VT. 05479

If the Vermont Service Center later sends you a Notice of Approval of your petition, you may apply at your local INS office to adjust your status as a lawful permanent resident.

**Public Service Information.** The National Domestic Violence Hotline povides information, crisis intervention and referrals to local service providers, including legal assistance organizations, to victims of domestic violence or anyone calling on their behalf at 1-800-799-7233 or TDD at 1-800-787-3244 TTD. The hotline services are available 24 hours a day seven (7) days a week, toll-free from anywhere in the United States, Puerto Rico or the Virgin Islands. The staff and volunteers speak both English and Spanish and have access to translators in 139 languages.

**Fee.**
The fee for this petition to $110.00, except that there is no fee if you are filing for an Amerasian. The fee must be submitted in the exact amount. It cannot be refunded. DO NOT MAIL CASH. All checks and money orders must be drawn on a bank or other institution located in the United States and must be payable in United States currency. The check or money order should be made payable to the Immigration and Naturalization Service, except that:

- If you live in Guam, and are filing this application in Guam, make your check or money order payable to the "Treasurer, Guam."
- If you live in the Virgin Islands, and are filing this application in the Virgin Islands, make your check or money order payable to the "Commissioner of Finance of the Virgin Islands."

Checks are accepted subject to collection. An uncollected check will render the application and any document issued invalid. A charge of $30.00 will be imposed if a check in payment of a fee is not honored by the bank on which it is drawn.

**Processing Information.**
*Rejection.* Any petition that is not signed or is not accompanied by the correct fee will be rejected with a notice that the petition is deficient You may correct the deficiency and resubmit the petition. However, a petition is not considered properly filed until accepted by the Service.

*Initial processing.* Once the petition has been accepted, it will be checked for completeness, including submission of the required initial evidence. If you do not completely fill out the form, or file it without required initial evidence, you will not establish a basis for eligibility and we may deny your petition.

**NOTE:** A self-petitioning battered or abused spouse or child of a U.S. citizen or lawful permanent resident may submit any relevant credible evidence in place of the suggested evidence.

***Requests for additional information or interview.*** We may request additional information or evidence or we may request that you appear at an INS office for an interview. We may also request that you submit the originals of any copy. We will return these originals when they are no longer required.

*Decision.* If you establish that the person this petition is for is eligible for the requested classification, we will approve the petition. We will send it to the U.S. Embassy/Consulate for visa issuance unless he or she is in the U.S. and appears eligible and intends to apply for adjustment to permanent resident status while here. If you do not establish eligibility, we will deny the petition. We will notify you in writing of our decision.

**Penalties.**
If you knowingly and willfully falsify or conceal a material fact or submit a false document with this request, we will deny the benefit you are filing for, and may deny any other immigration benefit. In addition, you will face severe penalties provided by law, and may be subject to criminal prosecution.

**Forms and Information.**

To request INS forms, call our toll free number at 1-800-870-3676. You may also obtain INS forms and information on immigration laws, regulations and procedures by telephoning our National Customer Service Center (NCSC) at 1-800-375-5283 or from the INS Internet website at www.ins.usdoj.gov.

**Privacy Act Notice.**

We ask for the information on this form, and associated evidence to determine if you have established eligibility for the immigration benefit you are seeking. Our legal right to ask for this information is in 8 USC 1154. We may provide this information to other government agencies. Failure to provide this information, and any requested evidence, may delay a final decision or result in denial of your request.

**Paperwork Reduction Act Notice.**

A person is not required to respond to a collection of information unless it displays a currently valid OMB control number. We try to create forms and instructions that are accurate, can be easily understood, and which impose the least possible burden on you to provide us with information. Often this is difficult because some immigration laws are very complex Accordingly, the reporting burden for this collection of information is computed as follows: (1) learning about the law and form, 15 minutes; (2) completing the form, 20 minutes; and (3) assembling and filing the application, 85 minutes for an estimated average of 2 hours per response. If you have comments regarding the accuracy of this estimate, or suggestions for making this form simpler, you can write to the Immigration and Naturalization Service, HQPDI, 425 I Street N.W., Room 4034, Washington, D.C. 20536; OMB No. 1115-0117. **DO NOT MAIL YOUR COMPLETED APPLICATION TO THIS ADDRESS.**

**U.S. Department of Justice**
Immigration and Naturalization Service

# Petition for Amerasian, Widow(er), or Special Immigrant

## START HERE - Please Type or Print

### Part 1. Information about person or organization filing

**this petition.** (Individuals should use the top name line; organizations should use the second line.) If you are a self-petitioning spouse or child and do not want INS to send notices about this petition to your home, you may show an alternate mailing address here. If you are filing for yourself and do not want to use an alternate mailing address, skip to part 2.

| Family Name | Given Name | Middle Initial |
|---|---|---|
| | | |

Company or Organization Name

**Address** - C/O

| Street Number and Name | | Apt. # |
|---|---|---|
| City | State or Province | |
| Country | Zip/Postal Code | |

| U.S. Social Security # | A # | IRS Tax # (if any) |
|---|---|---|
| | | |

### Part 2. Classification Requested (check one):

a. ☐ Amerasian
b. ☐ Widow(er) of a U.S. citizen who died within the past two (2) years
c. ☐ Special Immigrant Juvenile
d. ☐ Special Immigrant Religious Worker
e. ☐ Special Immigrant based on employment with the Panama Canal Company, Canal Zone Government or U.S. Government in the Canal Zone
f. ☐ Special Immigrant Physician
g. ☐ Special Immigrant International Organization Employee or family member
h. ☐ Special Immigrant Armed Forces Member
i. ☐ Self-Petitioning Spouse of Abusive U.S. Citizen or Lawful Permanent Resident
j. ☐ Self-Petitioning Child of Abusive U.S. Citizen or Lawful Permanent Resident
k. ☐ Other, explain: _____

### Part 3. Information about the person this petition is for.

| Family Name | Given Name | Middle Initial |
|---|---|---|
| | | |

**Address** - C/O

| Street Number and Name | | Apt. # |
|---|---|---|
| City | State or Province | |
| Country | Zip/Postal Code | |

| Date of Birth (Month/Day/Year) | Country of Birth |
|---|---|
| | |

| U.S. Social Security # | A # (if any) |
|---|---|
| | |

Marital Status: ☐ Single ☐ Married ☐ Divorced ☐ Widowed

Complete the items below if this person is in the United States:

| Date of Arrival (Month/Day/Year) | I-94# |
|---|---|
| | |
| Current Nonimmigrant Status | Expires on (Month/Day/Year) |

### FOR INS USE ONLY

| Returned | Receipt |
|---|---|
| | |
| Resubmitted | |
| | |
| Reloc Sent | |
| | |
| Reloc Rec'd | |
| | |

☐ Petitioner/ Applicant Interviewed
☐ Benefitiary Interviewed

☐ I-485 Filed Concurrently
☐ Bene "A" File Reviewed

Classification

Consulate

Priority Date

Remarks:

Action Block

**To Be Completed by**
*Attorney or Representative, if any*
☐ Fill in box if G-28 is attached to represent the applicant

VOLAG#

ATTY State License #

*Continued on back.*

# Part 4. Processing Information.

Below give to United States Consulate you want notified if this petition is approved and if any requested adjustment of status cannot be granted.

| American Consulate: City | Country |
|---|---|
| | |

If you gave a United States address in Part 3, print the person's foreign address below. If his/her native alphabet does not use Roman letters, print his/her name and foreign address in the native alphabet.

| Name | Address |
|---|---|
| | |

| | | |
|---|---|---|
| Sex of the person this petition is for. | ☐ Male | ☐ Female |
| Are you filing any other petitions or applications with this one? | ☐ No | ☐ Yes (How many? _____ ) |
| Is the person this petition is for in exclusion or deportation proceedings? | ☐ No | ☐ Yes (Explain an a separate sheet of paper) |
| Has the person this petition is for ever worked in the U.S. without permission? | ☐ No | ☐ Yes (Explain an a separate sheet of paper) |
| Is an appilication for adjustment of status attached to this petition? | ☐ No | ☐ Yes |

# Part 5. Complete only if filing for an Amerasian.

### Section A. Information about the mother of the Amerasian

| Family Name | Given Name | Middle Initial |
|---|---|---|
| | | |

Living? ☐ No (Give date of death _____ ) ☐ Yes (complete address line below) ☐ Unknown (attach a full explanation)

Address

### Section B. Information about the father of the Amerasian: If possible, attach a notarized statement from the father regarding parentage.
Explain on separate paper any question you cannot fully answer in the space provided on this form.

| Family Name | Given Name | Middle Initial |
|---|---|---|
| Date of Birth (Month/Day/Year) | Country of Birth | |

Living? ☐ No (give date of death _____ ) ☐ Yes (complete address line below) ☐ Unknown (attach a full explanation)

Home Address

| Home Phone # | Work Phone # |
|---|---|
| | |

At the time the Amerasian was conceived:

☐ The father was in the military (indicate branch of service below - and give service number here): _____

    ☐ Army    ☐ Air Force    ☐ Navy    ☐ Marine Corps    ☐ Coast Guard

☐ The father was a civilian employed abroad. Attach a list of names and addresses of organizations which employed him at that time.

☐ The father was not in the military, and was not a civilian employed abroad. (Attach a full explanation of the circumstances.)

# Part 6. Complete only if filing for a Special Immigrant Juvenile Court Dependent.

### Section A. Information about the Juvenile

List any other names used.

Answer the following questions regarding the person this petition is for. If you answer "no," explain on a separate sheet of paper.

Is he or she still dependent upon the juvenile court or still legally committed to or under the custody of an agency or department of a state?    ☐ No    ☐ Yes

Does he/she continue to be eligible for long term foster care?    ☐ No    ☐ Yes

*Continued on next page.*

# Part 7. Complete only if filing as a Widow/Widower, a Self-petitioning Spouse of an Abuser, or as a Self-petitioning Child of an Abuser.

**Section A.** Information about the U.S. citizen husband or wife who died or about the U.S. citizen or lawful permanent resident abuser.

| Family Name | | Given Name | | Middle Initial |
|---|---|---|---|---|

| Date of Birth *(Month/Day/Year)* | Country of Birth | | Date of Death *(Month/Day/Year)* |
|---|---|---|---|

He or she is now, or was at time of death a (check one):

☐ U.S. citizen born in the United States.
☐ U.S. citizen born abroad to U.S. citizen parents.

☐ U.S. citizen through Naturalization *(Show A #)* _____
☐ U.S. lawful permanent resident (Show A #) _____
☐ Other, explain _____

**Section B. Additional Information about you.**

| How many times have you been married? | How many times was the person in Section A married? | Give the date and place you and the person in Section A were married. *(If you are a self-petitioning child, write: "N/A")* |
|---|---|---|

When did you live with the person named in Section A? From *(Month/Year)*_____ until *(Month/Year)* _____

If you are filing as a widow/widower, were you legally separated at the time of to U.S citizens's death? ☐ No ☐ Yes, *(attach explanation)*.

Give the last address at which you lived together with the person named in Section A, and show the last date that you lived together with that person at that address:

If you we filing as a self-petitioning spouse, have any of your children filed separate self-petitions? ☐ No ☐ Yes *(show child(ren)'s full names)*:

# Part 8. Information about the spouse and children of the person this petition is for. A widow/widower or a self-petitioning spouse of an abusive citizen or lawful permanent resident should also list the children of the deceased spouse or of the abuser.

| A. Family Name | Given Name | Middle Initial | Date of Birth *(Month/Day/Year)* |
|---|---|---|---|
| Country of Birth | Relationship ☐ Spouse ☐ Child | | A # |
| B. Family Name | Given Name | Middle Initial | Date of Birth *(Month/Day/Year)* |
| Country of Birth | Relationship ☐ Child | | A # |
| C. Family Name | Given Name | Middle Initial | Date of Birth *(Month/Day/Year)* |
| Country of Birth | Relationship ☐ Child | | A # |
| D. Family Name | Given Name | Middle Initial | Date of Birth *(Month/Day/Year)* |
| Country of Birth | Relationship ☐ Child | | A # |
| E. Family Name | Given Name | Middle Initial | Date of Birth *(Month/Day/Year)* |
| Country of Birth | Relationship ☐ Child | | A # |
| F. Family Name | Given Name | Middle Initial | Date of Birth *(Month/Day/Year)* |
| Country of Birth | Relationship ☐ Child | | A # |

| G. Family Name | Given Name | Middle Initial | Date of Birth (Month/Day/Year) |
|---|---|---|---|
| Country of Birth | Relationship ☐ Child | A# | |
| H. Family Name | Given Name | Middle Initial | Date of Birth (Month/Day/Year) |
| Country of Birth | Relationship ☐ Child | A# | |

## Part 9. Signature.

*Read the information on penalties in the instructions before completing this part. If you are going to file this petition at an INS office in the United States, sign below. If you are going to file it at a U.S. consulate or INS office overseas, sign in front of a U.S. INS or consular official.*

I certify, or, if outside the United States, I swear or affirm, under penalty of perjury under the laws of the United States of America, that this petition and the evidence submitted with it is all true and correct. If filing this on behalf at an organization, I certify that I am empowered to do so by that organization. I authorize the release of any information from my records, or from the petitioning organization's records, which the Immigration and Naturalization Service needs to determine eligibility for the benefit being sought.

| Signature | Date |
|---|---|

| Signature of INS or Consular Official | Print Name | Date |
|---|---|---|

Please Note: If you do not completely fill out this form or fail to submit required documents listed in the instructions, the person(s) filed for may not be found eligible for a requested benefit and it may have to be denied.

## Part 10. Signature of person preparing form if other than above. (sign below)

I declare that I prepared this application at the request of the above person and it is based on all information of which I have knowledge.

| Signature | Print Your Name | Date |
|---|---|---|

| Firm Name and Address | | |
|---|---|---|

## Purpose of This Form.

This form is used by a person who is in the United States to apply to the Immigration and Naturalization Service (INS) to adjust to permanent resident status or register for permanent residence. It may also be used by certain Cuban nationals to request a change in the date their permanent residence began.

## Who May File.

**Based on an immigrant petition.** You may apply to adjust your status if:

- an immigrant visa number is immediately available to you based on an approved immigrant petition; or

- you are filing this application with a complete relative, special immigrant juvenile or special immigrant military petition, which if approved, would make an immigrant visa number immediately available to you.

**Based on being the spouse or child (derivative) at the time another adjustment applicant (principal) files to adjust status or at the time a person is granted permanent resident status in an immigrant category that allows derivative status for spouses and children.**

- **If the spouse or child is in the United States**, the individual derivatives may file their Form I-485 adjustment of status applications concurrently with the Form I-485 for the principal beneficiary, or file the Form I-485 at anytime after the principal is approved, if a visa number is available.

- **If the spouse or child is residing abroad**, the person adjusting status in the United States should file the **Form I-824, Application for Action on an Approved Application or Petition, concurrently** with the principal's adjustment of status application to allow the derivates to immigrate to the United States without delay, if the principal's adjustment of status application is approved. **No I-824 fee will be refunded if the principal's adjustment is not granted.**

**Based on admission as the fiance(e) of a U. S. citizen and subsequent marriage to that citizen.** You may apply to adjust status if you were admitted to the U. S. as the K-1 fiance(e) of a U. S. citizen and you married that citizen within 90 days of your entry. If you were admitted as the K-2 child of such a fiance(e), you may apply based on your parent's adjustment application.

**Based on asylum status.** You may apply to adjust status if you have been granted asylum in the U. S. after being physically present in the U. S. for one year after the grant of asylum, if you still qualify as an asylee or as the spouse or child of a refugee.

**Based on Cuban citizenship or nationality.** You may apply to adjust status if:

- you are a native or citizen of Cuba, were admitted or paroled into the U.S. after January 1, 1959, and thereafter have been physically present in the U.S. for at least one year; or
- you are the spouse or unmarried child of a Cuban described above, and regardless of your nationality, you were admitted or paroled after January 1, 1959, and thereafter have been physically present in the U.S. for at least one year.

**Based on continuous residence since before January 1, 1972.** You may apply for permanent residence if you have continuously resided in the U.S. since before January 1, 1972.

**Applying to change the date your permanent residence began.** If you were granted permanent residence in the U. S. prior to November 6, 1966, and are a native or citizen of Cuba, his or her spouse or unmarried minor child, you may ask to change the date your lawful permanent residence began to your date of arrival in the U. S. or May 2, 1964, whichever is later.

**Other basis of eligibility.** If you are not included in the above categories, but believe you may be eligible for adjustment or creation of record of permanent residence, contact your local INS office.

## Persons Who Are Ineligible.

Unless you are applying for creation of record based on continuous residence since before January 1, 1972, or adjustment of status under a category in which special rules apply (such as asylum adjustment, Cuban adjustment, special immigrant juvenile adjustment or special immigrant military personnel adjustment), **you are not eligible for adjustment of status if any of the following apply to you:**

- you entered the U.S. in transit without a visa;
- you entered the U.S. as a nonimmigrant crewman;
- you were not admitted or paroled following inspection by an immigration officer;
- your authorized stay expired before you filed this application; you were employed in the U.S. prior to filing this application, without INS authorization; or you otherwise failed to maintain your nonimmigrant status, other than through no fault of your own or for technical reasons, unless you are applying because you are an immediate relative of a U.S. citizen (parent, spouse, widow, widower or unmarried child under 21 years old), a K-1 fiance(e) or K-2 fiance(e) dependent who married the U.S. petitioner within 90 days of admission or an "H" or "I" or special

immigrant (foreign medical graduates, international organization employees or their derivative family members);

- you are or were a J-1 or J-2 exchange visitor, are subject to the two-year foreign residence requirement and have not complied with or been granted a waiver of the requirement;

- you have an A, E or G nonimmigrant status, or have an occupation which would allow you to have this status, unless you complete Form I-508 (I-508F for French nationals) to wave diplomatic rights, privileges and immunities, and if you are an A or G nonimmigrant, unless you submit a complete Form I-566;
- you were admitted to Guam as a visitor under the Guam visa waiver program;
- you were admitted to the U.S. as a visitor under the Visa Waiver Pilot Program, unless you are applying because you are an immediate relative of a U.S. citizen (parent, spouse, widow, widower or unmarried child under 21 years old);
- you are already a conditional permanent resident;
- you were admitted as a K-1 fiance(e) but did not marry the U.S. citizen who filed the petition for you, or were admitted as the K-2 child of a fiance(e) and your parent did not marry the U.S. citizen who filed the petition.

## General Filing Instructions.

Please answer all questions by typing or clearly printing in black ink. Indicate that an item is not applicable with **"N/A."** If the answer is **"none,"** write **"none."** If you need extra space to answer any item, attach a sheet of paper with your name and your alien registration number (A#), if any, and indicate the number of the item to which the answer refers.You must file your application with the required **Initial Evidence** described below, beginning on this page. Your application must be properly signed and filed with the correct fee. If you are under 14 years of age, your parent or guardian may sign your application.

**Translations.** Any foreign language document must be accompanied by a full English translation which the translator has certified as complete and correct, and by the translator's certification that he or she is competent to translate the foreign language into English.

**Copies.** If these instructions state that a copy of a document may be filed with this application, and you choose to send us the original, we may keep the original for our records.

## Initial Evidence.

You must file your application with the following evidence:

- **Birth certificate.** Submit a copy of your foreign birth certificate or other record of your birth that meets the provisions of secondary evidence found in 8 CFR 103.2(b)(2).

- **Copy of passport page with nonimmigrant visa.** If you have obtained a nonimmigrant visa(s) from an American consulate abroad within the last year, submit a photocopy(ies) of the page(s) of your passport with the visa(s).

- **Photos.** Submit two (2) identical natural color photographs of yourself, taken within 30 days of the application. Photos must have a white background, be unmounted, printed on thin paper and be glossy and unretouched. They must show a three-quarter frontal profile showing the right side of your face, with your right ear visible and with your head bare. You may wear a headdress if required by a religious order of which you are a member. The photos must be no larger than 2 X 2 inches, with the distance from the top of the head to just below the chin about 1 and 1/4 inches. Lightly print your A# (or your name if you have no A#) on the back of each photo, using a pencil.

- **Fingerprints.** If you are between the ages of 14 and 75, you must be fingerprinted. After filing this application, INS will notify you in writing of the time and location where you must go to be fingerprinted. Failure to appear to be fingerprinted may result in denial of your application.

- **Police clearances.** If you are filing for adjustment of status as a member of a special class described in an I-485 supplement form, please read the instructions on the supplement form to see if you need to obtain and submit police clearances, in addition to the required fingerprints, with your application.

- **Medical examination (Section 232 of the Act).** When required, submit a medical examination report on the form you have obtained from INS.

-- **A. Individuals applying for adjustment of status through the INS Service Center: 1) General:** If you are filing your adjustment of status application with the INS Service Center, include your medical exam report with the application, unless you are a refugee or asylee. **2) Refugees:** If you are applying for adjustment of status one year after you were admitted as a refugee, you only need to submit a vaccination supplement with your adjustment of status application, not the entire medical report, **unless** there were medical grounds of inadmissibility that arose during the initial exam you had overseas.

-- **B. Individuals applying for adjustment of status through the local INS office and asylees applying for adjustment of status through the Service Center:** If you are filing your adjustment of status application with the local INS office, or if you are an asylee filing an adjustment of status application with the Service Center, one year after you were granted asylum, do not submit a medical report with your adjustment of status application. Wait for further instructions from INS about how and where to take the medical exam and submit the medical exam report.

-- **Fiance(e)s:** If you are a K-1 fiance(e) or K-2 dependent who had a medical exam within the past year as required for the nonimmigrant fiance (e) visa, you only need to submit a vaccination supplement, not the entire medical report. You may include the vaccination supplement with your adjustment of status application.

-- **Individuals not required to have a medical exam:** The medical report is not required if you are applying for creation of a record of admission as a lawful permanent resident under section 249 of the Act as someone who has continuously resided in the United States since January 1, 1972 (registry applicant).

• **Form G-325A, Biographic Information Sheet.** You must submit a completed G-325A if you are between 14 and 79 years of age.

• **Evidence of status.** Submit a copy of your Form I-94, Nonimmigrant Arrival/Departure Record, showing your admission to the U.S. and current status, or other evidence of your status.

• **Affidavit of Support/Employment Letter.**

-- **Affidavit of Support.** Submit the Affidavit of Support (Form I-864) if your adjustment of status application is based on your entry as a fiance(e), or a relative visa petition (Form I-130) filed by your relative or on an employment based visa petition (Form I-140) based on a business that is five percent or more owned by your family.

-- **Employment Letter.** If your adjustment of status application is based on an employment based visa petition (Form I-140), you must submit a letter on the letterhead of the petitioning employer which confirms that the job on which the visa petition is based is still available to you. The letter must also state the salary that will be paid.

(Note: The affidavit of support and/or employment letter are not required if you applying for creation of record based on continuous residence since before January 1, 1972, asylum adjustment, or a Cuban or a spouse or unmarried child of a Cuban who was admitted after January 1, 1959.)

• **Evidence of eligibility.**

-- **Based on an immigrant petition.** Attach a copy of the approval notice for an immigrant petition which makes a visa number immediately available to you, or submit a complete relative, special immigrant juvenile or special immigrant military petition which, if approved, will make a visa number immediately available to you.

-- **Based on admission as the K-1 fiance(e) of a U.S. citizen and subsequent marriage to that citizen.** Attach a copy of the fiance(e) petition approval notice, a copy of your marriage certificate and your Form I-94.

-- **Based on asylum status.** Attach a copy of the letter or Form I-94 which shows the date you were granted asylum.

-- **Based on continuous residence in the U.S. since before January 1, 1972.** Attach copies of evidence that shows continuous residence since before January 1, 1972.

-- **Based on Cuban citizenship or nationality.** Attach evidence of your citizenship or nationality, such as a copy of your passport, birth certificate or travel document.

-- **Based on derivative status as the spouse or child of another adjustment applicant or person granted permanent residence based on issuance of an immigrant visa.** File your application with the application of that other applicant, or with evidence that it is pending with the Service or has been approved, or evidence that your spouse or parent has been granted permanent residence based on an immigrant visa and:

• If you are applying as the spouse of that person, also attach a copy of your marriage certificate and copies of documents showing the legal termination of all other marriages by you and your spouse;

• If you are applying as the child of that person, also attach a copy of your birth certificate, and if the other person is not your natural mother, copies of evidence (such as a marriage certificate and documents showing the legal termination of all other marriages and an adoption decree) to demonstrate that you qualify as his or her child.

• **Other basis for eligibility.** Attach copies of documents proving that you are eligible for the classification.

**Where to File.**
File this application at the INS office having jurisdiction over your place of residence.

**Fee.** The fee for this application is **$220**, except that it is **$160** if you are less than 14 years old. There is no application fee if you are filing as a refugee under section 209(a) of the Act. If you are between the ages of 14 and 75, there is a $25 fingerprinting fee in addition to the application fee. For example, if your application fee is $220 and you are between the ages of 14 and 75, the total fee you must pay is $245. You may submit one check or money order for both the application and fingerprinting fees. Fees must be submitted in the exact amount. **DO NOT MAIL CASH.** Fees cannot be refunded. All checks and money orders must be drawn on a bank or other institution located in the United States and must be payable in United States currency. The check or money order should be made payable to the Immigration and Naturalization Service, except that:

-- if you live in Guam and are filing this application in Guam, make your check or money order payable to the "Treasurer, Guam."

-- if you live in the U.S. Virgin Islands and are filing this application in the U.S. Virgin Islands, make your check or money order payable to the "Commissioner of Finance of the Virgin Islands."

Checks are accepted subject to collection. An uncollected check in payment of an application fee will render the application and any document issued invalid. A charge of $30 will be imposed if a check in payment of a fee is not honored by the bank on which it is drawn.

**Processing Information.**

**Acceptance.** Any application that is not signed, or is not accompanied by the correct application fee, will be rejected with a notice that the application is deficient. You may correct the deficiency and resubmit the application. An application is not considered properly filed until accepted by the INS.

**Initial Processing.** Once an application has been accepted, it will be checked for completeness, including submission of the required initial evidence. If you do not completely fill out the form, or file it without required initial evidence, you will not establish a basis for eligibility, and we may deny your application.

**Requests for More Information.** We may request more information or evidence. We may also request that you submit the originals of any copy. We may return these originals when they are no longer required.

**Interview.** After you file your application you will be notified to appear at an INS office to answer questions about the application. You will be required to answer these questions under oath or affirmation. You must bring your Arrival-Departure Record (Form I-94) and any passport to the interview.

**Decision.** You will be notified in writing of the decision on your application.

**Selective Service Registration.** If you are a male at least 18 years old, but not yet 26 years old, and required according to the Military Selective Service Act to register with the Selective Service System, the INS will help you register. When your signed application is filed and accepted by the INS, we will transmit your name, current address, Social Security number, date of birth and the date you filed the application to the Selective Service to record your registration as of the filing date. If the INS does not accept your application, and if still so required, you are responsible to register with the Selective Service by other means, provided you are under 26 years of age. If you have already registered, the Selective Service will check its records to avoid any duplication. (**Note: men 18 through 25 years old, who are applying for student financial aid, government employment or job training benefits should register directly with the Selective Service or such benefits may be denied. Men can register at a local post office or on the Internet at http://www.sss.gov**).

**Travel Outside the U.S. for Adjustment of Status Applicants Under Sections 209 and 245 of the Act and Registry Applicants Under Section 249 of the Act.** Your departure from the U.S. (including brief visits to Canada or Mexico) constitutes an abandonment of your adjustment of status application, unless you are granted permission to depart and you are inspected upon your return to the U.S. Such permission to travel is called "advance parole." To request advance parole, you must file Form I-131, with fee, with the INS office where you applied for adjustment of status.

-- **Exceptions: 1) H and L nonimmigrants:** If you are an H or L nonimmigrant who continues to maintain his or her status, you may travel on a valid H or L visa without obtaining advance parole.

**2) Refugees and Asylees:** If you are applying for adjustment of status one year after you were admitted as a refugee or one year after you were granted asylum, you may travel outside the United States on your valid refugee travel document, if you have one, without the need to obtain advance parole.

-- **WARNING:** Travel outside of the U.S. may trigger the 3-and 10-year bars to admission under section 212(a)(9)(B)(i) of the Act for adjustment applicants, but not registry applicants. This ground of inadmissibility is triggered if you were unlawfully present in the U.S. (i.e., you remained in the United States beyond the period of stay authorized by the Attorney General) for more than 180 days before you applied for adjustment of status, and you travel outside of the U.S. while your adjustment of status application is pending. (**Note:** Only unlawful presence that accrued on or after April 1, 1997, counts towards the 3-and 10-year bars under section 212 (a)(9) (B)(i) of the Act.)

-- If you become inadmissible under section 212(a)(9)(B)(i) of the Act while your adjustment of status application is pending, you will need a waiver of inadmissibility under section 212(a)(9)(B)(v) of the Act before your adjustment of status application can be approved. This waiver, however, is granted on a case-by-case basis and in the exercise of discretion. It requires a showing of extreme hardship to your U.S. citizen or lawful permanent resident spouse or parent, unless you are a refugee or asylee. For refugees and asylees, the waiver may be granted for humanitarian reasons, to assure family unity or if it is otherwise in the public interest.

**Penalties.** If you knowingly and willfully falsify or conceal a material fact or submit a false document with this request, we will deny the benefit you are filing for and may deny any other immigration benefit. In addition, you will face severe penalties provided by law and may be subject to criminal prosecution.

**Privacy Act Notice.** We ask for the information on this form and associated evidence to determine if you have established eligibility for the immigration benefit you are seeking. Our legal right to ask for this information is in 8 USC 1255 and 1259. We may provide this information to other government agencies, including the Selective Service System. Your failure to provide this information on this form and any requested evidence may delay a final decision or result in denial of your application.

**Paperwork Reduction Act Notice.** A person is not required to respond to a collection of information unless it displays a current valid OMB number. We try to create forms and instructions that are accurate, can be easily understood and which impose the least possible burden on you to provide us with information. Often this is difficult because some immigration laws are very complex. The estimated average time to complete and file this application is computed as follows: (1) 20 minutes to learn about the law and form; (2) 25 minutes to complete the form and (3) 270 minutes to assemble and file the application, including the required interview and travel time -- for a total estimated average of 5 hours and 15 minutes per application. If you have comments regarding the accuracy of this estimate or suggestions to make this form simpler, you should write to the Immigration and Naturalization Service, 425 I Street, N.W., Room 5307, Washington, D.C. 20536; OMB No. 1115-0053. **DO NOT MAIL YOUR COMPLETED APPLICATION TO THIS ADDRESS.**

**U.S. Department of Justice**
Immigration and Naturalization Service

# Form I-485, Application to Register Permanent Resident or Adjust Status

## START HERE - Please Type or Print

### Part 1. Information About You.

| Family Name | Given Name | Middle Initial |
|---|---|---|

Address - C/O

| Street Number and Name | Apt. # |
|---|---|

City

| State | Zip Code |
|---|---|

| Date of Birth (month/day/year) | Country of Birth |
|---|---|

| Social Security # | A # (if any) |
|---|---|

| Date of Last Arrival (month/day/year) | I-94 # |
|---|---|

| Current INS Status | Expires on (month/day/year) |
|---|---|

### Part 2. Application Type. (check one)

**I am applying for an adjustment to permanent resident status because:**

a. ☐ an immigrant petition giving me an immediately available immigrant visa number has been approved. (Atttach a copy of the approval notice-- or a relative, special immigrant juvenile or special immigrant military visa petition filed with this application that will give you an immediately available visa number, if approved.)

b. ☐ my spouse or parent applied for adjustment of status or was granted lawful permanent residence in an immigrant visa category that allows derivative status for spouses and children.

c. ☐ I entered as a K-1 fiance(e) of a U.S. citizen whom I married within 90 days of entry, or I am the K-2 child of such a fiance(e). [Attach a copy of the fiance(e) petition approval notice and the marriage certificate.]

d. ☐ I was granted asylum or derivative asylum status as the spouse or child of a person granted asylum and am eligible for adjustment.

e. ☐ I am a native or citizen of Cuba admitted or paroled into the U.S. after January 1, 1959, and thereafter have been physically present in the U.S. for at least one year.

f. ☐ I am the husband, wife or minor unmarried child of a Cuban described in (e) and am residing with that person, and was admitted or paroled into the U.S. after January 1, 1959, and thereafter have been physically present in the U.S. for at least one year.

g. ☐ I have continuously resided in the U.S. since before January 1, 1972.

h. ☐ Other basis of eligibility. Explain. (If additional space is needed, use a separate piece of paper.)
_____
_____

**I am already a permanent resident and am applying to have the date I was granted permanent residence adjusted to the date I originally arrived in the U.S. as a nonimmigrant or parolee, or as of May 2,1964, whichever date is later, and:** (Check one)

i. ☐ I am a native or citizen of Cuba and meet the description in (e), above.

j. ☐ I am the husband, wife or minor unmarried child of a Cuban, and meet the description in (f), above.

### FOR INS USE ONLY

| Returned | Receipt |
|---|---|
| | |

| Resubmitted | |
|---|---|
| | |

| Reloc Sent | |
|---|---|
| | |

| Reloc Rec'd | |
|---|---|
| | |

| Applicant Interviewed | |
|---|---|

**Section of Law**
☐ Sec. 209(b), INA
☐ Sec. 13, Act of 9/11/57
☐ Sec. 245, INA
☐ Sec. 249, INA
☐ Sec. 2 Act of 11/2/66
☐ Sec. 2 Act of 11/2/66
☐ Other _____

**Country Chargeable**

**Eligibility Under Sec. 245**
Approved Visa Petition
Dependent of Principal Alien
Special Immigrant
Other _____

**Preference**

**Action Block**

**To be Completed by Attorney or Representative, if any**
☐ Fill in box if G-28 is attached to represent the applicant.
VOLAG #

ATTY State License #

# Part 3. Processing Information.

| **A.** City/Town/Village of Birth | Current Occupation |
|---|---|
| Your Mother's First Name | Your Father's First Name |

Give your name exactly how it appears on your Arrival /Departure Record (Form 1-94)

| Place of Last Entry Into the U.S. (City/State) | In what status did you last enter? *(Visitor, student, exchange alien, crewman, temporary worker, without inspection, etc.)* |
|---|---|
| Were you inspected by a U.S. Immigration Officer?  ☐ Yes  ☐ No | |
| Nonimmigrant Visa Number | Consulate Where Visa Was Issued |

| Date Visa Was Issued (month/day/year) | Sex: ☐ Male ☐ Female | Marital Status  ☐ Married  ☐ Single  ☐ Divorced  ☐ Widowed |
|---|---|---|

Have you ever before applied for permanent resident status in the U.S.? ☐ No ☐ Yes  If you checked "Yes," give date and place of filing and final disposition.

**B.** List your present husband/wife and all your sons and daughters. (If you have none, write "none."  If additional space is needed, use a separate piece of paper.)

| Family Name | Given Name | Middle Initial | Date of Birth (month/day/year) |
|---|---|---|---|
| Country of Birth | Relationship | A # | Applying with You? ☐ Yes  ☐ No |
| Family Name | Given Name | Middle Initial | Date of Birth (month/day/year) |
| Country of Birth | Relationship | A # | Applying with You? ☐ Yes  ☐ No |
| Family Name | Given Name | Middle Initial | Date of Birth (month/day/year) |
| Country of Birth | Relationship | A # | Applying with You? ☐ Yes  ☐ No |
| Family Name | Given Name | Middle Initial | Date of Birth (month/day/year) |
| Country of Birth | Relationship | A # | Applying with You? ☐ Yes  ☐ No |
| Family Name | Given Name | Middle Initial | Date of Birth (month/day/year) |
| Country of Birth | Relationship | A # | Applying with You? ☐ Yes  ☐ No |

**C.** List your present and past membership in or affiliation with every political organization, association, fund, foundation, party, club, society or similar group in the United States or in other places since your 16th birthday.  Include any foreign military service in this part.  If none, write "none."  Include the name(s) of the organization(s), location(s), dates of membership from and to, and the nature of the organization (s).  If additional space is needed, use a separate piece of paper.

_____

_____

_____

_____

_____

# Part 3. Processing Information. (*Continued*)

Please answer the following questions. (If your answer is **"Yes"** to any one of these questions, explain on a separate piece of paper. Answering **"Yes"** does not necessarily mean that you are not entitled to adjust your status or register for permanent residence.)

1. Have you ever, in or outside the U. S.:

   a. knowingly committed any crime of moral turpitude or a drug-related offense for which you have not been arrested?    ☐ Yes ☐ No

   b. been arrested, cited, charged, indicted, fined or imprisoned for breaking or violating any law or ordinance, excluding traffic violations?    ☐ Yes ☐ No

   c. been the beneficiary of a pardon, amnesty, rehabilitation decree, other act of clemency or similar action?    ☐ Yes ☐ No

   d. exercised diplomatic immunity to avoid prosecution for a criminal offense in the U. S.?    ☐ Yes ☐ No

2. Have you received public assistance in the U.S. from any source, including the U.S. government or any state, county, city or municipality (other than emergency medical treatment), or are you likely to receive public assistance in the future?    ☐ Yes ☐ No

3. Have you ever:

   a. within the past ten years been a prostitute or procured anyone for prostitution, or intend to engage in such activities in the future?    ☐ Yes ☐ No

   b. engaged in any unlawful commercialized vice, including, but not limited to, illegal gambling?    ☐ Yes ☐ No

   c. knowingly encouraged, induced, assisted, abetted or aided any alien to try to enter the U.S. illegally?    ☐ Yes ☐ No

   d. illicitly trafficked in any controlled substance, or knowingly assisted, abetted or colluded in the illicit trafficking of any controlled substance?    ☐ Yes ☐ No

4. Have you ever engaged in, conspired to engage in, or do you intend to engage in, or have you ever solicited membership or funds for, or have you through any means ever assisted or provided any type of material support to, any person or organization that has ever engaged or conspired to engage, in sabotage, kidnapping, political assassination, hijacking or any other form of terrorist activity?    ☐ Yes ☐ No

5. Do you intend to engage in the U.S. in:

   a. espionage?    ☐ Yes ☐ No

   b. any activity a purpose of which is opposition to, or the control or overthrow of, the government of the United States, by force, violence or other unlawful means?    ☐ Yes ☐ No

   c. any activity to violate or evade any law prohibiting the export from the United States of goods, technology or sensitive information?    ☐ Yes ☐ No

6. Have you ever been a member of, or in any way affiliated with, the Communist Party or any other totalitarian party?    ☐ Yes ☐ No

7. Did you, during the period from March 23, 1933 to May 8, 1945, in association with either the Nazi Government of Germany or any organization or government associated or allied with the Nazi Government of Germany, ever order, incite, assist or otherwise participate in the persecution of any person because of race, religion, national origin or political opinion?    ☐ Yes ☐ No

8. Have you ever engaged in genocide, or otherwise ordered, incited, assisted or otherwise participated in the killing of any person because of race, religion, nationality, ethnic origin or political opinion?    ☐ Yes ☐ No

9. Have you ever been deported from the U.S., or removed from the U.S. at government expense, excluded within the past year, or are you now in exclusion or deportation proceedings?    ☐ Yes ☐ No

10. Are you under a final order of civil penalty for violating section 274C of the Immigration and Nationality Act for use of fradulent documents or have you, by fraud or willful misrepresentation of a material fact, ever sought to procure, or procured, a visa, other documentation, entry into the U.S. or any immigration benefit?    ☐ Yes ☐ No

11. Have you ever left the U.S. to avoid being drafted into the U.S. Armed Forces?    ☐ Yes ☐ No

12. Have you ever been a J nonimmigrant exchange visitor who was subject to the two-year foreign residence requirement and not yet complied with that requirement or obtained a waiver?    ☐ Yes ☐ No

13. Are you now withholding custody of a U.S. citizen child outside the U.S. from a person granted custody of the child?    ☐ Yes ☐ No

14. Do you plan to practice polygamy in the U.S.?    ☐ Yes ☐ No

# Part 4.   Signature.   *(Read the information on penalties in the instructions before completing this section. You must file this application while in the United States.)*

I certify, under penalty of perjury under the laws of the United States of America, that this application and the evidence submitted with it is all true and correct. I authorize the release of any information from my records which the INS needs to determine eligibility for the benefit I am seeking.

**Selective Service Registration. The following applies to you if you are a man at least 18 years old, but not yet 26 years old, who is required to register with the Selective Service System:** I understand that my filing this adjustment of status application with the Immigration and Naturalization Service authorizes the INS to provide certain registration information to the Selective Service System in accordance with the Military Selective Service Act. Upon INS acceptance of my application, I authorize INS to transmit to the Selective Service System my name, current address, Social Security number, date of birth and the date I filed the application for the purpose of recording my Selective Service registration as of the filing date. If, however, the INS does not accept my application, I further understand that, if so required, I am responsible for registering with the Selective Service by other means, provided I have not yet reached age 26.

| *Signature* | *Print Your Name* | *Date* | *Daytime Phone Number* |
|---|---|---|---|

*Please Note:*   *If you do not completely fill out this form or fail to submit required documents listed in the instructions, you may not be found eligible for the requested benefit and this application may be denied.*

# Part 5.   Signature of Person Preparing Form, If Other Than Above. *(Sign Below)*

I declare that I prepared this application at the request of the above person and it is based on all information of which I have knowledge.

| *Signature* | *Print Your Name* | *Date* | *Daytime Phone Number* |
|---|---|---|---|

*Firm Name and Address*

**U.S. Department of Justice**
Immigration and Naturalization Service

# Supplement A to Form I-485
## Adjustment of Status Under Section 245(i)

*Only use this form if you are applying to adjust status to that of a lawful permanent resident under section 245(i) of the Immigration and Nationality Act.*

## What Is the Purpose of This Form?

Section 245 of the Immigration and Nationality Act (the Act) allows the Attorney General, in his or her discretion, to adjust the status of an alien to that of a lawful permanent resident (LPR), in lieu of consular visa processing, while the alien remains in the United States. In order to be eligible, the alien must have been inspected and admitted or paroled, be eligible for an immigrant visa and admissible for permanent residence, have an immigrant visa immediately available and, with some exceptions, have maintained lawful nonimmigrant status. The alien must also not have engaged in unauthorized employment and must not be ineligible to adjust status under section 245(c) of the Act. **If you meet all of these requirements, you do not have to submit this form when applying for adjustment of status to that of LPR.**

Section 245(i) of the Act allows certain aliens to file for adjustment of status upon payment of a penalty fee of $1,000, even though some of the conditions required by section 245(a) and (c) of the Act are not met. **Aliens in the United States who have an immigrant visa immediately available, but who entered the United States without inspection, remained in the United States past the period of admission, worked unlawfully, or are otherwise ineligible for adjustment of status under section 245(c) of the Act must submit this form along with Form I-485, Application to Register Permanent Residence or Adjust Status.**

**NOTE:** If you are applying to adjust as the spouse or unmarried minor child of a U.S. citizen or the parent of a U.S. citizen child at least 21 years of age, and if you were inspected and lawfully admitted to the United States, you do not need to file this form.

## Who May Use Supplement A to Adjust Status to That of LPR Under Section 245(i)?

You may apply for adjustment of status to that of LPR under section 245(i) if you:

- are physically present in the United States when the application is submitted; and
- have an immigrant visa number immediately available; and
- are admissible to the United States for permanent residence; and
- are the beneficiary of an approvable-when-filed visa petition, or an application for labor certification filed on or before April 30, 2001; and
- pay a $1,000 fee (unless exempted).

In addition, the alien must fall within one of the below categories:

- alien crewmen;
- aliens who work without authorization;
- aliens in unlawful immigrant status;
- aliens who fail to continuously maintain a lawful status since entry into the United States;
- aliens who were admitted in transit without visa;
- aliens admitted as nonimmigrant visitors under section 212(l) of the Act or under the Visa Waiver Program;
- aliens admitted as nonimmigrant described in section 101(a)(15)(S) of the Act; or
- aliens seeking employment-based adjustment of status who are not in lawful nonimmigrant status.

## What Documentation Must You Include If You Are Submitting This Form With Form I-485?

You do not need to submit documentation in addition to the documentation required by the instructions to Form I-485 unless you are the beneficiary of a visa petition or application for labor certification properly filed on your behalf after January 14, 1998, and on or before April 30, 2001. **Aliens using section 245(i) because they are beneficiaries of a visa petition or application for labor certification filed after January 14, 1998, and on or before April 30, 2001, should submit documentation along with this form that demonstrates physical presence in the United States on December 21, 2000.**

## What Documentation Demonstrates Your Physical Presence on December 21, 2000?

Documentation of your physical presence in the United States on December 21, 2000, can consist of federal, state or local government-issued documents or other documents establishing your physical presence on that date. If one document does not establish your physical presence, you should submit documentation establishing your physical presence in the United States prior to and after December 21, 2000. In some cases, a single document may suffice to establish the applicant's physical presence on December 21, 2000. In most cases, however, the alien may need to submit several documents, because most applicants may not possess documentation that contains the exact date of December 21, 2000. In such instances, the applicant should submit sufficient documentation establishing the applicant's physical presence in the United States prior to, and after December 21, 2000. If you submit affidavits, they should be accompanied by supporting documentation. The Immigration and Naturalization Service (INS) will evaluate all documentation on a case-by-case basis.

## Who Does Not Need to Use Supplement A to Form I-485?

You do not have to submit Supplement A to Form I-485 if you:

- are already an LPR; or
- have continuously maintained lawful immigration status in the United States since November 5, 1986; or
- are applying to adjust status as the spouse or unmarried minor child of a United States citizen or the parent of a United States citizen child at least 21 years of age, and you were inspected and lawfully admitted to the United States.

In addition, you do not have to submit Supplement A to Form I-485, if you are filing for an immigration benefit other than adjustment of status to that of LPR or if you are applying for adjustment of status to that of LPR because you:

- were granted asylum in the United States; or
- have continuously resided in the United States since January 1, 1972; or
- entered as a K-1 finance'(e) of a United States citizen; or
- have an approved Form I-360, Petition for Amerasian, Widow(er), or Special Immigrant, and are applying for adjustment as a special immigrant juvenile court dependent, or as a special immigrant who has served in the United States armed forces, or as a battered spouse or child; or
- are a special immigrant retired international organization employee or family member; or
- are a special immigrant physician; or
- are a public interest parolee, who was denied refugee status, and is from the former Soviet Union, Vietnam, Laos or Cambodia (a "Lautenberg Parolee" under Public Law 101-167); or
- are eligible under the Immigration Nursing Relief Act.

## What Is the Filing Fee for the Supplement A to Form I-485 and Form I-485 Filed Together?

The total fee for this form when filed along with Form I-485 is:

- **$ 255** Fee required with Form I-485
- **$ 50** Fingerprint Service Fee. (Applicants younger than 14 or older than 79 do not have to pay this fee.)
- **$ 1,000** Fee required with Supplement A to Form I-485

If you filed Form I-485 separately, attach a copy of your filing receipt and pay only the additional sum of **$1,000**.

There are two categories of applicants who do not need to pay the **$1,000** fee associated with Supplement A to Form I-485:

1. applicants under the age of 17 years; and
2. applicants who are an unmarried son or daughter of a legalized alien and less than 21 years of age or the spouse of a legalized alien, and have attached a copy of a receipt or an approval notice for a properly filed Form I-817, Application for Voluntary Departure under the Family Unity Program.

## Where Should You File This Form?

You must file this form at the same location where you must file the related Form I-485.

## What Are the Penalties for Perjury?

All statements contained in response to questions in this application are declared to be true and correct under penalty of perjury. Title 18 of the United States Code, Section 1546, provides in part:

> Whoever knowingly makes under oath, or as permitted under penalty of perjury under 1746 of Title 28 of the United States Code, knowingly subscribes as true, any false statement with respect to a material fact in any application, affidavit, or other document required by the immigration laws or regulations prescribed thereunder, or knowingly presents any such application, affidavit or other document containing any such false statement--shall be fined in accordance with this title or imprisoned not more than five years, or both.

## What Is Our Authority for Collecting This Information?

We request the information on the form to carry out the immigration laws contained in Title 8 of the United States Code, Section 1154(a). We need this information to determine whether you are eligible for immigration benefits. This information you provide may also be disclosed to other Federal, state, local and foreign law enforcement and regulatory agencies. Furnishing this information on this form is voluntary. However, if you do not give some or all of the information, your application may be denied.

## Paperwork Reduction Act Notice.

An agency may not conduct or sponsor an information collection and a person is not required to respond to an information collection unless it contains a currently valid OMB control number. We try to create forms that are accurate, can easily be understood and that impose the least possible burden on you to provide us with the information. Often this is difficult because some immigration laws are very complex. The public reporting burden for this information collection beyond the time to complete the parent form is estimated to average 13 minutes which includes learning about the form and understanding the instructions; collecting the necessary supporting documents; completing the form; and traveling to and waiting at a preparer's office (e.g., attorney or voluntary agency). If you have comments regarding the accuracy of this estimate or suggestions for making this form simpler, you can write to the Immigration and Naturalization Service, 425 I Street, N.W., Room 4034, Washington, DC 20536; OMB No. 1115-0053. **DO NOT MAIL YOUR COMPLETED APPLICATION TO THIS ADDRESS.**

## Checklist.

☐ I have signed the form at Part E.

☐ I have included the appropriate fee (if any) as determined by Part D.

☐ If I checked box c or box d in question 1, Part A, I have included evidence of my physical presence in the United States on December 21, 2000.

**U.S. Department of Justice**
Immigration and Naturalization Service

# Supplement A to Form I-485
## Adjustment of Status Under Section 245(i)

**Only use this form if you are applying to adjust status to that of a lawful permanent resident under Section 245(i) of the Immigration and Nationality Act.**

| Part A.    Information about you. | | | INS Use Only |
|---|---|---|---|
| Last<br>Name | First<br>Name | Middle<br>Initial | |
| Address:<br>*In care of -* | | | |
| Street Number<br>and Name | | Apt # | |
| City | State | Zip<br>Code | |
| A # *(If any)* | Date of Birth *(MM/DD/YYYY)* | Country<br>of Birth | |

## Part B. Eligibility. *(Check the correct response.)*

1. **I am filing Supplement A to Form I-485 because:**

   a. ☐ I am the beneficiary of a visa petition filed on or before January 14, 1998.

   b. ☐ I am the beneficiary of a visa petition filed on or after January 15, 1998.

   c. ☐ I am the beneficiary of an application for labor certification filed on or before January 14, 1998, and before April 30, 2001.

   d. ☐ I am the beneficiary of an application for labor certification filed on or after January 15, 1998,  and on or before April 30, 2001.

   *If you checked box c or d on question one, you must submit evidence demonstrating that you were physically present in the United States on December 21, 2000.*

2. **And I fall into one or more of these categories:**  *(Check all that apply to you.)*

   a. ☐ I entered the United States as an alien crewman;

   b. ☐ I have accepted employment without authorization;

   c. ☐ I am in unlawful immigration status because I entered the United States without inspection or I remained in the United States past the expiration of the period of my lawful admission;

   d. ☐ I have failed (except through no fault of my own or for technical reasons) to maintain, continuously, unlawful status;

   e. ☐ I was admitted to the United States in transit without a visa;

   f. ☐ I was admitted as a nonimmigrant visitor without a visa;

   g. ☐ I was admitted to the United States as a nonimmigrant in the S classification; or

   h. ☐ I am seeking employment-based adjustment of status and am not in lawful nonimmigrant status.

## Part C. Additional eligibility information.

1. **Are you applying to adjust status based on any of the below reasons?**

   a. You were granted asylum in the United States;

   b. You have continuously resided in the United States since January 1, 1972;

   c. You entered as a K-1 fiance'(e) of a United States citizen;

   d. You have an approved Form I-360, Petition for Amerasian, Widow(er), or Special Immigrant, and are applying for adjustment as a special immigrant juvenile court dependent or a special immigrant who has served in the United States armed forces, or a battered spouse or child;

   e. You are a native or citizen of Cuba, or the spouse or child of such alien, who was not lawfully inspected or admitted to the United States;

   f. You are a special immigrant retired international organization employee or family member;

   g. You are a special immigrant physician;

   h. You are a public interest parolee, who was denied refugee status, and are from the former Soviet Union, Vietnam, Laos or Cambodia (a "Lautenberg Parolee" under Public Law 101-167); or

   i. You are eligible under the Immigration Nursing Relief Act.

   ☐ **NO.**   I am not applying for adjustment of status for any of these reasons. *(Go to next question.)*

   ☐ **YES.**   I am applying for adjustment of status for any one of these reasons. *(If you answered "YES", do not file this form.)*

## Part C.  Additional eligibility information *(Continued)*.

**2.  Do any of the following conditions describe you?**

    a.  You are already a lawful permanent resident of the United States.

    b.  You have continuously maintained lawful immigration status in the United States since November 5, 1986.

    c.  You are applying to adjust status as the spouse or unmarried minor child of a United States citizen or the parent of a U.S. citizen child at least 21 years of age, and you were inspected and lawfully admitted to the United States.

    ☐ **NO.**  None of these conditions describe me.  *(Go to next question.)*

    ☐ **YES.**  *If you answered "YES", <u>do not file this form.</u>*

## Part D.  Fees.

**Aliens filing this form with Form I-485\* need to pay the following fees:**

    $   255  Fee required with Form I-485 and

    $    50  Fingerprint Service Fee. (Applicants younger than 14 or older than 79 years of age do not have to pay this fee.)

    $ 1,000  Fee required with Supplement A to Form I-485

If you filed Form I-485 separately, attach a copy of your filing receipt and pay only the additional sum of $1,000.

There are two categories of applicants using this form who do not need to pay the $1,000 fee:

    1.  appliants under the age of 17 years; and

    2.  applicants who are an unmarried son or daughter of a legalized alien and less than 21 years of age or the spouse of a legalized alien, and have attached a copy of a receipt or an approval notice showing that a Form I-817, Application for Voluntary Departure under the Family Unity Program, has been properly filed.

## Part E.  Signature.  *Read the information on penalties in the instructions before completing this section.*

I certify, under penalty of perjury under the laws of the United States of America, that this application and the evidence submitted with it is all true and correct.  I authorize the release of any information from my records which the Immigration and Naturalization Service needs to determine eligibility for the benefit being sought.

| Signature | Print Name | Date |
|---|---|---|
| | | |

## Part F.  Signature of person preparing form, if other than above.  *Read the information on penalties in the instructions before completing this section.*

I certify, under penalty of perjury under the laws of the United States of America, that I prepared this form at the request of the above person and that to the best of my knowledge the contents of this application are all true and corect.

| Signature | Print Name | Date |
|---|---|---|
| | | |

| Firm Name and Address | Daytime Phone Number *(Area Code and Number)* |
|---|---|
| | Fax Number *(Area Code and Number)* |

## INSTRUCTIONS

### Purpose of This Form.

This form is for use by an entrepreneur to petition to the Bureau of Citizenship and Immigration Services (BCIS) for status as an immigrant to the United States pursuant to section 203(b)(5) of the Immigration and Nationality Act, as amended. That section of the law pertains to immigrant visas for an investor in a new commercial enterprise. The BCIS is comprised of offices of the former Immigration and Naturalization Service.

### Who May File.

You may file this petition for yourself if you have established a new commercial enterprise:

- in which you will engage in a managerial or policy-making capacity, and

- in which you have invested or are actively in the process of investing the amount required for the area in which the enterprise is located, and

- which will benefit the United States ecomomy, and

- which will create full-time employment in the United States for at least ten U.S. citizens, permanent residents, or other immigrants authorized to be employed, other than yourself, your spouse, your sons or daughters, or any nonimmigrant aliens.

The establishment of a new commercial enterprise may include:

- creation of a new business;

- the purchase of an existing business with simultaneous or subsequent restructuring or reorganization resulting in a new commercial enterprise; or

- the expansion of an existing business through investment of the amount required, so that a substantial change (at least 40 percent) in either the net worth, number of employees, or both, results.

The amount of investment required in a particular area is set by regulation. Unless adjusted downward for targeted areas or upward for areas of high employment, the amount of investment shall be **$1,000,000 (one million dollars)**. You may obtain additional information from a BCIS field office in the United States or at a American embassy or consulate abroad.

### General Filing Instructions.

Please answer all questions by typing or clearly printing in black ink. Indicate that an item is not applicable with "N/A." If an answer to a question is "none," please write "none." If you need extra space to answer any item, attach a sheet of paper with your name and your A#, if any, and indicate the number of the item. Your petition must be properly signed and filed with the correct fee.

### Initial Evidence Requirements.

The following evidence must be filed with your petition:

- Evidence that you have established a lawful business entity under the laws of the jurisdiction in the United State in which it is located, or, if you have made an investment in an existing business, evidence that your investment has caused a substantial (at least 40 percent) increase in the net worth of the business, the number of employees, or both.

  Such evidence shall consist of copies of articles of incorporation, certificate of merger or consolidation, partnership agreement, certificate of limited partnership, joint venture agreement, business trust agreement, or other similar organizational document; a certificate evidencing authority to do business in a state or municipality, or if such is not required, a statement to that effect; or evidence that the required amount of capital was transferred to an existing business resulting in a substantial increase in the net worth or number of employees, or both.

  This evidence must be in the form of stock purchase agreements, investment agreements, certified financial reports, payroll records or other similar instruments, agreements or documents evidencing the investment and the resulting substantial change.

- Evidence, if applicable, that your enterprise has been established in a targeted employment area. A targeted employment area is defined as a rural area or an area which has experienced high unemployment of at least 150 percent of the national average rate. A rural area is an area not within a metropolitan statistical area or not within the outer boundary of any city or town having a population of 20,000 or more.

- Evidence that you have invested or are actively in the process of investing the amount required for the area in which the business is located.

  Such evidence may include, but need not be limited to, copies of bank statements, evidence of assets that have been purchased for use in the enterprise, evidence of property transferred from abroad for use in the enterprise, evidence of monies transferred or committed to be transferred to the new commercial enterprise in exchange for shares of stock, any loan or mortgage, promissory note, security agreement, or other evidence of borrowing that is secured by assets of the petitioner.

- Evidence that capital is obtained through lawful means. The petition must be accompanied, as applicable, by: foreign business registration records, tax returns of any kind filed within the last five years in or outside the United States, evidence of other sources of capital, or certified copies of any judgment, pending governmental civil or criminal actions, or private civil actions against the petitioner from any court in or outside the United States within the past 15 years.

- Evidence that the enterprise will create at least ten full-time positions for U.S. citizens, permanent residents, or aliens lawfully authorized to be employed (except yourself, your spouse, sons, or daughters, and any nonimmigrant aliens). Such evidence may consist of copies of relevant tax records, Forms I-9, or other similar documents, if the employees have already been hired, or a business plan showing when such employees will be hired within the next two years.

- Evidence that you are or will be engaged in the management of the enterprise, either through the exercise of day-to-day managerial control or through policy formulation. Such evidence may include a statement of your position title and a complete description of your duties, evidence that you are a corporate officer or hold a seat on the board of directors, or, if the new enterprise is a partnership, evidence that you are engaged in either direct management or policy-making activities.

## Processing Information.

*Acceptance.* Any petition that is not signed or accompanied by the correct fee will be rejected with a notice that it is deficient. You may correct the deficiency and resubmit the petition. However, a petition is not considered properly filed until accepted by the BCIS.

*Initial processing.* Once the petition has been accepted, it will be checked for completeness, including submission of the required initial evidence. If you do not completely fill out the form or file it without required initial evidence, you will not establish a basis for eligibility and we may deny your petition.

*Requests for more information or interview.* We may request more information or evidence or we may request that you appear at a BCIS office for an interview. We may also request that you submit the originals of any copy. We will return these originals when they are no longer required.

*Approval.* If you have established that you qualify for investor status, the petition will be approved. If you have requested that the petition be forwarded to an American embassy or consulate abroad, the petition will be sent there unless that consulate does not issue immigrant visas. If you are in the United States and state that you will apply for adjustment of status, and the evidence indicates you are not eligible for adjustment, the petition will be sent to an American embassy or consulate abroad. You will be notified in writing of the approval of the petition and where it has been sent, and the reason for sending it to a place other than the one requested, if applicable.

*Meaning of petition approval.* Approval of a petition shows only that you have established that you have made a qualifying investment. It does not guarantee that the American embassy or consulate will issue the immigrant visa. There are other requirements that must be met before a visa can be issued. The American embassy or consulate will notify you of those requirements. Immigrant status granted based on this petition will be conditional. Two years after entry, the conditional investor will have to apply for the removal of conditions based on the ongoing nature of the investment.

*Denial.* If you have not established that you qualify for the benefit sought, the petition will be denied. You will be notified in writing of the reasons for the denial.

## Copies.

If these instructions state that a copy of a document may be filed with this application and you choose to send us the original, we may keep that original for our records.

## Where to File.

If the new commercial enterprise is located, or will principally be doing business in: Alabama, Arkansas, Connecticut, Delaware, District of Columbia, Florida, Georgia, Kentucky, Louisiana, Mississippi, Maine, Maryland, Massachusetts, New Hampshire, New Jersey, New Mexico, New York, North Carolina, South Carolina, Oklahoma, Pennsylvania, Puerto Rico, Rhode Island, Tennessee, or Texas, Vermont, the U.S. Virgin Islands, Virginia or West Virginia, mail the petition to:

**BCIS Texas Service Center**
**P.O. Box 852135**
**Mesquite, TX 75185-2135**

If the new commercial enterprise is located, or will principally be doing business in: Alaska, Arizona, California, Colorado, Guam, Hawaii, Idaho, Illinois, Indiana, Iowa, Kansas, Michigan, Minnesota, Missouri, Montana, Nebraska, Nevada, North Dakota, Ohio, Oregon, South Dakota, Utah, Washington, Wisconsin or Wyoming, mail the petition to:

**BCIS California Service Center**
**P.O. Box 10140**
**Laguna Niguel, CA 92607-0526**

## Fees.

The fee for this petition is **$400.00**. The fee must be submitted in the exact amount. it cannot be refunded. DO NOT MAIL CASH. All checks and money orders must be drawn on a bank or other institution located in the United States and must be payable in United States currency. The check or money order should be made payable to the Bureau of Citizenship and Immigration Services (do not use initials), except that:

- If you live in Guam and are filing this application there, make your check or money order payable to the "Treasurer, Guam."

- If you live in the U.S. Virgin Islands and are filing this application there, make your check or money order payable to the "Commissioner of Finance of the Virgin Islands."

Checks are accepted subject to collection. A check returned due to insufficient funds will render the application and any document issued invalid. A charge of $30.00 will be imposed if a check in payment of a fee is not honored by the bank on which it is drawn.

## Information and BCIS Forms.

For informaton on immigration laws, regulations and procedures or to order BCIS forms, call our National Customer Service Center at **1-800-375-5283** or visit our website at **www.bcis.gov.**

## Penalties.

If you knowingly and willfully falsify or conceal a material fact or submit a false document with this request, we will deny the benefit you are seeking and may deny any other immigration benefit. In addition, you will face severe penalties provided by law and may be subject to criminal prosecution.

## Privacy Act Notice.

We ask for the information on this form and associated evidence to determine if you have established eligibility for the immigration benefit you are seeking. Our legal right to ask for this information is in 8 USC 1184, 1255 and 1258. We may provide this information to other government agencies. Failure to provide this information and any requested evidence may delay a final decision or result in denial of your petition.

## Paperwork Reduction Act Notice.

A person is not required to respond to a collection of information unless it displays a currently valid OMB control number. We try to create forms and instructions that are accurate, can be easily understood and that impose the least possible burden on you to provide us with information. Often this is difficult because some immigration laws are very complex. Accordingly, the reporting burden for this collection of information is computed as follows: (1) learning about the law and form, 15 minutes; (2) completing the form, 25 minutes; and (3) assembling and filing the application, 35 minutes, for an estimated average of 1 hour and 15 minutes per response. If you have comments regarding the accuracy of this estimate or suggestions for making this form simpler, you may write to the Bureau of Citizenship and Immigration Services, HQRFS, 425 I Street, N.W., Room 4034, Washington, DC 20536; OMB No.1615-0026. **DO NOT MAIL YOUR COMPLETED PETITION TO THIS ADDRESS.**

**DO NOT WRITE IN THIS BLOCK - FOR BCIS USE ONLY (Except G-28 Block Below)**

| Classification | Action Block | Fee Receipt |
|---|---|---|
| _____ | | |
| Priority Date | | |
| _____ | | **To be completed by Attorney or Representative, if any** <br> ☐ G-28 is attached <br> Attorney's State License No. _____ |

Remarks:

**START HERE -  Type or Print in Black Ink.**

## Part 1.    Information about you.

Family Name [                ]  Given Name [                ]  Middle Name [                ]

Address:
In care of [                ]

Number and Street [                ]  Apt. # [    ]

City [        ]  State or Province [        ]  Country [        ]  Zip/Postal Code [    ]

Date of Birth (mm/dd/yyyy) [        ]  Country of Birth [        ]  Social Security # (if any) [        ]  A # (if any) [        ]

**If you are in the United States, provide the following information:**  Date of Arrival (mm/dd/yyyy) [        ]  I-94 # [        ]

Current Nonimmigrant Status [        ]  Date Current Status Expires (mm/dd/yyyy) [        ]  Daytime Phone # (    ) - with Area Code

## Part 2.    Application type (Check one).

a. ☐  This petition is based on an investment in a commercial enterprise in a targeted employment area for which the required amount of capital invested has been adjusted downward.

b. ☐  This petition is based on an investment in a commercial enterprise in an area for which the required amount of capital invested has been adjusted upward.

c. ☐  This petition is based on an investment in a commercial enterprise that is not in either a targeted area or in an upward adjustment area.

## Part 3.    Information about your investment.

Name of commercial enterprise in which funds are invested [                ]

Street Address [                ]

Phone # with Area Code [        ]  Business organized as (corporation, partnership, etc.) [        ]

Kind of business (e.g. furniture manufacter) [        ]  Date established (mm/dd/yyyy) [        ]  IRS Tax # [        ]

RECEIVED: _____  RESUBMITTED: _____  RELOCATED: SENT _____  REC'D _____

## Part 3. Information about your investment. (continued)

Date of your initial investment (mm/dd/yyyy)

Amount of your initial investment $

Your total capital investment in the enterprise to date $

Percentage of the enterprise you own

If you are not the sole investor in the new commercial enterprise, list on separate paper the names of all other parties (natural and non-natural) who hold a percentage share of ownership of the new enterprise and indicate whether any of these parties is seeking classification as an alien entrepreneur. Include the name, percentage of ownership and whether or not the person is seeking classification under section 203(b)(5). **NOTE:** A "natural" party would be an individual person and a "non-natural" party would be an entity such as a corporation, consortium, investment group, partnership, etc.

If you indicated in **Part 2** that the enterprise is in a targeted employment area or in an upward adjustment area, name the county and state:

County

State

## Part 4. Additional information about the enterprise.

**Type of Enterprise (check one):**

[ ] New commercial enterprise resulting from the creation of a new business.

[ ] New commercial enterprise resulting from the purchase of an existing business.

[ ] New commercial enterprise resulting from a capital investment in an existing business.

**Composition of the Petitioner's Investment:**

Total amount in U.S. bank account .......................................................................................... $

Total value of all assets purchased for use in the enterprise............................................. $

Total value of all property transferred from abroad to the new enterprise...................... $

Total of all debt financing........................................................................................................ $

Total stock purchases............................................................................................................... $

Other (explain on separate paper)......................................................................................... $

**Total** $

**Income:**

When you made the investment.......... Gross $       Net $

Now........................................... Gross $       Net $

**Net worth:**

When you made investment................. Gross $       Now $

## Part 5. Employment creation information.

**Number of full-time employees in the enterprise in U.S.** (excluding you, your spouse, sons and daughters)

When you made your initial investment? [          ]     Now [          ]     Difference [          ]

How many of these new jobs were created by your investment? [          ]     How many additional new jobs will be created by your additional investment? [          ]

What is your position, office or title with the new commercial enterprise?

[                                                                            ]

Briefly describe your duties, activities and responsibilities.

[                                                                            ]

What is your salary? $ [                    ]     What is the cost of your benefits? $ [                    ]

## Part 6. Processing information.

**Check One:**

☐ The person named in **Part 1** is now in the United States and an application to adjust status to permanent resident will be filed if this petition is approved.

☐ If the petition is approved and the person named in **Part 1** wishes to apply for an immigrant visa abroad, complete the following for that person:

Country of nationality: [                              ]

Country of current residence or, if now in the United States, last permanent residence abroad: [                              ]

If you provided a United States address in **Part 1**, print the person's foreign address:

[                                                                            ]

If the person's native alphabet is other than Roman letters, write the foreign address in the native alphabet:

[                                                                            ]

Is a Form I-485, Application for Adjustment of Status, attached to this petition?     ☐ Yes     ☐ No

Are you in deportation or removal proceedings?     ☐ Yes (Explain on separate paper)     ☐ No

Have you ever worked in the United States without permission?     ☐ Yes (Explain on separate paper)     ☐ No

## Part 7. Signature. *Read the information on penalties in the instrucitons before completing this section.*

I certify, under penalty of perjury under the laws of the United States of America, that this petition and the evidence submitted with it is all true and correct. I authorize the release of any information from my records which the Bureau of Citizenship and Immigration Services needs to determine eligibility for the benefit I am seeking.

Signature [                              ]     Date [                    ]

**Please Note:** *If you do not completely fill out this form or fail to the submit the required documents listed in the instructions, you may not be found eligible for the immigration benefit you are seeking and this petition may be denied.*

## Part 8. Signature of person preparing form, if other than above. (Sign below)

I declare that I prepared this application at the request of the above person and it is based on all information of which I have knowledge.

Signature [                    ]     Print Your Name [                    ]     Date [          ]

Firm Name [                    ]     Daytime phone # with area code ( [    ] ) – [        ]

Address [                    ]

## Purpose of This Form.

You should use this form if you are one of the nonimmigrants listed below and wish to apply to the Immigration and Naturalization Service (INS) for an extension of stay or a change to another nonimmigrant status. In certain situations, you may be able to use this form to apply for an initial nonimmigrant status.

You may also use this form if you are a nonimmigrant F-1 or M-1 student applying for reinstatement.

## Who May File/Initial Evidence.

### Extension of Stay or Change of Status:

Nonimmigrants in the United States may apply for an extension of stay or a change of status on this form, except as noted in these instructions under the heading, "Who May Not File."

### Multiple Applicants.

You may include your spouse and your unmarried children under age 21 years as co-applicants in your application for the same extension or change of status, if you are all now in the same status or they are all in derivative status.

### Required Documentation - Form I-94, Nonimmigrant Arrival/ Departure Record.

You are required to submit with your Form I-539 application the original or copy, front and back, of Form I-94 of each person included in your application. If the original Form I-94 or required copy cannot be submitted with this application, include a Form I-102, Application for Replacement/Initial Nonimmigrant Arrival/Departure Document, with the required fee.

### Valid Passport.

If you were required to have a passport to be admitted into the United States, you must maintain the validity of your passport during your nonimmigrant stay. If a required passport is not valid when you file the Form I-539 application, submit an explanation with your form.

### Additional Evidence.

You may be required to submit additional evidence noted in these instructions.

### Nonimmigrant Categories.

This form may be used by the following nonimmigrants listed in alphabetical order:

- **An A, Ambassador, Public Minister, or Career Diplomatic or Consular Officer** and their immediate family members.

  You must submit a copy, front and back, of the Form I-94 of each person included in the application and a Form I-566, Interagency Record of Individual Requesting Change, Adjustment to, or from, A to G Status; or Requesting A, G or NATO Dependent Employment Authorization, certified by the Department of State to indicate your accredited status.

**NOTE:** An A-1 or A-2 nonimmigrant is not required to pay a fee with the I-539 application.

- **An A-3, Attendant or Servant of an A nonimmigrant** and the A-3's immediate family members.

  You must submit a copy, front and back, of the Form I-94 of each person included in the application.

  The application must be filed with:

  -- a copy of your employer's Form I-94 or approval notice demonstrating A status;

  -- an original letter from your employer describing your duties and stating that he or she intends to personally employ you; and arrangements you have made to depart the U.S.; and

  -- an original Form I-566, certified by the Department of State, indicating your employer's continuing accredited status.

- **A B-1, Visitor for Business or B-2, Visitor for Pleasure.**

  If you are filing for an extension/change, you must file your application with the original Form I-94 of each person included in your application. In addition, you must submit a written statement explaining in detail:

  -- the reasons for your request;

  -- why your extended stay would be temporary, including what arrangements you have made to depart the United States; and

  -- any effect the extended stay may have on your foreign employment or residency.

- **Dependents of an E, Treaty Trader or Investor.**

  If you are filing for an extension/change of status as the dependent of an E, this application must be submitted with:

  -- the Form I-129, Petition for Alien Worker, filed for that E or a copy of the filing receipt noting that the petition is pending with INS;

  -- a copy of the E's Form I-94 or approval notice showing that he or she has already been granted status to the period requested on your application; and

  -- evidence of relationship (example: birth or marriage certificate).

**NOTE:** An employer or investor should file Form I-129 to request an extension/change to E status for an employee, prospective employee, or the investor. Dependents of E employees should file for an extension/change of status on this form, not Form I-129.

- **An F-1, Academic Student.**

  To request a change to F-1 status or to apply for reinstatement as an F-1 student, you must submit your original Form I-94, as well as the original Form I-94 of each person included in the application.

Your application must include your original Form I-20 (Certificate of Eligibility for Nonimmigrant Student) issued by the school where you will study. To request either a change or reinstatement, you must submit documentation that demonstrates your ability to pay for your studies and support yourself while you are in the United States.

### *F-1 Extensions:*

Do not use this form to request an extension. For information concerning extensions, contact your designated school official at your institution.

### *F-1 Reinstatement:*

You will only be considered for reinstatement as an F-1 student if you establish:

- that the violation of status was due solely to circumstances beyond your control or that failure to reinstate you would result in extreme hardship;
- you are pursuing or will pursue a full course of study;
- you have not been employed without authorization; and
- you are not in removal proceedings.

- **A G, Designated Principal Resident Representative of a Foreign Government** and his or her immediate family members.

   You must submit a copy, front and back, of the Form I-94, of each person included in the application, and a Form I-566, certified by the Department of State to indicate your accredited status.

   **NOTE:** A G-1 through G-4 nonimmigrant is not required to pay a fee with the I-539 application.

- **A G-5, Attendant or Servant of a G nonimmigrant** and the G-5's immediate family members.

   You must submit a copy, front and back, of the Form I-94 of each person included in the application.

   The application must also be filed with:

- a copy of your employer's Form I-94 or approval notice demonstrating G status;
- an original letter from your employer describing your duties and stating that he or she intends to personally employ you; and arrangements you have made to depart the U.S.; and
- an original Form I-566, certified by the Department of State, indicating your employer's continuing accredited status.

- **Dependents of an H, Temporary Worker.**

   If you are filing for an extension/change of status as the dependent of an employee who is an H temporary worker, this application must be submitted with:

- the Form I-129 filed for that employee or a copy of the filing receipt noting that the petition is pending with INS;
- a copy of the employee's Form I-94 or approval notice showing that he or she has already been granted status to the period requested on your application; and

- evidence of relationship (example: birth or marriage certificate).

   **NOTE:** An employer should file Form I-129 to request an extension/change to H status for an employee or prospective employee. Dependents of such employees should file for an extension/change of status on this form, not on Form I-129.

- **A J-1, Exchange Visitor.**

   If you are requesting a change of status to J-1, your application must be filed with an original Form IAP-66, Certificate of Eligibility for Exchange Visitor Status, issued by your program sponsor. You must also submit your original Form I-94, as well as the original Form I-94 of each person included in the application.

   **NOTE:** A J-1 exchange visitor whose status is for the purpose of receiving graduate medical education or training, who has not received the appropriate waiver, is ineligible for any change of status. Also, a J-1 subject to the foreign residence requirement, who has not received a waiver of that requirement, is only eligible for a change of status to A or G.

### *J-1 Extensions:*

If you are seeking an extension, contact the responsible officer of your program for information about this procedure.

### *J-1 Reinstatement:*

If you are a J-1 exchange visitor seeking reinstatement, you may need to apply for such approval by the Department of State's Office of Education and Cultural Affairs. Contact the responsible officer at your sponsoring program for information on the reinstatement filing procedure.

- **Dependents of an L, Intracompany Transferee.**

   If you are filing for an extension/change of status as the dependent of an employee who is an L intracompany transferee, this application must be submitted with:

- the Form I-129 filed for that employee or a copy of the filing receipt noting that the petition is pending with INS;
- a copy of the employee's Form I-94 or approval notice showing that he or she has already been granted status to the period requested on your application; and
- evidence of relationship (example: birth or marriage certificate).

   **NOTE:** An employer should file Form I-129 to request an extension/change to L status for an employee or prospective employee. Dependents of such employees should file for an extension/change of status on this form, not on Form I-129.

- **An M-1, Vocational or Non-Academic Student.**

   To request a change to or extension of M-1 status, or apply for reinstatement as an M-1 student, you must submit your original Form I-94, as well as the original Form I-94 of each person included in the application.

   Your application must include your original Form I-20 issued by the school where you will study. To request either extension/change or reinstatement, you must submit documentation that demonstrates your ability to pay for your studies and support yourself while you are in the United States.

### M-1 Reinstatement:

You will only be considered for reinstatement as an M-1 student if you establish:

- -- that the violation of status was due solely to circumstances beyond your control or that failure to reinstate you would result in extreme hardship;

- -- you are pursuing or will pursue a full course of study;

- -- you have not been employed without authorization; and

- -- you are not in removal proceedings.

**NOTE:** If you are an M-1 student, you are not eligible for a change to F-1 status and you are not eligible for a change to any H status, if the training you received as an M-1 helps you qualify for the H status. Also, you may not be granted a change to M-1 status for training to qualify for H status.

- **An N-1 or N-2, Parent or Child of an Alien Admitted as a Special Immigrant** under section 101(a)(27)(I) of the Immigration and Nationality Act (I&NA).

  You must file the application with a copy, front and back, of your Form I-94 and a copy of the special immigrant's permanent resident card and proof of the relationship (example: birth or marriage certificate).

- **Dependents of an O, Alien of Extraordinary Ability or Achievement.**

  If you are filing for an extension/change of status as the dependent of an employee who is classified as an O nonimmigrant, this application must be submitted with:

  - -- the Form I-129 filed for that employee or a copy of the filing receipt noting that the petition is pending with INS;

  - -- a copy of the employee's Form I-94 or approval notice showing that he or she has already been granted status to the period requested on your application; and

  - -- evidence of relationship (example: birth or marriage certificate).

  **NOTE:** An employer should file Form I-129 to request an extension/change to an O status for an employee or prospective employee. Dependents of such employees should file for an extension/change of status on this form, not on Form I-129.

- **Dependents of a P, Artists, Athletes and Entertainers.**

  If you are filing for an extension/change of status as the dependent of an employee who is classified as a P nonimmigrant, this application must be submitted with:

  - -- the Form I-129 filed for that employee or a copy of the filing receipt noting that the petition is pending with INS;

  - -- a copy of the employee's Form I-94 or approval notice showing that he or she has already been granted status to the period requested on your application; and

  - -- evidence of relationship (example: birth or marriage certificate).

  **NOTE:** An employer should file Form I-129 to request an extension/change to P status for an employee or prospective employee. Dependents of such employees should file for an extension/change of status on this form, not on Form I-129.

- **Dependents of an R, Religious Worker.**

  If you are filing for an extension/change of status as the dependent of an employee who is classified as an R nonimmigrant, this application must be submitted with:

  - -- the Form I-129 filed for that employee or a copy of the filing receipt noting that the petition is pending with INS;

  - -- a copy of the employee's Form I-94 or approval notice showing that he or she has already been granted status to the period requested on your application; and

  - -- evidence of relationship (example: birth or marriage certificate).

- **TD Dependents of TN Nonimmigrants.**

  TN nonimmigrants are citizens of Canada or Mexico who are coming as business persons to the United States to engage in business activities at a professional level, pursuant to the North American Free Trade Agreement (NAFTA). The dependents (spouse or unmarried minor children) of a TN nonimmigrant are designated as TD nonimmigrants. A TD nonimmigrant may accompany or follow to join the TN professional. TD nonimmigrants may not work in the United States.

  The Form I-539 shall be used by a TD nonimmigrant to request an extension of stay or by an applicant to request a change of nonimmigrant status to TD classification.

  - -- If applying for an extension of stay at the same time as the TN professional, the TD dependent shall file Form I-539 along with the Form I-129, for the TN professional. This filing procedure is also followed if the applicant is applying for a change of nonimmigrant status to TD at the same time that the professional is applying for a change of nonimmigrant status to TN.

  - -- If the applicant is not applying for an extension of stay at the same time that the TN professional is applying for an extension, or applying for a change of nonimmigrant status to TD after the nonimmigrant obtains status, the applicant must present a copy of the TN's Form I-94 to establish that the TN is maintaining valid nonimmigrant status.

- **A V, Spouse or Child of a Lawful Permanent Resident.**

  Use this Form I-539 if you are physically present in the United States and wish to request initial status or change status to a V nonimmigrant, or to request an extension of your current V nonimmigrant status.

  Applicants should follow the instructions on this form and the attached instructions to Supplement A to Form I-539, Filing Instructions for V Nonimmigrants. The supplement contains additional information and the location where V applicants must file their applications.

**Notice to V Nonimmigrants.**

The Legal Immigration Family Equity Act (LIFE), signed into law on December 21, 2000, created a new V visa. This nonimmigrant status allows certain persons to reside legally in the United States and to travel to and from the United States while they wait to obtain lawful permanent residence.

In order to be eligible for a V visa, all of the following conditions must be met:

- you must be the spouse or the unmarried child of a lawful permanent resident;
- a Form I-130, Petition for Alien Relative, must have been filed for you by your permanent resident spouse on or before December 21, 2000; and
- you must have been waiting for at least three years after the Form I-130 was filed for you;

Or you must be the unmarried child (under 21 years of age) of a person who meets the three requirements listed above.

V visa holders will be eligible to adjust to lawful permanent resident status once an immigrant visa becomes available to them. While they are waiting, V visa holders may be authorized to work following their submission and INS approval of their Form I-765, Application for Employment Authorization.

**WARNING:** Be advised that persons in V status who have been in the United States illegally for more than 180 days may trigger the grounds of inadmissibility regarding unlawful presence (for the applicable 3-year or 10-year bar to admission) if they leave the United States. Their departure may prevent them from adjusting status as a permanent resident.

### Who May Not File.

You may not be granted an extension or change of status if you were admitted under the Visa Waiver Program or if your current status is:

- an alien in transit (C) or in transit without a visa (TWOV);
- a crewman (D); or
- a fiance'(e) or dependent of a fiance'(e) (K)(1) or (K)(2).

A spouse (K-3) of a U.S. citizen and their children (K-4), accorded such status pursuant to the LIFE Act, may not change to another nonimmigrant status.

**EXCEPTION:** A K-3 and K-4 are eligible to apply for an extension of status. They should file for an extension during the processing of the Form I-130 filed on their behalf and up to completion of their adjustment of status application.

**NOTE:** Any nonimmigrant (A to V) may not change their status to K-3 or K-4.

### General Filing Instructions.

Please answer all questions by typing or clearly printing in black ink. Indicate that an item is not applicable with "N/A." If the answer is "none," please so state. If you need extra space to answer any item, attach a sheet of paper with your name and your alien registration number (A#), if any, and indicate the number of the item to which the answer refers. Your application must be filed with the required initial evidence. Your application must be properly signed and filed with the correct fee. If you are under 14 years of age, your parent or guardian may sign your application.

*Copies.*
If these instructions state that a copy of a document may be filed with this application and you choose to send us the original, we will keep that original document in our records.

*Translations.*
Any foreign language document must be accompanied by a full English translation that the translator has certified as complete and correct, and by the translator's certification that he or she is competent to translate the foreign language into English.

## When and Where to File.

You must submit an application for extension of stay or change of status before your current authorized stay expires. We suggest you file at least 45 days before your stay expires, or as soon as you determine your need to change status. Failure to file before the expiration date may be excused if you demonstrate when you file the application that:

- the delay was due to extraordinary circumstances beyond your control;
- the length of the delay was reasonable;
- you have not otherwise violated your status;
- you are still a bona fide nonimmigrant; and
- you are not in removal proceedings.

If you are filing as a V applicant, follow the instructions on the Supplement A to Form I-539, Filing Instructions for V Nonimmigrants, on where to file your application.

If you are filing for reinstatement as an **F-1** or **M-1** student, submit this application at your local INS office.

If you are a **TD** filing for an extension of stay or requesting a change to a nonimmigrant **TD** status, mail your application to: **USINS Nebraska Service Center, P.O. Box 87539, Lincoln, NE 68501-7539.**

If you are an **E dependent** filing for an extension of stay and you live in Alabama, Arkansas, Connecticut, Delaware, District of Columbia, Florida, Georgia, Kentucky, Louisiana, Maine, Maryland, Massachusetts, Mississippi, New Hampshire, New Jersey, New Mexico, New York, North Carolina, Oklahoma, Pennsylvania, Puerto Rico, Rhode Island, South Carolina, Tennessee, Texas, the U.S. Virgin Islands, Vermont, Virginia or West Virginia, mail your application to: **USINS Texas Service Center, Box 851182, Mesquite, TX 75185-1182.**

If you are an **E dependent** filing for an extension of stay and you live anywhere else in the United States, mail your application to: **USINS California Service Center, P.O. Box 10539, Laguna Niguel, CA 92607-1053.**

**In all other instances,** mail your application to the INS Service Center having jurisdiction over where you live in the United States.

If you live in Connecticut, Delaware, District of Columbia, Maine, Maryland, Massachusetts, New Hampshire, New Jersey, New York, Pennsylvania, Puerto Rico, Rhode Island, the U.S. Virgin Islands, Vermont, Virginia or West Virginia, mail your application to: **USINS Vermont Service Center, 75 Lower Welden Street, St. Albans, VT 05479-0001.**

If you live in Alabama, Arkansas, Florida, Georgia, Kentucky, Louisiana, Mississippi, New Mexico, North Carolina, Oklahoma, South Carolina, Tennessee or Texas, mail your application to: **USINS Texas Service Center, Box 851182, Mesquite, TX 75185-1182.**

If you live in Arizona, California, Guam, Hawaii or Nevada, mail your application to: **USINS California Service Center, P.O. Box 10539, Laguna Niguel, CA 92607-1053.**

If you live elsewhere in the United States, mail your application to: **USINS Nebraska Service Center, P.O. Box 87539, Lincoln, NE 68501-7539.**

## Fee.

The fee for this application is $120.00, except for certain A and G nonimmigrants who are not required to pay a fee, as noted in these instructions. The fee must be submitted in the exact amount. It cannot be refunded. **DO NOT MAIL CASH.**

All checks and money orders must be drawn on a bank or other institution located in the United States and must be payable in U.S. currency.

The check or money order should be made payable to the Immigration and Naturalization Service, except that:

-- if you live in Guam and are filing this application in Guam, make your check or money order payable to the "Treasurer, Guam."

-- if you live in the U.S. Virgin Islands and are filing this application in the U.S. Virgin Islands, make your check or money order payable to the "Commissioner of Finance of the Virgin Islands."

Checks are accepted subject to collection. An uncollected check will render the application and any document issued invalid. A charge of $30.00 will be imposed if a check in payment of a fee is not honored by the bank on which it is drawn.

## Processing Information.

### Acceptance.

Any application that is not signed or is not accompanied by the correct fee will be rejected with a notice that the application is deficient. You may correct the deficiency and resubmit the application. An application is not considered properly filed until accepted by INS.

### Initial Processing.

Once the application has been accepted, it will be checked for completeness. If you do not completely fill out the form, or file it without the required initial evidence, you will not establish a basis for eligibility and we may deny your application.

### Requests for More Information or Interview.

We may request more information or evidence or we may request that you appear at an INS office for an interview. We may also request that you submit the originals of any copy. We will return these originals when they are no longer required.

### Decision.

An application for extension of stay, change of status, initial status or reinstatement, may be approved at the discretion of INS. You will be notified in writing of the decision on your application.

## Penalties.

If you knowingly and willfully falsify or conceal a material fact or submit a false document with this application, we will deny the benefit you are seeking and may deny any other immigration benefit. In addition, you will face severe penalties provided by law and may be subject to criminal prosecution.

## Privacy Act Notice.

We ask for the information on this form and associated evidence to determine if you have established eligibility for the immigration benefit you are seeking. Our legal right to ask for this information is in 8 U.S.C. 1184 and 1258. We may provide this information to other government agencies. Failure to provide this information and any requested evidence may delay a final decision or result in denial of your request.

## Information and Forms.

For information on immigration laws, regulations and procedures and to order INS forms, call our **National Customer Service Center** toll-free at **1-800-375-5283** or visit the INS internet web site at **www.ins.gov.**

## Paperwork Reduction Act Notice.

An agency may not conduct or sponsor an information collection and a person is not required to respond to a collection of information unless it displays a currently valid OMB control number. We try to create forms and instructions that are accurate, can easily be understood and which impose the least possible burden on you to provide us with information. Often this is difficult because some immigration laws are very complex. The estimate average time to complete and file this application is as follows: (1) 10 minutes to learn about the law and form; (2) 10 minutes to complete the form; and (3) 25 minutes to assemble and file the application; for a total estimated average of 45 minutes per application. If you have comments regarding the accuracy of this estimate, or suggestions for making this form simpler, you can write to Immigration and Naturalization Service, HQPDI, 425 I Street, N.W., Room 4034, Washington, D.C. 20536; OMB No. 1115-0093. **DO NOT MAIL YOUR COMPLETED APPLICATION TO THIS ADDRESS.**

---

**Mailing Label - Complete the following mailing label and submit this page with your application if you are required to submit your original Form I-94.**

**Name and address of applicant.**

Name

Street Number and Name

City, State, and Zip Code

Your Form I-94, Arrival/Departure Record is attached. It has been amended to show the extension of stay/change of status granted.

U.S. Department of Justice

Immigration and Naturalization Service

OMB No. 1115-0093; Expires 7/31/04

# Application to Extend/Change Nonimmigrant Status

**START HERE - Please Type or Print.**

FOR INS USE ONLY

## Part 1.    Information about you.

| Family Name | Given Name | Middle Initial |
|---|---|---|

Address - In care of -

| Street Number and Name | | Apt. # |
|---|---|---|

| City | State | Zip Code | Daytime Phone # |
|---|---|---|---|

| Country of Birth | Country of Citizenship |
|---|---|

| Date of Birth (MM/DD/YYYY) | Social Security # (if any) | A # (if any) |
|---|---|---|

| Date of Last Arrival Into the U.S. | I-94 # |
|---|---|

| Current Nonimmigrant Status | Expires on (MM/DD/YYYY) |
|---|---|

| Returned | Receipt |
|---|---|
| Date | |
| Resubmitted | |
| Date | |
| Reloc Sent | |
| Date | |
| Reloc Rec'd | |
| Date | |

## Part 2.    Application type. *(See instructions for fee.)*

1. I am applying for: *(Check one.)*
   - a. ☐ An extension of stay in my current status.
   - b. ☐ A change of status. The new status I am requesting is: _____
   - c. ☐ Other: *(Describe grounds of eligibility.)* _____
2. Number of people included in this application: *(Check one.)*
   - a. ☐ I am the only applicant.
   - b. ☐ Members of my family are filing this application with me.
     The total number of people (including me) in the application is: _____
     *(Complete the supplement for each co-applicant.)*

☐ Applicant Interviewed on

_____
Date

☐ *Extension Granted to (Date):*
_____

*Change of Status/Extension Granted*
New Class:   From *(Date)*: _____
_____    To *(Date)*: _____

## Part 3.    Processing information.

1. I/We request that my/our current or requested status be extended until (MM/DD/YYYY): _____
2. Is this application based on an extension or change of status already granted to your spouse, child or parent?
   ☐ No ☐ Yes, Receipt # _____
3. Is this application based on a separate petition or application to give your spouse, child or parent an extension or change of status? ☐ No ☐ Yes, filed with this I-539.
   ☐ Yes, filed previously and pending with INS. INS receipt number: _____
4. If you answered "Yes" to Question 3, give the name of the petitioner or applicant:

   _____

   If the petition or application is pending with INS, also give the following information:

   Office filed at _____  Filed on (MM/DD/YYYY) _____

If Denied:
☐ Still within period of stay
☐ S/D to: _____
☐ Place under docket control

**Remarks:**

**Action Block**

## Part 4.    Additional information.

1. For applicant #1, provide passport information: Valid to: (MM/DD/YYYY)
   Country of Issuance

2. Foreign Address: Street Number and Name | Apt. #

| City or Town | State or Province |
|---|---|

| Country | Zip/Postal Code |
|---|---|

**To be Completed by**
***Attorney or Representative, if any***

☐ Fill in box if G-28 is attached to represent the applicant.

ATTY State License #

Form I-539 (Rev. 09/04/01)N *Prior versions may be used until 3/30/02*

## Part 4. Additional information.

| 3. Answer the following questions. If you answer "Yes" to any question, explain on separate sheet of paper. | Yes | No |
|---|---|---|
| a. Are you, or any other person included on the application, an applicant for an immigrant visa? | | |
| b. Has an immigrant petition ever been filed for you or for any other person included in this application? | | |
| c. Has a Form I-485, Application to Register Permanent Residence or Adjust Status, ever been filed by you or by any other person included in this application? | | |
| d. Have you, or any other person included in this application, ever been arrested or convicted of any criminal offense since last entering the U.S.? | | |
| e. Have you, or any other person included in this application, done anything that violated the terms of the nonimmigrant status you now hold? | | |
| f. Are you, or any other person included in this application, now in removal proceedings? | | |
| g. Have you, or any other person included in this application, been employed in the U.S. since last admitted or granted an extension or change of status? | | |

- If you answered "Yes" to Question 3f, give the following information concerning the removal proceedings on the attached page entitled "**Part 4. Additional information. Page for answers to 3f and 3g.**" Include the name of the person in removal proceedings and information on jurisdiction, date proceedings began and status of proceedings.

- If you answered "No" to Question 3g, fully describe how you are supporting yourself on the attached page entitled "**Part 4. Additional information. Page for answers to 3f and 3g.**" Include the source, amount and basis for any income.

- If you answered "Yes" to Question 3g, fully describe the employment on the attached page entitled "**Part 4. Additional information. Page for answers to 3f and 3g.**" Include the name of the person employed, name and address of the employer, weekly income and whether the employment was specifically authorized by INS.

## Part 5. Signature. *(Read the information on penalties in the instructions before completing this section. You must file this application while in the United States.)*

I certify, under penalty of perjury under the laws of the United States of America, that this application and the evidence submitted with it is all true and correct. I authorize the release of any information from my records which the Immigration and Naturalization Service needs to determine eligibility for the benefit I am seeking.

| Signature | Print your Name | Date |
|---|---|---|
| | | |

***Please note:*** *If you do not completely fill out this form, or fail to submit required documents listed in the instructions, you may not be found eligible for the requested benefit and this application will have to be denied.*

## Part 6. Signature of person preparing form, if other than above. *(Sign below.)*

I declare that I prepared this application at the request of the above person and it is based on all information of which I have knowledge.

| Signature | Print your Name | Date |
|---|---|---|
| | | |

| Firm Name and Address | Daytime Phone Number *(Area Code and Number)* |
|---|---|
| | Fax Number *(Area Code and Number)* |

***(Please remember to enclose the mailing label with your application.)***

## Part 4. Additional information. Page for answers to 3f and 3g.

**If you answered "Yes" to Question 3f** in Part 4 on page 3 of this form, give the following information concerning the removal proceedings. Include the name of the person in removal proceedings and information on jurisdiction, date proceedings began and status of procedings.

**If you answered "No" to Question 3g** in Part 4 on page 3 of this form, fully describe how you are supporting yourself. Include the source, amount and basis for any income.

**If you answered "Yes" to Question 3g** in Part 4 on page 3 of this form, fully describe the employment. Include the name of the person employed, name and address of the employer, weekly income and whether the employment was specifically authorized by INS.

## Supplement -1
### Attach to Form I-539 when more than one person is included in the petition or application.
*(List each person separately.  Do not include the person named in the form.)*

| Family Name | Given Name | Middle Name | Date of Birth (MM/DD/YYYY) |
|---|---|---|---|
| Country of Birth | Country of Citizenship | Social Security # (if any) | A # (if any) |
| Date of Arrival (MM/DD/YYYY) | | I-94 # | |
| Current Nonimmigrant Status: | | Expires On (MM/DD/YYYY) | |
| Country Where Passport Issued | | Expiration Date (MM/DD/YYYY) | |

| Family Name | Given Name | Middle Name | Date of Birth (MM/DD/YYYY) |
|---|---|---|---|
| Country of Birth | Country of Citizenship | Social Security # (if any) | A # (if any) |
| Date of Arrival (MM/DD/YYYY) | | I-94 # | |
| Current Nonimmigrant Status: | | Expires On (MM/DD/YYYY) | |
| Country Where Passport Issued | | Expiration Date (MM/DD/YYYY) | |

| Family Name | Given Name | Middle Name | Date of Birth (MM/DD/YYYY) |
|---|---|---|---|
| Country of Birth | Country of Citizenship | Social Security # (if any) | A # (if any) |
| Date of Arrival (MM/DD/YYYY) | | I-94 # | |
| Current Nonimmigrant Status: | | Expires On (MM/DD/YYYY) | |
| Country Where Passport Issued | | Expiration Date (MM/DD/YYYY) | |

| Family Name | Given Name | Middle Name | Date of Birth (MM/DD/YYYY) |
|---|---|---|---|
| Country of Birth | Country of Citizenship | Social Security # (if any) | A # (if any) |
| Date of Arrival (MM/DD/YYYY) | | I-94 # | |
| Current Nonimmigrant Status: | | Expires On (MM/DD/YYYY) | |
| Country Where Passport Issued | | Expiration Date (MM/DD/YYYY) | |

| Family Name | Given Name | Middle Name | Date of Birth (MM/DD/YYYY) |
|---|---|---|---|
| Country of Birth | Country of Citizenship | Social Security # (if any) | A # (if any) |
| Date of Arrival (MM/DD/YYYY) | | I-94 # | |
| Current Nonimmigrant Status: | | Expires On (MM/DD/YYYY) | |
| Country Where Passport Issued | | Expiration Date (MM/DD/YYYY) | |

### If you need additional space, attach a separate sheet(s) of paper.
*Place your name, A # if any, date of birth, form number and application date at the top of the sheet(s) of paper.*

# Instructions for Form I-589
## Application for Asylum and for Withholding of Removal

## Purpose of This Form.

This form is used to apply for asylum in the United States (U.S.) and for withholding of removal (formerly called "withholding of deportation"). This application may also be used to apply for protection under the Convention Against Torture. You may file this application if you are physically present in the United States and you are not a United States citizen.

**NOTE:** You **must** submit an application for asylum within one (1) year of arriving in the United States, unless there are changed circumstances that materially affect your eligibility for asylum or extraordinary circumstances directly related to your failure to file within one (1) year. (See Instructions, Part 1: Filing Instructions, Section V, "Completing the Form," Part C, for further explanation.)

You may include in your application your spouse and your unmarried children who are under 21 years of age and physically present in the United States. Married children and children 21 years of age or older must file a separate Form I-589 application. If you are granted asylum, you may file a petition Form I-730, Refugee and Asylee Relative Petition, OMB No. 1115-0121, for your spouse and/or any unmarried children under the age of 21 whom you did not include in your application.

This instruction pamphlet is divided into two (2) sections. The first section has filing instructions. It discusses basic eligibility criteria and will guide you through filling out and filing the application. The second section describes how your application will be processed. This section also describes potential interim benefits while your application is pending.

Please read these instructions carefully. The instructions will help you complete your application and understand how it will be processed. If you have questions about your eligibility, completing the form, or the asylum process, you may wish to consult an attorney or other qualified person to assist you. (See Instructions, Part I, Filing Instructions, Section IV, "Right to Counsel.")

Additional information concerning asylum and withholding of removal is available on the following websites: Immigration and Naturalization Service: http://www.ins.usdoj.gov and Executive Office for Immigration Review: http://www.usdoj.gov/eoir/.

---

*WARNING:* **Applicants who are in the United States illegally are subject to removal if their asylum or withholding claims are not granted by an Asylum Officer or an Immigration Judge. Any information provided in completing this application may be used as a basis for the institution of, or as evidence in, removal proceedings, even if the application is later withdrawn. Applicants determined to have knowingly made a frivolous application for asylum will be permanently ineligible for any benefits under the Immigration and Nationality Act (Act). See Section 208(d)(6) of the Act and 8 CFR 208.20.**

## TABLE OF CONTENTS

## PART 1:  FILING INSTRUCTIONS

### I.   Who May Apply and Filing Deadlines

You may apply for asylum irrespective of your immigration status, and even if you are in the United States unlawfully.

**You MUST file this application within one (1) year after you arrived in the United States, unless you can show that there are changed circumstances that materially affect your eligibility for asylum or extraordinary circumstances directly related to your failure to file within one (1) year.  (See Instructions, Part 1:  Filing Instructions, Section V, "Completing the Form," Part C, for further explanation of this requirement.)**

If you have previously been denied asylum by an Immigration Judge or the Board of Immigration Appeals, you must show that there are changed circumstances that affect your eligibility for asylum.

The determination of whether you are permitted to apply for asylum will be made once you have had an asylum interview with an Asylum Officer or a hearing before an Immigration Judge.  Even if you are not eligible to apply for asylum for the reasons stated above, you may still be eligible to apply for withholding of removal under section 241(b)(3) of the Immigration and Nationality Act (Act) or the Convention Against Torture before the Immigration Court.

### II.  Basis of Eligibility

### A.  Asylum

In order to qualify for asylum, you must establish that you are a refugee.  A refugee is a person who is unable or unwilling to return to his or her country of nationality, or last habitual residence in the case of a person having no nationality, because of persecution or a well-founded fear of persecution on account of race, religion, nationality, membership in a particular social group, or political opinion.

If you are granted asylum, you and any eligible dependents included in your application will be permitted to remain and work in the United States and may eventually adjust to lawful permanent resident status.  **If you are not granted asylum, the Immigration and Naturalization Service (INS) may use the information you provide in this application to establish that you are removable from the United States.**

## B. Withholding of Removal

Your asylum application is also considered to be an application for withholding of removal under section 241(b)(3) of the Act, as amended. It may also be considered an application for withholding of removal under the Convention Against Torture if you checked the box at the top of page 1 of this application. If asylum is not granted, you may still be eligible for withholding of removal. Regardless of the basis for the withholding application, you will not be eligible for withholding if you 1) assisted in Nazi persecution or engaged in genocide, 2) have persecuted another person, 3) have been convicted by a final judgment of a particularly serious crime and therefore represent a danger to the community of the United States, 4) are considered for serious reasons to have committed a serious non-political crime outside the United States, or 5) represent a danger to the security of the United States. (See section 241(b)(3) of the Act; 8 CFR 208.16.)

### i. Withholding of Removal under Section 241 (b)(3) of the Act

In order to qualify for withholding of removal under section 241(b)(3) of the Act, you must establish that it is more likely than not that your life or freedom would be threatened on account of race, religion, nationality, membership in a particular social group, or political opinion, in the proposed country of removal.

If you obtain an order withholding your removal, you cannot be returned to the country in which your life or freedom would be threatened. This means that you may be removed to a third country in which your life or freedom would not be threatened. Withholding of removal does not apply to any spouse or child included in the application. They would have to apply for such protection on their own. If you are granted withholding of removal, this would not give you the right to bring dependents to the United States. It also would not give you the right to become a lawful permanent resident of the United States.

### ii. Withholding of Removal under the Convention Against Torture

The Convention Against Torture refers to the United Nations Convention Against Torture and other Cruel, Inhuman or Degrading Treatment or Punishment.

To be granted withholding of removal to a country under the Convention Against Torture, you must show that it is more likely than not that you would be tortured in that country.

"Torture" is defined in Article 1 of the Convention Against Torture and at 8 CFR 208.18(a). For an act to be considered torture, it must be an extreme form of cruel and inhuman treatment; it must cause severe physical or mental pain and suffering; and it must be intended to cause severe pain and suffering. Torture is an act inflicted for such purposes as obtaining from the victim or a third person information or a confession, punishing the victim for an act he or she or a third person has committed or is suspected of having committed, or intimidating or coercing the victim or a third person, or for any reason based on discrimination of any kind. Torture must be inflicted by or at the instigation of a public official or someone acting in an official capacity, or it must be inflicted with the consent or acquiescence of a public official or person acting in an official capacity. The victim must be in the custody or physical control of the torturer. Torture does not include pain or suffering that arises from or is incidental to lawful sanctions.

Form I-589, Application for Asylum and for Withholding of Removal, will be considered an application for withholding of removal under the Convention Against Torture if you tell the Immigration Judge that you would like to be considered for withholding of removal under the Convention Against Torture or if it is determined that the evidence you present indicates you may be tortured in the country of removal. To apply for withholding of removal under the Convention Against Torture, you must check the box at the top of page one (1) of the application and fully complete the Form I-589. You should include a detailed explanation of why you fear torture in response to Part B, Question 4 of the application. In your response you should write about any mistreatment you experienced or any threats made against you by a government or somebody connected to a government.

Only Immigration Judges and the Board of Immigration Appeals may grant withholding of removal or deferral of removal under the Convention Against Torture. If you have applied for asylum, the Immigration Judge will first determine whether you are eligible for asylum under section 208 of the Act and for withholding of removal under section 241(b)(3) of the Act. If you are not eligible for either asylum or withholding of removal under section 241(b)(3) of the Act, the Immigration Judge will determine whether the Convention Against Torture prohibits your removal to a country in which you fear torture.

Article 3 of the Convention Against Torture prohibits the United States from removing you to a country in which it is more likely than not that you would be subject to torture. The Convention Against Torture does not prohibit the United States from returning you to any other country where you would not be tortured. This means that you may be removed to a third country, in which you would not be tortured. Withholding of removal does not allow you to adjust to lawful permanent resident status or to petition to bring family members to come to, or remain in, the United States.

### C. Deferral of Removal under the Convention Against Torture.

If it is more likely than not that you will be tortured in a country but you are ineligible for withholding of removal, your removal will be deferred under 8 CFR 208.17(a). Deferral of removal does not confer any lawful or permanent immigration status in the United States and does not necessarily result in release from detention. Deferral of removal is effective only until it is terminated. Deferral of removal is subject to review and termination if it is determined that it is no longer more likely than not that you would be tortured in the country to which your removal is deferred or if you request that your deferral be terminated.

### D. Legal Sources Relating to Eligibility

The documents listed below are some of the legal sources relating to asylum, withholding of removal under section 241(b)(3) of the Act, and withholding of removal or deferral of removal under the Convention Against Torture. These sources are provided for reference only. You do not need to refer to them in order to complete your application.

- Section 101(a)(42) of the Act, 8 U.S.C. 1101(a)(42) (defining "refugee");

- Section 208 of the Act, 8 U.S.C. 1158 (regarding eligibility for asylum);

- Section 241(b)(3) of the Act, 8 U.S.C. 1231 (b)(3) (regarding eligibility for withholding of removal);

- Title 8 of the Code of Federal Regulations, section 208, et. seq.;

- Article 3 of the Convention Against Torture and Other Cruel, Inhuman or Degrading Treatment or Punishment as ratified by Sec. 2242(b) of the Foreign Affairs Reform and Restructuring Act of 1998 and 8 CFR 208 as amended by the Regulations Concerning the Convention Against Torture: Interim Rule, 64 FR 8478-8492 (February 19, 1999) (effective March 22, 1999); 64 FR 13881 (March 23, 1999);

- The 1967 United Nations Protocol Relating to the Status of Refugees;

- The 1951 Convention Relating to the Status of Refugees; and

- Office of the United Nations High Commissioner for Refugees, Handbook on Procedures and Criteria for Determining Refugee Status (Geneva, 1992).

### III. Confidentiality

The information collected will be used to make a determination on your application. It may also be provided to other government agencies (federal, state, local and/or foreign) for purposes of investigation or legal action on criminal and/or civil matters and for issues arising from the adjudication of benefits. However, no information indicating that you have applied for asylum will be provided to any government or country from which you claim a fear of persecution. Regulations at 8 CFR 208.6 protect the confidentiality of asylum claims.

### IV. Right to Counsel

Immigration law concerning asylum and withholding of removal or deferral of removal is complex. You have a right to provide your own legal representation at an asylum interview and during immigration proceedings before the Immigration Court, at no cost to the United States Government. If you need, or would like, help in completing this form and preparing your written statements, assistance from pro bono (free) attorneys and/or voluntary agencies may be available. Voluntary agencies may help you for no fee or for a reduced fee and attorneys on the list may take your case for no fee. If you have not already received from INS or the Immigration Court a list of attorneys and accredited representatives, you may obtain a list by calling 1-800-870-FORM (3676) or visiting the United States Department of Justice, Executive Office for Immigration Review (EOIR) website at: http://www.usdoj.gov/eoir/probono/states.htm.

Representatives of the United Nations High Commissioner for Refugees (UNHCR) may be able to assist you in identifying persons to help you complete the application. The UNHCR website provides useful country conditions information and also has links to other reliable sources. You may also, if you wish, forward a copy of your application and other supporting documents to the UNHCR. (For instructions on where to file the original, please see Instructions, Part 1: Filing Instructions, Section XII. "Where to File." The current address of the UNHCR is:

United Nations High Commissioner for Refugees
1775 K Street, NW, Suite 300
Washington, DC 20006
Telephone: (202) 296-5191
Website: http://www.unhcr.ch

Calls from Detention Centers and Jails: Between the hours of 2:00 and 5:00 p.m. (Eastern Standard Time), Monday through Friday, asylum-seekers in detention centers and jails may call UNHCR collect at (202) 296-5191 or may call UNHCR's toll-free number at (888) 272-1913.

## V. Completing the Form

Type or print all of your answers in black ink on the Form I-589. Your answers must be completed in English. Forms completed in a language other than English will be returned to you.

Provide the specific information requested about you and your family. **Answer ALL of the questions asked.** If any question does not apply to you or you do not know the information requested, answer "none," "not applicable," or "unknown." Provide detailed information and answer the questions as completely as possible. If you need more space, attach the Supplement A or B Forms (included in the application package) and/or an additional sheet(s) indicating the question number(s) you are answering. You are strongly urged to attach additional written statements and documents that support your claim. Your written statements should include events, dates, and details of your experiences that relate to your claim for asylum.

NOTE: Please put your Alien Registration Number (A#), (if any), name (exactly as it appears in Part A.I. of the form), signature, and date on each supplemental sheet and on the cover page of any supporting documents.

You will be permitted to amend or supplement your application at the time of your asylum interview before an Asylum Officer and at your hearing in Immigration Court by providing additional information and explanations about your asylum claim.

## Part A. I. Information about You

This Part asks for basic information about you. Alien Registration Number (A#) refers to your INS file number. If you do not already have an A#, the INS will assign one to you. You must provide your residential street address in the United States in Part A. I., Question 7, of the asylum application. You may also provide a mailing address, if different from the address where you reside, in Question 8. In Question 12, use the current name of the country. Do not use historical, ethnic, provincial, or other local names.

If you entered the country with inspection, the I-94#, referred to in Question 18b, is the number on Form I-94, Arrival-Departure Record, OMB No. 1115-0077, given to you when you entered the United States. In Question 18c, enter the date and status as it appears on the Form I-94. If you did not receive a Form I-94, write "None". If you entered without being inspected by an immigration officer, write "No Inspection" in Question 18c in the current status or status section.

## Part A. II. Spouse and Children

You should list your spouse and all your children in this application regardless of their age, marital status, whether they are in the United States, or whether or not they are included in this application or filing a separate asylum application.

You may ask to have included in your asylum application your spouse and/or any children who are under the age of 21 and unmarried, if they are in the United States. Children who are married and/or children who are 21 years of age or older must file separately for asylum by submitting their own asylum application (Form I-589).

If you apply for asylum while in proceedings before the Immigration Court, the Immigration Judge may not have authority to grant asylum to any spouse or child included in your application who is not also in proceedings.

When including family members in your asylum application, you MUST submit one additional copy of your completed asylum application and primary documentary evidence establishing your family relationship, for each family member, as described below.

- If you are including your spouse in your application, submit three (3) copies of your marriage certificate, and three (3) copies of proof of termination of any prior marriages.

- If you are including any unmarried children under 21 years of age in your application, submit three (3) copies of each child's birth certificate.

If you do not have and are unable to obtain these documents, you must submit secondary evidence. Secondary evidence includes, but is not limited to, medical records, religious records, and school records. You may also submit an affidavit from at least one (1) person for each event you are trying to prove. Affidavits may be provided by relatives or others. Persons providing affidavits need not be United States citizens or lawful permanent residents.

### Affidavits must:

- fully describe the circumstances or event(s) in question and fully explain how the person acquired knowledge of the event(s);

- be sworn to, or affirmed by, persons who were alive at the time of the event(s) and have personal knowledge of the event(s) (date and place of birth, marriage, etc.) that you are trying to prove; and

- show the full name, address, date, and place of birth of each person giving the affidavit, and indicate any relationship between you and the person giving the affidavit.

If you submit secondary evidence or affidavits, you must explain why primary evidence (e.g., birth or marriage certificate) is unavailable. You may explain the reasons primary evidence is unavailable using the Supplement B Form or additional sheets of paper. Attach this explanation to your secondary evidence or affidavits.

If you have more than four (4) children, complete the Supplement A Form for each additional child, or attach additional pages and documentation providing the same information asked in Part A. II. of the Form I-589.

## Part A. III. Information about Your Background

Please answer questions 1 through 5, providing details as requested for each question. Your responses to the questions concerning the places you have lived, your education, and employment histories should be in reverse chronological order starting with your current residence, education, and employment, working back in time.

## Part B. Information about Your Application

This Part asks specific questions relevant to eligibility for asylum, for withholding of removal under section 241(b)(3) of the Act, or for withholding of removal under the Convention Against Torture. At question 1, please check the box(es) next to the reason(s) that you are completing this application. For all other questions, please check "Yes" or "No" in the box provided. If you answer "Yes" to any question, explain in detail using the Supplement B Form or additional sheets of paper as needed. You should clearly describe any of your experiences, or those of family members or others who have had similar experiences, that may show that you are a refugee.

If you have experienced harm that is difficult for you to write down and express, you should be aware that these experiences may be very important to the decision-making process regarding your request to remain in the United States. At your interview with an Asylum Officer or hearing with an Immigration Judge, you will need to be prepared to discuss the harm you have suffered. If you are having trouble remembering or talking about past events, it is suggested that you talk to a lawyer, an accredited representative, or a health professional who may be able to help you explain your experiences and current situation.

## Part C. Additional Information about Your Application

Check "Yes" or "No" in the box provided for each question. If you answer "Yes" to any question, explain in detail using the Supplement B Form or additional sheets of paper as needed.

If you answer "Yes" to question 5, you must explain why you did not apply for asylum within the first year after you arrived in the United States. The government will accept as an explanation certain changes in the conditions in your country, certain changes in your own circumstances, and certain other events that may have prevented you from applying earlier. For example, some of the events the government might consider as valid explanations include, but are not limited to, the following:

- You have learned that human rights conditions in your country have worsened since you left;

- Because of your health, you were not able to submit this application within a year after you arrived;

- You previously submitted an application, but it was returned to you because it was not complete, and you submitted a complete application within a reasonable amount of time.

Federal regulations specify some of the other types of events that may also qualify as valid explanations for why you filed late. These regulations are found at 8 CFR 208.4. The list in the regulations is not all-inclusive, and the government recognizes that there are many other circumstances that might be acceptable reasons for filing more than one year after arrival.

If you are unable to explain why you did not apply for asylum within the first year after you arrived in the United States, or your explanation is not accepted by the government, you may not be eligible to apply for asylum, but you could still be eligible for withholding of removal.

## Part D. Your Signature

You must sign your application in Part D and respond to the questions concerning any assistance you received to complete your application, providing the information requested. Sign after you have completed and reviewed the application.

**If it is determined that you have knowingly made a frivolous application for asylum, you can be permanently ineligible for any benefits under the Immigration and Nationality Act.** According to regulations at 8 CFR 208.20, an application is frivolous if any of its material elements is deliberately fabricated. (See Instructions, Part 1: Filing Instructions, Section IV, "Right to Counsel," in the event that you have any questions.)

## Part E. Signature of Person Preparing Form If Other than You

Any person, other than an immediate family member (your spouse, parent(s), or children) who helped prepare your application must sign the application in Part E and provide the information requested.

**Penalty for Perjury.** All statements in response to questions contained in this application are declared to be true and correct under penalty of perjury. You and anyone, other than an immediate family member, who assists you in preparing the application must sign the application under penalty of perjury. Your signature is evidence that you are aware of the contents of this application. Any person assisting you in preparing this form, other than an immediate family member, must include his or her name, address, telephone number, and sign the application where indicated in Part E. Failure of the preparer to sign will result in the application being returned to you as an incomplete application. If the INS later learns that you received assistance from someone other than an immediate family member and the person who assisted you **willfully** failed to sign the application, this may result in an adverse ruling against you.

Title 18, United States Code, Section 1546, provides in part:

> Whoever knowingly makes under oath, or as permitted under penalty of perjury under Section 1746 of Title 28, United States Code, knowingly subscribes as true, any false statement with respect to a material fact in any application, affidavit, or other document required by the immigration laws or regulations prescribed thereunder, or knowingly presents any such application, affidavit, or other document containing any such false statement shall be fined in accordance with this title or imprisoned not more than five years, or both.

If you knowingly provide false information on this application, you or the preparer of this application may be subject to criminal penalties under Title 18 of the United States Code and to civil penalties under Section 274C of the Immigration and Nationality Act, 8 U.S.C. 1324c.

## Part F.  To Be Completed at Interview or Hearing

Do not sign your application in Part F before filing this form.  You will be asked to sign your application in this space at the conclusion of the interview regarding your claim.

NOTE:  You must, however, sign Part D of the application.

## VI.  Required Documents and Required Number of Copies that You Must Submit with Your Application

You must submit the following documents to apply for asylum and withholding of removal:

- **The completed, signed original and two (2) copies of your completed application** Form I-589, and the original and two (2) copies of any supplementary sheets and supplementary statements.  If you choose to submit additional supporting material (See Instructions, Part 1:  Filing Instructions, Section VII, "Additional Documents that You Should Submit," page 9), you MUST include three (3) copies of each document.  You should make and keep one (1) additional copy of the completed application for your own records.

- **One (1) color passport-style photo** of yourself and each family member listed in Part A. II. who is included in your application.  These photos should be taken no more than 30 days before submission of your application to the INS.

Using a pencil, lightly write each person's complete name and INS A number, if known, on the the back of his or her photos.  The photos must:

- be taken with a white background, be un-mounted, be printed on thin paper, have a glossy finish, and not be retouched;

- not be larger than 1 1/2 x 1 1/2 inches, with the distance from the top of the head to just below each person's chin about 1 1/4 inches.

- **Three (3) copies of all passports or other travel documents** (cover to cover) in your possession, and three (3) copies of any U.S. Immigration documents, such as an I-94 Arrival-Departure Record, for you and each family member who you want included in your application, if you have such documents.

- If you have **other identification documents** (for example, birth certificate, military or national identification card, driver's license, etc.), it is recommended that you submit three (3) copies with your application and bring the original(s) with you to the interview.

- **Three (3) copies of primary or secondary evidence of relationship**, such as birth or school records of your children, marriage certificate, or proof of termination of marriage, for each family member listed in Part A. II. who you want to have included in your application.

  NOTE:  If you submit an affidavit, you must submit the original and two (2) copies. (For affidavit requirements, see Instructions, Part 1: Filing Instructions, Section V, "Completing the Form," Part A. II., page 6.)

- **One additional copy of your completed application** Form I-589, with supplementary sheets and supplementary statements, for each family member listed in Part A. II. who you want to have included in your application.

It is recommended that any documents filed with this application be photocopies but, please be advised, if you choose to send an original document, the INS or Immigration Court may keep that original document for its records.

**Translation of documents not in English is required.** Any document in a language other than English must be accompanied by an adequate English translation that the translator has certified as complete and correct, and by the translator's certification that he or she is competent to translate into English the language used in the document.

## VII. Additional Documents that You Should Submit

If they are available to you, you should submit documents evidencing (1) the general conditions in the country from which you are seeking asylum, and (2) the specific facts on which you are relying to support your claim. If documents supporting your claim are not available or you are not providing them at this time, you must explain why using the Supplement B Form or additional sheets of paper. Supporting documents may include, but are not limited to country condition reports, newspaper articles, affidavits of witnesses or experts, medical and/or psychological records, doctors' statements, periodicals, journals, books, photographs, official documents, or personal statements.

If you have difficulty discussing harm you have suffered in the past, you may wish to submit a health professional's report explaining this difficulty.

## VIII. Fee

There is no fee for filing this application.

## IX. Fingerprints

Applicants for asylum are subject to a check of all appropriate records and other information databases maintained by the Attorney General and by the Secretary of State. You and all of your dependents fourteen (14) years of age or older listed on your asylum application must be fingerprinted and photographed. You and your dependents will be given instructions on how to complete this requirement.

You will be notified in writing of the time and location of the Application Support Center or the designated Law Enforcement Agency where you must go to be fingerprinted and photographed. Failure to appear for a scheduled fingerprinting may delay eligibility for work authorization and/or result in an Asylum Officer dismissing your asylum application or referring it to an Immigration Judge. For applicants before an Immigration Judge, such failure will make the applicant ineligible for asylum and may delay eligibility for work authorization.

## X. Organizing Your Application

Put your application together in the following order, forming one (1) complete package (if possible, secure with binder clips and rubber bands so that material may be easily separated):

- Your original Form I-589, with all questions completed, and the application signed by you in Part D, and signed by any preparer, in Part E; and

- One (1) passport-style photograph of you stapled to the form at Part D, page 9.

Behind your original Form I-589, attach in the following order:

- One (1) Form G-28 Notice of Entry of Appearance as Attorney or Representative, signed by you and the attorney/representative if you are represented by an attorney or other representative;

- The original of all supplemental sheets and supplementary statements submitted with your application;

- All passports, other travel or identification documents;

- One (1) copy of the evidence of your relationship to your spouse and unmarried children under 21 years of age who you want included in your application, if any; and

- Supporting documents, if available, such as but not limited to, country condition reports, newspaper articles, affidavits of witnesses or experts, medical and/or psychological records, doctors' statements, etc.

Behind this original complete package include two (2) additional copies of all the items listed above except for your photograph.

If you are including family members in your application, attach one (1) additional package as specified below for each family member. Arrange each family member's package as follows:

- One (1) copy of pages 1,2,3 (including Supplement A Form I-589 as needed) and 9 of the principal's Form I-589 application;

- On Part D, page 9 of your family member's copy of the Form I-589 staple in the upper right corner one (1) passport-style photo of the family member to be included.

- One (1) copy of the proof of relationship to the principal applicant; and

- One (1) copy of the Form G-28, if any.

For example, if you include your spouse and two (2) children, you should submit your original package, plus two (2) duplicates for you, plus one (1) package for your spouse, plus one (1) package for each child, for a total of six (6) packages. Be sure each has the appropriate documentation.

NOTE: Any additional pages submitted should include your printed name (exactly as it appears in Part A.I. of the form), A# (if any), signature and date.

## XI. Incomplete Asylum Applications

An asylum application that is incomplete will be returned to you by mail within thirty (30) days of receipt of the application by the INS. An application that has not been returned to you within thirty (30) days of having been received by the INS will be considered complete and you will receive written acknowledgement of receipt from the Service.

The filing of a complete application starts the 150-day period you must wait before you may apply for employment authorization. If your application is not complete and is returned to you, the 150-day period will not begin until you resubmit a complete application. (See Instructions, Part 2: Information Regarding Post-Filing Requirements, Section V, "Employment Authorization while Your Application is Pending," for further information regarding eligibility for employment authorization.) The starting date of the 150-day waiting period is listed at the end of the first sentence in the I-589 Acknowledgement of Receipt Notice sent to you by the Service.

This notice informs you that your application was received by the Service and is pending as of that date.

An application will be considered incomplete in each of the following cases:

- The application does not include a response to each of the questions contained in the Form I-589;

- The application is unsigned;

- The application is submitted without the required photographs;

- The application is sent without the appropriate number of copies for any supporting materials submitted; or

- You indicated in Part D that someone prepared the application other than yourself or an immediate family member and the preparer failed to complete Part E of the asylum application.

## XII. Where to File

Although the INS will confirm in writing its receipt of your application, you may wish to send the completed forms by registered mail (return receipt requested) for your own records.

### *If you are in proceedings in Immigration Court:*

If you are currently in proceedings in Immigration Court (that is, if you have been served with Form I-221, Order to Show Cause and Notice of Hearing; Form I-122, Notice to Applicant for Admission Detained for Hearing Before an Immigration Judge; Form I-862, Notice to Appear; or Form I-863, Notice of Referral to Immigration Judge), you are required to file your Form I-589, Application for Asylum and for Withholding of Removal, with the Immigration Court having jurisdiction over your case.

### *If you are NOT in proceedings in Immigration Court:*

You are to mail your completed application for Asylum and for Withholding of Removal, Form I-589, and any other additional information, to the INS Service Center as indicated below.

If you live in Alabama, Arkansas, Colorado, Commonwealth of Puerto Rico, District of Columbia, Florida, Georgia, Louisiana, Maryland, Mississippi, New Mexico, North Carolina, Oklahoma, western Pennsylvania in the jurisdiction of the Pittsburgh Suboffice*, South Carolina, Tennessee, Texas, United States Virgin Islands, Utah, Virginia, West Virginia, or Wyoming, mail your application to:

> USINS Texas Service Center
> Attn: Asylum
> P.O. Box 851892
> Mesquite, TX 75185-1892

If you live in Alaska, northern California*, Idaho, Illinois, Indiana, Iowa, Kansas, Kentucky, Michigan, Minnesota, Missouri, Montana, Nebraska, northern Nevada in the jurisdiction of the Reno Suboffice*, North Dakota, Ohio, Oregon, South Dakota, Washington, or Wisconsin, mail your application to:

> USINS Nebraska Service Center
> P.O. Box 87589
> Lincoln, NE 68501-7589

If you live in Arizona, southern California*, Hawaii, southern Nevada in the jurisdiction of the Las Vegas Suboffice*, or the Territory of Guam, mail your application to:

> USINS California Service Center
> P.O. Box 10589
> Laguna Niguel, CA 92607-0589

If you live in Connecticut, Delaware, Maine, Massachusetts, New Hampshire, New Jersey, New York, eastern Pennsylvania excluding the jurisdiction of the Pittsburgh Suboffice*, Rhode Island, or Vermont, mail your application to:

> USINS Vermont Service Center
> Attn: Asylum
> 75 Lower Welden Street
> St. Albans, VT 05479-0589

*For applicants in the states of California, Nevada and Pennsylvania who may be unsure of which Service Center to use for mailing applications, you may call the National Customer Service Center or your local asylum office for more specific information. The National Customer Service Center and the asylum offices serving those states are listed below with their public information numbers:

The National Customer Service Center:

| | |
|---|---|
| Toll Free Number | 800-375-5283 |
| TDD Hearing Impaired | 800-767-1833 |

For California or Nevada:

| | |
|---|---|
| Los Angeles Asylum Office | 714-808-8199 |
| San Francisco Asylum Office | 415-744-8419 |

For Pennsylvania:

| | |
|---|---|
| Newark Asylum Office | 201-531-0555 |
| Arlington Asylum Office | 703-525-8141 |

Information concerning asylum offices and where to file asylum applications is also available on the INS website at: http://www.ins.usdoj.gov.

## PART 2: INFORMATION REGARDING POST-FILING REQUIREMENTS

### I. Notification Requirements when Your Address Changes

If you change your address you must inform the INS in writing within ten (10) days of moving.

**While your asylum application is pending before the asylum office, you MUST notify the asylum office on Form AR-11 (Change of Address Form) or by a signed and dated letter of any changes of address within ten (10) days after you change your address.** The address that you provide on the application, or the last change of address notification you submitted, will be used by the INS for mailing. Any notices mailed to that address will constitute adequate service, except that personal service may be required for the following: Notice to Alien Detained for Hearing by an Immigration Judge (Form I-122), Notice to Appear (Form I-862), Notice of Referral to Immigration Judge (Form I-863), and a Notice and Order of Expedited Removal (Form I-860).

**If you are already in proceedings in Immigration Court, you MUST notify the Immigration Court on Form EOIR 33 (Change of Address Form) or by a signed and dated letter of any changes of address within five (5) days of the change in address.** You must send the notification to the Immigration Court having jurisdiction over your case.

## II. Asylum Interview Process

If you are not in proceedings in Immigration Court, you will be notified by the INS asylum office of the date, time and place (address) of a scheduled interview. The INS suggests that you bring a copy of your Form I-589, asylum application, with you when you have your asylum interview. An Asylum Officer will interview you under oath and make a determination concerning your claim. In most cases, you will not be notified of the decision in your case until a date after your interview. You have the right to legal representation at your interview, at no cost to the United States Government. (See Instructions, Part 1: Filing Instructions, Section IV, "Right to Counsel.") You also may bring witnesses with you to the interview to testify on your behalf.

**If you are unable to proceed with the asylum interview in fluent English, you must provide at no expense to the INS, a competent interpreter fluent in both English and a language that you speak fluently.** Your interpreter must be at least 18 years of age. The following persons cannot serve as your interpreter: your attorney or representative of record; a witness testifying on your behalf at the interview; or a representative or employee of your country. Quality interpretation may be crucial to your claim. Such assistance must be obtained, at your expense, prior to the interview.

**Failure without good cause to bring a competent interpreter to your interview may be considered an unexcused failure to appear for the interview. Any unexcused failure to appear for an interview may prevent you from receiving work authorization, and your asylum application may be dismissed or referred directly to the Immigration Court.**

If available, you must bring some form of identification to your interview, including any passport(s), other travel or identification documents, or Form I-94 Arrival-Departure Record. You may bring to the interview any additional available items documenting your claim that you have not already submitted with your application.

If members of your family are included in your application for asylum, they must also appear for the interview and bring any identity or travel documents they have in their possession.

## III. Status while Your Claim Is Pending

While your case is pending, you will be permitted to remain in the United States. After your asylum interview, if you have not been granted asylum and appear to be deportable under Section 237 of the Act, 8 U.S.C. 1227, or inadmissible under Section 212 of the Act, 8 U.S.C. 1182, your application will be filed with the Immigration Court upon referral by the asylum office.

## IV. Travel Outside the United States

If you leave the United States without first obtaining advance parole from the INS using Form I-131, Application for a Travel Document, OMB No. 1115-0005, it will be presumed that you have abandoned your application. If you obtain advance parole and return to the country of claimed persecution, it will be presumed that you abandoned your application, unless you can show that there were compelling reasons for your return.

NOTE: The application process for advance parole varies depending on your personal circumstances. Check with your local INS District Office for application instructions.

## V. Employment Authorization while Your Application is Pending

You will be granted permission to work if your asylum application is granted.

Simply filing an application for asylum does not entitle you to work authorization. You may request permission to work if your asylum application is pending and 150 days have lapsed since your application was accepted by the INS or the Immigration Court. See 8 CFR 208.7(a)(1). Any delay in the processing of your asylum application that you request or cause shall not be counted as part of the 150-day period. If your asylum application has not been denied within 180 days from the date of filing a complete asylum application, you may be granted permission to work by filing an Application for Employment Authorization, Form I-765 (OMB No. 1115-0163), with the Service. Follow the instructions on that application and submit it with a copy of evidence as specified in the instructions that you have a pending asylum application. Each family member you have asked to have included in your application who also wants permission to work must submit a separate Form I-765. You may obtain a Form I-765 by calling 1- 800-870-FORM (3676), or from the INS website at http://www.ins.usdoj.gov.

## VI. Privacy Act Notice

The authority to collect this information is contained in Title 8 of the United States Code. Furnishing the information on this form is voluntary; however, failure to provide all of the requested information may result in the delay of a final decision or denial of your request.

## VII. Paperwork Reduction Act Notice

Under the Paperwork Reduction Act an agency may not conduct or sponsor an information collection and a  person is not required to respond to a collection of information unless it displays a currently valid OMB control number.  We try to create forms and instructions that are accurate, can be easily understood, and which impose the least possible burden on you to provide us with information.  Often this is difficult because some immigration laws are very complex.  The estimated average time to complete and file this application is as follows:  (1) 2 hours to learn about the form;

(2) 5 hours to complete the form; and (3) 5 hours to assemble and file the application; for the total estimated average burden hours of 12 hours per application.  The estimated time to complete the form will vary depending on the complexity of your individual circumstances.  If you have comments regarding the accuracy of this estimate or suggestions for making this form simpler, you can write to the Immigration and Naturalization Service, Policy Directives and Instructions Branch,  425 I Street, N.W., Room 4034, Washington, DC  20536, OMB No. 1115-0086.  **DO NOT MAIL YOUR COMPLETED APPLICATION TO THIS ADDRESS.**

## SUPPLEMENTS TO THE FORM I-589

**Form I-589, Supplement A**  -  for use in completing Part A. II.

**Form I-589, Supplement B**  -  for use in completing Parts B, C, and to provide additional information for any other part of the application.

# Application for Asylum and for Withholding of Removal

*Start Here - Please Type or Print.* **USE BLACK INK. SEE THE SEPARATE INSTRUCTION PAMPHLET FOR INFORMATION ABOUT ELIGIBILITY AND HOW TO COMPLETE AND FILE THIS APPLICATION.** (Note: There is NO filing fee for this application.)

*Please* check the box if you also want to apply for withholding of removal under the Convention Against Torture. ☐

## PART A. I.   INFORMATION ABOUT YOU

| 1. Alien Registration Number(s)(A#'s)*(If any)* | 2. Social Security No. *(If any)* |
|---|---|
| 3. Complete Last Name | 4. First Name | 5. Middle Name |

6. What other names have you used? *(Include maiden name and aliases.)*

| 7. Residence in the U.S. C/O | Telephone Number |
|---|---|
| Street Number and Name | Apt. No. |
| City | State | ZIP Code |

| 8. Mailing Address in the U.S., if other than above | Telephone Number |
|---|---|
| Street Number and Name | Apt. No. |
| City | State | ZIP Code |

9. Sex ☐ Male ☐ Female    10. Marital Status: ☐ Single ☐ Married ☐ Divorced ☐ Widowed

| 11. Date of Birth *(Mo/Day/Yr)* | 12. City and Country of Birth |
|---|---|

| 13. Present Nationality (Citizenship) | 14. Nationality at Birth | 15. Race, Ethnic or Tribal Group | 16. Religion |
|---|---|---|---|

17.    *Check the box, a through c that applies:*    a. ☐  I have never been in immigration court proceedings.
b. ☐ I am now in immigration court proceedings.    c. ☐ I am **not** now in immigration court proceedings, but I have been in the past.

18. *Complete 18 a through c.*
a. When did you last leave your country? *(Mo/Day/Yr)* _____    b. What is your current I-94 Number, if any? _____

c. Please list each entry to the U.S. beginning with your most recent entry.
*List date (Mo/Day/Yr), place, and your status for each entry. (Attach additional sheets as needed.)*

Date _____ Place _____ Status _____ Date Status Expires _____
Date _____ Place _____ Status _____
Date _____ Place _____ Status _____
Date _____ Place _____ Status _____

| 19. What country issued your last passport or travel document? | 20. Passport # Travel Document # | 21. Expiration Date *(Mo/Day/Yr)* |
|---|---|---|
| 22.    What is your native language? | 23. Are you fluent in English? ☐ Yes ☐ No | 24. What other languages do you speak fluently? |

| **FOR EOIR USE ONLY** | **FOR INS USE ONLY** |
|---|---|
| | **Action:** Interview Date: _____ **Decision:** __ Approval Date: _____ — Denial Date: _____ — Referral Date: _____ Asylum Officer ID# _____ |

Form I-589 (Rev. 10/18/01)N

## PART A. II.   INFORMATION ABOUT YOUR SPOUSE AND CHILDREN
**Your Spouse.** ☐ I am not married. (Skip to *Your Children*, below.)

| 1. Alien Registration Number (A#) *(If any)* | 2. Passport/ID Card No. *(If any)* | 3. Date of Birth *(Mo/Day/Yr)* | 4. Social Security No. *(If any)* |
|---|---|---|---|
| 5. Complete Last Name | 6. First Name | 7. Middle Name | 8. Maiden Name |
| 9. Date of Marriage *(Mo/Day/Yr)* | 10. Place of Marriage | 11. City and Country of Birth | |
| 12. Nationality *(Citizenship)* | 13. Race, Ethnic or Tribal Group | 14. Sex ☐ Male ☐ Female | |

15. Is this person in the U.S.? ☐ Yes *(Complete blocks 16 to 24.)*  ☐ No *(Specify location)*

| 16. Place of last entry in the U.S.? | 17. Date of last entry in the U.S. *(Mo/Day/Yr)* | 18. I-94 No. *(If any)* | 19. Status when last admitted *(Visa type, if any)* |
|---|---|---|---|
| 20. What is your spouse's current status? | 21. What is the expiration date of his/her authorized stay, if any? *(Mo/Day/Yr)* | 22. Is your spouse in immigration court proceedings? ☐ Yes ☐ No | 23. If previously in the U.S., date of previous arrival *(Mo/Day/Yr)* |

24. If in the U.S., is your spouse to be included in this application? *(Check the appropriate box.)*

☐ Yes *(Attach one (1) photograph of your spouse in the upper right hand corner of page 9 on the extra copy of the application submitted for this person.)*
☐ No

**Your Children.** Please list **ALL** of your children, regardless of age, location, or marital status.

☐ I do not have any children. *(Skip to Part A. III., Information about Your Background.)*
☐ I do have children. Total number of children _____

*(Use Supplement A Form I-589 or attach additional pages and documentation if you have more than four (4) children.)*

| 1. Alien Registration Number (A#) *(If any)* | 2. Passport/ID Card No. *(If any)* | 3. Marital Status *(Married, Single, Divorced, Widowed)* | 4. Social Security No. *(If any)* |
|---|---|---|---|
| 5. Complete Last Name | 6. First Name | 7. Middle Name | 8. Date of Birth *(Mo/Day/Yr)* |
| 9. City and Country of Birth | 10. Nationality *(Citizenship)* | 11. Race, Ethnic or Tribal Group | 12. Sex ☐ Male ☐ Female |

13. Is this child in the U.S.? ☐ Yes *(Complete blocks 14 to 21.)*  ☐ No *(Specify Location)*

| 14. Place of last entry in the U.S.? | 15. Date of last entry in the U.S.? *(Mo/Day/Yr)* | 16. I-94 No. *(If any)* | 17. Status when last admitted *(Visa type, if any)* |
|---|---|---|---|
| 18. What is your child's current status? | 19. What is the expiration date of his/her authorized stay, if any?*(Mo/Day/Yr)* | 20. Is your child in immigration court proceedings? ☐ Yes ☐ No | |

21. If in the U.S., is this child to be included in this application? *(Check the appropriate box.)*
☐ Yes *(Attach one (1) photograph of your child in the upper right hand corner of page 9 on the extra copy of the application submitted for this person.)*
☐ No

## PART A. II. INFORMATION ABOUT YOUR SPOUSE AND CHILDREN Continued

| 1. Alien Registration Number (A#) *(If any)* | 2. Passport/IDCard No. *(If any)* | 3. Marital Status *(Married, Single, Divorced, Widowed)* | 4. Social Security No. *(If any)* |
|---|---|---|---|
| 5. Complete Last Name | 6. First Name | 7. Middle Name | 8. Date of Birth *(Mo/Dayl/Yr)* |
| 9. City and Country of Birth | 10. Nationality *(Citizenship)* | 11. Race, Ethnic or Tribal Group | 12. Sex ☐ Male ☐ Female |

13. Is this child in the U.S.? ☐ Yes *(Complete blocks 14 to 21.)* ☐ No *(Specify Location)*

| 14. Place of last entry in the U.S.? | 15. Date of last entry in the U.S. ? *(Mo/Day/Yr)* | 16. I-94 No. *(If any)* | 17. Status when last admitted *(Visa type, if any)* |
|---|---|---|---|
| 18. What is your child's current status? | 19. What is the expiration date of his/her authorized stay,*(if any)? (Mo/Day/Yr)* | 20. Is your child in immigration court proceedings? ☐ Yes ☐ No | |

21. If in the U.S., is this child to be included in this application? *(Check the appropriate box.)*
   ☐ Yes *(Attach one (1) photograph of your child in the upper right hand corner of page 9 on the extra copy of the application submitted for this person.)*
   ☐ No

| 1. Alien Registration Number (A#) *(If any)* | 2. Passport/ID Card No.*(If any)* | 3. Marital Status *(Married, Single, Divorced, Widowed)* | 4. Social Security No. *(If any)* |
|---|---|---|---|
| 5. Complete Last Name | 6. First Name | 7. Middle Name | 8. Date of Birth *(Mo/Day/Yr)* |
| 9. City and Country of Birth | 10. Nationality *(Citizenship)* | 11. Race, Ethnic or Tribal Group | 12. Sex ☐ Male ☐ Female |

13. Is this child in the U.S. ? ☐ Yes *(Complete blocks 14 to 21.)* ☐ No *(Specify Location)*

| 14. Place of last entry in the U.S.? | 15. Date of last entry in the U.S.? *(Mo/Day/Yr)* | 16. I-94 No. *(If any)* | 17. Status when last admitted *(Visa type, if any)* |
|---|---|---|---|
| 18. What is your child's current status? | 19. What is the expiration date of his/her authorized stay, if any? *(Mo/Day/Yr)* | 20. Is your child in immigration court proceedings? ☐ Yes ☐ No | |

21. If in the U.S., is this child to be included in this application? *(Check the appropriate box.)*
   ☐ Yes *(Attach one (1) photograph of your child in the upper right hand corner of page 9 on the extra copy of the application submitted for this person.)*
   ☐ No

| 1. Alien Registration Number (A#) *(If any)* | 2. Passport/ID Card No. *(If any)* | 3. Marital Status *(Married, Single, Divorced, Widowed)* | 4. Social Security No. *(If any)* |
|---|---|---|---|
| 5. Complete Last Name | 6. First Name | 7. Middle Name | 8. Date of Birth *(Mo/Day/Yr)* |
| 9. City and Country of Birth | 10. Nationality *(Citizenship)* | 11. Race, Ethnic or Tribal Group | 12. Sex ☐ Male ☐ Female |

13. Is this child in the U.S.? ☐ Yes *(Complete blocks 14 to 21.)* ☐ No *(Specify Location)*

| 14. Place of last entry in the U.S.? | 15. Date of last entry in the U.S.? *(Mo/Day/Yr)* | 16. I-94 No. *(If any)* | 17. Status when last admitted *(Visa type, if any)* |
|---|---|---|---|
| 18. What is your child's current status? | 19. What is the expiration date of his/her authorized stay, if any? *(Mo/Day/Yr)* | 20. Is your child in immigration court proceedings? ☐ Yes ☐ No | |

21. If in the U.S., is this child to be included in this application? *(Check the appropriate box.)*
   ☐ Yes *(Attach one (1) photograph of your child in the upper right hand corner of page 9 on the extra copy of the application submitted for this person.)*
   ☐ No

## PART A. III.    INFORMATION ABOUT YOUR BACKGROUND

1.   Please list your last address where you lived before coming to the U.S.  If this is not the country where you fear persecution, also list the last address in the country where you fear persecution. *(List Address, City/Town, Department, Province, or State, and Country.)  (Use Supplement B Form I-589 or additional sheets of paper if necessary.)*

| Number and Street *(Provide if available)* | City/Town | Department, Province or State | Country | Dates From *(Mo/Yr)* | To *(Mo/Yr)* |
|---|---|---|---|---|---|
| | | | | | |
| | | | | | |

2.   Provide the following information about your residences during the last five years.  List your present address first. *(Use Supplement Form B or additional sheets of paper if necessary.)*

| Number and Street | City/Town | Department, Province or State | Country | Dates From *(Mo/Yr)* | To *(Mo/Yr)* |
|---|---|---|---|---|---|
| | | | | | |
| | | | | | |
| | | | | | |
| | | | | | |
| | | | | | |

3.   Provide the following information about your education, beginning with the most recent. *(Use Supplement B Form I-589 or additional sheets of paper if necessary.)*

| Name of School | Type of School | Location (Address) | Attended From *(Mo/Yr)* | To *(Mo/Yr)* |
|---|---|---|---|---|
| | | | | |
| | | | | |
| | | | | |
| | | | | |

4.   Provide the following information about your employment during the last five years.  List your present employment first. *(Use Supplement Form B or additional sheets of paper if necessary.)*

| Name and Address of Employer | Your Occupation | Dates From *(Mo/Yr)* | To *(Mo/Yr)* |
|---|---|---|---|
| | | | |
| | | | |
| | | | |
| | | | |
| | | | |

5.   Provide the following information about your parents and siblings (brother and sisters).  Check box if the person is deceased. *(Use Supplement B Form I-589 or additional sheets of paper if necessary.)*

| Name | City/Town and Country of Birth | Current Location |
|---|---|---|
| *Mother* | | ☐ Deceased |
| *Father* | | ☐ Deceased |
| *Siblings* | | ☐ Deceased |
| | | ☐ Deceased |

## PART B.   INFORMATION ABOUT YOUR APPLICATION

*(Use Supplement B Form I-589 or attach additional sheets of paper as needed to complete your responses to the questions contained in PART B.)*

When answering the following questions about your asylum or other protection claim (withholding of removal under 241(b)(3) of the Act or withholding of removal under the Convention Against Torture) you should provide a detailed and specific account of the basis of your claim to asylum or other protection. To the best of your ability, provide specific dates, places, and descriptions about each event or action described. You should attach documents evidencing the general conditions in the country from which you are seeking asylum or other protection and the specific facts on which you are relying to support your claim. If this documentation is unavailable or you are not providing this documentation with your application, please explain why in your responses to the following questions. Refer to Instructions, Part 1: Filing Instructions, Section II, "Basis of Eligibility," Parts A - D,  Section V, "Completing the Form," Part B, and Section VII, "Additional Documents that You Should Submit" for more information on completing this section of the form.

1. Why are you applying for asylum or withholding of removal under section 241(b)(3) of the Act, or for withholding of removal under the  Convention Against Torture?  Check the appropriate box (es) below and then provide detailed answers to questions A and B below:

    I am seeking asylum or withholding of removal based on

    ☐ Race
    ☐ Religion
    ☐ Nationality
    ☐ Political opinion
    ☐ Membership in a particular social group
    ☐ Torture Convention

    A. Have you, your family, or close friends or colleagues ever experienced harm or mistreatment or threats in the past by anyone?

    ☐ No   ☐ Yes  If your answer is "Yes," explain in detail:

    1) What happened;
    2) When the harm or mistreatment or threats occurred;
    3) Who caused the harm or mistreatment or threats; and
    4) Why you believe the harm or mistreatment or threats occurred.

    B. Do you fear harm or mistreatment if you return to your home country?

    ☐ No   ☐ Yes  If your answer is "Yes," explain in detail:

    1) What harm or mistreatment you fear;
    2) Who you believe would harm or mistreat you; and
    3) Why you believe you would or could be harmed or mistreated.

**PART B.   INFORMATION ABOUT YOUR APPLICATION Continued**

2.  Have you or your family members ever been accused, charged, arrested, detained, interrogated, convicted and sentenced, or imprisoned in any country other than the United States?

☐ No   ☐ Yes  If "Yes," explain the circumstances and reasons for the action.

3. A.   Have you or your family members ever belonged to or been associated with any organizations or groups in your home country, such as, but not limited to, a political party, student group, labor union, religious organization, military or paramilitary group, civil patrol, guerrilla organization, ethnic group, human rights group, or the press or media?

☐ No   ☐ Yes  If "Yes," describe for each person the level of participation, any leadership or other positions held, and the length of time you or your family members were involved in each organization or activity.

B.   Do you or your family members continue to participate in any way in these organizations or groups?

☐ No   ☐ Yes  If "Yes," describe for each person, your or your family members' current level of participation, any leadership or other positions currently held, and the length of time you or your family members have been involved in each organization or group.

4.  Are you afraid of being subjected to torture in your home country or any other country to which you may be returned?

☐ No   ☐ Yes  If "Yes," explain why you are afraid and describe the nature of the torture you fear, by whom, and why it would be inflicted.

## PART C.    ADDITIONAL INFORMATION ABOUT YOUR APPLICATION

*(Use Supplement B Form I-589 or attach additional sheets of paper as needed to complete your responses to the questions contained in Part C.)*

1.    Have you, your spouse, your child(ren), your parents, or your siblings ever applied to the United States Government for refugee status, asylum, or withholding of removal?    ☐ No ☐ Yes

   If "Yes" explain the decision and what happened to any status you, your spouse, your child(ren), your parents, or your siblings received as a result of that decision.  Please indicate whether or not you were included in a parent or spouse's application.  If so, please include your parent or spouse's A- number in your response.  If you have been denied asylum by an Immigration Judge or the Board of Immigration Appeals, please describe any change(s) in conditions in your country or your own personal circumstances since the date of the denial that may affect your eligibility for asylum.

2.    A.  After leaving the country from which you are claiming asylum, did you or your spouse or child(ren), who are now in the United States, travel through or reside in any other country before entering the United States?    ☐ No    ☐ Yes

   B.  Have you, your spouse, your child(ren), or other family members such as your parents or siblings ever applied for or received any lawful status in any country other than the one from which you are now claiming asylum?    ☐ No    ☐ Yes

   If "Yes" to either or both questions (2A and/or 2B), provide for each person the following: the name of each country and the length of stay; the person's status while there; the reasons for leaving; whether the person is entitled to return for lawful residence purposes; and whether the person applied for refugee status or for asylum while there, and, if not, why he or she did not do so.

3.    Have you, your spouse, or child(ren) ever ordered, incited, assisted, or otherwise participated in causing harm or suffering to any person because of his or her race, religion, nationality, membership in a particular social group or belief in a particular political opinion?

   ☐ No    ☐ Yes  If "Yes," describe in detail each such incident and your own or your spouse's or child(ren)'s involvement.

**PART C.   ADDITIONAL INFORMATION ABOUT YOUR APPLICATION Continued**

4.   After you left the country where you were harmed or fear harm, did you return to that country?

☐ No   ☐ Yes   If "Yes," describe in detail the circumstances of your visit (for example, the date(s) of the trip(s), the purpose(s) of the trip(s), and the length of time you remained in that country for the visit(s)).

5.   Are you filing the application more than one year after your last arrival in the United States?

☐No   ☐Yes   If "Yes," explain why you did not file within the first year after you arrived.   You should be prepared to explain at your interview or hearing why you did not file your asylum application within the first year after you arrived.   For guidance in answering this question, see Instructions, Part 1:  Filing Instructions, Section V. "Completing the Form," Part C.

6.   Have you or any member of your family included in the application ever committed any crime and/or been arrested, charged, convicted and sentenced for any crimes in the United States?

☐   No   ☐   Yes   If "Yes," for each instance, specify in your response what occurred and the circumstances; dates; length of sentence received; location; the duration of the detention or imprisonment; the reason(s) for the detention or conviction; any formal charges that were lodged against you or your relatives included in your application; the reason(s) for release.   Attach documents referring to these incidents, if they are available, or an explanation of why documents are not available.

## PART D.   YOUR SIGNATURE

*After reading the information regarding penalties in the instructions, complete and sign below. If someone helped you prepare this application, he or she must complete Part E.*

I certify, under penalty of perjury under the laws of the United States of America, that this application and the evidence submitted with it are all true and correct. Title 18, United States Code, Section 1546, provides in part: "Whoever knowingly makes under oath, or as permitted under penalty of perjury under Section 1746 of Title 28, United States Code, knowingly subscribes as true, any false statement with respect to a material fact in any application, affidavit, or knowingly presents any such application, affidavit, or other document required by the immigration laws or regulations prescribed thereunder, or knowingly presents any such application, affidavit, or other document containing any such false statement or which fails to contain any reasonable basis in law or fact - shall be fined in accordance with this title or imprisoned not more than five years, or both." I authorize the release of any information from my record which the Immigration and Naturalization Service needs to determine eligibility for the benefit I am seeking.

> Staple your photograph here or the photograph of the family member to be included on the extra copy of the application submitted for that person.

**WARNING:** Applicants who are in the United States illegally are subject to removal if their asylum or withholding claims are not granted by an Asylum Officer or an Immigration Judge. Any information provided in completing this application may be used as a basis for the institution of, or as evidence in, removal proceedings even if the application is later withdrawn. Applicants determined to have knowingly made a frivolous application for asylum will be permanently ineligible for any benefits under the Immigration and Nationality Act. See 208(d)(6) of the Act and 8 CFR 208.20.

| Print Complete Name | Write your name in your native alphabet |
|---|---|
|  |  |

Did your spouse, parent, or child(ren) assist you in completing this application?  ☐ No  ☐ Yes *(If "Yes," list the name and relationship.)*

_____  _____    _____  _____
         *(Name)*                         *(Relationship)*                      *(Name)*                       *(Relationship)*

Did someone other than your spouse, parent, or child(ren) prepare this application?  ☐ No  ☐ Yes *(If "Yes," complete Part E)*

Asylum applicants may be represented by counsel. Have you been provided with a list of persons who may be available to assist you, at little or no cost, with your asylum claim?   ☐ No   ☐ Yes

Signature of Applicant *(The person in Part A. I.)*

[ _____ ]                    _____
   Sign your name so it all appears within the brackets                                 Date *(Mo/Day/Yr)*

## PART E.   DECLARATION OF PERSON PREPARING FORM IF OTHER THAN APPLICANT, SPOUSE, PARENT OR CHILD

I declare that I have prepared this application at the request of the person named in Part D, that the responses provided are based on all information of which I have knowledge, or which was provided to me by the applicant and that the completed application was read to the applicant in his or her native language or a language he or she understands for verification before he or she signed the application in my presence. I am aware that the knowing placement of false information on the Form I-589 may also subject me to civil penalties under 8 U.S.C. 1324(c).

| Signature of Preparer | Print Complete Name | | |
|---|---|---|---|
| Daytime Telephone Number ( ) | Address of Preparer: Street Number and Name | | |
| Apt. No. | City | State | ZIP Code |

## PART F.   TO BE COMPLETED AT INTERVIEW OR HEARING

*You will be asked to complete this Part when you appear before an Asylum Officer of the Immigration and Naturalization Service (INS), or an Immigration Judge of the Executive Office for Immigration Review (EOIR) for examination.*

I swear (affirm) that I know the contents of this application that I am signing, including the attached documents and supplements, that they are all true to the best of my knowledge taking into account correction(s) numbered _____ to _____ that were made by me or at my request.

Signed and sworn to before me by the above named applicant on:

_____          _____
           Signature of Applicant                                           Date *(Mo/Day/Yr)*

_____          _____
   Write Your Name in Your Native Alphabet                    Signature of Asylum Officer or Immigration Judge

| A # *(If available)* | Date |
| --- | --- |
| Applicant's Name | Applicant's Signature |

## LIST ALL OF YOUR CHILDREN, REGARDLESS OF AGE OR MARITAL STATUS.

*(Use this form and attach additional pages and documentation as needed to your application if you have more than four (4) children.)*

| 1. Alien Registration Number (A#)*(If any)* | 2. Passport/ID Card No. *(If any)* | 3. Marital Status *(Married, Single, Divorced, Widowed)* | 4. Social Security No. *(If any)* |
| --- | --- | --- | --- |
| 5. Complete Last Name | 6. First Name | 7. Middle Name | 8. Date of Birth *(Mo/Day/Yr)* |
| 9. City and Country of Birth | 10. Nationality *(Citizenship)* | 11. Race, Ethnic or Tribal Group | 12. Sex ☐ Male ☐ Female |

13. Is this child in the U.S.? ☐ Yes *(Complete blocks 14 to 21.)* ☐ No *(Specify Location)*

| 14. Place of last entry in the U.S.? | 15. Date of last entry in the U.S.? *(Mo/Day/Yr)* | 16. I-94 No. *(If any)* | 17. Status when last admitted *(Visa type, if any)* |
| --- | --- | --- | --- |
| 18. What is your child's current status? | 19. What is the expiration date of his/her authorized stay, if any? *(Mo/Day/Yr)* | 20. Is your child in immigration court proceedings? ☐ Yes ☐ No | |

21. If in the U.S., is this child to be included in this application? *(Check the appropriate box.)*
☐ Yes *(Attach one (1) photograph of your child in the upper right hand corner of page 9 on the extra copy of the application submitted for this person.)*
☐ No

| 1. Alien Registration Number (A#)*(If any)* | 2. Passport/ID Card No. *(If any)* | 3. Marital Status *(Married, Single, Divorced, Widowed)* | 4. Social Security No. *(If any)* |
| --- | --- | --- | --- |
| 5. Complete Last Name | 6. First Name | 7. Middle Name | 8. Date of Birth *(Mo/Day/Yr)* |
| 9. City and Country of Birth | 10. Nationality *(Citizenship)* | 11. Race, Ethnic or Tribal Group | 12. Sex ☐ Male ☐ Female |

13. Is this child in the U.S.? ☐ Yes *(Complete blocks 14 to 21.)* ☐ No *(Specify Location)*

| 14. Place of last entry in the U.S.? | 15. Date of last entry in the U.S.? *(Mo/Day/Yr)* | 16. I-94 No. *(If any)* | 17. Status when last admitted *(Visa type, if any)* |
| --- | --- | --- | --- |
| 18. What is your child's current status? | 19. What is the expiration date of his/her authorized stay, if any? *(Mo/Day/Yr)* | 20. Is your child in immigration court proceedings? ☐ Yes ☐ No | |

21. If in the U.S., is this child to be included in this application? *(Check the appropriate box.)*
☐ Yes *(Attach one (1) photograph of your child in the upper right hand corner of page 9 on the extra copy of the application submitted for this person.)*
☐ No

OMB No. 1115-0086

## ADDITIONAL INFORMATION ABOUT YOUR CLAIM TO ASYLUM.

| A # *(If available)* | Date |
|---|---|
| Applicant's Name | Applicant's Signature |

*Use this as a continuation page for any information requested. Please copy and complete as needed.*

**PART** _____

**QUESTION** _____

**U.S. Department of Justice**
Immigration and Naturalization Service

# Petition to Classify Orphan as an Immediate Relative

## 1. Eligibility.

**A. Child.** Under immigration law, an orphan is an alien child who has no parents because of the death or disappearance of, abandonment or desertion by, or separation or loss from both parents. An orphan is also a child who has only one parent who is not capable of taking care of the orphan and who has, in writing, irrevocably released the orphan for emigration and adoption. A petition to classify an alien as an orphan may not be filed in behalf of a child in the United States, unless that child is in parole status and has not been adopted in the United States. The petition must be filed before the child's 16th birthday.

**B. Parent(s).** The petition may be filed by a married United States citizen and spouse or unmarried United States citizen at least twenty-five years of age. The spouse does not need to be a United States citizen.

**C. Adoption abroad.** If the orphan was adopted abroad, it must be established that both the married petitioner and spouse or the unmarried petitioner personally saw and observed the child prior to or during the adoption proceedings. The adoption decree must show that a married petitioner and spouse adopted the child jointly or that an unmarried petitioner was at least 25 years of age at the time of the adoption.

**D. Proxy adoption abroad.** If both the petitioner and spouse or the unmarried petitioner did not personally see and observe the child prior to or during the adoption proceedings abroad, the petitioner (and spouse, if married) must submit a statement indicating the petitioner's (and, if married, the spouse's) willingness and intent to readopt the child in the United States. If requested, the petitioner must submit a statement by an official of the state in which the child will reside that readoption is permissible in that state. In addition, evidence of compliance with the preadoption requirements, if any, of that state must be submitted.

**E. Preadoption requirements.** If the orphan has not been adopted abroad, the petitioner and spouse or the unmarried petitioner must establish that the child will be adopted in the United States by the petitioner and spouse jointly or by the unmarried petitioner and that the preadoption requirement, if any, of the state of the orphan's proposed residence have been met.

## 2. Filing petition for known child.

An orphan petition for a child who has been identified must be submitted on a completed Form I-600 with the certification of petitioner executed and the required fee. If the petitioner is married, the Form I-600 must also be signed by the petitioner's spouse. The petition must be accompanied by the following:

### A. Proof of United States citizenship of the petitioner.

(1) If the petitioner is a citizen by reason of birth in the United States, submit a copy of the petitioner's birth certificate, or if birth certificate is unobtainable, a copy of petitioner's baptismal certificate under the seal of the church, showing place of birth, (baptism must have occurred within two months after birth), or if a birth or baptismal certificate cannot be obtained, affidavits of two United States citizens who have personal knowledge of petitioner's birth in the United States.

(2) If the petitioner was born outside the United States and became a citizen through the naturalization or citizenship of a parent or husband and and has not been issued a certificate of citizenship in his or her own name, submit evidence of the citizenship and marriage of the parent or husband, as well as termination of any prior marriages.

Also, if petitioner claims citizenship through a parent, submit petitioner's birth certificate and a separate statement showing the date, place, and means of all his or her arrivals and departures into and out of the United States.

(3)  If petitioner's naturalization occurred within 90 days immediately preceding the filing of this petition, or if it occurred prior to September 27, 1906, the naturalization certificate must accompany the petition.

(4)  An unexpired U.S. passport initially issued for ten years may also be submitted.

**B.  Proof of marriage of petitioner and spouse.**
The married petitioner should submit a certificate of the marriage and proof of termination of all prior marriages of himself or herself and spouse. In the case of an unmarried petitioner who was previously married, submit proof of termination of all prior marriages. **NOTE:** If any change occurs in the petitioner's marital status while the case is pending, the district director should be notified immediately.

**C.  Proof of age of orphan.**
Petitioner should submit a copy of the orphan's birth certificate if obtainable; if not obtainable, submit an explanation together with the best available evidence of birth.

**D.  Copies of the death certificate(s) of the child's parent(s), if applicable.**

**E.  A certified copy of adoption decree together with certified translation,** if the orphan has been lawfully adopted abroad.

**F.  Evidence that the sole or surviving parent is incapable of providing for the orphan's care** and has, in writing, irrevocably released the orphan for emigration and adoption, if the orphan has only one parent.

**G.  Evidence that the orphan has been unconditionally abandoned to an orphanage,** if the orphan has been placed in an orphanage by his/her parent or parents.

**H.  Evidence that the preadoption requirements, if any, of the state of the orphan's proposed residence have been met,** if the child is to be adopted in the United States. If it is not possible to submit this evidence upon initial filing of the petition under the laws of the state of proposed residence, it may be submitted later. The petition, however, will not be approved without it.

**I.  A home study** with a statement or attachment recommending or approving of the adoption or proposed adoption signed by an official of the responsible state agency in the state of the child's proposed residence or of an agency authorized by that state, or, in the case of a child adopted abroad, of an appropriate public or private adoption agency which is licensed in the United States. Both individuals and organizations may qualify as agencies. If the recommending agency is a licensed agency, the recommendation must set forth that it is licensed, the state in which it is licensed, its license number, if any, and the period of validity of its license. The research, including interviewing, however, and the preparation of the home study may be done by an individual or group in the United States or abroad satisfactory to the recommending agency. A responsible state agency or licensed agency can accept a home study made by an unlicensed agency can accept a home study made by an unlicensed or foreign agency and use that home study as a basis for a favorable recommendation. The home study must contain, but is not limited to, the following elements:

(1)  the financial ability of the adoptive or prospective parent or parents to read and educate the child.

(2)  a detailed description of the living accommodations where the adoptive or prospective parent or parents currently reside.

(3)  a detailed description of the living accommodations where the child will reside.

(4)  a factual evaluation of the physical, mental, and moral capabilities of the adoptive or prospective parent or parents in relation to rearing and educating the child.

**J. Fingerprints.**

Each member of the married prospective adoptive couple or the married prospective adoptive parent, and each additional adult member of the prospective adoptive parents' household must be fingerprinted in connection with this petition.

*Petitioners residing in the United States.* After filing this petition, INS will notify each person in writing of the time and location where they must go to be fingerprinted. Failure to appear to be fingerprinted may result in denial of the petition.

*Petitioners residing abroad.* Completed fingerprint cards (Forms FD-258) must be submitted with the petition. Do not bend, fold, or crease completed fingerprint cards. Fingerprint cards must be prepared by a United States consular office or a United States military installation.

## 3. Filing Petition for Known Child Without Full Documentation on Child or Home Study.

When a child has been identified but the documentary evidence relating to him/her or the home study is not yet available, an orphan petition may be filed without that evidence or home study. The evidence outlined in Instructions 2A and 2B, however, must be submitted. If the necessary evidence relating to the child or the home study is not submitted within one year from the date of submission of the petition, the petition will be considered abandoned and the fee will not be refunded. Any further proceeding will require the filing of a new petition.

## 4. Submitting an Application for Advance Processing of an Orphan Petition in Behalf of a Child Who Has Not Been Identified.

A prospective petitioner may request advance processing when the child has not been identified or when the prospective petitioner and/or spouse are or is going abroad to locate or adopt a child. If unmarried, the prospective petitioner must be at least 24 years of age, provided that he or she will be at least 25 at the time of the adoption and the completed petition in behalf of a child is filed. The request must be on Form I-600A, Application for Advance Processing of Orphan Petition, and must be accompanied by the evidence required by that form. After a child or children are located and/or identified, a separate Form I-600, Petition to Classify Orphan as an Immediate Relative, must be filed for each child. A new fee is not required if only one Form I-600 is filed, provided the form is filed within one year of completion of all advance

processing in a case where there has been a favorable determination concerning the prospective petitioner's ability to care for a beneficiary orphan.

## 5. When Child/Children Located and/or Identified.

A separate form I-600, Petition to Classify Orphan as an Immediate Relative, must be filed for each child. A new fee is not required if only one form I-600 is filed and it is filed within one year of completion of all advance processing in a case where there has been a favorable determination concerning the beneficiary orphan.

Normally, Form I-600 should be submitted to the INS office where the advance processing application was filed. The Immigration and Naturalization Service has offices in the following countries: Austria, China, Cuba, Denmark, Dominican Republic, Ecuador, El Salvador, Germany, Ghana, Great Britain, Greece, Guatemala, Haiti, Honduras, India, Italy, Jamaica, Kenya, Korea, Mexico, Pakistan, Panama, Peru, Philippines, Russia, Singapore, South Africa, Spain, Thailand, and Vietnam. A prosepective petitioner who is going abroad to adopt or locate a child in one of these countries should file Form I-600 at the INS office having jurisdiction over the place where the child is residing or will be located unless the case is being retained at the stateside office.

However, a prospective petitioner who is going abroad to any other country to adopt or locate a child should file Form I-600 at the American embassy or consulate having jurisdiction over the place where the child is residing or wil be located unless the case is being retained at the stateside office.

The case may be retained at the stateside office, if the petitioner requests it and if it appears that the case will be processed more quickly in that manner. Form I-600 must be accompanied by all the evidence required on the instruction sheet of that form, except that the evidence required by and submitted with this form need not be furnished.

## 6. General Filing Instructions.

**A.** Type or print legibly in ink.

**B.** If extra space is needed to complete any item, attach ¿ continuation sheet, indicate the item number, and date and sign each sheet.

C. **Translations.** Any foreign language document must be accompanied by a full English translation, which the translator has certified as complete and correct, and by the translator's certification that he or she is competent to translate the foreign language into English.

D. **Copies.** If these instruction state that a copy of a document may be filed with this petition and you choose to send us the original, we may keep that original for our records.

## 7. Submission of petition.

A petitioner residing in the United States should send the completed petition to the INS office having jurisdiction over his/her place of residence. A petitioner residing outside the United States should consult the nearest American embassy or consulate designated to act on the petition.

## 8. Fee. Read instructions carefully.

A fee of four hundred and sixty dollars ($460) must be submitted for filing this petition. There is a fifty dollar ($50) per person, fingerprinting fee, in addition to the petition fee for each person residing in the United States and required to be fingerprinted. For example, if a petition is filed by a married couple residing in the United States with one additional adult member in their household, the total of fees that must be submitted is $610. However, if a petition is filed by a married couple residing abroad, only the petition fee of $460 must be submitted.

One check or money order may be submitted for both the petition fee and the fingerprinting fees. It cannot be refunded regardless of the action taken on the petition. **Do not mail cash. All fees must be submitted in the exact amount.** Payment by a check or money order must be drawn on a bank or other institution located in the United States and be payable in United States currency.

If the petitioner resides in Guam, the check or money order must be payable to the "Treasurer, Guam."

If the petitioner resides in the Virgin Islands, check or money order must be payable to the "Commissioner of Finance of the Virgin Islands."

All other petitioners must make the check or money order payable to the "Immigration and Naturalization Service." When a check is drawn on the account of a person other than the petitioner, the name of the petitioner must be entered on the face of the check.

If petition is submitted from outside the United States, remittance may be made by a bank international money order or foreign draft drawn on a financial institution in the United States and payable to the Immigration and Naturalization Service in United States currency. Personal checks are accepted subject to collectibility. An uncollectible check in payment of a petition fee will render the petition and any document issued invalid. A charge of $30.00 will be imposed if a check in payment of a fee is not honored by the bank on which it is drawn. When more than one petition is submitted by the same petitioner in behalf of orphans who are siblings, only one set of petition and fingerprinting fees is required.

## 9. Assistance.

Assistance may be obtained from a recognized social agency or from any public or private agency. The following recognized social agencies, which have offices in many of the principal cities of the United States, have agreed to furnish assistance:

**Bethany Christian Services.**
2600 Fivemile Road NE
Grand Rapids, MI. 419525
Tel: (616) 224-7446
Fax: (616) 224-7585

**Catholic Legal Immigration Network, Inc., (CLINIC).**
415 Michigan Avenue, NE., Suite 150
Washington, DC 20017
Tel: (202) 635-2556
Fax: (202) 635-2649

**International Social Services/U.S. of America Branch**
700 Light Street
Baltimore, MD. 21230
Tel: (410) 230-2734
Fax: (410) 230-2741

**United States Catholic Conference Migration and Refugee Services (USCC/MRS).**
3211 4th Street, NE
Washington, DC 20017
Tel: (202) 541-3352
Fax: (202) 722-8800

## 10. Penalties.

Willful false statements on this form or supporting documents can be punished by fine or imprisonment. U.S. Code, Title 18, Sec. 1001 (formerly Sec. 80.)

## 11 Authority.

8 USC 1154(a). Routine uses for disclosure under the Privacy Act of 1974 have been published in the Federal Register and are available upon request. INS will use the information to determine immigrant eligibility. Submission of the information is voluntary, but failure to provide any or all of the information may result in denial of the petition.

## 12 Reporting Burden.

A person is not required to respond to a collection of information unless it displays a currently valid OMB control number. Public reporting burden for this collection of information is estimated to average 30 minutes per response, including the time for reviewing instructions, searching existing data sources, gathering and maintaining the data needed, and completing and reviewing the collection of information. Send comments regarding this burden estimate or any other aspect of this collection of information, including suggestions for reducing this burden, to: Immigration and Naturalization Service, HQPDI, 425 I Street, N.W., Room 4034, Washington, DC 20536; OMB No. 1115-0049. **DO NOT MAIL YOUR COMPLETED APPLICATION TO THIS ADDRESS.**

# Petition to Classify Orphan as an Immediate Relative

**U.S. Department of Justice**
Immigration and Naturalization Service

[Section 101 (b)(1)(F) of the Immigration and Nationality Act, as amended.]

## Please do not write in this block.

TO THE SECRETARY OF STATE;
The petition was filed by:

☐ Married petitioner    ☐ Unmarried petitioner

The petition is approved for orphan:

☐ Adopted abroad    ☐ Coming to U.S. for adoption. Preadoption requirements have been met.

Remarks:

Fee Stamp

File number

DATE OF ACTION

DD

DISTRICT

## Please type or print legibly in ink. Use a separate petition for each child.

*Petition is being made to classify the named orphan as an immediate relative.*

### BLOCK I - Information about prospective

1. My name is: (Last)    (First)    (Middle)

2. Other names used (including maiden name if appropriate):

3. I reside in the U.S.    (C/O if appropriate)    (Apt. No.)

   (Number and street)    (Town or city)    (State)    (Zip Code)

4. Address abroad (if any)(Number and street)    (Apt. No.)

   (Town or city)    (Province)    (Country)

5. I was born on:    (Month)    (Day)    (Year)

   In: (Town or City)    (State or Province)    (Country)

6. My phone number is: (Include Area Code)

7. My marital status is:
   ☐ Married
   ☐ Widowed
   ☐ Divorced
   ☐ Single
      ☐ I have never been married.
      ☐ I have been previously married _____ time(s).

8. If you are now married, give the following information:

   Date and place of present marriage

   Name of present spouse (include maiden name of wife)

   Date of birth of spouse    Place of birth of spouse

   Number of prior marriages of spouse

   My spouse resides ☐ With me    ☐ Apart from me
   (provide address below)
   (Apt. No.)    (No. and street)    (City)    (State)    (Country)

9. I am a citizen of the United States through:
   ☐ Birth    ☐ Parents    ☐ Naturalization
   If acquired through naturalization, give name under which naturalized, number of naturalization certificate, and date and place of naturalization:

   If not, submit evidence of citizenship. See Instruction 2.a(2).

   If acquired through parentage, have you obtained a certificate in your own name based on that acquisition?
   ☐ No    ☐ Yes

   Have you or any person through whom you claimed citizenship ever lost United States citizenship?
   ☐ No    ☐ Yes (If yes, attach detailed explanation.)

*Continue on reverse.*

| Received | Trans. In | Ret'd Trans. Out | Completed |
|---|---|---|---|
|  |  |  |  |

## BLOCK II - Information about orphan beneficiary

**10.** Name at birth  (First)  (Middle)  (Last)

**11.** Name at present  (First)  (Middle)  (Last)

**12.** Any other names by which orphan is or was known.

**13.** Sex  ☐ Male  **14.** Date of birth (Month/Day/Year)
☐ Female

**15.** Place of birth  (City)  (State or Province)  (Country)

**16.** The beneficiary is an orphan because (check One)
☐ He/she has no parents.
☐ He/she has only one parent who is the sole or surviving

**17.** If the orphan has only one parent, answer the following
a. State what has become of the other parent:

b. Is the remaining parent capable of providing for the orphan's
support?  ☐ Yes  ☐ No
c. Has the remaining parent, in writing, irrevocably released
orphan for emigration and adoption? ☐ Yes  ☐ No

**18.** Has the orphan been adopted abroad by the petitioner and
jointly or the unmarried petitioner?  ☐ Yes  ☐ No

If yes, did the petitioner and spouse or unmarried petitioner
personally see and observe the child prior to or during the
adoption proceedings?  ☐ Yes  ☐ No

Date of adoption

Place of adoption

**19.** If either answer in question 18 is "No", answer the following:
a. Do petitioner and spouse jointly or does the unmarried
intend to adopt the orphan in the United States?
☐ Yes  ☐ No
b. Have the preadoption requirements, if any, of the orphan's
proposed state of residence been met?
☐ Yes  ☐ No
c. If b. is answered "No", will they be met later?
☐ Yes  ☐ No

**20.** To petitioner's knowledge, does the orphan have any physical or
affliction?  ☐ Yes  ☐ No
If "Yes", name the affliction.

**21.** Who has legal custody of the child?

**22.** Name of child welfare agency, if any, assisting in this case:

**23.** Name of attorney abroad, if any, representing petitioner in this

Address of above.

**24.** Address in the United States where orphan will reside.

**25.** Present address of orphan.

**25.** If orphan is residing in an institution, give full name of institution.

**26.** If orphan is not residing in an institution, give full name of person
whom orphan is residing.

**27.** Give any additional information necessary to locate orphan such
as name of district, section, zone or locality in which orphan
resides.

**28.** Location of American Consulate where application for visa will
be made.
(City in Foreign Country)  (Foreign Country)

---

**Certification of prospective petitioner**
I certify under penalty of perjury under the laws of the United
States of America that the foregoing is true and correct and that
I will care for an orphan/orphans properly if admitted to the
United States.

*(Signature of Prospective Petitioner)*

Executed on (Date)

**Certification of married prospective petitioner's spouse**
I certify under penalty of perjury under the laws of the United
States of America that the foregoing is true and correct and that
my spouse and I will care for an orphan/orphans properly if
admitted to the United States.

*(Signature of Prospective Petitioner)*

Executed on (Date)

---

**Signature of person preparing form, if other than petitioner**
I declare that this document was prepared by me at the request of the
prospective petitioner and is based on all information of which I have
any knowledge.

*(Signature)*

Address

Executed on (Date)

**U.S. Department of Justice**
Immigration and Naturalization Service

# Application for Advance Processing of Orphan Petition (8CFR 204.1(b)(3))

Advanced processing is a procedure for completing the part of an orphan petition relating to the petitioner before an orphan is located so that there will be no unnecessary delays in processing the petition after an orphan is located.
**USE THIS FORM ONLY IF YOU WISH TO ADOPT AN ORPHAN WHO HAS NOT YET BEEN LOCATED AND IDENTIFIED OR YOU AND/OR YOUR SPOUSE, IF MARRIED, ARE/IS GOING ABROAD TO ADOPT OR LOCATE A CHILD.**
This application is not a petition to classify orphan as an immediate relative (Form I-600).

## 1. Eligibility.

**A. Eligibility for advance processing application (Form I-600A).** An application for advance processing may be filed by a married United States citizen and spouse. The spouse does not need to be a United States citizen. It may also be filed by an unmarried United States citizen at least 24 years of age provided that he or she will be at least 25 at the time of the adoption and of filing an orphan petition in behalf of a child.

**B. Eligibility for Orphan Petition (Form I-600).** In addition to the requirements concerning the citizenship and age of the petitioner described in Instruction 1a, when a child is located and identified, the following eligibility requirements will apply:

(1) **Child.** Under immigration law, an orphan is an alien child who has no parents because of the death or disappearance of, abandonment or desertion by, or separation or loss from both parents. An orphan is also a child who has only one parent who is not capable of taking care of the orphan and who has, in writing, irrevocably released the orphan for emigration and adoption. A petition to classify an alien as an orphan may not be filed in behalf of a child in the United States unless that child is in parole status and has not been adopted in the United States. The petition must be filed before the child's 16th birthday.

(2) **Adoption abroad.** If the orphan was adopted abroad, it must be established that both the married petitioner and spouse or the unmarried petitioner personally saw and observed the child prior to or during the adoption proceedings. The adoption decree must show that a married petitioner and spouse adopted the child jointly or that an unmarried petitioner was at least 25 years of age at the time of the adoption.

(3) **Proxy adoption abroad.** If both the petitioner and spouse or the unmarried petitioner did not personally see and observe the child prior to or during the adoption proceedings abroad, the petitioner (and spouse, if married) must submit a statement indicating the petitioner's (and, if married, the spouse's) willingness and intent to readopt the child in the United States. If requested, the petitioner must submit a statement by an official of the state in which the child will reside that readoption is permissible in that state. In addition, evidence of compliance with the preadoption requirements, if any, of that state must be submitted.

(4) **Preadoption requirements.** If the orphan has not been adopted abroad, the petitioner and spouse or the unmarried petitioner must establish that the child will be adopted in the United States by the petitioner and spouse jointly or by the unmarried petitioner and that the preadoption requirement, if any, of the state of the orphan's proposed residence have been met.

## 2. Filing Advance Processing Application.

An advance processing application must be submitted on Form I-600A with the certification of prospective petitioner executed and the required fee. If the prospective petitioner is married, the Form I-600A must also be signed by the prospective petitioner's spouse. The application must be accompanied by:

**A. Proof of United States citizenship of the prospective petitioner.**

(1) If the petitioner is a citizen by reason of birth in the United States, submit a copy of the petitioner's birth certificate, or if birth certificate is unobtainable, a copy of petitioner's baptismal certificate under seal of the church, showing place of birth, (baptism must have occurred within two months after birth), or if a birth or baptismal certificate cannot be obtained, affidavits of two United States citizens who have personal knowledge of petitioner's birth in the United States.

(2) If the petitioner was born outside the United States and became a citizen through the naturalization or citizenship of a parent or husband and has not been issued a certificate of citizenship in his or her own name, submit evidence of the citizenship and marriage of the parent or husband, as well as termination of any prior marriages. Also, if petitioner claims citizenship through a parent, submit a copy of the petitioner's birth certificate and a separate statement showing the date, place, and means of all his/her arrivals and departures into and out of the United States.

(3) If petitioner's naturalization occurred within 90 days immediately preceding the filing of this petition, or if it occurred prior to September 27, 1906, a copy of the naturalization certificate must accompany the petition.

(4) An unexpired U.S. passport initially issued for ten years may also be submitted.

**B. Proof of marriage of petitioner and spouse.**
The married petitioner should submit a copy of the certificate of the marriage and proof of termination of all prior marriages of himself or herself and spouse. In the case of an unmarried petitioner who was previously married, submit proof of termination of all prior marriages. **NOTE:** If any change occurs in the petitioner's marital status while the case is pending, the district director should be notified immediately.

**C. A home study** with a statement or attachment recommending or approving of the adoption or proposed adoption signed by an official of the responsible state agency in the state of the child's proposed residence or of an agency authorized by that state, or, in the case of a child adopted abroad, of an appropriate public or private adoption agency which is licensed in the United States. Both individuals and organizations may qualify as agencies. If the recommending agency is a licensed agency, the recommendation must set forth that it is licensed, the state in which it is licensed, its license number, if any, and the period of validity of its license. The research, including interviewing, however, and the preparation of the home study may be done by an individual or group in the United States or abroad satisfactory to the recommending agency. A responsible state agency or licensed agency can accept a home study made by an unlicensed or foreign agency and use that home study as a basis for a favorable recommendation. The home study must contain, but is not limited to, the following elements:

(1) the financial ability of the adoptive or prospective parent or parents to rear and educate the child.

(2) a detailed description of the living accommodations where the adoptive or prospective parent or parents currently reside.

(3) A detailed description of the living accommodations where the child will reside.

(4) A factual evaluation of the physical, mental, and moral capabilities of the adoptive or prospective parent or parents in relation to rearing and educating the child.

**D. Fingerprints.**
Each member of the married prospective adoptive couple or the married prospective adoptive parent, and each additional adult member of the prospective adoptive parents' household must be fingerprinted in connection with this petition.

(1) *Petitioners residing in the United States.* After filing this petition, INS will notify each person in writing of the time and location where they must go to be fingerprinted. Failure to appear to be fingerprinted may result in denial of the petition.

(2) *Petitioners residing Abroad.* Completed fingerprint cards (Forms FD-258)

must be submitted with the petition. Do not bend, fold, or crease completed fingerprint cards. Fingerprint cards must be prepared by a United States consular office or a United States military installation.

## 3. General Filing Instructions.

**A. Type or print legibly in ink.**

**B. If extra space is needed** to complete any item, attach a continuation sheet, indicate the item number, and date and sign each sheet.

**C. Translations.** Any foreign language document must be accompanied by a full English translation, which the translator has certified as complete and correct, and by the translator's certification that he or she is competent to translate the foreign language into English.

**D. Copies.** If these instructions state that a copy of a document may be filed with this petition and you choose to send us the original, we may keep that original for our records.

## 4. Submission of Application.

A prospective petitioner residing in the United States should send the completed application to the office of this Service having jurisdiction over his or her place of residence. A prospective petitioner residing outside the United States should consult the nearest American consulate for the overseas or stateside INS office designated to act on the application.

## 5. Fee. (Read instructions carefully.)

A fee of four hundred and sixty dollars ($460) must be submitted for filing this petition. There is a fifty dollar ($50) per person fingerprinting fee in addition to the petition fee for each person residing in the United States and required to be fingerprinted. For example, if a petition is filed by a married couple residing in the United States with one additional adult member in their household, the total of fees that must be submitted is $610. However, if a petition is filed by a married couple residing abroad, only the petition fee of $460 must be submitted.

One check or money order may be submitted for both the petition fee and the fingerprinting fees. All fees must be submitted in the exact amount. Payment by check or money order must be drawn on a bank or other institution located in the United States and be payable in United States currency.

If petitioner resides in Guam, the check or money order must be payable to the "Treasurer, Guam."

If petitioner resides in the Virgin Islands, the check or money order must be payable to the "Commissioner of Finance of the Virgin Islands."

All other petitioners must make the check or money order payable to the "Immigration and Naturalization Service." When a check is drawn on the account of a person other than the petitioner, the name of the petitioner must be entered on the face of the check.

If petition is submitted from outside the United States, remittance may be made by bank international money order or foreign draft drawn on a financial institution in the United States and payable to the Immigration and Naturalization Service in United States currency. Personal checks are accepted subject to collectibility. An uncollectible check in payment of a petition fee will render the petition and any document issued invalid. A charge of $30.00 will be imposed if a check in payment of a fee is not honored by the bank on which it is drawn.

**When more than one petition is submitted by the same petitioner in behalf of orphans who are siblings, only one set of petition and fingerprinting fees is required.**

## 6. When Child/Children Located and/or Identified.

A separate Form I-600, Petition to Classify Orphan as an Immediate Relative, must be filed for each child. A new fee is not required if only one form I-600 is filed and it is filed within one year of completion of all advance processing in a case where there has been a favorable determination concerning the beneficiary orphan.

Normally, Form I-600 should be submitted to the INS office where the advance processing application was filed. The immigration and Naturalization Service has offices in the following countries: Austria, China, Cuba, Denmark, Domincan Republic, Ecuador, El Salvador, Germany, Ghana, Great Britain, Greece, Guatemala, Haiti, Honduras, India, Italy, Jamaica, Kenya, Korea, Mexico, Pakistan, Panama, Peru, Philippines, Russia, Singapore, South Africa, Spain, Thailand, and Vietnam. A prospective petitioner who is going abroad to adopt or locate a child in one of these countries should file Form I-600 at the INS office having jurisdiction over the place where the child is residing or will be located, unless the case is being retained at the stateside office.

However, a prospective petitioner who is going abroad to any other country to adopt or locate a child should file Form I-600 at the American consulate or embassy having jurisdiction over the place where the child is residing or will be located unless the case is being retained at the stateside office.

The case may be retained at the stateside office, if the petitioner requests it and if it appears that the case will be processed more quickly in that manner. Form I-600 must be accompanied by all the evidence required on the instruction sheet of that form, except that the evidence required by and submitted with this form need not be furnished.

## 7. Assistance.

Assistance may be obtained from a recognized social agency or from any public or private agency. The following recognized social agencies, which have offices in many of the principal cities of the United States, have agreed to furnish assistance:

**Bethany Christian Services.**
2600 Fivemile Road NE
Grand Rapids, MI. 49525
Tel: (616) 224-7446
Fax: (616) 224-7585

**Catholic Legal Immigration Network, Inc. (CLINIC)**
415 Michigan Avenue, NE., Suite 150
Washington, DC 20017
Tel: (202) 635-2556
Fax: (202) 632-2649

**International Social Services/U.S. of America Branch.**
700 Light Street
Baltimore, MD. 21230
Tel: (410) 230-2734
Fax: (410) 230-2741

**United States Catholic Conference Migration and Refugee Services (USCC/MRS).**
3211 4th Street, NE
Washington, DC 20017
Tel: (202) 541-3352
Fax: (202) 722-8800

## 8. Penalties.

Willful false statements on this form or supporting documents can be punished by fine or imprisonment. U.S. Code, Title 18, Sec. 1001 (Formerly Sec. 80.)

## 9. Authority.

8 U.S.C 1154(a). Routine uses for disclosure under the Privacy Act of 1974 have been published in the Federal Register and are available upon request. The Immigration and Naturalization Service will use the information to determine immigrant eligibility. Submission of the information is voluntary, but failure to provide any or all of the information may result in denial of the petition.

## 10. Reporting Burden.

A person is not required to respond to a collection of information unless it displays a currently valid OMB control number. Public reporting burden for this collection of information is estimated to average 30 minutes per response, including the time for reviewing instructions, searching existing data sources, gathering and maintaining the data needed, and completing and reviewing the collection of information. Send comments regarding this burden estimate or any other aspect of this collection of information, including suggestions for reducing this burden, to: Immigration and Naturalization Service, HQPDI, 425 I Street, N.W., Room 4034, Washington, DC 20536; OMB No. 1115-0049. **DO NOT MAIL YOUR COMPLETED APPLICATION TO THIS ADDRESS.**

OMB No. 1115-0049

**U.S. Department of Justice**
Immigration and Naturalization Service

# Application for Advance Processing of Orphan Petition [8CFR 204.1(b)(3)]

## Please do not write in this block.

It has been determined that the

☐ Married            ☐ Unmarried

Fee Stamp

There

☐ are            ☐ are not

preadoptive requirements in the state of the child's proposed residence.

The following is a description of the preadoption requirements, if any, of the state of the child's proposed residence:

_____

_____

DATE OF FAVORABLE DETERMINATION

DD

DISTRICT

The preadoption requirements, if any,

☐ have been met.            ☐ have not been met.

File number of petitioner, if applicable

## Please type or print legibly in ink.

*Application is made by the named prospective petitioner for advance processing of an orphan petition.*

**BLOCK I - Information about prospective petitioner**

1. My name is: (Last)    (First)    (Middle)

2. Other names used (including maiden name if appropriate):

3. I reside in the U.S. at:    (C/O if appropriate)    (Apt. No.)

   (Number and street)    (Town or city)    (State)    (ZIP Code)

4. Address abroad (if any):    (Number and street)    (Apt. No.)

   (Town or city)    (Province)    (Country)

5. I was born on:    (Month)    (Day)    (Year)

   In:    (Town or City)    (State or Province)    (Country)

6. My phone number is:    (Include Area Code)

7. My marital status is:

   ☐ Married
   ☐ Widowed
   ☐ Divorced
   ☐ Single

   ☐ I have never been married.
   ☐ I have been previously married _____ time(s).

8. If you are now married, give the following information:

   Date and place of present marriage

   Name of present spouse (include maiden name of wife)

   Date of birth of spouse    Place of birth of spouse

   Number of prior marriages of spouse

   My spouse resides ☐ With me    ☐ Apart from me (provide address below)

   (Apt. No.)    (No. and street)    (City)    (State)    (Country)

9. I am a citizen of the United States through:
   ☐ Birth    ☐ Parents    ☐ Naturalization

   If acquired through naturalization, give name under which naturalized, number of naturalization certificate, and date and place of naturalization.

   If not, submit evidence of citizenship.  See Instruction 2.a(2).

   If acquired through parentage, have you obtained a certificate in your own name based on that acquisition?
   ☐ No    ☐ Yes

   Have you or any person through whom you claimed citizenship ever lost United States citizenship?
   ☐ No    ☐ Yes (If yes, attach detailed explanation.)

*Continue on reverse.*

| Received | Trans. In | Ret'd Trans. Out | Completed |
|----------|-----------|------------------|-----------|
|          |           |                  |           |

**BLOCK II - General information**

10. Name and address of organization or individual assisting you in locating or identifying an orphan

(Name)

_____

(Address)

11. Do you plan to travel abroad to locate or adopt a child?

☐ Yes ☐ No

12. Does your spouse, if any, plan to travel abroad to locate or adopt a child?

☐ Yes ☐ No

13. If the answer to question 11 or 12 is "yes," give the following information:

a. Your date of intended departure _____

b. Your spouse's date of intended departure _____

c. City, province _____

14. Will the child come to the United States for adoption after compliance with the preadoption requirements, if any, of the state of proposed residence?

☐ Yes ☐ No

15. If the answer to question 14 is "no," will the child be adopted abroad after having been personally seen and observed by you and your spouse, if married?

☐ Yes ☐ No

16. Where do you wish to file your orphan petition?

The service office located at

_____

The American Embassy or Consulate at

_____

17. Do you plan to adopt more than one child?

☐ Yes ☐ No

If "Yes", how many children do you plan to adopt?

---

**Certification of prospective petitioner**

I certify, under penalty of perjury under the laws of the United States of America, that the foregoing is true and correct and that I will care for an orphan/orphans properly if admitted to the United States.

_____
(Signature of Prospective Petitioner)

_____
Executed on (Date)

**Certification of married prospective petitioner's spouse**

I certify, under penalty of perjury under the laws of the United States of America, that the foregoing is true and correct and that my spouse and I will care for an orphan/orphans properly if admitted to the United States.

_____
(Signature of Prospective Petitioner)

_____
Executed on (Date)

---

**Signature of person preparing form, if other than petitioner**

I declare that this document was prepared by me at the request of the prospective petitioner and is based on all information of which I have any knowledge.

(Signature)

Address

Executed on (Date)

## Purpose of This Form.

This form is for a conditional resident who obtained such status through marriage to petition to the Immigration and Naturalization Service (INS) to remove the conditions on his or her residence.

## Who May File.

If you were granted conditional resident status through marriage to a U.S. citizen or permanent resident, use this form to petition for the removal of those conditions. Your petition should be filed jointly by you and the spouse through whom you obtained conditional status if you are still married. However, you may apply for a waiver of this joint filing requirement on this form if:

- you entered into the marriage in good faith, but your spouse subsequently died;
- you entered into the marriage in good faith, but the marriage was later terminated due to divorce or annulment;
- you entered into the marriage in good faith, and remain married, but have been battered or subjected to extreme cruelty by your U.S. citizen or permanent resident spouse; or
- the termination of your status and removal would result in extreme hardship.

You may include your conditional resident children in your petition, or they may file separately.

## General Filing Instructions.

Please answer all questions by typing or clearly printing in black ink. Indicate that an item is not applicable with "N/A." If an answer is "none," write "none." If you need extra space to answer any item, attach a sheet of paper with your name and your alien registration number (A#), and indicate the number of the item to which the answer refers. You must file your petition with the required initial evidence. Your petition must be properly signed and accompanied by the correct fee. If you are under 14 years of age, your parent or guardian may sign the petition on your behalf.

*Translations.* Any foreign language document must be accompanied by a full English translation that the translator has certified as complete and correct, and by the translator's certification that he or she is competent to translate the foreign language into English.

*Copies.* If these instructions state that a copy of a document may be filed with this petition and you choose to send us the original, we may keep that original for our records.

## Initial Evidence.

*Permanent Resident Card.* You must file your petition with a copy of your permanent resident or alien registration card, and a copy of the permanent resident or alien registration card of any of your conditional resident children you are including in your petition.

*Evidence of the Relationship.* Submit copies of documents indicating that the marriage upon which you were granted conditional status was entered into in "good faith" and was not for the purpose of circumventing immigration laws. You should submit copies of as many documents as you wish to establish this fact and to demonstrate the circumstances of the relationship from the date of the marriage to the present date, and to demonstrate any circumstances surrounding the end of the relationship, if it has ended. The documents should cover as much of the period since your marriage as possible. Examples of such documents are:

- birth certificate(s) of child(ren) born to the marriage.

- lease or mortgage contracts showing joint occupancy and/or ownership of your communal residence.

- financial records showing joint ownership of assets and joint responsibility for liabilities, such as joint savings and checking accounts, joint federal and state tax returns, insurance policies that show the other spouse as the beneficiary, joint utility bills, joint installments or other loans.

- other documents you consider relevant to establish that your marriage was not entered into in order to evade the immigration laws of the United States.

- affidavits sworn to or affirmed by at least two people who have known both of you since your conditional residence was granted and have personal knowledge of your marriage and relationship. (Such persons may be required to testify before an immigration officer as to the information contained in the affidavit.) The original affidavit must be submitted and also contain the following information regarding the person making the affidavit: his or her full name and address; date and place of birth; relationship to you or your spouse, if any; and full information and complete details explaining how the person acquired his or her knowledge. Affidavits must be supported by other types of evidence listed above.

*If you are filing to waive the joint filing requirement due to the death of your spouse,* also submit a copy of the death certificate with your petition.

*If you are filing to waive the joint filing requirement because your marriage has been terminated,* also submit a copy of the divorce decree or other document terminating or annulling the marriage with your petition.

*If you are filing to waive the joint filing requirement because you and/or your conditional resident child were battered or subjected to extreme cruelty,* also file your petition with the following:

- Evidence of the physical abuse, such as copies of reports or official records issued by police, judges, medical personnel, school officials, and representatives of social service agencies, and original affidavits as described under *Evidence of the Relationship;* or

- Evidence of the abuse, such as copies of reports or official records issued by police, courts, medical personnel, school officials, clergy, social workers and other social service agency personnel. You may also submit any legal documents relating to an order of protection against the abuser or relating to any legal steps you may have taken to end the abuse. You may also submit evidence that you sought safe haven in a battered women's shelter or similar refuge, as well as photographs evidencing your injuries.

- A copy of your divorce decree, if your marriage was terminated by divorce on grounds of physical abuse or extreme cruelty.

*If you are filing for a waiver of the joint filing requirement because the termination of your status, and removal would result in "extreme hardship,"* you must also file your petition with evidence your removal would result in hardship significantly greater than the hardship encountered by other aliens who are removed from this country after extended stays. The evidence must relate only to those factors that arose since you became a conditional resident.

*If you are a child filing separately from your parent,* also file your petition with a full explanation as to why you are filing separately, along with copies of any supporting documentation.

## When to File.
*Filing jointly.* If you are filing this petition jointly with your spouse, you must file it during the 90 days immediately before the second anniversary of the date you were accorded conditional resident status. This is the date your conditional residence expires. However, if you and your spouse are outside the United States on orders of the U.S. Government during the period in which the petition must be filed, you may file it within 90 days of your return to the United States.

*Filing with a request that the joint filing requirement be waived.* You may file this petition at any time after you are granted conditional resident status and before you are removed.

*Effect of Not Filing.* If this petition is not filed, you will automatically lose your permanent resident status as of the second anniversary of the date on which you were granted this status. You will then become removable from the United States. If your failure to file was through no fault of your own, you may file your petition late with a written explanation and request that INS excuse the late filing. Failure to file before the expiration date may be excused if you demonstrate when you file the application that the delay was due to extraordinary circumstances beyond your control and that the length of the delay was reasonable.

## Where to File.
If you live in Connecticut, Delaware, District of Columbia, Maine, Maryland, Massachusetts, New Hampshire, New Jersey, New York, Pennsylvania, Puerto Rico, Rhode Island, Vermont, Virgin Islands, Virginia or West Virginia, mail your petition to:

**USINS Vermont Service Center,**
**75 Lower Welden Street**
**St. Albans, VT 05479-0001.**

If you live in Alabama, Arkansas, Florida, Georgia, Kentucky, Louisiana, Mississippi, New Mexico, North Carolina, Oklahoma, South Carolina, Tennessee or Texas, mail your petition to:

**USINS Texas Service Center,**
**P.O. Box 850965,**
**Mesquite,TX 75185-0965.**

If you live in Arizona, California, Guam, Hawaii or Nevada, mail your petition to:

**USINS California Service Center,**
**P.O. Box 10751**
**Laguna Niguel, CA 92607-0751.**

If you live in elsewhere in the U.S., mail your petition to:

**USINS Nebraska Service Center,**
**P.O. Box 87751**
**Lincoln, NE 68501-7751.**

## Fee.
The fee for this petition is $145.00. The fee must be submitted in the exact amount. It cannot be refunded. **DO NOT MAIL CASH.**

All checks and money orders must be drawn on a bank or other institution located in the United States and must be payable in United States currency. The check or money order should be made payable to the Immigration and Naturalization Service, except that:

- if you live in Guam and are filing this petition in Guam, make your check or money order payable to the "Treasurer, Guam."

- if you are living in the Virgin Islands and are filing this application in the Virgin Islands, make your check or money order payable to the "Commissioner of Finance of the Virgin Islands."

Checks are accepted subject to collection. An uncollected check will render the application and any document issued invalid. A charge of $30.00 will be imposed if a check in payment of a fee is not honored by the bank on which it is drawn.

## Processing Information.
*Acceptance.* Any petition that is not signed or accompanied by the correct fee, will be rejected with a notice that the petition is deficient. You may correct the deficiency and resubmit the petition. A petition is not considered properly filed until accepted by INS.

*Initial processing.* Once a petition has been accepted, it will be checked for completeness, including submission of the required initial evidence. If you do not completely fill out the form, or file it without required initial evidence, you will not establish a basis for eligibility and we may deny your petition.

*Requests for more information or interview.* We may request more information or evidence, or we may request that you appear at an INS office for an interview. We may also request that you submit the originals of any copy. We will return these originals when they are no longer required.

*Decision.* You will be advised in writing of the decision on your petition.

## Penalties.
If you knowingly and willfully falsify or conceal a material fact or submit a false document with this request, we will deny the benefit you are filing for and may deny any other immigration benefit. In addition, you will face severe penalties provided by law and may be subject to criminal prosecution.

## Privacy Act Notice.
We ask for the information on this form and associated evidence, to determine if you have established eligibility for the immigration benefit you are seeking. Our legal right to ask for this information is in 8 USC 1184, 1255 and 1258. Failure to provide this information and any requested evidence may delay a final decision or result in denial of your request.

All the information provided on this form, including addresses, are protected by the Privacy Act and the Freedom of Information Act. This information may be released to another government agency. However, the information will not be released in any form whatsoever to a third party who requests it without a court order, or without your written consent, or, in the case of a child, the written consent of the parent or legal guardian who filed the form on the child's behalf.

## Paperwork Reduction Act Notice.

We try to create forms and instructions that are accurate, can be easily understood and that impose the least possible burden on you to provide us with information. Often this is difficult because some immigration laws are very complex. The estimated average time to complete and file this application is as follows: (1) 15 minutes to learn about the law and form; (2) 15 minutes to complete the form; and (3) 50 minutes to assemble and file the petition; for a total estimated average of 1 hour and 20 minutes per petition. If you have comments regarding the accuracy of this estimate, or suggestions for making this form simpler, you may write to the Immigration and Naturalization Service, HQPDI, 425 I Street, N.W., Room 4034, Washington, DC 20536; OMB No. 1115-0145. **DO NOT MAIL YOUR COMPLETED APPLICATION TO THIS ADDRESS.**

## Do You Need Help or INS Forms?

If you need information on immigration laws, regulations or procedures or INS forms, call our National Customer Service Center at **1-800-375-5283**, or visit the INS Internet website at **www.ins.usdoj.gov**.

U.S. Department of Justice
Immigration and Naturalization Service

OMB No. 1115-0145

# Petition to Remove the Conditions on Residence

## START HERE - Please Type or Print

### Part 1.  Information about you.

| Family Name | Given Name | Middle Initial |
|---|---|---|

Address - C/O:

| Street Number and Name | | Apt. # |
|---|---|---|

| City | State or Province |
|---|---|

| Country | ZIP/Postal Code |
|---|---|

| Date of Birth (month/day/year) | Country of Birth |
|---|---|

| Social Security # (if any) | A# |
|---|---|

Conditional residence expires on (month/day/year)

Mailing address if different from address listed above:

| Street Number and Name | | Apt. # |
|---|---|---|

| City | State or Province |
|---|---|

| Country | ZIP/Postal Code |
|---|---|

### Part 2.  Basis for petition (check one).

a. ☐ My conditional residence is based on my marriage to a U.S. citizen or permanent resident, and we are filing this petition together.

b. ☐ I am a child who entered as a conditional permanent resident and I am unable to be included in a Joint Petition to Remove the Conditional Basis of Alien's Permanent Residence (Form I-751) filed by my parent(s).

My conditional residence is based on my marriage to a U.S. citizen or permanent resident, but I am unable to file a joint petition and I request a waiver because: (check one)

c. ☐ My spouse is deceased.

d. ☐ I entered into the marriage in good faith, but the marriage was terminated through divorce/annulment.

e. ☐ I am a conditional resident spouse who entered into the marriage in good faith, or I am a conditional resident child, who has been battered or subjected to extreme cruelty by my citizen or permanent resident spouse or parent.

f. ☐ The termination of my status and removal from the United States would result in an extreme hardship.

### Part 3.  Additional information about you.

| Other Names Used (including maiden name): | Telephone # |
|---|---|

| Date of Marriage | Place of Marriage |
|---|---|

If your spouse is deceased, give the date of death. (month/day/year)

- Are you in removal or deportation proceedings?    ☐ Yes  ☐ No

- Was a fee paid to anyone other than an attorney in connection with this petition?    ☐ Yes  ☐ No

*Continued on back.*

Form I-751 (Rev. 06/05/02)Y Page 1

## Part 3. Additional information about you. (continued)

- Since becoming a conditional resident, have you ever been arrested, cited, charged, indicted, convicted, fined or imprisoned for breaking or violating any law or ordinace (excluding traffic regulations), or committed any crime for which you were not arrested?  ☐ Yes ☐ No

- If you are married, is this a different marriage than the one through which conditional residence status was obtained?  ☐ Yes ☐ No

- Have you resided at any other address since you became a permanent resident? *(If yes, attach a list of all addresses and dates.)*  ☐ Yes ☐ No

- Is your spouse currently serving with or employed by the U.S. government and serving outside the United States?  ☐ Yes ☐ No

## Part 4. Information about the spouse or parent through whom you gained your conditional residence.

| Family Name | Given Name | Middle Initial | Phone Number |
|---|---|---|---|
| | | | |

| Address | | | |
|---|---|---|---|

| Date of Birth (month/day/year) | Social Security # (if any) | A# |
|---|---|---|
| | | |

## Part 5. Information about your children. *List all your children. Attach another sheet(s) if necessary.*

| Name | Date of Birth (month/day/year) | If in U.S., give A number, current immigration status and U.S. address. | Living with you? |
|---|---|---|---|
| 1. | | | ☐ Yes ☐ No |
| 2. | | | ☐ Yes ☐ No |
| 3. | | | ☐ Yes ☐ No |
| 4. | | | ☐ Yes ☐ No |

## Part 6. Signature. *Read the information on penalties in the instructions before completing this section. If you checked block " a" in Part 2, your spouse must also sign below.*

I certify, under penalty of perjury under the laws of the United States of America, that this petition and the evidence submitted with it is all true and correct. If conditional residence was based on a marriage, I further certify that the marriage was entered into in accordance with the laws of the place where the marriage took place and was not for the purpose of procuring an immigration benefit. I also authorize the release of any information from my records that the Immigration and Naturalization Service needs to determine eligibility for the benefit sought.

| Signature | Print Name | Date |
|---|---|---|
| | | |
| Signature of Spouse | Print Name | Date |
| | | |

**Please note:** If you do not completely fill out this form or fail to submit any required documents listed in the instructions, you cannot be found eligible for the requested benefit and this petition may be denied.

## Part 7. Signature of person preparing form, if other than above.

I declare that I prepared this petition at the request of the above person and it is based on all information of which I have knowledge.

| Signature | Print Name | Date |
|---|---|---|
| | | |

Firm Name and Address

## Instructions for
## Application for Employment Authorization

**The Immigration and Naturalization Service (INS) recommends that you retain a copy of your completed application for your records.**

### Index

---

### Part 1. General.

**Purpose of the Application.** Certain aliens who are temporarily in the United States may file a Form I-765, Application for Employment Authorization, to request an Employment Authorization Document (EAD). Other aliens who are authorized to work in the United States without restrictions should also use this form to apply to the INS for a document evidencing such authorization. Please review Part 2: Eligibility Categories to determine whether you should use this form.

If you are a Lawful Permanent Resident, a Conditional Resident, or a nonimmigrant authorized to be employed with a specific employer under 8 CFR 274a.12(b), please do **NOT** use this form.

#### Definitions

**Employment Authorization Document (EAD):** Form I-688, Form I-688A, Form I-688B, Form I-766, or any successor document issued by the INS as evidence that the holder is authorized to work in the United States.

**Renewal EAD:** an EAD issued to an eligible applicant at or after the expiration of a previous EAD issued under the same category.

**Replacement EAD:** an EAD issued to an eligible applicant when the previously issued EAD has been lost, stolen, mutilated, or contains erroneous information, such as a misspelled name.

**Interim EAD:** an EAD issued to an eligible applicant when the INS has failed to adjudicate an application within 90 days of receipt of a properly filed EAD application or within 30 days of a properly filed initial EAD application based on an asylum application filed on or after January 4, 1995. The interim EAD will be granted for a period not to exceed 240 days and is subject to the conditions noted on the document.

---

### Part 2. Eligibility Categories.

The INS adjudicates a request for employment authorization by determining whether an applicant has submitted the required information and documentation, and whether the applicant is eligible. In order to determine your eligibility, you must identify the category in which you are eligible and fill in that category in question 16 on the Form I-765. Enter only **one** of the following category numbers on the application form. For example, if you are a refugee applying for an EAD, you should write "(a)(3)" at question 16.

For easier reference, the categories are subdivided as follows:

#### *Asylee/Refugee Categories*

**Refugee--(a)(3).** File your EAD application with either a copy of your Form I-590, Registration for Classification as Refugee, approval letter or a copy of a Form I-730, Refugee/Asylee Relative Petition, approval notice.

**Paroled as a Refugee--(a)(4).** File your EAD application with a copy of your Form I-94, Departure Record.

**Asylee (granted asylum)--(a)(5).** File your EAD application with a copy of the INS letter, or judge's decision, granting you asylum. It is not necessary to apply for an EAD as an asylee until 90 days before the expiration of your current EAD.

**Asylum Applicant (with a pending asylum application) who Filed for Asylum on or after January 4, 1995--(c)(8).** (For specific instructions for applicants with pending asylum claims, see page 5).

## Nationality Categories

**Citizen of Micronesia, the Marshall Islands or Palau--(a)(8).** File your EAD application if you were admitted to the United States as a citizen of the Federated States of Micronesia (CFA/FSM), the Marshall Islands (CFA/MIS), or Palau, pursuant to agreements between the United States and the former trust territories.

**Deferred Enforced Departure (DED) / Extended Voluntary Departure--(a)(11).** File your EAD application with evidence of your identity and nationality.

**Temporary Protected Status (TPS)--(a)(12).** File your EAD application with Form I-821, Application for Temporary Protected Status. If you are filing for an initial EAD based on your TPS status, include evidence of identity and nationality as required by the Form I-821 instructions.

**Temporary treatment benefits --(c)(19).** For an EAD based on 8 CFR 244.5. Include evidence of nationality and identity as required by the Form I-821 instructions.

- Extension of TPS status: include a copy (front and back) of your last available TPS document: EAD, Form I-94 or approval notice.

- Registration for TPS only without employment authorization: file the Form I-765, Form I-821, and a letter indicating that this form is for registration purposes only. No fee is required for the Form I-765 filed as part of TPS registration. (Form I-821 has separate fee requirements.)

**NACARA Section 203 Applicants who are eligible to apply for NACARA relief with INS--(c)(10).** See the instructions to Form I-881, Application for Suspension of Deportation or Special Rule Cancellation of Removal, to determine if you are eligible to apply for NACARA 203 relief with INS.

If you are eligible, follow the instructions below and submit your Form I-765 at the same time you file your Form I-881 application with INS:

- If you are filing a Form I-881 with INS, file your EAD application at the same time and at the same filing location. Your response to question 16 on the Form I-765 should be "(c)(10)."

- If you have already filed your I-881 application at the service center specified on the Form I-881, and now wish to apply for employment authorization, your response to question 16 on Form I-765 should be "(c)(10)." You should file your EAD application at the Service Center designated in Part 5 of these instructions.

- If you are a NACARA Section 203 applicant who previously filed a Form I-881 with the INS, and the application is still pending, you may renew your EAD. Your response to question 16 on Form I-765 should be "(c)(10)." Submit the required fee and the EAD application to the service center designated in Part 5 of these instructions.

**Dependent of TECRO E-1 Nonimmigrant--(c)(2).** File your EAD application with the required certification from the American Institute in Taiwan if you are the spouse, or unmarried dependent son or daughter of an E-1 employee of the Taipei Economic and Cultural Representative Office.

## Foreign Students

**F-1 Student Seeking Optional Practical Training in an Occupation Directly Related to Studies--(c)(3)(i).** File your EAD application with a Certificate of Eligibility of Nonimmigrant (F-1) Student Status (Form I-20 A-B/I-20 ID) endorsed by a Designated School Official within the past 30 days.

**F-1 Student Offered Off-Campus Employment under the Sponsorship of a Qualifying International Organization-- (c)(3)(ii).** File your EAD application with the international organization's letter of certification that the proposed employment is within the scope of its sponsorship, and a Certificate of Eligibility of Nonimmigrant (F-1) Student Status--For Academic and Language Students (Form I-20 A-B/I-20 ID) endorsed by the Designated School Official within the past 30 days.

**F-1 Student Seeking Off-Campus Employment Due to Severe Economic Hardship--(c)(3)(iii).** File your EAD application with Form 1-20 A-B/I-20 ID, Certificate of Eligibility of Nonimmigrant (F-1) Student Status--For Academic and Language Students; Form I-538, Certification by Designated School Official, and any evidence you wish to submit, such as affidavits, which detail the unforeseen economic circumstances that cause your request, and evidence you have tried to find off-campus employment with an employer who has filed a labor and wage attestation.

**J-2 Spouse or Minor Child of an Exchange Visitor--(c)(5).** File your EAD application with a copy of your J-1's (principal alien's) Certificate of Eligibility for Exchange Visitor (J-1) Status (Form IAP-66). You must submit a written statement, with any supporting evidence showing, that your employment is not necessary to support the J-1 but is for other purposes.

**M-1 Student Seeking Practical Training after Completing Studies--(c)(6).** File your EAD application with a completed Form I-538, Application by Nonimmigrant Student for Extension of Stay, School Transfer, or Permission to Accept or Continue Employment, Form I-20 M-N, Certificate of Eligibility for Nonimmigrant (M-1) Student Status--For Vocational Students endorsed by the Designated School Official within the past 30 days.

## Eligible Dependents of Employees of Diplomatic Missions, International Organizations, or NATO

### Dependent of A-1 or A-2 Foreign Government Officials--(c)(1).

Submit your EAD application with Form I-566, Inter-Agency Record of Individual Requesting Change/Adjustment to, or from, A or G Status; or Requesting A, G, or NATO Dependent Employment Authorization, through your diplomatic mission to the Department of State (DOS). The DOS will forward all favorably endorsed applications directly to the Nebraska Service Center for adjudication.

### Dependent of G-1, G-3 or G-4 Nonimmigrant--(c)(4).

Submit your EAD application with a Form I-566, Inter-Agency Record of Individual Requesting Change/Adjustment to or from A or G Status; or Requesting A, G, or NATO Dependent Employment Authorization, through your international organization to the Department of State (DOS). [In New York City, the United Nations (UN) and UN missions should submit such applications to the United States Mission to the UN (USUN).] The DOS or USUN will forward all favorably endorsed applications directly to the Nebraska Service Center for adjudication.

### Dependent of NATO-1 through NATO-6--(c)(7).

Submit your EAD application with Form I-566, Inter-Agency Record of Individual Requesting Change/Adjustment to, or from, A or G Status; or Requesting A, G or NATO Dependent Employment Authorization, to NATO SACLANT, 7857 Blandy Road, C-027, Suite 100, Norfolk, VA 23551-2490. NATO/SACLANT will forward all favorably endorsed applications directly to the Nebraska Service Center for adjudication.

## Employment-Based Nonimmigrant Categories

### B-1 Nonimmigrant who is the personal or domestic servant of a nonimmigrant employer--(c)(17)(i).

File your EAD application with:

- Evidence from your employer that he or she is a B, E, F, H, I, J, L, M, O, P, R, or TN nonimmigrant and you were employed for at least one year by the employer before the employer entered the United States or your employer regularly employs personal and domestic servants and has done so for a period of years before coming to the United States; and

- Evidence that you have either worked for this employer as a personal or domestic servant for at least one year or, evidence that you have at least one year's experience as a personal or domestic servant; and

- Evidence establishing that you have a residence abroad which you have no intention of abandoning.

### B-1 Nonimmigrant Domestic Servant of a U.S. Citizen-- (c)(17)(ii).

File your EAD application with:

- Evidence from your employer that he or she is a U.S. citizen; and

- Evidence that your employer has a permanent home abroad or is stationed outside the United States and is temporarily visiting the United States or the citizen's current assignment in the United States will not be longer than four (4) years; and

- Evidence that he or she has employed you as a domestic servant abroad for at least six (6) months prior to your admission to the United States.

### B-1 Nonimmigrant Employed by a Foreign Airline--(c)(17)(iii).

File your EAD application with a letter from the airline fully describing your duties and indicating that your position would entitle you to E nonimmigrant status except for the fact that you are not a national of the same country as the airline or because there is no treaty of commerce and navigation in effect between the United States and that country.

### Spouse of an E-1/E-2 Treaty Trader or Investor--(a)(17).

File your EAD application with evidence of your lawful status and evidence you are a spouse of a principal E-1/E-2, such as your I-94. (Other relatives or dependents of E-1/E-2 aliens who are in E status are not eligible for employment authorization and may not file under this category.)

### Spouse of an L-1 Intracompany Transferee--(a)(18).

File your EAD application with evidence of your lawful status and evidence you are a spouse of a principal L-1, such as your I-94. (Other relatives or dependents of L-1 aliens who are in L status are not eligible for employment authorization and may not file under this category.)

## Family-Based Nonimmigrant Categories

### K-1 Nonimmigrant Fiance(e) of U.S. Citizen or K-2 Dependent--(a)(6).

File your EAD application if you are filing within 90 days from the date of entry. This EAD cannot be renewed. Any EAD application other than for a replacement must be based on your pending application for adjustment under (c)(9).

### K-3 Nonimmigrant Spouse of U.S. Citizen or K-4 Dependent--(a)(9).

File your EAD application along with evidence of your admission such as copies of your Form I-94, passport, and K visa.

**Family Unity Program--(a)(13).** File your EAD application with a copy of the approval notice, if you have been granted status under this program. You may choose to file your EAD application concurrently with your Form I-817, Application for Voluntary Departure under the Family Unity Program. The INS may take up to 90 days from the date upon which you are granted status under the Family Unity Program to adjudicate your EAD application. If you were denied Family Unity status solely because your legalized spouse or parent first applied under the Legalization/SAW programs after May 5, 1988, file your EAD application with a new Form I-817 application and a copy of the original denial. However, if your EAD application is based on continuing eligibility under (c)(12), please refer to **Deportable Alien Granted Voluntary Departure.**

**LIFE Family Unity--(a)(14).** If you are applying for initial employment authorization pursuant to the Family Unity provisions of section 1504 of the LIFE Act Amendments, or an extension of such authorization, you should not be using this form. Please obtain and complete a Form I-817, Application for Family Unity Benefits. If you are applying for a replacement EAD that was issued pursuant to the LIFE Act Amendments Family Unity provisions, file your EAD application with the required evidence listed in Part 3.

**V-1, V-2 or V-3 Nonimmigrant--(a)(15).** If you have been inspected and admitted to the United States with a valid V visa, file this application along with evidence of your admission, such as copies of your Form I-94, passport, and K visa. If you have been granted V status while in the United States, file this application along with evidence of your V status, such as an approval notice. If you are in the United States but you have not yet filed an application for V status, you may file this application at the same time as you file your application for V status. INS will adjudicate this application after adjudicating your application for V status.

### *EAD Applicants Who Have Filed For Adjustment of Status*

**Adjustment Applicant--(c)(9).** File your EAD application with a copy of the receipt notice or other evidence that your Form I-485, Application for Permanent Residence, is pending. You may file Form I-765 together with your Form I-485.

**Adjustment Applicant Based on Continuous Residence Since January 1, 1972--(c)(16).** File your EAD application with your Form I-485, Application for Permanent Residence; a copy of your receipt notice; or other evidence that the Form I-485 is pending.

### *Other*

**N-8 or N-9 Nonimmigrant--(a)(7).** File your EAD application with the required evidence listed in Part 3.

**Granted Withholding of Deportation or Removal --(a)(10).** File your EAD application with a copy of the Immigration Judge's order. It is not necessary to apply for a new EAD until 90 days before the expiration of your current EAD.

**Applicant for Suspension of Deportation--(c)(10).** File your EAD application with evidence that your Form I-881, Application for Suspension of Deportation, or EOIR-40,is pending.

**Paroled in the Public Interest--(c)(11).** File your EAD application if you were paroled into the United States for emergent reasons or reasons strictly in the public interest.

**Deferred Action--(c)(14).** File your EAD application with a copy of the order, notice or document placing you in deferred action and evidence establishing economic necessity for an EAD.

**Final Order of Deportation--(c)(18).** File your EAD application with a copy of the order of supervision and a request for employment authorization which may be based on, but not limited to the following:

- Existence of a dependent spouse and/or children in the United States who rely on you for support; and
- Existence of economic necessity to be employed;
- Anticipated length of time before you can be removed from the United States.

**LIFE Legalization applicant--(c)(24).** We encourage you to file your EAD application together with your Form I-485, Application to Regsiter Permanent Residence or Adjust Status, to facilitate processing. However, you may file Form I-765 at a later date with evidence that you were a CSS, LULAC, or Zambrano class member applicant before October 1, 2000 and with a copy of the receipt notice or other evidence that your Form I-485 is pending.

**T-1 Nonimmigrant--(a)(16).** If you are applying for initial employment authorization as a T-1 nonimmigrant, file this form only if you did not request an employment authorization document when you applied for T nonimmigrant status. If you have been granted T status and this is a request for a renewal or replacement of an employment authorization document, file this application along with evidence of your T status, such as an approval notice.

**T-2, T-3, or T-4 Nonimmigrant--(c)(25).** File this form with a copy of your T-1's (principal alien's) approval notice and proof of your relationship to the T-1 principal.

## Part 3.  Required Documentation

All applications must be filed with the documents required below, in addition to the particular evidence required for the category listed in Part 2, **Eligibility Categories**, with fee, if required.

If you are required to show economic necessity for your category (See Part 2), submit a list of your assets, income and expenses.

Please assemble the documents in the following order:

Your application with the filing fee. See Part 4, **Fee** for details.

If you are mailing your application to the INS, you must also submit:

- A copy of Form I-94 Departure Record (front and back), if available.
- A copy of your last EAD (front and back).
- 2 photos with a white background taken no earlier than 30 days before submission to the INS.  They should be unmounted, glossy, and unretouched.  The photos should show a three-quarter front profile of the right side of your face, with your right ear visible.  Your head should be bare unless you are wearing a headdress as required by a religious order to which you belong.  The photo should not be larger than 1½ X 1 ½ inches, with the distance from the top of the head to just below the chin about 1 1/4 inches.  Lightly print your name and your A#, if known, on the back of each photo with a pencil.

### *Special filing instructions for those with pending asylum applications ((c)(8))*

**Asylum Applicant (with a pending asylum application) who Filed for Asylum on or after January 4, 1995.** *You must wait at leat 150 days following the filing of your asylum claim before you are eligible to apply for an EAD. If you file your EAD application early, it will be denied. File your EAD application with:*

- A copy of the INS acknowledgement mailer which was mailed to you; or
- Other evidence that your Form I-589 was filed with the INS; or
- Evidence that your Form I-589 was filed with an Immigration Judge at the Executive Office for Immigration Review (EOIR); or
- Evidence that your asylum application remains under administrative or judicial review.

**Asylum Applicant (with a pending asylum application) who Filed for Asylum and for Withholding of Deportation Prior to January 4, 1995 and is *NOT* in Exclusion or Deportation Proceedings.** You may file your EAD application at any time; however, it will only be granted if the INS finds that your asylum application is not frivolous. File your EAD application with:

- A complete copy of your previously filed Form I-589; AND
- A copy of your INS receipt notice; or
- A copy of the INS acknowledgement mailer; or
- Evidence that your Form I-589 was filed with EOIR; or
- Evidence that your asylum application remains under administrative or judicial review; or
- Other evidence that you filed an asylum application.

**Asylum Applicant (with a pending asylum application) who Filed an Initial Request for Asylum Prior to January 4, 1995, and *IS IN* Exclusion or Deportation Proceedings.**  If you filed your Request for Asylum and Withholding of Deportation (Form I-589) prior to January 4, 1995 and you ARE IN exclusion or deportation proceedings, file your EAD application with:

- A date-stamped copy of your previously filed Form I-589; or
- A copy of Form I-221, Order to Show Cause and Notice of Hearing, or Form I-122, Notice to Applicant for Admission Detained for Hearing Before Immigration Judge; or
- A copy of EOIR-26, Notice of Appeal, date stamped by the Office of the Immigration Judge; or
- A date-stamped copy of a petition for judicial review or for *habeas corpus* issued to the asylum applicant; or
- Other evidence that you filed an asylum application with EOIR.

**Asylum Application under the ABC Settlement Agreement--(c)(8).**  If you are a Salvadoran or Guatemalan national eligible for benefits under the ABC settlement agreement, American Baptist Churches v. Thornburgh, 760 F. Supp. 976 (N.D. Cal. 1991), please follow the instructions contained in this section when filing your Form I-765.

You must have asylum application (Form I-589) on file either with INS or with an immigration judge in order to receive work authorization.  Therefore, please submit evidence that you have previously filed an asylum application when you submit your EAD application.  You are not required to submit this evidence when you apply, but it will help INS process your request efficiently.

If you are renewing or replacing your EAD, you must pay the filing fee.

Mark your application as follows:

- Write "ABC" in the top right corner of your EAD application.  You must identify yourself as an ABC class member if you are applying for an EAD under the ABC settlement agreement.
- Write "(c)(8)" in Section 16 of the application.

You are entitled to an EAD without regard to the merits of your asylum claim. Your application for an EAD will be decided within 60 days if: (1) you pay the filing fee, (2) you have a complete, pending asylum application on file, and (3) write "ABC" in the top right corner of your EAD application. If you do not pay the filing fee for an initial EAD request, your request may be denied if INS finds that your asylum application is frivolous. However, if you cannot pay the filing fee for an EAD, you may qualify for a fee waiver under 8 CFR 103.7(c). See Part 4 concerning fee waivers.

---

## Part 4. Fee

Applicants must pay a fee of **$120** to file this form unless noted below. If a fee is required, it will not be refunded. Pay in the exact amount. Checks and money orders must be payable in U.S. currency. Make check or money order payable to **"Immigration and Naturalization Service."** If you live in Guam make your check or money order payable to **"Treasurer, Guam."** If you live in the U.S. Virgin Islands make your check or money order payable to **"Commissioner of Finance of the Virgin Islands."** A charge of $30.00 will be imposed if a check in payment of a fee is not honored by the bank on which it is drawn. Please do **not** send cash in the mail.

***Initial EAD:*** If this is your initial application and you are applying under one of the following categories, a filing fee is not required:

- (a)(3) Refugee;
- (a)(4) Paroled as Refugee;
- (a)(5) Asylee;
- (a)(7) N-8 or N-9 nonimmigrant;
- (a)(8) Citizen of Micronesia, Marshall Islands or Palau;
- (a)(10) Granted Withholding of Deportation;
- (a)(11) Deferred Enforced Departure;
- (a)(16) Victim of Severe Form of Trafficking (T-1);
- (c)(1), (c)(4), or (c)(7) Dependent of certain foreign government, international organization, or NATO personnel; or
- (c)(8) Applicant for asylum [an applicant filing under the special ABC procedures must pay the fee].

***Renewal EAD:*** If this is a renewal application and you are applying under one of the following categories, a filing fee is not required:

- (a)(8) Citizen of Micronesia, Marshall Islands, or Palau;
- (a)(10) Granted Withholding of Deportation;
- (a)(11) Deferred Enforced Departure; or
- (c)(l), (c)(4), or (c)(7) Dependent of certain foreign government, international organization, or NATO personnel.

***Replacement EAD:*** If this is your replacement application and you are applying under one of the following categories, a filing fee is not required:

- (c)(l), (c)(4), or (c)(7) Dependent of certain foreign government, international organization, or NATO personnel.

You may be eligible for a fee waiver under 8 CFR 103.7(c).

The INS will use the Poverty Guidelines published annually by the Department of Health and Human Services as the basic criteria in determining the applicant's eligibility when economic necessity is identified as a factor.

The Poverty Guidelines will be used as a guide, but not as a conclusive standard, in adjudicating fee waiver requests for employment authorization applications requiring a fee.

---

## Part 5. Where to File

If your response to question 16 is: **(a)(3), (a)(4), (a)(5), (a)(7), or (a)(8)** mail your application to:

**INS Service Center**
P.O. Box 87765
Lincoln, NE 68501-7765

---

If your response to question 16 is **(a)(9)**, mail your application to:
**USINS**
P.O. Box 7218
Chicago, IL 60680-7218

---

If your response to question 16 is **(a)(15)**, mail your application to:
**USINS**
P.O. Box 7216
Chicago, IL 60680-7216

---

If your response to question 16 is **(a)(14)** or **(c)(24)**, mail your application to:
**USINS**
P.O. Box 7219
Chicago, IL 60680-7219

---

If your response to question 16 is: **(a)(16)** or **(c)(25)** mail your application to:
**INS Service Center**
75 Lower Welden St.
St. Albans, VT 05479-0001

---

If your response to question 16 is: **(a)(10), (c)(11), (c)(12), (c)(14), (c)(16), (c)(18),**

apply at the local INS office having jurisdiction over your place of residence.

---

If your response to question 16 is: **(a)(12)** or **(c)(19)**, file your EAD application according to the instructions in the Federal Register notice for your particular country's TPS designation.

---

If your response to question 16 is **(c)(1), (c)(4)**, or **(c)(7)**, submit your application through your principal's sponsoring organization. Your application will be reviewed and forwarded by the DOS, USUN, or NATO/SACLANT to the Nebraska Service Center following certification of your eligibility for an EAD.

If your response to question 16 is **(c)(8)** under the special ABC filing instructions and you are filing your asylum and EAD applications together, mail your application to the office where you are filing your asylum application.

If your response to question 16 is **(c)(9)**, file your application at the <u>same local INS office or Service Center where you submitted your adjustment of status application.</u>

If your response to question 16 is:

**(a)(6), (a)(11), (a)(13), (a)(17), (a)(18), (c)(2), (c)(3)(i), (c)(3)(ii), (c)(3)(iii), (c)(5), (c)(6), (c)(8),(c)(17)(i), (c)(17)(ii), or (c)(17)(iii):**

mail your application based on your address to the appropriate **Service Center**. The correct **Service Center** is based on the state or territory in which you live.

| If you live in: | | Mail your application to: |
|---|---|---|
| Connecticut<br>D.C.<br>Maryland<br>New Hampshire<br>New York<br>Puerto Rico<br>Vermont<br>West Virginia | Delaware<br>Maine<br>Massachusetts<br>New Jersey<br>Pennsylvania<br>Rhode Island<br>Virginia<br>U.S.V.I. | **INS Service Center**<br>75 Lower Welden Street<br>St. Albans, VT<br>05479-0001 |
| Arizona<br>Guam<br>Nevada | California<br>Hawaii | **INS Service Center**<br>P.O. Box 10765<br>Laguna Niguel, CA<br>92607-1076 |
| Alabama<br>Florida<br>Kentucky<br>Mississippi<br>North Carolina<br>South Carolina<br>Texas | Arkansas<br>Georgia<br>Lousiana<br>New Mexico<br>Oklahoma<br>Tennessee | **INS Service Center**<br>P.O. Box 851041<br>Mesquite, TX<br>75185-1041 |
| Alaska<br>Idaho<br>Indiana<br>Kansas<br>Minnesota<br>Montana<br>North Dakota<br>Oregon<br>Utah<br>Wisconsin | Colorado<br>Illinois<br>Iowa<br>Michigan<br>Missouri<br>Nebraska<br>Ohio<br>South Dakota<br>Washington<br>Wyoming | **INS Service Center**<br>P.O. Box 87765<br>Lincoln, NE |

If your response to question 16 is **(c)(10)**, and you are a NACARA 203 applicant eligible to apply for relief with the INS, or if your I-881 application is still pending with INS and you wish to renew your EAD, mail your EAD application with the required fee to the appropriate INS service center below:

- If you live in Alabama, Arkansas, Colorado, Connecticut, Delaware, the District of Columbia, Florida, Georgia, Louisiana, Maine, Maryland, Massachusetts, Mississippi, New Hampshire, New Jersey, New Mexico, New York, North Carolina, Oklahoma, Pennsylvania, Puerto Rico, Rhode Island, South Carolina, Tennessee, Texas, Utah, the U.S. Virgin Islands, Vermont, Virginia, West Virginia or Wyoming, mail your application to:

    **INS Service Center**
    75 Lower Welden St.
    St. Albans, VT  05479-0001

- If you live in Alaska, Arizona, California, the Commonwealth of Guam, Hawaii, Idaho, Illinois, Indiana, Iowa, Kansas, Kentucky, Michigan, Minnesota, Missouri, Montana, Nebraska, Nevada, North Dakota, Oregon, Ohio, South Dakota, Washington, or Wisconsin, mail your application to:

    **INS Service Center**
    P.O. Box 10765
    Laguna Niguel, CA 92607-1076

You should submit the fee for the EAD application on a separate check or money order. Do not combine your check or money order with the fee for the Form I-881.

If your response to question 16 is **(c)(10) and you are not eligible to apply for NACARA 203 relief with INS,** but you are eligible for other deportation or removal relief, apply at the local INS office having jurisdiction over your place of residence.

## Part 6. Processing Information

**Acceptance.** If your application is complete and filed at an INS Service Center, you will be mailed a Form I-797 receipt notice. However, an application filed without the required fee, evidence, signature or photographs (if required) will be returned to you as incomplete. You may correct the deficiency and resubmit the application; however, an application is not considered properly filed until the INS accepts it.

**Approval.** If approved, your EAD will either be mailed to you or you may be required to appear at your local INS office to pick it up.

**Request for evidence.** If additional information or documentation is required, a written request will be sent to you specifying the information or advising you of an interview.

**Denial.** If your application cannot be granted, you will receive a written notice explaining the basis of your denial.

**Interim EAD.** If you have not received a decision within 90 days of receipt by the INS of a properly filed EAD application or within 30 days of a properly filed initial EAD application based on an asylum application filed on or after January 4, 1995, you may obtain interim work authorization by appearing in person at your local INS district office. You must bring proof of identity and any notices that you have received from the INS in connection with your application for employment authorization.

## Part 7. Other Information

**Penalties for Perjury.** All statements contained in response to questions in this application are declared to be true and correct under penalty of perjury. Title 18, United States Code, Section 1546, provides in part:

**...** Whoever knowingly makes under oath, or as permitted under penalty of perjury under 1746 of Title 28, United States Code, knowingly subscribes as true, any false statement with respect to a material fact in any application, affidavit, or other document required by the immigration laws or regulations prescribed thereunder, or knowingly presents any such application, affidavit, or other document containing any such false statement-shall be fined in accordance with this title or imprisoned not more than five years, or both.

The knowing placement of false information on this application may subject you and/or the preparer of this application to criminal penalties under Title 18 of the United States Code. The knowing placement of false information on this application may also subject you and/or the preparer to civil penalties under Section 274C of the Immigration and Nationality Act (INA), 8 U.S.C. 1324c. Under 8 U.S.C. 1324c, a person subject to a final order for civil document fraud is deportable from the United States and may be subject to fines.

**Authority for Collecting this Information.** The authority to require you to file Form I-765, Application for Employment Authorization, when applying for employment authorization is found at sections 103(a) and 274A(h)(3) of the Immigration and Nationality Act. Information you provide on your Form I-765 is used to determine whether you are eligible for employment authorization and for the preparation of your Employment Authorization Document if you are found eligible. Failure to provide all information as requested may result in the denial or rejection of this application. The information you provide may also be disclosed to other federal, state, local and foreign law enforcement and regulatory agencies during the course of the INS investigations.

**Paperwork Reduction Act.** An agency may not conduct or sponsor an information collection and a person is not required to respond to a collection of information unless it displays a currently valid OMB control number. The Immigration and Naturalization Service (INS) tries to create forms and instructions which are accurate and easily understood. Often this is difficult because immigration law can be very complex. The public reporting burden for this form is estimated to average three (3) hours and twenty-five (25) minutes per response, including the time for reviewing instructions, gathering and maintaining the data needed, and completing and reviewing the collection of information. The INS welcomes your comments regarding this burden estimate or any other aspect of this form, including suggestions for reducing this burden to Immigration and Naturalization Service, HQPDI, 425 I Street, N.W., Room 4034, Washington, DC 20536; OMB No. 1115-0163. **DO NOT MAIL YOUR COMPLETED APPLICATION TO THIS ADDRESS.**

OMB No. 1115-0163; Expires 04/30/05

# Application for Employment Authorization

**Do Not Write in This Block.**

| Remarks | Action Stamp | Fee Stamp |
|---|---|---|
| A# | | |
| Applicant is filing under §274a.12 _____ | | |

☐ Application Approved. Employment Authorized / Extended *(Circle One)* until _____ (Date).

_____ (Date).

Subject to the following conditions: _____

☐ Application Denied.
   ☐ Failed to establish eligibility under 8 CFR 274a.12 (a) or (c).
   ☐ Failed to establish economic necessity as required in 8 CFR 274a.12(c)(14), (18) and 8 CFR 214.2(f)

I am applying for:
☐ Permission to accept employment.
☐ Replacement *(of lost employment authorization document).*
☐ Renewal of my permission to accept employment *(attach previous employment authorization document).*

1. Name (Family Name in CAPS) (First) (Middle)

2. Other Names Used (Include Maiden Name)

3. Address in the United States (Number and Street) (Apt. Number)

(Town or City) (State/Country) (ZIP Code)

4. Country of Citizenship/Nationality

5. Place of Birth (Town or City) (State/Province) (Country)

6. Date of Birth    7. Sex ☐ Male ☐ Female

8. Marital Status ☐ Married ☐ Single ☐ Widowed ☐ Divorced

9. Social Security Number (Include all Numbers you have ever used) (if any)

10. Alien Registration Number (A-Number) or I-94 Number (if any)

11. Have you ever before applied for employment authorization from INS?
☐ Yes (If yes, complete below)    ☐ No
Which INS Office?     Date(s)

Results (Granted or Denied - attach all documentation)

12. Date of Last Entry into the U.S. (Month/Day/Year)

13. Place of Last Entry into the U.S.

14. Manner of Last Entry (Visitor, Student, etc.)

15. Current Immigration Status (Visitor, Student, etc.)

16. Go to Part 2 of the Instructions, Eligibility Categories. In the space below, place the letter and number of the category you selected from the instructions (For example, (a)(8), (c)(17)(iii), etc.).

Eligibility under 8 CFR 274a.12

(    ) (    ) (    )

## Certification.

**Your Certification:** I certify, under penalty of perjury under the laws of the United States of America, that the foregoing is true and correct. Furthermore, I authorize the release of any information which the Immigration and Naturalization Service needs to determine eligibility for the benefit I am seeking. I have read the Instructions in Part 2 and have identified the appropriate eligibility category in Block 16.

*Signature*      Telephone Number      Date

## Signature of Person Preparing Form, If Other Than Above: I declare that this document was prepared by me at the request of the applicant and is based on all information of which I have any knowledge.

Print Name      Address      *Signature*      Date

| Initial Receipt | Resubmitted | Relocated | | Completed | | |
|---|---|---|---|---|---|---|
| | | Rec'd | Sent | Approved | Denied | Returned |
| | | | | | | |

Form I-765 (Rev. 5/09/02)Y

# Application - Alternative Inspection Services

## INSTRUCTIONS

*Read carefully -- fee will be not refunded. Failure to follow instructions may require return of your application and delay final action.*

**1. Preparation of Application.** Fill in application in single copy only, by typewriter, or print in block letters using only dark ink. Do not use pencil or red ink. Do not leave any question unanswered. Mark any question which does not apply to you "N/A".

**2. Who Can Apply.**

Citizens and lawful permanent residents of the United States, citizens of Canada and Landed Canadian immigrants who are citizens of British Commonwealth countries are eligible to apply for all programs. Additional eligibility criteria for each program are indicated below:

   **A.** *Dedicated Commuter Lane Program ("DCL")* - Certain citizens of Mexico and certain non-immigrants.

   **B.** *Automated Permit Port Program ("APP")* - Certain non-immigrants.

   **C.** *INSPASS Airport* - Citizens of Visa Waiver Program countries or any other country approved for participation by the Commissioner, Immigration and Naturalization Service (INS).

Each participant in each program must submit a separate application. Persons under 14 years of age may not enroll in either INSPASS Program.

**3. Where to Submit This Application.** Applications may be submitted in person or by mail to the U.S. port of entry sponsoring the DCL for which you are applying, or at the port of entry having jurisdiction over the APP for which you request access. INSPASS applicants may apply at any INSPASS port of entry in person or by mail.

**4. Submission of Application.** Each application must be supported by evidence of citizenship, legal resident status, or other documention as applicable, including but not limited to proof of employment or residence, vehicle registration and insurance. Original documention must be presented at the time of the personal interview. Personal identifiers, i.e., voice print or other biometrics, may be required for participation.

**5. Final Approval.** Your application will be reviewed and an interview may be scheduled prior to acceptance. You will be required to produce your original evidence of eligibility at that time. Approval for participation is valid for one year unless otherwise revoked. The pass may not be used for purposes other than those involved in this application and approved by the INS.

**6. Denial.** An application for participation in a program may be denied at the discretion of the District Director without appeal. All applicants denied shall be so notified. Applications submitted without the required documentation or which are incomplete will be returned without action.

All applicants who have been denied permission to participate in the DCL or APP programs, or who have had their permission to participate in either program revoked for any reason, must wait 90 days from the date of denial or revocation to reapply.

**7. Fees**.

   **A. Application or Replacement Card Fee.**

   (1) The application fee for the DCL program is $25 (U.S.)., with a maximum amount payable by a family (husband wife, and any minor children) of $50 (U.S.). If fingerprints are required, an additional fee equal to the amount of the current FBI fee for conducting fingerprints checks will be required at the time of application. The fee for a replacement card for the DCL program is $25.

   (2) Presently, there are no application fees for the APP program, or for either INSPASS program.

   **B. System Costs Fee.**

   (1) A non-refundable fee of $80 (U.S.) will be assessed on all approved applicants for DCLs located at certain ports of entry, with the maximum payable by family (husband, wife and any minor children ) of $160 (U.S.). If an approved participant wishes to register more than one vehicle for use in the lane, he/she may be assessed an additional $42, also non refundable, for each additional vehicle.

   (2) Presently, there is no System Costs Fee for the APP program or for either INSPASS Program.

Payment may be made by check or money order in the exact amount. All checks and money orders must be payable in U.S. currency at a financial institution in the United States. Make check or money order payable to "Immigration and Naturalization Service." A charge of $30.00 will be imposed if a check in payment of a fee is not honored by the bank on which it is drawn. At some port of entries, payment may be made by credit card.

**8. Privacy Act Statement.** The authority to collect this information is contained in Title 8, United States Code. Furnishing the information on this form is voluntary; however, failure to provide all of the requested information may result in the delay of a final decision or denial of your request. The information collected will be used to make a determination on your application. It may also be provided to other government agencies (Federal, state, local and/or foreign). All applicants are subject to a check of criminal information databases in order to determine eligibility.

**9. Penalties for False Statements in Applications.** Severe penalties are provided by law for knowingly and willfully falsifying or concealing a material fact or using any false document in the submission of this application. Also, a false representation may result in the denial of this application and any other application you may make for any benefit under the immigration laws of the United States.

**10. Random compliance checks.** Periodic random checks will be conducted to ensure compliance with the conditions of each program.

11. Applicant acknowledges and agrees that should he/she violate any condition(s) of this program(s), or any law or regulation of any Federal inspection service, or is otherwise determined to be inadmissible to the U.S., his/her participation in this program may be revoked and he/she may be subject to other applicable sanctions. Such sanctions may include, but are not limited to, criminal prosecution, exclusion or deportation proceedings, imposition of civil monetary penalties, and seizure of merchandise and/or vehicles. Conditions by which the applicant must abide include, but are not limited to, the following.

A) Adherence to all Federal, state, and local laws regarding the importation of alcohol and agricultural products; possession and importation of controlled substances, and all other laws and regulations under the jurisdiction of any federal agency.

B) Adherence to all requirements of the Immigration and Nationality Act, as amended, and all INS regulations, regarding documentary requirements.

**12. Reporting Burden.** A person is not required to respond to a collection of information unless it displays a currently valid OMB control number. We try to create forms and instructions that are accurate, can be easily understood, and which impose the least possible burden on you to provide us with information. Often this is difficult because some immigration laws are very complex. Accordingly, the reporting burden for this collection of information is computed as follows: 1) learning about the form, and reading and understanding U.S. INS Publications 28 minutes; 2) completing the form, 8 minutes; 3) fingerprinting 30 minutes; and 4) assembling and mailing the application, 4 minutes, for an estimated average of 70 minutes per response. If you have comments regarding the accuracy of this estimate, or suggestions for making this form simpler, you can write to the Immigration and Naturalization Service, HQPDI, 425 I Street, N.W; Room 4034, Washington, DC 20536, OMB No. 1115-0174. **Do not mail your completed application to this address.**

**U.S. Department of Justice**
Immigration and Naturalization Service

OMB No. 1115-0174

# Application - Alternative Inspection Services

## START HERE - PLEASE TYPE OR PRINT

**Application Type:** *(Check one)* ☐ Dedicated Commuter Lane Program ☐ Automated Permit Port Program ☐ INSPASS Airport

| 1. Name: *(Last)* *(First)* *(Middle Name)* | 2. Date of Birth: *(MM/DD/YYYY)* |
|---|---|

| 3. U.S. Alien Registration No. *(If applicable)* | 4. Gender: ☐ Male ☐ Female |
|---|---|

5. Place of Birth: *(City)* *(State)* *(Country)*

6. Permanent Address *(Street Number and Name):*

| City: | State/Province/Country: | Zip/Postal Code: | 8. Country of Citizenship: |
|---|---|---|---|

7. Usual purpose of Entry:

8. Port of entry where you intend to enter the United States:

9. Have you ever been:

    a. Arrested or convicted of a criminal offense, anywhere?    Yes ☐ No ☐

    b. Granted a conditional discharge or pardon?    Yes ☐ No ☐

    c. Found to be in violation of any immigration law?    Yes ☐ No ☐

    d. Found to be in violation of any customs law?    Yes ☐ No ☐

    e. Refused admission to the United States?    Yes ☐ No ☐

    f. Denied any other immigration benefit, whether you applied for the benefit directly, or the benefit was sought on your behalf?    Yes ☐ No ☐

        If yes, please explain: _____

10. Occupation: _____

    Employer: _____

    Employer Address: _____

    Employer Phone #: _____ Employer Point of Contact: _____

11. Admission Classification

    ☐ United States Citizen

    ☐ Lawful Permanent Resident

    ☐ Other (specify) _____

*Continue on Back*

12. Citizenship and Admissibility

For completion by U.S. citizens only

Passport #: _____ Expiration Date: _____

Other evidence of U.S. Citizenship: _____

For completion by non-U.S. citizens

Passport #: _____ Expiration Date:_____

Issuing Country:_____

**AND**

Form I-551, Permanent Resident Card #: _____

**OR**

Visa Classification:_____ Visa #: _____

Place of Issuance: _____ Expiration Date:_____

**OR**

Border Crossing Card #:_____

Expiration Date: _____

**TRANSPORTING UNDOCUMENTED ALIENS NARCOTICS, UNDECLARED MERCHANDISE, FIREARMS CONTRABAND, OR DECLARED CURRENCY IN EXCESS OF $10,000 ARE VIOLATIONS OF UNITED STATES LAW THAT WILL BE PROSECUTED AND PUNISHABLE BY IMPRISONMENT AND FINE.**

**For Government Use Only**

Identification Document(s) Presented _____ Expiration Date:_____

Type of Application: ☐ Initial ☐ Renewal ☐ Replacement Card

Remarks: _____

_____

_____

# Application - Alternative Inspection Services

## AUTOMATED PERMIT PORT APPLICATIONS

1. Applicant acknowledges that (s)he is a citizen or lawful permanent resident of the U.S., or non-immigrant as determined eligible by the Commissioner of the Service. Applicant acknowledges that he or she must be in possession of all documentation required by the Immigration and Nationality Act and implementing regulations at all times when using the Automated Permit Port (APP). When in the U.S., a non-U.S. citizen applicant acknowledges that (s)he must remain otherwise eligible to enter the U.S. at time of each use of the APP.

2. Applicant agrees to a full inspection of each vehicle presented for registration in the APP prior to approval of his/her application, and at any time during use of the APP. The applicant acknowledges and agrees to be responsible for all contents of the vehicle s(he) occupies when using the APP, whether or not that vehicle is owned by or registered to the applicant.

3. Applicant acknowledges that vehicle registration and insurance must be current when using the APP, and documentation evidencing same must be made made available to the Service upon request. If the vehicle is owned or registered to someone other than the applicant, evidence permitting use of the vehicle in the APP must be made available to the Service upon request.

4. Applicant acknowledges and agrees that by submitting this application, (s)he will be subject to a check of criminal information databases prior to and during each use of the APP.

5. Applicant acknowledges that s(he) may only use the APP when occupying the specific vehicle inspected and authorized by the Service for the applicants use of the APP.

6. Applicant acknowledges and agrees that all devices, decals, or other equipment, methodology, or technology used to identify or inspect persons or vehicles remains the property of the U.S. government, and must be surrendered upon request.

7. If the registered owner is not the applicant, then written proof must be provided that the applicant has authorization to register and use the vehicle in the APP.

   A. Vehicle License Number: _____     A. State/Province: _____
       Vehicle Identification Number: _____     Vehicle Make/Model: _____
       Vehicle Year: _____     Vehicle Color: _____
       Vehicle Insurance Number: _____     Registered Owner: _____

   B. Vehicle License Number: _____     B. State/Province: _____
       Vehicle Identification Number: _____     Vehicle Make/Model: _____
       Vehicle Year: _____     Vehicle Color: _____
       Vehicle Insurance Number: _____     Registered Owner: _____

   C. Vehicle License Number: _____     C. State/Province: _____
       Vehicle Identification Number: _____     Vehicle Make/Model: _____
       Vehicle Year: _____     Vehicle Color: _____
       Vehicle Insurance Number: _____     Registered Owner: _____

8. Driver's License #: _____

   Issuing Country and State/Province: _____

   Expiration Date: _____

9. Will you be the sole occupant of the vehicle? *(All occupants of a vehicle used in the APP must have current participation authorization.)*
(check one) ☐ YES ☐ NO
If no, who else might be in the vehicle?_____

10. Contact in the United States *(name, address, and phone number):*

_____

_____

_____

## CERTIFICATION:

I certify that I have read, understood, and agree to abide by all conditions required for use of the APP. I also certify that the information provided is true and complete. I understand that all information provided may be shared with other government agencies.

_____        _____
*(Signature of Applicant)*             *(Date)*

## INSPASS AIRPORT PARTICIPANTS

1. Applicant acknowledges he/she is a citizen or permanent resident of the United States, a citizen of Canada, a Landed Canadian Immigrant who is a citizen of a British Commonwealth country, a citizen of a Visa Waiver Program country, or any other country approved for participation by the Commissioner, Immigration and Naturalization Service.

2. Applicant may not use the INSPASS card when entering the United States for a purpose other than that stated in this application.

3. Applicant will not be exempt from the normal examination process when entering for any other purpose.

**CERTIFICATION:** *(All applicants must sign)*

I certify that I have read, understood, and agree to abide by all conditions listed above for use of the INSPASS. I also certify that the information is true and complete. I understand that any information may be shared with other government agencies.

_____          _____
*(Signature of Applicant)*                                      *(Date)*

### VISA WAIVER PARTICIPANTS *(To be completed by Visa Waiver Program Applicants Only)*

|  | YES | NO |
|---|---|---|
| A. Do you have a communicable disease, physical or mental disorder; or are you a drug abuser or addict? | ☐ | ☐ |
| B. Have you ever been arrested or convicted for an offense or crime involving moral turpitude or a violation related to a controlled substance; or been arrested or convicted for two or more offenses for which the aggregate sentence to confinement was five years or more; or been a controlled substance trafficker; or are you seeking entry to engage in criminal or immoral activities? | ☐ | ☐ |
| C. Have you ever been or are you now involved in espionage or sabotage; or in terrorist activities; or genocide; or were you involved, in any way, between 1933 and 1945 in persecutions associated with Nazi Germany or its allies? | ☐ | ☐ |
| D. Are you seeking to work in the United States; or have you ever been excluded and deported or previously removed from the United States; or have you ever procured or attempted to procure a visa or entry into the United States by fraud or misrepresentation? | ☐ | ☐ |
| E. Have you ever detained, retained, or withheld custody of a child from a United States citizen granted custody of the child? | ☐ | ☐ |
| F. Have you ever been denied a United States visa or entry into the United States or had a United States visa cancelled? | ☐ | ☐ |

If yes, when? _____      Where? _____

| G. Have you ever asserted immunity from prosecution? | ☐ | ☐ |

I understand that I am not entitled to any review or appeal of an immigration officer's determination as to my admissibility, nor am I entitled to contest any determination of deportability other than on the basis of an application for asylum.

_____          _____
*(Signature of Applicant)*                                      *(Date)*

**WARNING:** You may not accept unauthorized employment; or attend school; or represent the foreign information media during your visit under this program. You are authorized to stay in the United States for 90 days or less. You may not apply for: 1) a change of nonimmigrant status; 2) adjustment of status to temporary or permanent resident, unless eligible under section 201(b) of the Immigration and Nationality Act (Act); or 3) an extension of stay. Violation of these terms will subject you to deportation.

## DEDICATED COMMUTER LANE PARTICIPANTS

☐ New Application ☐ Application for Replacement Card ☐ Renewal

1. Applicant acknowledges that he/she is a citizen or lawful permanent resident of the U.S., or non-immigrant as determined eligible by the Commissioner, INS. Applicant acknowledges that he/she must be in possession of all documentation required the Immigration and Nationality Act and implementing regulations at all times when using the Dedicated Commuter Lane (DCL). When in the U.S., a non-U.S.citizen applicant acknowledges that he/she must remain otherwise eligible to enter the U.S. at time of each use of the DCL.

2. Applicant agrees to a full inspection of each vehicle presented for registration in the DCL prior to approval of his/her application, and at any time during use of the DCL. The applicant acknowledges and agrees to be responsible for all contents of the vehicle he/she occupies when using the APP, whether or not that vehicle is owned by or registered to the applicant.

3. Applicant acknowledges that vehicle registration and insurance must be current when using the DCL, and documentation evidencing same must be made made available to the INS upon request. If the vehicle is owned or registered to someone other than the applicant, evidence permitting use of the vehicle in the DCL must be made available to the INS upon request.

4. Applicant acknowledges and agrees that by submitting this application, he/she will be subject to a check of criminal information databases prior to and during each use of the DCL.

5. Applicant acknowledges and agrees that by submitting this application, he/she may only use the DCL when occupying the specific vehicle inspected and authorized by the INS for the applicants, use of the DCL.

6. Applicant acknowledges and agrees that he/she has been made aware of the nature and amount of all fees associated with participating in the DCL, including a fingerprint fee, system costs fee, and additional vehicle fee.

7. Applicant acknowledges and agrees that all devices, decals, or other equipment, methodology, or technology used to identify, inspect persons or vehicles remains the property of the U.S. government, and must be surrendered upon request.

8. If the registered owner of the vehicle is not the applicant, then written proof must be provided that the applicant has authorization to register and use the vehicle in the DCL.

A. Vehicle License Number: _____  A. State/Province: _____
   Vehicle Identification Number: _____  Vehicle Make/Model: _____
   Vehicle Year: _____  Vehicle Color: _____
   Vehicle Insurance Number: _____  Registered Owner: _____

B. Vehicle License Number: _____  B. State/Province: _____
   Vehicle Identification Number: _____  Vehicle Make/Model: _____
   Vehicle Year: _____  Vehicle Color: _____
   Vehicle Insurance Number: _____  Registered Owner: _____

C. Vehicle License Number: _____  C. State/Province: _____
   Vehicle Identification Number: _____  Vehicle Make/Model: _____
   Vehicle Year: _____  Vehicle Color: _____
   Vehicle Insurance Number: _____  Registered Owner: _____

9. Driver's License #: _____

   Issuing Country and State/Province: _____

   Expiration Date: _____

10. Will you be the sole occupant of the vehicle? *(All occupants of a vehicle used in the DCL must have current participation authorization.)*

    (check one) ☐ YES ☐ NO

    If no, who else might be in the vehicle? _____

11. Contact in the United States *(name, address, and phone number):*

_____
_____
_____

## CERTIFICATION:

I certify that I have read, understood, and agree to abide by all conditions required for use of the DCL. I also certify that the information provided is true and complete. I understand that all information provided may be shared with other government agencies.

_____          _____
*(Signature of Applicant)*                        *(Date)*

**U.S. Department of Homeland Security**
Bureau of Citizehsip and Immigration Services

# I-824, Application for Action on an Approved Application or Petition

**START HERE - Please Type or Print**

**FOR BCIS USE ONLY**

**Part 1.** **Information about the person that filed the original application or petition.** (Individuals use the top name line. Organizations use the second line.)

| Family Name | Given Name | Middle Name |
|---|---|---|
| | | |

Company or Organization Name

**Address** - In care of -

| Street Number and Name | | Apt./Suite # |
|---|---|---|
| | | |

| City | State or Province | Zip/Postal Code | Country |
|---|---|---|---|
| | | | |

| Date of Birth (mm/dd/yyyy) | Country of Birth |
|---|---|
| | |

| Social Security # (if any) | A # (if any) | IRS Tax # (if any) |
|---|---|---|
| | | |

**Part 2.** **Application type.** (check one)

a. ☐ I am applying for a duplicate approval notice.

b. ☐ I am requesting that a new U.S. Consulate or Port of Entry be notified of the previous approval of a petition. Please notify the U.S. Consulate or Port of Entry at:

c. ☐ I am requesting that a U.S. Consulate be notified that my status has been adjusted to permanent resident. Please notify the U.S. Consulate at:

**Part 3.** **Processing information.**

| Type of Petition/Application (Form #) | Filing Receipt # |
|---|---|
| | |

| Date of Filing (mm/dd/yyyy) | Date of Approval (mm/dd/yyyy) |
|---|---|
| | |

**If petition is filed for another person, give the following information about the person you filed for:**

| Family Name | Given Name | Middle Name |
|---|---|---|
| | | |

| Date of Birth (mm/dd/yyyy) | Country of Birth | A # (if any) |
|---|---|---|
| | | |

**Part 4.** **Signature.** *Read the information on penalties in the instructions before completing this section.*

I certify, under penalty of perjury under the laws of the United States of America, that this application and the evidence submitted with it are all true and correct. I authorize the release of any information from my records which the Bureau of Citizenship and Immigration Services needs to determine eligibility for the benefit I am seeking.

| Signature | Print or Type Your Name | Daytime Phone # (with A/C) | Date (mm/dd/yyyy) |
|---|---|---|---|
| | | | |

**Part 5.** **Signature of person preparing form, if other than above.** (Sign below)

I declare that I prepared this application at the request of the above person and it is based on all information of which I have knowledge.

| Signature | Print or Type Your Name | Fax Number (if any) | Date (mm/dd/yyyy) |
|---|---|---|---|
| | | | |

| Firm Name and Address | Daytime Telephone Number (with A/C) |
|---|---|
| | |

**FOR BCIS USE ONLY** (right column)

| Returned | Receipt |
|---|---|
| Date | |
| Date | |
| Resubmitted | |
| Date | |
| Date | |
| Reloc Sent | |
| Date | |
| Date | |
| Reloc Rec'd | |
| Date | |
| Date | |

☐ Applicant Interviewed on _____

☐
☐

☐

**Action Block**

**To Be Completed By**
*Attorney or Representative*, if any.
☐ Fill in box if G-28 is attached to represent the applicant.

**ATTY State License #**

Form I-824 (Rev. 04/04/031)N (Prior versions may be used until 09/30/03)

**U.S. Department of Homeland Security**
Bureau of Citizehsip and Immigration Services

# I-824, Application for Action on an Approved Application or Petition

# INSTRUCTIONS

## Purpose of This Form.

This form is used to apply to the Bureau of Citizenship and Immigration Services (BCIS) to request further action on a previously approved petition or application. The BCIS is comprised of offices of the former Immigration and Naturalization Service.

## Who May File.

If you filed an application or petition that has been approved, use this form during the validity of the approved application or petition to:

- request a duplicate approval notice;
- request that another U.S. embassy or consulate be notified of the approval of the petition; or
- request that a U.S. embassy or consulate be notified that your status has been adjusted to permanent resident, so your spouse and children may apply for immigrant visas.

You should enclose a copy of the original approval notice. It may speed the processing of your request.

## General Filing Instructions.

Please answer all questions by typing or clearly printing in black ink. Indicate that an item is not applicable with "N/A." If an answer is "none," write "none." If you need extra space to answer any item, attach a sheet of paper with your name and your alien registration number (A#), if any, and indicate the number of the item to which the answer refers. Your application must be properly signed and filed with the correct fee. If you are under 14 years of age, your parent or guardian may sign the application.

## Where to File.

File this application with the office that approved the original application or petition.

## Fee.

The fee for this application is **$140.00**. The fee must be submitted in the exact amount. It cannot be refunded. **DO NOT MAIL CASH.**

All checks and money orders must be drawn on a bank or other institution located in the United States and must be payable in United States currency. The check or money order should be made payable to the Bureau of Citizenship and Immigration Services, except that:

- If you live in Guam and are filing this application in Guam, make your check or money order payable to the "Treasurer, Guam."
- If you live in the U.S. Virgin Islands and are filing this application in the Virgin Islands, make your check or money order payable to the "Commissioner of Finance of the Virgin Islands."

Checks are accepted subject to collection. An uncollected check will render the application and any document issued invalid. A charge of $30.00 will be imposed if a check in payment of a fee is not honored by the bank on which it is drawn.

## Processing Information.

*Acceptance.* Any application that is not signed or is not accompanied by the correct fee will be rejected with a notice that the application is deficient. You may correct the deficiency and resubmit the application. However, an application is not considered properly filed until accepted by the BCIS.

*Initial processing.* Once the application has been accepted, it will be checked for completeness. If you do not completely fill out the form, you will not establish a basis for eligibility and we may deny your application.

*Requests for more information or interview.* We may request more information or evidence or request that you appear at a BCIS office for an interview. We may also request that you submit the originals of any copy. We will return these originals when they are no longer required.

*Decision.* You will be notified in writing of the decision on your application.

## Penalties.

If you knowingly and willfully falsify or conceal a material fact or submit a false document with this request, we will deny the benefit you are seeking and may deny any other immigration benefit. In addition, you will face severe penalties provided by law and may be subject to criminal prosecution.

## Privacy Act Notice.

We ask for the information on this form and associated evidence to determine if you have established eligibility for the immigration benefit you are seeking. Our legal right to ask for this information is in 8 USC 1103. We may provide this information to other government agencies. Failure to provide this information and any requested evidence may delay a final decision or result in denial of your request.

## Paperwork Reduction Act Notice.

A person is not required to respond to an information collection unless it displays a currently valid OMB control number. We try to create forms and instructions that are accurate, can be easily understood and that impose the least possible burden on you to provide us with information. Often this is difficult because some immigration laws are very complex. The estimated average time to complete and file this application is as follows: (1) 5 minutes to learn about the law and form; (2) 5 minutes to complete the form; and (3) 15 minutes to assemble and file the application; for a total estimated average of 25 minutes per application. If you have comments regarding the accuracy of this estimate, or suggestions for making this form simpler, you can write to the Bureau of Citizenship and Immigration Services, HQRFS, 425 I Street, N.W., Room 4034, Washington DC, 20536; OMB No. 1615-0044. **DO NOT MAIL YOUR COMPLETED APPLICATION TO THIS ADDRESS.**

# I-829, Petition by Entrepreneur to Remove Conditions

## Purpose of This Form.

This form is for a conditional permanent resident who obtained such status through entrepreneurship to petition to the Bureau of Citizenship and Immigration Services (BCIS) to remove the conditions on his or her residence. The BCIS is comprised of offices of the former Immigration and Naturalization Service.

## Who May File.

If you were granted conditional permanent resident status through entrepreneurship, use this form to petition for the removal of those conditions. You may include your conditional permanent resident spouse and children in your petition, or they may file separately subsequent to your petition. If filing subsequently, attach a copy of the Form I-797, Notice of Action, relating to the principal's petition.

If you obtained conditional permanent resident status through your entrepreneur spouse or parent and your spouse or parent has died, you may use this form for removal of the conditions.

## General Filing Instructions.

Please answer all questions by typing or clearly printing in black ink. Indicate that an item is not applicable with "N/A." If an answer is "none," write "none." It you need extra space to answer any item, attach a sheet of paper with your name and your alien registration number (A#), and indicate the number of the item to which the answer refers. You must file your petition with the required initial evidence. Your petition must be properly signed and accompanied by the correct fee. If you are under 14 years of age, your parent or guardian may sign the petition on your behalf.

### Translations.

Any foreign language document must be accompanied by a full English translation that the translator has certified as complete and correct, and by the translator's certification that he or she is competent to translate the foreign language into English.

### Copies.

If these instructions state that a copy of a document may be filed with this petition and you choose to send us the original, we may keep that original for our records.

## Initial Evidence.

### Permanent Resident Card (Form I-551).

You must file your petition with:
- a copy of your permanent resident, and, if applicable,
- a copy of the permenent resident card of your conditional permanent resident spouse and each of your conditional permanent resident children included in your petition.

### Evidence of the Commercial Enterprise.

Submit the following types of evidence with your petition: (Please label each type of evidence.)

- Evidence that you established a commercial enterprise. Such evidence includes, but is not limited to, federal tax returns;
- Evidence that you invested or were actively in the process of investing the amount of capital required for the location of your enterprise. Such evidence includes, but is not limited to, an audited financial statement; and

- Evidence that you sustained your enterprise and your investmen in that business throughout your period of conditional permanen residence. Examples of such evidence include:
  -- invoices and receipts,
  -- bank statements,
  -- contracts,
  -- business licenses, and
  -- federal or state income tax returns or quarterly tax statements.
- Evidence of the number of full-time employees at the beginning of the investment and at present. Such evidence includes but is not limited to:
  -- payroll records,
  -- relevant tax documents, and
  -- I-9 Forms.

If you are filing as a spouse or child whose entrepreneur spouse or parent has died, submit the following with your petition:
- your spouse's permanent resident card;
- your spouse's death certificate, and
- evidence that the conditions set forth above in "Evidence of the Commercial Enterprise" have been met.

## When to File.

You must file this petition during the 90 days immediately before the second anniversary of the date that you obtained conditional permanent resident status. This is the date your conditional permanent residence expires.

## Effect of Filing.

Filing this petition extends your conditional permanent residence for six months. You will receive a filing receipt that you should carry with your permanent resident card. If you travel outside the United States during this period, you may present your permanet resident card and the filing receipt in order to be readmitted.

## Effect of Not Filing.

If this petition is not filed, you will automatically lose your permanent resident status as of the second anniversary of the date that you were granted conditional status. As a result, you will become removable from the United States. If your failure to file was for good cause and due to extenuating circumstances, you may file your petition late with a written explanation and request that BCIS excuse the late filing.

## Where to File.

If the new commercial enterprise is located or will be doing business principally in Alabama, Arkansas, Connecticut, Delaware, District of Columbia, Florida, Georgia, Kentucky, Louisiana, Mississippi, Maine, Maryland, Massachusetts, New Hampshire, New Jersey, New Mexico, New York, North Carolina, South Carolina, Oklahoma, Pennsylvania, Puerto Rico, Rhode Island, Tennessee, Texas, Vermont, U.S. Virgin Islands, Virginia or West Virginia, mail the petition to:

**BCIS Texas Service Center**
**P.O. Box 852135**
**Mesquite, TX 75185-2135**

If the new commercial enterprise is located or will be doing business principally in Alaska, Arizona, California, Colorado, Guam, Hawaii, Idaho, Illinois, Indiana, Iowa, Kansas, Michigan, Minnesota, Missouri, Montana, Nebraska, Nevada, North Dakota, Ohio, Oregon, South Dakota, Utah, Washington, Wisconsin or Wyoming, mail the petition to:

**BCIS California Service Center**
**P.O. Box 10526**
**Laguna Niguel, CA 92607-0526**

## Fee.

The fee for filing this petition is **$395.00.** The fee must be submitted in the exact amount. It cannot be refunded. DO NOT MAIL CASH.

All checks and money orders must be drawn on a bank or other institution located in the United States and must be payable in United States currency. The check or money order should be made payable to the Bureau of Citizenship and Immigration Services (do not use the initials), except that:

- if you live in Guam and are filing this petition in Guam, make your check or money order payable to the "Treasurer, Guam."

- if you are living in the U.S. Virgin Islands and are filing this petition in the Virgin Islands, make your check or money order payable to the "Commissioner of Finance of the Virgin Islands."

Checks are accepted subject to collection. An uncollected check will render the application and any document issued invalid. A charge of $30.00 will be imposed if a check in payment of a fee is not honored by the bank on which it is drawn.

## Processing Information.

### Acceptance.

Any petition that is not signed or accompanied by the correct fee will be rejected with a notice that the petition is deficient. You may correct the deficiency and resubmit the petition. A petition is not considered properly filed until accepted by the BCIS.

### Initial processing.

Once a petition has been accepted, it will be checked for completeness, including submission of the required initial evidence. If you do not completely fill out the form or file it without the required initial evidence, you will not establish a basis for eligibility and we may deny your petition.

### Requests for more information or interview.

We may request more information or evidence or request that you appear at a BCIS office for an interview. We may also request that you submit the originals of any copy. We will return these originals when they are no longer required.

### Decision.

You will be advised in writing of the decision on your petition.

## Penalties.

If you knowingly and willfully falsify or concede a material fact or submit a false document with this request, we will deny the benefit you are seeking and may deny any other immigration benefit. In addition, you will face severe penalties provided by law and may be subject to criminal prosecution.

## Privacy Act Notice.

We ask for the information on this form and associated evidence to determine if you have established eligibility for the immigration benefit you are seeking. Our legal right to ask for this information is in 8 USC 1184, 1255 and 1258. Failure to provide this information and any requested evidence may delay a final decision or result in denial of your request.

All the information provided on this form, including addresses, is protected by the Privacy Act and the Freedom of Information Act. This information may be released to another government agency. However, the information will not be released in any form whatsoever to a third party who requests it without a court order or without your written consent, or in the case of a child, the written consent of the parent or legal guardian who filed the form on the child's behalf.

## Information and BCIS Forms.

For information on immigration laws, regulations and procedures or to order BCIS forms, call our National Customer Service Center at **1-800-375-5283** or visit our website at **www.bcis.gov.**

## Paperwork Reduction Act Notice.

A person is not required to respond to a collection of information unless it displays a currently valid OMB control number. We try to create forms and instructions that are accurate, can be easily understood and that impose the least possible burden on you to provide us with information. Often this is difficult because some immigration laws are very complex. The estimated average time to complete and file this application is as follows: (1) 15 minutes to learn about the law and form; (2) 15 minutes to complete the form; and (3) 35 minutes to assemble and file the petition; for a total estimated average of 1 hour and 5 minutes per petition. If you have comments regarding the accuracy of this estimate, or suggestions for making this form simpler, you can write to the Bureau of Citizenship and Immigration Services, HQRFS, 425 I Street, N.W., Room 4034 Washington, DC 20536; OMB No. 1115-0190. **DO NOT MAIL YOUR COMPLETED APPLICATION TO THIS ADDRESS.**

## START HERE - Please Type or Print

### DO NOT WRITE IN THIS BLOCK - FOR BCIS USE ONLY (Except G-28 Block Below)

☐ Applicant Interviewed

**Action**

**Fee Receipt**

**To be completed by Attorney or Representative, if any**

☐ G-28 is attached

Attorney's State License No. _____

Remarks:

**START HERE - Type or Print in Black Ink.**

## Part 1.  Information about you.

A # (if any) [____]  Form I-526 Receipt Number [____]

Family Name [____]  Given Name [____]  Middle Name [____]

Address:
In care of [____]

Number and Street [____]  Apt. # [____]

City [____]  State or Province [____]

Country [____]  Zip/Postal Code [____]  Daytime Phone # [____]

Date of Birth (mm/dd/yyyy) [____]  Country of Birth [____]  Social Security # (if any) [____]

Since becoming a conditional permanent resident, have you ever been arrested, cited, charged, indicted, convicted, fined or imprisoned for breaking or violating any law or ordinance (excluding traffic regulations), or committed any crime for which you were not arrested?
☐ Yes  ☐ No  (If yes, explain on separate sheet(s) of paper, including disposition, if any.)

## Part 2. Basis for petition.  (Check one)

a. ☐ My conditional permanent residence is based on an investment in a commercial enterprise.

b. ☐ I am a conditional permanent resident spouse or child of an entrepreneur, and I am unable to be included in a Petition by Entrepreneur to Remove Conditions (Form I-829) filed by my conditional resident spouse or parent.

c. ☐ I am a conditional permanent resident spouse or child of an entrepreneur who is deceased.

## Part 3. Information about your husband or wife.

Family Name [____]  Given Name [____]  Middle Name [____]

Gender  ☐ Male  ☐ Female  Date of Birth (mm/dd/yyyy) [____]  Date of Marriage (mm/ddy/yyyy) [____]

Other names used (including maiden name or aliases) [____]

A# (If any) [____]  Current Immigration Status [____]  Is your current immigration status based on the petitioner's current status?  ☐ Yes  ☐ No

RECEIVED: _____  RESUBMTTED: _____  RELOCATED:  SENT _____  REC'D ____

## Part 4. Children. *(List all your children. Attach another sheet(s), if necessary.)*

| Family Name | | Given Name | | Middle Name | |
|---|---|---|---|---|---|
| A# (if any) | Current Immigration Status | | Date of Birth (mm/dd/yyyy) | | Living with you? ☐ Yes ☐ No |

| Family Name | | Given Name | | Middle Name | |
|---|---|---|---|---|---|
| A# (if any) | Current Immigration Status | | Date of Birth (mm/dd/yyyy) | | Living with you? ☐ Yes ☐ No |

| Family Name | | Given Name | | Middle Name | |
|---|---|---|---|---|---|
| A# (if any) | Current Immigration Status | | Date of Birth (mm/dd/yyyy) | | Living with you? ☐ Yes ☐ No |

| Family Name | | Given Name | | Middle Name | |
|---|---|---|---|---|---|
| A# (if any) | Current Immigration Status | | Date of Birth (mm/dd/yyyy) | | Living with you? ☐ Yes ☐ No |

| Family Name | | Given Name | | Middle Name | |
|---|---|---|---|---|---|
| A# (if any) | Current Immigration Status | | Date of Birth (mm/dd/yyyy) | | Living with you? ☐ Yes ☐ No |

| Family Name | | Given Name | | Middle Name | |
|---|---|---|---|---|---|
| A# (if any) | Current Immigration Status | | Date of Birth (mm/dd/yyyy) | | Living with you? ☐ Yes ☐ No |

## Part 5. Information about your commercial enterprise.

**Type of Enterprise** *(Check one)*:

☐ New commercial enterprise resulting from the creation of a new business.

☐ New commercial enterprise resulting from the reorganization of an existing business.

☐ New commercial enterprise resulting from a capital investment in an existing business.

**Kind of Business** *(Be as specific as possible)*:

**Date Business Established** (mm/dd/yyyy)          Amount of Initial Investment

**Date of Initial Investment** (mm/dd/yyyy)          % of Enterprise You Own

**Number of full-time employees in enterprise in United States (excluding you, your spouse, sons and daughters):**

At the time of your initial investment:          Presently:          Difference:

**How many of these new jobs were created by your investment?**

## Part 5. Information about your commercial enterprise (continued).

**Subsequent Investment in the Enterprise:**

| Date of Investment | Amount of Investment | Type of Investment |
|---|---|---|
|  |  |  |
|  |  |  |
|  |  |  |

Provide the gross and net incomes generated annually by the commercial enterprise since your initial investment. Include all income generated up to date during the present year.

| Year | Gross Income | Net Income |
|---|---|---|
|  |  |  |
|  |  |  |
|  |  |  |

Has your commercial enterprise filed for bankruptcy, ceased business operations, or have any changes in its business organization or ownership occurred since the date of your initial investment? ☐ Yes (Explain on separate sheet) ☐ No

Has your commercial enterprise sold any corporate assets, shares, property, or had any capital withdrawn since the date of your initial investment? ☐ Yes (Explain on separate sheet) ☐ No

## Part 6. Signature. (Read the information on penalties in the instructions before completing this section.)

I certify, under penalty of perjury under the laws of the United States of America, that this petition and the evidence submitted with it is all true and correct. I further certify that the investment was made in accordance with the laws of the United States and was not for the purpose of evading United States immigration laws. I also authorize the release of any information from my records which the Bureau of Citizenship and Immigration Services needs to determine eligibility for the benefit being sought.

| Signature of Applicant | Print Name | Date |
|---|---|---|
|  |  |  |

**Please note: If you do not completely fill out this form or fail to submit any required documents listed in the instructions, you cannot be found eligible for the requested benefit and this petition may be denied.**

## Part 6. Signature of person preparing form, if other than above.

I declare that I prepared this petition at the request of the above person and it is based on all information of which I have knowledge.

| Signature | Print Name | Date |
|---|---|---|
|  |  |  |

Firm Name and Address

## INSTRUCTIONS

### Purpose of this Form

This form is required to show that an intending immigrant has adequate means of financial support and is not likely to become a public charge.

### Sponsor's Obligation

The person completing this affidavit is the sponsor. A sponsor's obligation continues until the sponsored immigrant becomes a U.S. citizen, can be credited with 40 qualifying quarters of work, departs the United States permanently, or dies. Divorce does not terminate the obligation. By signing this form, you, the sponsor, agree to support the intending immigrant and any spouse and/or children immigrating with him or her and to reimburse any government agency or private entity that provides these sponsored immigrants with Federal, State, or local means-tested public benefits.

### General Filing Instructions

Please answer all questions by typing or clearly printing in black ink only. Indicate that an item is not applicable with "N/A". If an answer is "none," please so state. If you need extra space to answer any item, attach a sheet of paper with your name and Social Security number, and indicate the number of the item to which the answer refers.

You must submit an affidavit of support for each applicant for immigrant status. You may submit photocopies of this affidavit for any spouse or children immigrating with an immigrant you are sponsoring. For purposes of this form, a spouse or child is immigrating with an immigrant you are sponsoring if he or she is: 1) listed in Part 3 of this affidavit of support; and 2) applies for an immigrant visa or adjustment of status within 6 months of the date this affidavit of support is originally completed and signed. The signature on the affidavit must be notarized by a notary public or signed before an Immigration or a Consular officer.

You should give the completed affidavit of support with all required documentation to the sponsored immigrant for submission to either a Consular Officer with Form OF-230, Application for Immigrant Visa and Alien Registration, or an Immigration Officer with Form I-485, Application to Register Permanent Residence or Adjust Status. You may enclose the affidavit of support and accompanying documents in a sealed envelope to be opened only by the designated Government official. The sponsored immigrant must submit the affidavit of support to the Government within 6 months of its signature.

### Who Needs an Affidavit of Support under Section 213A?

This affidavit must be filed at the time an intending immigrant is applying for an immigrant visa or adjustment of status. It is required for:

- All immediate relatives, including orphans, and family-based immigrants. (Self-petitioning widow/ers and battered spouses and children are exempt from this requirement); and

- Employment-based immigrants where a relative filed the immigrant visa petition or has a significant ownership interest (5 percent or more) in the entity that filed the petition.

### Who Completes an Affidavit of Support under Section 213A?

- For immediate relatives and family-based immigrants, the family member petitioning for the intending immigrant must be the sponsor.

- For employment-based immigrants, the petitioning relative or a relative with a significant ownership interest (5 percent or more) in the petitioning entity must be the sponsor. The term "relative," for these purposes, is defined as husband, wife, father, mother, child, adult son or daughter, brother, or sister.

- If the petitioner cannot meet the income requirements, a joint sponsor may submit an additional affidavit of support.

A sponsor, or joint sponsor, must also be:

- A citizen or national of the United States or an alien lawfully admitted to the United States for permanent residence;

- At least 18 years of age; and

- Domiciled in the United States or its territories and possessions.

### Sponsor's Income Requirement

As a sponsor, your household income must equal or exceed 125 percent of the Federal poverty line for your household size. For the purpose of the affidavit of support, household size includes yourself, all persons related to you by birth, marriage, or adoption living in your residence, your dependents, any immigrants you have previously sponsored using INS Form I-864 if that obligation has not terminated, and the intending immigrant(s) in Part 3 of this affidavit of support. The poverty guidelines are calculated and published annually by the Department of Health and Human Services. Sponsors who are on active duty in the U.S. Armed Forces other than for training need only demonstrate income at 100 percent of the poverty line *if* they are submitting this affidavit for the purpose of sponsoring their spouse or child.

If you are currently employed and have an *individual* income which meets or exceeds 125 percent of the Federal poverty line or (100 percent, if applicable) for your household size, you do not need to list the income of any other person. When determining your income, you may include the income generated by individuals related to you by birth, marriage, or adoption who are living in your residence, if they have lived in your residence for the previous 6 months, or who are listed as dependents on your most recent Federal income tax return whether or not they live in your residence. For their income to be considered, these household members or dependents must be willing to make their income available for the support of the sponsored immigrant(s) if necessary, and to complete and sign Form I-864A, Contract Between Sponsor and Household Member. However, a household member who is the immigrant you are sponsoring only need complete Form I-864A if his or her income will be used to determine your ability to support a spouse and/or children immigrating with him or her.

If in any of the most recent 3 tax years, you and your spouse each reported income on a joint income tax return, but you want to use only your own income to qualify (and your spouse is not submitting a Form I-864A), you may provide a separate breakout of your individual income for these years. Your individual income will be based on the earnings from your W-2 forms, Wage and Tax Statement, submitted to IRS for any such years. If necessary to meet the income requirement, you may also submit evidence of other income listed on your tax returns which can be attributed to you. You must provide documentation of such reported income, including Forms 1099 sent by the payer, which show your name and Social Security number.

You must calculate your household size and total household income as indicated in Parts 4.B. and 4.C. of this form. You must compare your total household income with the minimum income requirement for your household size using the poverty guidelines. For the purposes of the affidavit of support, determination of your ability to meet the income requirements will be based on the most recent poverty guidelines published in the Federal Register at the time the Consular or Immigration Officer makes a decision on the intending immigrant's application for an immigrant visa or adjustment of status. Immigration and Consular Officers will begin to use updated poverty guidelines on the first day of the second month after the date the guidelines are published in the Federal Register.

If your total household income is equal to or higher than the minimum income requirement for your household size, you do not need to provide information on your assets, and you may *not* have a joint sponsor unless you are requested to do so by a Consular or Immigration Officer. If your total household income does not meet the minimum income requirement, the intending immigrant will be ineligible for an immigrant visa or adjustment of status, unless:

- You provide evidence of assets that meet the requirements outlined under "Evidence of Assets" below; and/or

- The immigrant you are sponsoring provides evidence of assets that meet the requirements under "Evidence of Assets" below; or

- A joint sponsor assumes the liability of the intending immigrant with you. A joint sponsor must execute a separate affidavit of support on behalf of the intending

immigrant and any accompanying family members. A joint sponsor must individually meet the minimum requirement of 125 percent of the poverty line based on his or her household size and income and/or assets, including any assets of the sponsored immigrant.

The Government may pursue verification of any information provided on or in support of this form, including employment, income, or assets with the employer, financial or other institutions, the Internal Revenue Service, or the Social Security Administration.

### Evidence of Income
In order to complete this form you must submit the following evidence of income:

- A copy of your complete Federal income tax return, as filed with the Internal Revenue Service, for each of the most recent 3 tax years. If you were not required to file a tax return in any of the most recent 3 tax years, you must provide an explanation. If you filed a joint income tax return and are using only your own income to qualify, you must also submit copies of your W-2s for each of the most recent 3 tax years, and if necessary to meet the income requirement, evidence of other income reported on your tax returns, such as Forms 1099.

- If you rely on income of any members of your household or dependents in order to reach the minimum income requirement, copies of their Federal income tax returns for the most recent 3 tax years. These persons must each complete and sign a Form I-864A, Contract Between Sponsor and Household Member.

- Evidence of current employment or self-employment, such as a recent pay statement, or a statement from your employer on business stationery, showing beginning date of employment, type of work performed, and salary or wages paid. You must also provide evidence of current employment for any person whose income is used to qualify.

### Evidence of Assets
If you want to use your assets, the assets of your household members or dependents, and/or the assets of the immigrant you are sponsoring to meet the minimum income requirement, you must provide evidence of assets with a cash value that equals at least five times the difference between your total household income and the minimum income requirement. For the assets of a household member, other than the immigrant(s) you are sponsoring, to be considered, the household member must complete and sign Form I-864A, Contract Between Sponsor and Household Member.

All assets must be supported with evidence to verify location, ownership, and value of each asset. Any liens and liabilities relating to the assets must be documented. List only assets that can be readily converted into cash within one year. Evidence of assets includes, but is not limited to the following:

- Bank statements covering the last 12 months, *or* a statement from an officer of the bank or other financial institution in which you have deposits, including deposit/withdrawal history for the last 12 months, and current balance;

- Evidence of ownership and value of stocks, bonds, and certificates of deposit, and date(s) acquired;

- Evidence of ownership and value of other personal property, and date(s) acquired; and

- Evidence of ownership and value of any real estate, and date(s) acquired.

### *Change of Sponsor's Address*

You are required by 8 U.S.C. 1183a(d) and 8 CFR 213a.3 to report every change of address to the Immigration and Naturalization Service and the State(s) in which the sponsored immigrant(s) reside(s). You must report changes of address to INS on Form I-865, Sponsor's Notice of Change of Address, within 30 days of any change of address. You must also report any change in your address to the State(s) in which the sponsored immigrant(s) live.

### *Penalties*

If you include in this affidavit of support any material information that you know to be false, you may be liable for criminal prosecution under the laws of the United States.

If you fail to give notice of your change of address, as required by 8 U.S.C. 1183a(d) and 8 CFR 213a.3, you may be liable for the civil penalty established by 8 U.S.C. 1183a(d)(2). The amount of the civil penalty will depend on whether you failed to give this notice because you were aware that the immigrant(s) you sponsored had received Federal, State, or local means-tested public benefits.

### *Privacy Act Notice*

Authority for the collection of the information requested on this form is contained in 8 U.S.C. 1182(a)(4), 1183a, 1184(a), and 1258. The information will be used principally by the INS or by any Consular Officer to whom it is furnished, to support an alien's application for benefits under the Immigration and Nationality Act and specifically the assertion that he or she has adequate means of financial support and will not become a public charge. Submission of the information is voluntary. Failure to provide the information will result in denial of the application for an immigrant visa or adjustment of status.

The information may also, as a matter of routine use, be disclosed to other Federal, State, and local agencies or private entities providing means-tested public benefits for use in civil action against the sponsor for breach of contract. It may also be disclosed as a matter of routine use to other Federal, State, local, and foreign law enforcement and regulatory agencies to enable these entities to carry out their law enforcement responsibilites.

### *Reporting Burden*

A person is not required to respond to a collection of information unless it displays a currently valid OMB control number. We try to create forms and instructions that are accurate, can be easily understood, and which impose the least possible burden on you to provide us with information. Often this is difficult because some immigration laws are very complex. The reporting burden for this collection of information on Form I-864 is computed as follows: 1) learning about the form, 63 minutes; 2) completing the form, 105 minutes; and 3) assembling and filing the form, 65 minutes, for an estimated average of 3 hours and 48 minutes minutes per response. The reporting burden for collection of information on Form I-864A is computed as: 1) learning about the form, 20 minutes; 2) completing the form, 55 minutes; 3) assembling and filing the form, 30 minutes, for an estimated average of 1 hour and 45 minutes per response. If you have comments regarding the accuracy of this estimates, or suggestions for making this form simpler, you can write to the Immigration and Naturalization Service, HQPDI, 425 I Street, N.W., Room 4034, Washington, DC 20536. **DO NOT MAIL YOUR COMPLETED AFFIDAVIT OF SUPPORT TO THIS ADDRESS.**

## CHECK LIST

**The following items must be submitted with Form I-864, Affidavit of Support Under Section 213A:**

**For *ALL* sponsors:**

☐ This form, the **I-864, completed and signed** before a notary public or a Consular or Immigration Officer.

☐ Proof of **current employment** or self employment.

☐ Your individual Federal **income tax returns for the most recent 3 tax years,** or an explanation if fewer are submitted. Your **W-2s** for any of the most recent 3 tax years for which you filed a joint tax return but are using only your own income to qualify. Forms 1099 or evidence of other reported income *if* necessary to qualify.

**For *SOME* sponsors:**

☐ *If the immigrant you are sponsoring is bringing a spouse or children,* **photocopies of the immigrant's affidavit of support** for each spouse and/or child immigrating with the immigrant you are sponsoring.

☐ *If you are on active duty in the U.S. Armed Forces and are sponsoring a spouse or child using the 100 percent of poverty level exception,* **proof of your active military status.**

*If you are using the income of **persons in your household or dependents** to qualify,*

☐ A separate **Form I-864A** for each person whose income you will use. A sponsored immigrant/household member who is not immigrating with a spouse and/or child **does not need to complete Form I-864A.**

☐ Proof of their **residency and relationship** to you if they are not listed as dependents on your income tax return for the most recent tax year.

☐ Proof of their **current employment** or self-employment.

☐   Copies of their individual Federal **income tax returns for the 3 most recent tax years,** or an explanation if fewer are submitted.

*If you use your assets or the assets of the sponsored immigrant to qualify,*

☐   **Documentation of assets** establishing location, ownership, date of acquisition, and value. Evidence of any liens or liabilities against these assets.

☐   A separate **Form I-864A** for each household member other than the sponsored immigrant/household member.

*If you are a joint sponsor or the relative of an employment-based immigrant requiring an affidavit of support,* **proof of your citizenship status.**

☐   For U.S. citizens or nationals, a copy of your birth certificate, passport, or certificate of naturalization or citizenship.

☐   For lawful permanent residents, a copy of both sides of your I-551, Permanent Resident Card.

**U.S. Department of Justice**
Immigration and Naturalization Service

# Affidavit of Support Under Section 213A of the Act

**START HERE - Please Type or Print**

## Part 1.  Information on Sponsor  (You)

| Last Name | First Name | Middle Name |
|---|---|---|

| Mailing Address *(Street Number and Name)* | Apt/Suite Number |
|---|---|

| City | State or Province |
|---|---|

| Country | ZIP/Postal Code | Telephone Number |
|---|---|---|

| Place of Residence if different from above *(Street Number and Name)* | Apt/Suite Number |
|---|---|

| City | State or Province |
|---|---|

| Country | ZIP/Postal Code | Telephone Number |
|---|---|---|

| Date of Birth *(Month, Day, Year)* | Place of Birth *(City, State, Country)* | Are you a U.S. Citizen? ☐ Yes ☐ No |
|---|---|---|

| Social Security Number | A-Number *(If any)* |
|---|---|

**FOR AGENCY USE ONLY**

| This Affidavit | Receipt |
|---|---|
| [  ] Meets | |
| [  ] Does not meet | |

Requirements of Section 213A

_____
Officer or I.J. Signature

_____
Location

_____
Date

## Part 2.  Basis for Filing Affidavit of Support

I am filing this affidavit of support because *(check one)*:

a. ☐  I filed/am filing the alien relative petition.

b. ☐  I filed/am filing an alien worker petition on behalf of the intending

immigrant, who is related to me as my _____ .
*(relationship)*

c. ☐  I have ownership interest of at least 5% _____ .
*(name of entity which filed visa petition)*
which filed an alien worker petition on behalf of the intending

immigrant, who is related to me as my _____ .
*(relationship)*

d. ☐  I am a joint sponsor willing to accept the legal obligations with any other sponsor(s).

## Part 3.  Information on the Immigrant(s) You Are Sponsoring

| Last Name | First Name | Middle Name |
|---|---|---|

| Date of Birth *(Month, Day, Year)* | Sex ☐ Male  ☐ Female | Social Security Number *(If any)* |
|---|---|---|

| Country of Citizenship | A-Number *(If any)* |
|---|---|

| Current Address  *(Street Number and Name)* | Apt/Suite Number | City |
|---|---|---|

| State/Province | Country | ZIP/Postal Code | Telephone Number |
|---|---|---|---|

List any spouse and/or children immigrating with the immigrant named above in this Part:   *(Use additional sheet of paper if necessary.)*

| Name | Relationship to Sponsored Immigrant | | | Date of Birth | | | A-Number *(If any)* | Social Security *(If any)* |
|---|---|---|---|---|---|---|---|---|
| | Spouse | Son | Daughter | Mo. | Day | Yr. | | |
| | | | | | | | | |
| | | | | | | | | |
| | | | | | | | | |
| | | | | | | | | |

Form I-864 (Rev. 11/05/01)Y

## Part 4.    Eligibility to Sponsor

To be a sponsor you must be a U.S. citizen or national or a lawful permanent resident.  If you are not the petitioning relative, you must provide proof of status.  To prove status, U.S. citizens or nationals must attach a copy of a document proving status, such as a U.S. passport, birth certificate, or certificate of naturalization, and lawful permanent residents must attach a copy of both sides of their Permanent Resident Card (Form I-551).

The determination of your eligibility to sponsor an immigrant will be based on an evaluation of your demonstrated ability to maintain an annual income at or above 125 percent of the Federal poverty line (100 percent if you are a petitioner sponsoring your spouse or child and you are on active duty in the U.S. Armed Forces).  The assessment of your ability to maintain an adequate income will include your current employment, household size, and household income as shown on the Federal income tax returns for the 3 most recent tax years.  Assets that are readily converted to cash and that can be made available for the support of sponsored immigrants if necessary, including any such assets of the immigrant(s) you are sponsoring, may also be considered.

The greatest weight in determining eligibility will be placed on current employment and household income.  If a petitioner is unable to demonstrate ability to meet the stated income and asset requirements, a joint sponsor who *can* meet the income and asset requirements is needed.  Failure to provide adequate evidence of income and/or assets or an affidavit of support completed by a joint sponsor will result in denial of the immigrant's application for an immigrant visa or adjustment to permanent resident status.

### A. Sponsor's Employment

I am:    1 .    ☐  Employed by _____ *(Provide evidence of employment)*

Annual salary _____ or hourly wage $ _____ *(for _____ hours per week)*

2.    ☐  Self employed _____ *(Name of business)*

Nature of employment or business    _____

3.    ☐  Unemployed or retired since    _____

### B. Sponsor's Household Size

**Number**

1. Number of persons (related to you by birth, marriage, or adoption) living in your residence, including yourself *(Do NOT include persons being sponsored in this affidavit.)*    _____

2. Number of immigrants being sponsored in this affidavit *(Include all persons in Part 3.)*    _____

3. Number of immigrants **NOT** living in your household whom you are obligated to support under a previously signed Form I-864.    _____

4. Number of persons who are otherwise dependent on you, as claimed in your tax return for the most recent tax year.    _____

5. Total household size. *(Add lines 1 through 4.)*    **Total**    _____

List persons below who are included in lines 1 or 3 for whom you previously have submitted INS Form I-864, *if your support obligation has not terminated.*

*(If additional space is needed, use additional paper)*

| Name | A-Number | Date Affidavit of Support Signed | Relationship |
|---|---|---|---|
|  |  |  |  |
|  |  |  |  |
|  |  |  |  |
|  |  |  |  |
|  |  |  |  |
|  |  |  |  |

## Part 4. Eligibility to Sponsor *(Continued)*

### C. Sponsor's Annual Household Income

Enter total unadjusted income from your Federal income tax return for the most recent tax year below. If you last filed a joint income tax return but are using only your *own* income to qualify, list total earnings from your W-2 Forms, or, *if* necessary to reach the required income for your household size, include income from other sources listed on your tax return. If your *individual* income does not meet the income requirement for your household size, you may also list total income for anyone related to you by birth, marriage, or adoption currently living with you in your residence if they have lived in your residence for the previous 6 months, or any person shown as a dependent on your Federal income tax return for the most recent tax year, even if not living in the household. For their income to be considered, household members or dependents must be willing to make their income available for support of the sponsored immigrant(s) and to complete and sign Form I-864A, Contract Between Sponsor and Household Member. A sponsored immigrant/household member only need complete Form I-864A if his or her income will be used to determine your ability to support a spouse and/or children immigrating with him or her.

*You must attach evidence of current employment and copies of income tax returns as filed with the IRS for the most recent 3 tax years for yourself and all persons whose income is listed below. See "Required Evidence" in Instructions.* Income from all 3 years will be considered in determining your ability to support the immigrant(s) you are sponsoring.

- ☐ I filed a single/separate tax return for the most recent tax year.
- ☐ I filed a joint return for the most recent tax year which includes only my own income.
- ☐ I filed a joint return for the most recent tax year which includes income for my spouse and myself.
    - ☐ I am submitting documentation of my individual income (Forms W-2 and 1099).
    - ☐ I am qualifying using my spouse's income; my spouse is submitting a Form I-864A.

### Indicate most recent tax year

_____
*(tax year)*

Sponsor's individual income      $ _____

**or**

Sponsor and spouse's combined income      $ _____
*(If spouse's income is to be considered, spouse must submit Form I-864A.)*

Income of other qualifying persons.
*(List names; include spouse if applicable. Each person must complete Form I-864A.)*

_____    $ _____

_____    $ _____

_____    $ _____

_____    $ _____

### Total Household Income      $ _____

Explain on separate sheet of paper if you or any of the above listed individuals were not required to file Federal income tax returns for the most recent 3 years, or if other explanation of income, employment, or evidence is necessary.

### D. Determination of Eligibility Based on Income

1.   ☐ I am subject to the 125 percent of poverty line requirement for sponsors.
      ☐ I am subject to the 100 percent of poverty line requirement for sponsors on active duty in the U.S. Armed Forces sponsoring their spouse or child.
2.   Sponsor's total household size, from Part 4.B., line 5   _____ .
3.   Minimum income requirement from the Poverty Guidelines chart for the year of _____ is $ _____
      for this household size.        *(year)*

**If you are currently employed and your household income for your household size is equal to or greater than the applicable poverty line requirement (from line D.3.), you do not need to list assets (Parts 4.E. and 5) or have a joint sponsor (Part 6)** unless you are requested to do so by a Consular or Immigration Officer. You may skip to Part 7, Use of the Affidavit of Support to Overcome Public Charge Ground of Admissibility. **Otherwise, you should continue with Part 4.E.**

## Part 4.    Eligibility to Sponsor    *(Continued)*

### E. Sponsor's Assets and Liabilities

Your assets and those of your qualifying household members and dependents may be used to demonstrate ability to maintain an income at or above 125 percent (or 100 percent, if applicable) of the poverty line *if* they are available for the support of the sponsored immigrant(s) and can readily be converted into cash within 1 year. The household member, other than the immigrant(s) you are sponsoring, must complete and sign Form I-864A, Contract Between Sponsor and Household Member. List the cash value of each asset *after* any debts or liens are subtracted. Supporting evidence must be attached to establish location, ownership, date of acquisition, and value of each asset listed, including any liens and liabilities related to each asset listed. See "Evidence of Assets" in Instructions.

| Type of Asset | Cash Value of Assets *(Subtract any debts)* |
|---|---|
| Savings deposits | $ |
| Stocks, bonds, certificates of deposit | $ |
| Life insurance cash value | $ |
| Real estate | $ |
| Other *(specify)* | $ |
| **Total Cash Value of Assets** | $ _____ |

## Part 5.    Immigrant's Assets and Offsetting Liabilities

The sponsored immigrant's assets may also be used in support of your ability to maintain income at or above 125 percent of the poverty line *if* the assets are or will be available in the United States for the support of the sponsored immigrant(s) and can readily be converted into cash within 1 year.

The sponsored immigrant should provide information on his or her assets in a format similar to part 4.E. above. Supporting evidence must be attached to establish location, ownership, and value of each asset listed, including any liens and liabilities for each asset listed. See "Evidence of Assets" in Instructions.

## Part 6.    Joint Sponsors

If household income and assets do not meet the appropriate poverty line for your household size, a joint sponsor is required. There may be more than one joint sponsor, but each joint sponsor must individually meet the 125 percent of poverty line requirement based on his or her household income and/or assets, including any assets of the sponsored immigrant. By submitting a separate Affidavit of Support under Section 213A of the Act (Form I-864), a joint sponsor accepts joint responsibility with the petitioner for the sponsored immigrant(s) until they become U.S. citizens, can be credited with 40 quarters of work, leave the United States permanently, or die.

## Part 7.    Use of the Affidavit of Support to Overcome Public Charge Ground of Inadmissibility

Section 212(a)(4)(C) of the Immigration and Nationality Act provides that an alien seeking permanent residence as an immediate relative (including an orphan), as a family-sponsored immigrant, or as an alien who will accompany or follow to join another alien is considered to be likely to become a public charge and is inadmissible to the United States unless a sponsor submits a legally enforceable affidavit of support on behalf of the alien. Section 212(a)(4)(D) imposes the same requirement on an employment-based immigrant, and those aliens who accompany or follow to join the employment- based immigrant, if the employment-based immigrant will be employed by a relative, or by a firm in which a relative owns a significant interest. Separate affidavits of support are required for family members at the time they immigrate if they are not included on this affidavit of support or do not apply for an immigrant visa or adjustment of status within 6 months of the date this affidavit of support is originally signed. The sponsor must provide the sponsored immigrant(s) whatever support is necessary to maintain them at an income that is at least 125 percent of the Federal poverty guidelines.

> *I submit this affidavit of support in consideration of the sponsored immigrant(s) not being found inadmissible to the United States under section 212(a)(4)(C) (or 212(a)(4)(D) for an employment-based immigrant) and to enable the sponsored immigrant(s) to overcome this ground of inadmissibility. I agree to provide the sponsored immigrant(s) whatever support is necessary to maintain the sponsored immigrant(s) at an income that is at least 125 percent of the Federal poverty guidelines. I understand that my obligation will continue until my death or the sponsored immigrant(s) have become U.S. citizens, can be credited with 40 quarters of work, depart the United States permanently, or die.*

### Notice of Change of Address.

Sponsors are required to provide written notice of any change of address within 30 days of the change in address until the sponsored immigrant(s) have become U.S. citizens, can be credited with 40 quarters of work, depart the United States permanently, or die.  To comply with this requirement, the sponsor must complete INS Form I-865.  Failure to give this notice may subject the sponsor to the civil penalty established under section 213A(d)(2) which ranges from $250 to $2,000, unless the failure to report occurred with the knowledge that the sponsored immigrant(s) had received means-tested public benefits, in which case the penalty ranges from $2,000 to $5,000.

> *If my address changes for any reason before my obligations under this affidavit of support terminate, I will complete and file INS Form I-865, Sponsor's Notice of Change of Address, within 30 days of the change of address.  I understand that failure to give this notice may subject me to civil penalties.*

### Means-tested Public Benefit Prohibitions and Exceptions.

Under section 403(a) of Public Law 104-193 (Welfare Reform Act), aliens lawfully admitted for permanent residence in the United States, with certain exceptions, are ineligible for most Federally-funded means-tested public benefits during their first 5 years in the United States.  This provision does not apply to public benefits specified in section 403(c) of the Welfare Reform Act or to State public benefits, including emergency Medicaid; short-term, non-cash emergency relief; services provided under the National School Lunch and Child Nutrition Acts; immunizations and testing and treatment for communicable diseases; student assistance under the Higher Education Act and the Public Health Service Act; certain forms of foster-care or adoption assistance under the Social Security Act; Head Start programs; means-tested programs under the Elementary and Secondary Education Act; and Job Training Partnership Act programs.

### Consideration of Sponsor's Income in Determining Eligibility for Benefits.

If a permanent resident alien is no longer statutorily barred from a Federally-funded means-tested public benefit program and applies for such a benefit, the income and resources of the sponsor and the sponsor's spouse will be considered (or deemed) to be the income and resources of the sponsored immigrant in determining the immigrant's eligibility for Federal means-tested public benefits.  Any State or local government may also choose to consider (or deem) the income and resources of the sponsor and the sponsor's spouse to be the income and resources of the immigrant for the purposes of determining eligibility for their means-tested public benefits.  The attribution of the income and resources of the sponsor and the sponsor's spouse to the immigrant will continue until the immigrant becomes a U.S. citizen or has worked or can be credited with 40 qualifying quarters of work, provided that the immigrant or the worker crediting the quarters to the immigrant has not received any Federal means-tested public benefit during any creditable quarter for any period after December 31, 1996.

> *I understand that, under section 213A of the Immigration and Nationality Act (the Act), as amended, this affidavit of support constitutes a contract between me and the U.S. Government. This contract is designed to protect the United States Government, and State and local government agencies or private entities that provide means-tested public benefits, from having to pay benefits to or on behalf of the sponsored immigrant(s), for as long as I am obligated to support them under this affidavit of support. I understand that the sponsored immigrants, or any Federal, State, local, or private entity that pays any means-tested benefit to or on behalf of the sponsored immigrant(s), are entitled to sue me if I fail to meet my obligations under this affidavit of support, as defined by section 213A and INS regulations.*

### Civil Action to Enforce.

If the immigrant on whose behalf this affidavit of support is executed receives any Federal, State, or local means-tested public benefit before this obligation terminates, the Federal, State, or local agency or private entity may request reimbursement from the sponsor who signed this affidavit.  If the sponsor fails to honor the request for reimbursement, the agency may sue the sponsor in any U.S. District Court or any State court with jurisdiction of civil actions for breach of contract. INS will provide names, addresses, and Social Security account numbers of sponsors to benefit-providing agencies for this purpose. Sponsors may also be liable for paying the costs of collection, including legal fees.

## Part 7.   Use of the Affidavit of Support to Overcome Public Charge Grounds   *(Continued)*

*I acknowledge that section 213A(a)(1)(B) of the Act grants the sponsored immigrant(s) and any Federal, State, local, or private agency that pays any means-tested public benefit to or on behalf of the sponsored immigrant(s) standing to sue me for failing to meet my obligations under this affidavit of support.  I agree to submit to the personal jurisdiction of any court of the United States or of any State, territory, or possession of the United States if the court has subject matter jurisdiction of a civil lawsuit to enforce this affidavit of support.  I agree that no lawsuit to enforce this affidavit of support shall be barred by any statute of limitations that might otherwise apply, so long as the plaintiff initiates the civil lawsuit no later than ten (10) years after the date on which a sponsored immigrant last received any means-tested public benefits.*

## Collection of Judgment.

*I acknowledge that a plaintiff may seek specific performance of my support obligation.  Furthermore, any money judgment against me based on this affidavit of support may be collected through the use of a judgment lien under 28 U.S.C 3201, a writ of execution under 28 U.S.C 3203, a judicial installment payment order under 28 U.S.C 3204, garnishment under 28 U.S.C 3205, or through the use of any corresponding remedy under State law.  I may also be held liable for costs of collection, including attorney fees.*

## Concluding Provisions.

*I, _____ , certify under penalty of perjury under the laws of the United States that:*

*(a) I know the contents of this affidavit of support signed by me;*

*(b) All the statements in this affidavit of support are true and correct,*

*(c) I make this affidavit of support for the consideration stated in Part 7, freely, and without any mental reservation or purpose of evasion;*

*(d) Income tax returns submitted in support of this affidavit are true copies of the returns filed with the Internal Revenue Service; and*

*(e) Any other evidence submitted is true and correct.*

_____        _____
*(Sponsor's Signature)*                                                          *(Date)*

Subscribed and sworn to (or affirmed) before me this

_____ day of _____ , _____
                                    *(Month)*                   *(Year)*

at  _____ .

My commission expires on  _____ .

_____
*(Signature of Notary Public or Officer Administering Oath)*

_____
*(Title)*

## Part 8.   If someone other than the sponsor prepared this affidavit of support, that person must complete the following:

I certify under penalty of perjury under the laws of the United States that I prepared this affidavit of support at the sponsor's request, and that this affidavit of support is based on all information of which I have knowledge.

| Signature | Print Your Name | Date | Daytime Telephone Number |
|---|---|---|---|
| | | | |

Firm Name and Address

OMB No. 1115-0214

# Contract Between Sponsor and Household Member

| Sponsor's Name *(Last, First, Middle)* | Social Security Number | A-Number (If any) |
|---|---|---|
| | | |

## General Filing Instruction

Form I-864A, Contract Between Sponsor and Household Member, is an attachment to Form I-864, Affidavit of Support Under Section 213A of the Immigration and Nationality Act (the Act). The sponsor enters the information above, complete Part 2 of this form, and signs in Part 5. The household member completes Parts 1 and 3 of this form and signs in Part 6. A household member who is also the sponsored immigrant completes Parts 1 and 4 (instead of Part 3) of this form and signs i Part 6. The Privacy Act Notice and information on penalties for misrepresentation or fraud are included on the instructions to Form I-864.

The signatures on the I-864A must be notarized by a notary public or signed before an immigration or consular officer. A separate form must be used for each household member whose income and/or assets are being used to qualify. This blank form may be photocopied for that purpose. A sponsored immigrant who qualifies as a household member is only required to complete this form if he or she has one or more family members immigrating with him or her and is making his or her *income* available for their support. Sponsored immigrants who are using their *assets* to qualify are not required to complete this form. This completed form is submitted with Form I-864 by the sponsored immigrant with an application for an immigrant visa or adjustment of status.

## Purpose

This contract is intended to benefit the sponsored immigrant(s) and any agency of the Federal Government, any agency of a State or local government, or any private entity to which the sponsor has an obligation under the affidavit of support to reimburse for benefits granted to the sponsored immigrant, and these parties will have the right to enforce this contract in an court with appropriate jurisdiction. Under Section 213A of Act, this contract must be completed and signed by the sponsor and any household member, including the sponsor's spouse, whose income is included as household income by a person sponsoring one or more immigrants. The contract must also be completed if a sponsor is relying on the assets of a househo member who is not the sponsored immigrant to meet the income requirements. If the sponsored immigrant is a household member immigrating with a spouse or children, and is using his or her income to assist the sponsor in meeting the income requirement, he or she must complete and sign this contract as a "sponsored immigrant/household member."

By signing this form, a household member, who is not a sponsored immigrant, agrees to make his or her income and/or assets available to the sponsor to help support the immigrant(s) for whom the sponsor has filed an affidavit of support and to be responsible, along with the sponsor, to pay any debt incurred by the sponsor under the affidavit of support. A sponsored immigrant/household member who signs this contract agrees to make his or her income available to the sponsor to help support any spouse or children immigrating with him or her and to be responsible, along with the sponsor, to pay any debt incurred by the sponsor under the affidavit of support. The obligations of the household member and the sponsored immigrant/household member under this contract terminate when the obligations of the sponsor under the affidavit of support terminate. For additional information see section 213A of the Act, part 213a of title 8 of the Code of Federal Regulations, and Form I-864, Affidavit of Support Under Section 213A of the Act.

## Definitions:

1) An "affidavit of support" refers to Form I-864, Affidavit of Support Under Section 213A of the Act, which is complete and filed by the sponsor.

2) A "sponsor" is a person, either the petitioning relative, the relative with a significant ownership interest in the petitionin entity, or another person accepting joint and several liability with the sponsor, who completes and files the Affidavit of Support under Section 213A of the Act on behalf of a sponsored immigrant.

3) A "household member" is any person (a) sharing a residence with the sponsor for at least the last 6 months who is related to the sponsor by birth, marriage, or adoption, *or* (b) whom the sponsor has lawfully claimed as a dependent or the sponsor's most recent federal income tax return even if that person does not live at the same residence as the sponsor, *and* whose income and/or assets will be used to demonstrate the sponsor's ability to maintain the sponsored immigrant(s) at an annual income at the level specified in section 213A(f)(1)(E) or 213A(f)(3) of the Act.

4) A "sponsored immigrant" is a person listed on this form on whose behalf an affidavit of support will be completed and filed.

5) A "sponsored immigrant/household member" is a sponsored immigrant who is also a household member.

## Part 1. Information on Sponsor's Household Member or Sponsored Immigrant/Household Member

| Last Name | First Name | Middle Name |
|---|---|---|

| Date of Birth *(Month, Day, Year)* | Social Security Number *(Mandatory for non-citizens; voluntary for U.S. citizens)* | A-Number *(If any)* |
|---|---|---|

| Address *(Street Number and Name)* Apt Number | City | State/Province | ZIP/Postal Code |
|---|---|---|---|

| Telephone Number<br>(     ) | Relationship to Sponsor: _____<br>I am: ☐ The sponsor's household member. *(Complete Part 3.)*<br>☐ The sponsored immigrant/household member. *(Complete Part* | Length of residence with sponsor<br>_____ years, _____ months) |
|---|---|---|

## Part 2. Sponsor's Promise

**I, THE SPONSOR,** _____ , in consideration of the household member's promise to support the
*(Print name of sponsor)*
sponsored immigrant(s) and to be jointly and severally liable for any obligations I incur under the affidavit of support,
promise to complete and file an affidavit of support on behalf of the following _____ sponsored immigrant(s):
*(Indicate number)*

| Name of Sponsored Immigrant<br>*(First, Middle, Last)* | Date of Birth<br>*(Month, Day, Year)* | Social Security Number<br>*(If any)* | A-Number<br>*(If any)* |
|---|---|---|---|
| | | | |
| | | | |
| | | | |
| | | | |
| | | | |

## Part 3. Household Member's Promise

**I, THE HOUSEHOLD** _____ , in consideration of the sponsor's
*(Print name of household member)*
promise to complete and file the affidavit of support on behalf of the sponsored immigrant(s):

1) Promise to provide any and all financial support necessary to assist the sponsor in maintaining the sponsored immigrant(s) at or above the minimum income provided for in section 213A(a)(1)(A) of the Act (not less than 125 percent of the Federal Poverty Guidelines) during the period in which the affidavit of support is enforceable;

2) Agree to be jointly and severally liable for payment of any and all obligations owed by the sponsor under the affidavit of support to the sponsored immigrant(s), to any agency of the Federal Government, to any agency of a state or local government, or to any private entity;

3) Agree to submit to the personal jurisdiction of any court of the United States or of any state, territory, or possession of the United States if the court has subject matter jurisdiction of a civil lawsuit to enforce this contract or the affidavit of support; and

4) Certify under penalty of perjury under the laws of the United States that all the information provided on this form is true and correct to the best of my knowledge and belief and that the income tax returns I submitted in support of the sponsor affidavit are true copies of the returns filed with the Internal Revenue Service.

## Part 4. Sponsored Immigrant/Household Member's Promise

**I, THE SPONSORED IMMIGRANT/HOUSEHOLD** _____

*(Print name of sponsored immigrant)*

in consideration of the sponsor's promise to complete and file the affidavit of support on behalf of the sponsored immigrant(s) accompanying me:

1) Promise to provide any and all financial support necessary to assist the sponsor in maintaining any sponsored immigrant(s) immigrating with me at or above the minimum income provided for in section 213A(a)(1)(A) of the Act (not less than 125 percent of the Federal Poverty Guidelines) during the period in which the affidavit of support is enforceable;

2) Agree to be jointly and severally liable for payment of any and all obligations owed by the sponsor under the affidavit of support to any sponsored immigrant(s) immigrating with me, to any agency of the Federal Government, to any agency of a state or local government, or to any private entity;

3) Agree to submit to the personal jurisdiction of any court of the United States or of any state, territory, or possession of the United States if the court has subject matter jurisdiction of a civil lawsuit to enforce this contract or the affidavit of support; and

4) Certify under penalty of perjury under the laws of the United States that all the information provided on this form is tru and correct to the best of my knowledge and belief and that the income tax returns I submitted in support of the sponsor's affidavit of support are true copies of the returns filed with the Internal Revenue Service.

## Part 5. Sponsor's Signature

_____     Date: _____
*Sponsor's Signature*

Subscribed and sworn to *(or affirmed)* before me this_____     day of _____ , _____

(Month)                    (Year)

at _____ .     My commission expires on_____ .

_____     _____
*Signature of Notary Public or Officer Administering Oath*                    *Title*

## Part 6. Household Member's or Sponsored Immigrant/Household Member's Signature

_____     Date: _____
*Household Member's or Sponsored Immigrant/Household Member's Signature*

Subscribed and sworn to *(or affirmed)* before me this_____     day of _____ , _____

(Month)                    (Year)

at _____ .     My commission expires on_____ .

_____     _____
*Signature of Notary Public or Officer Administering Oath*                    *Title*

# 2003 Poverty Guidelines*
## Minimum Income Requirement For Use in Completing Form I-864

### For the 48 Contiguous States, the District of Columbia, Puerto Rico, the U.S. Virgin Islands, and Guam:

| Sponsor's Household Size | 100% of Poverty Line — For sponsors on active duty in the U.S. Armed Forces who are petitioning for their spouse or child. | 125% of Poverty Line — For all other sponsors |
|---|---|---|
| 2 | $12,120 | $15,150 |
| 3 | 15,260 | 19,075 |
| 4 | 18,400 | 23,000 |
| 5 | 21,540 | 26,925 |
| 6 | 24,680 | 30,850 |
| 7 | 27,820 | 34,775 |
| 8 | 30,960 | 38,700 |
| | Add $3,140 for each additional person. | Add $3,925 for each additional person. |

| Sponsor's Household Size | For Alaska — 100% of Poverty Line — For sponsors on active duty in the U.S. Armed Forces who are petitioning for their spouse or child | For Alaska — 125% of Poverty Line — For all other sponsors | For Hawaii — 100% of Poverty Line — For sponsors on active duty in the U.S. Armed Forces who are petitioning for their spouse or child | For Hawaii — 125% of Poverty Line — For all other sponsors |
|---|---|---|---|---|
| 2 | $15,140 | $18,925 | $13,940 | $17,425 |
| 3 | 19,070 | 23,837 | 17,550 | 21,937 |
| 4 | 23,000 | 28,750 | 21,160 | 26,450 |
| 5 | 26,930 | 33,662 | 24,770 | 30,962 |
| 6 | 30,860 | 38,575 | 28,380 | 35,475 |
| 7 | 34,790 | 43,487 | 31,990 | 39,987 |
| 8 | 38,720 | 48,400 | 35,600 | 44,500 |
| | Add $3,930 for each additional person. | Add $4,912 for each additional person. | Add $3,610 for each additional person. | Add $4,512 for each additional person. |

## Means-tested Public Benefits

**Federal Means-tested Public Benefits.** To date, Federal agencies administering benefit programs have determined that Federal means-tested public benefits include Food Stamps, Medicaid, Supplemental Security Income (SSI), Temporary Assistance for Needy Families (TANF), and the State Child Health Insurance Program (SCHIP).

**State Means-tested Public Benefits.** Each State will determine which, if any, of its public benefits are means-tested. If a State determines that it has programs which meet this definition, it is encouraged to provide notice to the public on which programs are included. Check with the State public assistance office to determine which, if any, State assistance programs have been determined to be State means-tested public benefits.

**Programs Not Included:** The following Federal and State programs are *not* included as means-tested benefits: emergency Medicaid; short-term, non-cash emergency relief; services provided under the National School Lunch and Child Nutrition Acts; immunizations and testing and treatment for communicable diseases; student assistance under the Higher Education Act and the Public Health Service Act; certain forms of foster-care or adoption assistance under the Social Security Act; Head Start Programs; means-tested programs under the Elementary and Secondary Education Act; and Job Training Partnership Act programs.

\* **These poverty guidelines remain in effect for use with the Form I-864 Affidavit of Support from April 1, 2003 until new poverty guidelines go into effect in the Spring of 2004.**

# Sponsor's Notice of Change of Address

**START HERE - Please Type or Print     Answer all Questions**

## Part 1.     Information about Sponsor

| Last Name | First Name | Middle Name |
|---|---|---|

| Date of Birth *(Month, Day, Year)* | Place of Birth *(City, State, Country)* |
|---|---|

| A-Number *(If any)* | Social Security Number |
|---|---|

| My **New** Mailing Address *(Street Number and Name)* | Apt/Suite Number |
|---|---|

| City | State or Province |
|---|---|

| Country | ZIP/Postal Code | Telephone Number |
|---|---|---|

**FOR AGENCY USE ONLY**

Receipt

| My **New** Place of Residence if different from above *(Street Number and Name)* | Apt/Suite Number |
|---|---|

| City | State or Province |
|---|---|

| Country | ZIP/Postal Code | Telephone Number |
|---|---|---|

Effective Date of Change of Address

## Part 2.     Sponsor's Signature

I certify under penalty of perjury under the laws of the United States of America that all information on this notice is true and correct.

| Signature | Date | Daytime Telephone |
|---|---|---|

## Part 3.     Signature of person preparing notice if other than sponsor

I declare I prepared this application at the request of the above person and it is based on information of which I have knowledge.

| Signature | Date | Daytime Telephone |
|---|---|---|

| Last Name *(Print)* | First name | Middle Initial |
|---|---|---|

Firm Name and Address *(Print)*

**U.S. Department of Justice**
Immigration and Naturalization Service

OMB No. 1115-0009

# Application for Naturalization

Print clearly or type your answers using **CAPITAL** letters. Failure to print clearly may delay your application. Use black or blue ink.

## Part 1. Your Name *(The Person Applying for Naturalization)*

Write your INS "A"- number here:

A __ __ __ __ __ __ __ __ __

A. Your current legal name.

Family Name *(Last Name)*

Given Name *(First Name)*　　　Full Middle Name *(If applicable)*

**FOR INS USE ONLY**

| Bar Code | Date Stamp |
|---|---|

B. Your name **exactly** as it appears on your Permanent Resident Card.

Family Name *(Last Name)*

Given Name *(First Name)*　　　Full Middle Name *(If applicable)*

Remarks

C. If you have ever used other names, provide them below.

| Family Name *(Last Name)* | Given Name *(First Name)* | Middle Name |
|---|---|---|
|  |  |  |
|  |  |  |
|  |  |  |

D. Name change *(optional)*

Please read the Instructions before you decide whether to change your name.

1. Would you like to legally change your name?　☐ Yes　☐ No

2. If "Yes," print the new name you would like to use. Do not use initials or abbreviations when writing your new name.

Family Name *(Last Name)*

Given Name *(First Name)*　　　Full Middle Name

Action

## Part 2. Information About Your Eligibility　*(Check Only One)*

I am at least 18 years old **AND**

A. ☐ I have been a Lawful Permanent Resident of the United States for at least 5 years.

B. ☐ I have been a Lawful Permanent Resident of the United States for at least 3 years, AND I have been married to and living with the same U.S. citizen for the last 3 years, AND my spouse has been a U.S. citizen for the last 3 years.

C. ☐ I am applying on the basis of qualifying military service.

D. ☐ Other *(Please explain)* _____

Form N-400 (Rev. 07/23/02)N

**Part 3. Information About You**

A. Social Security Number

__ __ __ - __ __ - __ __ __ __

B. Date of Birth *(Month/Day/Year)*

__ __ / __ __ / __ __ __ __

C. Date You Became a Permanent Resident *(Month/Day/Year)*

__ __ / __ __ / __ __ __ __

D. Country of Birth

E. Country of Nationality

F. Are either of your parents U.S. citizens? *(if yes, see Instructions)* ☐ Yes ☐ No

G. What is your current marital status? ☐ Single, Never Married ☐ Married ☐ Divorced ☐ Widowed

☐ Marriage Annulled or Other *(Explain)* _____

H. Are you requesting a waiver of the English and/or U.S. History and Government requirements based on a disability or impairment and attaching a Form N-648 with your application? ☐ Yes ☐ No

I. Are you requesting an accommodation to the naturalization process because of a disability or impairment? *(See Instructions for some examples of accommodations.)* ☐ Yes ☐ No

If you answered "Yes", check the box below that applies:

☐ I am deaf or hearing impaired and need a sign language interpreter who uses the following language: _____

☐ I use a wheelchair.

☐ I am blind or sight impaired.

☐ I will need another type of accommodation. Please explain: _____

**Part 4. Addresses and Telephone Numbers**

A. Home Address - Street Number and Name *(Do NOT write a P.O. Box in this space)* | Apartment Number

| City | County | State | ZIP Code | Country |
|------|--------|-------|----------|---------|
|      |        |       |          |         |

B. Care of | Mailing Address - Street Number and Name *(If different from home address)* | Apartment Number

| City | State | ZIP Code | Country |
|------|-------|----------|---------|
|      |       |          |         |

C. Daytime Phone Number *(If any)*

( )

Evening Phone Number *(If any)*

( )

E-mail Address *(If any)*

## Part 5. Information for Criminal Records Search

Write your INS "A"- number here:

A __ __ __ __ __ __ __ __ __

**Note:** The categories below are those required by the FBI. See Instructions for more information.

A. Gender

☐ Male  ☐ Female

B. Height

| Feet | Inches |

C. Weight

| | Pounds |

D. Are you Hispanic or Latino?  ☐ Yes  ☐ No

E. Race *(Select one or more.)*

☐ White  ☐ Asian  ☐ Black or African American  ☐ American Indian or Alaskan Native  ☐ Native Hawaiian or Other Pacific Islander

F. Hair color

☐ Black  ☐ Brown  ☐ Blonde  ☐ Gray  ☐ White  ☐ Red  ☐ Sandy  ☐ Bald (No Hair)

G. Eye color

☐ Brown  ☐ Blue  ☐ Green  ☐ Hazel  ☐ Gray  ☐ Black  ☐ Pink  ☐ Maroon  ☐ Other

## Part 6. Information About Your Residence and Employment

A. Where have you lived during the last 5 years? Begin with where you live now and then list every place you lived for the last 5 years. If you need more space, use a separate sheet of paper.

| Street Number and Name, Apartment Number, City, State, Zip Code and Country | Dates *(Month/Year)* | |
| --- | --- | --- |
| | From | To |
| Current Home Address - Same as Part 4.A | __ __ /__ __ __ __ | Present |
| | __ __ /__ __ __ __ | __ __ /__ __ __ __ |
| | __ __ /__ __ __ __ | __ __ /__ __ __ __ |
| | __ __ /__ __ __ __ | __ __ /__ __ __ __ |
| | __ __ /__ __ __ __ | __ __ /__ __ __ __ |

B. Where have you worked (or, if you were a student, what schools did you attend) during the last 5 years? Include military service. Begin with your current or latest employer and then list every place you have worked or studied for the last 5 years. If you need more space, use a separate sheet of paper.

| Employer or School Name | Employer or School Address *(Street, City and State)* | Dates *(Month/Year)* | | Your Occupation |
| --- | --- | --- | --- | --- |
| | | From | To | |
| | | __ __ /__ __ __ __ | __ __ /__ __ __ __ | |
| | | __ __ /__ __ __ __ | __ __ /__ __ __ __ | |
| | | __ __ /__ __ __ __ | __ __ /__ __ __ __ | |
| | | __ __ /__ __ __ __ | __ __ /__ __ __ __ | |
| | | __ __ /__ __ __ __ | __ __ /__ __ __ __ | |

Write your INS "A"- number here:

A __ __ __ __ __ __ __ __ __

A. How many total days did you spend outside of the United States during the past 5 years? ☐ days

B. How many trips of 24 hours or more have you taken outside of the United States during the past 5 years? ☐ trips

C. List below all the trips of 24 hours or more that you have taken outside of the United States since becoming a Lawful Permanent Resident. Begin with your most recent trip. If you need more space, use a separate sheet of paper.

| Date You Left the United States (Month/Day/Year) | Date You Returned to the United States (Month/Day/Year) | Did Trip Last 6 Months or More? | Countries to Which You Traveled | Total Days Out of the United States |
|---|---|---|---|---|
| __ __ / __ __ / __ __ __ __ | __ __ / __ __ / __ __ __ __ | ☐ Yes ☐ No | | |
| __ __ / __ __ / __ __ __ __ | __ __ / __ __ / __ __ __ __ | ☐ Yes ☐ No | | |
| __ __ / __ __ / __ __ __ __ | __ __ / __ __ / __ __ __ __ | ☐ Yes ☐ No | | |
| __ __ / __ __ / __ __ __ __ | __ __ / __ __ / __ __ __ __ | ☐ Yes ☐ No | | |
| __ __ / __ __ / __ __ __ __ | __ __ / __ __ / __ __ __ __ | ☐ Yes ☐ No | | |
| __ __ / __ __ / __ __ __ __ | __ __ / __ __ / __ __ __ __ | ☐ Yes ☐ No | | |
| __ __ / __ __ / __ __ __ __ | __ __ / __ __ / __ __ __ __ | ☐ Yes ☐ No | | |
| __ __ / __ __ / __ __ __ __ | __ __ / __ __ / __ __ __ __ | ☐ Yes ☐ No | | |
| __ __ / __ __ / __ __ __ __ | __ __ / __ __ / __ __ __ __ | ☐ Yes ☐ No | | |
| __ __ / __ __ / __ __ __ __ | __ __ / __ __ / __ __ __ __ | ☐ Yes ☐ No | | |

**Part 8. Information About Your Marital History**

A. How many times have you been married (including annulled marriages)? ☐ If you have NEVER been married, go to Part 9.

B. If you are now married, give the following information about your spouse:

1. Spouse's Family Name *(Last Name)*    Given Name *(First Name)*    Full Middle Name *(If applicable)*

2. Date of Birth *(Month/Day/Year)*    3. Date of Marriage *(Month/Day/Year)*    4. Spouse's Social Security Number

__ __ / __ __ / __ __ __ __    __ __ / __ __ / __ __ __ __    __ __ __ - __ __ - __ __ __ __

5. Home Address - Street Number and Name    Apartment Number

City    State    ZIP Code

## Part 8. Information About Your Marital History *(Continued)*

C. Is your spouse a U.S. citizen?  ☐ Yes  ☐ No

D. If your spouse is a U.S. citizen, give the following information:

    1. When did your spouse become a U.S. citizen?  ☐ At Birth  ☐ Other

    If "Other," give the following information:

    2. Date your spouse became a U.S. citizen

    __ __/__ __/__ __ __ __

    3. Place your spouse became a U.S. citizen *(Please see Instructions)*

                                     City and State

E. If your spouse is NOT a U.S. citizen, give the following information :

    1. Spouse's Country of Citizenship

    2. Spouse's INS "A"- Number *(If applicable)*

    A __ __ __ __ __ __ __ __ __

    3. Spouse's Immigration Status

    ☐ Lawful Permanent Resident  ☐ Other _____

F. If you were married before, provide the following information about your prior spouse. If you have more than one previous marriage, use a separate sheet of paper to provide the information requested in questions 1-5 below.

    1. Prior Spouse's Family Name *(Last Name)*    Given Name *(First Name)*    Full Middle Name *(If applicable)*

    2. Prior Spouse's Immigration Status

    ☐ U.S. Citizen

    ☐ Lawful Permanent Resident

    ☐ Other _____

    3. Date of Marriage *(Month/Day/Year)*

    __ __/__ __/__ __ __ __

    4. Date Marriage Ended *(Month/Day/Year)*

    __ __/__ __/__ __ __ __

    5. How Marriage Ended

    ☐ Divorce  ☐ Spouse Died  ☐ Other _____

G. How many times has your current spouse been married (including annulled marriages)?  ☐

If your spouse has EVER been married before, give the following information about **your spouse's** prior marriage.
If your spouse has more than one previous marriage, use a separate sheet of paper to provide the information requested in questions 1 - 5 below.

    1. Prior Spouse's Family Name *(Last Name)*    Given Name *(First Name)*    Full Middle Name *(If applicable)*

    2. Prior Spouse's Immigration Status

    ☐ U.S. Citizen

    ☐ Lawful Permanent Resident

    ☐ Other _____

    3. Date of Marriage *(Month/Day/Year)*

    __ __/__ __/__ __ __ __

    4. Date Marriage Ended *(Month/Day/Year)*

    __ __/__ __/__ __ __ __

    5. How Marriage Ended

    ☐ Divorce  ☐ Spouse Died  ☐ Other _____

## Part 9. Information About Your Children

A. How many sons and daughters have you had? For more information on which sons and daughters you should include and how to complete this section, see the Instructions.

B. Provide the following information about all of your sons and daughters. If you need more space, use a separate sheet of paper.

| Full Name of Son or Daughter | Date of Birth (Month/Day/Year) | INS "A"- number (if child has one) | Country of Birth | Current Address (Street, City, State & Country) |
|---|---|---|---|---|
| | __ __ / __ __ / __ __ __ __ | A__ __ __ __ __ __ __ __ __ | | |
| | __ __ / __ __ / __ __ __ __ | A__ __ __ __ __ __ __ __ __ | | |
| | __ __ / __ __ / __ __ __ __ | A__ __ __ __ __ __ __ __ __ | | |
| | __ __ / __ __ / __ __ __ __ | A__ __ __ __ __ __ __ __ __ | | |
| | __ __ / __ __ / __ __ __ __ | A__ __ __ __ __ __ __ __ __ | | |
| | __ __ / __ __ / __ __ __ __ | A__ __ __ __ __ __ __ __ __ | | |
| | __ __ / __ __ / __ __ __ __ | A__ __ __ __ __ __ __ __ __ | | |
| | __ __ / __ __ / __ __ __ __ | A__ __ __ __ __ __ __ __ __ | | |

## Part 10. Additional Questions

Please answer questions 1 through 14. If you answer "Yes" to any of these questions, include a written explanation with this form. Your written explanation should (1) explain why your answer was "Yes," and (2) provide any additional information that helps to explain your answer.

### A. General Questions

1. Have you **EVER** claimed to be a U.S. citizen *(in writing or any other way)*? ☐ Yes ☐ No

2. Have you **EVER** registered to vote in any Federal, state, or local election in the United States? ☐ Yes ☐ No

3. Have you **EVER** voted in any Federal, state, or local election in the United States? ☐ Yes ☐ No

4. Since becoming a Lawful Permanent Resident, have you **EVER** failed to file a required Federal, state, or local tax return? ☐ Yes ☐ No

5. Do you owe any Federal, state, or local taxes that are overdue? ☐ Yes ☐ No

6. Do you have any title of nobility in any foreign country? ☐ Yes ☐ No

7. Have you ever been declared legally incompetent or been confined to a mental institution within the last 5 years? ☐ Yes ☐ No

Write your INS "A"- number here:

A __ __ __ __ __ __ __ __ __

## B. Affiliations

8. a. Have you **EVER** been a member of or associated with any organization, association, fund, foundation, party, club, society, or similar group in the United States or in any other place?  ☐ Yes ☐ No

b. If you answered "Yes," list the name of each group below. If you need more space, attach the names of the other group(s) on a separate sheet of paper.

| Name of Group | Name of Group |
|---|---|
| 1. | 6. |
| 2. | 7. |
| 3. | 8. |
| 4. | 9. |
| 5. | 10. |

9. Have you **EVER** been a member of or in any way associated *(either directly or indirectly)* with:

  a. The Communist Party?  ☐ Yes ☐ No

  b. Any other totalitarian party?  ☐ Yes ☐ No

  c. A terrorist organization?  ☐ Yes ☐ No

10. Have you **EVER** advocated *(either directly or indirectly)* the overthrow of any government by force or violence?  ☐ Yes ☐ No

11. Have you **EVER** persecuted *(either directly or indirectly)* any person because of race, religion, national origin, membership in a particular social group, or political opinion?  ☐ Yes ☐ No

12. Between March 23, 1933, and May 8, 1945, did you work for or associate in any way *(either directly or indirectly)* with:

  a. The Nazi government of Germany?  ☐ Yes ☐ No

  b. Any government in any area (1) occupied by, (2) allied with, or (3) established with the help of the Nazi government of Germany?  ☐ Yes ☐ No

  c. Any German, Nazi, or S.S. military unit, paramilitary unit, self-defense unit, vigilante unit, citizen unit, police unit, government agency or office, extermination camp, concentration camp, prisoner of war camp, prison, labor camp, or transit camp?  ☐ Yes ☐ No

## C. Continuous Residence

Since becoming a Lawful Permanent Resident of the United States:

13. Have you **EVER** called yourself a "nonresident" on a Federal, state, or local tax return?  ☐ Yes ☐ No

14. Have you **EVER** failed to file a Federal, state, or local tax return because you considered yourself to be a "nonresident"?  ☐ Yes ☐ No

### D. Good Moral Character

For the purposes of this application, you must answer "Yes" to the following questions, if applicable, even if your records were sealed or otherwise cleared or if anyone, including a judge, law enforcement officer, or attorney, told you that you no longer have a record.

15. Have you **EVER** committed a crime or offense for which you were NOT arrested? ☐ Yes ☐ No

16. Have you **EVER** been arrested, cited, or detained by any law enforcement officer (including INS and military officers) for any reason? ☐ Yes ☐ No

17. Have you **EVER** been charged with committing any crime or offense? ☐ Yes ☐ No

18. Have you **EVER** been convicted of a crime or offense? ☐ Yes ☐ No

19. Have you **EVER** been placed in an alternative sentencing or a rehabilitative program (for example: diversion, deferred prosecution, withheld adjudication, deferred adjudication)? ☐ Yes ☐ No

20. Have you **EVER** received a suspended sentence, been placed on probation, or been paroled? ☐ Yes ☐ No

21. Have you **EVER** been in jail or prison? ☐ Yes ☐ No

If you answered "Yes" to any of questions 15 through 21, complete the following table. If you need more space, use a separate sheet of paper to give the same information.

| Why were you arrested, cited, detained, or charged? | Date arrested, cited, detained, or charged *(Month/Day/Year)* | Where were you arrested, cited, detained or charged? *(City, State, Country)* | Outcome or disposition of the arrest, citation, detention or charge *(No charges filed, charges dismissed, jail, probation, etc.)* |
|---|---|---|---|
|  |  |  |  |
|  |  |  |  |
|  |  |  |  |

Answer questions 22 through 33. If you answer "Yes" to any of these questions, attach (1) your written explanation why your answer was "Yes," and (2) any additional information or documentation that helps explain your answer.

22. Have you **EVER:**

    a. been a habitual drunkard? ☐ Yes ☐ No

    b. been a prostitute, or procured anyone for prostitution? ☐ Yes ☐ No

    c. sold or smuggled controlled substances, illegal drugs or narcotics? ☐ Yes ☐ No

    d. been married to more than one person at the same time? ☐ Yes ☐ No

    e. helped anyone enter or try to enter the United States illegally? ☐ Yes ☐ No

    f. gambled illegally or received income from illegal gambling? ☐ Yes ☐ No

    g. failed to support your dependents or to pay alimony? ☐ Yes ☐ No

23. Have you **EVER** given false or misleading information to any U.S. government official while applying for any immigration benefit or to prevent deportation, exclusion, or removal? ☐ Yes ☐ No

24. Have you **EVER** lied to any U.S. government official to gain entry or admission into the United States? ☐ Yes ☐ No

Write your INS "A"- number here:

A __ __ __ __ __ __ __ __ __

### E. Removal, Exclusion, and Deportation Proceedings

25.  Are removal, exclusion, rescission or deportation proceedings pending against you? ☐ Yes  ☐ No

26.  Have you **EVER** been removed, excluded, or deported from the United States? ☐ Yes  ☐ No

27.  Have you **EVER** been ordered to be removed, excluded, or deported from the United States? ☐ Yes  ☐ No

28.  Have you **EVER** applied for any kind of relief from removal, exclusion, or deportation? ☐ Yes  ☐ No

### F. Military Service

29.  Have you **EVER** served in the U.S. Armed Forces? ☐ Yes  ☐ No

30.  Have you **EVER** left the United States to avoid being drafted into the U.S. Armed Forces? ☐ Yes  ☐ No

31.  Have you **EVER** applied for any kind of exemption from military service in the U.S. Armed Forces? ☐ Yes  ☐ No

32.  Have you **EVER** deserted from the U.S. Armed Forces? ☐ Yes  ☐ No

### G. Selective Service Registration

33.  Are you a male who lived in the United States at any time between your 18th and 26th birthdays
in any status except as a lawful nonimmigrant? ☐ Yes  ☐ No

If you answered "NO", go on to question 34.

If you answered "YES", provide the information below.

If you answered "YES", but you did NOT register with the Selective Service System and are still under 26 years of age, you
must register before you apply for naturalization, so that you can complete the information below:

Date Registered (Month/Day/Year) [                    ]  Selective Service Number __ __ / __ __ __ __ __ __ __ / __

If you answered "YES", but you did NOT register with the Selective Service and you are now 26 years old or older, attach a
statement explaining why you did not register.

### H. Oath Requirements *(See Part 14 for the text of the oath)*

Answer questions 34 through 39.  If you answer "No" to any of these questions, attach (1) your written explanation why the answer was
"No" and (2) any additional information or documentation that helps to explain your answer.

34.  Do you support the Constitution and form of government of the United States? ☐ Yes  ☐ No

35.  Do you understand the full Oath of Allegiance to the United States? ☐ Yes  ☐ No

36.  Are you willing to take the full Oath of Allegiance to the United States? ☐ Yes  ☐ No

37.  If the law requires it, are you willing to bear arms on behalf of the United States? ☐ Yes  ☐ No

38.  If the law requires it, are you willing to perform noncombatant services in the U.S. Armed Forces? ☐ Yes  ☐ No

39.  If the law requires it, are you willing to perform work of national importance under civilian
direction? ☐ Yes  ☐ No

| Part 11. Your Signature | Write your INS "A"- number here: |
|---|---|
| | A __ __ __ __ __ __ __ __ __ |

I certify, under penalty of perjury under the laws of the United States of America, that this application, and the evidence submitted with it, are all true and correct. I authorize the release of any information which INS needs to determine my eligibility for naturalization.

Your Signature

Date *(Month/Day/Year)*

__ __ / __ __ / __ __ __ __

## Part 12. Signature of Person Who Prepared This Application for You *(if applicable)*

I declare under penalty of perjury that I prepared this application at the request of the above person. The answers provided are based on information of which I have personal knowledge and/or were provided to me by the above named person in response to the *exact questions* contained on this form.

Preparer's Printed Name

Preparer's Signature

Date *(Month/Day/Year)*

__ __ / __ __ / __ __ __ __

Preparer's Firm or Organization Name *(If applicable)*

Preparer's Daytime Phone Number

( )

Preparer's Address - Street Number and Name

City

State

ZIP Code

## Do Not Complete Parts 13 and 14 Until an INS Officer Instructs You To Do So

## Part 13. Signature at Interview

I swear (affirm) and certify under penalty of perjury under the laws of the United States of America that I know that the contents of this application for naturalization subscribed by me, including corrections numbered 1 through _____ and the evidence submitted by me numbered pages 1 through _____ , are true and correct to the best of my knowledge and belief.

Subscribed to and sworn to (affirmed) before me

Officer's Printed Name or Stamp         Date *(Month/Day/Year)*

Complete Signature of Applicant

Officer's Signature

## Part 14. Oath of Allegiance

If your application is approved, you will be scheduled for a public oath ceremony at which time you will be required to take the following oath of allegiance immediately prior to becoming a naturalized citizen. By signing , you acknowledge your willingness and ability to take this oath:

I hereby declare, on oath, that I absolutely and entirely renounce and abjure all allegiance and fidelity to any foreign prince, potentate, state, or sovereignty, of whom or which which I have heretofore been a subject or citizen;

that I will support and defend the Constitution and laws of the United States of America against all enemies, foreign and domestic;
that I will bear true faith and allegiance to the same;
that I will bear arms on behalf of the United States when required by the law;
that I will perform noncombatant service in the Armed Forces of the United States when required by the law;
that I will perform work of national importance under civilian direction when required by the law; and
that I take this obligation freely, without any mental reservation or purpose of evasion; so help me God.

Printed Name of Applicant

Complete Signature of Applicant

## Instructions
### (Tear off this instruction sheet before filling out this form)

This form must be filled in completely. Print the answers in ink or use typewriter. If any question does not apply to this application, please print "N/A" in the answer line. If you do not have enough room for any answer or if the instructions tell you to use a separate sheet of paper, use another sheet this size, giving the answer the same number as the number of the question, and attach it to the application. You will later be notified to appear for an examination before an officer of the Immigration and Naturalization Service (INS). You may be requested to bring a relative or other witness to provide additional testimony.

**AGE OF APPLICANT**- Applicants 14 years of age or over must sign their full names in the space provided on page 3 of this application. If under 14 years, only the parent or guardian must sign his or her name and only in the space provided on page 3.

**FEE** - A fee of one hundred and sixty dollars ($160) must be paid for filing this application. It cannot be refunded, regardless of the action taken on the application. **DO NOT MAIL CASH. ALL FEES MUST BE SUBMITTED IN THE EXACT AMOUNT.** Payment by check or money order must be drawn on a bank or other institution located in United States and be payable in United States currency. If the applicant resides in Guam, the check or money order must be payable to the "Treasurer, Guam." If the applicant resides in the U.S. Virgin Islands, the check or money order must be payable to the "Commissioner of Finance of the Virgin Islands." All other applicants must make the check or money order payable to the "Immigration and Naturalization Service." When a check is drawn on account of a person other than the applicant, the name of the applicant must be entered on the face of the check. If the application is submitted from outside the United States, remittance may be made by a bank international money order or foreign draft drawn on a financial institution in the United States and payable to the Immigration and Naturalization Service in United States currency. Personal checks are accepted subject to collectibility. An uncollectible check will render the application and any document issued pursuant thereto invalid. A charge of $30.00 will be imposed if a check in payment of a fee is not honored by the bank on which it is drawn.

**PHOTOGRAPHS** - With this application, you are required to send three identical unglazed, colored photographs of yourself taken within 30 days of the date of this application. These photographs must be 2 x 2 inches in size, and the distance from top of head to point of chin should be approximately 1 1/4 inches; must *not* be pasted on a card or mounted in any other way; must be on thin paper, have a light background, and clearly show a three-quarter profile view of the features of the applicant with head bare (unless the applicant is wearing a headdress as required by a religious order of which he or she is a member.) Snapshots, groups or full - length portraits or machine - made photographs will not be accepted. **YOUR PHOTOGRAPHS MUST NOT BE SIGNED**, but you should print your name and alien registration number, if any, in the center of the *back* of each photograph lightly with a soft lead pencil. taking care not to mutilate the photograph.

**FACTS CONCERNING ARRIVAL IN THE UNITED STATES** - Detailed information should be given in Statement 3 regarding your first arrival in the United States for permanent residence in this country. The information regarding the number of the passport and date and place of issuance does not need to be given unless you traveled on a *United States* passport at that time. If you do not know the exact date of arrival or name of the vessel or port and cannot obtain this information, give the facts of your arrival to the best of your ability. If you have a permanent resident card or alien registration receipt card, immigrant identification card, ship's card or baggage labels, they will help you to give this information.

**NAME TO BE SHOWN ON CERTIFICATE** - The certificate will be issued only in a name that you have a legal right to use.

**DOCUMENTS** - If your birth abroad, or the birth abroad of any person through whom citizenship is claimed, was registered with an American Consul abroad, submit with this application any registration form that was issued. **If any required documents were submitted to and RETAINED by the American Consul in connection with such registration, or in connection with the issuance of a United States passport or in any other official matter, and you wish to use such documents in connection with this application instead of submitting duplicate copies, merely list the documents in Statement 14 of the application and give the location of the Consulate.** If you wish to make similar use of required documents contained in any INS file, list them in Statement 14 and identify the file by name, number and location. Otherwise, the documents as mentioned in the box on page 6 applicable to your case (see over) must accompany your application and, for any required document not furnished, you must explain why, what efforts you have made to get it, and if possible, enclose a statement from the official custodian of such records showing that the document is not available. You should also forward for consideration, in lieu of that document, a record or the affidavits described under **SECONDARY EVIDENCE**, on the reverse of this page.

If any person through whom citizenship is claimed became a citizen through his or her parent(s), but does not have a certificate of citizenship (with a number preceded by an A or AA) in his or her own name, communicate with the INS for information as to additional documents that must be submitted.

**REPORTING BURDEN.** An agency may not conduct or sponsor an information collection and a person is not required to respond to a collection of information unless it displays a currently valid OMB control numbers. Public reporting burden for this collection of information is estimated to average one (1) hour per response, including the time for reviewing instructions, searching existing data sources, gathering and maintaining the data needed, and completing and reviewing the collection of information. Send comments regarding this burden estimate or any other aspect of this collection of information, including suggestions for reducing this burden, to U.S. Department of Justice, Immigration and Naturalization Service, HQPDI, 425 I Street N.W., Room 4034, Washington, DC 20536. OMB No. 1115-0018. **DO NOT MAIL YOUR COMPLETED APPLICATION TO THIS ADDRESS.**

# INSTRUCTIONS (Continued)

Any document in a foreign language must be accompanied by a translation in English. The translator must certify that he or she is competent to translate and that the translation is accurate. Do not send a Certificate of Naturalization or Citizenship and do not make any copy of such a certificate. An interview in connection with your application will be scheduled before an officer of the Immigration and Naturalization Service, and any Certificate of Naturalization or Citizenship may be presented in person at that time. If the law does not prohibit the making of copies, send a legible copy of any document that you submit with the application, but bring the original of any submitted copy with you to the interview. The original will be returned to you and the copy retained. You may be called upon to present proof of a parent's residence or physical presence in the United States.

## IF CLAIMING CITIZENSHIP THROUGH FATHER (OR BOTH PARENTS)

1. Applicant's birth certificate.
2. Marriage certificate of applicant's parents.
3. If applicant's parents were married before their marriage to each other, death certificate or divorce decree showing the termination of any previous marriage of each parent.
4. If applicant is a woman and has ever been married, her marriage certificate(s).
5. If applicant's parent(s) became citizen(s) at birth, birth certificate(s) of parent(s).
6. Death certificate(s) of applicant's parent(s), if deceased.
7. If applicant is an adopted child, applicant's adoption decree.

## IF CLAIMING CITIZENSHIP THROUGH MOTHER

1. Applicant's birth certificate.
2. Marriage certificate(s) of applicant's mother.
3. If applicant is a woman and has ever been married, her marriage certificate(s).
4. If applicant's mother became a citizen of the United States at birth, mother's birth certificate.
5. If applicant is claiming citizenship through mother's marriage before September 22, 1922, to applicant's stepfather, death certificate or divorce decree showing termination of any previous marriage(s) of mother and stepfather.
6. If applicant is claiming citizenship through mother's marriage before September 22, 1922, to applicant's stepfather and stepfather became a citizen of the United States at birth, stepfather's birth certificate.
7. Death certificate of applicant's mother, if deceased.

## IF CLAIMING CITIZENSHIP THROUGH HUSBAND
### (NOTE: APPLICABLE ONLY IF MARRIAGE OCCURRED PRIOR TO SEPTEMBER 22, 1922.)

1. If husband through whom citizenship is claimed became a citizen of the United States at birth, husband's birth certificate.
2. Applicant's marriage certificate(s).
3. If either applicant or the husband through whom she is claiming citizenship was married before their marriage to each other, death certificate or divorce decree showing the termination of each such prior marriage(s).
4. If applicant's marriage to the husband through whom she is claiming citizenship has terminated, death certificate or divorce decree showing such a termination.

## SECONDARY EVIDENCE

If it is not possible to obtain any one of the required documents or records shown above, the following may be submitted for consideration:

1. *Baptismal certificate.* - A certificate under the seal of the church where the baptism occurred, showing date and place of the child's birth, date of baptism, the names of the godparents, if known.
2. *School record.* - A letter from the school authorities having jurisdiction over school attended (preferably the first school), showing the date of admission to the school, child's date of birth or age at that time, place of birth, and the names and places of birth of parents, if shown in the school records.
3. *Census record.* - State or Federal census record showing the name(s) and place(s) of birth, and date(s) of birth or age(s) of the person(s) listed.
4. *Affidavits.*- Notarized affidavits of two persons who were living at the time and who have personal knowledge of the event you are trying to prove - for example, the date and place of a birth, marriage or death. The persons making the affidavits may be relatives and need not be citizens of the United States. Each affidavit should contain the following information regarding the person making the affidavit: his or her full name and address date and place of birth, relationship to you, if any; full information concerning the event, and complete details concerning how he or she acquired knowledge of the event.

**U.S. Department of Justice**
Immigration and Naturalization Service

# Application for
# Certificate of Citizenship

**FEE STAMP**

Take or mail this application to:
**IMMIGRATION AND NATURALIZATION SERVICE**

*(Print or type)*

Date _____

_____ nee _____
(Full, True Name, without Abbreviations)                (Maiden name, if any)

_____
(Apartment number, Street address, and if appropriate, "in care of")

**ALIEN REGISTRATION**

NO._____

_____
(City)      (Country)      (State)      (Zip Code)

_____
(Telephone Number)

# (SEE INSTRUCTIONS. BE SURE YOU UNDERSTAND EACH QUESTION BEFORE YOU ANSWER IT.)

I hereby apply to the Commissioner of Immigration and Naturalization for a certificate showing that I am a citizen of the United States of America.

(1) I was born in _____ on _____
                        (City) (State or Country)                      (Month) (Day) (Year)

(2) My personal description is: Gender _____ ; height _____ feet _____ inches;

Marital status: ☐ Single; ☐ Married; ☐ Divorced; ☐ Widow(er).

(3) I arrived in the United States at _____ on _____
                                              (City and State)                    (Month) (Day) (Year)

under the name _____ by means of _____
                                                                        (Name of ship or other means of arrival)

☐ on U. S. Passport No._____ issued to me at _____ on _____
                                                                                                      (Month) (Day) (Year)

☐ on an Immigrant Visa. ☐ Other (specify)_____

(4) FILL IN THIS BLOCK ONLY IF YOU ARRIVED IN THE UNITED STATES BEFORE JULY 1, 1924.

(a) My last permanent foreign residence was _____
                                                                    (City)                            (Country)

(b) I took the ship or other conveyance to the United States at _____
                                                                                    (City)                        (Country)

(c) I was coming to _____ at _____
                              (Name of person in the United States)      (City and State where this person was living)

(d) I traveled to the United States with _____
                                                      (Names of passengers or relatives with whom you traveled, and their relationship to you, if any)

(5) Have you been out of the United States since you first arrived? ☐ Yes ☐ No; If "Yes," fill in the following information for every absence.

| DATE DEPARTED | DATE RETURNED | Name of airlines or other means used to return to the United States | Port of return to the United States |
|---|---|---|---|
|  |  |  |  |
|  |  |  |  |
|  |  |  |  |
|  |  |  |  |

(6) I_____ filed a petition for naturalization. *(If "have," attach full explanation.)*
     (have) (have not)

**TO THE APPLICANT. - Do not write between the double lines below. Continue on next page.**

**ARRIVAL RECORDS EXAMINED**

Card index _____

Index books _____

Manifest _____

_____

**ARRIVAL RECORD FOUND**

Place _____ Date _____

Name _____

Manner _____

Marital status _____ Age _____

_____
(Signature of person making search)

Form N-600 (Rev. 10/11/00)Y

**(CONTINUE HERE)**

**(7) I claim United States citizenship through my** *(check whichever applicable)* ☐ **father;** ☐ **mother;** ☐ **both parents;**

☐ **adoptive parent(s);** ☐ **husband**

**(8) My father's name is** _____ ; he was born on _____
(Month)   (Day)   (Year)

at _____ ; and resides at _____
(City)                              (State or Country)                              (Street address, city and State or country. If dead, write

_____ He became a citizen of the United States by ☐ birth; ☐ naturalization on _____
"dead" and date of death.)                                                                                          (Month)   (Day)   (Year)

in the _____ Certificate of Naturalization No. _____
(Name of court, city and State)

☐ through his parent(s), and _____ **issued Certificate of Citizenship No. A or AA** _____
(was)   (was not)

(If known) His former Alien Registration No. was _____

He _____ lost United States citizenship. *(If citizenship lost, attach full explanation.)*
(has)   (has not)

He resided in the United States from _____ to _____ ; from _____ to _____ ; from _____ to _____
(Year)   (Year)                              (Year)   (Year)                              (Year)   (Year)

from _____ to _____ ; from _____ to _____ ; I am the child of his _____ marriage.
(Year)   (Year)                 (Year)   (Year)                                          (1st, 2d, 3d, etc.)

**(9) My mother's present name is** _____ ; her maiden name was _____ ;

she was born on _____ ; at _____ ; she resides
(Month)  (Day)  (Year)                              (City)   (State or country)

at _____ . She became a citizen of the
(Street address, city, and State or country. If dead, write "dead" and date of death.)

United States by ☐ birth; ☐ naturalization under the name of _____

on _____ in the _____ ;
(Month) (Day) (Year)                              (Name of court, city, and State)

Certificate of Naturalization No. _____ ; ☐ through her parent(s), and _____ issued Certificate of
(was) (was not)

Citizenship No. A or AA _____ (If known) Her former Alien Registration No. was _____ .

She _____ lost United States citizenship. *(If citizenship lost, attach full explanation.)*
(has)  (has not)

She resided in the United States from _____ to _____ ; from _____ to _____ ; from _____ to _____ ;
(Year)   (Year)                              (Year)   (Year)                              (Year)   (Year)

from _____ to _____ ; from _____ to _____ ; I am the child of her _____ marriage.
(Year)   (Year)                 (Year)   (Year)                                          (1st, 2d, 3d, etc.)

**(10) My mother and my father were married to each other on** _____ at _____
(Month) (Day) (Year)                  (City)   (State or country)

**(11) If claim is through adoptive parent(s):**

I was adopted on _____ in the _____
(Month) (Day) (Year)                              (Name of Court)

at _____ by my _____ who were not United States citizens at that time.
(City or town) (State) (Country)                  (mother, father, parents)

**(12) My** _____ served in the Armed Forces of the United States from _____ to _____ and _____
(father) (mother)                                                      (Date)         (Date)            (was) (was not)

honorably discharged.

**(13) I** _____ lost my United States citizenship. *(If citizenship lost, attach full explanation.)*
(have)  (have not)

**(14) I submit the following documents with this application:**

*Nature of Document*                                        *Names of Persons Concerned*

_____                    _____

_____                    _____

_____                    _____

_____                    _____

_____                    _____

(15) Fill in this block if your brother, sister, mother or father ever applied to the INS for a certificate of citizenship.

| NAME OF RELATIVE | RELATIONSHIP | DATE OF BIRTH | WHEN APPLICATION SUBMITTED | CERTIFICATE NO. AND FILE NO., IF KNOWN, AND LOCATION OF OFFICE |
|---|---|---|---|---|
| | | | | |
| | | | | |
| | | | | |
| | | | | |

(16) Fill in this block only if you are now or ever have been a married woman.  I have been married _____ time(s), as follows:
(1, 2, 3 etc.)

| DATE MARRIED | NAME OF HUSBAND | CITIZENSHIP OF HUSBAND | IF MARRIAGE HAS BEEN TERMINATED: | |
|---|---|---|---|---|
| | | | Date Marriage Ended | How Marriage Ended *(Death or Divorce)* |
| | | | | |
| | | | | |

(17) Fill in this block only if you claim citizenship through a husband. *(Marriage must have occurred prior to September 22, 1922.)*

Name of citizen husband _____ ; he was born on _____
(Give full and complete name)                                                                 (Month) (Day) (Year)

at _____ ; and resides at _____ He became a citizen of the
(City) (State or country)                        (Street address, city, and State or country. If dead, write "dead" and date of death.)

United States by ☐ birth; ☐ naturalization on _____ in the _____ Certificate of
(Month) (Day) (Year)                (Name of court, city, and state)

Naturalization No. _____ ; ☐ through his parent(s), and _____ issued Certificate of Citizenship No. A or AA
(was) (was not)

_____ . He _____ since lost United States citizenship. *(If citizenship lost, attach full explanation.)*
(has) (has not)

I am of the _____ race.  Before my marriage to him, he was married _____ time(s), as follows:
(1,2, 3,etc.)

| DATE MARRIED | NAME OF WIFE | IF MARRIAGE HAS BEEN TERMINATED: | |
|---|---|---|---|
| | | Date Marriage Ended | How Marriage Ended *(Death or Divorce)* |
| | | | |
| | | | |

(18) Fill in this block only if you claim citizenship through your stepfather. *(Applicable only if mother married U. S. Citizen prior to September 22, 1922.)*

The full name of my stepfather is _____ ; he was born on _____ at _____ ;
(Month) (Day) (Year)     (City) (State or country)

and resides at _____ He became a citizen of the United States by ☐ birth;
(Street address, city, and State or country.  If dead, write "dead" and date of death.)

☐ naturalization on _____ in the _____ Certificate of Naturalization No. _____ ;
(Month) (Day) (Year)        (Name of court, City and State)

☐ through his parent(s), and _____ issued Certificate of Citizenship No. A or AA _____ He _____ since lost United
(was) (was not)                                                                                         (has) (has not)

States citizenship. *(If citizenship lost, attach full explanation.)* He and my mother were married to each other on _____ at _____
(Month) (Day) (Year)   (City and State or

_____ My mother is of the _____ race. She _____ issued Certificate of Citizenship No. A _____
country)                                                         (was) (was not)

Before marrying my mother, my stepfather was married _____ time(s), as follows:
(1, 2, 3,etc.)

| DATE MARRIED | NAME OF WIFE | IF MARRIAGE HAS BEEN TERMINATED: | |
|---|---|---|---|
| | | Date Marriage Ended | How Marriage Ended *(Death or Divorce)* |
| | | | |
| | | | |

(19) I _____ previously applied for a certificate of citizenship on _____ , at _____
(have) (have not)                                                                 (Date)                              (Office)

(20) Signature of person preparing form, if other than applicant. I declare that this document was prepared by me at the request of the applicant and is based on all information of which I have any knowledge.

SIGNATURE _____

(SIGN HERE) _____

| ADDRESS: | DATE |
|---|---|

(Signature of applicant or parent or guardian)

## AFFIDAVIT

I, the _____ , do swear
(Applicant, parent, guardian)
that I know and understand the contents of this application, signed by me, and
of attached supplementary pages numbered (      ) to (      ), inclusive;
that the same are true to the best of my knowledge and belief; and that
corrections numbered (      ) to (      ) were made by me or at my request.

Subscribed and sworn to before me upon examination of the applicant
(parent, guardian) at _____,
this _____ day of _____ , _____
and continued solely for:

_____
(Signature of applicant, parent, guardian)

_____
(Officer's Signature and Title)

## REPORT AND RECOMMENDATION ON APPLICATION

On the basis of the documents, records, and persons examined, and the identification upon personal appearance of the underage beneficiary, I find that
all the facts and conclusions set forth under oath in this application are _____ true and correct; that the applicant did _____ derive or acquire United
States citizenship on _____ , through
(Month) (Day) (Year)

and that (s)he _____ been expatriated since that time. I recommend that this application be _____ and that
( has) (has not )                                                                                                                          (granted)   (denied)
_____ Certificate of citizenship be _____ issued in the name of _____
(A) (AA)
In addition to the documents listed in Item 14, the following documents and records have been examined:

| Person Examined | Address | Relationship to Applicant | Date Testimony Heard |
|---|---|---|---|
| _____ | _____ | _____ | _____ |
| | _____ | | |
| _____ | _____ | _____ | _____ |
| | _____ | | |

Supplementary Report(s) No.(s) _____ Attached.
Date _____ , _____

_____
(Officer's Signature and Title)

I do _____ concur in the recommendation

Date _____ , _____

_____
(Signature of District Director or Officer in Charge)

# Index

# Remember:

Little publishers have big ears.
We really listen to you.

*Take 2 Minutes & Give Us Your 2 cents*

**Y**our comments make a big difference in the development and revision of Nolo books and software. Please take a few minutes and register your Nolo product—and your comments—with us. Not only will your input make a difference, you'll receive special offers available only to registered owners of Nolo products on our newest books and software. Register now by:

**PHONE**
1-800-728-3555

**FAX**
1-800-645-0895

**EMAIL**
cs@nolo.com

or **MAIL** us
this registration card

fold here

---

# Registration Card

NAME _____  DATE _____

ADDRESS _____

_____

CITY _____  STATE _____ ZIP _____

PHONE _____  E-MAIL _____

WHERE DID YOU HEAR ABOUT THIS PRODUCT? _____

WHERE DID YOU PURCHASE THIS PRODUCT? _____

DID YOU CONSULT A LAWYER? (PLEASE CIRCLE ONE)   YES   NO   NOT APPLICABLE

DID YOU FIND THIS BOOK HELPFUL?   (VERY)   5   4   3   2   1   (NOT AT ALL)

COMMENTS _____

_____

_____

WAS IT EASY TO USE?   (VERY EASY)   5   4   3   2   1   (VERY DIFFICULT)

We occasionally make our mailing list available to carefully selected companies whose products may be of interest to you.

❏   If you do not wish to receive mailings from these companies, please check this box.

❏   You can quote me in future Nolo promotional materials.
    Daytime phone number _____.

**GRN 5.2**

## Nolo
*in the*
## NEWS

"Nolo helps lay people perform legal tasks without the aid—or fees—of lawyers."

**—USA TODAY**

Nolo books are ..."written in plain language, free of legal mumbo jumbo, and spiced with witty personal observations."

**—ASSOCIATED PRESS**

"...Nolo publications...guide people simply through the how, when, where and why of law."

**—WASHINGTON POST**

"Increasingly, people who are not lawyers are performing tasks usually regarded as legal work... And consumers, using books like Nolo's, do routine legal work themselves."

**—NEW YORK TIMES**

"...All of [Nolo's] books are easy-to-understand, are updated regularly, provide pull-out forms...and are often quite moving in their sense of compassion for the struggles of the lay reader."

**—SAN FRANCISCO CHRONICLE**

fold here

- - - - - - - - - - - - - - - - - - - - - - - - - - - - - - - - - - - - - - - - - -

Place
stamp here

## NOLO  **Nolo**
**950 Parker Street**
**Berkeley, CA 94710-9867**

**Attn:** GRN 5.2